# STRANGERS IN THE WEST

Wedding photo of Adelia Shahdan and Gabriel Saba, 1902
(courtesy Frank Saba).

# STRANGERS IN THE WEST

## THE SYRIAN COLONY OF NEW YORK CITY, 1880–1900

LINDA K. JACOBS

NEW YORK

ISBN: 978-0-9835392-5-4
Library of Congress Control Number: 2015904081



Inquiries should be sent to:
info@KalimahPress.com

Art Direction: Liliana Zavaleta
Cover and text design: Francisca Toral R.

Cover photo: Barbara and Antoine Sadallah, ca.1901. Courtesy of Carl Antoun.

Printed in the United States

For my mother, Violet Evelyn Jabara Jacobs
(Born, 1915, Brooklyn, New York; Died, 2015, Pasadena, California)

For the one who has departed with no regrets and no desire to retrace his steps, the place he has just left has little importance in comparison to the place where he is going.... Like the nomad, he will be at home wherever he goes.

–Vera Linhartova (trans. Tala Hadid)

There is no question but that the Syrian tree planted in American soil will grow and flourish and blossom out into as good fruit as that of any other nationality.

–*Kawkab America*, April 29, 1892

"Many of those more fortunate ones," said a Syrian, "have become lost forever to the Syrians. They have joined Protestant churches and have assumed names like Jones, Smith and Johnson. Their children know more English than Arabic and the next generation will be so thoroughly American that they will not believe that their grandparents came from the Holy Land."

–*New-York Tribune*, March 13, 1898

# Contents

## FIGURES

## MAPS

## ACKNOWLEDGMENTS

This book, although written mostly in solitude, would not have been possible without the help of others. Most importantly, my late mother, her late brother, my late father, and my late grandmother told me the stories that started me on the path to discovering the Syrian Colony in New York. The rest of the family—immediate and extended—and all of the new friends found through my genealogical work helped me fill in the gaps. Helen Samhan, a member of my extended family, deserves special thanks for her generosity with material and knowledge about the past. Gail O'Keefe Edson, a descendant of an important Colony member, provided hospitality and a treasure trove of nineteenth-century artifacts; every Oussani photograph and document that appears in this book belongs to her.

My research assistant, Gina Shedid, who signed on for six months and ended up working on this project for three years, was invaluable, both for her Arabic and for her insights. My other assistants/translators, Rudy Kazan in Beirut and Adham el Kady and Zeina Sayyegh here, helped me cut through the sometimes impenetrable thicket of Arabic newspaper writing.

The former Middle Eastern librarian at New York University, Peter Magierski, assisted me in large ways and small, tracking down obscure sources and getting me access to them. Bobst Library was an invaluable asset in this research. Him Mistry and Krista White did the GIS mapping, and Manuela Garreton designed the maps. Madeleine Adams edited the manuscript with panache and realism.

Liliana Zavaleta and Francisca Toral designed the book—a Chilean dream team.

## A NOTE ON SOURCES AND CITATIONS

The title of this book is taken from Mikhail Rustum's *Al Gharib fi al Gharb* (Stranger in the West), published in New York in 1895.

Newspaper articles are listed only in the footnotes and not repeated in the bibliography. The following abbreviations are used: *NYT* for the *New York Times*, *NYH* for the *New York Herald* and *BDE* for the *Brooklyn Daily Eagle*. The *New York Times* archive online does not include page numbers. The first four years of *Kawkab Amīrkā* (America), 1892–1896, are available online: http://lccn.loc.gov/sn2007058045. The first reel of the microform copy of *Al Hoda*, representing the years 1898–1900 can be found at the Center for Research Libraries, Chicago, and Bibliothèque Orientale, Université St. Joseph, Beirut. One year (July 1899-June 1900) is missing. The New York Public Library holds a complete set of the *Syrian-American Commercial Magazine*, published by Salloum Mokarzel (Issues 1–8, 1918–1926).

The following abbreviations refer to archives of unpublished documents:

*Naff Interview*. The Faris and Yemna Naff Arab-American Collection, held at the Archives Center of the National Museum of American History, Smithsonian Institution, Washington, D.C.

*Archdiocese Letters*. A collection of correspondence to and from Archbishop Michael Augustine Corrigan held at the Archives of the Archdiocese of New York, St. Joseph's Seminary at Dunwoodie, Yonkers, NY.

*Presbyterian Letters*. Collection of letters to the Board of Foreign Missions in New York from the Presbyterian missionaries in Syria, held at the Presbyterian Historical Society, Philadelphia, PA.

*Trials*. Original documents of civil cases involving Syrians, held at the County Clerk's Office, New York and Brooklyn. Microform transcripts of criminal cases (Zreik, Karam, and Tahar), held at the John Jay College of Law Library, New York.

*Oussani Letters*. Letters and documents held by Gail O'Keefe Edson (Joseph Oussani's great- granddaughter), Cape Cod, MA.

All maps and charts are based on data collected by the author. The spreadsheets described in chapter 1 are accessible on Google Docs at the following URL: http://bit.ly/LJacobs. Comments and corrections are welcome.

# STRANGERS IN THE WEST

# INTRODUCTION

The New York Syrian[1] Colony, located during the nineteenth century primarily around Washington Street on the Lower West Side of Manhattan, was thought of by many Syrians as the "Mother Colony." It was the home of many of the most prominent Arab-American intellectuals, the birthplace of almost three dozen Arabic-language newspapers, the locus of Syrian Christian religious practice in the New World, and the center of Syrian economic life in North America. It was also probably the largest agglomeration of Syrians in North America. It was where "it all started," as many second- and third-generation immigrants said, and where a few Arabs continue to live to this day, despite the community's obliteration by the financial district and the construction of the Brooklyn–Battery Tunnel.

It is not entirely accurate to say that the Syrians' American experience started in New York, since Syrians were settling in other parts of the United States at the same time they settled in New York. In fact, if we accept the idea that the family of Yusef Arbeely was the first to come to the United States to stay, we are forced to conclude that the very first Syrian settlement was in Maryville, Tennessee! Most of the Syrian communities around the country were established in the mid-1880s, as was New York's. Although the Port of New York was the most popular landing place, other American ports—Boston, Providence, Philadelphia, and New Orleans—were important points of entry, as were the Canadian and Mexican borders, and most people who came into these other ports went and settled elsewhere. But New York was the place from which much of the intellectual and economic energy of the Syrian diaspora radiated, and Syrians in other parts of the country thought of it as their center, if only because the Arabic newspapers that reached them

[1] I must say a word about the use of the term "Syrian" here. I have been chastised by Lebanese scholars who say that the use of the word will lead to the wrong impression by modern readers—implying that the book is about people from present-day Syria. I cannot change the past. This term may have been imposed on them by outsiders (as Kayal and Kayal 1975 insist), but the terms "Syrian" and the "Syrian Colony" were used quite early by the Colonists themselves (for example, in the first issue of *Kawkab America*), although they also used the terms "sons of Ottomans," "our countrymen," or simply "our people" to refer to themselves. The term "Syrian" continued to be used until the mid-twentieth century by the community, whereas the other terms fell by the wayside. By and large, "Syrian" describes the Colony best, and I use the term unapologetically (and without quotation marks) throughout this book. However, it should be noted that this book also deals with other Arabic-speaking people in New York City; although they comprise a very small percentage of the whole, they are still important to the narrative.

wherever they were living originated in New York and reported on the community there.

New York City was the gateway city for most immigrants from Western and Eastern Europe and the Middle East, and many of them stayed; in 1900 more than one-third of the city's population was foreign born.[2] The Syrians who came to New York in the nineteenth century, however, were true pioneers, especially those who came in the 1880s. There were few forerunners to show them the way; they built their home lives and their businesses by instinct; and they welcomed others who came after them. Their residence pattern followed that of many other immigrant groups: living in a tightly bounded community in their first years, they moved out into other areas once they had made good, although they tended to live together in these new neighborhoods as well. The Brooklyn colonies of the 1910s through 1930s were a product of these first successes, as were, to a certain extent, the communities in other parts of New York, New Jersey, and Connecticut. Their numbers were small enough in the nineteenth century to ensure that they were never fully isolated—at least physically—from other immigrant groups, particularly the Irish. Their language and customs, however, kept them apart. Many of them consciously emphasized and used their "exoticism" to sell goods, to entertain, and to educate the public, and they practiced a certain amount of what Civantos calls "auto-Orientalism."[3] At the same time, and from the very first, there was a drive to assimilate, which was so successful that they are difficult to identify in these days of identity politics.

How did these first visitors (and many thought of themselves as visitors) negotiate the challenges of being in a completely foreign environment? Some of them were products of American Presbyterian missionary schools or British schools in Syria and arrived knowing English and something about America, but many did not. Salloum Mokarzel claimed the immigrants were "destitute" of capital, experience, and any knowledge of English.[4] Not only did they need to learn American ways (language, business practices, social mores), but also most of them were thrown directly from their villages in Mount Lebanon into an intense urban maelstrom. These villages were not isolated; from at least the mid-nineteenth century there was interaction with foreigners, and many villagers traveled to and from Beirut, Tripoli, or Damascus on a regu-

[2] Foner 2008: 52.
[3] Civantos 2006: 128.
[4] Mokarzel 1927: 6.

lar basis. Many of the immigrants had been born or lived in those cities. It is, nevertheless, a testimony to their fortitude, flexibility, inventiveness, and ambition that they adapted as well and as quickly as they did. The New York Colony was not only the center of American Syrians' economic life, but the issues all Syrians faced here—acculturation, assimilation, business practices, preservation of their culture, political choices (both Ottoman and American)—were hotly debated in the newspapers, coffeehouses, and associations on Washington Street. The debates were carried around the country by the peddlers who traveled from one coast to the other and by the Arabic newspapers, which had a wide circulation.

Yet no one has written a definitive history of the New York Colony. When I began researching my family genealogy—all of my grandparents were Syrian immigrants and lived in New York City—I was surprised to find almost nothing written about this community. Many articles and books have treated the general phenomenon of Arab immigration to the United States, with the New York Colony necessarily playing a role in the story; how could it not? Monographs of other Arab-American communities, from Fall River, Massachusetts, to North Dakota, have appeared.[5] Some attention has been paid to Arabs in New York (for example, the 2002 exhibition at the Museum of the City of New York, which dealt mostly with the modern diaspora, the 2011 centennial of the Book of Khalid by Ameen Rihani, and the 2013 "Little Syria" exhibition by the Arab American National Museum in Dearborn, Michigan). But the nineteenth-century Mother Colony has yet to be fully explored or described.

Known as the "Syrian Colony" or the "Syrian Quarter," first by American newspapermen and then by the Syrians themselves, lower Washington Street was not that different from other nineteenth-century tenement neighborhoods; it was crowded, decrepit, dirty, and noisy—and self-contained. Unlike those neighborhoods, however, it was little noticed by New Yorkers. There was no attention paid to the misery there; no crusading photographers like Jacob Riis arrived to take pictures of the slums; and no muckraking articles appeared in the press, much less a book like Riis's *How the Other Half Lives*.[6] Unless there was violence in the neighborhood or a reporter ventured downtown to gawk at this strange "other" ("red-fezzed heads and dark languorous eyes" was a typical headline) the Syrian Colony did not exist for New Yorkers. This paucity of attention is a testimony, I think, to the success and the speed with which the Colonists

[5] For example, Zelditch 1936; Tannous 1943; Boosahda 2003; Sherman et al. 2002.
[6] Riis 1890.

assimilated into American society, despite the fact that they came from a culture quite different from that which they encountered here. Who were these men and women (and children) who traveled five thousand miles from their villages in Syria to settle in the heart of urban America?

I have set out to write a social geography of the nineteenth-century community, looking at individual residents, families, and the community as a whole. It is meant to be descriptive, not theoretical, and quite narrow in scope, concentrating solely on the Arabic-speaking residents of the five boroughs of New York up to and including 1900. Although the focus of the book is the Syrian Colony, it would not do justice to the nineteenth-century city if I did not include other Arab residents. There were very few, but they were a colorful and interesting lot and should be remembered. Those left out of this study who might have been included are other Ottoman subjects, such as the Armenians, who came in greater numbers and earlier than the Syrians and came from many of the same cities, but who, in the main, did not live with them, partner with them, or intermarry. Syrian Jews did not, in general, mix with the Syrians; they lived with their coreligionists on the Lower East Side or far uptown. A few individuals from each of these communities were deeply involved in the Syrian Colony and, therefore, form part of this story.

In addition to these "ethnic" boundaries, I have limited the geographic and temporal boundaries of the study for several reasons. The sheer size and difficulty of the task of reconstructing the Colony militated against a larger focus, although the Syrians in Atlantic City, New Jersey, for example, should by rights be included in this survey; their lives also revolved around Washington Street. A group of about 120 Syrians lived in Dutchess County, New York, employed by the brickyards in Dutchess Junction and Fishkill. Muossa Daoud, who worked in the brickyards when he arrived and became one of the spokesmen of the New York Colony, considered these workers to be New Yorkers, "because if work failed in the brickyard in Dutchess, they would return to New York."[7] Many of them married or had their children baptized here. Only the fact that these Syrians lived in a different city puts them outside the scope of this study; nevertheless, they do appear in our narrative when appropriate.

The 1900 census provided a convenient (if artificial) temporal endpoint for the self-contained Manhattan Colony. Although all businesses remained in Manhattan, one-quarter of the Syrians already lived in Brooklyn in 1900.

[7] "A Syrian Trick," *Cleveland Leader*, June 17, 1894.

The year 1900 can also be seen as the (symbolic) point in the life of the Colony when the Syrians ceased being struggling immigrants, many of whom had come intending to return to Syria, and began to experience success and settle down. Most of those who arrived in the nineteenth century and were still in New York when the twentieth century dawned had made up their minds to stay. Many of the companies established in the nineteenth century continued to exist well into the twentieth. After 1900, there were fewer changes in partnerships and more specialization in business. Of course these were processes which had begun much earlier—in fact, only a few years after the first immigrants arrived—and continued well into the twentieth century, but the year can serve as the tipping point, after which there was no going back. As the twentieth century dawned, the immigrants had become men and women of substance and property—in short, they had become Americans.

Despite the limits imposed on this study, it has been a daunting task to build a database of all the nineteenth-century Syrian Colonists. It would of course have been much more daunting before the Internet, since much of the information is now online. However, nothing can make up for the fact that the 1890 federal census was destroyed in a fire. This is the bane of every modern demographer and genealogist, but for the historian of Syrian immigration, it is nearly fatal, because the decade 1880–1890 saw the beginnings of the first influx of Arabic-speaking people to this country and to New York City. The missing census would have been a crucial bookend to the 1900 census in defining the community as it established itself. Without such a guide, however, it became my mission to reconstruct the Colony by "main strength," one name at a time. It seemed vital that the names of these first Colonists not be forgotten.

My methodology for doing so is described in the first section of chapter 1, and the problems inherent in such a methodology are discussed in the second section. The reader should bear in mind that every number given in this discussion is as close an approximation as could be gleaned from the data; the discussion of the gaps in the data will show that the margin of error can be quite large. Absolute numbers, therefore, should be taken with a large grain of salt. In fact, practically every day I stumble on the name of someone whom I had not known about or a new fact about someone already in the database. By the same token, many names that pop up are ones already in the database, making credible my claim to having uncovered most of the names of the Colonists.

Following the discussion of sources, methodology, and gaps in the data, chapter 2 summarizes existing theories on the reasons why Syrians began their great emigration and then describes what greeted them when they stepped off the boat in New York Harbor. Lower Washington Street, where they settled, was in many ways unique, being at the tip of Manhattan and one block from the Hudson River. Yet it also had many similarities with other immigrant neighborhoods, and those differences and similarities are discussed in chapter 3. There I concentrate on the physical aspects of the neighborhood: what a new resident saw when he or she looked around. Chapter 4 looks at the characteristics of the group: their origins, religion, gender, age, and literacy.

Work, which was the defining aspect of every male Syrian's life, is described in chapters 5 through 9, concentrating particularly on the progress from "peddler to capitalist," the trajectory that is the founding myth of the Syrian Colony. In chapter 5, I describe several world's fairs that took place in the 1890s, the most important of which was the Chicago fair of 1893. These fairs gave the Syrian businessmen who were already here access to a huge market and served as an introduction to the market for those who came from the Middle East.

As is well known, many—but not all—of the immigrants peddled after they arrived, and that occupation is discussed in chapter 6. Both men and women peddled, but women peddlers are discussed in chapter 10. After peddling, most men settled down to trade in goods—either as retailer, wholesaler, manufacturer, or importer. These businesses are described in chapter 7. Chapter 8 treats the small minority of service professionals: doctors, lawyers, pharmacists, and restaurateurs, as well as an important but neglected profession, entertainers. The nineteenth-century Arabic press in New York was vibrant, spawning a half dozen newspapers and several books before the turn of the century. Literary men (and some women) wrote for these publications, and grievances were aired in them as well. These publications circulated throughout the diaspora and in the Ottoman lands, a fact that contributed to the yearly increase in the number of immigrants. Chapter 9 describes this literary world.

Women contributed significantly to the overall economic well-being of the Syrian Colony in the nineteenth century, but much of that work is undocumented, and therefore hidden. The workingwomen we know about represent only a small proportion of the female workforce in the nineteenth century; their lives and professions will be discussed in chapter 10. Chapter 11, on the emerging Brooklyn Colony, will show that the Syrians' early successes led to their moving to Brooklyn in larger numbers and much earlier than had been supposed, even though their businesses remained in Manhattan.

The violence that erupted sporadically in the Colony, both between

Syrians and outsiders and among the Syrians themselves, was covered extensively in American newspapers. Although relatively infrequent, these outbursts took on the coloration of factional discord that residents supposedly brought from the old country, although it is equally plausible that the fighting resulted from the tensions of living in such close quarters in a foreign land. These battles occurred intermittently for more than a decade. Surprisingly, at least to me, is how quickly the Syrians adapted to and took advantage of the American legal system: they often summoned the police to quell disturbances in the Colony, and they took their fellow Syrians and non-Syrians to court with some frequency. They became citizens, registered to vote, and fought in the Spanish-American War. Chapter 12 describes their ways of adapting to the American legal landscape and explores their reputation for being law-abiding citizens.

Chapter 13 describes a nascent civil society in the Syrian Colony, putting to rest the assertion (by Syrians themselves) that Syrians were unable to work cooperatively. In chapter 14, I summarize some of the conflicting forces evident in the Colony—coming and going; success and failure; the conflicts between women and men; assimilation and resistance—and the dramas played out among the residents as they struggled to define their new world and their place in it.

Most of this work is data driven and inductive in the sense that the collection of facts (names, addresses, dates, and so on) drove the conclusions, rather than the reverse. This strategy has its own problems, the most important being the large gaps in the data, discussed in chapter 1.

Despite these caveats, the value of such a study should be evident:

- It is the first study that identifies by name most of the earliest residents of the Colony; any further studies of the Colony, whether in greater depth or through a longer time frame, can use these data as a baseline.
- It provides information about the gender, age, and religious affiliation of the early immigrants, which can help us understand the makeup of the community.
- One can get a sense of the mobility, or lack thereof, of members of the Colony by looking at their residence and business addresses over time.
- The range of occupations within the Colony and over time can tell us whether the businesses were as homogeneous as we were led to believe.
- This research tries to evaluate the myths surrounding the Syrian "immigrant story" by looking at disparities in wealth, economic success and failure, and social striving.

• Relationships between and among Syrians and non-Syrians can be discerned from business partnerships, marriages, club memberships, and conflict.

I would hope and expect that the data I've amassed will be a jumping-off point for further research into each of these families and will be reworked creatively by other scholars better versed than I in the geographic and sociological methods that might be usefully applied to them. Another book remains to be written about the Colony in its heyday—from 1900 to 1945—and in-depth studies of different aspects of Colony life (including religion, political attitudes, intellectual ferment, and the like) all remain to be done. In addition, oral histories should be gathered from the Colonists' descendants, some of whom are still in New York and many of whom have memories and artifacts that would provide material for another book—or two.

Despite the gaps in the data and the limited scope of the project, I trust that this study will be not only a contribution to immigrant and New York history, but also a much-needed antidote to the stereotyping and negative press that Arabs in this country are subjected to now. There was a time when they came to New York in large numbers, learned English quickly, acquired wealth in their own businesses, and turned themselves into true patriotic Americans—all in the span of one generation.

Chapter 1

# Sources

## Methodology

This book is an attempt to reconstruct the New York Syrian Colony from its beginnings in about 1880 through 1900.[1] A few Syrians came in the first five years of the 1880s, but the real influx began in mid-decade. I had two goals: to construct a database of every person who lived in the Colony in the nineteenth century in order to know who the pioneers were, and to describe, as completely as possible, what their life was like. "Lived" is of course a relative term and one that is applied here loosely to anyone who seemed to be a resident in New York in the nineteenth century, no matter for what span of time.

In building the database of individuals who settled in New York in those years, I utilized the following sources (roughly in the order in which I conducted the research):

- The 1900 federal census. The census delineated not only residents' birthplaces, but those of their parents as well. In the case of new immigrants, all three columns were usually identical. We entered the search terms Syria, Turkey (which also brought up Turkey in Asia and Turkey in Europe), Egypt, Palestine, Morocco, Assyria, and Persia, as well as the names of possible origin cities: Damascus, Beirut, Alexandria, Cairo, Tunis, Jerusalem, Tripoli, Aleppo, and Algiers. The place name Lebanon was not used in the 1900 census. Clearly some people would have fallen between the cracks (for example, Arabs who were not identified by any of these origin places), but we believe we have identified the majority of Arabs in the 1900 census.

[1] It should be noted that when I use the term "nineteenth century" in this book, I include the year 1900.

- Other censuses. Given the missing 1890 census, I searched the 1880 census in case there were Arabs in New York that early, using the same criteria mentioned above. Because that census did not distinguish among Syrians, Greeks, Jews, or Armenians from the Ottoman Empire (all being categorized under Turkey), it was difficult to know how many might be hidden. I found only a very few recognizable Arab names in the whole of the United States: the famous Arbeelys living in Maryville, Tennessee (much more will be said about this family later, as they played an important role in the New York Colony, as well as being the "first immigrant Syrian family"); some cavalry soldiers in Providence, Rhode Island; a diplomat from the Ottoman Porte in Washington, DC, (who was in fact Turkish); and a Joseph "Abemader" (Abi Nader) in Philadelphia, probably someone who had stayed after the Philadelphia Centennial fair in 1876. No Syrians were found in New York, even though one or two of our individuals claimed to have immigrated in 1879 and "should" have been in the 1880 census. We also searched the fragmentary 1890 Police Census for Manhattan, the very spotty 1892 census, which includes some parts of Brooklyn and Queens, and the 1905 census for Manhattan and Brooklyn. When a person who we knew was a member of the nineteenth-century Colony did not appear on any of these censuses, we looked at later censuses—1910 and 1920—to collect information such as birthdates and arrival dates (those facts that did not change through time).
- Arabic newspapers. We read every pre-1900 issue of the earliest Arabic-language newspaper published in New York, *Kawkab America* (Star of America), which began publication in 1892. The issues of the first four years survive (and are now online), but none of the later issues. We recorded every individual's name mentioned in connection with New York (whether in articles or advertisements) and any other relevant data about the person, thus building a preliminary database of pre-1900 census names and addresses. Since most early Syrian businesses were named for their owners, we could add these names and addresses to the list of individuals we were compiling. The earliest issues of *Al Hoda* (The Guidance, 1898–1900), although first published in Philadelphia, contributed a significant number of New York names and other information. As I don't read Arabic, I had an assistant who helped me read these.

- Passport and naturalization applications. We looked at every one that included the word Syria, Turkey, Egypt, Palestine, or Morocco on it and added those names, addresses, and occupations to the list, along with the date of the document. We searched applications dated as late as 1905, since most of these people arrived in the nineteenth century. Their dates of arrival and dates of birth are, at best, approximations (most people did not know their birth dates and could not remember their arrival dates) and, at worst, lies. But we recorded them as given, knowing that these would at least be approximately accurate and might be confirmed or refuted by other sources. These documents gave us information not only about the individual who filed the application, but also about other Syrians living in New York at the same time since one other person, usually a fellow Syrian, witnessed each document. We added the witness's name, address, and occupation to the list, along with the date of the document. These documents are available on ancestry.com and fold3.com.
- American newspapers, not only in New York, but countrywide. We used search terms such as Syrian, the names of Colonists, and occasionally events. We added names that appeared in the articles, despite the fact that American reporters regularly mangled them. As we added more names to our list from other sources, we were often able to go back and identify those in the American newspaper articles. As in most newspapers, however, negative articles far outnumbered positive ones, and that means that the people mentioned were often marginal in the Colony and not represented in other sources. Newspaper articles, despite their bias, put "meat on the bones" of the data we collected (providing concrete dates for events, for example, or eyewitness accounts—however biased—of the Colony). Taken collectively, they gave one a sense of how Americans viewed the Colony. Most of these newspapers are online at various sites such as Fultonhistory.com, Genealogy Bank, and the Chronicling America site at the Library of Congress.
- Arrival announcements and ship manifests. The Arabic newspaper *Kawkab America* published the names of Syrians arriving at the Port of New York in a few of its early issues, but soon gave up the practice; perhaps there were just too many to list. The newspaper also had a regular feature called "Coming and Going," which would mention the arrival or departure of businessmen (and sometimes their

families). We also looked at ships' manifests to search for names of early arrivals. These records are available at ancestry.com and ellisisland.org. As a source for names of members of the Colony, these lists are problematic because one is never certain whether the people who arrived in New York actually settled here. Even though some were asked their intended destination when they landed—and many said New York—we cannot be sure they stayed. For these individuals, settlement in New York had to be confirmed by at least one other piece of evidence; otherwise they were not included. New York friends or relatives who were used as references in some of the manifests, whether or not the passengers themselves settled here, were New York residents, and their names (and, occasionally, addresses) were added to the list.

- Vital Records and Archives. With a preliminary list thus built, we merged the names from all of the above-mentioned sources with the 1900 census. The merged list became the basis on which we searched for the names (and their variants) in New York birth, marriage, and death records in the Municipal Archives of New York City. Indexes of these records are online at www.italiangen.org, but copies of the actual certificates are available only at the archives themselves. I also searched for Syrian names in the files of the County Clerk's offices in Brooklyn and Manhattan, looking for matrimonial and legal disputes. These few records not only gave us information about these important events—so crucial to understanding the lives of the nineteenth-century Syrians—but also sometimes provided new names (for example, of witnesses, parents, or defendants) and addresses of Colonists. These documents are not online. Transcripts of some criminal trials are on microfilm at John Jay College of Law; these provided a wealth of information.
- City directories and other documents. We took each name (and all its known variants) and searched for any mention of the name in any other documents at ancestry.com, fold3.com, and FamilySearch.org. These searches often produced entries in early city directories, which gave business names and addresses and/or residence addresses, and sometimes these sources provided copies of important original records (for example, naturalization papers) that had not turned up in our original search.
- Name sweep. We entered "typical" Arab names (and their variants) in all these databases that might uncover new people (for example, Abdallah, Labiba, Malake, Salim, Iskandar, Khalil, Mohammed, Tannous).

- Family genealogies. I constructed basic genealogies for about thirty families of the Colony, including my own, following them not only in the nineteenth century but also, if possible, through the death of the patriarch or matriarch. These give a sense of how the lives of the nineteenth-century residents unfolded, adding a retrospective understanding to the events of their lives previously. Because of the endogamous nature of the community, many of these genealogies overlap. In the course of this research, I collected family stories and photographs from my family and from the descendants of some of the other families in the database.
- Church records. Our Lady of Lebanon Maronite Church in Brooklyn had baptismal records going back to 1897, when St. Joseph's Maronite Church was in Manhattan. Its wedding registry, however, included only four marriages prior to 1901. St. Nicholas Orthodox Cathedral, also in Brooklyn, had a fire and had moved twice before settling in its present location, so had no early records.[2] Nor did the Antiochian Archdiocese in Englewood, New Jersey, or the Antiochian Museum in Bolivar, Pennsylvania. The Melkite Church of the Virgin Mary in Brooklyn gave me access to an English translation of its earliest baptisms and weddings, going back to 1890. It is an incomplete translation and the original in Arabic has been lost, but it added many names to our list and helped, as well, to identify the Melkites in the community.
- Googling a name occasionally led us to obscure citations about a person, such as court cases, real estate transactions, college graduations, patent applications, and so forth. These were rare, although in the course of writing this book, much more became available through this means than there had been earlier.
- Serendipity. In searching for names on the list, we sometimes happened upon other names nearby that were Arabic (for example, in early city directories that listed dry goods dealers).

The results of this search produced three separate spreadsheets under the collective title, *The Syrian Colony in New York City, 1880-1900*: 1)*Arabs Who Lived in New York*, 2)*Arabs in the 1900 Census*, and 3)*Source Data*. The first is a list of every identified member of the Colony (along with the few other

[2] Father Thomas Zein, personal communication (hereafter, p.c.).

New York Arabs) with his or her family ties and other vital data that would not have changed through time. This list provides a "snapshot" of each family as it existed in 1900 or before. The census spreadsheet is self-explanatory: every presumed Arab name unearthed in the 1900 census was transcribed with all its accompanying data. The Source Data spreadsheet contains the raw data attached to each name, including newspaper articles, city directory entries, baptisms, and the like. There are multiple entries for each name in this spreadsheet because each piece of information was treated as a separate entry. Many bits of data were redundant (or outside our time and space parameters) but were included because they helped confirm the accuracy of the information. Some told us nothing except that the person was present in New York on a certain date, but each entry helped build a diachronic picture of the resident's life.[3]

On these three spreadsheets, we have some or all of the following information for each resident through time:

- Name. Names of members of the Colony, including first and last name, and maiden names of many of the married women.
- Family Relationships. We traced sibling relationships by the middle name or initial, which was usually the first name of their father: thus we know that Nahoum Daher Merhige and Solomon Daher Merhige were brothers. A woman sometimes used her father's first name as a middle name, changing her middle name to her husband's first name when she married. My grandmother, Katherine George Milkie, became Katherine Frederick Jabara when she married. This identifies the father-daughter and husband-wife relationships in some cases. We included children who were born in the Colony in the nineteenth century, but not those born after. We could sometimes identify more distant relationships as well, such as in-laws and cousins.
- Address. It is difficult to tease out the residents' home addresses, especially in the early years of the Colony, when people often lived and worked in the same building, or even the same room. A much more detailed description of these housing arrangements will be given in chapter 3, but suffice it to say that a person's business and residence were in most cases the same. It was only as people became successful that they began to separate workplace and home. The census gave only home addresses, and city directories usually gave only the business address.

[3] These spreadsheets are accessible on Google Docs at the following URL: http://bit.ly/LJacobs.

Occasionally the city directories gave both addresses, specifying which was a home and which was a business address. Passport applications required a mailing address, and again it was impossible to know whether these were home or business addresses (or neither: some applicants gave the address of a friend, lawyer, or nearby business). They moved frequently; we have several entries for each individual as he or she changed residences over the twenty years of the study.

- Gender.
- Marital status and year of marriage.
- Birthdate.
- Hometown.
- Date of immigration.
- Immigration status—whether alien, naturalized, or native (born here). If naturalized, the year of naturalization.
- Occupation, business sector, and name and address of business.[4]
- Religion.
- Date of death.
- Source and date of information.

## Problems and Gaps in the Data

### *Names*

Much collating and correcting needed to be done to rationalize the wild variation in spelling of names. The problems of transcription and transliteration of names are familiar to anyone who has worked in fields involving Arabic. Every immigrant gave her or his name as well as he or she could to a ship's purser or immigration authority. None of the authorities understood Arabic, and they would have had no clue how to transliterate the sounds they were hearing. The immigrants, for their part, could not articulate their names for an American ear. This meant that for the Syrians, as for other immigrants, names were changed arbitrarily or written down as they were heard, and what was written might have no relation to the actual transliteration. In addition, once the Syrians became literate in English and started their own businesses,

[4] I use the term "occupation" to signify the role one played in business and the term "sector" for the field in which the person worked. Thus an occupation is storeowner; the sector is groceries.

they spelled their names as they saw fit, and they often Anglicized them as well. We have in our database, for example, Coory, Coury, Khouri, Khoury, Koory, Kouri, Elcouri, el-Khoury, and Kahoori. If we encountered the name in Arabic, we had to decide which transliteration to use. If we had two or more spellings for the same person or family, we used one spelling for the whole family—the one that appeared most often. But if two different families spelled their names consistently differently, we left them as they were spelled. For first names, too, we have many variants (for example Khalil, Kaleel, Kalil, Calil, Kali, and Charles). First names were more often Anglicized than last names. If we had variant names for the same person, we changed them to the one used most often or latest. To add to the confusion, some of the Syrians, particularly the Maronites, used French spelling for their names. Tannous Sadallah was called Thomas, Antoine, and Antonio in various documents. In business documents, he was known as "A.J." American newspapers spelled names in ways that made it difficult to recognize them at all, much less correlate them with names we had.

Another issue, and one more rarely recognized, was the tendency of the Syrians to use their father's first name as their last name, coming of course directly out of the tradition of calling someone Yusef ibn (son of) Ya'oub or Katherine bint George. When it is used as a middle name it is useful for us because it identifies the person's father. But when used as a last name it can be confusing. We see this occurring on marriage documents, for example, where the bride's name is given as Farideh Moses, and her father's name as Moses Salibi. There's no difficulty in this case, since we know the father's name, but what about the times when we don't? Men also did this, using their father's first name as a last name on early documents and then, perhaps when they learned the custom in the United States, changing their name to their father's last name later.[5] All of those Syrians with last names such as Joseph, Michael, Simon, and Gabriel are those who never changed back. My paternal grandfather claimed (as did thousands of immigrants) that his name, unbeknownst to him, had been changed at Castle Garden from Yusef ibn Ya'oub Maroun to Joseph Jacobs. It's possible, and perhaps even likely, that he came up with the name himself, which the ship's purser or the immigration officer transcribed, perhaps adding the "s" at the end.

Baptismal names, which were given to Maronite and Melkite children, were often taken as their names henceforward, or were used interchangeably with their given names.

[5] Julee Milham 2012: p.c.

Louis Farshee's family, which he describes in his memoir, presents an almost comical case in which different members of his close family adopted three different surnames as well as innumerable given names, sometimes changing their names in adulthood.[6]

## *Numbers*

The problems and gaps in the data used in determining the number of individuals in New York are myriad. As mentioned earlier, the 1890 federal census was destroyed by fire. A copy of the 1890 Police Census of Manhattan is lodged at the Municipal Archives in New York. Unfortunately, about half of the census of the First Ward (where the Syrian Colony was located) is missing. In the parts we do have, the information given for each resident is minimal: name, gender, address, and (approximate) age. No nationality or ethnicity is given. Because the census taker's rendering of a name often made it indecipherable, we had to guess whether someone was an Arab; this guess was based on the similarity of first or last name to an Arab name, presence of other Arabs in the building, and the address. Sometimes, after we had constructed a list of names from other sources, we were able to go back and identify Arabs whom we hadn't recognized as Arabs the first time around. We have identified only 91 (probable) Syrians in the 1890 census; we have addresses for an additional six from other documents, and documentary evidence (but no addresses) for another fifty: a total of 147 documented residents in 1890. We know that this number is too low, since there are a number of individuals who were in New York immediately before and after 1890 and must have been here in 1890, but we simply don't have a document for that particular year, so they don't show up on our 1890 list or on the 1890 map (see chapter 3). No 1895 census exists for Manhattan so the map for Syrian residences for that year is based solely on other documentation and is, therefore, underpopulated. We can assume a steady increase in the number of Syrians every year.

Syrians were distinguished from other citizens of the Ottoman Empire for the first time in the 1900 federal census, making their identification much easier. As mentioned, each census taker noted their place of birth as he or she thought appropriate: by the old designation, "Turkey in Asia" or "Turkey," the new designation, "Syria," or numerous other possibilities, such as Assyria,

[6] Farshee 2010.

Arabia, city names, and so forth. A small number of duplications within the census were also noted: two entire families were listed twice, and a number of individuals were listed in two cities. The most common duplication occurred with children who were listed in orphanages and at home. Since the names were fluidly transcribed and our bias was not to eliminate names if there was any possibility that they represented different people, there are probably duplications we did not find. But the most salient error is not duplication but the opposite: people missing from the census.

The Immigration Commission *Report* of 1901 states that "the immigration of Syrians commenced to attain significance about 10 years ago, and has grown steadily until at the present time there, are probably 25,000 of these people in the United States, of whom 6,000 claim a residence in greater New York."[7] We do not know what was meant by "greater New York," but assume it was what we now call the five boroughs. If that is the case, this estimate is wildly overblown. Note the use of the words "probably" and "claim"; they were not sure of their numbers. Estimates by the American press also were wildly divergent. An 1893 article estimated the New York population at 1,000.[8] In an 1896 article in the *New York Press,* an otherwise relatively well-informed piece, the reporter gives the number of Syrians in the Quarter as "nearly 5,000."[9] This number was repeated in an article in the *New-York Tribune* in 1898.[10]

The estimates of their numbers by the Syrians themselves also varied widely. In 1898, for example, on the occasion of the establishment of the Syrian-American Club, the founders stated unequivocally that there were "7,000 Syrians in the City of New York and about 200,000 in the U.S."[11] It was of course sometimes advantageous to exaggerate their numbers. In most cases, New York Syrians estimated their population to be around 1,000, which according to our data is much more accurate.[12] For all of the nineteenth century, from 1880 to 1900 inclusive, we have a total of about 3,130 individuals resident in New York for some period of time, which means that the total number of Syrians living in the Colony at any one time probably never exceeded 1,500. In the early years, there were considerably fewer.

---

[7] Industrial Commission on Immigration 1901: 442.

[8] "Oriental New York," *The* (NY) *Press,* January 8, 1893.

[9] "Thousands Inhabit the Turkish Quarter, But Not a Single Turk," *New York Press,* December 27, 1896.

[10] "New-York's Syrian Colony," *New-York Tribune,* March 13, 1898.

[11] *New York Times* (hereafter, *NYT*), February 6, 1898.

[12] See for example, "The New Syrian Society Has a School," *Brooklyn Daily Eagle* (heareafter *BDE), May* 3, 1892, where Ameen Haddad estimates the number of Syrians in New York as 1,000, and the February 24, 1893, issue of *Kawkab America,* which gives the same number.

In the 1900 census, we were able to identify 1,229 Arab residents in the (present-day) five boroughs of New York: 878 (71.4 percent) in Manhattan, 323 (26.3 percent) in Brooklyn, and the remaining 28 individuals scattered in the Bronx (10), Staten Island (10), and Queens (8). We use the word "Arab" because a few of the people identified were North Africans rather than Syrians; they are included because they form an interesting, if minor, part of our story. Some of those we have classified as Syrians may not be Syrians at all: there are people in the census who were born in Turkey or Syria but who have names that may or may not be Arabic; they may be missionaries or other nationalities from the Ottoman Empire; we have tried to eliminate these names. The total number of Syrians we've found in the census, however, may be even smaller than stated.

How does that number compare to Lucius Hopkins Miller's door-to-door survey of the New York Syrian communities conducted three years later?[13] He estimated a total population of 2,482 Syrians, of whom 1,891 (76 percent) were "actually seen" (Miller's phrase).[14] Another 91 were "located," and the rest were "missed" or "out of city." The 1900 census was taken in June 1900 when, as every summer, a large number of the Syrian community had left the city to peddle, thus reducing the number in the Colony. Indeed, documents attest to an additional 303 Syrians who were not in the census but who we know were living in New York in 1900, a margin of error close to 20 percent, a percentage close to Miller's "missed" residents. If we add 24 percent (the number missed in Miller's survey) to our census number, we would get a total of about 1,524 residents in 1900. The difference between his estimated total and ours is still very large (2,482 vs. 1,524).

How might we explain this discrepancy? We do not know the margin of error in the censuses of this period, but we do know that in our case, the census had myriad errors: duplicated names, incomplete addresses, and missing at least one building in which we know Syrians were living: Number 71 Washington Street. But census error cannot explain a 25 percent increase between 1900 and 1903.

The most obvious explanation is that we missed a significant number of people, a problem that has already been alluded to in our discussion of the lacunae in the data. A second possibility is that there was a large influx of Arabic-speaking immigrants in the years between 1900 and 1903. Although

[13] Miller 1903 has been a point of reference for every part of this study.

[14] Miller 1903: 6.

a 1902 article in the *New York Times* stated, "Within the last couple of years, the Syrian immigration through ports of the United States has dwindled until it amounts comparatively to nothing, and the Syrians who do get into the country are now slipping in through Canada,"[15] in fact, more than 8,000 Syrians landed in New York between 1900 and 1902, 3,267 of whom gave New York as their final destination.[16] We don't know how many of these people actually stayed in New York, but less than a third of them would be needed to make up the difference between Miller's count and ours.

Although we have identified more than 3,200 individuals who were in New York sometime in the last two decades of the nineteenth century, only about 1,500 were living there in 1900, probably more than had lived in New York at any time previously. What happened to the other 1,700 people? The disappearance of these people may indicate that the story told about the early immigrants was true, that they came to make a "quick buck" and then went back to Syria. Certainly the story that the immigrants told was of a longing to return: "The eyes and hearts of the elders are fixed on Lebanon, and while some adopt American ways and customs with American citizenship, the great majority are birds of passage."[17]

As Khater notes, we do not know how many emigrants ultimately returned to Syria. In a long discussion with mostly anecdotal evidence, he concludes, "Perilously extrapolating from these numbers, we reach a rate of return of about 45 percent."[18] Based on Ottoman sources, Karpat estimates that about one-third of the immigrants returned home. He also cites a Syrian publisher in Marseilles who was paid to provide the Ottoman government with information about the comings and goings of the Syrians, who also estimated that one-third had returned.[19] One of the express purposes of the Syrian Ladies' Aid Society, founded in 1907, was to provide funds to those Syrians who wanted to return home but couldn't pay their passage, so there must have been a need. After five years, however, the Society reported that it had assisted a total of eighty-five returnees,[20] an average of seventeen per year—a very small percentage of those who had come. Whether this small number reflected a lack of funds or a lack of demand is not made clear.

[15] "Crowding Ellis Island," *NYT*, April 13, 1902.

[16] Miller 1903: 4.

[17] "Turkish Life in New York," *The* (NY) *Evening Telegram*, September 5, 1903.

[18] Khater 2001: ch. 5.

[19] Karpat 1985: 185.

[20] Letter from the Syrian Ladies' Aid Society to Commissioner Williams, reproduced in Felton 1912: 22–23.

In 1926, the magazine *The Syrian World* published a table taken from the pages of the Beirut newspaper *Lisan al Hal*, which gave the number of Syrian émigrés from the Ottoman Empire and the number of returnees for the previous four and a half years. The percentage of returnees was very high—between 54 percent and 60 percent.[21] Of course these numbers were based on the total number of people who had obtained exit papers and all those who entered the country, whether or not they planned to stay or were simply visiting. From our point of view, the number of returnees is huge; from the Ottoman point of view, the *population* was decreasing alarmingly, with a net loss of many thousands of persons every year.

We do have some anecdotal information about members of the New York Colony returning to Syria for good, but this information concerns only those prominent enough in the community to warrant notice. David Biskinty, who went back to Syria for health reasons, never returned, leaving his brother Constantine in charge of their store. George Abdoo Coudsy, who came with his wife in 1892, partnered with Alexander Andalaft to do business at the Chicago fair (they won a bronze medal for the quality of their goods). After the close of the fair, the partners came back to New York and continued in business, setting up a store on West 23rd Street, an unusual choice of location. In August 1895, Coudsy and his wife returned to Syria for good (cheered off by the newspaper, *Kawkab America*), presumably with a sizable nest egg.

Immigrating in 1891 (not in steerage, but in second class), Moussa Zalka immediately set up shop as "M. Zalka & Co." at 66 Trinity Place, importing Oriental goods; he was a partner with his brother Elias, who remained in Syria. He then took goods to the Columbian Exposition. When he returned, he opened a store at 29 Broadway and in 1898 announced that he had gone into partnership with Selim Marrash, remaining in the Oriental goods business at 29 Broadway. He had no relatives here—perhaps his immediate family stayed in Syria—and he was never naturalized. After 1901, we have no record of him anywhere in the United States; it seems he went home.

The older brother of Ghattas Faris, who arrived in the nineties and then brought his brother over, went back to Syria before the turn of the century and stayed. According to the *Syrian-American Commercial Magazine*, Beshara Ganim's father immigrated in 1887 from Baskinta. After Beshara joined him, the father returned to Syria and did not return to the United States,

[21] *The Syrian World*, November, 1926: 57.

leaving Beshara his dry goods business. Doumit Abu Sama'an, after setting up a business with George Ishie, left for Syria in about 1898 and never returned. Adele Younis mentions that Thomas Abalan was inspired to come to New York after Mansour Sharbel returned to Baskinta from New York.[22] Wadie Macsoud, Saleem Macsoud's son, immigrated in 1899 and lived in New York for a short time, but ended up in Tacoma, Washington, the owner of a dry goods store. In 1924, he returned to Zahleh with his wife and son and died there in 1940. But these examples barely scratch the surface of an assumed 30–40 percent return of immigrants. If a sizable percentage of peddlers returned home after a few years, with or without their fortune made, we know nothing about them.

James Ansara cites a Syrian toast, which was common, he says, among the early immigrants: "May your return home be soon," to which the response was, "In your company."[23]

There was an inherent contradiction in the settlers' expressed desire to return to their homeland. On the one hand, if they were successful in the United States, they might be loath to leave their businesses to return to Syria. On the other hand, many must have felt that if they did not go back with a fortune, it would have been humiliating; they therefore stayed on, trying to make that fortune, and ended up not going back. In addition, those who didn't make it might not have been able to pay their passage home and were thus stuck in the United States or forced to apply to an aid society to obtain the passage home.

The immigrants who went home for a visit talked about the many people they met who had been to America and returned home for good.[24] One imagines that a higher proportion of the earliest immigrants returned permanently as they must have suffered more than did the later immigrants from loneliness, isolation, and homesickness. Even though the absolute number of returnees may have been small in those years, they caused a huge ripple effect, inspiring hundreds and then thousands to follow in their footsteps to America. Nineteenth-century immigrants told of people coming back to the village, showing the $1,000 they had earned in their two years' peddling, and firing up other villagers. Younis quotes an 1893 letter from a Protestant missionary who described the back-and-forth movement of immigrants: "The Sheikh of

[22] Younis 1995: 128.
[23] Ansara 1931: 50.
[24] For example, in Al Akl 1945.

this village [Hadath] has been to the United States five times."[25] This must have often been the case; and how does one distinguish a visit home from a protracted sojourn (to use the Immigration Commission's language)?

Morris Zelditch, in his 1936 thesis on the Syrians of Pittsburgh, interviewed the patriarch or matriarch of each of the ten pioneer families there; all had arrived in Pittsburgh in the nineteenth century. One man in Zelditch's study described going back to his village with $10,000 in his pocket in 1889 (surely an exaggeration, as he had been peddling for only two years). He planned to stay home. But his family and friends were so struck by his fortune that they persuaded him to accompany them back to America. Three brothers and fifteen friends moved to Pittsburgh with him in 1890; none ever returned to Syria.[26] Of Zelditch's ten interviewees, only one went back to Syria to stay; his son later brought him back to the United States. Two others went back to Syria intending to stay, but found themselves dissatisfied with the life in Syria and returned to the United States. Two more went back to find wives. The others never made it back at all. Zelditch emphasized the fact, however, that all had intended to go back or said they had intended to go back. Unfortunately, he did not ask about people who might have gone back and stayed.

There were, then, at least four levels of interaction with the home country: those who came to the United States as "birds of passage" and returned with whatever capital they had managed to accumulate; those who went back and forth, spending a couple of years making money peddling in the United States and then returning to the home country repeatedly to build their houses; those who definitely settled in the United States, became citizens, and kept in touch by letters or visits to their hometowns; and those who cut all ties. That there was a net loss of population in Mount Lebanon in these years does not obviate the fact that all of these forces were in play.

Did any of the women who came over alone ever go back for good? This is a question that as far as I know has never been studied. In the cases that we know about of women coming alone to New York, none went back. They sent for their families, married here, and settled down, or lived with their relatives until their deaths. Again, the paucity of information about women (and the complete absence of information on any women who might have gone back to Syria after a stint of peddling) makes any conclusion suspect. A study of

[25] Younis 1995: 135.
[26] Zelditch 1936: 66.

the returnees, though labor-intensive, would be a valuable contribution to immigrant studies.

Another confounding problem in gathering accurate numbers (a bane in all historical research) is that those who stayed here but didn't "make it" are as invisible as those who left, because they leave little or no documentary evidence. They were not business owners so were rarely listed in city directories. They traveled less than the wealthy or not at all, so did not apply for passports, and since they didn't need passports, they did not often apply for naturalization. They were rarely involved in lawsuits. They appear only in catchall documents such as the census, church records, or birth, death, and marriage certificates, which are, as we will see, dismally incomplete where it comes to the Syrians. Only deep family research will uncover the presence of these men and women.

One shorthand way of getting at this issue is to look at the number of records attached to each of the more than 3,200 names in our database. Obviously, their presence in the list at all means that they were mentioned in at least one document, while many others must be completely absent. Of these 3,200 names, only about 600 have more than one data entry, meaning that more than 80 percent of the individuals may have come and gone or been low-profile (unsuccessful?) enough to have had almost nothing written about them. Some of them appear in post-1900 documents (which we have not yet thoroughly studied), so not all of these absences are revealing, but the large percentage of single entries is striking. Of course a number of these single-entry individuals are women and children about whom the data are by definition minimal.

A woman was naturalized by virtue of her husband's or father's naturalization so did not fill out forms. By the same token, women did not often travel alone so did not apply for passports on their own. Men made up the majority of business owners and were listed in city directories; women's names rarely appear. Of the 408 New York business owners or professionals in the 1909 *Syrian Business Directory*, for example, only seven were women. Women were mentioned in birth, death, marriage, and divorce documents. The witness or attendant of the bride or godmother of the baptized child could be added to the list. Women were also listed in ship manifests, but as I said, it is impossible to know without corroborating evidence if these passengers stayed in New York or moved on elsewhere. Women are only occasionally mentioned in newspaper articles about the Colony.

To get an idea whether our dataset is missing women in large numbers, we looked at a sample of 755 Syrian immigrants in a group of 1892 ships' manifests; of those whose gender was given, 31.1 percent were females. The Immigration Commission reported that 38 percent of all Syrian immigrants who arrived between 1895 and 1899 were females.[27] In our overall pre-1900 data (1880–1899), 36.5 percent are women and girls, with females making up more of the population in the later years than the earlier ones. In the 1900 census, 44 percent were female. As a further comparison, of the 1,891 individuals "actually seen" by Miller, 869 (45.9 percent) were women.[28] These numbers indicate that in fact we do seem to have tracked down most of the women, although the jump from our pre-1900 percentage and that of the census is a large one and probably misleading. The increasing proportion of women through time is a reflection of the fact that women were arriving in greater numbers as the original immigrants got settled and were ready to start families or bring their existing families over. We unfortunately do not have enough data to do a year-by-year analysis of the female population of the Colony; a more finely tuned analysis of Colony women will follow in chapters 2, 4, 10, and 13.

As far as children are concerned, all of the same limitations in the sources pertain as they do to the women. Children were naturalized by virtue of their fathers' naturalizations, and many were born here, making them citizens by right. Birth certificates in the municipal archives, represent only a fraction of the births that took place in New York. The baptismal records are spotty. Children of course didn't appear in business directories or apply for passports. The only places they appear are in ship manifests, the census, and birth, baptismal, and death records.

### Dates

As mentioned earlier, dates of birth and dates of immigration are also problematic. People lied about both if they thought it would help them obtain naturalization papers or a passport, or for other more obscure reasons. They may simply not have known their date of birth or forgotten the date of their arrival since decades may have separated their arrival from the application for naturalization. Rather than admit ignorance, many would arbitrarily choose

[27] Industrial Commission on Immigration 1901: 303.
[28] Miller 1903: 46.

a day, month, or year. Particularly obvious were the months and dates they chose in order to fill in the blanks of a naturalization application: the fourth of July showed up often, as did the 15th of a month which fell in the more or less correct season of their birth or arrival. Some were honest and admitted they didn't know or remember. Michael Shadid, an immigrant from Jdeideh Marjayoun, who became a well-known doctor and the founder of the first cooperative hospital in Oklahoma, spelled out this confusion very well: "There was as little regard for vital statistics as for sanitation in Judeidet, and since my mother could neither read nor write, there was no record of the year of my birth. Later, when I had to give a definite date, I arbitrarily chose January 1, 1882, for my mother, to whom the seasons rather than the calendar were a guide, had told me that I was born during the winter and that I was eleven years old when we moved to Beirut in 1893."[29] His guess was more accurate than most.

There are of course sources other than an immigrant's memory, which, when taken with the immigrant's statements, can provide some assurance of the accuracy of a date. If one can find his or her name on a ship manifest on a date that generally fits with the date the immigrant has provided, one has an incontrovertible piece of evidence. But because the immigrants' memories were usually faulty both as to the date they arrived and the name of the ship, it is close to impossible to find the correct manifest, except by luck.[30] The dates given in the census are often the only ones we have; they are of course also problematic because the residents themselves provided them to the census taker. Sometimes newspaper articles mentioned the age of a person or the number of years he or she had been in the United States, but the reporter got those figures from the person him- or herself. Occasionally a reporter would say that a person gave his age as nineteen, although to the reporter he looked thirty, which is disconcerting. Newspaper articles about Colony events are invaluable, because they were usually written a day or two after the event took place, and are not in that sense subject to debate. Nevertheless, the day, month, and even the year of any life event have to be approached with skepticism.

[29] Shadid 1939: 18–19.

[30] Searching for the name in the ship manifest on the Ellis Island database is difficult, because the Ellis Island documents are poorly indexed.

Chapter 2

# Syrian Immigration to New York

*A Talk with Syrian Beggars* (1882)
*Syrian Impostor to Be Sent Home* (1883)
*Arabs Unwilling to Go Home* (1884)
*A Parabolic Pilgrimage* (1885)
*A Few More Paupers* (1887)
*Not Wanted as Citizens* (1887)
*Arabs Not Wanted* (1888)
*Syrians Must Go Back* (1889)
*Arabs to Be Returned* (1889)
*Forty-two Syrians Detained* (1889)
*More Arab Immigrants* (1889)
*A Motley Crew of Arabs, Armenians, and Syrians* (1891)
*Troubles at Ellis Island* (1897)
*Syrian Peddlers Deported* (1897)[1]

## Why They Came

There are many theories regarding why the Syrians left Syria and came to the United States at this time—usually divided into push and pull theories. First among the "push" theories is one that is commonly retailed in our families: that the Christian Syrians wanted to get away from the oppression of their Muslim overlords, the Ottoman Turks. Yusef Arbeely, the "first" Syrian immigrant, gave this reason when he was interviewed on arrival, and his eldest son, Abraham, echoed him by saying, "Well you see we are Christians…and we were subjected to great persecution at the hands of the Turks."[2] Abraham even

[1] Headlines from various newspapers regarding the reception of Syrian immigrants at New York.
[2] (St. Louis, MO) *Globe-Democrat*, July 22, 1880. A transcription of the entire article can be found here: http://orthodoxhistory.org/2009/11/30/the-first-syrians-in-america/.

added that they had escaped the Ottoman lands by applying for permission to go to the Paris World's Fair of 1889 and then sailing from there to New York.[3] Zelditch cites such stories from several of his sources, one of whom was one hundred years old in 1934.[4] My paternal grandfather told his children that he had to leave Syria because he killed an Ottoman official who had tried to arrest him. Many immigrants talked about the Ottoman tax collector coming around to tax the Christians into penury. Others cited the Druse-Maronite wars of the 1860s and the wholesale slaughter of the Christians of Mount Lebanon. Syrian women who went out on the lecture circuit talked about their oppression at the hands of the "Turk."

Although these stories may have been true, it is also true that Syrians quickly learned that such a story played well to Americans, who were only too eager to think the worst of the Ottoman Turks. "Official Ottoman documents suggest that claiming religious intolerance or oppression was a favored ploy of illegal emigrants seeking legal admission to the United States."[5]

Economic hardship was another push. For example, the silk industry, for which hundreds of farmers gave up subsistence farming in order to take advantage of the boom market in silk, was devastated first by a disease that killed off many of the silkworms, and later by falling prices caused by the increasing availability of cheap Asian silk. In 1881, a newspaper predicted, "the culture of silk will finally be abandoned in that country altogether."[6] Afif Tannus poignantly described the ruined silk mills that he observed in his native village of Bishmezzine when he returned in 1938 to research his dissertation.[7] The five family-run mills that had been built in the late nineteenth century had been abandoned one generation later.

The sectarian conflict in 1860 forced many Christians to flee Mount Lebanon. Some went to Cairo, Beirut, Alexandria, or Damascus, settling down and starting businesses in these cities, which later became jumping-off points for those who came to the United States. The long period of peace that followed this conflict was a mixed blessing since peace, along with better health and a high birth rate, brought the population of Mount Lebanon to a point where the land could not sustain it.[8]

[3] "Syrian Immigration," *The* (NY) *Evening Telegram,* August 19, 1880 (citing a July 19, 1880, article in the *Kansas City Times).*

[4] Zelditch 1936: 8.

[5] Ipek and Caglayan 2008: 32.

[6] "Syrian Hope," *Philadelphia Inquirer,* August 23, 1881.

[7] Tannus 1940.

[8] Khater 2001: ch. 3.

Apparently much more compelling were the "pull" factors toward emigration: primarily the promise of making one's fortune in America. The presence of American missionaries in many areas of Mount Lebanon in the nineteenth century gave peasants—both boys and girls—their first taste of American values, language, and culture. In 1890, there were 117 Presbyterian village schools alone, with a total enrollment of 5,200 pupils, of whom almost 1,800 were girls.[9] Three seminaries (high schools) for girls, in Beirut, Sidon, and Tripoli, and a number of seminaries and academies for boys, in Abeih, Suq el Gharb, Sidon, and Beirut, were established in the mid-nineteenth century to continue the children's educations. And finally, the Syrian Protestant College (now the American University of Beirut) educated many young Syrian men who later came to the United States.[10] In teaching English and modeling American values and behavior, the teachers encouraged the children to think well of America. Michael Shadid mentions the presence of three elementary schools in his small village in 1882: Greek Orthodox, Roman Catholic, and Protestant, the last of which was considered heretical by many of the villagers.[11]

Many accounts describe agents of steamship companies traveling in Mount Lebanon luring people to foreign parts, but the American missionaries played a large part in the exodus as well. Although they lamented the "thirst for American gold," which in their view was a "disease" that struck all classes of Syrians,[12] the missionaries had taught the students all they knew about America and even paid for their schooling. Now the students were leaving in droves, abandoning the mission and all it stood for to pursue crass lucre. Those who stayed were equally "unsettled," demanding raises and striking if they were refused. The departures were "instances of the grossest ingratitude," and they happened over and over again; the best and the brightest were leaving. One can hear in the missionaries' angry prose the hurt feelings as these ungrateful "children" rebelled against their "parents" and went their own way. Yet the missionaries themselves were the proximate cause of this exodus.

Other pulls, such as the American democratic political system and the lure of living in a Christian country, may have influenced some people, but

[9] Women's Foreign Missionary Society for the Presbyterian Church 1891: 311.
[10] Women's Foreign Missionary Society for the Presbyterian Church 1891: 312–313.
[11] Shadid 1939: 20.
[12] *Presbyterian Letters,* Harris to Ellinwood, September 25, 1893.

these attractions, as Hatab points out, were probably limited to the educated elite among the immigrants.[13] Khater concluded, "Each emigrant had an individual tale of the events that led him or her out of the village and onto roads to foreign lands."[14]

Until 1896, the Ottoman government officially prohibited emigration, but the prohibition was widely ignored both because Ottoman officials apparently were easy to bribe, and because they made scant effort to enforce the law. Emigration prevention was a problem with which the government grappled as they watched Mount Lebanon become depopulated. They refused to issue passports for foreign ports, but they continued to issue permits for travel within the Empire, albeit in increasingly limited numbers. Foreign steamship companies, travel agents, and others in Beirut would board Syrians onto ships supposedly headed for some port within the Empire, and then continue on to Europe. Soon the government got wind of this scheme and forbade foreign shipping companies to dock in Beirut, which simply meant that the ships anchored in international waters and Syrian passengers were brought out on small craft. Passengers who came from Lebanon or Egypt were able to obtain Ottoman passports at the consulates in Marseilles or Barcelona; the Ottomans, in response, increased their fees in an effort to slow the flood of emigrants. That the travel ban did not work is attested by the fact that as early as 1893, Ottoman consular reports estimated the number of Ottomans living in the Americas at 200,000.[15] In 1896/97, the travel ban was abolished, in part because the government realized that the remittances from Syrian emigrants bolstered the Ottoman economy.[16] One condition that led to conflicts between the government and the diaspora was the government's requirement that emigrants retain Ottoman citizenship. When Syrians who had become American citizens returned home, they were treated ipso facto as Ottoman subjects by the government, while the emigrants expected to be under the protection of the American consulate. This led to many diplomatic incidents.

[13] Hatab 1975: 46.
[14] Khater 2001: 52.
[15] Karpat 1985: 184.
[16] Karpat 1985: 189.

## On Arriving

Although Younis did stellar research in showing that Arabs had been coming to this country as early as the American Civil War,[17] the first true Syrian immigration occurred when, after a thirty-two-day journey, Yusef Arbeely and his large family arrived at the Port of New York on August 23, 1878.[18] A reporter from the *New York Herald* was on hand when they disembarked. "They assert," he wrote, "that a large number of families in Syria are anxious to emigrate to this country, and will do so if they [the Arbeelys] succeed in getting on well here."[19] It is fortunate that the first Syrian family spoke English, and interesting that Arbeely and the reporter were fully aware that he was a pioneer and catalyst for the forthcoming immigration. Two days after their arrival, they took out their naturalization papers.[20]

Two weeks later, however, the same newspaper claimed that Arbeely had deceived the public: all the while he had been "piteously" appealing to the public for work, he actually had "$1,200 on deposit at the Howard Savings Institution at Newark, besides some Turkish and Roumelian railway bonds."[21] Was this revelation an expression of relief that he would not become a public charge, or was it an allusion to his duplicity? In any case, the accusation makes little sense. How had Arbeely managed to deposit money in a New Jersey bank, when he apparently had not yet left Manhattan? Did he really have $1,200 when he arrived? And why on earth would he own, much less bring, "Roumelian railway bonds" with him? The Arbeelys left New York on September 11 with the alleged assistance of the Emigration Commission, which contributed half the expense for their transport in order to encourage them to leave New York.[22] Again, why would they need assistance if they had $1,200 in a bank in New Jersey?

One can already glimpse in these early articles the beginnings of impatience with these new immigrants, as well as the often nonsensical reporting.

[17] Younis (1995) makes clear that Syrians had been coming to the United States for many years, and their presence at the 1876 Centennial Exposition in Philadelphia is well documented. Syrians had been in the United States even earlier of course; see, for example, the article in the October 19, 1859, issue of the *Morning Courier and New-York Enquirer,* which mentions that a member of the Ethnological Society recommends a young Syrian in New York, Naseef Jimmal, as a teacher of Arabic. However, the Arbeelys seem to have the distinction of being the first Syrian *family* to immigrate.

[18] "Syrian Emigrants," *New York Herald* (hereafter, *NYH*), August 23, 1878.

[19] "Syrian Emigrants," *NYH,* August 23, 1878.

[20] "City and Suburban News," *NYT,* August 25, 1878.

[21] "Not So Very Poor," *NYH*, September 8, 1878.

[22] "Departure of the Syrian Family," *NYH,* September 11, 1878.

The Americans' goodwill did not last even a month. There was such a contrast, it seemed, between the Syrians of the Orientalists' imagination and the real thing!

The Arbeelys went to Maryville, Tennessee, of all places. Yusef claimed that he had written to the governors of seven states, asking for information in regard to business conditions.[23] It's hard to imagine that he received replies from any of these august men, but it was a different time, so perhaps he did. However he found the place (perhaps through one of the missionaries in Beirut with whom he was on friendly terms), the job that Yusef took up—teaching Arabic at the Christian Maryville College—was very far removed from "business." He was a learned man in both English and Arabic and had taught at the Greek Patriarchal College in Damascus before heading the Patriarchal College in Beirut. He reportedly assisted Cornelius Van Dyke in translating the Bible into Arabic. His two older sons were graduates of the Syrian Protestant College, but all continued their studies here.

In Yusef's very first interview in New York, he told the reporter that he wanted his children educated in American schools and married to American women, both of which they succeeded in doing. All of his sons became professionals (two were doctors, two were dentists, and two were lawyers), and two of them married "American" (non-Syrian) women named Mary (also the name of the sons' mother). Two of his sons—Abraham and Nageeb—played an important role in the New York Colony, where they founded the first Arabic-language newspaper; they will be described more fully in later chapters. Jamilie, the niece who traveled with them from Beirut, married Yusef's third son; they settled down in Atlanta, Georgia.

After his wife died in 1880, Yusef moved his family to Monrovia, California, perhaps in response to a call for missionaries issued by the Presbyterian Church.[24] In the 1880s and 1890s, he was a well-known lecturer, taking one or two of his sons around the country to give talks about and demonstrations of "Life in the Holy Land." He wrote a delightful essay (in English) for an early issue of his sons' newspaper, comparing an exciting and pleasurable trip on the Santa Fe Railroad from California to Chicago to a journey by camel from Damascus to Baghdad, in which he exclaimed, "How different the

[23] "The Syrian Colony in New York an Interesting Element There," *Springfield* (MA) *Republican,* March 26, 1899.

[24] The classic family portrait, which appears in every book on Syrian immigration, includes an empty chair in memory of his recently deceased wife.

Palace Car from the ship of the desert!"[25] A lifelong learner, Yusef attended dental school in Atlanta with his son Habeeb, both earning their degrees the same year. His obituary also claims he took degrees in medicine, law, and theology here,[26] which is hard to credit, but perhaps possible. He became an American booster, praising the people, the political system, and everything about America to anyone who would listen. He died in Glendora, California, in 1894 at the age of 73.

2-1. A group of immigrants, probably from Egypt, at Ellis Island, ca. 1905 (Photography Collection, Miriam and Ira D. Wallach Division of Art, Prints and Photographs, The New York Public Library, Astor, Lenox and Tilden Foundations).

Yusef had told reporters that he planned to write letters back to the people he knew at home, encouraging them to come to the United States. Whether he did so or whether these letters were a catalyst for Syrian immigration is doubtful; in fact, we have no evidence that his coming had any influence at all on the forthcoming flood. In all the references to "immigration fever" in the letters of American missionaries in Syria, for example, the Arbeelys are never mentioned. In a sense, their moving to Tennessee removed them from view, and it was not until Yusef's sons moved to New York and started a newspaper that they became influential in the Syrian diaspora.

[25] *Kawkab America* (English), April 29, 1892.
[26] *Kawkab America,* August 24, 1894.

According to our data, Syrian immigration did not start in earnest until the mid-1880s; we have evidence for only twelve people who settled in New York between 1880 and 1885. Whether the earliest immigrants returned home, as many said, and left no documentary evidence, or whether the data are faulty is unclear. Karpat gives a tantalizing hint that there were more early immigrants in New York than we have information about: "As early as 1880, it was calculated [by the Ottoman government] that each Syrian in New York saved about $50 a month."[27] The fact that the government was already counting the earnings and/or remittances of people in New York implies that there was a significant number there. There may be some ambiguity in Karpat's (or the Ottoman consul's) use of the word "Syrian," and the comment may actually refer to earlier immigrants from the Ottoman Empire, such as Armenians or Greeks. The first mention of emigration as an issue in the Protestant missionaries' correspondence was in 1885, but this was concerned with emigration to Egypt. It was not until 1892 that American fever struck, at least as far as the missionaries were concerned. In the summary data for the foreign-born immigrants in New York in the 1890 census, no Syrians (or Turks, Greeks, or Armenians) are named.[28] Some of them were no doubt included in the "all others" category—about 1.5 percent of the foreign-born immigrants—but if so, their numbers were tiny.

In those early years, Americans regarded the new arrivals with both fascination and horror. The newspapers played an important role in stirring up American fear and loathing of these newcomers, while adoring (and exploiting) their exoticism. Early newspaper stories described them as indigent beggars who threatened to become a burden on American society. The immigration authorities were constantly threatening to send them back and often did so.

Under the innocuous heading of "Political Jottings," a squib printed in the *Boston Journal* in 1888 encapsulates this attitude of fear and loathing: "Last Sunday thirty Syrian Arabs were landed at Castle Garden. This makes about 3,000 of these people who have thus far come in. Most of them are devoted to one of two industries—thieving and begging. It is time the bars were put up."[29]

And the bars were put up. The Ford Committee of 1889 proposed to Congress that undesirables be turned back. An undesirable was defined as

[27] Karpat 1985: 192.
[28] http://tenant.net/Community/LES/clag1.html.
[29] *Boston Journal*, February 23, 1888.

anyone who "is an idiot, insane, a pauper, or liable to become a public charge, or who has been legally convicted of a felony, other infamous crime, or misdemeanor involving moral turpitude, or who is a polygamist, anarchist or socialist, or who is afflicted with any loathsome disease, or who has entered into contract, express or implied, oral or written, to perform labor or service... or whose passage is paid on a promise to labor."[30] These restrictions were used to deny entry to those who failed any one of these tests.

An unnamed source at the Barge Office described a vast conspiracy involving merchants on Washington Street and the immigrants coming from the East. The New York merchants had representatives in Syria arranging passage for would-be émigrés, and getting money from them on the installment plan. Contradicting himself, the source stated, "We are convinced that some of the Syrians are sent for and their passage money paid by the merchants who employ them." Which was it? Did the immigrant pay or the merchant? Finally, when they reached America, a woman often obtained "an immigration husband" and a man "an immigration wife."[31] A story titled "Four Husbands Failed to Pass" described the attempts by a Syrian woman and her fifteen-year-old daughter to present four different men as husband and father. None passed muster, even after she presented a marriage certificate for the fourth one; it seems that the certificate had other names on it and had been used before. She and the girl were detained at the Barge Office.[32]

Until 1890, immigrants were processed at Castle Garden, then for one and a half years at the Barge Office at the southeastern end of Battery Park, and then finally, from 1892, at Ellis Island (except for an interval of two and a half years, from 1897 to 1900, when the Barge Office was again used after the building on Ellis Island burned down). The "processing" assessed the immigrants based on the criteria listed above. If one can believe the newspaper reports, these restrictive laws were used to reject a significant number of the Syrian arrivals, and the Syrians in America saw this as a huge problem. Naoum Mokarzel, in one of his earliest editorials in his newspaper *Al Hoda* (The Guidance), urged Syrian newspapers to stop encouraging emigration, as the immigrants would likely be turned back on arrival.[33] A poignant article reprinted from the *New York Sun* called the immigration officials who

30 "Putting Up Extra Bars," *BDE*, January 20, 1889.

31 "Come to Be Peddlers," *Daily* (Springfield) *Illinois State Journal*, January 9, 1898.

32 "Four Husbands Failed to Pass," *The New York Press*, June 16, 1898.

33 *Al Hoda*, March 14, 1898.

decided on the immigrants' fate "understudies to St. Peter," who must have had trouble sleeping at night. The article described the pen in which the debarred were held while they awaited their ship back; they were kept in ignorance of their fate so they would not panic or revolt. They must have known they were being sent back, however, since they watched other immigrants leave freely. When they arrived at the pier to board their return ship, the reporter continued, there was "swearing, and pleading, and lamentation in Yiddish, Polish, Italian, Syrian…there is wild sobbing in the international code of distress. There is resistance, sometimes even downright rebellion."[34]

Taking each of the disallowing criteria in turn, we will give examples of how each was used against the Syrian immigrant.

### *Likelihood of Becoming a Public Charge*

The most common reason for deportation was having too little money; authorities feared that the immigrant might become dependent on the state. Most of the deportations—and indeed most of the articles about the newly arrived immigrants—focused on their poverty. Many Americans equated peddling with begging, and, therefore, any immigrant who came with the stated intention of peddling was considered a pauper. It was not until much later that the entrepreneurship and energy required for peddling were recognized as virtues.

The immigrants were almost invariably described as poverty-stricken, dirty, and slothful. Yet there was some ambivalence even in the newspapers about whether this was, in fact, the case. It seems that some of them did come with money—or with goods to sell, which amounted to the same thing. Sometimes this fact was reported in the newspapers but, as always, the negative characterizations far outweighed the positive.

The first documented instance of sending Syrians back for the reason of poverty occurred in 1882. A *New York Times* reporter, who evidently spoke Arabic, approached a group of "Syrian beggars" who had just arrived at Castle Garden. Their names were Elias, Selim, and Khairallah—no last names given. All were said to be unskilled and penniless, and Khairallah was blind as well. When the reporter asked how they were going to get along, Elias, the spokesmen, said that they would ask people to help "the poor blind man." They were Catholics and wore several small crosses on their persons. The three seemed

[34] "Home of Despair," *Grand Rapids* (MI) *Press,* February 15, 1900.

to be in limbo, neither being allowed to leave Castle Garden nor being sent back.[35] A few days later, it was reported that the three, "Mense Salim, Elias Faddoux, and Kherallas Faddoux, the Syrian beggars who came here professedly on the part of a poverty stricken church at Mount Lebanon, have been sent back to Europe by the Commissioners of Emigration to prevent them becoming a burden upon the city."[36] This was also one of the earliest instances of a peddler claiming he was collecting money for a church or Christian school at home, or was trying to earn enough to pay his fees at such schools. Thus, deceit became part of a number of distasteful characteristics attributed to these foreigners. It is undoubtedly true, as attested in Syrian as well as American articles, that Syrians sometimes did use this ploy to sell goods. We will see examples of this ruse in subsequent chapters.

An 1885 article titled "A Parabolic Pilgrimage" described the "holding of noses" in the vicinity of Castle Garden when a group of six Syrians landed, saying that they had come to trade. They had a few beads but no money. When asked how they would survive, they said, "The Lord would provide." But the reporter surmised that the authorities would send them back since they obviously had no wish to add the Syrian tramps to all the other able-bodied men who begged in the city. "The Lebanon tough might just as well save his passage money and do his begging on his native heath. He can't beg here."[37] The names of the six young men are difficult to read on the ship manifest, but they boarded together at Liverpool so may have been friends. Were they sent back?

New immigrants were often referred to as "mendicants" to call up images of poverty, wandering, begging, and lying. Sometimes violence was added to the characterization: one article reported that, "It took a Roundsman and ten patrolmen to conduct sixteen poor Syrians from Castle Garden to the Rotterdam."[38] Unsurprisingly, they didn't want to be sent back.

"Twenty-four Syrians, whose unwashed condition was their mark of genuineness, were among the steerage passengers of the steamship Rotterdam, which came in from Rotterdam yesterday. They had no money and no friends in this country. Some of them had been here before, and they piloted the others through Castle Garden."[39] Each of the men of this group swore he was the master of some trade and had anywhere between $50 and $100 in his

[35] "A Talk with Three Syrian Beggars," *NYT,* July 7, 1882.
[36] "City News Items," *NYH,* July 11, 1882.
[37] "A Parabolic Pilgrimage," *NYH,* August 15, 1885.
[38] "Gotham Gossip," *Times-Picayune* (New Orleans, LA), June 24, 1887.
[39] "A Few More Paupers," *NYH,* December 27, 1887.

possession, but when asked to show the money, the immigrants refused, afraid it would be confiscated. Four Syrian businessmen then appeared with "pockets full of gold coins" to post bond for the Syrians. The four men—Beshara Safi, Antonio Saadi, Mansour Sharbel, and a man puzzlingly called Elwyne—said they would furnish bonds in the amount of $27,000.[40] The amount seems incredible since this suggests that a bond of $1,000 per person was required. The article alludes to the craftiness of the immigrants ("they had been here before, and they piloted the others"), which was a recurring theme in newspaper articles about the Syrians. Their fate is not known.

The same week, the *Chateau Léoville* brought seventy Syrians to New York from Bordeaux; forty-two were held as paupers and were to be sent back. The *New York Evening Telegram* sent a reporter to Castle Garden, where the immigrants were being held until the return voyage of the *Léoville.* Although the reporter called them a "motley group," a customs officer was quoted as saying, "The statements made about these people are entirely wrong. They are as clean as you could wish. Every mother's son and daughter of them, babies included, washed this morning.... They are all able to work. What they have for sale are trinkets, beads, plants, earth, &c., from the Holy Land."[41] Nageeb Arbeely, Yusef's son, acted as interpreter for this group, and perhaps he was the customs officer who gave the reporter such a positive assessment of the immigrants. He told a second reporter, "These people have no right to be sent back, as they are perfectly able to sustain themselves." He went on, "They are decidedly a more industrious class than many of the emigrants that are allowed to land in this country and I think that if Collector Magone insists on sending them back he will have cause to repent it."[42]

The group was finally allowed to land when a lawyer presented to the Collector a written guarantee accompanied by a $15,000 bond to ensure they would not become public charges.[43] Fifteen thousand dollars! Again, that seems excessive and perhaps a figment of the reporter's imagination. It is fascinating that as early as 1888, Syrians were using the law to fight back. Clearly someone already here hired the lawyer, perhaps one of the wealthy men mentioned above. Why would these men go to so much trouble and expense if they didn't see the new immigrants as an investment?

---

[40] "Those Detained Syrians," *NYH,* December 31, 1887.

[41] "The Syrian Arabs," *The* (NY) *Evening Telegram,* December 28, 1887.

[42] "The Syrians Must Go Back," *The* (NY) *Weekly Press,* December 29, 1887.

[43] "The Syrians to Remain," *NYH,* January 1, 1888.

The answer to that question may lie in an article that appeared a week later. "That batch of forty-two Arab immigrants brought from Bordeaux on the Chateau Léoville turned up yesterday as a continued source of trouble and annoyance to the Castle Garden authorities." It was actually a story of them being cheated by John Abd-el-Nour[44] and his henchman Beshara Safi (the same man who came to the "rescue" of those immigrants who arrived on the *Rotterdam,* mentioned earlier). Safi, at whose hotel the Bordeaux immigrants were staying, allegedly swindled them out of $300 by telling them that they would each have to pay two Napoleons (about $4.00) for their release from confinement at Ellis Island.[45] But no sympathy was extended to the poor immigrants; they were simply blamed for being an annoyance to the authorities because they protested their treatment at the hands of Abd-el-Nour. If Safi and Abd-el-Nour had paid for the lawyer and put up the bond for the immigrants, the immigrants did owe them something. "The fact that Abd-el-Nour, the manufacturer of holy earth and relics, which the Arabs were imported to peddle, gave a bond for them, convinced the authorities that they were imported simply as Abd-el-Nour's henchmen,"[46] or contract laborers.

These two incidents involving the immigrants on the *Rotterdam* and the *Chateau Léoville* point up the ambiguity of the role of the merchants of the Colony vis-à-vis the new immigrants. Since the incidents took place in the same week and both involved Beshara Safi, perhaps Abd-el-Nour and the others were sponsoring the whole lot (twenty-four on the *Rotterdam* and forty-two on the *Chateau Léoville*). Were they using the same pockets of gold to guarantee both groups? Were these men (Safi and the rest) saviors or swindlers? Were they rescuing the poor immigrants or indenturing them?

Thirty-five Arabs, including fourteen women and children, were sent back on the *Leerdam* in January 1888.[47] The newspaper reports that they were distraught, tearing their hair and beating their breasts. John Abd-el-Nour weighed in once again, this time declaring, "I consider the treatment these poor people have received nothing short of barbarous. Why, despotic Turkey herself would not abuse a stranger who visited her shores in this manner. Since their incarceration at the Garden on Monday not one of their relatives or friends in this city has been permitted to see them. What is the complaint

[44] His name is often spelled Abdelnour in the American press, but he mostly used the hyphenated form.

[45] "Those Syrians Again," *NYH,* January 8, 1888.

[46] "Backsheesh Extorted from Them," *The* (NY) *Sun,* January 8, 1888.

[47] "The Arabs Must Go," *NYH,* January 14, 1888.

against these people? Not that they are paupers, but that they peddle."[48] He claimed that not one Syrian had ever been arrested in this country, nor had they ever become public charges. "While the criminal and pauper dregs of Europe are given the freedom of these shores without question, these sober, honest, industrious and law abiding folks find the door slammed in their faces."[49] In 1889, twenty-eight Arabs from Mount Lebanon were returned as well, "as it is thought that there are about all the peddlers in this country that are needed at present."[50]

Another early article reported that twenty one Arabs and Armenians, who had been ordered to return on the *Leerdam* to Rotterdam, fought back. Deeb Lutfy, the son of New York merchant Abdow Lutfy, filed a writ of habeas corpus with the Supreme Court of the City of New York requiring the Emigration Commissioner and Collector to show cause why they should not be allowed to stay.[51] In it, he named seventeen Syrians and an Armenian family, asserting forcefully that they had broken no laws and were not paupers.[52] He filed the writ on the day the *Leerdam* was scheduled to sail, and a special hearing was set for February 25 at "10½ A.M.," two days later. The outcome of the hearing, if it indeed took place, is not known. Although several of the travelers eventually did settle in New York, none gave 1889 as their immigration date, and one can surmise that they were sent back as scheduled, some of them repeating the voyage two or three years later.

That same year, the Immigration Commission detained forty-two of forty-eight Syrians. As usual, the newspaper referred to their stock as "cheap trinkets and jewelry," which they intended to peddle. "Their poverty and nomadic intentions seem likely to reduce them to the condition of paupers."[53] These Syrians, too, fought back. Joining with others who had been debarred, they (or someone) hired a lawyer to fight their deportation. Several resident Syrians (including Said Jureidini) attested to the fact that they were able bodied and that there was plenty of work for them.[54] Judge Lacombe of the United States Circuit Court ordered that the Board of Commissioners reexamine the case.

---

[48] "The Pilgrims from Lebanon", *The* (NY) *Press*, January 14, 1888.
[49] "The Pilgrims from Lebanon", *The* (NY) *Press*, January 14, 1888.
[50] "Arabs to Be Returned,"*NYH,* August 24, 1889.
[51] Although Lutfy signed it, the document was actually written by one Jacob Meyer.
[52] *Trials,* Geha, George v. Superintendent of Emigration et al., February 23, 1889: WR B-1781; "The Arabs Are Still Here," *NYH,* February 24, 1889.
[53] *NYT*, August 23, 1889.
[54] "The Syrian Immigrants Apply for a Writ of Habeas Corpus," *Times-Picayune* (New Orleans, LA), August 30, 1889.

One week later, perhaps as a result of the lawyer's work, the *Times* did a complete about-face with regard to these same detainees. A reporter wrote, "These immigrants are, in reality, among the most thrifty and profitable to the country who arrive here."[55] It was reported that one of them, Hammon Mukkaddem, had letters of reference from two prominent Englishmen in Beirut. At least twenty-five of the forty-two were allowed to land, and Mukkaddem became a fixture on the American lecture circuit. But this was a rare admission by an American newspaper that some of the Syrians at least might not be destitute or undesirable. Only three weeks later, the *Brooklyn Daily Eagle* complained that ten more Syrians had landed and that "they were in a filthy and dirty state and apparently entirely destitute."[56]

In order to prevent immigrants from becoming a charge on the public purse, each was supposed to have sufficient means to support him or herself and/or give the name of someone as a reference. Most of these references were legitimate; it was usually a relative or friend who would, in theory if not in fact, take responsibility for the new immigrant. Many people, however, would give the name of someone they did not actually know, someone whose name had been passed on through the grapevine. Often the passenger would offer a nameless "friend" accompanied by an address on Washington Street, or give the name of a boardinghouse owner[57] whom they didn't know but had heard about. Muossa[58] Daoud, a merchant and boardinghouse owner from Zahleh, was one of those names; one sees his name recurring regularly in ships' manifests. Using his name was a safe bet, as he was unlikely to admit that he didn't know the person; after all, every traveler was a potential customer both for his boardinghouse and his dry goods business. He also served as a kind of godfather to new immigrants; Abraham Rihbany describes Daoud finding him his first job as a clerk.[59] Not everyone was as eager to support the new immigrants as Daoud; other "references" given to the immigration officials disclaimed acquaintance with an immigrant once the heat of the immigration office was turned on the reference. Elias Reesha, a dry goods merchant, did decline acquaintance with the sixteen Syrians who came in 1888. Most of these small deceptions by the immigrants were not caught (because who of

[55] "Allowed to Land," *NYT,* September 1, 1889.

[56] "More Arab Immigrants," *BDE*, September 20, 1889.

[57] "Owner" is used figuratively, as none of these men actually owned the building. They probably rented a building or several floors of a tenement and rented rooms to fellow Syrians.

[58] His name most often appears with this spelling, but Moussa was also used.

[59] Rihbany 1914: 208.

the immigration officials had the time to check on each immigrant's reference?), but sometimes one was unlucky.

During this period, the Immigration-Restriction League (IRL), whose name makes its aim evident, tried to make literacy a condition for admission. The League contended that illiterate immigrants were undesirable, and that they tended to settle disproportionately in urban areas, which meant that New York was unfairly burdened with them. The IRL examined a very small group of new immigrants in 1895 (there were only thirty-nine Syrians in a group of 1,000 immigrants examined) and found that the Syrians had a higher rate of illiteracy than other "races."[60] Whether this was illiteracy in Arabic or English was not mentioned. Based on these findings, the IRL tried and failed three times to get a literacy requirement passed (in 1896, 1897, and 1913); the Republican Senator Charles Fairbanks, Chairman of the Immigration Committee, delivered an address to the Senate supporting the effort in 1898.[61] The purpose of the proposed legislation was made clear: "It would tell most heavily against those classes of immigrants who now furnish the paupers, diseased, and criminals excluded by the existing law, and is therefore a continuance of the present policy."[62] The labor unions, of course, also supported it. It was not until 1917, however, that a literacy test was finally passed (over President Wilson's veto). The real root of the argument was of course race anxiety: the alarm caused by the increasing percentage of immigrants from Central and Eastern Europe at the supposed expense of those from Northern Europe. To his credit, a *Times* reporter was skeptical of the League's recommendations and felt that an immigrant's fitness for citizenship should be decided in the courts, not "from the steerage of the steamships."[63]

In 1900, the Immigration Commission itself put forth the IRL argument. It reported that 56.4 percent of the arriving Syrian immigrants fourteen years and older were illiterate; only the Turks and the Portuguese had higher rates of illiteracy.[64] Again, they made no mention of whether this was illiteracy in Arabic or English. The Immigration Commission claimed that immigrants from "southern" countries had a higher rate of illiteracy than those from the

[60] Report of the [Senate] Committee on Immigration, March 25, 1897: 7–9.

[61] "Immigration: Fairbanks of Indiana Makes a Strong Talk in the Senate," *The Daily Chronicle* (Spokane, WA), January 11, 1898.

[62] Report of the [Senate] Committee on Immigration, June 4, 1902.

[63] "Where the Immigrants Go," *NYT*, January 27, 1896: 72.

[64] Note that by 1900 "Turks" and "Syrians" were distinguished from each other in the census; previously they had not been.

north (meaning, of course, the north of Europe), and they then aggregated the data to prove that "Asiatics," including Syrians, had the highest rates of illiteracy of all.[65]

Due to previous failures to pass a literacy bill, the Commission went a step further than the IRL, claiming there was a close correlation between illiteracy and poverty among immigrants, thus cleverly eliding the literacy argument into the existing criterion for debarment: the likelihood of an immigrant becoming a public charge. In the case of the Syrians (whose illiteracy rate was supposedly so high), however, the amount of money in their possession was reported to average $14.31, which was actually the median amount for all "races," thus undermining the very correlation they were trying to establish. If the "experts" who compiled these data for the Commission were not in the employ of the IRL, they should have been.

These data suggest that the Syrian immigrants were not as poor as the press depicted them to be. Khater computed the amount of money an emigrant in 1911 would have had to spend to get to the United States, estimating that an average immigrant would have paid about $30 to reach his destination, a huge sum for a farmer from Mount Lebanon. And even with such expenditure, the average Syrian arrived in America with $31.85; this is twice the per capita wealth of new arrivals cited ten years earlier ($14.31).[66] According to Khater, then, the total amount an immigrant would have had in 1910 was about $80. Such an amount was equivalent, he says, to a year's tuition at an elite private school in Lebanon.[67]

In an attempt to weed out the poor, and to counter those Syrian merchants bringing their gold down to Ellis Island, the Emigration Commission began demanding that steamship companies ask the traveler how much money he or she was carrying, in addition to asking who had paid their fare. The column heading on a 1902 ship's manifest read, "Whether in possession of money, if so whether more than $30 and how much if $30 or less." There was no minimum amount that an immigrant had to show (until 1909, when the number was set at $25), so what the $30 figure meant in practice is a mystery. It was really up to the inspector at Ellis Island to determine how much

[65] Industrial Commission on Immigration 1901: 282.

[66] Khater 2001: 56. He took this number from the 1911 Industrial Commission on Immigration *Report* (Dillingham 1911), which explains the discrepancy between his number and that of the Industrial Commission on Immigration's 1901 *Report*.

[67] Khater 2001: 56.

was "enough."[68] In one example, a group of 57 Syrian passengers on the *Graf Wildensee* in 1902 averaged a respectable $11 per person. One merchant, George Nehmi, who was carrying $220, skewed this average. If he is removed from the equation, the Syrians averaged only $7.78 per person, much less than the $30 apparently called for. The odd thing about this particular case is that every amount of money was an even number: four, six, eight, or more dollars. Did people pass the same (two-dollar?) bills from one to another? Or were they in fact, as the officer said, prefunded by people in New York for whom they were to work? We don't know. There were certainly some occasions when merchants would surreptitiously provide checks or money to immigrants at the Barge Office, and there were apparently agents in Marseilles who would hand over funds, which were to be returned after the immigrant cleared Immigration. An unnamed Syrian, accompanied by a lawyer, gave checks for twenty-five dollars each to three immigrants whom he recognized as cousins of his employer. They were still deported, but each went home twenty-five dollars richer.[69]

Notwithstanding the common perception of Syrians coming penniless to this country and peddling goods taken on credit (which of course happened in many cases), many newspaper articles attested to the fact that some Syrians arrived with money and/or goods. Despite the fact that the immigrants looked like paupers to the New York press (who wouldn't, after more than two weeks in steerage?), it is well to remember that the majority of immigrants were not from the poorest classes but a step or two above.

### *Contract Labor*

The new U.S. ship manifest form adopted in 1893 asked two questions aimed at stemming the practice of immigrants who came over under contract to merchants in the United States. One asked, "Whether under Contract, express or implied to labor in the United States." And the second, "By whom was passage paid?" To the first question they always answered, "No," if they knew what was good for them, and to the second they answered, "self," or a relative back home, knowing full well they could not give the name of someone in New York.

[68] http://www.powayusd.com/online/usonline/worddoc/ellisislandsite.htm.
[69] "Three Lucky Immigrants," *NYT*, December 31, 1899.

The prohibition against contract labor was primarily aimed at Italian immigrants who, according to the Immigration Service, were brought over essentially indentured to their padrones. Such an arrangement was illegal and, when discovered, led to the deportation of the immigrant. Of course if a Syrian immigrant's way was paid by someone in the United States and he was expected to peddle that man's goods, it may have looked like contract labor to the officials. Since the new immigrant then owed the merchant the money for passage, probably money for lodging and food and for the goods he was given on credit, the immigrant was essentially indentured to the merchant. The emigration authorities imagined an organized syndicate centered in New York that controlled the movements of goods and peddlers all over the country, a very different proposition. It was not an accident that the authorities used the Italian word "padrone" for the Syrian merchant.

An 1889 article titled "Syrians Must Go Back" described the fate of sixteen Syrians (two of them women). Some of the sixteen apparently had come as contract labor for a dry goods merchant (Elias Reesha) in New York, for whom they were to work, presumably as peddlers. As he declined acquaintance with them, they were sent back.

Another case involved eight Syrians who were "detained on suspicion of being contract laborers. They made their escape today while General O'Beirne was arranging to have them photographed."[70] Their destination was Brooklyn. Several other examples appeared in the press of new immigrants who were destined for the silk mills of New Jersey or the brickyards of Fishkill, New York. Their fate went unreported.

John Abd-el-Nour was accused of violating the contract labor law when he "imported" thirty-two Arabs who landed in Philadelphia on the SS *Pennsylvania.* In fact a man claiming to be his brother, Ounas (Ohanes/Wanees) Abd-el-Nour, was the only person to say his passage had been paid by Abd-el-Nour, but the whole group was detained.[71] A second man on the ship, Michael Lattof (Lutfy?), was also caught in the net. His brother-in-law, Joseph Nohra of 19 Morris Street, New York City, said, "I paid the passage of my brother-in-law, and I do not know why he does not come right on here."[72] An article originating in the *San Francisco Chronicle*, but reprinted in several newspapers around the United States, referred to these immigrants as "Syrian

[70] "Immigrants Landed," *Philadelphia Inquirer,* June 10, 1890.
[71] "Must be Sued in New York," *Philadelphia Inquirer,* July 25, 1890.
[72] "Thirty-two Syrians Detained," *The World* (NY), July 24, 1890.

Chattels," and subtitled the article, "Oriental Serfs Who Are Really in Bondage to Padrones in This Country."[73]

The *Omaha World Herald* added an unusual wrinkle to this story of Syrian padrones by claiming that the Syrian system differed from that of the Italians in that Syrian merchants contracted with a large number of women. They were said to work for less than men and be less likely to strike out on their own.[74]

Testimony to the Industrial Commission on Immigration, presumably given by immigration officers, included a discussion of this issue: "As I said, it is very suspicious that large numbers of this class [Syrians] arrive here with a stated amount of American gold, and I think it is established beyond doubt that these people are controlled by a centralized body of notion peddlers, with general headquarters here in New York, and with branches all over the United States, and that these people are representatives of some branch of this padrone traffic."[75] We have seen that the amounts of money immigrants had were, in fact, suspicious, being all even numbers of dollars. So what the Immigration inspector said may have been true, but whether it was indentured servitude or simply the way people made their way to New York in the absence of their own funds is difficult to say.

It is obvious that no one, including the immigration officials themselves, could determine what exactly constituted contract labor or how to recognize it. It often came down to the supposed padrone having to convince an official that he had, in fact, no contract with the immigrant, but that they were friends for whom he had done a favor. An immigrant could be admitted or refused based on whether the official was convinced of the "contractor's" honesty. One reporter allowed if the friend named by the immigrant "is in reality a padrone or a padrone's agent, the immigration bureau has no way of proving it except by catching the immigrant in a lie," which was the job of the official or interpreter.[76] There were certainly men who met the ships with money in their pockets to get the immigrants cleared for landing, but their motives are murky.

A sad, if ironic, story concerned four Syrian immigrants who arrived in New York and were held on suspicion of being contract laborers. Nothing

[73] Reprinted, for example, in *The San Jose* (CA) *Evening News,* May 22, 1891, and *Jackson* (MI) *Citizen Patriot,* April 20, 1891.

[74] "Syrian Immigrants," *Omaha World Herald,* October 7, 1897.

[75] Industrial Commission on Immigration 1901: 88.

[76] "Irish Maids Are Easily Passed Through," *Denver Post,* May 10, 1899.

could be proven in this respect, so the accusation changed; they were sent back on the grounds that they were likely to become public charges since they didn't have jobs waiting for them.[77]

### *Loathsome Disease*

Health inspectors had about six seconds to inspect each immigrant. Stories passed through families about the mysterious mark that they made on the immigrant's coat in chalk—a mark that determined whether one was allowed to stay or was sent back. An "X" meant suspected mental defect; an X with a circle around it, definite signs of mental disease; a "CT," trachoma (an infectious eye disease often leading to blindness); and an "H," heart disease.[78] The marks were mysterious not only because immigrants didn't know their meaning, but because they were sometimes made on the backs of their coats where they couldn't be seen. My grandmother told me how terrified she had been as a child hearing about "the mark," which decided an immigrant's fate. Eighty years after her immigration, I could still hear the fear in her voice.

The most prevalent disease and the most common reason for being sent home was trachoma. Other diseases (such as pneumonia, leprosy, yellow fever, or cholera) condemned immigrants to a stay in the quarantine ward at best, or, at worst, a return to their port of embarkation. Those who were detained for health reasons had a special page devoted to them in the ship manifest, with one column headed "date of death."

A group of sixty-seven Syrians were turned away for trachoma in June 1899. They could not have all been ill, but all of the passengers traveling with the infected person would also be sent back. These sixty-seven were deported on a French liner, but the Immigration Bureau sent an urgent message to all ports warning them that these immigrants "have been supplied with money by Syrian importers of New York for the avowed purpose of effecting their return to this country via some other port."[79] The Bureau advised foreign steamships, sailing vessels, and trains from Canada to be on the lookout. It is easy to understand how the big men of the Syrian Colony could use their wealth to bring in those immigrants who were indigent, but it is difficult to see how

[77] *NYH*, July 3, 1890.
[78] http://www.powayusd.com/online/usonline/worddoc/ellisislandsite.htm.
[79] "Villainous Trick," *Boston Journal*, July 8, 1899.

money could "cure" trachoma to the satisfaction of the immigration officials.

In testimony to the Industrial Commission, a medical inspector (MI) at Ellis Island was asked:

> Do you know of any instance of a person deported for having a loathsome and dangerous contagious disease returning again to this country?
>
> MI: Several instances.
>
> Can you relate any of the instances?
>
> MI: The first is the case of Maria Laham [Rahaim?], 29, Syria, arrived April 11, 1899, per steamship Alesia (Fabre Line); deported for trachoma. Returned to the United States July 5, 1899, per steamship Spaarndam (Holland Line) under name of Martha Jousef Simon, and again deported for trachoma. In this case I understand the party admitted the fact of her identity."[80]

Martha and Maria may have been entirely different persons, but even if they were the same woman, one can imagine that the two names resulted from being simply misheard by the officials. Someone who wanted to deceive would not have revealed her name so readily. She must have turned around immediately when she reached the European port to return to New York. But how heartbreaking to have paid two fares, only to be sent back twice! And one wonders what happened to her when she reached Europe the second time.

The infamous episode of the cholera quarantine of 1892 affected a number of Syrians who were traveling in steerage on the SS *Rugia.* The panic that overtook the people of New York, the city, state, and federal health authorities, and all the newspapers led to the quarantining of dozens of ships, mostly those coming from Germany. The *Rugia,* a German steamship that sailed from Hamburg but stopped in Le Havre to pick up more than forty Syrians, was the second ship quarantined when it arrived on September 3. Forty-two cases of cholera were found, resulting in sixteen deaths. The ship was forced to stay in New York Harbor for several weeks while the health services essentially waited out the disease; all passengers were first kept in quarantine on Hoffman Island and then were taken to Fort Low in Sandy Hook, New Jersey. The cabin class passengers were finally released on Sep-

[80] Industrial Commission on Immigration 1901: 128.

tember 19; the steerage passengers were held until October 8.[81] Steerage passengers (particularly the Eastern European Jews) were considered to be the primary carriers of the disease, despite the fact that members of the cabin class also died.

In 1898, two Syrian children, Khalil Sussine and Hannas Yousef, came down with smallpox on the journey from Le Havre to New York. All of the steerage passengers on the ship were quarantined when they reached New York; their immigration fate was not reported.[82] Khalil died. A young Syrian man who had only recently arrived was also diagnosed with smallpox. The crowded tenement where he was lodging (27 Washington Street) had to be cleared and fumigated.[83] Jacob Couri, a Syrian man of twenty-three, was diagnosed with typhus when his ship docked. He was quarantined, along with his brother and all the other steerage passengers, and all of his possessions were burned. The cabin passengers were allowed to land.[84] Jamna Chadad (Yemna Haddad), although passed by the health inspectors who boarded her incoming ship, was later found to have leprosy when she landed at Ellis Island; she was immediately debarred and quarantined.[85] She was isolated at Ellis Island and was to have a cabin to herself on the return to Rotterdam, but was, to the horror of some, conducted to the ship on a public ferry. When he learned of this, the Immigration Superintendent said, "I have no doubt that sensitive persons would contract leprosy by merely looking upon Mrs. Chadad, did they know she was a leper."[86] No one knew what would become of her after the ship landed in Rotterdam.[87]

Skander Farah, a twenty-five-year-old Syrian, who allegedly became violently insane on the voyage, was taken to Bellevue Hospital and placed in the insane pavilion. He was there pronounced incurable. He was deported, as "he had not been in the country a year, and no one can become a charge on the country who has not been here a year."[88]

[81] Markel 1999: 130.
[82] "French Liner Brought Smallpox," *The New York Press,* November 22, 1898.
[83] "Smallpox in a Battery Tenement," *NYT,* October 10, 1899.
[84] "Had Fever on Board," *Chicago Herald,* April 20, 1891.
[85] "Mrs. Chadad to Go Back," *NYT,* July 11, 1892.
[86] "Leper Chadad in Transit," *NYH,* July 12, 1892.
[87] "Leper Jamna to Go Back," *NYH,* July 11, 1892.
[88] "Insane Syrian Deported," *BDE,* December 1, 1900.

## *Polygamy*

The law excluding polygamists from immigration, primarily aimed at Mormons living in Mexico, was passed in 1892. It was obviously used infrequently against Syrians since the vast majority of Syrian immigrants were Christians. In an article titled "Turks Can't Come Here,"[89] it was reported that a group of six Mohammedans were detained at the Barge Office and would probably be sent back to Turkey because of their belief in polygamy. They were headed to Toledo, Ohio, to try their hand at farming. It was Nageeb Arbeely again who quizzed the immigrants on their beliefs and reported them to the commissioner. Arbeely's contention was that a believer in a religion that condoned polygamy should be turned away whether or not he was actually a polygamist. Xenophon Baltazzi, the Turkish Consul-General, said he would appeal the case.

According to the *Times*, the six were deported without their case even being reviewed,[90] and apparently without giving the Turkish consul a chance to appeal. Only one newspaper protested their treatment: "a party of Mohammedan Syrians has been denied entrance to the country, not because any one of them has more than one wife, but because they are faithful to their religion which sanctions polygamy. One is a 15-year-old boy who has not reached the marrying age, but he stands by the prophet and can't get in. Is this the right way to interpret the law?"[91]

The question of whether belief in polygamy was grounds for deportation was a vexing one for Americans. An 1897 article in the *Dallas Morning News* was titled "Are Moslem Harems Possible Here?" For the reporter, this was not a theoretical question because a number of Muslims (he does not say how many) lived in the Midwest by that time. Apparently most of the Muslims who had already come were farmers or had set up businesses in farming communities,[92] just as those whose fate was being decided at the Barge Office were planning to do. A new ship manifest form adopted in 1893 asked whether the passenger was a polygamist (although the use of this new form was, at best, hit or miss). In addition, every applicant for naturalization had to swear that he was not a polygamist or a believer in the practice of polygamy. Would anyone in the know have ever answered, "yes" to these questions, regardless of their beliefs?

[89] *The* (NY) *Sun*, November 19, 1897.

[90] "Six Polygamists Shut Out," *NYT,* November 18, 1897.

[91] Editorial, *Springfield* (MA) *Republican*, November 20, 1897.

[92] "Are Moslem Harems Possible Here?" *Dallas Morning News,* December 5, 1897.

### *Unaccompanied Women*

Nageeb Arbeely asserted that unaccompanied women were also sent back. He repeatedly warned Syrians not to let their women come alone, and chastised the husbands who remained in Syria and "sent their wives to sell merchandise."[93] He cites the cases of ten unaccompanied women who were debarred over the course of two years, but we know that many unaccompanied women did come, and many were admitted. It may be that the bar was a little higher for them (that is, their references may have been more carefully checked, or their means, since a woman without any visible means of support would, in the Americans' view, likely turn to prostitution), but we have no evidence that they were routinely discriminated against. Arbeely took it upon himself to guarantee a number of arriving women, but he cautioned people that he could do only so much to "rescue" women who had been refused.

The steamship companies were required to provide return passage for those rejected (the American authorities thought that this would encourage the companies to screen passengers before they embarked), but only to the port of embarkation; many Syrians were left stranded in Marseilles, Le Havre, or Liverpool, with no money, no family, and no way to get home to Syria. In 1886, for example, it was reported that eleven Syrians were sent back to Le Havre because they were supposedly destitute. The French government refused to accept them and, after five weeks, they were put on a Cunard liner and sent to Liverpool, where they were put in the Liverpool workhouse. An editorial in the *New York Times* urged European countries to screen out undesirables before sending them to the United States so as not to impose "a burden from abroad that the taxpayers of this State have to bear."[94] The burden did not fall on the state but rather on the poor immigrant, left stranded in a European port.

As if these restrictions were not enough, there was even a feeling among some Americans that immigration should be completely eliminated, because "alien paupers" (i.e., Eastern European and Asian immigrants) were coming in such large numbers. Singled out in this diatribe were the Syrians, who were seen as "absolutely lazy and want only light employment such as peddling."[95] This movement gained no traction until immigration quota laws were put

[93] *Kawkab America*, June 1, 1894.
[94] "Syrian Emigrants in Bad Luck," *San Francisco Bulletin*, April 14, 1886; Editorial, *NYT*, April 12, 1886.
[95] "Low Standard," *Boston Daily Advertiser*, November 26, 1897.

into effect in 1924. Until that time, Syrians and other "undesirables" continued to come, and most were admitted.

## Those Who Succeeded in Being Admitted

Even though these stories and headlines imply that hundreds, if not thousands, of Syrians were sent back, the Industrial Commission on Immigration reported that during the year 1900, a mere 0.41 percent (120) of Syrians who arrived were barred from entering the United States: 71 for poverty, 48 for disease, and 1 for being a contract laborer.[96] Polygamy was not mentioned, nor were unaccompanied women. It may be that by 1900 the immigrants had become more savvy about the immigration process and were more frequently able to pass inspection, or it may be that the number of Syrians debarred was always small, at least compared to the number admitted.

Despite all the rejections and the negative press, the Syrians came and kept coming. Many of them told stories about making the trip two or three times before actually being admitted: some accomplished this by coming through Canada or Mexico, where the immigration procedures were more relaxed; others simply understood the system better the second time around and were able to meet the requirements. This knowledge was viewed in a sinister light by the press, who saw it as somehow manipulating the system, but in fact it was simply using hard-won knowledge to succeed in being admitted under these draconian and arbitrarily implemented laws.

They made their way from their hometowns to the port cities of Beirut, Tripoli, or Alexandria and then took ship to Europe, where they found passage west. They might spend a week or two in Marseilles or Le Havre until they found a ship. Some reported that when they embarked, they didn't know where the ship was headed and ended up in South America, the West Indies, or Mexico. It is said that there were, in fact, more Syrian immigrants in Latin America than in North America, but I have not seen any data supporting this statement. They certainly came by the score to New York, sailing mainly from Le Havre, Cherbourg, Bordeaux, or Liverpool. A few came from Havana, the West Indies, or South America; these places could have been simply transit points, but in some cases we know that an immigrant had settled there, made a life and a living, and then decided to push on to New York. Several

[96] Industrial Commission on Immigration 1901: 290.

immigrants gave their place of last residence as Haiti or Cuba, both of which had significant Syrian communities in the nineteenth century, and trade between Syrian businessmen in New York and the islands was brisk.

*Kawkab America* reported Syrian arrivals in their first few issues. In Issue 1 (April 15, 1892), twenty-one arrived; the next week, thirty; the following week, forty, and the week after that, one hundred and five. The SS *Rugia,* to give just one example, sailed from Bremen and Le Havre, and landed at New York Harbor on June 13, 1892. Of about 425 steerage passengers, 181 were Syrians (all of whom boarded at Le Havre). On the *Rugia*'s manifest, and on most of the early passenger lists, the names are nearly impossible to make out. The men were called cultivators, farmers, or laborers (the ditto marks went on for hundreds of lines); none were skilled workers. By the same token, women were labeled seamstresses or had no profession. It may be true that the vast majority of the early immigrants were farmers and seamstresses, or it may be that the pursers called them that out of laziness: only eight years after this ship landed, the Immigration Commission reported that fully 16.3 percent of the Syrians who came into the Port of New York were skilled workers.[97] Whether this increase in skilled workers is a reflection of a different kind of immigrant, a savvier immigrant, or simply an artifact of better record keeping is impossible to say.

## Finding a Home on Washington Street

After processing, if they were admitted, the Syrians either stayed in New York City or began to move west, south, or north to join fellow Syrians in other parts of the country. By the end of the nineteenth century, there were Syrian communities in all of the continental United States and Alaska. Significant communities existed in Virginia, Louisiana, Mississippi, and Texas; California and Washington; Michigan, Illinois, and the Great Plains; and upstate New York, Pennsylvania, and New England.

How many of the Syrians who landed at the Port of New York stayed? In just the two years between 1900 and 1902, for example, 41 percent (3,200) of the more than 8,000 Syrians who disembarked in New York said they planned to stay in New York.[98] But there were 1,000–1,500 already here,

[97] Industrial Commission on Immigration 1901: 303.
[98] Miller 1903: 4–5.

which would give a total population in 1902 of about 4,500–5,000 had they all stayed, yet the actual number of residents was less than half that. This fact alone would indicate that many more than the declared 60 percent did leave, notwithstanding what they told the immigration officials.

But hundreds did stay. Manhattan's First Ward—and specifically, the Lower West Side, centered on Washington Street—was the earliest hub of the Syrian Colony in New York because it was so close to the disembarkation point at Battery Place. Simon George (Simon Abuassaly), telling his story more than seventy years later to Dr. Alixa Naff, recalled that when he arrived at Castle Garden in the 1890s, Nageeb Arbeely met him at the Barge Office: "When an émigré had no family to come to, Mr. Arbeely would send them to Washington Street in New York, where there was a large Syrian community, until they found work or were directed to another area where they could earn a living amongst their own people, who would understand them."[99] When the new immigrant walked up Washington Street, he would have heard Arabic on every side. Many of the storefronts had signs in Arabic in the windows; there were men smoking water pipes in the cafés; and many of the men and women walking through the streets looked much as they did at home, notwithstanding their westernized clothing. The smells coming from the restaurants must have been comfortingly familiar, especially after the weeks at sea in steerage, and the new immigrant knew he would be able to find a bed in a Syrian-owned boardinghouse, a Syrian meal, work of some sort, and if he were lucky, he might even encounter a friend or relative from his hometown.

[99] *Naff Interview*, Simon George, n.d., 3.

## Chapter 3

# The Washington Street Neighborhood

*This district is one of the worst in New York, in the general condition of some of its tenements.*[1]

*The excessively high rents and generally wretched buildings of this district force them to live under unusually crowded and squalid conditions.*[2]

The Syrian Colony was bounded by West Street and the Hudson River on the west, Carlisle Street on the north, Greenwich Street on the east, and Battery Place on the south. The nineteenth-century Syrians were highly concentrated on lower Washington Street, with smaller enclaves on Battery Place, Morris, Rector, and Carlisle. Both their businesses and their homes were within these boundaries. There were outliers even in the earliest years, such as the Abo-Samras and the Halabys, who lived on Coenties Slip, the Arbeelys, who worked and lived at 45 Pearl Street, the Oussanis and a group of Moroccan entertainers who lived in the Tenderloin, and even a few who lived in Brooklyn. But the vast majority of the Colony lived and worked in and around Washington Street from their first arrival until well into the twentieth century.

The Syrians took the place of some of the earlier Irish and Italian immigrants who lived in the neighborhood; Eastern Europeans and the encroaching financial district, in turn, began to replace the Syrians in the first decades of the twentieth century. Although Syrians continued to live and work in Manhattan for many years, Miller's 1903 photograph of Washington Street from above already shows the taller financial buildings to the east looming over the low-rise houses on the street. The neighborhood was finally eradicated by the construction of the Brooklyn–Battery Tunnel, which began in 1946.

[1] Miller 1903: 7.
[2] Houghton 1911: I: 492.

What was it like living there? What kind of place did the Syrians find when they arrived, and how did they alter the neighborhood to suit their own needs? Was Washington Street really a slum, as many of the early accounts claimed? Did the presence of the Syrians make it worse or better?

## Tenements

The First Ward, an area of less than half a square mile, encompassed all of Manhattan below Maiden Lane. In 1890, it had an overall density of 26,962 people per square mile, much less than many other wards that included tenement districts.[3] A 1901 Immigration Commission *Report* indicated that the density of the ward had actually decreased between 1860 and 1890, as did the number of tenement buildings since they were falling prey to the new buildings of the financial district. Because of this, many of the earlier immigrants moved elsewhere, while the poorer and more recent immigrants (including Syrians) crowded into the remaining buildings. The average number of people living in each tenement increased by 5 percent.[4]

The same report found the most serious problems in the tenement neighborhoods to be lack of light and air (resulting in epidemic cases of tuberculosis);[5] danger from fire; lack of separate water closets (toilets) and washing facilities; overcrowding; and foul cellars and backyards. All of these conditions were to be found in the Syrian dwellings of lower Washington Street.

The Syrian tenements were probably not much different from other tenement districts in other parts of the city—crowded, dirty, and dark—but what set the Washington Street area apart was having water on two sides, which provided open space and a breeze in the summer, but which also meant cold winds and water in the cellars in the winter. The Syrians, like others before and after them, attempted to make these dreadful places into homes.

The great majority of Syrian residents lived in early- or mid-nineteenth-century single-family row houses that had been divided into numerous small rooms to house the incoming Irish and Italian immigrant population. The houses were on lots that were about twenty feet wide and ninety feet deep; the houses on the west side of Washington, backing onto the warehouses of the

[3] www.demographia.com/db-nyc-ward1800.htm.
[4] http://tenant.net/Community/LES/clag2.html.
[5] http://tenant.net/Community/LES/clag2.html.

shipping companies, generally took up the whole lot, while those on the east side (where most of the Syrians lived) were shallower, allowing for some outdoor space in the back. Since these houses shared a wall with the neighboring building on either side, the only light came from the front and back windows. When the building was divided up—depending on its size, there could be between eight and eighteen rooms per floor—only the front and back four rooms had windows, leaving up to fourteen windowless rooms that were rented out. In an early classified ad posted in the *New York Herald*, an unnamed Syrian looking for work as a tour guide in the Holy Land gave his address as "room 14, 2 Morris st."[6] This building, near the corner of Trinity and Morris, was small, about twenty feet wide and forty feet deep, but it apparently had at least fourteen rooms.

3-1. The Syrian district from above (Miller 1903).

Most of the buildings in the neighborhood were three to five stories tall, with or without habitable basements, and the privies, water standpipes, and sinks were jury-rigged in hallways or backyards. "The number of baths in the Syrian homes of this district can be counted on the fingers of one hand, and

[6] *NYH*, August 4, 1889.

there are very few private [water] closets. Some of the latter are in the hallways, but most of them are in the rear areas, and many are constructed in the illegal sink fashion."[7]

3-2. The heart of the Washington Street community (Miller 1903).

Miller conducted his survey of the Colony after the New Tenement Law of 1901 took effect, mandating that a certain amount of light and air had to penetrate all the tenement rooms. This law applied only to tenements built after the law was passed so it had no effect on those in which the Syrians were living. Miller was therefore very conscious of the substandard conditions of the Lower West Side tenements. He counted 179 Syrian families living in one dark room (having no window) and 38 families living in two dark rooms.[8] And of course this was before electricity was introduced into homes, so many of these residents lived in perpetual dark, or with single candles or lamps lighting their rooms. The halls and stairways were always dark ("as a wolf's mouth" as one reporter had it). This is in stark contrast to the conditions in the Brooklyn Syrian communities at the same time, where not one person was living in a dark room, according to Miller.

[7] Miller 1903: 9.
[8] Miller 1903: 9.

Miller also reported that seventeen of the houses in which Syrians lived had been reported to the Sanitary Commission the previous year for a number of unsanitary conditions, which, he said, were equal to the worst conditions of New York's Lower East Side. Miller blamed the owners rather than the residents for these slum-like dwellings, noting that the Syrians' rooms were generally cleaner than those of others who lived in the same tenements. "A twofold division according to cleanliness yields 68 per cent. clean' families," he reported.[9] A newspaperman from Worcester, Massachusetts, visiting the Manhattan neighborhood remarked on the numerous flowers and plants that grew in the windowsills. "One barber screens his shop from the public gaze with a cucumber vine."[10] An 1899 photograph of a coffeehouse and poolroom shows, on close examination, little herbs or flowers growing in cans on the windowsills above.[11]

3-3. Numbers 59 to 81 Washington Street from the south, 1942. Note the sign for Faour Bank at left, although it had folded a decade earlier (New-York Historical Society).

Others were not as kind. "The headquarters of these Maronite Arabs in this city are in the lower part of Washington and Greenwich Streets and the streets that cross those names. Some of their lodging houses are filthy in the extreme. Many of them pay as low as five cents for a night's lodging, and as

[9] Miller 1903: 9.
[10] "The Syrian Colony," *Worcester* (MA) *Daily Spy*, August 19, 1895.
[11] Cromwell Childe, "New York's Syrian Quarter," *NYT*, August 20, 1899.

many as ten or twelve men and women have been known to sleep on the floor in a single room.... There are a few respectable Arab merchants here and these are heartily ashamed of their countrymen and countrywomen."[12] The reporter, in addition to clearly being disgusted by the conditions these people lived in (by choice, he implies) makes reference to men and women sleeping in the same room, obliquely accusing the Syrians of licentiousness. Another article describes Muossa Daoud's tenement on Rector Street as "a dozen rooms or more...receiving placidly the dust of the street and the yard through disjointed doors and windows, a prey to indelible dirt. Piecemeal the partitions have lct fall the laths and the plaster of which they were formed."[13] The reporter claimed that if the tenants had not huddled in Muossa's store in the winter, they would have frozen to death. When the reporter visited, Daoud's building had been cited for numerous health violations. It is unclear whether these deplorable conditions were the result of landlords' neglect, as Miller would have it, or the responsibility of the person to whom the house (or the floor) was leased (in this case, Daoud), who then sublet rooms to other Syrians. Daoud's second boardinghouse was at 96 Greenwich, a small four-story tenement near the corner of Rector, which he leased and then re-rented to at least thirty Syrians. The elevated railroad thundered by the house. Among the boarders were a number of women heads of households who were scrubwomen; the other boarders were listed as peddlers, waitress, tailor, shoemaker, carpenter, and painter; no one called himself a "merchant." The rent must have been very low.

Abraham Rihbany described the two places he lived when he first arrived in New York in 1891: Abraham's (probably Ibrahim Khairallah's boardinghouse at 75 Washington), where the rent was fifteen cents a night, and Moses's (either Moses Abboud at 96 Washington, or more likely, Muossa Daoud at 17 Rector), where the rent was five cents a night. Rihbany was very poor, so he decided after one night at Abraham's to move to Moses's. The latter did away with the luxuries of soap, towels, bedding, and in fact, the room itself; Moses pointed out a space on the landing where Rihbany was supposed to sleep. But after Rihbany realized he had to share this meager space with two other men, he decided he would pay the 15 cents and return to the relative luxury of Abraham's.[14]

[12] "'Sanctified' Arab Tramps," *NYT*, May 25, 1890.

[13] "Moussa *[sic]* Daoud Their Leader," NYT, June 4, 1894.

[14] Rihbany 1914: 194.

3-4. Tenement, 25&27 Washington Street (Moss 1897). This tenement was exclusively Syrian.

Abdallah Jabbour, in an article written for *Kawkab America* in 1894, describes two classes of lodging house: those that charge a minimum of seven *rials*[15] a week and those that charge three to five *rials*. In the former class, there is the boardinghouse (*locanda*) where residents pay two *rials* a day for room and board and the lodging house (which serves no food) where residents pay one and a half *rials* a day. In the better-class house, Jabbour says, the landlady is careful about whom she accepts, making the residents a "kind of family," while at the lower-class establishments, anyone can rent a room, and the class of people at those places is very low.[16] He implies, but does not say, that Syrians lived in the second type of house, but should aspire to the first. Only two years later, the editor of *Kawkab America*, responding to a reader who

[15] A *rial*, or an "American *rial*" was equivalent to one dollar; twenty-eight *qurush* equaled one American *rial*. The Colonists continued to use these Arabic terms among themselves throughout the nineteenth century. In the two newspapers for which we have early copies, *Kawkab America* and *Al Hoda*, all dollar amounts are given in these terms. In a list of notions given in Rustum's book (1895), the prices are given in *rials* and *qurush*; he helpfully appends the conversion rate. Sometimes too the Syrians used the terms *dirhams*, *dinars*, or *liras* when they meant dollars and cents, or simply, money.

[16] *Kawkab America*, July 20, 1894.

was thinking about coming to New York, advised him that boardinghouses where you pay separately for food cost about fifty cents a night. A meal will cost about ten cents.[17] Arbeely was obviously referring to the lower class of boardinghouse.

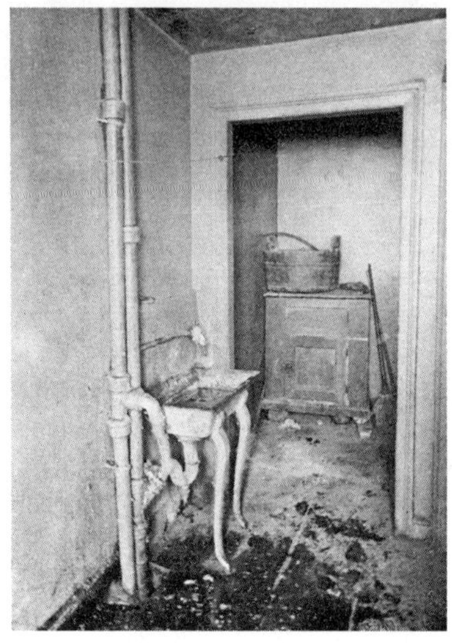

3-5. Hall sink in tenement, lower Washington Street (Trinity 1914).

"The poor Syrian contracts to pay $5 to $7 [per month] for two rooms, and as his family is usually a large one, and the rent out of proportion to his income, he resorts to overcrowding as a relief. Sometimes he is able to get one room for $4 a month, and proceeds to crowd his family of 7 persons into it."[18] In fact, the early Syrians' families were not, in the main, large, but they did likely crowd unrelated people into these rooms, just as poor immigrants do today in New York. It is difficult to fathom how unrelated men and women arranged themselves in these circumstances. A reporter who visited New York in 1894 for the *Omaha World Herald* asserted, "A few years ago about a dozen Syrians occupied the same room, but now they are more zealous for their personal comfort,"[19] but in reality, the Syrians did not materially improve their living conditions until they began to move to Brooklyn at the end of the century.

---

[17] *Kawkab America,* February 14, 1896.

[18] Industrial Commission on Immigration 1901: 444.

[19] Rufus R. Wilson, "Men From All Lands," *Omaha World Herald,* August 5, 1894.

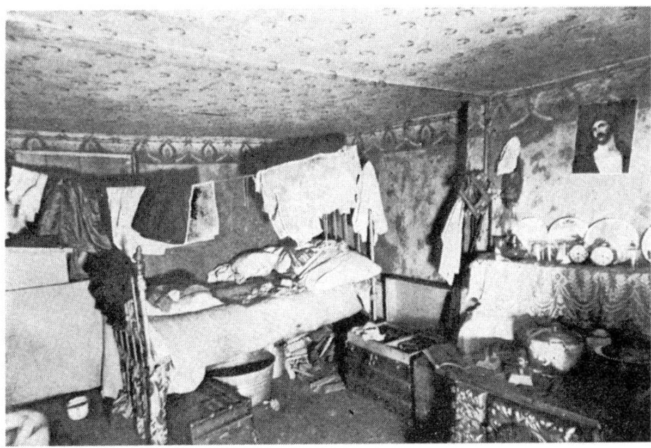

3-6. One-room apartment on lower Washington Street (Trinity 1914).

3-7. Outdoor toilets, Washington Street tenement (Trinity 1914). The doors are numbered (from right to left) 1–9.

In Miller's survey, 28 percent of the Manhattan residents still lived in one room, with an average of 2.4 people per room, while 44 percent lived in two rooms, with an average of 1.8 people per room. The former group paid $5.18 per month (about seventeen cents per night), while the latter paid $6.68 (about twenty-two cents per night). He went on to say that 39.2 percent of the families were living in "crowded" conditions, that is, more than two people per room.[20] He called these cohabitants "families,"

[20] Miller 1903: 9–10.

but it is just as likely that many were groups of unrelated men and women, as they were in the nineteenth century. Thus, the tenements in Manhattan continued to be occupied by new immigrants, and the conditions had not markedly improved.

By 1910, however, when the next Immigration Commission *Report* was published, the conditions of the Syrians in Manhattan had ameliorated. Although they continued to live in the same tenements, the average number of people per household had decreased to 3.78, and the average number of persons per room to 1.33. Most of the Syrians were still sharing hall sinks and toilets, but these were shared with one other family at the most, conditions quite different from a decade earlier.[21] Felton, in his 1912 master's thesis, says, "Nearly every Syrian in Manhattan has but two rooms for which the average rent is ten dollars per month."[22] The rents in the neighborhood had gone up almost 50 percent since Miller's survey. According to Felton, the front room, which had light, was generally clean, the dark back room "not so clean." The sanitary conditions were "deplorable," and Felton reports that fourteen buildings had been reported to the Sanitary Commission. He, like Miller, asserted that the Syrians themselves were clean, but the conditions they lived in were not, implying that it was the fault of the landlords, not the residents.

Trinity Church had as part of its mission to carry on charitable work in its neighborhood; to that end, its Men's Committee conducted a survey of the Washington Street District in 1913. By that time, many of the original Syrians had moved to Brooklyn, but new immigrants were still coming; 15 percent of the neighborhood residents were Syrians.[23] The Committee's assessment of the living conditions on Washington Street was still bleak: overcrowded, unsanitary conditions led to a large number of cases of tuberculosis; outdoor (backyard) toilets were still the norm (the authors charted the number of flights of stairs people had to descend or ascend in order to get to the toilets; some people had to go down five flights); the deplorable state of the hall sink shown in a photograph was certainly the cause of many of the illnesses rampant in the community, and adulterated milk sold by unscrupulous dairymen led to an abnormally high infant mortality rate. A photograph of a one-room apartment in one of the tenements shows a dark, low-ceilinged, apparently

---

[21] Dillingham 1911: Tables 279, 281, 292, and 293.

[22] Felton 1912: 10–11.

[23] Trinity Church Men's Committee 1914: 65.

unwindowed space just as unlivable as any in the more publicized district of the Lower East Side (Figure 3-6). A picture of Jesus hangs prominently on the wall above the stove.[24] All the common areas and facilities shown in the photographs—the sinks, stairways, standpipes, and backyard toilets—were filthy and decrepit. Whether these particular facilities or the conditions described in the 1913 study belonged to the Syrians is not stated, but they are certainly representative of how the Syrians lived in the nineteenth century, and apparently well into the twentieth century, in Manhattan.

## The 1890 Police Census

Although Syrians began settling in New York in the early 1880s, the 1890 Police Census is the earliest relevant census we have; it can serve as a starting point and a microcosm of the way the Syrians lived, as well as how they distributed themselves in the neighborhood. If we imagine the Syrians expanding out from the few addresses they inhabited in 1890 to a larger number of similar buildings on Washington and neighboring streets we will have an idea of the conditions under which they lived in the nineteenth century. The buildings where Syrians lived in this early census continued to be important in the lives of the Syrians throughout the decade and beyond, serving not only as residences but also as business addresses and churches. Thus, as we go through the 1890 census, we will tell the stories of the individual buildings up to 1900.

Unfortunately, essential parts of the census for the First Ward are missing, so Syrians whom we know were living in the Colony in 1890 are not included. Even some of those who lived at addresses that are included in the fragmentary census are missing. These residents may have been absent, perhaps on the road peddling.

We were able to identify 91 (probable) Syrians in the 1890 census. They were living at nineteen addresses, almost all on Washington Street, and of those, most were on the east (odd-numbered) side of the street—a preference that would be followed through the whole of their residence on Washington Street. Whether they chose this side because many of these buildings had backyards or because more of them had basements, or for some other reason, is not clear. The buildings were smaller on the east side because of the yards.

[24] Trinity Church Men's Committee 1914: 9.

In addition to privies, there were sometimes back tenements in the yards, which would narrow the open space behind the buildings to as little as ten feet but provide additional housing. All of these buildings—save one—continued to house Syrians throughout the decade.

The tenements on both sides of Washington Street sheltered other immigrants as well, and the Syrians were living cheek by jowl with them: primarily Irish, but also Italians, Germans, Greeks, and Scandinavians. Many of these immigrants were drawn to the work on the docks or catered to those workers. This close proximity to different nationalities led to frequent confrontations between groups; those incidents involving Syrians will be described below. The few Armenians who lived and worked on Washington Street meshed well with the Syrians and were often conflated with them in the American press.

The houses on the short east–west blocks (Morris, Rector, and Carlisle) were narrower and shallower than those on Washington, as if they were afterthoughts and built after all of the buildings on the major north–south thoroughfares had taken up most of the available space. Neighborhoods like the ones the Syrians lived in can still be seen all over New York in any district that has preserved its nineteenth-century character, but not on lower Washington Street itself, which has been completely destroyed.

Moving from south to north along Washington Street (that is, from the Battery northward) several addresses that would become important to later residents—Numbers 2, 3&5 (a double tenement), 11, and 24&26 (another double tenement)—housed no Syrians at all in 1890. Farther north, we find the first group of Syrians listed in the 1890 census at Numbers 25&27.[25] This was also a double tenement; whether the buildings were actually joined internally or were simply considered to be one is not clear. There is a photograph of the building in Moss's book (Figure 3-4).[26] The two tenements certainly look like one, presenting a six-story, fifty-six-foot brutally ugly, flat, and featureless frontage on Washington Street. No detailing remains around the doors or windows. Three narrow entrances give access to the upper floors. There are fire escapes festooned with drying laundry at every fourth window.

In the 1890 census, only two Syrians lived in each of the two buildings. We recognize the two at Number 27: Nicola Mallouk and his son Salim.

[25] I use the ampersand and no spaces because this is how the double tenements were designated in the censuses.

[26] Moss 1897.

Nicola's wife and five other children followed in 1892. Mallouk was a dealer in Oriental and fancy goods, and he soon moved his store to 105 Washington and his residence to 72 West Street. He died in 1899, but his sons Salim and Elias took over the business and became lace importers. Although there were only four Syrians there in 1890, Moss states that by 1897, "At Numbers 25 and 27 Washington Street are two filthy tenement houses that are crowded with them [Syrians],"[27] and indeed by 1900, both buildings were exclusively Syrian, 142 tenants in all.

In Moss' 1897 photograph, beaded curtains hang at four open street-level shops belonging, according to Moss, to "Calil Abraham and Saraya, and P. Khouri."[28] Kalil Abraham was a dry goods dealer, Peter Khoury dealt in novelties, and "Saraya" is either Najeeb Sawaya, who later became a manufacturer of mirrors and a newspaper editor, or Joseph Sawaya, who appeared in the 1890 census at 122 Washington. Najeeb had been in the United States only a couple of months when the book was written, and it seems unlikely that he would have already opened a shop. Other Syrian merchants who set up shops there over the decade included Assy Shaheen and Joseph Faris, jewelers; Beshara Nader and Nahoom Hatem, dry goods dealers; and the grocer Elias Faris.

Whether the men and boys standing on the street in the 1897 photo are Syrians is impossible to say, but they easily could be. They are well dressed in hats, waistcoats, and suits; there is not a *tarboush* (the classic red felt hat or *fez* worn by most Ottoman Turks at this time) to be seen. There are only four women in the photo: two are in the crowd of men at one of the entrances, a third stands down the street in front of one of the stores, and a fourth looks out a second-story window at the crowd of people posing for the photographer below. The crowd looks like any one would find in a nineteenth-century immigrant neighborhood. There are large metal trashcans lined up three deep blocking the sidewalks at each of the tenement entrances.[29] The only possible saving grace to this horrible place was the large back lot, but given what other tenement yards were like, it must have been filled with lean-tos that served as privies, refuse from being used as a dump, and the contents of chamber pots; having to travel down five flights of stairs to use the privy meant that people

[27] Moss 1897: 274.

[28] Moss 1897: 274.

[29] The editors of *Kawkab America* had urged Syrians to install trashcans on the street; the campaign seems to have succeeded.

regularly used chamber pots, and dumped them out the window if they were lucky enough to have a window.

Only three Syrians lived at 37 Washington, the next Syrian-occupied house listed in the 1890 census: Abraham and Saada Ashie and their seven-year-old son, Toufic. Abraham, who went on to sell notions in a succession of stores around lower Manhattan, was dealing in beads from his home at Number 37 in 1892. Toufic died in 1893,[30] but Saada gave birth to another son that year, who was named Toufic in honor of the dead boy. A daughter was born at home in 1898. A few Syrians continued to live at Number 37 through the years, but it was never a popular choice; there were none living there in the 1900 census.

Number 57 was a small brick building, probably a federal-style townhouse similar to the row at Numbers 71-79, described below. Measuring twenty-six by thirty feet, of three and half stories plus a basement, the building had about 780 square feet per floor. The inhabitable space was of course less, since a stairway would have taken a significant slice out of the floor area. We don't know if the basement at Number 57 was a full basement, having the same number of square feet as the other floors. This house had a small backyard. In the 1890 census, fifteen Syrians and two others who might have been Syrians lived in the house; they must have occupied the two and a half top floors. As in other tenement neighborhoods, even this "official" number of residents may be too low, as the Syrians were probably subletting space in their apartments to others in order to decrease the rent for each person, and some of the residents may have been out on the road peddling.

Some of those living at Number 57 in 1890 we know from later sources, among them Khalil Beshewate. The brother of the Melkite priest Abraham Beshewate (who is not listed in this census, although he had arrived in New York in 1889 at the same time as his brother), Khalil was a fruit and confectionery dealer all his life, and one imagines that he started his business here, selling from (and perhaps living in) the basement. Even if so, by 1894 he had a shop at the foot of Sixth Avenue at Broome Street. Joseph Ayoob and Mansour Sharbel also lived at Number 57. They had already formed a partnership and set up a store ("Sharbel & Ayoob") on the parlor floor, selling fancy goods and novelties. One reporter described their stock as "prayer beads and other articles of devotion."[31] We will hear much more about Joseph Ayoob in this

[30] *Kawkab America,* December 8, 1893.

[31] "New York's Syrian King," *Omaha World Herald,* October 16, 1889.

history. Sharbel also ran the house as a hotel and sent his Syrian boarders down to Castle Garden to greet new immigrants and "remove the new comers to Sharbel's Hotel."[32] A Syrian, whose name was transcribed as "Abraham Laadi," was probably Abraham Sahadi. His wife's name was written as "Iseen," nothing like her real name of Zakia.

In 1894, Lotfallah Atta, Elias Zreik, and George Shawi opened a restaurant on the parlor floor of Number 57 and advertised the high quality of their chef in *Kawkab America.*[33] Atta soon moved his restaurant to Number 71. A number of dry goods businesses were also housed at 57 throughout the decade, and in 1897, a Turkish coffeehouse opened on the parlor floor and a poolroom in the basement. The house finally became the headquarters for the Maronite Youth Association when their priest, Khairallah Stefan, moved there in 1900. It later became the Maronite church for Manhattan residents and/or workers after the main church was established in Brooklyn.

Number 59 Washington was a five-story building with a basement. It was thirty feet wide and fifty-five feet deep, making it larger than the majority of buildings on the street. Only five Syrians were listed at 59 Washington, but one, Salim Elias, a Maronite from Baskinta who had immigrated in 1885, became an important member of the community. He peddled for three years and brought his wife, Shamooney, over in 1888, starting his import–export business at Number 59 around 1889. Naoum Mokarzel lived there as well but had started a business with Abdow Rihani at Number 73 (Rihani's residence), since Elias may have already claimed Mokarzel's basement. Not listed in the census but also living at Number 59 were the three Ghiz brothers, Nohman, Salim, and Kalil. All three peddled when they first arrived, so perhaps they were out on the road when the census was taken. The building played an important role throughout the nineteenth century in the business lives of the Syrians, housing companies like "Petrus Saad & Bros." (fancy goods) and "Moshy Bros." (dry goods). In 1900, it was still home to three Syrian families, fifteen people in all.

Although we know that a number of Syrians were working at 63 Washington in 1890 (among them the Rahaim brothers, George Malhami, Kaisar Yamin, and Salim el Kuku), none are listed in the 1890 census. Perhaps it was a purely commercial building and not a residence, although this would be unusual for the time. The building, along with 60–62 Washington across the

[32] "New York's Syrian King," *Omaha World Herald,* October 16, 1889.

[33] *Kawkab America,* July 6, 1894.

street, continued to be a business center for these and other Syrians throughout the decade.

Syrians were also living at 71, 73, 77, and 79 Washington. Built between 1820 and 1825, 71–79 Washington had been a row of handsome Federal-style buildings, twenty feet wide and fifty feet deep (Number 75 was exceptional at thirty feet wide, because it included a covered driveway which led to a stable yard in the rear). All were three or three and a half stories with a basement. They had steeply pitched slate roofs in which dormer windows in front and back provided light to the half story. The doorways were graceful arches with handsome stone trim and brownstone steps; stone lintels decorated the six-over-six windows. Several of these houses still exist in the upper reaches of the street.[34] By the time the Syrians moved in, their handsome facades and interiors had been altered almost beyond recognition. Several of the arches had been filled in to make mean-looking rectangular doorways, the first-floor six-over-six windows had been replaced by (and sometimes enlarged to) plate glass windows for shops or broken through for new doorways; fire escapes defaced the facades. The beautiful arched driveway and porte cochère of Number 75 had been bricked in to make more rooms. The entrances to the coal cellars had, in some cases, been enlarged to give access to the basement from the street, and several had become shops. The one amenity—a continuous backyard stretching from Numbers 71 to 83—was taken up by backyard privies and a disused stable and was undoubtedly filthy with refuse.

In 1890, six of the twenty-eight residents in Number 71 were Syrians. All twenty-eight people were living on the two upper floors, which measured about 700 square feet each. One imagines all six of the Syrians might have lived in one room, but we have no way of knowing (heads of household and relationships were not labeled in the census). Two of the tenants, Habeeb Daoud and Tannous (Thomas in the census) Shishim, were a father-in-law and son-in-law from Zahleh. Shishim's wife, Sophie, who came with them from Zahleh in 1889, is not listed; she may have been peddling out of town. The two men also may have been peddlers in 1890, but only two years later they set up their own boardinghouse at 91 Washington. Yusef Balesh and Khalil Geha, Melkites from Zahleh, were also living at Number 71 in 1890; both "Balesh and Geha" (jewelry) and "Joseph Balesh" (novelties) were businesses listed at that address. Whether the two companies were the same or

[34] http://forgotten-ny.com/2007/11/in-search-of-washington-downtown-pieces-of-washington-street/

Balesh had two separate businesses is unclear. Perhaps they occupied both the basement and the street-level floors. In 1898, they moved their partnership to 77 Washington. Abdallah Hamati had arrived in 1885, and although not listed on the census, he was perhaps already running the upstairs rooms of Number 71 as a lodging house, which he continued to do for many years. Rasheed Safi opened a restaurant there in 1894, which Lotfalla Atta took over in 1897.

Out of a total of thirty-three residents listed in the 1890 census at Number 73, Abdow Rihani was the sole Syrian, although a second Syrian, T. Maroon, about whom we know nothing more, had a fancy goods business there in 1890 and probably lived there as well. Rihani came to the United States in 1888 with his eight-year-old nephew, Ameen Rihani, and Naoum Mokarzel—all three were Maronites from the village of Freike. Naoum was living at 59 Washington in 1890; Ameen was not listed in the census, perhaps because he was sent off to boardingschool shortly after they arrived.[35] Number 73 was another one of the handsome early-nineteenth-century row houses that had been heavily altered by successive waves of immigrants. The two windows on the first floor had been obliterated, and in their place was a wide shop window next to the entrance to a store. As at Number 71, the doorway to the rooms above was on the left of the building, but in this case, the handsome arched opening still existed. One entered the cellar under the shop window.[36]

If Maroon had his business on the parlor floor, Rihani and his partner Mokarzel must have set up their first shop, a variety shop, in the basement. They called it, grandly, "A. Rihani & Co." It was stocked with goods they had purchased in France, which means they must have carried a considerable amount of money with them from Syria. The shop was a "quick failure," according to Mokarzel's niece, Mary,[37] and soon after, Abdow joined forces with his brother Fares, who had just arrived, keeping the business at 73 Washington, while Mokarzel went on to other ventures. The store was renamed "F. & A. Rihani" (one wonders why Fares's name was listed first), but some years after Abdow's death in 1894, it was changed to the simpler "Fares Rihani."

[35] www.ameenrihani.org/index.php?page=biography.

[36] http://www.loc.gov/pictures/collection/hh/item/ny0590.photos.119790p/.

[37] Mokarzel 1968: 1.

3-8. The Rihani family in New York, ca. 1898 (The Ameen Rihani Museum, Freike, Lebanon). Seated, left to right: Fares Rihani, his daughter Adele, and Anissa Tomeh Rihani (Fares's wife); standing, left to right: Ameen, Sa'ada, Asa'ad, Joseph.

As is obvious, many of the early residents lived and worked in the same place—living above the store or in it. In his 1911 autobiographical novel, *The Book of Khalid*, Ameen Rihani, Fares's son, is eloquent on the subject of living and working in a basement in New York's Syrian Quarter in the nineteenth century:

> We rented a cellar, as deep and dark and damp as could be found.... In the front part of this cellar we had our shop; in the rear, our home. On the floor we laid our mattresses, on the shelves, our goods. And never did we stop to think who in this case was better off. The safety of our merchandise before our own. But ten days after we had settled down, the water issued forth from the floor and inundated our shop and home. It rose so high that it destroyed half of our capital stock and almost all our furniture. And yet, we continued to live in the cellar, because, perhaps, every one of our compatriot-merchants did so.[38]

The conditions were probably just as Ameen described. It is worth remembering that Greenwich used to be Manhattan's westernmost street; filling

[38] Rihani 2000 (1911): 41.

in the Hudson River created Washington and West Streets. The elevation on Washington Street (then as now just one block from the river) was no more than four feet above high tide level, so it's not surprising that the cellars would regularly flood. Notice that Rihani said the water "issued forth from the floor," which meant that the level of the river was simply rising, as it is wont to do. A 1940 Historic American Buildings Survey mentions that the cellars of these houses had dirt floors.[39] After Rihani moved his store, Najeeb N. Maloof and his cousin, Najeeb S. Maloof, who were silk importers, rented Number 73. Finally, at the end of the century the food importer Farjallah Zaloom and his son took over there.

No Syrians lived at Number 75 in 1890, at least according to the census, although Rasheed Safi opened his boardinghouse there around that time. In 1892, the boardinghouse was taken over by Ibrahim Khairallah, and it continued to be a boardinghouse until at least 1900, when it was exclusively Syrian, eighteen residents living on the two upper floors.

Among the six Syrians living at 77 Washington in 1890 were Abdow Lutfy and his wife, Tarkman (listed as Marta), Orthodox Christians from Zahleh who were already pillars of the Syrian community. He (or they) probably began as peddlers. Although there were no children listed with them in the 1890 census, they must have arrived together, because Abdow's son, Deeb Lutfy, signed the appeal for a writ of habeas corpus for a group of stranded Syrian immigrants in 1889. We know too that Ameen Batal, a peddler, was living at Number 77 at this time,[40] but he was not listed on the census; perhaps he too was out on the road. He was to play an important role in the establishment of the Melkite church in New York. My great-grandfather, Solomon Forzly, was also living at 77; his wife may have been listed as "Shozie Kezo." One unattached woman, Rosa Malfour (Maloof?), 35 years old, was among the residents; one wonders if indeed she was alone, or whether her husband or children were simply absent when the census was taken. If she was alone, how did she manage in this crowded, male-dominated space? Unfortunately, we know nothing more about her.

Number 77 played an important role in the Syrian Colony, not just in 1890 when a number of Syrians lived there, but for decades afterwards. It was a decidedly Orthodox building, attracting Orthodox tenants and

[39] http://www.loc.gov/pictures/resource/hhh.ny0590.sheet.00001a/?co=hh.

[40] Samra 2012: n.p.

businesses, culminating in the top two floors being converted into the Orthodox Chapel in 1895. The church will be fully described below. A wide variety of businesses successively established themselves at Number 77 in the nineteenth century. "Abdow Lutfy & Sons," which had probably been established even earlier, officially set up shop in 1892. So did the Tadross brothers—Nami and Antoni—who had a dry goods business there the same year. The "Tadross Brothers" house/store served as a center for Orthodox events. The Lutfys soon moved to 2 Carlisle and the Tadross brothers moved their dry goods business to 79 Washington, where they still regularly hosted Orthodox events. In 1895, when the upper two floors of the building were taken over by the church, the parlor floor and basement remained commercial.

An 1897 photograph shows the next business that took over Number 77: "Mallouk & Abo Samra." Nicola Mallouk and Nicola Abo Samra were importers of Oriental goods. The picture shows a façade completely altered from the original handsome front, with the arched doorway turned into a mundane rectangular door with a set of stairs leading up to it.[41] To the right, one of the first floor windows had been enlarged to make an entrance to the store, and the steps leading up to it have pulled away from the building and are canting down to the left. The one remaining first floor window has been changed from a six-over-six window to a plain single-pane double-hung window, which sits directly above a dark cellar entrance in which a young man stands with folded hands; only his upper half is visible above the level of the sidewalk. A sign above his head reads, "John Haddad, 77½ Washington St." Haddad had a small grocery shop in the basement. The three windows on the second floor retained their mullions and lintels but are obscured by a fire escape.

After Haddad vacated the basement, Yusef Balesh and Khalil Geha moved their dry goods business there, and in 1898, the two companies in the building merged to form "Mallouk, Balesh & Geha," which continued to import Oriental and Parisian goods and textiles from Constantinople. The company remained at Number 77 until 1900.[42] (Nicola Abo Samra went into partnership with Shakir Nasser, and they moved their Oriental importing business to 28 Rector.) The sons of Makhoul Boutross then took over the basement

[41] Moss 1897: n.p.

[42] *Al Hoda,* October 4, 1898.

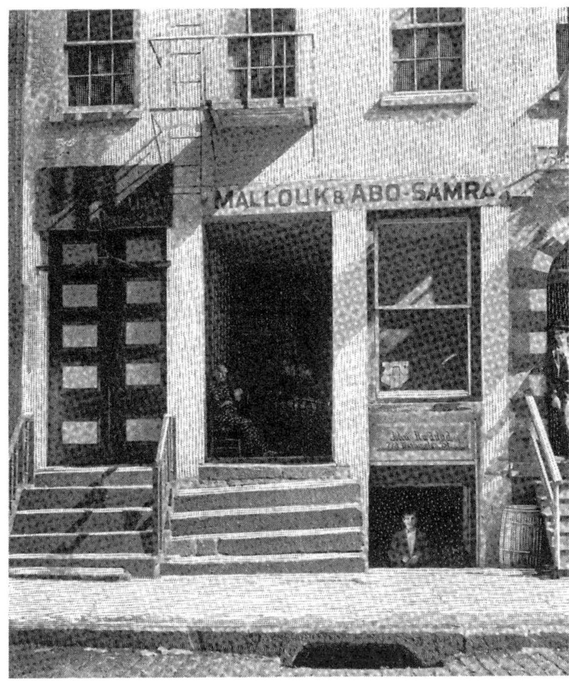


3-9. Mallouk & Abo-Samra Store, 77 Washington Street (Moss 1897). John Haddad is standing in the basement entrance of his grocery store, marked 77½.

space.[43] Although the Boutross family lived in Jersey City at that time and established an importing business on the Boardwalk in Atlantic City, three of the brothers—Abraham, George, and John Boutross—continued to have a business on Washington Street until at least the 1920s. By 1900, only two residents remained in the building: Ignatious Zouky and his wife, who occupied the basement alongside their fruit shop.

Number 79 Washington housed four Syrians in 1890. One of the residents, George Saba from Amioun, had joined with David G. Biskinty, who was living at Number 95, to open a dry goods business at 79. Saba and Biskinty soon parted ways; Saba went into partnership with Michael Isaac and continued to sell dry goods there, while David Biskinty set up a notions and fabric business at his own residence, Number 95. Lotfallah Atta opened his first restaurant on the parlor floor of Number 79 in 1894. In 1897 the building became wholly commercial, when Antoni Tadross took it over for

[43] Cromwell Childe, "New York's Syrian Quarter," *NYT,* August 20, 1899.

his dry goods business. The only residents remaining were the Syrian couple Kareemi and Nageeb Freije, who worked for Tadross.

Number 81 Washington became an important building for Maronite businesses later in the decade, but there were no Syrians living there in 1890, as far as we know. Joseph N. Maloof, who became the editor of *Al Ayyam* newspaper, opened a store that sold European fashions and accessories at 85 Washington in 1892. Although 91 Washington had no Syrians listed in the 1890 census, Habib Daoud and Tannous Shishim started their boarding-house and restaurant there in 1892.

Leaving his partnership with George Saba, David Biskinty set up a business at Number 95 in 1890, where he lived; he imported fancy goods from Europe and the Orient. In 1893, David brought in his brother Constantine as a partner, and David left soon after to go back to Syria for his health. He never returned to the United States. Constantine retained the business name, "David Biskinty & Co.," until 1900, by which time the company had relocated to 60–62 Washington Street. At this point he finally changed the name to "Constantine Biskinty," perhaps finally admitting to himself (and the world) that his brother wasn't coming back. It is said that David died young. Two other Syrians lived at Number 95 in 1890: Asad Milkie, my great-uncle from Bishmezzine, who immigrated in 1888, and was a clerk, printer, editor, and writer; and Ibrahim Farah, another dry goods merchant from Baskinta. From its earliest use as a Syrian residence, the building attracted Presbyterians. The Biskintys sold Presbyterian religious books in their dry goods store. In 1892, Ameen F. Haddad rented the second floor to house the Syrian Society School, displacing the residents, although Syrians continued to use the ground floor as a commercial space. Presbyterians worshipped upstairs in the later part of the century and continued to do so until they began to attend services in Brooklyn in 1908.

Three Syrians were living at 102 Washington in 1890 (Kalil Abraham, Anthony Elias and John Haidar), but very little is known about any of them. The location of 111½ Washington, where seventeen Syrians were living in 1890, is something of a mystery; there is no such address on either the 1885 or 1897 Manhattan map. In the 1890 census document itself, 111½ is sandwiched between 117 and 119 Washington; clearly the census taker missed it in his first run up the street and added it later. The main building at 111 was a five-story building with no basement, so the one-half cannot refer to a basement. The backyard had a small (apparently) two-story building along the back property line measuring about fifteen by twenty feet; this back tenement may have been 111½ Washington. If that is indeed the building, it was very crowded. One of the few large Syrian families from this early period, the seven El Hayek siblings, lived there. This Maronite family came from Baabda in 1888 and consisted of three older brothers (Souma, Said, and Touma), their older sister "Yatney" (Fatna/Fannie), and three younger siblings: Mary, Joseph, and Anissa. Presumably everyone peddled when they first arrived. In 1891 the brothers established "Said Hayek & Co.," a store selling jewelry and optical goods, at 3 Carlisle. In 1893, the company was renamed "El-Hayek Brothers."

In the same house (111½) resided three single, apparently unrelated, Syrian women, aged 35, 36, and 40. From the order in which they are listed, it may be that two of them were rooming together, but in such a small space, it must have been very difficult to maintain any privacy or modesty at all. How did these women manage with common water taps and privies? All women who lived in tenements all over the city had to contend with these conditions, but it seems impossible to imagine now.

Number 122, the northernmost Washington Street residence in which we find Syrians in the 1890 census, was located on the northwest corner of Washington and Carlisle. Nineteen Syrians lived there. It was the usual type of brick tenement with its short side facing Carlisle and its long side facing Washington, but it had a Washington Street address, which means that the entrance must either have been on the long side, an unusual configuration, or that there were two entrances, one on Carlisle and one on Washington. It was originally part of a row of similar houses on Carlisle and probably five stories high, twenty feet wide, and thirty-five feet deep. It was on a corner so it must have had more light than the other townhouses. Among the Syrians living there was the Melkite Basha family from Baalbek—six in all—including brothers Tanious and Joseph and their wives. Tanious had immigrated in 1885. After peddling Oriental jewelry, he opened a jewelry store at 6 Carlisle Street and was able to bring his family over in 1887.

As was true throughout his life, Muossa Daoud was living on his own at Number 122. By 1894, though, after a short interval at Number 111½, he became the proprietor of a boarding house *cum* notions supply house at 17 Rector. Also living alone at Number 122 was Salim Mikwee, who soon brought his family over and set up a dry goods business at 59 Washington (after Salim Elias had moved his business out). Number 122 was torn down early in the 1890s to make way for a public grammar school, which many of the Syrian children attended.

Said Jureidini lived at 2 Carlisle in 1890 and set up a dry goods and cutlery business there. Zahi Azar, another resident, was probably a peddler in 1890, but he established a variety store at 31 Washington in 1892. Shakir Nasser also lived at Number 2; in 1893 he set up an Oriental importing business with John Abd-el-Nour at 27 Rector, but by then he was living on West Street. Numbers 2 and 4 Carlisle, which were small federal-style houses in the middle of the block between Greenwich and Washington, continued to be important to Orthodox Syrians. Maronites lived and worked at Numbers 3 and 5. Although there are no Syrians listed at 5 Carlisle in 1890, we know that Maroon Fagher had a boarding house and dry goods business there perhaps as early as 1890, and he continued to live and work there until at least 1899.

Living at 20 Morris Street were the brothers Elias and Michael Abousleman, another Maronite family from Baabda, along with Elias's wife, Yasmine, and their son Nassif (although Michael, Yasmine, and Nassif are missing from the census). Elias and Michael claimed to have founded their dry goods business in 1889, the year they arrived, and their partnership was long-lasting and successful. An "Abraham Saib," who also lived at 20 Morris, may be Abraham Saba, whose son Daniel lived there for many years and ran his fancy goods business with Joseph Nohra next door at Number 18 for almost two decades. Although not listed in the census, several Syrians worked/lived at Number 19 Morris in 1890. Antoni Tadross, the Faour Brothers, Joseph Nohra, and Beshara Ganim and Antoine Sadallah all had early businesses there; some or all may have lived there as well.

Also missing from the 1890 census were several buildings that were in use quite early by the Syrians, but perhaps none were residences. Shakir Fihed and Abdou Hamrah established a wholesale jewelry business at 21 Rector in 1892. Michael Karam set up as a commission merchant at 71 Broadway and worked there from 1891 to 1895. John Abd-el-Nour had his fancy goods business at 39 Broadway from 1892 to 1905 (changing partners on a regular basis). Moussa Zalka and Selim Marrash imported Oriental goods at 29 Broadway; at the same time, Zalka had a sole proprietorship in Oriental goods at 66 Trinity Place. Joseph and Rasheed Ayoob had their Oriental goods business at 1 Trinity Place.

The three maps on the following pages show the residence patterns of the Syrians in 1890, 1895, and 1900, respectively.[44] The pattern is clear:

[44] Maps of business locations will be found in chapter 8.

Syrians lived mainly on the east side of Washington beginning in the first days of the Colony and continuing through 1900. They also lived on Carlisle, primarily east of Washington Street. The double tenements at 3&5, 25&27, and 24&26 Washington are clearly visible as concentrations of Syrian residents. As the Colony grew larger, Syrians began to expand to West, Morris, Rector, and Greenwich Streets. One lone outlier on Trinity Place housed the large Aleppan Hakim family, who were dealers in Oriental goods. Other outliers who are not on the maps at all will be discussed in subsequent chapters.

# MANHATTAN RESIDENCES, 1890.

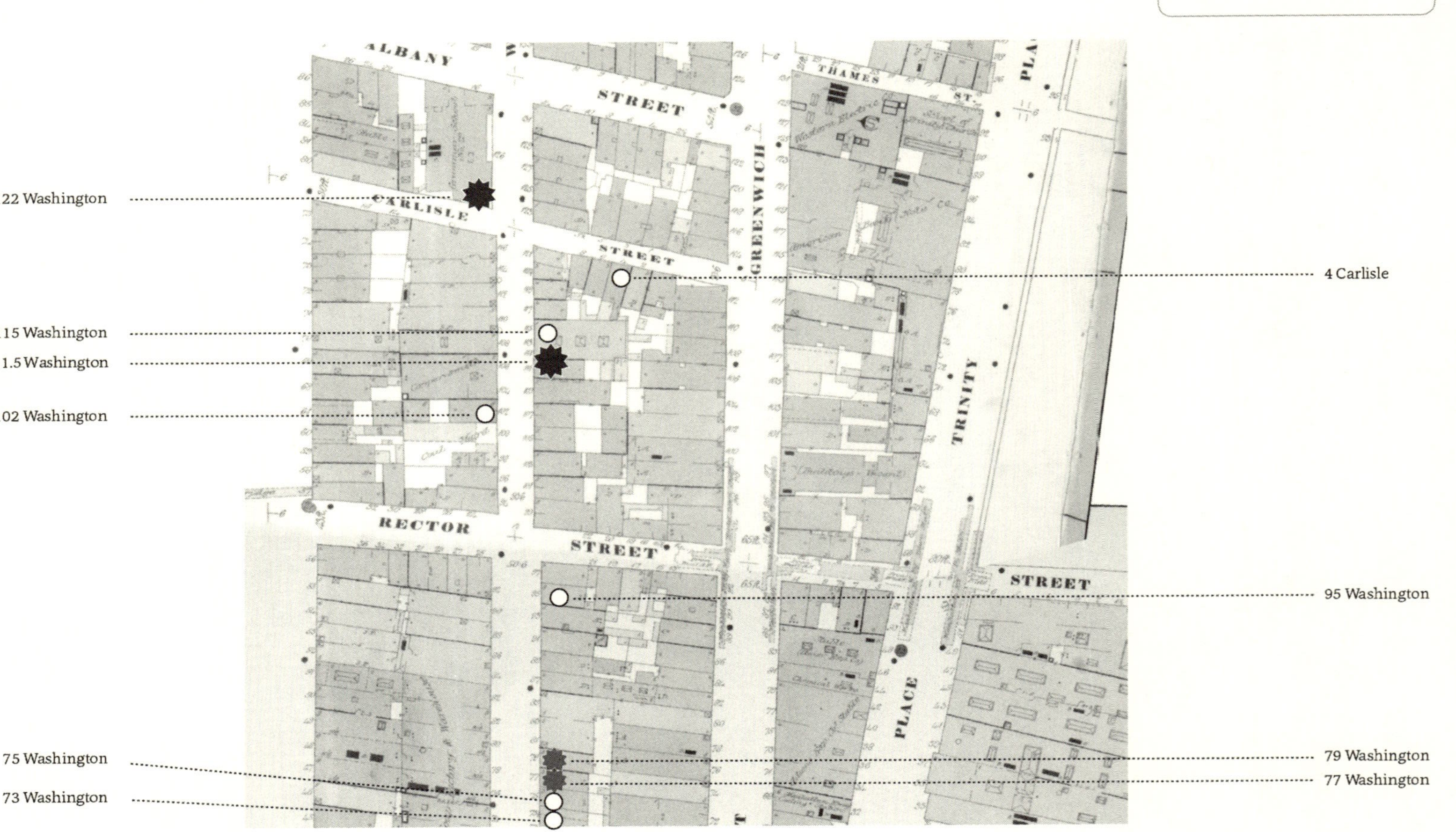

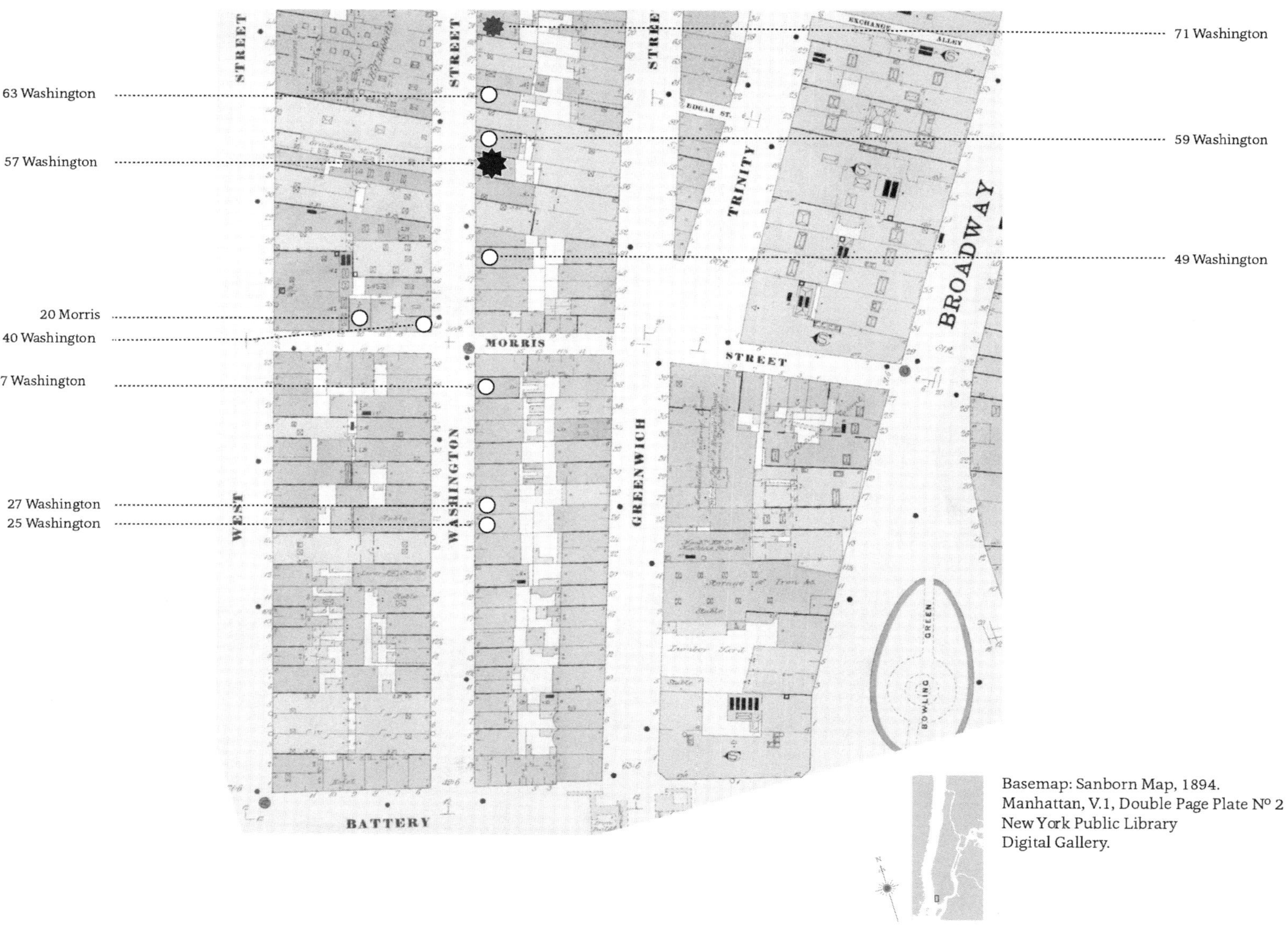


Basemap: Sanborn Map, 1894.
Manhattan, V.1, Double Page Plate Nº 2
New York Public Library
Digital Gallery.

# Manhattan residences, 1895.

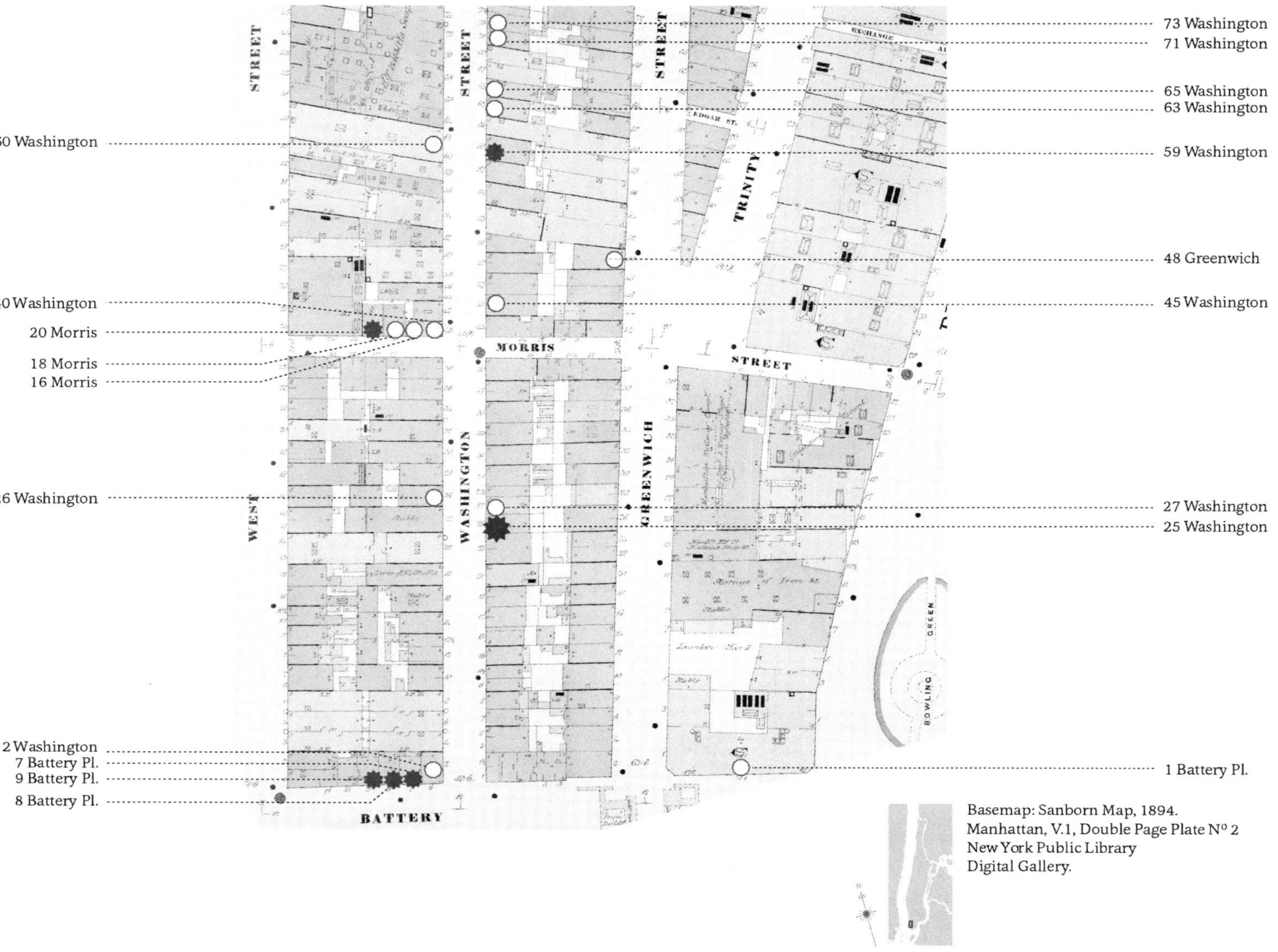


Basemap: Sanborn Map, 1894.
Manhattan, V.1, Double Page Plate Nº 2
New York Public Library
Digital Gallery.

# Manhattan residences, 1900.

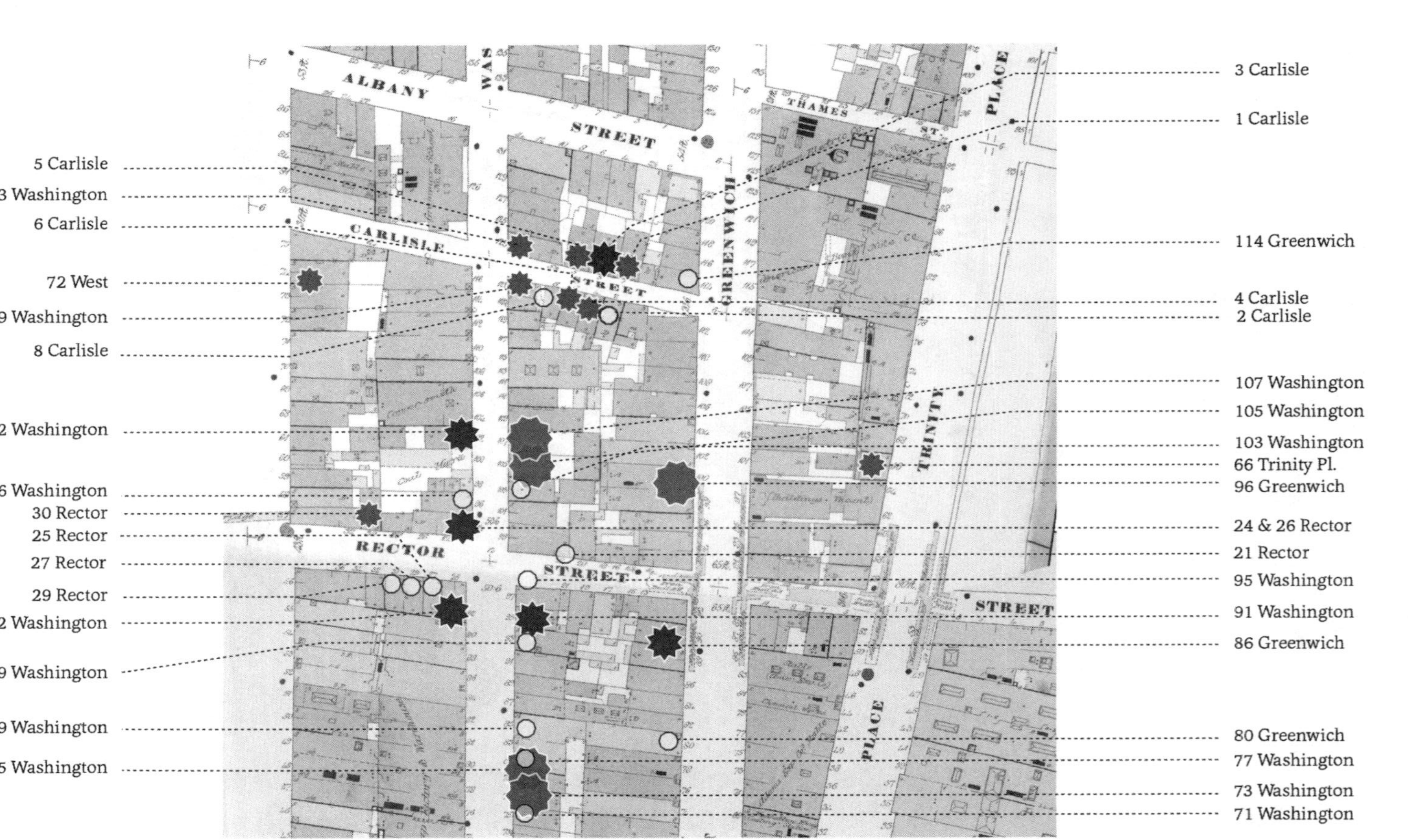

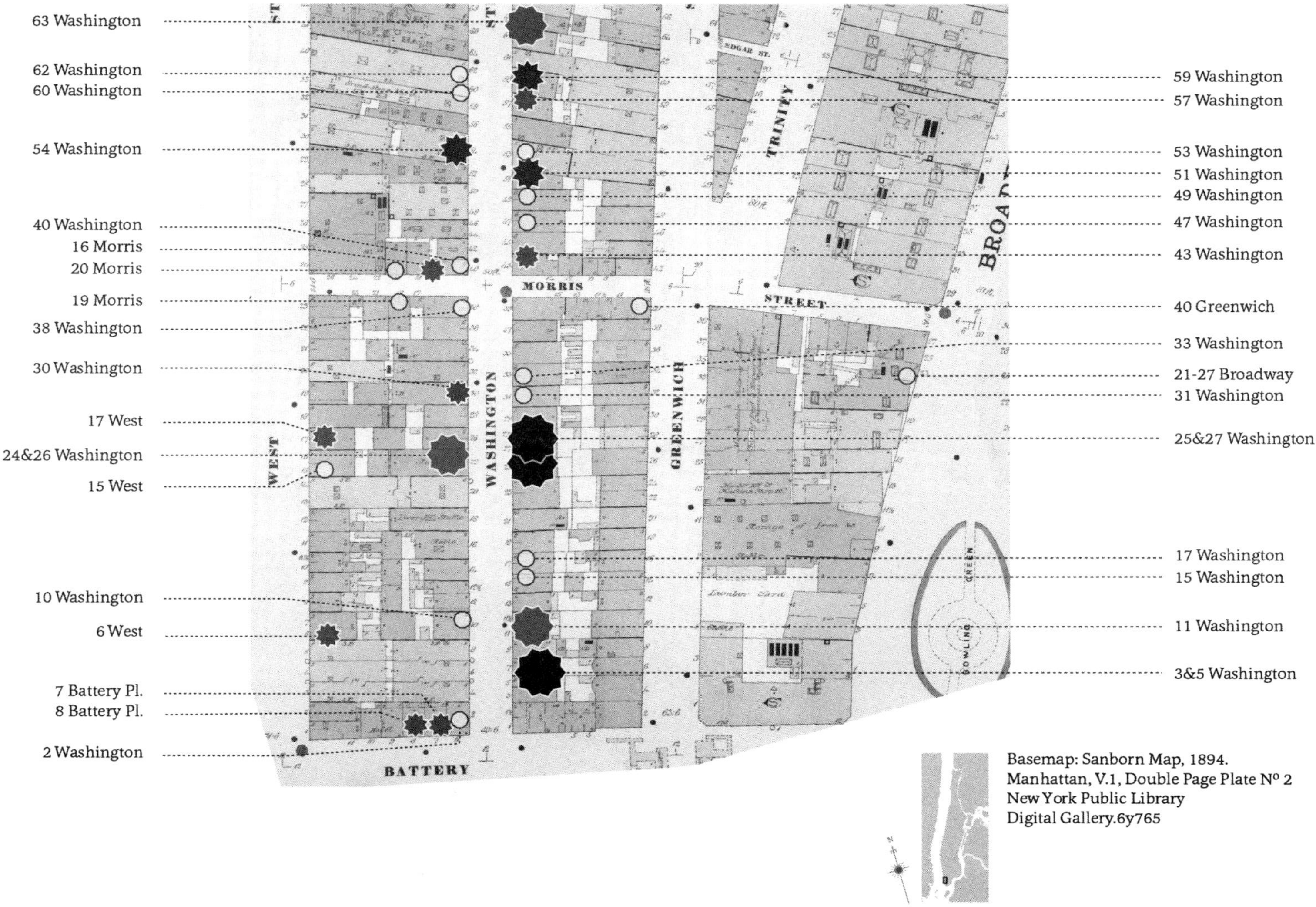


Basemap: Sanborn Map, 1894.
Manhattan, V.1, Double Page Plate Nº 2
New York Public Library
Digital Gallery.6y765

### Syrian-Owned Shops

Syrians quite early established a number of retail shops to serve other Syrians, as well as any tourists who might wander down to find something exotic in the neighborhood. An 1894 article noted "Its Forty Stores, Its Restaurants, Its Newspaper, School, Druggist and Doctors—American Words Among Arabic Signs—A Prosperous Community." The article detailed eighteen stores on Washington Street, five on Carlisle, three on Rector, three on Morris, and three on Broadway.[45] Restaurants, barbershops, fruit stands, and dozens of small shops were set up inside and in front of the row houses. None of these Syrian businesses were called out on contemporary maps; they did not yet own their property and were, it seems, too small to merit recognition. These small shops will be described in chapter 7.

### Non-Syrian Commercial Establishments

The Washington Street behemoth B.T. Babbitt's Soap Works dominated the neighborhood. It occupied parts of both sides of the street between Rector and Morris (Numbers 64, 65, 66, 67, 68, 69, 70, 72, 74, 76, 78, 80, 82, and 84) and extended all the way through to West Street,[46] covering twenty-three city lots in all. The noxious smells coming from the rendering of animal fat must have pervaded the neighborhood; an engraving of the factory from 1876 shows black smoke pouring out of the smokestacks.

Numbers 70, 72, and 74 Washington in the Babbitt complex were five-story buildings, while those on either side of them were lower; it looks as if Babbitt took over a block of row houses and joined them together to house his factory. The West Street side of the Soap Works had huge arched wooden doors opening directly onto the loading docks of the Hudson River steamship lines. The firm maintained a retail store at 65–67 Washington and its own stable from which a dozen draft horses and wagons delivered its soap to grocers all over the city.

In his 1870 *Grocers' Directory,* Babbitt bragged that the company produced five million pounds of soap per month. A fire in 1885 started when five hundred boxes of lard spontaneously burst into flames. In 1893, *Kawkab America*

[45] "Colonists from Lebanon," *The* (NY) *Sun,* April 22, 1894.

[46] Babbitt 1870; Bromley Manhattan Map 1897.

reported an explosion at the factory, which emitted plumes of smoke and dust. Many of the Syrians on the street and in the neighboring buildings thought the place was about to collapse and ran from their dwellings in a panic. Luckily, the firemen were able to put it out. The editors of *Kawkab America* urged the Syrians to move to a different street where they wouldn't be assailed by the stench or endangered by the fires and explosions.[47] No one took this advice.

Despite its hulking presence, we have no evidence of a single member of the Colony working at the soap factory. But according to an article in *The World,* the Syrians did take advantage of the factory in one way: the very long wooden awning in front of the building provided shade for the Syrians on Sundays in the heat of summer. The men would play backgammon and smoke *narghile*s (the Middle Eastern water pipe) at tables set up under the Babbitt awning, regularly sending their children for "bouzah, or ice-cream, and for kinafee, which is a delicious cake rolled around almonds."[48] Two sketches accompanying the article show men in fezzes or fedoras playing backgammon under the awning and, across the street, women and men standing in front of their shops. A breeze would blow up from the Battery, cooling the street.

P. Ballantine & Sons Brewery was up the street from Babbitt's, taking up the whole west side of Washington between Albany and Cedar streets, with its office at 134 Cedar. It may have been simply a bottling plant (since the company's main brewery was in Newark), but it too must have been a source of pungent odors wafting down the block. As far as we know, none of the Syrians worked there either.

The other large employers in the neighborhood, equally ignored by the Syrians, were the railroad and steamship companies that owned the piers on West Street: the Pennsylvania and Susquehanna Railroad, Iron Steamboat Company, Alexandre Steamship Line, New York & Baltimore Transportation Line, and the Lehigh Valley Line. An 1897 photograph of West Street looking north from Rector Street shows a chaotic street scene: horse-drawn streetcars running on tracks in two directions in the center of the street and dozens of loaded wagons driving on the outer edges. Scores of men are walking on the sidewalk on the east side of the street. About a dozen men are sitting on the ground in front of the buildings on the east side (perhaps they were day laborers waiting for work?). Boxes are stacked in one of the shipyards on the west side of the street, and the sign "Metropolitan Line to Boston" sits on

[47] *Kawkab America*, July 7, 1893.
[48] "Sunday in the Syrian Colony," *The* (NY) *World*, May 18, 1896.

top of one of the sheds. The only other legible sign reads "Rooms." This is such a contrast to the relatively quiet residential Washington Street one block to the east. Only a few Syrians ever lived on West Street; as far as we know, none had shops or stores there. The docks apparently offered them very little temptation or opportunity.

North of the Colony on the corner of Washington and Fulton was Washington Market, a thriving produce market, which, along with the Produce Exchange on Whitehall Street, just across Bowling Green from the neighborhood, must have provided the Syrian fruit sellers with their stock. Other non-Syrian commercial establishments on the street were those one would expect in any nineteenth-century New York neighborhood, with the added presence of businesses geared to the shipping industry one block west. There were stables at 14, 16, 18, 22, 30, 52, 87, 89, and 108 Washington, all belonging to Irishmen; storage warehouses (3–4, 84–86, and 110–112 Washington); a coal yard (98 Washington); R.P. Snowden Grindstones at 30 Washington; and the S.M. Bixby & Co. blacking (boot polish) business (174 Washington), plus a United States–bonded warehouse at 110–116 Washington and another at 52–60 Greenwich. Note that almost all these businesses were on the west side of the street. The newly built Grammar School 29 took up the west side of Washington between Carlisle and Albany. Springarn's Drugstore, first at the southwest corner of Rector and Greenwich and later at the southeast corner of Rector and Washington, was a focal point for many in the Syrian Colony. Louis Springarn called himself a licensed physician (although he was convicted of practicing medicine without a license in 1897) and sold drugs, as well. He treated many members of the Colony and served them as a notary public, and some of the residents used the drugstore as a mail drop.

Irish saloons and German beer parlors dotted the neighborhood, as did boardinghouses belonging to Irish, Germans, Greeks, and Swedes, both on the Battery and on Washington Street. Moss gives a good picture of the mixture of businesses on a single block of Washington between Rector and Carlisle: "George Forzly's Armenian bank, Hen Lee's Chinese laundry, Slevin's Irish liquor saloon, and J. Yamin's Syrian notion store. Close to them is J. Mahoney's boarding-house."[49]

At the southern end of Washington Street was Battery Park, where a constant stream of immigrants emerged from Castle Garden and later from the barges coming from Ellis Island. They were met by a cacophony of voices of

[49] Moss 1897: 275.

hucksters trying to fleece them of the little money they still had on them, as well as a hodge-podge of hotels, boardinghouses, bars, stores, and ticket agencies lining Battery Place. Moss reels off the names of Irish, Scandinavian, German, and Polish boardinghouses and the saloons that aimed to introduce newcomers to the phenomenon of the five-cent whiskey.[50]

## Public Transportation in the Neighborhood

Although there was no public transportation on Washington Street itself, the Manhattan Railway Company's elevated railroads took passengers from lower Manhattan to Midtown. Starting at the Battery, the line split at Morris Street, the 9th Avenue el going up Greenwich and the 6th Avenue el up Trinity Place. The els were screechingly noisy, causing nearby buildings to shake, dropping soot and cinders on pedestrians below, and intermittently blocking out the sun. They were sometimes dangerous as well: a Syrian woman named Mary Arians (Elias?) was seriously injured when her peddler's basket was caught in the door of a moving train; she was dragged more than twenty feet along the elevated tracks. A widow, she lived at Maroon Fagher's place at 5 Carlisle, and she "took goods" from him (he supplied her with the stock she peddled). He identified her and brought in the Maronite priest to administer last rites, but she did not die.[51] This happened several times over the course of the decade, and each time the victim had to decide whether to sue. In one case, the wife of one Boutross Helou won 600 *rials*, but others were not as lucky.

Mechanical shops, engineers' rooms, storage yards, a stable, lumberyards, and ticketing offices on Greenwich and Trinity serviced the els. The elevated stations at Battery Place, Rector, and Cortlandt (two stations at each corner—downtown and uptown) were elevated iron structures; their trestles narrowed the north–south streets and protruded onto the east–west ones. The el employed only two Syrian men: Abdul Fattali El Hoss as a guard and Alexander Haddad as a conductor. Haddad had started his working life in New York as a blacksmith, but moved to the job on the el in 1900. El Hoss later moved "up" from his job on the el to become a dry goods merchant. Public horse-drawn streetcars ran on tracks on West Street, moving people and goods between South Ferry and the piers farther north.

[50] Moss 1897: 271.
[51] "Mrs. Arians Will Not Die," *The* (NY) *Evening Telegram,* January 27, 1894.

## Battery Park

Notwithstanding the cacophony of joints, hucksters, and newcomers crowding the Battery, Battery Park was the place where people from the neighborhood went to get relief from the urban maelstrom. They could breathe fresh air or just look at the sky, the children could play unencumbered by traffic, and new immigrants might stare across the water thinking of home. Ameen Rihani, in his *Book of Khalid,* waxes lyrical about spending hours watching one of the beautiful milkmaids who plied her trade in Battery Park. Abraham Rihbany spent all his leisure hours there; it was there that he had the religious experience that set him on the road to the ministry. One editorial in *Kawkab America* complained that the air in Battery Park was polluted from the steam pipes and stacks associated with Castle Garden, but no one else noted this. A 1914 study by Trinity Church showed that it was a vital playground for the children of the neighborhood. Commuters from Brooklyn disembarked at its southeast corner and walked diagonally across it to reach their businesses on Washington Street.

## Churches

The development and assimilation of the four Christian sects of the immigrant Syrian community—Maronite, Melkite, Orthodox, and Protestant—have been well analyzed by Kayal and Kayal,[52] and the religious makeup of the New York community will be described in chapter 4. But the churches, which played such an important part in the spiritual lives of the Colonists, formed an important part of the physical landscape as well.

Two American churches served the earliest Syrian immigrants: Trinity Episcopal Church for the Orthodox and Protestants and St. Peter's Roman Catholic Church for the Melkites and Maronites. As it does today, Trinity Church and its yard took up the whole block between Trinity Place and Broadway and between Rector and Thames Streets. The church's February 1889 newsletter, *The Record,* noted the visit of an unnamed Syrian who was preparing himself for the (Presbyterian?) priesthood. He volunteered to work with his countrymen who, the church acknowledged, lived less than a half mile away. The note claimed, "Visiting and instruction has begun." The

[52] Kayal and Kayal 1975.

author appealed to the Trinity congregation to support this young man, as he was forbidden to take paid work while attending the seminary.[53] There is no evidence that these meetings or instruction actually occurred, at least not in subsequent issues of *The Record.*

Were the ties to Trinity anything other than ties of convenience? It may be that the Protestants worshipped there until their own priest arrived in 1899 (or even after, as Miller records them attending nearby churches for Sunday morning services, but attending the Syrian service on Sunday nights). Unfortunately, attendance at Sunday services was not recorded. The church's archives do make brief references to Syrians attending its various social service offerings, such as the school where girls were taught sewing; the night school that gave free instruction in English and other skills; and the Ladies' Employment Society, where women were given cloth that they made into school outfits for the Sunday school children. The women were paid for this work and were allowed to buy any clothes that weren't needed at the cost of the materials. They could take them home to their own children or sell them as they wished.[54] Although the number of women in this program never exceeded sixty, some number of them seem to have been Syrian. Two Syrian weddings and a few baptisms took place at Trinity. Christopher Jebbarah, a traveling Orthodox clergyman, performed one wedding there, but Trinity clergy performed the others.

Farther away sat St. Peter's Roman Catholic Church, on the corner of Barclay and Church streets. It was the closest Catholic Church; both the Maronite and Greek Catholic congregations held their services there in the early days of the Colony, and several Syrian weddings took place there. One can imagine the procession of Colonists in their "Sunday best" heading to the church every Sunday morning.

The Roman Catholic Church of the Epiphany, on 22nd Street and 2nd Avenue, hosted Arabic masses in 1881. One Reverend Joseph Memarbasci conducted the services, but to whom were they addressed?[55] St. Stephen's, a Catholic church on West 29th Street, was the venue for Joseph Oussani's wedding in 1896.

Even farther out of the neighborhood was St. Bartholomew's on 44th Street and Madison Avenue. Abraham Yohannon, an Assyrian from Persia, established St. Bart's Oriental Mission in 1897 to serve mostly the Armenians

[53] *The Record,* February 1889: 3.
[54] Trinity Church 1889: 27.
[55] "Rites from the Orient," *NYT,* January 7, 1881.

who lived in the neighborhood. Yohannon was fluent in several languages and also delivered religious instruction in Arabic, Syriac, and Persian. He provided help at Ellis Island to new immigrants and established workshops to employ women. In his 1901 report, he claims to have served Syrians as well as Armenians,[56] although to our knowledge no Syrians lived near the church, unless it attracted Arabic-speakers such as the Oussanis, who lived on the west side, in the Tenderloin.

Although these American churches served as stopgaps for the Syrian Christians, members of all four Christian sects yearned for their own place of worship in the neighborhood. There could be no Syrian church without a Syrian priest, and the arrival of the priest was the most important event in the history of the congregation. Each of the four Christian churches is described in the chronological order in which its priest arrived.

### *Melkite*

The Melkites and Maronites of New York had been attending services at the Roman Catholic Church of St. Peter's on Barclay Street, but the Melkites felt the need to have a priest to minister to them in their own language.[57] A group of them wrote to the Catholic archbishop of New York in 1889 requesting his permission to bring to New York a priest who spoke their language. They claimed there were 2,000 of them in New York: "women, ladies, girls, men, boys & babies living without a priest & very few [of] those…can understand english & the rest are ignorant." Ameen Batal, then living at 77 Washington Street, was apparently the person who sent in the petition. [58] The appeal for a priest was granted, but with the caveat that the diocese would not help them build a chapel, and they would have to use an existing church for their services.[59] St. Peter's would serve as their church.

Abraham Beshewate was identified as the ideal candidate. Although originally from Zahleh, he was living in Rome at the time. Archbishop Corrigan

[56] Anonymous 1901: 102.

[57] Samra 2012.

[58] *Archdiocese Letters,* (Presumably) Batal to Corrigan, n.d. (1889). The letter was not signed, but Batal's name and address are written in a different hand on the letter. The letter itself may have been transcribed or translated by a native English speaker, as the handwriting is fluent and native.

[59] *Archdiocese Letters*, Corrigan to (presumably) Batal (but addressed to "Very Rev. dear Sir") referring to his letter of November 20; December 3, 1889.

wrote to a Syrian prelate there, Isaac Saba, asking for his views on the appointment. Saba wrote back on December 20, 1889, giving Beshewate a ringing endorsement and saying that Beshewate was already on his way.[60] He arrived in time to preach a Christmas liturgy in St. Peter's basement on December 25, 1889. Thus, he became "the first permanent priest for the Syrian faithful."[61] When a reporter attended a service in mid-January; he counted about 600 people in the congregation.[62] The priest at St. Peter's was probably more realistic when he estimated the congregation at 100.[63] The first Melkite congregation in the United States was thus established as St. Peter's Syrian Roman Catholic Church, named after the church in which they held their first services.

On arrival, Beshewate settled at 151 Thompson Street (just south of Houston) with the Franciscan fathers who had charge of St. Anthony's Church on Sullivan Street, thus fulfilling Archbishop Corrigan's other condition that "no priest lives in his own house apart from the church."[64] Beshewate's first recorded baptism, of Rose Ganim Basha, and his first recorded marriage, of Nassif Mansour and Sultana Lutfy, both took place in April 1890,[65] either at St. Peter's or at St. Anthony's. Altogether, he officiated at 93 marriages and baptized 119 children between 1890 and 1900, but there is no indication in the records of where those ceremonies took place. For example, Beshewate officiated at Joseph Oussani's wedding, which was held at St. Stephen's Church on East 28th Street in 1896, but Bishop Colton of St. Stephen's signed the marriage certificate. At least once, Beshewate used St. Joseph's Maronite Church, located at 81 Washington, where he performed a wedding in 1893, and he assisted at several Maronite weddings performed by the Maronite priest.

There were troubles for Beshewate at the beginning. In 1891, some Syrians (their names are not known) signed a petition to have him recalled for misappropriation of funds and "frequenting saloons."[66] It may be that Ameen Batal, who had sent in the original petition, was behind the attempted recall, because a few months later he sued the priest for back wages. Father McGean, the priest of St. Peter's, testified that Batal had indeed worked for Beshewate,

[60] *Archdiocese Letters*, Saba to Corrigan, December 20, 1889.

[61] www.churchofthevirginmary.net/documents/church_his.htm.

[62] "Gotham Gossip," *Times-Picayune* (New Orleans, LA), January 17, 1890.

[63] Samra 2012: n.p.

[64] *Archdiocese Letters*, Corrigan to Batal, December 3, 1889.

[65] Samra 2012: n.p.

[66] "Arabs Want a Priest Recalled," *NYH*, March 26, 1891; "Dissatisfied with Their Priest," *The* (NY) *Sun*, February 12, 1891.

helping him serve mass. Batal had also served as Beshewate's interpreter, as the priest knew no English when he arrived. Beshewate claimed he had not been able to collect enough at offerings to pay Batal, but the judge ruled for Batal, and the congregation was forced to pay him $747.50 in back wages,[67] an extraordinary amount of money for one year's service. The *Sun* described all of the accusations against Beshewate as a "misunderstanding." After this fracas, Batal must have found himself persona non grata in the Melkite community of New York, and indeed, he soon moved to Lawrence, Massachusetts, and began lecturing in churches on "Life in Palestine."[68] The enmity he had earned in New York, however, followed him. In 1895, the governor of New York requested his extradition to answer an accusation of sodomy, which was supposed to have occurred in June 1892. The governor of Massachusetts refused to extradite him when it was proved that he was living with his wife in Massachusetts when the sodomy was supposed to have occurred.[69] Throughout his life, he continued to be embroiled in lawsuits, but he lived until the ripe age of eighty-eight.

Notwithstanding these stains on Beshewate's reputation, in 1892 the archbishop of New York wrote a letter of reference for Beshewate to introduce him to Catholic bishops in other American cities and to vouchsafe his raising money to build a chapel.[70] In 1895, Beshewate estimated his congregation at two hundred[71] and once again begged Archbishop Corrigan to allow him to raise money for a church. The priest must have agreed, because Beshewate sent out a fund-raising appeal to Catholics all over the country, enclosing Corrigan's 1892 letter of reference. Either the archbishop found out about this and asked Beshewate to cease this practice or the appeal was unsuccessful, because the Melkites continued to hold their services in the basement of St. Peter's until 1914, when they rented a floor of a house on Greenwich Street and converted it to become the St. George Syrian Catholic Church. Beshewate was then living at 19 Rector with his brother's family, and his niece Elsie served him as a bookkeeper. The congregation subsequently converted a tenement at 98 Washington and used it as their church until 1920, when the building was sold and demolished.[72] The congregation (with a substantial

67 "They Did Not Believe the Monk," *NYH,* September 22, 1891.
68 "*The Lowell* (MA) *Courier,* July 29, 1893.
69 "They Want Batal," *Boston Journal,* March 22, 1895.
70 *Archdiocese Letters*, Corrigan to bishops, February 15, 1892.
71 *Archdiocese Letters,* Beshewate to Corrigan, September 25, 1895.
72 Samra 2012: n.p.

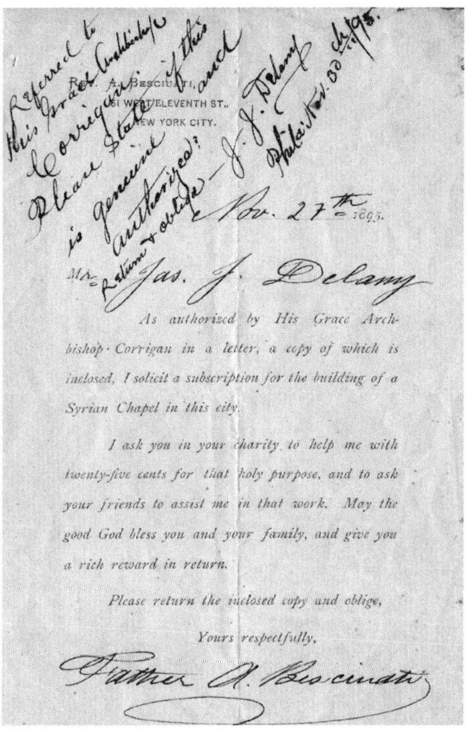

Rev. A. Besciutti,
61 West Eleventh St.,
New York City.

Nov. 27th 1895.

Mr. Jas. J. Delany

*As authorized by His Grace Archbishop Corrigan in a letter, a copy of which is inclosed, I solicit a subscription for the building of a Syrian Chapel in this city.*

*I ask you in your charity to help me with twenty-five cents for that holy purpose, and to ask your friends to assist me in that work. May the good God bless you and your family, and give you a rich reward in return.*

*Please return the inclosed copy and oblige,*

*Yours respectfully,*

Father A. Besciutti

3-10. Fund-raising letter from the Melkite priest Abraham Beshewate, 1895 (*Archdiocese Letters*). J.J. Delany wrote to Archbishop Corrigan asking if the letter "is genuine and authorized."

donation from George E. Bardwil) finally purchased the tenement at 103 Washington in 1920. The Syrian-American architect Harvey Farris Cassab, who was born in California and raised in Charleston, West Virginia, converted the building to the purpose. Rev. Beshewate served his flock in Manhattan for thirty-four years.

In 1908, a Melkite church was established at 83–85 Pacific Street, Brooklyn, which had its own priest and conducted services concurrently with the Manhattan church. It is the Brooklyn church that holds the early baptismal and marriage records. The church at 103 Washington Street, later converted to a bar, has now been landmarked as one of the last remnants of the Syrian community on the Lower West Side.

### *Maronite*

Peter Korkemas was born in Ghiballah, Mount Lebanon, in 1848. Ordained in 1874, he spent twelve years in Jerusalem before being sent to the United States to minister to American Maronites in New York in 1890. Yusef Yazbek, who subsequently earned a theology degree at Fordham, the first Maronite to be ordained in this country, accompanied him. After Yazbek's ordination, Archbishop Corrigan sent him to Boston, but he continued to play an important role in the New York Colony. In 1900, he began traveling around the United States ministering to the Syrian Catholics (both Maronites and Melkites); he maintained regular communication with Archbishop Corrigan about their situation.

The Maronites and Melkites had attended the Latin mass together at St. Peter's, but with the arrival of Beshewate, the Melkites moved downstairs, while the Maronites continued to attend mass in the main church. As soon as Korkemas arrived, however, he also began holding Arabic services downstairs. In 1891, a *New York Herald* article was headlined, "Novel High Masses in Oriental Tongues: St. Peter's Catholic Church the Scene of Three Celebrations of the Feast of the Epiphany." According to the article, the Latin mass was held at 9 A.M., the Melkite at 10, and the Maronite at 11.[73] Despite the synchronicity of the services, the priest of St. Peter's apparently felt that it was inadvisable to have both Syrian congregations meeting in the church; shortly after Korkemas arrived, he asked the Maronites to find a new home.[74]

Father Korkemas moved his flock out of St. Peter's and brought them to St. Leo's Home on Battery Park while he searched for a place to convert to a chapel. According to one article, the congregation secured a store at 26 Rector[75] and began to fit it out as a church, but apparently this attempt failed; the congregation ended up renting a room at 127 Washington, between Carlisle and Albany. St. Peter's rector, Father McGean, dedicated the new chapel. A reporter who attended the dedication was surprised that the congregation could respond in Latin.[76]

The chapel was described as "deep, narrow, and low, and lighted by what was a small show *[sic]* window, on which is this sign: 'Maronite Catholic

[73] "Novel High Masses in Oriental Tongues," *NYH,* January 7, 1891.

[74] Samra 2012: n.p.

[75] "Novel High Masses in Oriental Tongues," *NYH,* January 7, 1891.

[76] "Syrians of the Maronite Rite," *NYT,* January 19, 1891.

Chapel.'"[77] The building was five stories tall and sixty-three feet deep, with a bit of yard behind, and apparently light came into the chapel only from the front shop window, which implies that the floor was divided at least into a front and back space. The congregation was said to number 500 and was served by two Sunday masses. It's hard to imagine 250 people fitting into even a whole floor in that building.

3-11. St. Joseph's Maronite Chapel, located on the second floor of 81 Washington Street (Miller 1903).

The priest was living at 113 Washington, just down the street from the church, in "three very small rooms, second story back. They are very plain but very neat."[78] He soon moved around the corner into "three squalid rooms" at 1 Carlisle, upstairs from the Maronite El-Hayek Brothers' jewelry business,[79] next door to the Maronite midwife Mannie Shahdan at Number 3, and across the street from (Orthodox) Abdow Lutfy & Sons at Number 2. For the priest to have had three rooms for himself was exceptional in the

[77] "Syrian Worshippers," *The* (NY) *Sun*, April 26, 1891.
[78] "Syrian Worshippers," *The* (NY) *Sun,* April 26, 1891.
[79] "Forced in Illegal Marriage," *The (NY) Sun,* December 21, 1891.

crowded conditions of the Colony at that time; he may have needed them in order to have space in which to meet with his congregants. The writers at *The Rosary Magazine* of 1892 lamented, however, that the collections from the congregation were not enough to pay the rent for this "humble residence." They sought donations from other Catholics to defray some of the costs.[80]

After only two years at Number 127, the church moved to 81 Washington across from the soap works; it was called Mar Yusef (St. Joseph). The Rev. J.M. Farley (who later became the archbishop of New York) blessed the new chapel.[81] It was a relatively small five-story building (21 feet by 40 feet) with a small backyard. "Imagine a church on the top loft of an ancient four story *[sic]* brick building given up to wholesale business and storage. Yet such a building is No. 81 Washington street, and the Maronite Church is on the top floor."[82] A reporter called the chapel a "little hovel" and opined, "If there is a place in this world that resembles the Stable in Bethlehem, it is this chapel."[83] At one end of the large room "was a small altar, on which stood lighted candles and the various sacred ornaments seen in the Catholic Church."[84] On St. Maron's day in 1894, a reporter described how plain the church was: a simple altar framing a statue of Christ and statues of Mary and Joseph. Cheap paintings hung on the walls; there was a "little box of a confessional" and plain benches for pews.[85] A sketch of the chapel on that day, however, shows a rather grand altar with statues of saints on either side, Father Korkemas saying mass, and a dozen people sitting on wooden benches. Some of the congregation had apparently processed up Washington Street in "long cloaks of gay color floating over blouses and red, baggy trousers and Morocco boots, and curved scimitars that clanked in warlike style against the street lamp posts as they passed."[86] These men must have lent the chapel color, if not authenticity. Although they had been in this church only a year, Father Korkemas was already thinking of building his own church; he appealed for funds to all Catholic New Yorkers. "Donations will be received by Father Korkemas, 1 Carlisle street."[87] Korkemas's nephew, Father Gabriel M. Korkemas, joined him in November

[80] *The Rosary Magazine* 1892: 333.
[81] "To Bless a Catholic Maronite Chapel," *The* (NY) *Sun,* October 1, 1893.
[82] "St. Maron's Day Celebrated," *NYH,* February 10, 1894.
[83] "News from All Parts of the United States," *Irish World* (NY), October 7, 1893.
[84] "Syriac Wedding Service," *NYT,* October 29, 1894.
[85] "Our Syrian Christians," *Irish World* (NY), February 17, 1894.
[86] "St. Maron's Day Celebrated," *NYH,* February 10, 1894.
[87] "News from All Parts of the United States," *Irish World* (NY), October 7, 1893.

1893; they moved in together at 8 Carlisle Street, paying an astonishing $50 a month in rent.[88]

In 1895 or 1896, the congregation temporarily moved to 157 Cedar, which the Orthodox congregation had used earlier. Number 157 was a large (47′x 55′) five-story building on the northeast corner of Cedar and West Streets, a bit off the (Syrian) beaten path. "The Liberty Building," as it was called, was wholly commercial. On the ground floor were a café (or saloon) and cigar store; the floors above were open lofts. The size of the space must have been the attraction for both congregations. At this time, no other Syrian businesses were located there.

In 1897, the Korkemases moved the church back to 81 Washington Street, occupying the entire second floor.[89] Gabriel Korkemas appealed to Archbishop Corrigan for support of the church: "Our Congregation is so poor now that most of times I cannot have alms for Mass neither from them nor from outside the Congregation, and if I had any means in some way I will ornament our poor Chapel which is in #81 Washington St. It makes me deeply sorry, Eminence, to see our Chapel so poorly furnished and embellished while the Protestants and Greek schismatic churches are nicely furnished." He accompanied this appeal with a list of all the Maronite and Melkite children in the Colony ("66 in all") who were "like tender lambs" in danger of being devoured by Protestant wolves.[90] There is no evidence that the Catholic Church provided aid.

According to Moss, the top floor of 81 was a factory during the week, and the altar, crucifix, and picture of the Virgin were confined to one end.[91] In several articles, the building was described as an old warehouse, but Sahadi's store was on the ground floor, visible in a grainy photograph in Miller,[92] in which one can make out the *narghiles* and other Oriental goods displayed in the window, and a striped awning folded back above the door. Above the awning is a cross with a sign in English reading, "St. Joseph's," the sign a

[88] *Archdiocese Letters,* Peter Korkemas to Corrigan, 1897.

[89] "Maronites Honor Pastor," *NYT,* August 7, 1899. There is some confusion about this address: several articles place the church at 83 Washington, but city directories consistently give its address as 81. If 81 is correct, it is possible that the congregation moved to Cedar Street while the chapel was being renovated. Perhaps the two buildings were already joined to form a larger space, so that 81 and 83 were both correct addresses. The Maronite Faour Brothers converted Numbers 81–85 into a bank after the turn of the century.

[90] *Archdiocese Letters,* Gabriel Korkemas to Corrigan, 1897.

[91] Moss (1897: 272) says that Joseph Ayoob, in Number 81, "keeps the peace" between the Maronite Church at 83 and the Orthodox Church at 77.

[92] Miller 1903: 25.

gift from the Maronite Youth Association. Bunting decorates the fire escape above, which may have been left over from the celebration that took place in 1899 on the occasion of the twenty-fifth anniversary of Peter Korkemas's ordination.[93] Father Gabriel had again begun to collect money to build a Maronite church: not from the Syrians, or at least not only from the Syrians, but from wealthy Catholics in the city.[94]

Father Peter moved to 27 Rector (on the corner of Washington), where the furniture was "severely plain, the room untidy and void of attractive features."[95] Gabriel stayed at 8 Carlisle. The two priests were for a while assisted by another nephew of Peter's named Estefan Korkemas, but in 1898 Estefan was transferred to upstate New York, and Father Khairallah Stefan arrived in 1899 or 1900 to take his place. The three priests worked together and began again to raise money for a new church, and Father Khairallah was finally able to purchase a large brownstone at 295–297 Hicks Street in Brooklyn in 1902. In 1903, however, when Miller attended services, the Maronites were still meeting at 81 Washington; he estimated the attendance at one hundred men and ninety women.[96] Church services began in Brooklyn in 1904.[97] St. Joseph's Maronite Church survived into the 1930s at 57 Washington, serving new immigrants and those who continued to have their businesses in Manhattan.[98]

### *Orthodox*

In May 1893, an Orthodox priest named Archmandrite Christopher Jabara (his name was sometimes Hellenized to Christopherus) arrived in New York on his way to the World Congress of Religions at the Chicago fair. While he was in New York he officiated at the marriage of Nicola Abo-Samra and Mariam Abo Reehan in Trinity Church, and the following month, he consecrated an Orthodox chapel at 157 Cedar Street,[99] the same building that the Maronites later used for their temporary chapel. It was a bit out of the way, being

[93] "Maronites Honor Pastor," *NYT,* August 7, 1899.
[94] "Holding Mass in a Warehouse," *NYT,* August 21, 1897.
[95] "New York's Syrian Colony," *New-York Tribune*, March 13, 1898.
[96] Miller 1903: 25.
[97] http://www.ololc.org/about.html.
[98] Arida & Andria 1930: 45.
[99] *Kawkab America,* June 9, 1893.

at the corner of Cedar and West Streets, but *Kawkab America* described it as "a shop that was new and suitable and near the Syrian neighborhood."[100] The editors of the paper urged their fellow congregants to attend the first service. "Without this center," it said, "there could be no nation, no friendships, no success and no union. Earthly blessings are worth nothing without having a place to worship and a brotherhood of co-religionists.[101] Jabara, assisted by a Russian priest, conducted the first service on Sunday, June 11, 1893, and then departed for the Chicago fair.

3-12. Orthodox Chapel, located on the second floor of 77 Washington Street (Miller 1903).

Jabara gave a long presentation at the Congress, in which he advocated reconciliation between Islam and Christianity: "[When] the two great peoples, Christians and Mahometans, are also reconciled, the whole world will come into unity and all differences fade away."[102] After the fair he went back to Syria, leaving the Orthodox congregation with a church but no priest. Was his sojourn cut short after his controversial speech at the fair, as some people thought?[103] Perhaps so; otherwise why would he have dedicated a church in New York if he hadn't planned to return to it?

[100] *Kawkab America*, June 9, 1893.

[101] *Kawkab America*, June 9, 1893.

[102] www.orthodoxhistory.org/2009/11/24/fr-christopher-jabara-the-ultra-ecumenist/.

[103] Samra 2012.: n.p.

In 1894 a group of men incorporated themselves as the Syrian Orthodox Benevolent Society, and they named Dr. Abraham Arbeely (older brother of Nageeb and cofounder with him of *Kawkab America*) their president. On their behalf Arbeely wrote to Archmandrite Raphael Hawaweeny, who, like the Arbeelys, had been raised in Damascus and was probably an acquaintance.[104] Hawaweeny had written a long homily for the paper in 1893. When he received the request from New York, he was teaching and ministering in Russia, but Arbeely asked him to come to the United States as a permanent priest. In September 1895, the Russian Synod appointed him to the post. The full text of the letter was translated into Arabic and printed in *Kawkab America*. His salary and that of his deacon, Constantine Abi-Adel, were to be paid by the Synod (1,200 and 600 gold rubles, respectively).[105] An additional 500 gold rubles would be paid annually for traveling expenses to minister to the faithful in other parts of the United States (said to be "10,000 souls"), and 316 *chervonets* (about $900) were allocated for moving expenses for the two men.[106] They were to spend two months each summer and two months each winter ministering to the congregations of other cities.

Since more than two years had elapsed between the departure of Father Jabara and Hawaweeny's appointment, the congregation had given up the space at 157 Cedar and the Maronites had taken it over. In anticipation of Hawaweeny's arrival, the Orthodox rented the second floor of 77 Washington Street. Archmandrite Hawaweeny and Bishop Nicholas (bishop of Alaska and the Aleutian Islands and head of the Russian Orthodox Church in America) landed at Hoboken with great pomp in November 1895. Bishop Nicholas dedicated the chapel and introduced Hawaweeny to the congregation on November 17.[107] The Russian and U.S. flags hung on either side of the doorway for the occasion. Bishop Nicholas gave the address in Russian, which Hawaweeny translated into Arabic for the congregation. After blessing the water in a silver dish, the bishop used an olive branch to sprinkle the altar and walls of the room. Attending the service were not only members of the Syrian Orthodox community but also delegates from the Maronite congregation, a half-dozen "American" friends, and even

[104] The documentation for this event is a little confused; sometimes Nageeb is said to have been president and written the letter.

[105] "Bishop Nicholas Home," *The San Francisco Call*, December 1, 1895.

[106] "Minister for Syrians," *NYT*, September 15, 1895.

[107] *NYT*, November 18, 1895; *Kawkab America*, November 22, 1895.

the captain of a Russian ship that happened to be docked in the Port of New York.[108]

In describing the chapel, a reporter wrote, "A steep stairway leads to the room which corresponds in size with the store below and is divided into two parts, the larger part being the auditorium and the small part at the rear being reserved for the priest and his assistants."[109] Syrian Orthodox Benevolent Society had the flimsy room partitions removed to open up the space, and it was said that it could hold one hundred of the faithful, because most of the congregation stood. On the third floor was a medical dispensary run by the Benevolent Society that doubled as a meeting room;[110] it was there that the banquet following the dedication was held. That the Society could rent two floors speaks to the relative prosperity of the congregation. A partial list of contributors from outside New York showed that Syrians in Toledo and Fort Wayne together had contributed $7,400 to the Society in 1895, a handsome sum.[111] One can infer that the New Yorkers contributed more.

"No other sanctuary in New York is half so gorgeous and gay," one reporter said of the chapel.[112] A photograph of the interior shows a low-ceilinged room with two ornate chandeliers, floor-standing candlesticks, tapestries which demarcated a separate space, and double doors leading perhaps to a rear room. Five wooden chairs are visible. The walls, according to the reporter, were painted with bright murals of the agony of Christ and saints. "The room is full of dignity and does not lose its power."[113] It was said that Hawaweeny brought all these relics with him from Russia.

Hawaweeny conducted the services in the church, Abi-Adel assisted, and the businessman Abdow Lutfy served as choirmaster. Elias Zreik and Nayeff Saadi served as Hawaweeny's attendants at services and other ceremonies. In 1896, Hawaweeny, Abi-Adel, and Lutfy went on a pastoral trip across the United States from New York to San Francisco, spending several months baptizing, hearing confessions, and celebrating divine liturgies in the "crowded living rooms of the faithful."[114] One assumes that Lutfy also did business as he traveled with the priests. When they returned to New York, Abi-Adel

[108] "With Rich Ceremonial," *NYH,* November 18, 1895.
[109] "New York's Syrian Colony," *New-York Tribune,* March 13, 1898.
[110] "The Syrian Colony in New York an Interesting Element There," *Springfield* (MA) *Republican,* March 26, 1899.
[111] *Kawkab America,* November 15, 1895.
[112] "New York's Syrian Quarter," *NYT,* August 20, 1899.
[113] "New York's Syrian Quarter," *NYT,* August 20, 1899.
[114] Issa 1991: 20.

received notice that he had been transferred back to Russia, and Hawaweeny ministered alone for all of 1897. He married my paternal grandparents in the chapel at 77 Washington Street on a Wednesday in March 1897.

Hawaweeny lived at 7 Battery Place, where "an air of religious quiet and Oriental splendor pervades the little rooms."[115] This is quite a different description from the "three squalid rooms" of Korkemas cited above. We don't know whether he lived alone or had shared the space with Abi-Adel before the latter's departure. Hawaweeny made another pastoral trip across the United States in 1898, this trip lasting five months. Finally, a new priest, Nifon Shoohy of Homs, was sent to replace Abi-Adel.[116]

There were said to be 575 Orthodox Syrians in New York at this time.[117] Hawaweeny felt that the congregation should have a building of its own as well as its own parish cemetery, and he started to raise money toward those ends. The tsar of Russia was one of the first donors, contributing $1,017.[118] Another five-month-long trip, in which he visited forty-three cities, resulted in donations amounting to $5,000 toward the new church.[119] He eventually raised a total of $12,000.

Hawaweeny bought a large plot at Mt. Olivet Cemetery for the Orthodox faithful in 1901; a large number are buried there. Recognizing the trend of the Syrians moving to Brooklyn (having by then moved to 120 Pacific Street, Brooklyn, himself), Hawaweeny hired an architect, I.V. Bergezen, to design a new church "in Arabic style" in Brooklyn. Finding the cost prohibitive, Hawaweeny instead bought an existing church building at 301–303 Pacific Street and named it after St. Nicholas. It was dedicated on November 9, 1902. There was a splendid procession from Hawaweeny's home to the church, everyone dressed in their finest robes of office, and Hawaweeny and Bishop Tikhon of Alaska blessed the church. Then Rizq Haddad (a physician) and Nageeb Arbeely, Najeeb Diab, and Mansour J. Haddad (all newspaper editors) gave speeches. Rizq Haddad proclaimed, "In truth the building of a Syrian Arabic church in America is a very important and valuable task, all the more so since America has recently become a kind

[115] "New-York's Syrian Colony," *New-York Tribune,* March 13, 1898.

[116] Issa 1991: 22.

[117] *Al Hoda,* April 19, 1898. In a response to a query, Naoum Mokarzel wrote to all three religious leaders in New York to find out how many of each faith resided there. Only the Orthodox priest responded.

[118] Issa 1991: 25.

[119] Issa 1991: 33.

of promised land for all peoples."[120] The first wedding took place there in January 1903.

In 1904, the Russian Orthodox See was transferred from San Francisco to New York in recognition of the large numbers of Orthodox immigrants landing there, and Hawaweeny was named bishop of Brooklyn. Hawaweeny married my maternal grandparents in St. Nicholas Church in 1907, ten years after he married my other grandparents on Washington Street.

When Bishop Nicholas retired in 1899, he admonished the Orthodox Syrians not to let other churches proselytize to them. He also advised the Orthodox to take their children out of the public schools, "where they come out not only without the fear of God, but without a sense of shame."[121] Bishop Hawaweeny went even further when he issued a pastoral letter in 1912 forbidding the Orthodox to accept the ministrations of Episcopalian clergy.[122] Presumably these admonitions were aimed at Syrians in places where there was no Orthodox church, or perhaps the New York Syrians were drifting to other churches, but they speak to the fear of many Syrians that immigrants were losing their religion in the process of assimilation. In 1915, Bishop Hawaweeny died and was buried in a crypt under St. Nicholas Cathedral. The church later canonized him, and his remains were transferred to the Antiochian Village in Bolivar, Pennsylvania.

### *Protestant*

As early as 1891, H.H. Jessup, the Presbyterian missionary in Syria, advised the Presbyterian Board to hire someone "who knows Arabic to look after the religious interests of the Arab Colony in New York. The Maronites & Greek Catholics are sending priests to look after their people in Australia & America."[123] Nothing came of this until 1899, when Elias Saadi arrived. He settled in with his son John's family at 260 Greene Avenue in the Boerum Hill section of Brooklyn and began to conduct Sunday evening services at 95 Washington, a small four-story tenement (21 feet by 45 feet). Presbyterian Syrians had begun to live and work there starting in the 1880s: David

[120] Issa 1991: 41.
[121] "Russian Bishop Scores Schools," *The* (NY) *Evening Telegram,* January 2, 1899.
[122] Naff 1985: 295.
[123] *Presbyterian Letters,* H.H. Jessup to Mitchell, March 21, 1891.

Biskinty and then his brother Constantine had a store there until 1896, and in 1892, Ameen Haddad opened the Syrian Society school on the second floor, where, presumably, the services were also held. Miller called the church the "mission,"[124] because the Board of Foreign Missions of the Presbyterian Church supported it; we don't know what the congregation called it. Miller's 1903 photograph of the exterior of the building shows three of the four floors. It is a nondescript brick building with the entrance to Habeeb Srour's grocery store several steps below the sidewalk, and a shop window at street level. The second floor shows white curtains at the three windows—presumably the rooms shared by the church and school—and the third floor housed Srour's family. The windows have rather decrepit wooden shutters but do have curtains. Elias Reesha's Oriental Furnishings is next door at 93, and a butcher shop is on the other side, at 97.

Saadi came from Tripoli, where he taught Arabic. He had had some kind of religious experience in 1866, the year he married, and became a minister.[125] He was not a full-time preacher, as he owned rug stores in New York and Pittsburgh, the latter managed by his son Nessim. We do not know if he had duties other than delivering sermons. He is not listed in any of the pastoral lists in the Presbyterian records, so we must assume that he was a lay preacher. Whether he was paid is uncertain. The only obvious Protestant wedding in the nineteenth century, of Joseph Daas and Wadeah Deratany, was held at the Second Reformed Presbyterian Church in Manhattan in 1899, and Saadi did not officiate. Nahoum Daher Merhige and Minnie Kaydouh were also Protestants, but they were married at Trinity Church in an Episcopal ceremony performed by a Trinity clergyman.

Saadi hardly had time to make a mark; he died suddenly one Sunday in 1902 on his trip from Brooklyn to Manhattan to preach,[126] putting the survival of the Syrian mission in jeopardy. The Board of Foreign Missions, which had supported Saadi, apparently continued to sponsor a Sunday school for the children,[127] but the post of minister remained vacant. In 1903, Miller found "50 or 60 people attending the church on Sunday evenings, the sermons being supplied by members of the community."[128] Miller warned that although

[124] Miller 1903: 24.

[125] *Naff Interview,* Nabeah Shammas (Saadi's granddaughter), June 26, 1988.

[126] "Syrian Pastor Died Suddenly," *BDE,* November 24, 1902.

[127] The Presbyterian Mission also funded Miller's study of the Syrian community (Miller 1903) from which much of this information comes.

[128] Miller 1903: 25.

these Protestants' "rallying point" was the Sunday evening Arabic service at the Washington Street mission, they attended American churches on Sunday mornings. He urged the Board to find an Arabic-speaking preacher as soon as possible. He feared that, without one, the congregation would drift away.[129]

3-13. Presbyterian Mission, 95 Washington Street (Miller 1903).

Apparently, nothing was done until February 1907, when the Syrian Protestant Church was incorporated in Brooklyn; there were said to be sixty-five members, some of whom had been members of the "old church," some were new immigrants, and some were converts. They had only to wait for their minister, Anees Baroody, to graduate from college to take office.[130] Baroody began preaching in 1908 but resigned in 1909, and for many years after that, the congregation had neither church nor pastor. They attended services in local Presbyterian churches and held their meetings in the homes and offices of the members. They finally hired a pastor (Joseph Zeidan) in 1912, but still had no church of their own.

[129] For a full discussion of the role of religion in the American Syrian immigrant experience, see Kayal and Kayal 1975.

[130] *Presbyterian Letters*, "Minutes of the First Syrian Presbyterian Church of Brooklyn, N.Y.," March 1, 1908.

A decade later, Philip Hitti chastised American Protestant churches in New York for not doing enough to attract Syrians to their congregations and forcing Syrian Protestants to leave the Church altogether,[131] implying that the Syrian Presbyterian church in Brooklyn either had closed or was moribund. Whether moving to American churches or dropping out of religious life altogether, it seems to have been the case that the Protestants were the first to "assimilate" religiously, with the Orthodox not far behind. My maternal grandparents took their children out of the Syrian Orthodox church and sent them to Spencer Memorial Presbyterian Church in Brooklyn; in their case, it was a matter of the children not understanding enough Arabic to appreciate the service. But this was a part of the assimilation process that, writ large, was happening all across the Syrian diaspora.

[131] Hitti 2005 (1924): 112.

# Chapter 4

## Who Were the Syrians?

*When the Syrians first came to New York they had everything against them except their inherent resourcefulness and business ability. Of capital and experience or training they had none, and of any knowledge of the English language they were utterly destitute.*[1]

Who were the Syrians of the Syrian Colony? Lucius Hopkins Miller conducted the most complete survey of the Colony in 1903. Miller had been a Protestant missionary in Syria and came back with a profound love of the people. He was asked by the Board of Foreign Missions of the Presbyterian Church to report on the conditions of the Syrian Colony in New York; he did it with a thoroughness and enthusiasm that are still to be admired. He went door-to-door in the Manhattan, Brooklyn South Ferry (Atlantic Avenue), and South Brooklyn (Sunset Park) communities. He met with everyone he could find, and estimated the number of those he could not, defending the completeness of his count in strong and convincing terms. He asked them about their origins, religion, employment, literacy, whether their children were in school, and other equally nosy questions, which today would be greeted with suspicion, but apparently people were willing to talk with him. His knowledge of Arabic helped, I'm sure. He made two invaluable charts: the individual canvas and the family canvas, both of which were divided by neighborhood and block (not, unfortunately, by individual address), and which cross-referenced everything he thought meaningful.

Other early studies of the New York Colony include those of Louise Seymour Houghton (1911), Ralph A. Felton (1912), and Louise Ensign Catlin (1915). None of these works is as thorough as Miller's, and all used Miller's report as a point of departure (veering sometimes, in my view, close to plagiarism), some more successfully than others. Of the three, Houghton's is the best, but unfortunately she was concerned not just with New York, but

[1] Mokarzel 1927: 6.

with Syrian communities all over the United States, so her New York data are thinner than Miller's. However, she obviously had the most familiarity with the New York and Boston communities, and much of what she reported can be taken to refer to one of those cities. She, like Miller, generally avoided the use of names, but her photographs sometimes identified the subject. It is understandable that both researchers were reluctant to name names, since the people they were reporting on were still alive (in both cases, the report appeared less than a year after the research), but it is frustrating to those of us who are trying to identify individuals. The two other studies—both master's theses at Columbia—were of limited use, not only because of their derivative nature (cribbing liberally from Miller and Houghton), but also because Catlin's contempt for the Syrians damages her credibility as a researcher.

In the discussion that follows, I rely on Miller as a check on my figures whenever possible. And despite the fact that his survey took place between three and twenty years after my research focus, it is still relevant to our study, not least because most of the people in his study immigrated in the nineteenth century.

## Origins

The vast majority of "Syrian" immigrants to New York were indeed from Greater Syria.[2] We make no distinction (as they for the most part did not) between those from present-day Syria and those from present-day Lebanon. The sources for origin are scarce; we have origin data for less than one-fifth of the individuals in our database. The problems with even the ones we have were outlined in chapter 1.

The best sources are the two directories, the *Syrian Business Directory*[3] and the *Syrian American Directory Almanac*,[4] which in most cases list the village or town from which a business owner came. In the *Syrian-American Commercial Magazine* (published from 1919 to 1926), which printed a series of laudatory articles about Syrian businessmen in New York City, the owner's village of origin was sometimes given. Occasionally the village of origin is

[2] "Greater Syria" is used to designate the following *wilayets* (provinces) of the Ottoman Empire: Aleppo, Damascus, Beirut, Mount Lebanon, and Jerusalem.
[3] Mokarzel and Otash 1909.
[4] Arida and Andria 1930.

given in articles in *Kawkab America*. These sources are pretty much the only information we have. In most other instances, where birthplace was asked for—such as naturalization or passport applications, marriage certificates, and the like—people usually wrote "Turkey." Sometimes they gave the name of the nearest city or region, such as Homs, the Kura, or Mount Lebanon, or the name of their port of departure, such as Beirut, Tripoli, or Alexandria. It's possible of course that some number of those who gave these cities as their birthplace were actually born there, but their frequency makes them suspect. The significant exception to this tendency to generalize to the nearest city was that of people from Zahleh, who often named Zahleh as their place of origin. Some of these respondents were probably from villages near Zahleh rather than the town itself, but still, the information is more specific than most of what we have. It has been said that more than half the population of Zahleh emigrated, and one can certainly believe it if our database is any indication. Letters written by Presbyterian missionaries in Zahleh throughout the 1880s and 1890s lamented the number of people who were leaving for America. F.E. Hoskins, a new missionary in Zahleh, wrote in 1889 that "emigration fever" showed no signs of abating. "Hundreds go away every month," he said. "Zahleh has a population of about 18,000 and during the past 18 months at least 2,000 men have emigrated to English-speaking countries."[5] Those who had emigrated, he said, were the "bone and sinew" of the town.

Occasionally, too, American newspaper articles mentioned the place of origin of the protagonists, but these accounts are suspect since it is often clear from the context that the person(s) interviewed gave a hometown thought to be recognized by the reporter. In the case of the forty-two Syrians detained at Castle Garden in 1887, for example, all were said to come from Jerusalem. One had a tattoo of the "portals of Jerusalem" on his forearm.[6] This is in line with the tendency of the early immigrants to claim to be from the Holy Land, especially if they were in the business of selling Holy Land or Jerusalemite goods, but probably does not accurately reflect their birthplace.

In cases where the origin of one family member is known, we have assigned the whole family to that town. If their wives came with them to America, the wife was also assigned to the town. Although we know that she may have married in from another village, for our purposes it is enough to say that when she came to the United States, she came from that town.

[5] *Presbyterian Letters,* Hoskins to Mitchell, July 8, 1889.

[6] "The Syrian Arabs," *The Evening Telegram*, December 28, 1887.

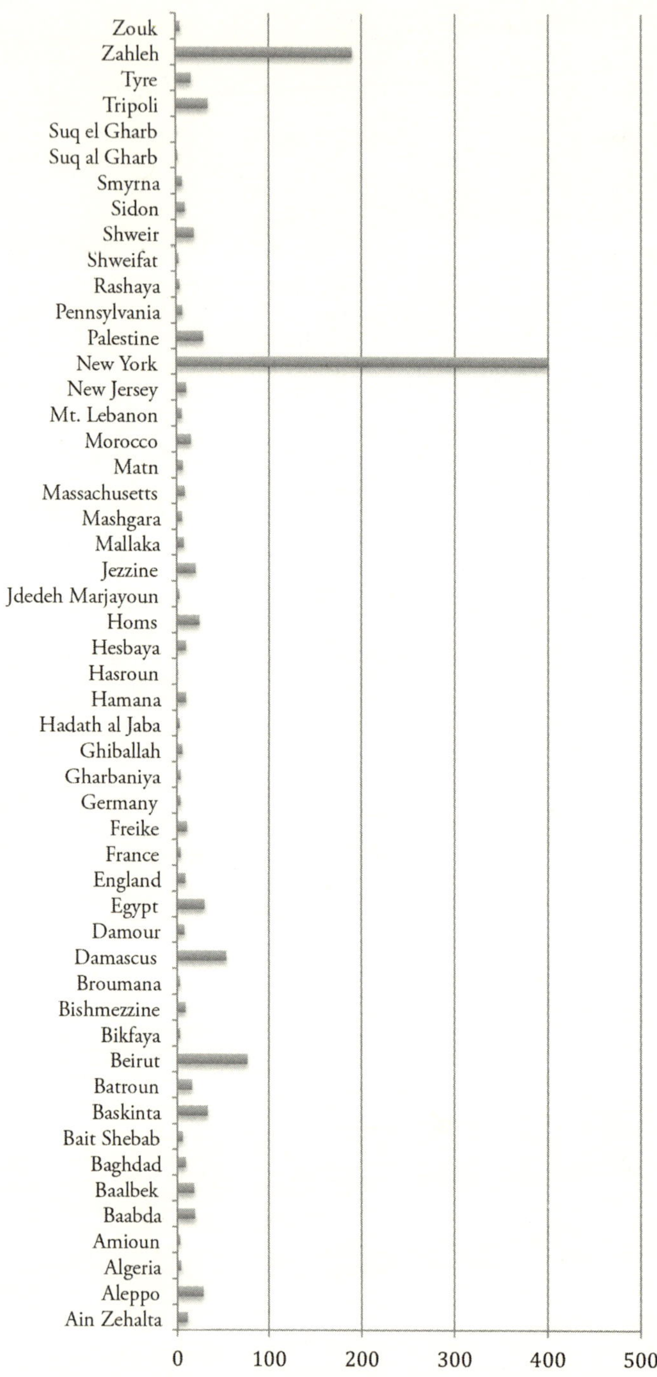
Places of Origin of Syrian Immigrants
n (total number) = 1235
Zouk
Zahleh
Tyre
Tripoli
Suq el Gharb
Suq al Gharb
Smyrna
Sidon
Shweir
Shweifat
Rashaya
Pennsylvania
Palestine
New York
New Jersey
Mt. Lebanon
Morocco
Matn
Massachusetts
Mashgara
Mallaka
Jezzine
Jdedeh Marjayoun
Homs
Hesbaya
Hasroun
Hamana
Hadath al Jaba
Ghiballah
Gharbaniya
Germany
Freike
France
England
Egypt
Damour
Damascus
Broumana
Bishmezzine
Bikfaya
Beirut
Batroun
Baskinta
Bait Shebab
Baghdad
Baalbek
Baabda
Amioun
Algeria
Aleppo
Ain Zehalta
0
100
200
300
400
500

The outliers—those not from the Syrian heartland—were a group of entertainers from North Africa (described more fully below), those from Egypt, and one family from Baghdad. The "Egyptians" were mostly Syrians from Mount Lebanon who moved to Cairo or Alexandria a generation or two before (or even in the 1880s) and then re-emigrated to America in the late nineteenth century. They were part of the Syrian Colony. The Moroccans did not live in the Colony, nor did the Oussani brothers, Chaldeans from Baghdad, who also stood out among the Syrian majority.

## Religion

Everyone who writes about the new immigrants talks about the preponderance of Christians among them: they were Maronites, Melkites, Greek Orthodox, or Protestant. But the diversity of the population is also described: how in the early days Muslims and Christians lived together in close proximity and amity.

### *Muslims in New York*

At the very beginning of this research, then, I set out to prove that some of the earliest Syrian immigrants from the Middle East were Muslims. All of these stories had to be based on some grain of truth! First, I searched for obviously Muslim names, such as Mohammed. In the entire database—from every source—there are only four Mohammeds loosely associated with the Syrians, but for none of them do we have sufficient information to guess their religion, nationality, or place of residence. There were about a dozen Moroccan entertainers who lived and worked in New York in the nineteenth century; most of them were probably Muslims. One of them, Hassan Ben Ali (about whom more will follow), claimed there were about 600 Muslims living in New York in 1896, and the lack of a mosque meant that they were in danger of converting to Christianity. He claimed he had already hired an architect to design a mosque.[7] In his peregrinations through the Syrian Colony in 1897, Frank Moss says, "Some of the people of this region are Mohammedans. There are in the City about six hundred of the 'Faithful,' and they are planning to erect

[7] "Planning to Build a Temple," *NYH,* December 18, 1896.

a mosque."[8] Perhaps Moss took his number from Ben Ali's earlier account. Nothing more was heard of this effort, nor of the 600 Muslims.

The second route in the search for Muslims was the examination of marriage and death certificates, which indicated the religion of the participants. All but three marriages were performed under Christian rites, and all burials took place at Christian cemeteries. Of course there were no Muslim cemeteries in New York at this time, so the burial place is not conclusive.

In the 1890s an American named Mohammed Alexander Russell Webb spearheaded an effort to convert Americans to Islam. He himself had converted to Islam after a stay in India. He affected a turban, thick beard, and mustache and wore Indian robes and footwear. It was said that Indian Muslims gave him "£40,000–£50,000" to open a Muslim "temple" (actually a lecture room) on West 20th Street, publish a magazine called *Moslem World*, and convert as many people as he could.[9] This generous gift notwithstanding, he spent years fundraising.[10] The year the temple opened, in 1893, a Syrian preacher named Anton F. Haddad gave a talk, in which he advised Americans to stop sending their missionaries to Syria. "They should be kept at home," he said, "and be subject to moral treatment themselves."[11] Haddad, apparently a Baha'i, came to New York several times, always with dire warnings for Americans. There is no record of why he was speaking in a Muslim temple or how many people were in attendance.

The editors of *Kawkab America* generally gave Webb measured if not favorable coverage in its English pages. Rather than dismissing him as a quack, they reported on his lectures and engaged seriously with his ideas, perhaps because he had hired the newspaper's Oriental Printing House to publish his book, *Islam in America,* in 1893. A long muckraking article written by Daoud Nakkhash in the Arabic section of *Kawkab America*, however, denied that Webb was a serious man. Although Nakkhash admitted Webb was "well-spoken," Webb knew no Arabic, and no one could be a follower of Islam or a scholar of the Qor'an without knowing Arabic. In fact, Nakkhash said, it seemed to be more of a moneymaking scheme than a religious effort. He warned Webb that the Syrians were keeping an eye on him.[12]

When a reporter visited Webb's fourth-floor mosque in 1895, he found

[8] Moss 1897: 274.

[9] "Fall of Islam in America," *NYT*, December 1, 1895.

[10] "The Islamic Propaganda," *NYT* May 28, 1893.

[11] "Luxury Loving Missionaries," *New York Sun,* October 15, 1893.

[12] *Kawkab America,* August 18, 1893.

not a Turk or Arab present and none of the Muslim customs observed.[13] Nevertheless, in 1901, the Ottoman sultan named Webb honorary consul general.[14] The mosque was never built, and Webb ended his days in New Jersey editing the newspaper *The Rutherford Times*. He died in 1916.

According to *Kawkab America*, Webb was not the only person to attempt to introduce Islam into America. Apparently a Muslim priest and doctor, who slaughtered his goats in the approved manner, lived on Elizabeth Street. The newspaper also mentioned an Oriental preacher who was arrested in Asbury Park, New Jersey, for preaching against Christianity. One Emin (Ameen?) L. Nabokov preached the Muslim faith from his home at 8 Union Square.[15] But who these men actually were is a mystery, and they were certainly not considered members of the Syrian Colony.

None of the Arabic newspapers had a Muslim orientation. They reported on Arab customs and culture, which ipso facto included Muslim customs and culture, but none were Muslim by ownership or outlook. *Kawkab America*, in one of its earliest issues, congratulated (in Arabic and English) its Mohammedan readers upon the end of Ramadan,[16] and the paper included the Hijra date (the date according to the Islamic calendar) in its masthead, but these touches were aimed at their readers in the Ottoman Empire, not here.

The few references to Muslims in the American press are mostly hysterical, and most dealt with people who lived outside New York. Like the Syrian Christians themselves, most Americans contrasted the Syrians with their presumed opposites, the Muslims. One New York reporter asserted, "There are a few veiled Moslem women in New York, living in seclusion and wearing the baggy trousers."[17] It is just as possible, however, that these women, if they existed at all, were Christians. The murder of a Syrian Christian in Binghamton, New York, in 1890 led the reporter to surmise that it was the work of a "fanatic" Mohammedan living in New York.[18] But he presented no evidence for this surmise.

Although we know that some Druse came early to the United States,[19] we have no evidence that there were any Druse in New York in the nineteenth century.

[13] "A Fourth-Floor Mosque," *NYT*, February 4, 1895.

[14] www.webbfound.org/about/.

[15] "Mahometanism and Woman," *New-York Daily Tribune*, December 18, 1893.

[16] "The Month of Ramadan," *Kawkab America*, April 29, 1892.

[17] "Are Moslem Harems Possible Here?" *Dallas Morning News*, December 5, 1897.

[18] "Probably the Work of Fanatics," *NYH*, September 6, 1890.

[19] "A Queer Sect of Turks," *NYH*, September 26, 1889. This article reported on the arrival of three Druse men. They "are fine looking men, and are evidently possessed of unusual intelligence." They were headed to Baltimore.

Miller identified a single Druse in New York in 1903. Once again, absence of evidence is not proof, but one imagines if there were Druse in New York, they would have been mentioned since they were reported on in other locales.

Karpat, however, contends that many more Muslims came to the United States, even during the nineteenth century, than is generally supposed. The Ottoman legation in Washington in 1892 recorded about 200 Muslims in the United States, many of them in Worcester, Massachusetts,[20] all of them Turks. Their Armenian neighbors, who had gone to Worcester earlier, had evidently influenced their choice of locale.[21] We know from other sources that there were some Muslims in the interior of the United States in the nineteenth century; the uproar about polygamy was sparked by the immigration of some Muslims who were headed to the Midwest. The same report by the Ottoman legation mentioned that Muslims often passed as Christians, feeling that they would thus be more easily accepted in the United States,[22] and therefore they would not have been recognized in the records as Muslims. Some of these, he says, kept "Christian coloration" to better succeed in America, and others actually converted to Christianity.[23] Karpat is a bit too offhand in his assertions that there were a significant number of these converts in New York in the nineteenth century, given the lack of hard data on either the Ottoman or the American side. Although there may have been 200 Muslims in the United States in 1892, by 1893 that number, as counted by the Ottoman authorities, had dropped to 100. There was a high rate of return (Muslims were loath to be buried in a Christian country),[24] and in 1893 the Ottoman minister in Washington reported to his superiors that "no single one among the approximately one hundred Muslims in the United States was actually happy."[25]

In 1894, at the request of the authorities, the Ottoman consul in New York prepared a list of Muslims living in the state. He submitted a list of the first names of thirteen men, none of whom seem to be in our database.[26] Whether these men were living elsewhere in the state or had, as Karpat insists, changed their names to blend in with the Christians is not clear.

[20] Karpat 1985: 182.
[21] Ekinci 2008: 49.
[22] Karpat 1985: 182.
[23] Karpat 1985: 183.
[24] Ipek and Caglayan 2008: 36.
[25] Ekinci 2008: 50.
[26] Ekinci 2008: 56.

## *The Syrian Christians*

Information on the religious affiliation of Syrian Christian immigrants in New York comes from a disparate range of sources: Maronite baptismal records, which go back only to 1898; Melkite baptismal and marriage records, which begin in 1890; the publication of various lists of Maronite and Orthodox immigrants in some of the Arabic newspaper articles; and birth, death, and marriage certificates, which sometimes indicate religious affiliation. The work is hampered by the absence of records from the Greek Orthodox Church, which were destroyed in a fire,[27] and the lack of an institutional Protestant presence before 1899 (and the death of the Protestant preacher three years later).

Keeping in mind the missing Orthodox records as well as the barely fifty percent of our residents whose religion is known, we have about 600 Maronites, 500 Melkites, 300 Orthodox and 60 Protestants. Several commentators stated that Maronites were in the clear majority. Two contemporary counts suggest that Maronites did outnumber Melkites. In 1895, Archbishop Corrigan sent out a call to bishops around the country to report on the numbers of Syrian Catholics and Greek Catholics in their dioceses. The New York bishop reported 400 Maronites and 200 Melkites in New York City.[28] Father Gabriel's 1897 list of sixty-six Catholic children in the New York Colony was made up of six percent Latin rite, thirty percent Greek Catholic, and sixty-four percent Maronite.[29] It seems likely that the Colony, however, was about equally divided among the three sects of Maronite, Melkite, and Orthodox, with Protestants a distant fourth. In 1898, an unnamed member of the Colony estimated that 35 percent of the Colony was Greek Orthodox, 30 percent Maronite, and 25 percent Greek Catholic, while ten percent had "drifted away from the Syrian Churches and now attend services in the Protestant Chapel near the Syrian Colony."[30] We know from a survey attempted by Naoum Mokarzel that there were 575 Orthodox in New York in 1898,[31] which would mean that

[27] Fr. Thomas Zain, p.c., 2012.

[28] "Greek and Oriental Catholics," *Archdiocese Letters,* n.d. (1895). The other dioceses reporting significant numbers of Maronites and Melkites were Boston, New Orleans, Cleveland, and Denver. The bishop for Cleveland reported, "It is almost impossible to give the exact number, as they are always wandering from one place to another."

[29] *Archdiocese Letters,* Gabriel Korkemas to Corrigan, n.d. (1897).

[30] "New York's Syrian Colony," *New-York Tribune,* March 13, 1898.

[31] *Al Hoda,* April 19, 1898.

the community was split about evenly among the three sects, with a small minority of Protestants.

Miller too found the community split about equally, but in his case, between Maronites (29.9 percent), Roman Catholics (31.1 percent), and Greek Orthodox (24.1 percent). He counted only 6.4 percent Greek Catholic (Melkite) and 6 percent Protestant, as well as a single Druse, Muslim, and Hebrew (one wonders about the stories of these last three—who they were, what they were doing in the Colony, etc.). The large number of Roman Catholics in Miller's count must mean that Maronites and Melkites were moving to the Roman Catholic Church as they settled down in America. A letter addressed to Catholic immigrants written by the pope in 1897 made American assimilation of the Syrian Catholics into the Roman Catholic Church nearly inevitable. In it, the pope ruled that Syrian Catholic priests could not insist that children of Syrians attend the native churches. If the English-speaking children of immigrants wished to attend American Catholic churches, no one could forbid it.[32] The Catholic Church foresaw (and looked forward to) the withering of the native churches as the immigrants assimilated.

As one of the epigraphs to this book suggests, many Syrians in New York viewed Protestantism with some suspicion. Notwithstanding the fact that Protestantism had been introduced into Syria with the establishment of the first American Protestant mission in Beirut in 1820, immigrants of other sects saw it as a defection from the Arab way of life and symptomatic of "Westoxification." Helen Uniss Khoury's story about her Protestant family living apart from the rest of the Syrians may be significant in this regard. Khoury, who had a Protestant mother and Greek Orthodox father, but was raised as a Protestant, said that the Unisses didn't live in the Syrian community. They were the only Syrians in their school in the Boerum Hill section of Brooklyn, just north of South Ferry.[33] Elias Saadi, the Presbyterian minister, and his family also lived in Boerum Hill, yet some of the Protestant families did live among the other Syrians, including Solomon Merhige, who moved his family from 92 Washington to Hicks Street in the South Ferry neighborhood in 1902.

The four Christian groups in Syrian New York permeate this book; how could they not when religion was a primary mode of self-definition? We have seen that several of the buildings in the Colony were used predominantly or exclusively by members of one sect. The arrival of their priests and

[32] "May Worship in English," *The* (NY) *Sun,* May 23, 1897.
[33] *Naff Interview*, with Helen Uniss Khoury, January 26, 1986.

establishment of their churches were outlined in chapter 3, their representation in the Arabic press is described in chapter 9, and the various sectarian associations and their activities are portrayed in chapter 13.[34]

## Women and Children

I put women and children together in the same section because the deficits in the documentary evidence are similar for both groups for similar reasons. Women were always in the minority in the nineteenth-century Syrian Colony. This is an artifact of both the sources of data and patterns of immigration. In the fragmentary 1890 census, 26.4 percent of the Syrians were females. In the decade following, 36.5 percent were women and girls, and in the 1900 census, 44 percent were female. The Industrial Commission on Immigration counted 47.1 percent females for all Syrians who came to this country in 1900.[35] Of the 1,891 individuals "actually seen" by Miller, 869 (45.9 percent) were women.[36] The increase in percentages through time is obviously the result of people settling down and starting families.

The nineteenth-century marriage records include twenty-five Syrian men who married "Americans" (although often the women were themselves immigrants from Europe), testifying perhaps to the relative paucity of single Syrian women in the early days, or perhaps it was another way of assimilating. We counted their children as Syrians. We have only two cases of Syrian women of the first generation marrying outside the community.

The history of Syrian women's immigration is another story yet to be told, although some new work has recently been done in this area.[37] Traditionally it has been assumed that the Syrian immigrant story followed the chain migration pattern: a single man came alone, made enough money to marry or send for his family, and the women and children would join him. And this seems, in large part, to be accurate. Of 295 separate households (that is, the number of individuals assigned the role of "head") in the 1900 census, only 35 (11 percent) had women heads. Of these, twenty were widowed, ten were married, and five were single.

[34] For a wide-ranging study on the evolution of the religious practices of the Syrian diaspora, see Kayal and Kayal 1975.
[35] Industrial Commission on Immigration 1901: 303.
[36] Miller 1903: 46.
[37] See, for example, Gualtieri 2004, Bier 2009, Shakir 1997.

There were many ways that the census-taker obscured the role of women in the household, thus adding to the persistent undervaluing of their economic and social contribution to the community. There were, for example, forty-six Syrian women who were called "boarders" and who may have been heads of households of one. Fourteen of these women were married (twelve had no husbands present), twenty-four were single, and eight widowed. The term "boarder" is in any case ambiguous: some of these women were related to the head of household and others were not; some were dependent on others in the household and others were not. My maternal great-grandmother immigrated with three of her daughters in 1897 to join her son and his growing family at 79 Washington Street. Everyone in the household had the same last name as the head, Asad Milkie, but their relationship to him was not specified; apart from Asad's immediate family, all were listed as boarders. At least two of my great-aunts, and perhaps my great-grandmother as well, were peddling and contributing to household expenses, although the "profession" category in each case was left blank. Even if she wasn't earning a living, perhaps my great-grandmother should have been called the head of the entire household (being the senior member) or at least the household that included her and her daughters. Or perhaps anyone who was earning her own living should have been called a "head." But adult males were privileged in the census and were often presumed to be the head, no matter who was paying the bills.

A woman's life was undoubtedly hard, especially if she were the sole head of a large family. The apparent ease with which some made their way in New York must be contrasted with those who were beset by hardship. The story of Anissa Lian could represent others. Her husband, Abdallah, immigrated from Zahleh in 1891. We know nothing about him except that he apparently returned to Syria at least once and sent for his wife and seven children in 1899. Their youngest was a year old. When the family arrived in New York, however, Abdallah had disappeared. Anissa did not know whether he had died, gone west, or, as some said, gone back to Syria for good. But here was Anissa, with seven children and no support. She made a logical choice: she put three of her children in the New York Juvenile Asylum, put two elsewhere, and kept her youngest and oldest with her, boarding at Muossa Daoud's boardinghouse at 96 Greenwich. She sent her oldest son, Abe, who was eighteen, out to peddle, and she took in washing and cared for her infant. In the 1900 census she declared herself a widow. She quickly retrieved her children; five appear in a family portrait of 1906. We know that one daughter had died, but we don't know what happened to the other one. By the time of the portrait, Abe Lian

4-1. Abdullah Lian, who later disappeared, ca. 1895 (top), and the Lian Family, ca. 1906. From left, front: Sahid (Sy), Anissa, Anissa's mother, Helen (Nabiha). Back row: William, Raji, and Abe (courtesy of Roger Lian).

and his brothers had already set up as dry goods salesmen, and in 1908 the brothers opened "Lian Brothers" grocery store on Atlantic Avenue in Brooklyn. After a few years, they started dealing in laces, which led to a successful partnership in kimono manufacturing that continued until their deaths. The baby, Sahid (Sy), joined the firm in 1920. Anissa lived with her son Raji until her death in 1925, after which he married.

Another woman, whose name we do not know, arrived in 1892 with her sixteen-year-old son. She had left her husband and four children—the youngest of whom was two-and-a-half—at home. She became ill and was unable to work and was forced to turn to a local charity for money for her return passage. She left her son in America. The charity hoped she would tell other "foolish and adventurous spirits" not to come.[38]

How do we define children in the nineteenth century? Today perhaps we would call anyone under sixteen a child, and using that as a benchmark, we have identified 689 children living in the Colony at some point during the years 1880–1900 (21 percent of the total), of whom 356 (54 percent) were born in the United States, the vast majority (329) in New York City. The 1900 census recorded 373 children fifteen or younger, 30 percent of the population. Forty-one percent (156) were born in the United States. The higher percentage of children in the latter part of the period clearly represents the process of settling down and having families.

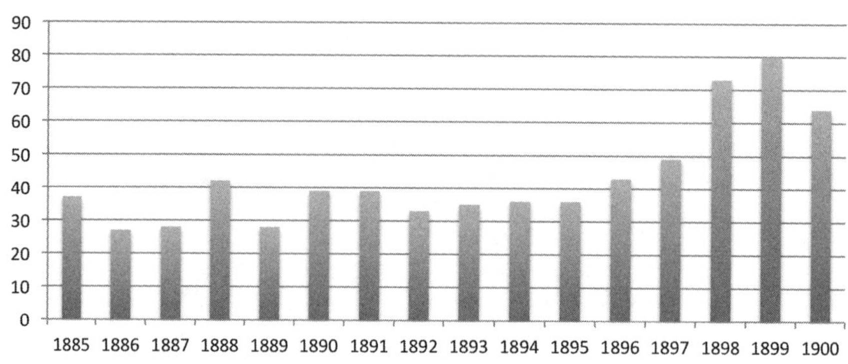


One can debate whether fifteen-year-olds should even be counted as children, and certainly the census shows a certain ambivalence on the part of the Syrians: of those whose "profession" was listed, half were already working, while the other half were in school. Most of the younger children were in school or had no profession listed, which may mean they were at work, like a few of their young cohort who were listed as working as apprentices or seamstresses.

Notwithstanding the almost universal assessment of Syrians as "taking care of their own," we have identified fifty-three Syrian children "in care" in public institutions in the 1900 census: twenty-nine girls and twenty-four boys. Even in the partial census of 1892, we have four young Syrian boys

[38] "The Land of Promise," *Boston Herald,* April 14, 1893.

living at St. John's Asylum in Brooklyn. There must have been other boys and girls in care in Manhattan in that year but, unfortunately, Manhattan was not included in the 1892 census.

In 1900, the New York Juvenile Asylum at 176th Street and Amsterdam had the largest number of Syrian children within its walls: fifteen. Its 1899 report noted about its Syrian inmates: "Up to the year 1889, but four children born in Turkey or Syria had been received; since then upwards of one hundred have entered the institution. Now it is a matter of common knowledge that the poorest of the self-supporting class in our city are those engaged in peddling, street vending, and similar occupations, and these trades, if trades they can be called, are largely followed by the Syrians and Russians, and from the families thus supported come most of the children received by us from these nationalities."[39] The number of Syrian children admitted to the Asylum is given in the following table:[40]

| Year | 1892 | 1893 | 1894 | 1895 | 1896 | 1897 | 1898 | 1899 | 1900 | Total |
|---|---|---|---|---|---|---|---|---|---|---|
| Number | 7 | 15 | 17 | 4 | 14 | 24 | 13 | 17 | 7 | 118 |

Syrian children made up less than 3 percent of the Asylum admissions, but this is much greater than their percentage in the general population of the city. We do not know why these Syrian children were committed to the Asylum, but we do know that their parents, rather than a judge, referred them all, which means that their parents voluntarily put them in care. Most were probably admitted for being destitute. It is comforting that none of them were considered "criminal or vicious."[41]

The children's education at the Asylum consisted of the three R's and vocational training, including shoemaking, printing, telegraphy, typewriting, and sewing. One of the institution's primary goals, however, was to outplace the children, who were "indentured" to farmers in Illinois and Iowa so that they could escape the corrupting influence of the city and find "a new environment with new ideals of life and its activities."[42] Many of these children had parents in New York; this forced separation must have been wrenching. We do not know if any of the Syrian children were sent away.

[39] New York Juvenile Asylum 1900: 17.
[40] New York Juvenile Asylum 1901: 103.
[41] New York Juvenile Asylum 1899: 72.
[42] New York Juvenile Asylum 1900: 18.

Lydia and Nabiha Merhige, ages ten and eleven, were inmates in the Asylum in 1900. Solomon Daher Merhige and his wife Mary had seven children at home at 92 Washington and claimed to have only seven living children, so these girls may not have been theirs; if they were not, we do not know to whom they belonged. Three of Anissa Lian's children were there, along with two Aoun siblings whose parents remain unidentified, and eight others.

Heartbreakingly, there were six Macksoud children in care at two different institutions in Brooklyn: the Home for Destitute Children and the Orphan Asylum. In January 1899, Manna Macksoud, a widowed sister-in-law of Elias Macksoud, arrived with four children, three of whom she put in care. In December of the same year, Saleem Macsoud—a cousin of Elias's—immigrated with his wife and their six children. They immediately put three in care, keeping their two older sons and a baby at home. Saleem's widowed cousin, Nazira Maloof, brought her seven-year-old son Michel on the same ship, and he was also put into care.

One of the North African entertainers, Hassan Ali, and his wife put two of their daughters into the Children's Fold on West 155th Street. They kept their sons with them. A similar case occurred in my family, where one of my relatives, a widower, had two children, a boy and a girl. After marrying again, he and his new wife put the girl in an orphanage, where she spent her entire childhood; they kept the boy at home. The family visited her on weekends.

Two Boutross girls—Hannie, 11, and Amelia, 4—were in care, Hannie at the New York Juvenile Asylum, and Amelia at the Randall's Island Asylum and School. Their parents and six siblings were living in Jersey City, and their mother was pregnant with her ninth child.

Lizzie Hammwy, four years old, was in the Messiah Home for Children in the Bronx in 1900. Her parents had immigrated with their oldest daughter, Catherine, in 1895; her mother, Salima, then had twins, one of whom was Lizzie. By 1900, as they were apparently unable to feed three children (and another was born in 1902), they put Lizzie in a home, but not her twin brother, Michael. As the family was not listed in the 1900 census, perhaps they were peddling and left Lizzie in care. Happily, Lizzie was able to rejoin them; she is listed in the 1910 census with her widowed mother and three siblings.

Hannah and Abraham Maloof had six children, but Abraham was listed as retired in 1900 (he was 38), and his wife and two of his daughters were doing fancy needlework to earn a living. Two other daughters, Adele and Emma, were in the Home for Friendless Women and Children in Brooklyn, although they were also listed as living at home with their parents on Amity Street;

perhaps the parents were ashamed and lied about their presence. By 1910, the two had apparently rejoined the family.

With the exception of the Lian boys, most of the boys in care had no parents that we could identify. It is impossible to know whether they were orphans, whether they were only temporarily in care (and if so, who rescued them?), or whether their parents had abandoned them. Two isolated cases of abandoned Syrian children were reported in news articles, but both were girls: a foundling who was left on the steps of 81 Washington Street in 1895, and a Syrian child, Delila, living at the Howard Mission and Home at 225 East 11th Street.[43]

The Industrial Commission on Immigration ascribed duplicitous motives to the parents of these children: "Cases have been known in which Syrian families of this class have applied for the commitment of 4 out of 5 children within 20 days after landing, all details as to alleged residence, widowhood, etc. being carefully 'fixed up' by hucksters common to the quarter."[44] This description could easily fit the case of Anissa Lian, except that we know she was in dire need, and that she retrieved her children as soon as she could.

A speech given by labor leader Edward F. McSweeney in 1902 was even more hostile: "The Syrians are the hardest proposition to deal with in the United States. I have known men of that race in New York worth $10,000, four of whose children were in the orphan asylum being cared for until they were able to be producers themselves."[45]

Malake Nafash, a midwife, adopted a boy born to a Syrian couple in Pawtucket, Rhode Island. We assume they were forced to give him up for economic reasons, and Malake, although she had two daughters of her own to support on a midwife's earnings, apparently felt she could afford to raise one more.[46] In any case, she had wanted a son. He was named after Malake's husband, who had stayed in Syria. For parents who could not afford to support their child, the choices were limited and heart wrenching. Putting children in a home until they could be retrieved must have seemed by far the best solution. Imagine, though, the mother who went to reclaim her child and found he had been sent to Iowa to live on a farm!

---

[43] *NYH,* November 21, 1895.

[44] Industrial Commission on Immigration 1901: 444.

[45] "Our Many New Races," *Boston Herald,* March 20, 1902.

[46] Renee Hoenig, p.c. 2011.

In 1902, some American girls of the Sunshine Club gave a party for "twenty poor children from the downtown slums," ten of whom were Syrians. "None of these girls had ever been to a party before and their delight was unbounded."[47] It's difficult to know whether the Syrian children were as deprived as the girls of the Sunshine Club thought. But we have to admit the possibility that from the vantage point of upper-class girls, the Syrian children's lives must have seemed dismal. Children from the Syrian Society School were taken on a "fresh-air" excursion sponsored by the *New York Herald*. Doubtless, there were Syrian children deserving of charity, their fathers' and mothers' strivings notwithstanding.

Some wives and daughters of prominent merchants founded the Syrian Women's Union in 1896, and in 1899 they opened a crèche for babies at 92 Washington Street, primarily as an effort to help those mothers who had to go out to work and could not care for their children. They had eight babies the first day. One of them was "Varida Stfan" (Farida Stefan), whose mother "has recently come from the old country, and is looking for something to do for her support. She left two children behind her when she emigrated." She may have actually put those two children (Rose and Tanous Stefan) in care. A second girl in the crèche, Amenie, had no father and "her mother makes a living selling goods around the city." "Shefel Morrono (Shafik Maroon?) is a healthy boy whose mother does machine stitching for a living."[48] By June, the women had twenty children in their care, "putting them into clean aprons, feeding them on bread and milk and eggs and employing a nurse to look after them."[49] This was day care only, very different from putting a child in a home. Women who had to peddle or otherwise work outside the home must have welcomed it.

The Syrian Society, which will be discussed in chapter 13, had plans to establish a home for children of women peddlers. The intention was to provide a place for children to live when their mothers left town for the summer or went to the Columbian fair. Houghton reports, however, that the effort was abandoned by the time of her report (1911) because "the need seemed not to exist, the mothers of children confining their industry to neighboring districts, setting out after the children had been sent to school and returning

[47] "Juniors Give a Party," *New-York Tribune*, February 7, 1902.

[48] "Nursery for Syrian Babes," *NYT,* May 21, 1899.

[49] "For Syrian Babies," *NYH,* June 9, 1899.

in time to prepare their supper."[50] In fact, the effort failed for lack of funds. In 1911, Houghton claimed she found no Syrian children in public institutions. If the putting of children into care was a passing phenomenon and ceased to be a problem in the later days of the Colony, this can be taken as another sign of the upward economic trajectory of the Colony as whole.

4-2. Syrian children (and some parents) in front of 77 Washington Street (Childe, *NYT*, 1899). Makhoul Boutross's store is in the basement, Mallouk & Abo Samra on the main floor.

## Age

As mentioned above, it is difficult to assign age to a Syrian with any confidence. Dates of birth or ages given by immigration officers or ships' pursers are all approximations. The census takers relied on the person's own testimony as to his or her age. For the midwife Malake Nafash, for example, we have birthdates of 1867, 1872, and 1877, presumably provided by her, from different sources. As a guess, I would choose the 1872 date given in the 1900 census, which would make her about 18 when she married, but both of the other two dates are also plausible; we have well-documented examples of girls marrying at thirteen and at twenty-three. Hers is not an isolated case. Even

[50] Houghton: III: 794.

given these discrepancies, it is possible to see patterns in the age range of the immigrants who settled in New York in the following table.

By far, the majority of immigrants were teenagers or young adults. This is not surprising given the rigors of the voyage and the courage it took to leave home and travel so far. The outliers were the very young, who came with a parent, and those of late middle age. Joseph Sadallah, one of those came alone in 1890 at the age of fifty-five to prepare the way for his sons. Perhaps he peddled when he first arrived, but by the time his son Tannous (Antoine) came in 1892, Joseph had apparently made it possible for him immediately to go into partnership with Beshara Ganim in the import/export business. Beshara's father had preceded him to America as well; when he returned to Syria he left his business in his son's hands. Yusef Arbeely was fifty-seven when he arrived in 1878 with his six sons and daughter; Abdow Lutfy came in 1888 at the age of forty-three, and when the midwife Mannie Shahdan arrived in 1887, she was forty-seven.

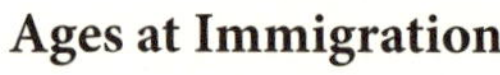

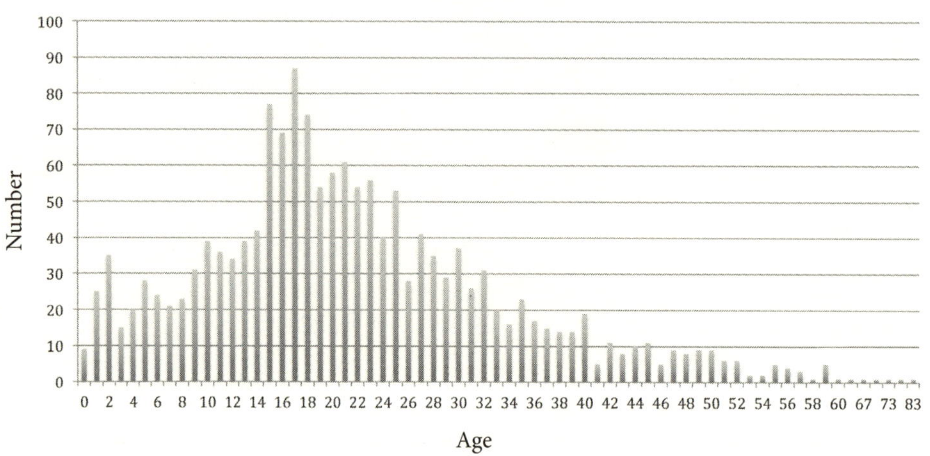


## Literacy and Education

Despite the Immigration Commission's efforts to prove the Syrians unfit for citizenship because of their high rates of illiteracy,[51] the 1900 census tells a different story. In addition to a column headed, "Attended school (in months)," the census had three categories related to language ability: "Can read," "Can write," "Can speak English." The first two do not specify the language of

[51] Industrial C ommission on Immigration 1901: 284.

literacy, but perhaps refer to English. One assumes that the census taker simply took people at their word, so that a person who was only literate in Arabic might have given a "Yes" answer, if he or she understood the question. Of the 1,163 Syrians in the 1900 census who answered these questions (the rest were left blank), 50 percent of the women and 62 percent of the men could both read and write, and 66 percent of the women and 74 percent of the men said they could speak English. These numbers cannot be accurate, however, because Miller's data starkly contradict them.

4-3. David A. Fuleihan, on his graduation from the Syrian Protestant College in 1885 (courtesy Julia Fuleihan).

In his 1903 study, he made a distinction between those literate in Arabic and those literate in English. He reported the following figures for literacy in Arabic: females over five years old: 27.8 percent; males over five years old: 60.9 percent. Although much lower than the figures in the census, these figures are still striking and explain the market for Arabic-language newspapers and books. The discrepancy between men's and women's literacy is large, reflecting a gap in their education in Syria.

In regard to English ability, Miller made a distinction between those who could read, write, and speak English and those who could speak but not read or write it. Of the males over five years old, 32.2 percent could speak, read and write English, while 27.7 percent could speak but not read or write.[52] The percentage of women who could read, write and speak English—23.6 percent—was not that much lower than the men's, and an additional 17.6 percent could speak it.

It is astonishing that one-third of the men and more than a quarter of the women were literate in English at this early date. These figures are supported by the contents of a letter written by my great-aunt Jamilie Milkie to the editors of the *Brooklyn Daily Eagle* in 1902, claiming that one of the benefits of peddling was learning to speak fluent English—"not simply to read it or write it, for most of us knew that before coming over."[53] The American missionary and British schools, which were the primary source of English-language learning in Syria, taught girls and boys, whereas the traditional Arabic-language schools taught boys almost exclusively. The men who went on for further study at the Syrian Protestant College were taught in English from 1883 on, making every graduate competent, if not fluent, in the language. The number of SPC graduates who emigrated in the nineteenth century was relatively small, however, so these numbers reflect the quality of the immigrants' education in Syria and/or their ability to rapidly acquire a new language.

Some immigrants (the Arbeely brothers, Ameen F. Haddad, David Sleem, Rizq Haddad, Antoine Haddad, Yusef Yazbek, Shukri Rizkallah, Ibrahim Khairallah, and a Syrian who went by the name of Najib Taky-Ud-Deen) obtained advanced degrees here in medicine, pharmacy, or theology not long after arriving, which meant that they must have been fluent in English when they arrived. Literate and/or bilingual men often served as interpreters and document translators, like Nageeb Arbeely, who worked as a full-time interpreter at Ellis Island. One reads in newspaper articles throughout the United States that literate Syrians often came to the aid of their less-educated countrymen. My paternal grandfather traveled from Fort Worth to Dallas, Texas, to interpret for a Syrian man accused of a crime. He read the documents and translated them for the court. This service notwithstanding, his English was said to be "so fragmentary that it was almost impossible to get at the truth."[54] Since he did not attend foreign schools in Syria, he must have learned adequate English in his less than two years in the United States.

[52] Miller 1903: 34–35.
[53] "Syrian Men Not Shirkers," *BDE*, September 23, 1902.
[54] *Dallas Morning News*, February 20, 1890.

These relatively high rates nothwithstanding, evidence for English illiteracy can be seen in many documents, including naturalization or passport applications and marriage certificates (which de facto included women), where one or both of the parties signed with his or her mark (an x or a +, symbolizing their Christian faith). Others signed in Arabic, with a transliteration supplied by the notary. In other cases, the notary or clerk who had filled out the rest of the form wrote the signature himself. The handwriting of most of the new immigrants was halting and awkward, as ours would be in Arabic, but still, the great majority could at least sign their names. Of course these documents were mostly filled out by men, and by the time they applied for citizenship or a passport, most of them had been in business for themselves for several years. They would have needed to know at least how to sign their name, even if they were not fully literate. In trial transcripts, an affidavit was often included asserting that one of the parties had read or had had someone read him the document.

The Zreik trial of 1906[55] also provides evidence that the ability to speak fluent English was not necessarily as widespread as the figures would indicate. Of the several witnesses, most had to have an interpreter, even those who had been in the United States for a decade or more. David Madower, for example, a witness for the prosecution, had been in the country for nine years and owned a dry goods business and a factory that produced kimonos and handkerchiefs. When asked by the prosecuting attorney if he needed an interpreter, he said, "Yes sir; I talk English, not much, just 'how much is this, how much cost,' I don't speak English except for business." If he only spoke this much English, would he have told the census taker that he was literate and/or could speak the language? Unfortunately, he is not in the 1900 census so we do not know.

George Howatt, a witness who had been in the United States for eighteen years, apparently could not speak English at all. Even the ones who didn't need an interpreter still spoke broken English, if one can believe the transcript. But we should remember that those who were witnesses in the trial were not the successful merchants of the Colony: they were mainly single men who were still trying to make their way in the world. Their lack of English matched their lack of material success; in general, the most successful businessmen and professional men spoke the most fluent English, both by necessity (they were more in contact with Americans than other Syrians) and by determination.

[55] *Trials,* People v. Zreik, 1906: #599.

For women the situation was even worse. Certainly English-language instruction for girls was spotty in Syria. My family again provides an example. My maternal grandmother and all her sisters were at least semiliterate in English and Arabic when they arrived, as Jamilie Milkie claimed. Their mother was not. None of the girls could have written essays in either language as their brother Asad did, but they certainly could read, write, and speak English. They all gave "yes" answers to the literacy questions on the census. My grandmother used to enjoy reading the novels of Marie Corelli before she married. My paternal grandmother, on the other hand, was illiterate in both languages, although she did learn to speak English. She spent more than sixty years in the United States and never learned to read or write in English or Arabic, yet in the 1900 census, she answered, "yes" to all three literacy questions. Both of her parents were illiterate as well, and despite this, her mother was able to run a confectionery store in Worcester, Massachusetts. Similarly, Miss David, a young woman who ran a restaurant on Whitehall Street, "doesn't know how to write English, but she talks it well."[56] It is rather amazing that illiterate men and women could run businesses.

In 1894, a reporter described the residents of Muossa Daoud's tenement on Rector Street:

> Trained by the skillful trainer, Misery, Daoud's tenants are seekers of truth, thinkers, intrepid students, determined to tame life, and, as they are weaned from every pleasure, have no other refuge than science. They study English, French, law, medicine, chemistry, history, and a great quantity of other indispensable branches of learning. They do not intend to remain peddlers, it is evident.[57]

Is it possible that every one of these peddlers was fluent enough in English to study these subjects? This kind of reporting fed the myths percolating through the community of the successful, assimilated, self-made man.

Most observers agreed that the Syrians put much faith in education, however, and that they pushed their children to attend school (at least when they weren't needed to earn a living). The editors of *Kawkab America* pleaded with the school authorities to offer Syrian children a class in English at Grammar School 29 so they could more quickly take advantage of American education.[58]

[56] "Yamin Says His Sister Objected," *The* (NY) *Sun,* July 15, 1893.

[57] "Moussa *[sic]* Daoud Their Leader," *NYT,* June 4, 1894.

[58] *Kawkab America,* September 30, 1892.

In the 1900 census, 163 out of 257 Syrian children aged five to fifteen (63.4 percent) were "at school," a number that includes the children in care, who were being given an education by fiat. Most of them were probably attending Grammar School 29, located on the corner of Washington and Carlisle. Others must have gone to parochial school and some (about thirty) attended the Syrian Society School at 95 Washington. Twenty-four other children (9 percent)—mostly the fifteen-year-olds—were working, the girls as seamstresses and cigarette makers, and the boys as messengers, peddlers, or helpers to blacksmiths or harness makers. One imagines that some number of children who had no profession listed were also at work.

Miller found that by 1903, 79 percent of the children in the Colony were in school: 45.5 percent of them in public school, 20.1 percent in Catholic day school, 14.7 percent in Protestant day school, 11.5 percent being taught at home, and 8.2 percent in night school (presumably those children working for their parents during the day).[59] The percentage of those in school was higher in Brooklyn than in Manhattan, as was to be expected as people became more prosperous and needed their children's labor less. One wonders, though, if "home schooling" was a euphemism for children working.

In his 1912 study, Felton reported that with the exception of forty children who were in parochial school, every Syrian child was enrolled in public school.[60] He admitted, however, that when a child was old enough (he did not specify the age), he or she was taken out of school to work. He cites the case of a man who worked in a restaurant, earning $30 per week. He had kept his oldest daughter out of school to work, but told Felton that the truant officer was after him.[61] Ameen Haddad, in his role as secretary of the Syrian Society, complained that parents would take their children out of school when the weather turned warm enough to peddle. The high numbers of children in school obviously do not tell the whole story of children's education in the early days of the Colony.

[59] Miller 1903: 32–33.
[60] Felton 1912: 15.
[61] Felton 1912: 16.

## What Did the Syrians Look Like?

Reporters wanted Syrian men and women to be exotic, especially in looks. One reporter described three scenes in the Syrian Colony, each of which featured a woman of exotic beauty. The first presented a woman about to have her ears pierced: "The woman had a dark olive skin, great black eyes with blackened lids, white, even teeth, black hair, and fine clear-cut features." The second described a woman sitting on the floor working, while a "pretty well-dressed man" looked on. This trope, of the indolent Middle Eastern husband letting (or forcing) his wife to work while he lazed about (usually smoking a *narghile*), was a common one in the American press, most often seen in stories about women peddlers. This article, however, adds that effeminate touch ("pretty") to the description, making the husband doubly despicable.

The third compared a woman and her naked baby to a Renaissance Madonna,[62] because of her veil. In almost every sketch of a Syrian woman in a newspaper, she is wearing a scarf and, often, a veil covering part of her face.[63] Some asserted that the women "do not go into the streets with their faces uncovered, nor do they wear hats, and with the shirt waist and the skirt there is the veil."[64] Sketches accompanying an 1894 *Herald* article show all the women in scarves, the older women more carefully covered than the younger, but no one with a face cover.[65] Most reporters would have us believe that the women used those "languorous eyes," to flirt with men over their veils. The Westerner's fascination with the veil is with us still.

In photographs of Syrian factories, the women workers wear Western clothes, no scarves, and certainly no veils. Some of the more objective American reporters, as well as contemporary photographs, noted that Syrian women were generally dressed in Western style. "The young girls are more Americanized than their elders. Occasionally one meets a girl whose ears are weighted with heavy gold hoops, and whose apparel savors strongly of the East, but stylishly made clothes of New York cut, and 'loves of bonnets' are the rule instead of the exception."[66] An article in an upstate New York newspaper described two young women who were peddling there. Both spoke "pure" English, without stooping to the use of slang. "Syrian women have come to

[62] "Three Oriental Scenes," *The* (NY) *Evening Post,* June 16, 1896.

[63] See, for example, the *NYT* article, "Foreign Types of New York Life," by E. Lyell Earle, August 28, 1898.

[64] "World of Women," *Utica* (NY) *Herald-Dispatch*, April 12, 1903.

[65] "Red Fezzed Heads; Languorous Eyes." *NYH,* November 18, 1894.

[66] "Sights and Characters of New York's 'Little Syria,'" *NYT,* March 23, 1903.

know the shirt waist and skirt—the universal costume,"[67] and have abandoned the use of kohl on their eyes and rouge on their cheeks, "not to their disadvantage, either."[68]

When Syrian women posed for studio photographs, all were dressed in the latest Western fashion, showing off not only their prosperity but also their modernity, but in an 1899 photograph of the customers in Yazaji's grocery store, the women are wearing Western clothes but had covered their heads (Figure 7-4). Many immigrant women—Italians, Jews, and Greeks, for example—wore scarves, something that distinguished them from their Western sisters, who wore hats. Two children who graced the cover of the Syrian Society School's *Financial Report* were dressed in miniature versions of this trope—the girl in a kerchief, the boy in a tiny fez.[69] Were they "dressed up" for the photo? In the few candid photos we have of children, none are wearing a scarf or a fez. A group of women's portraits in a 1903 article show three women with dark hair, heavy eyebrows and prominent noses. The dramatic lighting emphasized these features and their foreignness. They were not exotic either in their dress or their head coverings, except, perhaps, for being clearly dressed in home-sewn clothes, the clothing of the poor.[70]

In the same article, a portrait of an old man in profile could represent any nationality. As for men, many reporters commented on their "red-fezzed" heads, and an (Arabic) article in *Kawkab America* confirms that they wore them, advising readers, "If you're on Washington Street, you'll see it [the *fez*]."[71] Syrian men also supposedly wore "immense gunnybag pants" as they strolled around the street, but there is no evidence that this is true.[72] A reporter described "men whose slender frames and big eyed bearded faces seemed strangely out of place in cutaways and straight trousers—and tiny, swarthy women so timid of bearing as to suggest a covert longing for the muslin veil of their home."[73] It is clearly the reporter who longed for the muslin veil. In all the photographs we have of Syrian men, women, and children, nothing distinguishes them from other immigrants, save perhaps their Mediterranean features and the occasional *fez* or kerchief.

[67] "World of Women," *Utica* (NY) *Herald-Dispatch*, April 12, 1903.
[68] "Oriental New York," *The* (NY) *Press*, January 8, 1893.
[69] Syrian Society of the City of New York: 1898.
[70] "Children of Lebanon in Gotham," *NYH*, March 29, 1903.
[71] *Kawkab America,* October 14, 1892.
[72] "Red Fezzed Heads; Languorous Eyes." *NYH,* November 18, 1894.
[73] "Our Syrian Christians," *Irish World* (NY), February 17, 1894.

The same mixture of the old and the new can be seen in other aspects of Syrian appearance. Older women sometimes had tattoos on their faces; we have a few portraits taken both in Syria and in the United States of women with lines and dots on their faces, but no tattoos are seen on any women of middle age or younger. The practice may have died out in Syria before the immigrants left. A long article written about the Syrian Colony of Cincinnati, however, claimed that many of the "young Syrian women tattoo their hands and arms with flowers and birds in blue and red ink."[74] There is even a sketch of a woman's hand (captioned "the beauty mark") with a pattern of branches and squiggly lines running from the back of the hand up the forearm. Whether the tattooing was done here or there, whether these tattoos were only temporary tattoos drawn in henna, or whether this was all a figment of the reporter's imagination is not clear. Certainly the women ceased having their faces tattooed, but it is possible that the tradition of tattooing their arms and hands continued for a while after they arrived.

Apparently men were sometimes tattooed with Christian symbols. A reporter who boarded a steamship to meet some of the men and women who were coming to our shores noted tattoos on their hands and arms of crosses, rosaries, and other religious symbols. One man had the portals of the Temple of Jerusalem tattooed on his forearm.[75] It may have been a tradition adopted in the old country to distinguish themselves from Muslims, or the men may have done it simply to convince the immigration authorities that they were Christians. On two World War I registration cards, the men are described as having tattoos on their hands.

This mixture of Syrian tradition and American modernity must have reflected the age, class and gender of the individual, not to mention the sentiments they felt for their home or adopted land.

What about their physical appearance? Were they distinguishable at all from "Americans?" Reporters certainly thought so, or wanted their readers to think so. They were referred to as "Orientals" or "Asians," and often described as "swarthy" or "greasy." Notwithstanding the racism (or ethnic slur) evident in these terms, Syrians were categorized as white in the censuses, and their whiteness was apparently taken for granted by Americans, at least until the Syrians had to fight to be recognized as "white" in the twentieth century (sometimes, but by no means always, a fight over skin color). We should note

[74] "The 400," *Cincinnati Post,* September 3, 1892.

[75] "The Syrian Arabs," *New York Evening Telegram*, December 28, 1887.

as well that sometimes reporters described them in positive terms, as handsome or beautiful. Of course, these complimentary adjectives also make the person "other" but at least allow for the possibility of him or her eventually blending into the mainstream. The Syrian, to American eyes, looked like every other nineteenth-century Mediterranean immigrant: dark hair and eyes, luxuriant mustaches, and olive skin, features which could be ugly or beautiful, exotic or familiar, depending on the eye of the beholder.

## Chapter 5

# The Role of the World's Fairs: From Peddler to Capitalist

*Ethnology is a great "go" this summer.*[1]

*The advent of the Turkish and Syrian will be welcomed by those in search of something new and beautiful.*[2]

As Adele Younis pointed out, there were apparently Arab immigrants in the United States as early as the Civil War; she did an impressive job of winnowing out Arab names in land grant documents and ship manifests, which listed these occasional visitors. Some Syrian men came as homesteaders, so must have settled here, but we know little about them.[3] But she assumed, as have others, that the main events that brought Syrians here in significant numbers were the world's fairs in Philadelphia (the Centennial Exposition in 1876), Chicago (the Columbian Exposition in 1893), and St. Louis (the Louisiana Purchase Exposition in 1904). There were many local fairs as well in the intervening years, notably one in New York City in December 1893, which took place at Grand Central Palace, where many Syrian merchants set up concessions, and one in Buffalo in 1901. According to these accounts the fairs provided middle-class Americans a glimpse of Arab life, and Syrians discovered America. As origin myth, the fairs do not suffice. The Philadelphia fair, although the first to have Middle Eastern representation, had little lasting effect on Middle Eastern settlement in the United States. By the time of the Columbian Exposition, Syrians were already in the U.S. in large numbers, and many businesses were already established. Although each of the fairs had its impact, none was the precipitating factor in bringing Syrians here. The mere number of Syrian participants at the fairs attests to their importance,

[1] *The* (NY) *Press,* July 30, 1893.

[2] "Fads in Furniture," *Jersey Journal* (Jersey City, N.J.), October 13, 1893.

[3] Younis 1995: 112 et seq.

and among the fairs, none had the reach and influence of the Chicago fair. Although Syrian businessmen had been marketing Orientalism since their first contacts with Americans, the Middle Eastern components of the nineteenth-century fairs spectacularly demonstrated to Syrian businessmen that the market for Orientalism was huge and at the same time fueled that market among the American public.

## The Centennial Exposition (May–November 1876)

Younis exhaustively describes the Middle Eastern presence at the 1876 Centennial Exposition in Philadelphia.[4] Her research into original sources is exemplary. The Tunisian Pavilion, an Egyptian Court modeled after the Temple of Karnak, and a Turkish Pavilion represented the Middle East. The Turkish Coffee House and Bazaar in the Turkish Pavilion, "large and richly ornamented" consisted of four small bazaars, "in which a large stock of pipes, carpets, rich dresses, swords, daggers, jewelry, and other articles from the Turkish Empire were sold."[5] Inside the Horticultural Hall, the exhibition known as the Damascus Gate was on the main stage. The exhibit featured a *muezzin* sounding his call to prayer, a harem, a display of a man grinding grain on a millstone, and whirling dervishes.[6] The Syrians performed their interpretation of the Parable of the Ten Virgins.[7] For twenty-five cents one could sit in the Moorish Theater, drink a cup of Turkish coffee, and watch Tunisian musicians accompany a young woman dancer.

The official documents attested (and Younis apparently believes) that the primary motive for the countries that participated was national pride, not commerce. They supposedly sold goods only to defray some of the costs of the exhibits,[8] but if this were the case, the merchants were unaware of it. There were no fewer than seven "Palestine" bazaars that sold "all sorts of trinkets and many articles of practical value made of olive wood, gathered from the Mount of Olives, Bethany, the banks of the Jordan, Hebron, Bethlehem, and many other places familiar to Bible readers."[9] One visitor who had clearly

[4] Younis 1995: 142–149.
[5] McCabe 1975 (1876): 229.
[6] "Bazaar of the Nations," *Washington Review and Examiner* (Washington, PA), April 14, 1875.
[7] "Local Jottings," *Philadelphia Inquirer*, April 1, 1875.
[8] Younis 1995: 144.
[9] "What the Syrians Offer for Sale," *Commercial Advertiser* (NY), May 20, 1876.

been to the Holy Land opined that the Jerusalemite goods for sale there were genuine, in contrast to the objects in the other Middle Eastern venues, which were cheap and fake.[10] The Moorish Village he also declared genuine, and the articles for sale "had the true stamp of country and race."[11]

"It was generally remarked that the preponderance of articles from the Holy Land was so great that the visitor might well think Turkey had abandoned Mohammed and become a Christian country. Everything in the court was for sale."[12] One Oriental man complained that Americans were afraid of being cheated and had not the same interest in sacred relics as the Europeans he had met at other fairs.[13]

Many Middle Eastern goods received awards, according to Younis, but when the fair closed in November, "Turks, Moors, Algerines, and Syrians, genuine and bogus, were glad to accept one half the prices they demanded for their trumpery and trinkets."[14] Most of the Middle Easterners went home, contrary to what Younis says,[15] but they carried tales of American markets and American culture to their countrymen and countrywomen, adding fuel to the emigration fire that was already smoldering in Syria.

Following the Centennial Exposition several cities put on their own fairs, usually designed around their most famous agricultural or industrial product. The Southern Exposition in Louisville, Kentucky, was built around cotton. It had a five-year run, from 1883 to 1887. One Selah Mousur sold Jerusalemite goods.[16] John Abd-el-Nour, Fares Ferzan, E.F. Kettaneh, and Abraham Samaha all attended, showing Oriental goods. Abd-el-Nour was a New York merchant, while the other three had stores on the Boardwalk in Atlantic City, New Jersey. Ferzan went on to participate in the Minneapolis Industrial Exposition held in 1886. He demonstrated hand weaving of fine Oriental tapestries, claiming that the knowledge, loom, and materials had been in his family for hundreds of years.[17]

---

[10] "'Mussulmans' at the Centennial," *Cincinnati Daily Enquirer,* August 8, 1876.

[11] "World's Exposition," *NYH,* August 22, 1876.

[12] McCabe 1975: 155.

[13] "'Mussulmans' at the Centennial," *Cincinnati Daily Enquirer,* August 8, 1876.

[14] "Closing the Exhibition," *New-York Tribune,* November 18, 1876.

[15] "Many of the general working personnel from the Near East had stayed on in Philadelphia and elsewhere seeking jobs in industry" (Younis 1995: 149).

[16] Bush 2011: 70.

[17] "Sights and Scenes," *St. Paul* (MN) *Globe,* September 19, 1886.

## The Columbian Exposition (May–November 1893)

Chicago's great Columbian Exposition of 1893 fairly bristled with Middle Eastern displays. Syrians had begun to arrive as early as 1890 to prepare for the fair. A group of seventy silk weavers and decorative workers landed in New York in early December, 1890, more than two years before the fair was scheduled to open. They had plans to settle down in New York for the duration and use the time before the fair to produce the items they would exhibit there.[18] Whether or not they did stay in New York is unclear.

A Syrian from Damascus, Abraham Mouakad, was given the concession to build a replica of "A Street Called Straight" and other Biblical scenes; more to the point, he was to bring "a dozen of his countrymen engaged in embroidering, playing and singing national airs, and making and serving coffee in the Syrian style."[19] This concession was an early example of the layered character of the fair: an educational/scientific/patriotic veneer over a commercial core.

A year before the fair opened, Najeeb Maloof, writing from Camp Summit, Pennsylvania, warned those who would try their hand at selling at the fair that they should expect to spend a substantial amount in order to do so. He counted a round-trip ticket from Beirut to Chicago at 30 *rials*; renting a store at the fair for six months, 200 *rials*; room and board at 2 *rials*/day (an amount that seems way out of line, since peddlers in New York were paying 15 cents a day for lodging and 10 cents for a meal; perhaps prices were inflated because of the fair); 20 *rials* for advertising and other incidental expenses; 40 *rials* for furnishing and decorating the store; and 280 *rials* for entertainment (whatever that entailed). He came up with a total cost of 3,440 *rials*. Then there was the additional 10 percent fee that was charged by the Turkish government if one were renting in the Turkish section, which came to a total, according to Maloof, of 4,210 *rials*. The numbers don't add up, but one gets the idea. This outlay apparently did not even include the cost of goods. He insisted that those who wanted to come must do their homework, or they were liable to lose everything.[20] His warning, it turned out, was prescient. It is not clear what made Maloof an expert in these matters. Had he been to Chicago? Had he himself planned to show goods at the fair? Whether

[18] *Elkhart* (IN) *Daily Record*, December 3, 1890.
[19] "World's Fair Notes," *The Albany* (NY) *Times*, April 29, 1891.
[20] "Expenses to the Fair," *Kawkab America*, July 15, 1892.

his information was accurate or not, the amount of investment required was no doubt large. For that reason, almost every Syrian who participated in the fair did so in partnership with at least one other man; apparently the cost could not be borne alone.

5-1. Naoum Fuleihan (left) and friend (a Moghabghab?) perhaps on their way to the Chicago fair, 1893 (courtesy Nancy Fuleihan).

Hundreds of fair participants boarded steamships in the Middle East and began arriving in New York. On April 5, 1893, the *Guildhall* landed at New York harbor carrying 175 Egyptians: donkey boys, dancing girls, musicians, coffee men, waiters, wrestlers, jesters, torchbearers, farriers, and camel men. *Kawkab America* asserted, "A more interesting and picturesque crowd of Orientals had never passed the aisles of the registration department or faced the government examiners of immigrants."[21] All the entertainers, as well as the seven camels and twenty donkeys aboard, were bound for the Street of Cairo attraction at the fair. George Pangalo, the manager of the Egyptian Exhibition Company, accompanied them from Alexandria to New York. Born in Smyrna, educated at Robert College in Constantinople, a journalist in Bucharest, and finally manager of the Anglo-Egyptian bank in Cairo, Pangalo

[21] *Kawkab America* (English), April 7, 1893.

was a true cosmopolitan. He is credited with conceiving the idea of building Cairo Street.[22] He had enough foresight to deposit his troupe's return fares in his Cairo bank, in order to forestall any difficulty in getting his entertainers home. The managers of other concessions were not as perspicacious.

*Kawkab America* reported that the Ottoman Hamidie Company had chartered a special steamship of 4,000 tons to carry people and animals ("fifty Arabian horses and several dromedaries and camels") to the fair.[23] The *Cynthiana* duly brought 274 Syrians and their animals to New York from Beirut on April 26. Most of the passengers were described as performers, but there were also cooks, refreshment purveyors, servants, clerks, and waiters. Ameen Shakour and Abdullah Sayegh were in charge of the group. The American fever caused by the prospect of the fair, which had so many Syrians in its grip, distressed their American missionary friends: the missionaries were losing their teachers at an alarming rate and were having to increase salaries in an attempt to keep them. "We hope that after these people have had their fill of either fortune or misfortune at the Syrian department in the sales at the fair in Chicago, that they will settle down for a while. But who knows?"[24]

The fair was essentially divided into two sections: the fairgrounds themselves and the Midway Plaisance, a two-mile-long corridor outside the fair, which was perhaps the first amusement park. Inside the fairgrounds, the only Middle Eastern installation was the Turkish Building on the Street of All Nations; this was the Ottoman Empire's contribution to the intellectual/scientific/artistic pretensions of the fair. Emblematic of how seriously countries took these fairs, Sultan Abdul Hamid II declared that he himself would serve as patron and Taki Bey, commissioner to the fair, presided over the groundbreaking ceremony in which a sheep was ritually slaughtered and luncheon served to the guests in a tent erected for the purpose.[25] Inside the Turkish Building there were certainly booths run by Syrian merchants, but its displays were mainly educational and patriotic.

The real fun was outside the fairgrounds proper, in the Midway Plaisance. The Middle East was well represented in this amusement park: the Algerian and Tunisian Village, the Street in Cairo, the Moorish Palace, the Persian Concession, and the Turkish Village were supposed to represent the variety

---

[22] Anonymous 1894, *Portrait Types.*
[23] "Oriental Items," *Kawkab America,* February 17, 1893.
[24] *Presbyterian Letters,* Wm. Jessup to Mitchell, August 15, 1892.
[25] "Turkish Pavilion Dedicated," *NYT,* November 24, 1892.

of the "Mohammedan World," notwithstanding the fact that, according to the newspaper *Kawkab America,* most of these attractions were built and managed by Syrian Christians. The editors added that the prevalence of Syrians showed that "the Yankee spirit and enterprise of Americans have proven themselves too contagious for them to resist after a short residence in this country,"[26] implying that most of these merchants were already resident in the United States.

Moving from west to east along the Midway Plaisance, one first encountered the Algerian and Tunisian Village, constructed under the aegis of the French government. It was a large horseshoe-shaped building housing a large theater, souks, cafés, and kiosks, along with a Bedouin encampment set up on the grounds. Everyone working in the Village wore traditional (picturesque) clothing. In the theater, six Algerian dancers performed. The Village also included the reconstruction of a room of an Eastern sultan, made by the "greatest living Oriental designer and decorator," Betros Effendi Helweh, who designed it in Paris and brought it to the fair in forty large boxes.[27] One concern built a replica of an immense temple entirely of dried fruit.[28] Several Syrians had shops in the Tunisian section, including Selim Nahas (Oriental goods) and Selim Forzly (confectionery).

Joseph Oussani, a Chaldean from Baghdad, had been given a concession by two Syrian companies, Elia Souhami Sadullah & Cie. and S.K. Bistany & Cie., to bring over twelve persons to do business in the Ottoman section. The certificate was signed in Constantinople on February 1, 1893, in the presence of the American consul-general.[29] Oussani and his brother Yacoub claimed they built the Persian Palace at the fair, but whether this was under the aegis of the two companies or on their own is not clear. The Oussanis had been traders between Baghdad and Persia for many years and brought forty trunk loads of goods to sell at the fair on their own account. Joseph kept a diary of his trip from Baghdad to Marseilles with these trunks; it took him thirty-eight days.

The people Oussani brought over were called "artists" on the ship manifest, so they may have been entertainers in the Persian Palace. The Palace had disappointing attendance early in the fair, but finally the managers hit on the

[26] "Oriental Items," *Kawkab America,* February 17, 1893.
[27] "Wonderful Mosaic Kiosk," *The* (NY) *Evening World,* March 20, 1893.
[28] "In Regimentals," *Kawkab America,* July 15, 1892.
[29] *Oussani Letters.*

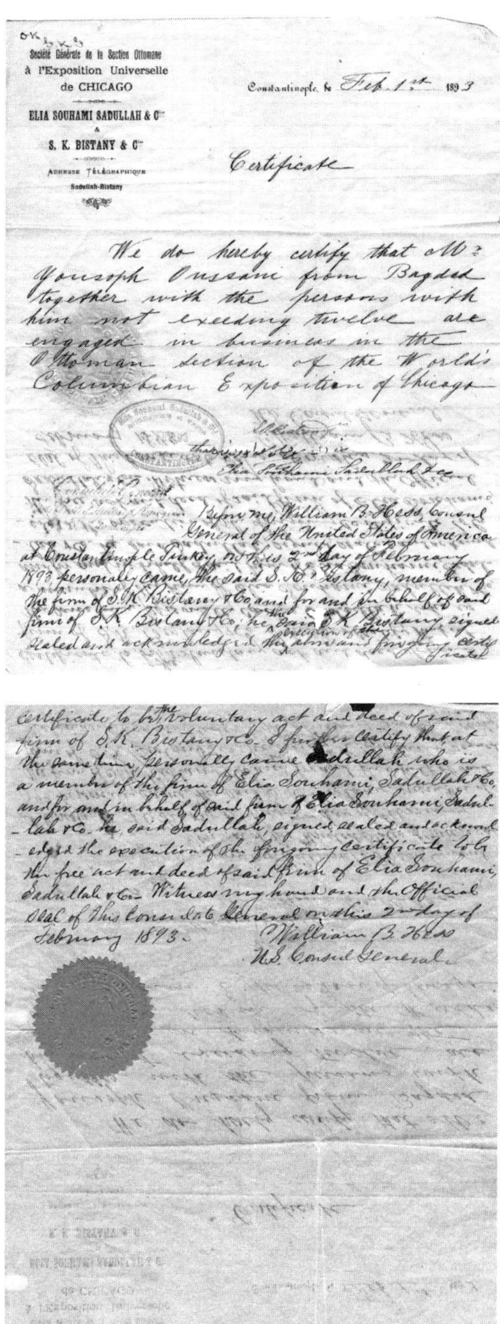

Société Générale de la Section Ottomane
à l'Exposition Universelle
de CHICAGO

ELIA SOUHAMI SADULLAH & Cie
&
S. K. BISTANY & Cie

Adresse Télégraphique
Sadullah-Bistany

Constantinople, le Feb. 1st 1893

Certificate

We do hereby certify that Mr. Yousoph Oussani from Bagdad together with the persons with him not exceeding twelve are engaged in business in the Ottoman section of the World's Columbian Exposition of Chicago

Elia Souhami Sadullah & Co.

Before me, William B. Hess, Consul General of the United States of America at Constantinople Turkey, on this 2nd day of February 1893 personally came the said S. K. Bistany, member of the firm of S. K. Bistany & Co. and for and in behalf of said firm of S. K. Bistany & Co. he the said S. K. Bistany signed sealed and acknowledged the execution of the above and foregoing certificate certificate to be the voluntary act and deed of said firm of S. K. Bistany & Co. I further certify that at the same time personally came Sadullah who is a member of the firm of Elia Souhami, Sadullah & Co. and for and in behalf of said firm of Elia Souhami, Sadullah & Co. he said Sadullah, signed sealed and acknowledged the execution of the foregoing certificate to be the free act and deed of said firm of Elia Souhami, Sadullah & Co. Witness my hand and the Official seal of this Consulate General on this 2nd day of February 1893.

William B. Hess
U.S. Consul General

5-2. Contract between Joseph Oussani and Sadullah and Bistany companies authorizing Oussani to take not more than twelve persons to the Ottoman section of the Chicago fair. Constantinople, February 1, 1893 (courtesy Gail O'Keefe Edson).

idea of importing French women from the Moulin Rouge to perform the can-can under the guise of Oriental entertainment. The attraction became wildly popular, despite (or because of) several attempts to shut it down. The building's name was changed, at least among the cognoscenti, to "The Persian Palace of Eros."

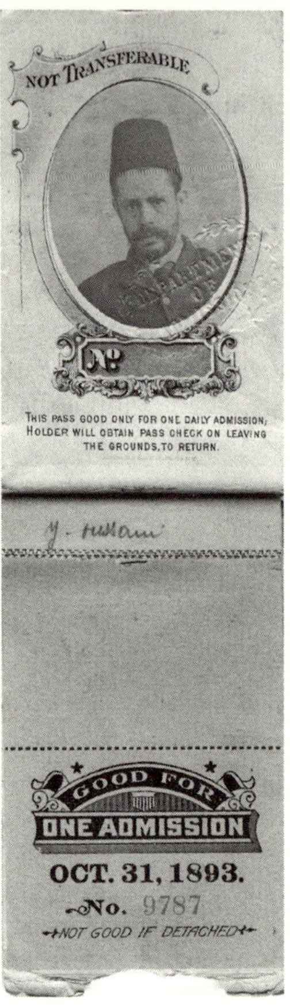


5-3. Joseph Oussani's identity card and ticket book for the Chicago fair, 1893 (courtesy of Gail O'Keefe Edson).

George Ferris's wheel made its first appearance at the fair. It was the tallest installation at the fair and the many bird's-eye views of the fair were taken from the top. It dwarfed the large Moorish Palace, a nearly square building with minarets at two of its corners and a dome above the entrance, which stood beside it. The Moorish Palace housed a restaurant, coffee shops, wax figures, and, in the center, a veritable forest of Alhambra-like arched corridors.

The Ottoman Empire was doubly represented, both by the high-minded Turkish Building inside the fair on the Street of All Nations and the much more theatrical Turkish Village on the Midway Plaisance. The Turkish Village covered a whole square block next to the Moorish Palace and consisted of fifteen buildings. Khalil Sarkis (the publisher of the Beirut newspaper *Lisan al Hal*) and seven other Syrian businessmen managed (and were investors in) the Hamidie Company that administered this, the largest of the Middle Eastern attractions. The company's managing directors were Sarkis, Raji Seikaly, Beshara Zaza (Geagea), Najeeb Sursock, Shukri Farjallah, Ameen Shakour, and Abdullah Sayegh (the last two having accompanied the group on the *Cynthiana*). They sought to protect their turf as any company would, even before the fair opened. A letter from the Turkish legation to the American secretary of state written in 1892, for example, protested the intention of Syrian Christians to build a mosque at the fair, to which they would charge admission. The legation asserted that it was an insult to the Muslim religion,[30] but the real reason was that they themselves intended to build a mosque, which was to be one of the tourist attractions in the Turkish Village. And of course, the people who wrote this letter were Syrian Christians themselves. The letter-writers were unsuccessful, and one can see the two competing mosques in bird's-eye photos of the Midway Plaisance. The company also asked the fair's managers to shut down the shops of some of the merchants in the Tunisian Pavilion who were selling Turkish goods under the guise of being Tunisian. They were, the company said, competing with legitimate Syrian merchants in the Turkish Village. Of course most of the merchants in the Tunisian section were also Syrian.

The Odeon Theater in the Turkish Village (25 and 50 cent admission fees, depending on the performance) presented plays in the Turkish language, farces, and traditional dance. Visitors could tour a mosque, a Persian tent, a Bedouin camp, a panorama of Syrian photographs, and a facsimile of an Egyptian temple for twenty-five cents each. At the café chantant, fairgoers could smoke water pipes, be served Turkish coffee, and enjoy native music.[31] All the employees of the Hamidie Company had a star and crescent emblazoned on their sleeves or chests, making them instantly recognizable. One can see that even here in the Midway Plaisance, the Hamidie Company was trying to hold on to the cultural high ground by presenting ethnographically

[30] *Daily Inter Ocean* (Chicago), November 15, 1892.
[31] Carlton 1994: 35.

"authentic" exhibits, while still earning money. At the same time, the redundancy of the "cultural" offerings in the various Middle Eastern buildings—Turkish coffee, dancing, reenactments, etc.—and the competition they must have engendered was a portent of difficulties to come.

5-4 and 5-5. Portrait of Joseph Oussani at the Chicago fair, 1893 (courtesy of Gail O'Keefe Edson). Yak Oussani (called "Mirza Yacob" (Persian)) at the Chicago fair, 1893 (*Portrait Types,* 1894).

The great majority of Syrian businessmen who were at the fair set up their booths in the Turkish Village. Most of them sold the same things: Oriental embroideries, Holy Land goods, woodwork, trinkets, and Turkish products. Yusef Waked sold Turkish tobacco, two Syrians sold Oriental photographs, and others sold dried fruit. These merchants not only had the huge setup costs outlined by Maloof, but were also required to pay a percentage of their income to the fair management as well as to the Hamidie Company—double taxation, as it were. Unlike most of the Middle Easterners there, the Syrians were not in the main entertainers, although they could be persuaded to dress up and perform as Persian swordsmen or Arab sheiks. But they more often managed others. A particularly telling photograph that purports to show a group of "European Turks" and "Asiatic Turks," actually represents a group of Syrians, half of whom dressed up for the photographer (Figure 5-6). Several of them can be seen in other photographs playing different roles.[32]

[32] Buel 1894.

5-6. "European and Asiatic Turks" at the Chicago fair (Buel 1894).

The biggest draw at the fair was Pangalo's "A Street in Cairo," modeled after a display of the same name at the Paris fair of 1889. Its importance to the success of the Chicago fair cannot be overstated. Cairo Street, as it came to be called by everyone, was by far the most popular attraction there, bringing in more than two and a half million visitors in less than six months.[33] It was a full-scale replica of a street in Cairo, complete with buildings with their protruding *mashrabiehs* (pierced wooden screens installed on the upper floors of Egyptian houses to allow women to gaze out at the street without being seen), a mosque, and coffeehouses and shops on each side. Visitors could ride a camel or a donkey up and down the street, watch a wedding procession twice a day, see swordplay by a Sudanese chief, enjoy Turkish smoking parlors, partake of exotic foods, and buy objects from the Holy Land ("Bethlehemite" or "Jerusalemite" goods). "Here indeed we met with life such as never before was seen in America and here was the opportunity for a study of national character of great variety. At one end of the street the old Temple of Luxor reminded us of ancient Egypt, while the architecture of the street and Mosque at the other end told of Cairo in its splendor."[34]

[33] Carlton 1994: 15.

[34] Anonymous 1894, *Portrait Types:* "Introduction" by F.W. Putnam.

The dozens of books of photographic views that appeared during and after the fair show the popularity of the Middle Eastern sections; no other region or group was so often photographed. In just one example, there were eleven postcard-size photos and a dozen full-page photographs of Middle Eastern "types,"[35] while other nationalities were shown one or two times at most (Figure 5-10). In a folio-size book of portraits from the Midway Plaisance, fully one-third showed people of Middle Eastern origin.[36]

5-7. Street of Cairo, Chicago fair, 1893. Almost everyone is in costume. Note the veiled women, the "bear" in the center front, and the camels tended by Egyptian camel drivers (Buel 1894).

There were some rocky moments in the first months of the fair; attendance disappointed everyone. The most important debate (carried on in the newspapers, in churches, by local guardians of morality, and among the fair managers) centered on whether the fair should be allowed to open on Sundays. It was finally decided to allow the fair to stay open, but the Oriental dance venues

[35] Buel 1894. The fascination with the exotic, together with the pseudo-scientific presentation of racial or ethnic types that underlay these exhibits, have been lucidly analyzed by Celik 1992.

[36] Anonymous 1894, *Portrait Types.*

were ordered closed on Sundays. This was met by a howl of protest from the Syrian merchants, but more effective than their protests was the fact that fair attendance on Sunday plummeted. The authorities halved the admission price for Sundays, and still the attendance was half that of weekdays. Merchants continued to complain and took the issue to court. A judge finally ruled that the entire fair should be open on Sundays.[37] But this seesawing of openings and closures hurt the merchants, and it took a while to recover.

5-8. "Ben Yakar (Egyptian)" at the Chicago fair. He was supposedly proprietor of thirty-five shops in Cairo Street (*Portrait Types,* 1894).

Despite these setbacks, attendance at the Chicago fair reached an astounding 27.5 million, more than a third of the entire population of the United States, and the fair ended in November 1893 with a $2.5 million surplus. The Midway Plaisance alone generated $4 million in revenues. *Kawkab America* reported on the profits of the Syrians at the fair each week. They steadily increased, as did the attendance. Particularly lucrative was the Street of Cairo, which was bringing in a profit of $2,000 a day, in contrast to the other large

[37] When the Presbyterian Mission in Syria heard of this decision, "it filled us all with shame and dismay." *Presbyterian Letters,* H.H. Jessup to Grant, May 31, 1893.

Oriental companies, which were bringing in between $200 and $500 a day.[38] This outsized amount for the Egyptian section was due entirely to the Egyptian belly dancers performing inside, attracting more than 12,000 visitors a day.[39] They were the subject of debates raging between the merchants and the moral police. As word of these arguments spread, the attendance figures only grew. The spillover from Cairo Street lifted the boats of all the other Middle Eastern concessions: revenues of $200–$500 a day earned by other concessions were still substantial, amounting to between $36,000 and $90,000 for the six months of the fair. We do not know how profitable they really were, since we do not know the extent of their expenses. If Malouf's estimates given in the beginning of this section were even close to accurate, the profits could be substantial.

Among the more successful concessions were the Arabic Coffee Company and the Ottoman Coffee Company, which together sold all of the Turkish coffee at the fair and ran the cafés. Also profitable were the wholesalers of drinks, companies that ran the Tunisian markets, and the confectionery dealers. The confectioners who sold deep-fried sweet dough became known for yelling "Hot! Hot!" to the passersby, and this became a byword for Cairo Street. Khalil Abdulaziz Bistany, who was in charge of the Egyptian theater and also acted in it, claimed he earned a profit of $15,000 at the fair.[40] Another merchant claimed a $4,000 profit.

A small but successful attraction was the Syrian fortune-teller, Sheikh Barakat, whose place was crowded with people from everywhere, "even intelligent ones."[41] He brought in a cool fifteen dollars a day,[42] which was pure profit. A writer (signed only "Tarek") in *Kawkab America* claimed that many of the Arabs on the Midway Plaisance—particularly the camel drivers and donkey "boys"—were constantly high on hashish and having the time of their lives as they raked in the cash.[43] One American reporter described a scene in which an Egyptian woman sold her baby for one dollar, and then demanded the baby be returned. When the buyer refused, she brought back "six or seven men of her race," who retrieved the baby. They walked away, and the woman

---

[38] *Kawkab America,* July 7, 1893. It is not entirely clear whether the amounts reported are real profits or revenues.

[39] Belly dancers at the fair and subsequently will be discussed fully in chapter 10.

[40] "A Thrifty Woman," *Repository* (Canton, OH), March 16, 1894.

[41] Rustum 1995 (1895): 36.

[42] *Kawkab America,* October 6, 1893.

[43] *Kawkab America,* October 6, 1893.

looked back at the sucker and said, "I have my baby and my dollar."[44] The story is ridiculous but probably did portray the scamming that was going on at every level at the fair.

A reporter described the excitement at a local bank after the fair closed in November 1893:

> The first arrival Tuesday was a donkey boy from Cairo Street. From some remote corner of his flowing robes he produced a tattered cloth, and, unrolling it, dumped $700 in silver on the counter. "Let me have French francs for it," he said through an interpreter. A camel driver followed, who wanted $1,000 changed. Along in quick succession came an Arab who bought a draft for $1,500 on Beyroot [Beirut], a Turk who had $600 to transfer, a Persian dancer with a fortune of $1,500 in American silver, and a Nubian soldier who unrolled $600 in bills.... The praises of Chicago will be sung in many lands this winter, because hundreds of families in the Orient will be in plenty with what their fathers have earned in trade and received in backsheesh.... They will be howling swells among their people.[45]

Hidden in this garden of apparent material success there were bound to be some worms. Note that none of the concessions earning high revenues or the howling swells mentioned above were actually merchants selling Oriental or Holy Land goods, and for a reason: the sellers of goods apparently did not do very well. Despite *Kawkab America*'s assertion that the Tunisian stores (most of which were run by Syrians) were successes, ten of them were closed in the second month of the fair for failing to pay their rental fees. One of the Syrian merchants in the Tunisian section (Elias Ghannoum) committed suicide because he had lost everything.[46] Some of the merchants who had opened on Sundays in defiance of the ban were fined $1,000 each, putting a large dent in their earnings and placing their enterprises in jeopardy. The Turkish Café and Theater sued the Ottoman section for encroaching on their market; the suit was settled by a payment of $1,000 to the Turkish Café. This dispute was part of a larger disagreement between the Syrian merchants on the Midway and those in the Turkish Building in the Street of All Nations inside the fair proper, who were selling similar goods and competing against one another.

[44] "Teresa Takes in the Midway by Moonlight," *Daily Inter Ocean* (Chicago), August 1, 1893.

[45] "Swells Will These Orientals Be When at Home," *Cincinnati Post,* November 17, 1893.

[46] *Kawkab America,* December 8, 1893.

5-9. "Persian" soldier, probably a Syrian, at the fair (Buel 1894).

Mikhail Rustum in his book *Stranger in the West*, which was published two years after the fair closed, and *Kawkab America*, writing during the fair, alluded to some of the failed enterprises. Rustum blamed these failures on the fact that the Middle Eastern section was run by a Jew (Robert Levi),[47] who, he said, assigned some of the worst positions to the Syrians. Perhaps Rustum himself lost money at the fair, which would explain his bitterness. In fact, *Kawkab America* reported that Levi responded positively to complaints from the merchants that he was depressing their sales by charging admission for some sections and not others; he agreed to level the playing field by removing all admission charges.[48] Levi's portrait taken at the fair shows a splendid Oriental gentleman in a tarboush embellished with the Hamidie star and crescent, two embroidered vests, embroidered Kurdish trousers, and a huge colorful cummerbund. He carries a sword at his waist and leans on an elaborately inlaid rifle.

Some or many of the merchants did lose money. A pathetic follow-up story in *Kawkab America* reported on the merchants trying to sell the buildings they had built but which they were forced to leave behind in Chicago. The 1,500-seat Turkish Theater, on which investors had spent $8,000, sold

[47] Rustum 1995 (1895): 40.

[48] *Kawkab America*, September 29, 1893.

for $25, the Turkish Café for $60.[49] Of course, there was no way they could take these buildings with them, but it must have been horribly disappointing to the merchants who had invested so much. The editors of *Kawkab America* were bitter about how the American buyers took advantage of the Syrians. Although no summary report appeared in *Kawkab America*, one can read between the lines to surmise that many of the Syrian merchants were disappointed, if not bankrupt.

5-10. Three Middle Eastern "types" at the fair (Buel 1894).

The most far-reaching and certainly the most shocking failure was that of the Hamidie Company, founded under the aegis of Sultan Abdul Hamid himself. It was a massive enterprise, costing hundreds of thousands of dollars—the biggest of the Middle Eastern concessions at the fair. It seemed to be cursed from the beginning: there was a disastrous fire in its stable in June, killing dozens of animals and destroying much of its stock. There were problems with the land it had leased, and it changed venues twice in an attempt to increase attendance, to no avail. *Kawkab America* wrote numerous articles about the company's progress from crown jewel of the Ottoman presence at the fair to ignominious failure. Correspondent Abdallah Jabbour wrote an excruciatingly detailed series of essays after the close of the fair, dissecting every aspect of the failure. He filled two to three columns every week from December 15, 1893, to May 4, 1894. His critiques were the critiques one could make of any failed business: top-heavy management, badly worded contracts, too many employees, a sclerotic structure that required approvals for every

[49] *Kawkab America,* November 24, 1893.

move, and so forth. In desperation, the company sent some of its entertainers to Canada and other states to perform while the fair was still open. These troupes did bring back profits, but not enough to save the company. The company probably could have saved itself by having belly dancers perform at its theater; instead it insisted on presenting the more high-minded folkloric troupes, which were a total washout with the American public.

At the close of the fair in November, the company admitted it was broke and in debt to the tune of about $30,000, leaving hundreds of Arab performers (not to mention horses, camels, and all their lavish trappings) stranded in Chicago with no way to get home. Unlike the manager of the Egyptian concession, the Hamidie Company's leaders had put nothing aside for the return fares. The very first drawdown from the United States' newly established Immigrant Fund, in fact, went to pay the passage back to his home country of a Syrian performer that the government feared was liable to become a public charge. A Mr. Hays from Kansas City helped the stranded Simon Tanous get back home. Simon had apparently been Hays's guide on a trip to the Holy Land the year before, and Hays was grateful enough to buy him a ticket. Tanous wrote a letter of thanks to Mr. Hays when he was happily back home, ensconced in the Hotel Khedival, Beirut.[50]

The Hamidie Company was put into receivership, but the question arose as to whether any of the objects, which belonged in theory, if not in fact, to the sultan, could be sold to make good the debts.[51] Some of the investors wrote bitterly that the goods held by the court were worth twice the debt. The seven Syrian investors lost everything. It is clear that apart from the Syrians' own failings as managers, the Americans were able to take advantage of their lack of knowledge of Chicago in particular and American ways of doing business in general, contradicting *Kawkab America*'s assertion that the Syrian merchants at the fair were so successful because they had learned the ways of American business very well. Of course the managers and investors in the Hamidie Company were Syrian Syrians who had come especially for the fair, and they apparently were not prepared for the sharper business practices of their American counterparts. The logistics of getting hundreds of people, animals, props, and tons of building materials from Beirut to Chicago in 1893, providing housing, food, and salaries for everyone, and then having to take care of their return, would have been a nightmare for anyone, Syrian or not.

[50] "Simon Is Home at Last," *Kansas City Star,* May 23, 1894.

[51] "Want Their Desert," *Daily Inter Ocean* (Chicago), November 10, 1893.

The merchants and investors entered into the spirit of the fair with great optimism, perhaps not entirely aware of how much they were risking. Jabbour's most telling comment was that the company "felt as a stranger in the land where they had expended so much money."[52]

## Copycat Fairs (1893–1895)

Several copycat fairs, which were specifically designed to exploit the success of the Chicago fair, opened soon after it closed. All seemed pale in comparison to the great original. The first was New York's exposition, which opened in December 1893 at the newly built Grand Central Palace on Lexington Avenue and 43rd Street. It advertised itself as featuring the prizewinners from the Chicago fair. All six floors of the Palace (400,000 square feet) were given over to the expo, with attractions from the Midway Plaisance on exhibit in the third gallery. There were more than three dozen Syrian merchants selling their wares and another "Streets of Cairo" attraction, as well as an Egyptian café and an Egyptian theater, in which were performed the "Torture Dance" (one of the many names given to erotic dancing) and the *danse du ventre*, that is, belly dancing.[53] It was in the Egyptian Theater that the scandals and arrests that are described in chapter 10 took place. That the expo was a disappointment—at least as far as the Syrian merchants were concerned—is clear from the increasingly disillusioned stories in *Kawkab America* reporting that the Syrians threatened to close their shops if the mayor, to whom they turned for help, could not better promote the exposition.

The California Midwinter International Exposition, which was erected in Golden Gate Park in San Francisco, opened its doors in January 1894. There was yet another Street of Cairo—this one much simplified, even cartoonish, compared to the one in Chicago, with camel and donkey rides on offer and a Bedouin wedding procession twice a day. Just as at the Columbian fair, one could recline on a divan, puff a cigarette made of genuine Turkish or Egyptian tobacco, and drink coffee prepared by "Hassan of Constantinople" at the Egyptian Café. The Egyptian Theater featured "the erotic dancer known as Little Egypt." A photograph of the interior of the Egyptian Theater shows a group of men and women, which, if their nationalities can be guessed by

[52] *Kawkab America,* December 29, 1893.
[53] "Exposition by Prize Winners," *NYT,* November 30, 1893.

their faces, included at least as many Americans as Middle Easterners. Syrian merchants opened more than sixty shops, "their dusky interiors glowing with tinted silks and embroidered muslins, jeweled weapons, brass and copper lamps, warm-hued rugs and silver filigree."[54] Most of these Syrian merchants, one would guess, were from the American Midwest and West, but we know that Abdow Lutfy, after closing up his shop at the New York expo, sent his sons, daughter, and sister out to San Francisco to set up a concession there; others from New York must have gone as well since *Kawkab America* reported extensively on the expo. Like the New York fair, the San Francisco expo disappointed the expectations of the Syrian merchants. They blamed the poor attendance on the entry fee charged by the Turkish Pavilion; violence erupted when the Syrian manager of the Pavilion—unlike Robert Levi at the Chicago fair—refused to eliminate the fee. The merchants demanded a refund of their rental fees, and many closed up shop early and went home.[55] Those who stayed open until the end, however, reported improved earnings and were generally satisfied.

Opening in May 1894, hard on the heels of the San Francisco fair, the Antwerp fair featured Egyptian and Turkish markets, a theater and café, and a Syrian market that attracted a number of merchants from New York, including David A. Fuleihan, Yousef Kanawati, Ibrahim el Rayyes, George and Tewfiq Wahsh, and Ameen Moatelany. Moatelany filed optimistic reports at the beginning, but by the time the fair closed in October, everyone expressed disappointment and most had lost money.[56] Other fairs, especially the Cotton States fair held in Atlanta in 1895, also attracted Syrian businessmen. Nageeb Arbeely had been given (or bought) the "privilege" of managing the Eastern Section and spent the year hyping the fair in *Kawkab America* in order to rent out spaces to his fellow countrymen. Someone, perhaps Arbeely, ran a classified ad in the newspaper for several weeks seeking a genuine Bedouin tent, a complete Bedouin costume, and "five camels, well-trained, like those that performed at Chicago" to take to Atlanta.[57] One wonders why the Syrians continued to attend these fairs when they and their fellow countrymen seemed to lose money at every one of them, or perhaps it was just that the results did not live up to their outsized expectations.

[54] Anonymous 1894, *Official Guide:* 114.

[55] *Kawkab America,* February 23, 1894.

[56] *Kawkab America,* October 5, 1894.

[57] *Kawkab America,* March 15, 1895.

No matter the sad stories retailed about the fairs, the dealers and entertainers who came from the Middle East to make a quick profit and return home—and those who were here already—did realize that they had uncovered (or created) a large market in the United States. The collective attendance at the fairs (more than forty million attendees all told) helped spur on the Orientalist craze that had begun in an earlier decade, this time among the American middle class. The objects on display began to take root in the popular imagination. This new market was a boon to those merchants who could provide the goods that were suddenly so popular. So-called Turkish rooms sprang up all over the country in middle-class and wealthy homes, and people began to buy Orientalia to furnish them. Sometimes these rooms were tricked out as Turkish smoking rooms, the décor including a *narghile* or two, long divans, and voluminous draperies. Words such as "narghile" and "divan" began to appear without quotation marks in newspaper articles.

The goods that were sold with such success at the fairs—tobacco, carpets, furniture, textiles, cutlery, jewelry, brass work, and religious goods—were those that Syrian merchants continued to specialize in. Many of those who came especially for the fairs decided to settle here (or were forced to if they could not afford passage home), while others went back to Syria, told their stories about the wealth awaiting anyone who was willing to work, and returned to the United States with a supply of goods. Their friends and families followed. Those who were already living here returned to their homes newly energized and set up businesses that capitalized on what they had learned at the fairs. New Yorkers who had participated, including Abdow Lutfy, Yusef Balesh, Nicola Abo Samra, John Abd-el-Nour, Alexander Andalaft, and dozens of others, built large businesses selling the goods that had proved so popular.

Along with goods, the live attractions featured at the fairs were also transported to venues all over the country; the dancers, camel drivers, acrobats, and other performers formed their own troupes, joined the circus, moved to Coney Island, or became entertainers in minstrel shows or on vaudeville stages. Joseph Oussani, George Jabour, and Hajji Tahar were among those who made a good living on the backs of Arab entertainers. Middle Easterners were soon usurped by American imitators in most of these venues, but some Arabs continued to perform and make a living for decades after the fairs closed.

All the merchants had made a large capital outlay to participate in the fairs, and although some may have suffered losses, the investment paid off in the lessons learned about what did and did not sell. They were able to capitalize on this knowledge in the ensuing years.

## Chapter 6

# Peddlers

*The Syrian pedler's* [sic] *motto is: "He cannot rest who will succeed."*[1]

The classic immigrant story, not just for Syrians but also for Jews and others, has the new immigrant begin his work life in the United States by peddling. In the Syrian case, the data bear out this stereotyped picture. Almost every life story that I have reconstructed includes a blank period between immigration and the first known business; these were the peddling years. The exceptions are few enough to be detailed in subsequent chapters. In the list we compiled with 5,000 data entries for the period from 1880 to 1899, the word "peddler" appears as a profession just fifty-four times. It is only in the 1900 census that this profession shows up in its true strength, where 190 men and women peddlers represented 23.6 percent of those who listed a profession. If we assume that those calling themselves "salesmen" were actually peddlers, the percentage increases to 26 percent. One can only imagine that for the earlier years, the percentage was much higher; by 1900, many people had moved up from peddling into running their own business. There were always new immigrants to fill the vacancies.

In an illustrated supplement, the *New-York Tribune* charted the Syrian's progress from peddler to capitalist, by first showing four different "stages" of peddling: a cheerful young man standing at the counter of a supplier having his *keshi* (a wooden box with a leather shoulder strap) filled with notions before going out on the road; an older peddler with his *keshi* beside him on the ground (later reproduced in Miller's book), who is no longer an itinerant and has, the author says, a small amount of capital; a slightly more prosperous pushcart owner, "now fairly on the road to prosperity"; and fourth, a man with a horse and wagon filled to overflowing with dozens of barrels:

[1] "Victims of the Turk Finding Homes Here," *New-York Tribune Illustrated Supplement,* October 11, 1903.

"he no longer tramps the ground with weary feet."[2] Syrians were mainly pack peddlers who went door-to-door, carrying a *keshi*, a *shenta* (a shoulder bag or satchel), a basket, or a dress suitcase, which they called *jezdan harir* (silk bag).

6-1. Bashara K. Forzley with his *shenta* and *keshi* in Boston, 1898 (Faris and Yamna Naff Collection, National Museum of American History).

The new immigrant, or so the story goes, arrived in America and was immediately sent to someone who would supply him with goods on credit. Bashara Kalil (B.K.) Forzley described his first day on the job: "Cousin Farrah, proprietor of a dry goods store, put five dollars' worth of goods into a basket, looped it over my arm, and gently prodded me out into the strange world to sell from house to house."[3] Naff describes the experience of "Mike H." who, upon his arrival, was directed to Washington Street where he stayed in a Syrian hotel and bought "$40 worth of goods" from a Syrian wholesaler.[4] Whether he had $40 with him or took the goods on credit is not stated. Simon George was directed to the Faour Brothers to get his first stock of goods. My paternal grandfather, a Maronite, was sent to George J. Malhami, another Maronite, for his first load.

[2] "Victims of the Turk Finding Homes Here," *New-York Tribune Illustrated Supplement,* October 11, 1903.
[3] Forzley 1958: 8.
[4] Naff 1985: 134.

New immigrants went to suppliers with whom they had a connection: men from the same town, the same family, or the same religion. Suppliers' names were spread by word of mouth. The most important point of these stories of the first experiences of the peddlers is the faith the wholesaler demonstrated in the new immigrant. The risks were really quite small since the Syrians' horror of a debt unpaid was well known. After paying back the supplier for that first load, the peddler would go out again with a slightly larger inventory, until he was forced, like Beshara Forzley, to buy a suitcase and a *keshi* to replace his first basket. A famous photograph shows Forzly at the age of twelve in 1898 with his *shenta* and *keshi*, a jaunty hat on his head and a sweet smile on his face.[5] Naff describes the load that one "Wadi N." carried: a heavy pack strapped on his back with a hook attached to the strap in front, from which hung a notions case, which alone could weigh thirty pounds.[6]

Some of these men and women went far afield; the more they could carry, the less frequently they would have to come back to restock their cases. Naff divides these peddling journeys into three kinds: long-term, where the peddler would be gone for months and venture far from his suppliers; mid-range, where the person would be gone for one or two weeks; and short-term, where the person would be gone only for the day and then return home. Suppliers would send goods by train to far-off depots to which the long-term peddler would return periodically to restock his or her pack.[7] Surely the longest peddling trip on foot was reported in *Kawkab America*, which claimed that a Syrian man had walked from New York to Mexico, selling goods all along the way. The newspaper asserted he had the strength to do so because he had been a muleteer in Mount Lebanon.[8]

New York peddlers were mainly mid-range and short-term peddlers. Some sold goods during the day in the city; others traveled to nearby towns by train. Some would go farther afield, perhaps to upstate New York in the summer, when they would move from town to town, selling. Sometimes they would be gone the entire summer. My maternal grandmother, for example, spent the summer of 1907 with her mother and one of her sisters selling goods in the watering holes of Clifton Springs, Niagara Falls, and Geneva, New York. They were, perhaps, selling the laces imported by her husband-to-be, F.M. Jabara.

[5] Forzley 1958: 6.
[6] Naff 1985: 163.
[7] Naff 1985: 167.
[8] "Oriental Items of Interest," *Kawkab America,* August 26, 1892.

From very early the Syrians made a distinction between the *keshi* peddlers and the *jezdan harir* peddlers, and we know, contrary to the stories told by our parents, that "silk bag" peddling was actually an entry-level option for some peddlers. Silk bag peddlers carried finer goods: white goods, Oriental tapestries, or silks.[9] Zelditch cites an early immigrant to Pittsburgh on his first day of peddling: "Mr. A had a store on Washington Place. I was taken there and he fitted me out with a complete line of fancy goods and religious notions."[10] The line between notions peddlers and fancy goods peddlers was not strictly drawn; some peddlers sold both. The distinction was clear; each peddler was characterized as mainly selling one or the other type of goods.

Rustum, in his 1895 book *Stranger in the West*, published two useful charts for the would-be peddler: the wholesale prices of notions that a *kesha* salesman might carry, and the prices of the fine tapestries and cloths that the *jezdan harir* peddler would carry. The *keshi*, which had to be made by a carpenter, cost serious money (two *rials* fifty).[11] We have several carpenters in our database who must have been providing these boxes to peddlers or to wholesalers who loaned them to the peddlers. The *keshi* contained notions: pins, shoelaces, brushes, or collar buttons, whose wholesale prices ranged from five cents to forty cents a dozen. The *jezdan harir* goods were expensive items in silk and satin, imported from the Middle East. Rustum lists a large tablecloth, for example, made of satin with gold embroidery, whose wholesale price was fifteen *rials*. No European items were found on his list, although we know that there were a number of Syrian wholesalers selling Parisian goods by at least 1892. It is doubtful, however, that Syrian peddlers carried European goods, so these wholesalers must have been selling to retail stores.

John Abd-el-Nour said in an 1888 interview, "every wholesale house in New York has 30 or 40 peddlers or drummers in its pay."[12] These numbers of course included peddlers in other states who were "employed" by the New York wholesale houses, but even at this early date, the number of peddlers in New York itself must have been large. Twelve years later, when the census was taken, the number of wholesalers had probably tripled, and so too the number of peddlers, yet only 190 individuals declared themselves peddlers.

[9] Ansara 1931: 87.
[10] Zelditch 1936: 33.
[11] Rustum 1995 (1895): 24.
[12] "The Pilgrims from Lebanon," *The* (NY) *Press*, January 14, 1888.

There were no peddlers at all in the Brooklyn census, signifying the upwardly mobile character of the Brooklyn community. This, however, was an ephemeral situation. My own grandfather's history, as well as the data from Miller (1903), show that as new immigrants began to bypass Manhattan altogether and go straight to the burgeoning community in Brooklyn, a concomitant number of peddlers appeared there. Thus, Miller reports that 18.2 percent of the Brooklyn South Ferry immigrants were peddling.[13] The Immigration Commission *Report* of 1911 stated that more than 50 percent of the Syrians living in the Washington Street neighborhood were still peddlers.[14] The Syrian population of Washington Street had gotten much smaller and poorer, as the newly wealthy moved away, so the proportion of peddlers was greater.

The reluctance to call oneself a peddler might be attributable to the negative connotation the term had for many Americans. They tended to equate peddling with begging. Here is an excerpt from a long, vitriolic newspaper article about peddlers in the Syrian Colony: "The Emigration Commissioners began sending back these Lebanon tramps on their arrival, but these were not to be defeated as easily. They assumed new names, Jerusalemites and Bethlehemites, and brought with them sacred trinkets, as rosaries, crucifixes and the like, and gave themselves out as peddlers. Under this guise they could not easily be kept out, and they again started on begging tours, holding a bunch of rosaries in one hand, which they pretended to sell, whenever a policeman was in sight."[15] It was a common belief that peddlers were only pretending to sell things and were really just beggars. As mentioned, the word "mendicant" was often used as a synonym for peddler, with all the negative connotations implied by that word. The Immigration Commission *Report* of 1901, after admitting that "business was the Syrians' lodestar," added, "Notwithstanding the superficial scope of his enterprise, an unstable, too versatile, and constitutionally indolent temperament tends to restrict his energies to the nomadic and parasitic pursuits rather than those truly useful to the community."[16] The attitude toward women peddling was even more hostile; this will be described more fully in chapter 10.

Even Syrians realized that some of their countrymen used questionable tactics to sell their wares. Writing to the editors of *Kawkab America*, one

[13] Miller 1903: 14.

[14] Dillingham 1911: Table 300.

[15] "'Sanctified' Arab Tramps: Wretched Maronite Beggars Infest This Country," *NYT*, May 25, 1890.

[16] Industrial Commission on Immigration 1901: XV: 442.

man claimed that some peddlers lied to potential customers saying, "My husband (or wife) died, leaving me with five or six children. I'm hungry and I'm poor." He accused them of having learned these phrases in English by rote, which they repeated at every house, which might easily be true, as was his assumption that peddlers thought such tactics gained them sympathy and thereby increased sales. The writer urged them to be honest and protect the reputation of all the Syrians.[17] The quotation at the beginning of this chapter from a letter sent from one Presbyterian missionary to another shows that this tactic was well known. We shall see how many people made a living by falsely claiming to be raising money for Christians in Syria. Naff, in her laconic way, concurs: "The business probity of the Syrian peddler was by no means ideal, but neither does it seem exceptional."[18]

An Arabic editorial in *Kawkab America* titled "WARNING" was an effort to deflect some of the negative impressions of Americans toward Syrian peddlers. The editors urged peddlers to refrain from getting angry and cursing, apparently in response to articles like one in the *Cleveland Leader* reporting that one Elias Mouakad (a peddler from New York) became abusive toward a customer when she refused to buy. To make matters worse, he spit on her windows as he left. A friend who spoke on his behalf to the judge tried to say that these were customs of the East, but the judge did not buy the argument.[19] Several women in Massachusetts claimed that peddlers whose wares they did not buy had abused them; one peddler allegedly drew a gun! According to *Kawkab America*, peddlers thought they could get away with this behavior because the customers did not understand Arabic, but the editors admonished them, "They are always watching you, looking for your bad behavior." To help curb this practice, the editors threatened to publish the names of any peddlers who used inappropriate language. This would not only serve to embarrass the offender, but would prove to Americans that other Syrians did not approve of this behavior (although the number of Americans who read *Kawkab America* in Arabic must have been vanishingly small).[20] The newspaper never did publish names of the offenders.

The next step for the Syrian peddler, as described in the *Tribune*,[21] was pushcart peddling. The photograph of the pushcart peddler in the article

[17] *Kawkab America,* September 1, 1893.

[18] Naff 1985: 179.

[19] "A Damascus Loafer," *Cleveland Leader,* February 28, 1891.

[20] "Warning," *Kawkab America,* June 9, 1893.

[21] "Victims of the Turks Finding Homes Here," *New-York Tribune Illustrated Supplement,* October 11, 1903.

shows a man alongside a cart overflowing with vegetables, fruits, and canned goods. A photograph of an ice cream seller on wheels[22] may indicate that this method of selling was more common than we know. Another article described a fire on Greenwich Street that destroyed a building in which a number of pushcarts belonging to Syrians were being stored. If these accounts were accurate, it would put the Syrians squarely in the tradition of all urban peddlers, particularly those on the Lower East Side, where streets were crowded with pushcarts every day. The fact that the Brooklyn-to-Manhattan ferry had a special fare for people with pushcarts is indirect evidence that Syrians may have been taking these carts to Manhattan each day.

A 1900 article described the many New York Syrian businesses on wheels: "You may buy a platter or a set of dishes from the owner of a perambulating crockery store. You may get a bit of Turkish tobacco from a tobacconist's booth on wheels. You may select a soup bone and a handful of vegetables from the pushcart of an enterprising tradesman. Little bakery shops are trundled here and there, and steaming hot from within wicker baskets are the big, thick pancakes, a foot and a half in diameter.... Even the shoemaker will stop at your very door and repair your footwear while you wait."[23] Not everyone went through the stages described in the article; we know that most people jumped straight from door-to-door peddling to opening a store or shop.

The peddler's life was fraught with hardship and danger. One very real danger to a person out alone was the threat of robbery or murder. The nineteenth-century press reported a number of murders of Syrian peddlers, none of which took place in New York City. These were opportunistic robberies, nothing more, carried out on lonely country roads. Reports of peddlers being set upon by American drunks or thugs were also common. Sometimes this was an attempt to rob them, but sometimes it was harassment or race hatred pure and simple. *Kawkab America*, in its continuing efforts to justify Americans to Syrians (as opposed to justifying Syrians to Americans, which it also did), said that these acts of violence were not representative of the American people in general, but simply the work of bad apples.[24] One notable exception to this sunny attitude was a long 1894 letter from Mitry Garzouzi in Louisiana. After describing the murder of two Syrians, one in Mississippi and one in Louisiana, he warned prospective émigrés that, despite all the good things they were told

[22] Cromwell Childe, "New York's Syrian Quarter," *NYT,* August 20, 1899.
[23] "The Syrian Colony," *Bay City* (MI) *Times*, June 22, 1900.
[24] *Kawkab America,* August 19, 1892.

about America, this was the kind of danger they faced: as "a moth is attracted to the light that burns it." He advised peddlers never to travel alone, for safety's sake.[25] In many of these cases, Garzouzi complained, the murderer escaped or was arrested and then released by the police, underlining the favoritism Americans showed toward their own. Perhaps more disturbing was the tale of three Syrian peddlers in Pennsylvania, two of whom murdered the third, took his money, and fled.[26] The danger was real, and the stories circulated widely in the Syrian community, both in the Arabic press and by word of mouth.

Police harassment was a constant thorn in the peddler's side. Did he or she need a license? It depended on the locale. How was one to know? Peddlers and merchants wrote letters to *Kawkab America* trying to advise others of the risks. In some places, selling without a license was a minor offense; one man reported that the police simply took him down to the license bureau where he paid his fine and returned the same day to peddling. But others reported being arrested or even forced to cease their peddling until they were arraigned in court and fined, putting a huge dent in their earnings. One man, Joseph Sharbel, was sentenced to 100 days in a New York prison or a $100 fine for peddling without a license. His jailers reportedly threatened to shave his mustache.[27] A couple of Syrians whose names are difficult to decipher were arrested for peddling on Broadway and sent to Castle Garden to await deportation. They were released when the immigration authorities found that they had money.[28] License requirements were constantly changing, as one letter writer reported bitterly in *Kawkab America*: a new tax in the form of a $50 license fee had been imposed on Syrian and Indian pushcart peddlers in New Jersey. This fee had been enacted under pressure from merchants and property owners who complained that peddlers were selling in front of their shops, driving business away,[29] a complaint still heard today in New York City. Sometimes policemen had to be bribed to let them work, as was the case in Texas when a peddler was forced to pay $14 to a policeman to leave him alone. Naff lists the other hardships that peddlers had to contend with, which were myriad.[30]

Despite the negative press and the hardships and dangers encountered on the road, the rewards of peddling definitely outweighed the disadvantages. It

---

[25] *Kawkab America,* September 28, 1894.
[26] *Kawkab America*, June 3, 1892.
[27] "Wanted to Save His Mustache," *BDE,* August 24, 1886.
[28] "Turkish Peddlers Released," *BDE,* August 18, 1889.
[29] *Kawkab America*, July 1, 1892.
[30] Naff 1985: 183.

was work that allowed one who knew little English to survive and even prosper. It satisfied the entrepreneurial spirit of many of them: one's profit depended on one's own efforts. It gave men and women freedom: the ability to set their own schedules and sometimes decide on their own inventory. The 1903 *Tribune* article describes the peddler bargaining with the wholesaler over the goods the peddler has chosen to buy.[31] No boss could tell them what to do, at least when they were out peddling. They felt the exhilaration of the open road and, possibly, an escape from the strictures of what must have seemed a very conservative society, at least to the young people now surrounded by an American culture very different from their own. Notwithstanding the web of indebtedness to the supplier and his apparent control over routes and stock, the peddler held his head up high because he considered himself to be "in business," that is, self-employed.

Most important, peddling was lucrative. Naff estimated a peddler's weekly profits to be between $30 and $50;[32] Houghton estimated a bit less.[33] Miller, on the other hand, thought peddlers made no more than $10–12 per week for "average gross returns."[34] This last figure is contradicted by every story told by immigrants. Michael Shadid, who became a well-known Midwestern doctor, claimed that after two years of pack peddling in and around New York (in 1898), he was able to pay back the debt to the uncle who had paid for his transportation, send $1,000 back to his mother to bring her to America, and put aside $2,000 toward his medical studies.[35] When he discovered that his savings, which had been left in the care of relatives, had been lost in an ill-conceived business venture, Shadid went back to peddling, and in another two years had saved $5,000 toward medical school.

Another immigrant, John Nohrer (Nohra), went to Pittsburgh with his wife and daughter in 1890 and became a peddler. In two years, he had saved about $2,000, enough to take him home to Tripoli.[36] One reporter said that the sale of two silk handkerchiefs in the high-class resorts made the peddler more money than a week's work in town.[37]

Naff's interviews with a number of peddlers all over the United States

[31] "Victims of the Turk Finding Homes Here," *New-York Tribune Illustrated Supplement,* October 11, 1903.
[32] Naff 1985: 194.
[33] Houghton 1911: II: 663.
[34] Miller 1903: 29.
[35] Naff 1985: 193.
[36] "His Daughter and His Ducats Gone," *NYH,* May 8, 1892.
[37] "Strangers Who Get Along," *St. Louis Republic,* February 27, 1894.

confirmed this impression, as did Zelditch's in Pittsburgh; recall the immigrant who claimed he went back to Syria with $10,000. This was much more money than could be made in a factory, where salaries were about four dollars a week, or working in another Syrian's store. If these figures are accurate, it makes the six dollars monthly rent for two rooms in the tenement seem quite affordable. Yet the immigrants continued to live in these crowded conditions: why? The Syrians, like most new immigrants, were extremely frugal, and it took them about a decade to have enough money to feel comfortable spending on themselves, a confidence symbolized by the move to Brooklyn at the end of the century. One of Naff's informants confirms this assessment by scoffing at the idea that anyone living in one of the peddlers' hostels would waste money on buying a bed. It was not that they couldn't afford beds, but rather that they didn't see the need to spend the money.[38] The suggestion that many of the Syrians chose to live in the conditions previously described, long past the time when they could afford better, is difficult to accept yet easy to understand, and it earned for them a reputation for probity (or stinginess) and shrewdness.

As men began to start their own businesses, including factories for making kimonos and other textiles, there were new jobs to be had in Syrian-owned factories, which, if less lucrative, allowed the new immigrant to stay home. Smaller Syrian-owned businesses too might take on one or two assistants, who were invariably Syrian.

Miller attributed the decline in peddling to the fact that "it does not pay,"[39] but as we have seen, peddling did pay. And it never entirely disappeared; it remained an important entry-level job for Syrian immigrants well into the twentieth century. Many people told stories to Naff and others about going back out on the road when times were tough, and as the 1911 Commission report stated, 50 percent of the (declining) population of Washington Street were still peddlers.

Many articles assert that the New York merchants controlled peddlers in all parts of the country. It's true that a peddler took goods from only one supplier and that the peddler-supplier relationship tended to be of long duration. This relationship must have been based on some combination of family connection, loyalty, convenience, habit, debt, and coercion. Joseph Mahfouz, for example, was a "drummer" (peddler) for the dry goods firm of Salim Elias

[38] Naff 1985: 207.
[39] Miller 1903: 29.

& T. Abdoo. Like other peddlers he considered himself self-employed, saying, "I sleep in Brooklyn and my business is at New York."[40] People who were employed by others said they "worked," whereas those who considered themselves self-employed (even if by our lights they would be considered employees) said they were "in business."

The number of suppliers and business owners expanded as the century drew to a close. Peddlers not only wanted to stop wandering but they wanted to own their own businesses, like their suppliers. Although there was a seemingly endless supply of new immigrants to take up the *keshi* or *jezdan harir*, the number of the self-employed grew faster. Soon enough the Syrian peddler became a rare breed, and the Syrian businessmen had to expand their market to Americans. This they did with alacrity.

[40] *Trials,* People v. Zreik, 1906: #599.

## Chapter 7

# Men in Trade

*What could be more of a business romance than the record of a penniless, almost illiterate immigrant who, in the course of a decade, rises from the humble rank of a peddler to the exalted position of an international merchant prince, directing from his office in New York the humming industries he controls across the waters of both the Atlantic and the Pacific?*[1]

## Employees: Men Who Worked for Others

First we must touch on those men who did not follow the Syrian dream: those who were in the employ of others. The numbers of documented cases of men working for others in New York is very small. This is not true in other cities, where Syrian men in large numbers worked in brickyards, textile mills, and shoe factories. Although in our database we have Syrian waiters and cooks, bookkeepers and clerks, guards, carpenters, printers and writers, cigarette makers, silk weavers, factory workers, truckmen, and the most ambiguous profession of all—salesmen—we know almost nothing about where they were employed or about their working conditions. It is only luck if we find out.

Newspaper articles and city directories naturally concentrate on the owners of businesses; employees are not mentioned. We know that every Syrian company for which we have documentation (beyond the mom-and-pop stores) must have had employees, and that a majority of them must have been Syrians. It can probably be assumed that more women than men worked for others, since many of the manufacturers were in textiles; this would partially explain the paucity of documentation about them. Women employees will be discussed in chapter 10. The little information we do have about Syrian men working for others follows.

[1] "History of the Syrians in New York," *The Syrian World*, November 1927.

In the fragmentary 1892 census, more than two dozen silk weavers from Turkey were living in Flushing, Queens. They were almost all Armenians, but a few of the names were odd and may have been Syrian: Dartly (Thomas, Sarah, and Anton), Asfer (Asfour?), (S.), and See and Kate Rado, but we know almost nothing about them. In the 1900 census there were seven Syrians living in Queens (including Anton Dartly), of whom four were male silk weavers or silk ribbon weavers. Perhaps these workers were employed in one of the silk mills at College Point, the largest of which was the Myhnepo (the name of the owner, A. Openhym, spelled backwards) Ribbon Mills. There were a number of strikes at his mills during the late nineteenth century, primarily a reaction to drastic reductions in wages in the 1890s.

The Liberty Silk Company, one of the few non-Syrian companies where we know at least one Syrian was employed, was located at 548 W. 57th Street in Manhattan. Incorporated in 1892, by 1901 the company ran 400 looms. Liberty was probably the employer of the seven Syrian silk workers who lived on West 57th and 60th Streets in the 1900 census. A loom mechanic and six silk weavers, they must have learned their trades in Mount Lebanon and carried them to the New World. A bitter letter, signed by an anonymous "Wage Slave," outlined the inhumane treatment the workers received at Liberty, including this: "7. A Syrian had a few mispicks and a little dirt on his piece (a piece is about 60 yards)...they fined him $2. Nearly one-half of his whole week's pay."[2] In 1899, 1900, and 1901, the workers at Liberty Silk threatened to strike for higher wages and better conditions; each time, they went to arbitration and reached a compromise. The company, however, went bankrupt in 1906.

The few Syrian silk workers who lived in the downtown Colony could have been employed by any one of the more than a hundred silk manufacturers in New York City at that time (none owned by Syrians); most of the factories were located in lower Manhattan. We should not forget that there were several Syrian-owned silk mills in New Jersey, and these must have employed a significant number of Syrians, but we have no evidence that residents of the Colony commuted from New York to work in them; they therefore fall outside our geographic parameters. If the Syrian silk weaver was making a bit over $4 a week—and working in such horrible conditions—one can see the attraction of peddling, which was so much more lucrative. A tantalizing snippet alludes to "red capped young men who work at rugs in the windows of the Broadway stores by day and smoke cigarettes and drink

[2] "Liberty Silk Work Again," *People* (NY), May 7, 1899.

wine in the Syrian restaurants at night,"[3] but we don't know by whom they were employed.

The lengthy trial of Elias Zreik[4] provides a rare picture of the world of workers (as opposed to owners) in the Colony, a picture that is woefully underdocumented. Apart from the arresting officers and the medical experts in the trial, all the witnesses were Syrians, and most worked for others.[5] Although the trial took place outside our temporal limit (in 1906), it is invaluable in understanding the fluidity of the working lives of the Colonists in this early period. It appears that they changed jobs, residences, and even cities at the drop of a hat. Six or eight months in one position seemed to be the rule.

A few snippets from the trial transcript provide a picture of the life of four Syrian men who were employed by others: John Hassoun, Selim Kirshy, Philip Joseph Lahood, and Menheem Ghabryel. Hassoun, a witness for the prosecution, had been in the country ten years in 1906. He had always worked for other people, but apart from stints in a factory and grocery store, we don't know who his employers were. At the time of the events leading to the trial, he had been working for Boutross & Son, the grocery store at 81 Washington Street, for five or six months. When he was subpoenaed for the trial, however, he had to travel down from Fall River, Massachusetts, where he was working as a weaver in a textile mill.

Having emigrated from Damascus in 1902, another witness, Selim Kirshy, peddled for a while, "taking" goods from Nicola Awad. He then worked as a freelance carpenter, doing jobs for "people" (meaning Syrians) up and down Washington Street, and finally he went to work as a glass polisher for the American company Simon Bache & Co., which is where he was working in 1906.

Philip Joseph Lahood, who in 1906 was lodging at 71 Washington Street, had also been in the United States for only three years, part of that time in New Orleans. Now he was spending his summers working in a cotton mill in Warren, Rhode Island, and winters peddling in New York. Menheem Ghabryel worked as a salesman for Machenbach Importing Company at 50 Howard Street, an importer of European fancy goods such as shawls, laces, and drawn linen work—another non-Syrian employer.

This fluidity in employment was matched by fluidity in residence.

---

[3] "Red Fezzed Heads; Languorous Eyes," *NYH,* November 18, 1894.

[4] *Trials,* People v. Zreik, 1906: #599.

[5] The crime took place in a restaurant, and if, in 1906, one were still eating in a restaurant it meant that one was single, a new immigrant who came without a wife, or not doing well financially (as one's wife would be out peddling).

Another witness, the peddler Joseph Mahfouz, whom we met in chapter 6, had moved so recently to Brooklyn that, when asked where he lived, he gave his former Manhattan address; when pressed, he couldn't remember his present address on Henry Street. Ghabryel had been in the country eight years when the trial took place. In the previous eight months he had lived at three addresses: 81 Washington, 7 State Street in Brooklyn, and Columbia Place, also in Brooklyn.

These employees were relatively recent arrivals without families and so were living as all new arrivals did, in tenements, rooming with strangers (men and women), and eating in their local restaurant. All of this was normal for them; no one spoke of hardship, discomfort, or unhappiness. It was just the way one lived when trying to make one's way in New York. Their matter-of-fact attitude hints at the possibility that working for others was neither particularly rare nor universally despised. Unfortunately we know little else about these men.

Almost all Syrians aspired to be in business for themselves, and those who made it—whether small shopkeepers or big men—were held in high esteem.

## Small Shopkeepers: "What Business Are You In?"[6]

As soon as he could—again, according to the prevailing story, these were mostly men—the peddler went into business for himself, moving either horizontally, that is by simply giving up the open road to open a small (or sometimes large) shop selling the same goods that he had peddled; or vertically, by moving "upstream" to become a wholesaler, importer, or manufacturer. The Syrians called both these business types "stores," causing great confusion among Americans who thought a store was a retail nook on a street corner. As we will show, however, the Syrian store was often a hybrid: a large wholesale and retail business, and of course the word has both meanings in English as well: a warehouse as well as a retail establishment. Sometimes a businessman would simply call it "the place" (*mahal* in Arabic); this referred to an office where business was done, but which might not sell to the public. For the sake of clarity, I have appropriated the word "shop" for

[6] This phrase comes from my father's book (Jacobs 1991: 22) in which he claims that the first question any Syrian asked another Syrian was not "What do you do for a living?" or "Where do you work?" but "What business are you in?"

the small retail stores that dotted the neighborhood (the Syrians did not use the word) and reserved the word "store" for the wholesalers, but the reader should always keep in mind that the difference between them was a matter of degree rather than kind.

7-1. Shaheen Maroon's notions shop at 40 Washington Street on the corner of Morris (Miller 1903).

The transition to owning a shop or store took about the same amount of time: three years from the time of arrival. In the progression from peddler to capitalist outlined in the *New-York Tribune*, the shopkeeper was one step above the man with a horse and wagon.[7] In most cases men went directly from peddling to ownership without following the path outlined in the article.

The small shopkeepers primarily served other Syrian residents; the grocers, bakers, fruit dealers, and shoemakers provided the necessities to their neighbors. They were usually located in the basements of Washington Street tenements. The retail notions/novelties/variety dealers could fall into this category as well, since every person occasionally needs shoelaces, string, shoe polish, or a sewing needle, but these shops also catered to "Americans."

[7] "Victims of the Turk Finding Homes Here," *New-York Tribune Illustrated Supplement,* October 11, 1903.

Zahi Azar provides an example: he came to this country before 1890, apparently settling at 4 Carlisle. He owned small variety stores in a number of different venues in the 1890s, including at Numbers 31, 40, 75, 107, and 113 Washington. His last place was shut down for nonpayment of a debt to Assy Shaheen in 1897, and he never reopened. Miller has a photograph of a retail notions shop belonging to Shaheen Maroon at 40 Washington Street, on the northwest corner of Morris and Washington. It is a tiny place with a single window on Washington. It undoubtedly served only people in the neighborhood.

Retail grocery shops could be tiny fruit stands in a basement or larger general stores, which almost always sold wholesale as well as retail. Both of these types dotted Washington Street, at (from south to north) Numbers 25 (Alex Ayoob & Elias Faris), 33 (Ameen Shamoun), 45 (Hanna Sarboukh), 51 (Farjallah Zaloom & Sons) 53 (Alexander Yazaji), 57 (Habeeb Srour), 71 (Rahal & Ackel), 75 (Namen Saba, and later F. Zaloom), 77½ (John Haddad), 81½ (Tannous el Sayyegh), 83 (Abraham Sahadi), and 95 (Srour, after he left 57). Najeeb Azar had a fruit stand at 27 Rector/92 Washington, where Sahadi later opened his store. Many of these addresses the reader will recognize as also being tenements, but there were often two commercial establishments on the main floor, one on each side of the entrance, and a third in the basement. Residents slept upstairs or behind the shops.

The photograph in the 1903 *Tribune* article illustrating this stage of small shopkeeper shows a beefy Syrian standing with (presumably) his two sons on the steps going down to his basement store. He has fruit and vegetables on display, a large milk can on the sidewalk, and he is holding a cleaver, which means he was also a butcher. In Miller's 1903 photo of the exterior of Rahal & Ackel, a similarly modest shop at 71 Washington, one sees fruit and vegetables on a stand in front of the shop, which also occupies the basement. Access to this store was only a few steps down from the street, unlike other establishments, which were truly deep and dark. The fact that the parlor floor was on a level several steps above the street meant that the basement had a reasonable amount of headroom. A proprietor (Elias Rahal?) stands next to his produce display on the sidewalk in front of 71, while three Syrian men loll in the doorway. Lotfallah Atta's restaurant was on the parlor floor of this building; five wooden steps with wooden handrails gave access to it. His part of the facade was painted white, and a large awning provided shade both to the restaurant and to the fruit stand below. Atta (along with Wadie Mejdelani) managed the rest of the building as a boardinghouse, but we don't know whether he also sublet the basement to Rahal and Ackel. It should be remembered that these basements regularly flooded, so the rent must have been substantially lower than for the parlor floors that the more ambitious and successful grocers like Sahadi and Yazaji occupied.

7-2. Rahal & Ackel Grocery, 71 Washington Street (Miller 1903).

An 1899 illustrated supplement in the *New York Times* features photographs of Sahadi's and Yazaji's stores. They show similarly large interiors (perhaps the front and back parlors of the original townhouse had been knocked together), with bottled and canned goods piled up to the high ceiling. The reporter described the goods in Sahadi's shop: "native wines and liqueurs, American groceries, swords and lamps, glass bracelets of many colors, Oriental embroideries, water pipes (hubble bubbles) and their 'fixings.'"[8] Abraham Sahadi and his wife, Zakia, stand behind the counter in their store; Abraham is looking at the camera. He is already balding and has the serious look of the man in charge. He is in shirtsleeves and has his hand on one of the *narghile*s for sale. Zakia is wearing a mutton-sleeve dress with her hands folded in front of her, smiling at the sole customer, a woman in a shirtwaist and skirt. There are brass scales on the counter and glass bins behind. Save for the *narghile*s

[8] Cromwell Childe, "New York's Syrian Quarter," *NYT*, August 20, 1899.

and brass trays for sale—and presumably the contents of those boxes, cans, and bottles (many of which surely contained Sahadi-brand *'araq*, an anise-flavored liqueur)—it could be any nineteenth-century American grocery store.

7.3. Interior, Sahadi's store at 92 Washington (Childe, *NYT,* 1899).

In the photograph of Alexander Yazaji's store at 53 Washington, the man behind the counter in the photograph may not be Yazaji, as Yazaji was only twenty-five in 1899, and this man looks older. He is beefy, already balding, wearing spectacles and dressed in shirtsleeves and a waistcoat. Yazaji moved to Florida in 1899 and may have recently sold his shop lock, stock, and barrel to this man, who had not had time to change the name on the window. This store has more Oriental bric-a-brac than Sahadi's: more than a dozen pierced brass lanterns hang from the ceiling, and a half dozen *narghile*s sit on a shelf. These items may have been aimed at tourists, but the customers look like Syrians: an oldish woman in a headscarf, skirt, and blouse and a slightly younger woman—also in a kerchief—with (presumably) her children. They must be buying the mundane goods held in the bins behind the counter and barrels sitting on the floor. Interestingly, there are two men with their sons visible outside the glass front doors, looking in as the photographer took his picture.[9]

[9] Cromwell Childe, "New York's Syrian Quarter," *NYT,* August 20, 1899.

7-4. Interior, Alexander Yazaji's store at 53 Washington (Childe, *NYT,* 1899).

By 1908, there were thirty Syrian-owned groceries in the neighborhood.

Syrians opened other small retail establishments including cigar/cigarette stores. Assad George Khoury immigrated in 1885 and after presumably peddling for a few years, opened a cigar store at Avenue A and 12th Street. After a few years, he moved it to a four-story brick townhouse at 154 8th Avenue (at 17th Street), obviously catering to an American clientele. He soon moved into manufacturing his own cigars, while still running the retail store. Like Joseph Oussani, he parlayed a tobacco fortune into real estate. He began to buy and sell property in 1894, and by 1896, he was wealthy enough to buy ten contiguous building lots in the Bronx. Dozens of his real estate transactions are listed in the *New York Times* from 1894 through 1901.

Michael D. Kaydouh, after being in the dry goods business for several years (he partnered with John Abd-el-Nour at the 1893 New York expo, then went out on his own at 89 Washington), opened a cigar store in the Whitehall Building on Battery Place after the family moved to Brooklyn. Miller includes a photograph of the Whitehall shop in his book. Despite the seeming modesty of such an enterprise, he apparently made a very good living (it is possible that he was also selling liquor), and he became one of the more prominent members of the community: the Kaydouh weddings were celebrated in the Syrian and American press, his family lived in well-appointed digs in Brooklyn, and in the first decade of the twentieth century, he opened two restaurants in Manhattan.

7-5. Michael D. Kaydouh's cigar and candy store, Whitehall Building on the Battery (Miller 1903).

Several men operated barbershops in the neighborhood, including Beshara Daher and Cesar Abdelnour. Not content with simply being a barber, Daher and his partner, Yusef Zeidan, also offered fresh pastries, baked to order, from their barbershop at 73 Washington Street.[10] The shop is pictured next to Rahal and Ackel's grocery in Miller's photograph: the barbershop is on the parlor floor, with a big shop window advertising the name, and a barber pole above. Another fruit stand or grocery store occupies the basement below, perhaps Saba Bros. and Dibs, Oriental Grocers. Daher later moved his barbershop to 81 Washington, again occupying the parlor floor.

George Jureidini was the only baker that we know about, but there must have been many others to supply all the bread and baklava going to the Syrian

[10] Advertisement, *Kawkab America,* October 27, 1893.

restaurants. It is possible that restaurants baked their own bread and pastries. At one point, *Kawkab America* castigated an unnamed baker at 91 Washington (where Tannous Shishim had his restaurant) for holding the community hostage to his expensive bread. A group of merchants got together to hire a baker, rent a store, and sell bread at a lower price.[11] We do not know whether this scheme succeeded in forcing the "tyrant" to lower his prices.

Another small Syrian-owned business was that of truckman or expressman. Several men, including Habib Wahby, Yusef Kherbati, and George Shweiry, had carts (or wagons) and horses for hire. The horses and carts were kept in one of the stables on Washington Street owned by the Syrians' Irish neighbors—either Clancy's at 14 Washington or the stable at Number 56. They may have leased both horse and cart from the stable or owned them. We know that Shweiry also had an office at 95 Washington in which he prepared bills of lading to put goods on ships, so he was not just an expressman but a shipping agent as well. The companies of A.H. Mouakad & Co. (at 29 Broadway) and A.M. Arachtingi and S. Shea (at 43 Washington) were ticket agencies for French steamship lines. Lian Kattini became the exclusive agent for Wagons-Lits, a European train operator. These companies catered to Syrians, Armenians, and Greeks and sold passage all the way to Beirut. In the early years of the twentieth century, several other Syrians became shipping and ticketing agents, including Muossa Daoud, Pedro Caram, A.K. Hitti, and Constantine Biskinty. These men sold tickets while continuing their trade in goods or their services as expressmen.

We might also include in this category of small businesses the half-dozen Syrian carpenters and masons who worked for other members of the community. They must have been employed building the cheap partitions that divided the tenement rooms in the boardinghouses, adapting the tenements for commercial use, constructing *keshi*, and doing general repairs.

We could think of all these men as small business owners, deserving of respect from other members of the community because they were self-employed, however modest their income. Unlike the careers of the wealthier businessmen, the paths to these small businesses were generally straightforward: one peddled, saved up enough money, and opened a store or business with all or some of the same goods one had sold as a peddler; usually the wife helped out every step of the way and the store became the couple's lifetime career.

[11] *Kawkab America,* August 23, 1895.

## "Big Men": Importers, Wholesalers, and Manufacturers

*One of the big men of the quarter does an annual business of almost half a million. He not only has a good share of local trade, but he exports goods to South America and Australia as well.*[12]

Moving from peddler to large storeowner, wholesaler, importer, or manufacturer was much less straightforward than moving from peddler to simple shop owner. For one thing, the distance was greater. One needed a larger amount of capital. The route was often circuitous, filled with risks, involving multiple partners and configurations, and always one faced the specter of bankruptcy. Yet for those whose success is known to us, it seems preordained.

Almost everyone had the same goal: opening a business of one's own. Despite the twists and turns, the transition from one stage to another was often quite rapid, at least in comparison with today's career paths. Peddlers usually set up their first businesses as wholesalers, dealers, and/or storeowners about three years after arriving. After that, the changes in partnerships, businesses, and residences came thick and fast. Some people of course came with enough to set up immediately in business (such as Abdow Rihani and Naoum Mokarzel, Azeez Khayat, or Tannous Azeez, all discussed below), but these instances did not make it into the immigrant myth, in which every immigrant had to have a rags-to-riches story. Nevertheless, the route to business success was more circuitous than our family stories would have us believe. Most of the merchants we know about changed partners, businesses, suppliers, and residences many times before at last settling down in a business and a home.

The testimonies in two criminal trials bring to light this zigzag path to success more vividly than other documents. The first case is the trial of Elias Zreik in 1906, which has already been mentioned and which will be described fully in chapter 12. Here we use it simply to illustrate a number of roads that a Syrian might have taken to the point of owning a business.

Two of the witnesses in Zreik's trial were in partnership together, George Joseph Nohra and George M. Ganim. Their company was called "Khouri, Nohra & Ganim, Commission Merchants." It was a new company, having been founded only six months earlier; we don't know how long it survived. The stories that Ganim and Nohra told about how they came to form the

[12] "From the Orient: Merchants in New York Who Deal in Strange Wares," *Evening Star* (Washington, DC), October 22, 1898.

partnership are instructive. Nohra had immigrated in 1888, Ganim in 1890. Both started out as peddlers. Nohra then acquired a "truck" (horse and wagon) and carried, in a freelance manner, goods from one part of Manhattan Island to another. The trucking company was called "George Joseph,"[13] Joseph being, of course, his father's first name. Both men were Maronites, and they went to work for the (Maronite) Faour Brothers (bankers and dry goods suppliers), which is probably where they met. Ganim was a bookkeeper, Nohra a salesman or peddler. Finally, after fifteen years, they had saved enough money to start their own business.

A second criminal trial further illustrates the sometimes-halting path taken to self-employment. This was a trial for attempted arson brought against Kalil Matta and Elias Karam.[14] They had a skirt (petticoat) manufacturing business on the fourth floor of 157 Cedar (the same building in which the Orthodox and Maronite churches had earlier been housed) under the name "The New Petticoat Manufacturing Company." Matta had been in the country fourteen years in 1905, and up until the summer of 1904 had worked in Boston, first as a carpenter, and then as a lumber surveyor at an American company, Davis & Sargent. He was able to save up about $1,500 and decided to go into business for himself. Again, when you compare this amount with the $2,000 that Michael Shadid was able to make in two years peddling, it is surprising that people ever worked for others. Matta invited his cousin Elias Karam, who had been a cutter in a shirtwaist factory in Boston, to join him in setting up his New York factory, using Matta's money and Karam's expertise. Karam's three sisters (who had also worked in textile factories in Boston) were employed in Matta's factory, along with several other Syrian women and girls. None of the Karams received wages, so Karam must have been given a piece of the business in exchange for his family's labor and experience; as co-owners, both Karam and Matta were defendants in the suit. At the time of the trial (March 15, 1905), the factory had been in business for five months.

These two examples show that people who went into partnerships had often done many things between peddling and starting their own businesses, and our rule of thumb—three years from immigration to self-employment—is not hard and fast. Partnerships formed and dissolved in the span of a mo-

[13] Women and men, in the early immigrant years, often used their father's first name as a last name. This practice diminished over the years, and some who had followed it changed their last names to their father's last name at some later date, as Nohra did.
[14] *Trials*, People v. Zreik, 1906: #599.

ment. Although these partnerships seem to have been serendipitous for the most part, we have one small piece of evidence from *Kawkab America* that alerts us to the fact that sometimes people went out looking for partners with some specific business in mind. An unnamed Syrian placed a classified ad in the newspaper looking for someone with whom to open a *locanda* (boardinghouse) and restaurant. He claimed he was a good cook and wished to also offer Oriental sweets for sale. He had some capital of his own, but he was looking for someone to invest additional funds.[15]

Moving up the ladder required a certain amount of capital to buy goods and rent a shop or warehouse, although suppliers were able to buy on credit from (non-Syrian) wholesalers, just as peddlers were. The supplier had to figure out where he would buy his goods: whether they were available in the United States, or if not, should he import them or manufacture them here, and if so, where? Every issue of *Kawkab America* featured a full page of ads of "American" wholesalers of notions, dry goods, or twine—anything that a Syrian wholesaler might buy and resell to his peddlers. Peddlers did not take goods from non-Syrians, but the men upstream did—both in this country and abroad.

If a merchant decided to import goods, this added an extra layer of complexity to the task of setting up a business since the merchant had to set up international networks. How did he do it? He must have had relatives and/or friends who would supply him with goods, even in the nineteenth century when the Syrian diaspora was still quite small. Considering the glacial speed of international travel in those years, the rapidity of this process is astonishing. In an 1894 article about the Colony, a reporter wrote, "The principal Syrian merchants have their own agents and buyers in Europe, and act both as exporters and importers, sending out American goods for sale in Europe and Asia and bringing Oriental and European goods to be disposed of in this country."[16] It had been only a decade and a half since the first Syrian family had landed on our shores, and the Syrians already had an extensive network of suppliers and customers. A few Syrians also established factories in the nineteenth century, although the great majority of factories were begun in the early twentieth; these early forays into manufacturing will be described below.

The move from peddling to ownership took many paths, but it was straight in one sense: one can trace the contents of the peddler's *keshi* or *jezdan harir* in almost all of these businesses. From peddlers of Jerusalemite

[15] *Kawkab America,* January 19, 1894.

[16] "Men of All Lands," *Omaha World Herald,* August 6, 1894.

goods came the religious goods dealers and manufacturers like the Rahaims and the Malhamis. The notions peddlers became owners of novelty or variety stores or dry goods dealers, and/or supplied notions to peddlers. The towels and linens that came to occupy more and more of the peddlers' packs were imported and/or manufactured by the Syrians. Cutlery in the form of scissors, knives, and razors, which were carried to farmsteads around the country, became an important sector for Syrian importers and wholesalers. Those who sold "Oriental" goods became manufacturers of such goods or importers of fine textiles, antiques, or rugs.

The business always had the immigrant's name on the door. He most often joined forces with a partner, with whom he would pool resources and buy stock. To give an idea of the variety of forms these companies could take, we give just a few examples of nineteenth-century company names: "Abraham Mouakad" (Oriental silk embroideries); "D.J. Faour and Brothers" (dry goods and later, a bank); "Ganim & Sadallah" (novelties); "Abdow Lutfy & Sons" (Oriental goods); "Habeeb Daoud & Company" (boardinghouse/restaurant). Most of these company names are self-explanatory; the last example is ambiguous. In this case, "& Company" meant Daoud's son-in-law, Tannous Shishim, but the term was often used to exaggerate the size or importance of a single-owner business. We do not know the exact role each of the named partners took in these businesses, whether the first name was the larger investor, the person who did the work, neither, or both. It must have varied from company to company.

These partnerships were constantly shifting; our most extreme example, in terms of the number of partnerships he forged in the nineteenth century, was John Abd-el-Nour. He was one of the earliest immigrants, arriving in 1880, only two years after the Arbeelys. He may have peddled when he arrived but his profession on the ship manifest was listed as "Merchant," which implies that he was already well off, so he may have come with a nest egg in the form of cash or goods. Like every other Syrian, though, he traveled in steerage. He probably worked alone as an importer of Oriental goods during his first few years in New York. He, along with three Syrians who had stores on the Boardwalk in Atlantic City, New Jersey, attended the Southern expositions in Louisville, Kentucky, in 1883 and 1885 to sell Oriental goods.[17] It is not clear whether the four were partners or simply traveling companions. Abd-el-Nour claimed to have opened the first Syrian store in the United States in 1885.

[17] "The Cotton Exposition," *Times-Picayune* (New Orleans, LA), October 31, 1883; "An Oriental Picnic," *Kansas City Star,* October 1, 1885. The others were Fares Ferzan, Abraham Samaha, and E.F. Kettaneh.

# Manhattan businesses, 1886–1895.

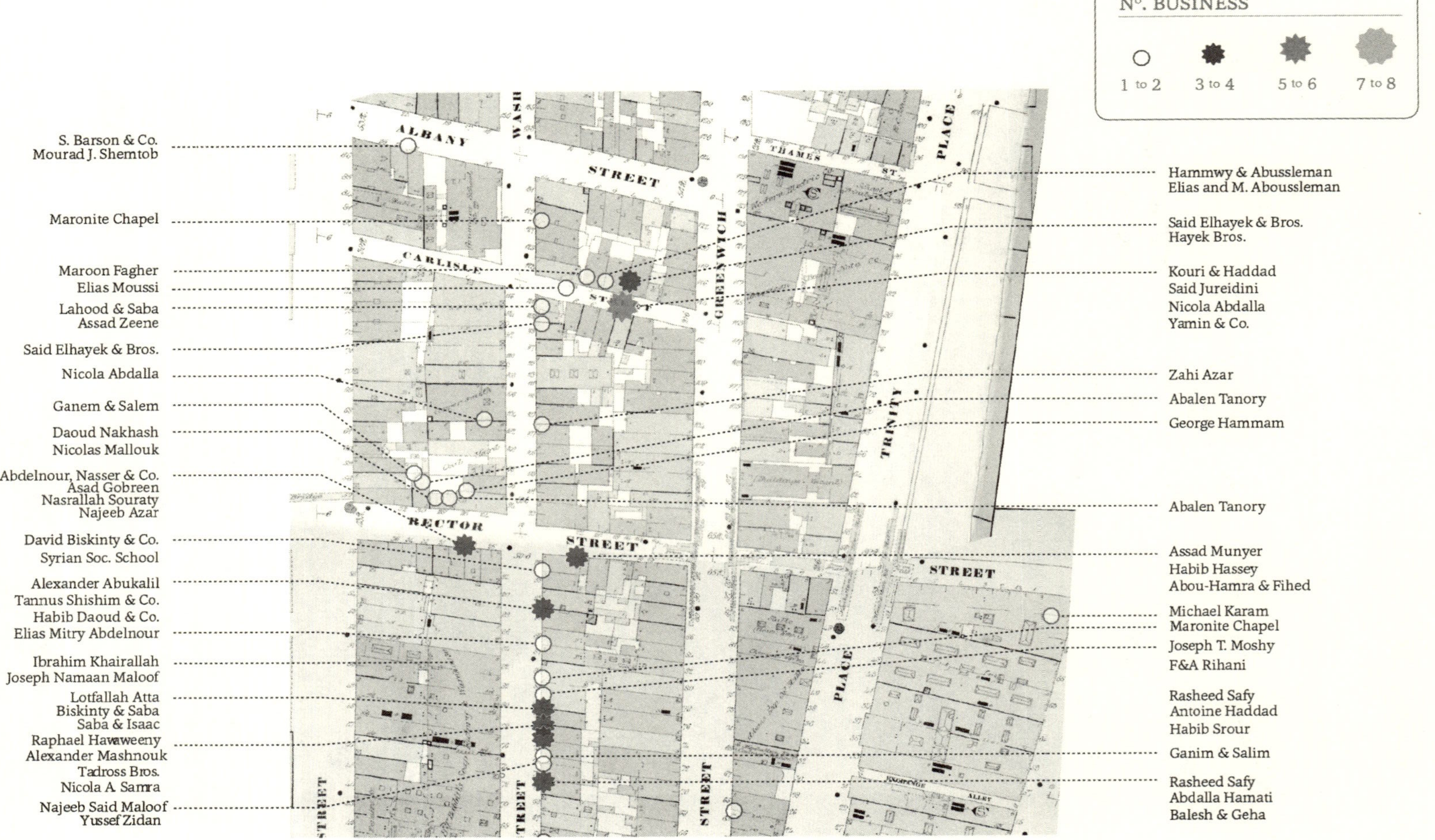

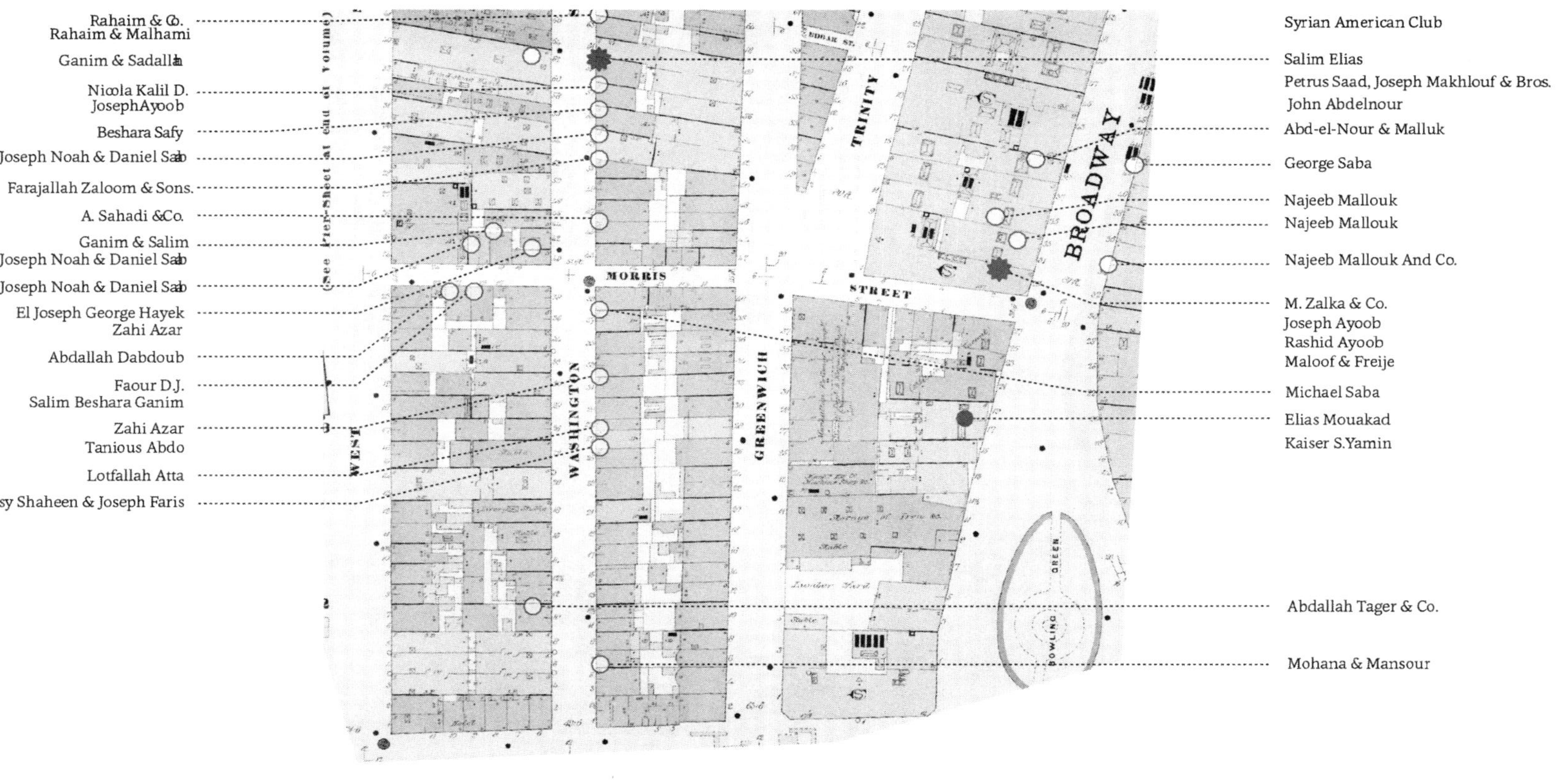


Basemap: Sanborn Map, 1894.
Manhattan, V.1, Double Page Plate Nº 2
New York Public Library
Digital Gallery.

# Manhattan businesses, 1896–1900.

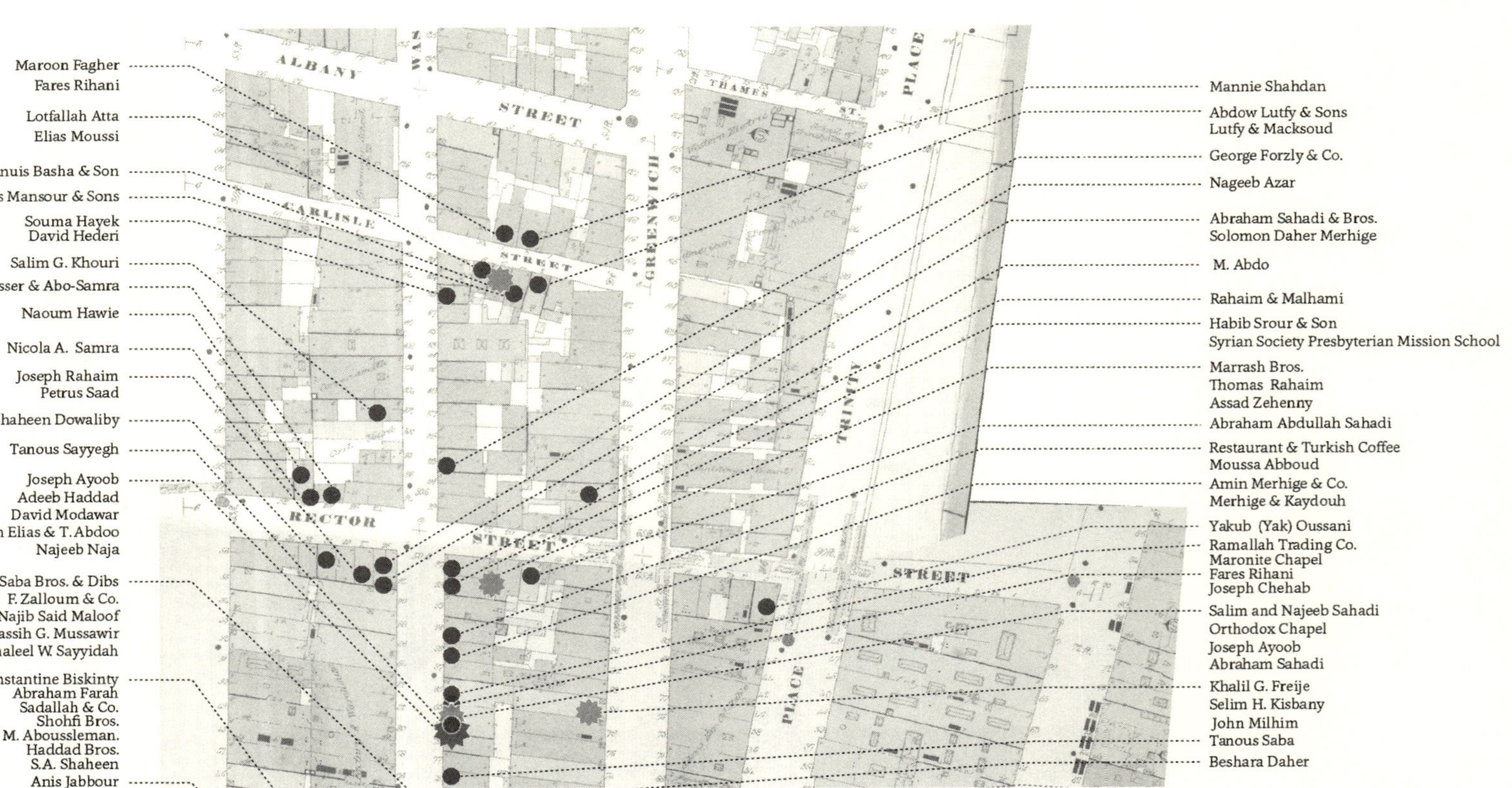

Basemap: Sanborn Map, 1894.
Manhattan, V.1, Double Page Plate Nº 2
New York Public Library
Digital Gallery.

In 1890, he was doing business under the name "John Abd-el-Nour & Co., Dealers in Oriental Goods." We don't know whether he had partners or whether he was the sole proprietor. He took goods to the Chicago fair in 1893 and made it quite clear in several notes to *Kawkab America* that he had no partners in this endeavor because there was some confusion about a different Abdelnour who was also at the fair. Then came a series of short-lived partnerships: one with Michael Kaydouh ("Abd-el-Nour and Kaydouh"), formed to sell goods at the New York Exposition of 1893, and in that same year, with Shakir Nasser ("Abd-el-Nour, Nasser & Co.") to import fine textiles. These simultaneously formed partnerships may have been two different concessions at the New York fair, or one for the fair and one for another purpose. In 1894, he had at least three partnerships apparently simultaneously: importing embroideries with his brother-in-law, Assad Gobreen ("Abd-el-Nour & Ghobreen"), with Joseph Ayoob, and with his brother, Elias Abd-el-Nour. He established a partnership with Najeeb Mallouk in 1895 ("Abd-el-Nour and Malluk"). In that year, he is listed at three different business locations—one on Broadway, one on Hudson, and one on Washington Street—perhaps representing three different businesses. In 1899, he joined forces with Habib N. Maloof ("Abd-el-Nour and Maloof"), importing Parisian and Oriental goods, a partnership that survived until 1905. He then entered into a partnership with Abraham Jabaly, "Abd-el-Nour & Jabaly," that was dissolved after a short time. Apparently Abd-el-Nour then began to work on his own again, claiming in 1910 to be the owner of a goldmine. He traveled back and forth to Asia in the teens and twenties, representing (or owning) a company called the "Philippine Embroidery Company." In the late 1920s, he and his son went into partnership with an American horticulturalist to start a huge silkworm enterprise in San Diego, California.

Although Abd-el-Nour's case was perhaps extreme, many of the Syrian business partnerships of the nineteenth century were, at least from the perspective of the twenty-first century, rather casually entered into and casually dissolved. Many were short-lived, conceived and executed for a specific purpose (such as exhibiting at a world's fair), and then abandoned. They were not registered in any official way with the city or the state, so there was no red tape to go through in either the establishment or dissolution of the partnership. In the 1906 trial of Elias Zreik, one of the witnesses was asked whether he and his partners had written a contract when they went into business together. At first he was puzzled by the question and asked the prosecutor to clarify. When it was explained to him, he answered, "Why, it is not necessary to make any contract to go into business."[18] Most of the early partnerships were between men from the same village, the same extended family, or at least the same religion. We do not know whether they knew each other in the old country or met here; ship manifests rarely show them traveling together, which would be our only indication of their prior acquaintanceship.

The exceptions to this ever-shifting pattern of partnerships were family firms, which seemed to survive longer than the others. Father-son(s) partnerships, however, ended when the father retired or died, and sibling partnerships, which started out with great optimism, often fell apart with acrimony. Rarely did these cases get into the courts; it was seemingly too shaming for a family to display their dirty linen in this way, but many family stories of betrayal were passed down through the generations. We have circumstantial evidence of some of these breakups: a brother moving to a different state or into a different or competing line of business. In one starkly documented example, Abdow Lutfy announced in print that his son Ameen's business was completely separate from his,[19] probably to protect himself from a lawsuit that Ameen was involved in in Montreal. Some sibling partnerships were conspicuous in their longevity, often lasting well into the twentieth century. These intertwining—and often simultaneous—businesses involving a man and his sons, brothers, sons-in-law, brothers-in-law, or cousins are confusing to us but apparently weren't to them.

The men who founded these firms were proud to have their names on the door. It is lucky for us that they did since the names tell us so much about relationships in the community. As the years went by, however, more and more companies took on nonpersonal names, such as "European Fashion and Accessories" or "Pyramid Playing Cards," a part of the assimilation process that included giving their children names like Florence and Patrick.

As most of the Syrians were in the business of buying and selling, the most common occupations listed in documents were merchant, commission merchant, importer, salesman, dealer, and commercial traveler, in order of frequency. Each of these is self-explanatory yet vague, making it difficult to figure out what the individual actually did in the way of business. A salesman, for example, could be a glorified name for a peddler, someone working in a shop or the owner. A commercial traveler could also mean a peddler; a dealer could mean just about anything, from being a middleman in an export-import

[18] *Trials,* People v. Zreik, 1906: #599.

[19] *Kawkab America,* November 17, 1893.

business to owning a shop; and a merchant could encompass owning a large-scale import-export business to running a tiny shop selling notions.

The commission merchant was a different type of middleman; rather than buy outright from a wholesaler, the commission merchant received goods on consignment and sold them on commission. He had physical control of the goods but not title. Most commission merchants dealt in basic commodities such as cotton, wool, and foodstuffs, but at the end of the nineteenth century, there was a growing niche for commission merchants for dry goods, which is where the Syrians fit in. In the 1909 *Syrian Business Directory*, the category "Commission Merchant" was used interchangeably with "Dry Goods." This arrangement limited the risk for the supplier, did not tie up large amounts of capital, and allowed a larger inventory. It also limited the up side, because he was paid a fixed commission on goods sold rather than owning them and making whatever profit he could. In an 1898 ad in *Al Hoda*, the Khoury Brothers (Antoine and Habeeb) at 60–62 Washington Street claimed to be the only Syrian commission merchants in New York.[20] This was patently false, as we have more than a dozen men calling themselves commission merchants in our database.

In addition to the vagueness of the categories of occupation, the sectors in which a person worked were often unspecified. If someone called himself a wholesale merchant in the documents, what kind of goods did he sell? Often we are not told, and if we are told, the category is so vague that it is minimally informative (such as dry goods). Conversely, sometimes the sector is specified (e.g., Holy Land goods) but not how the person was involved in that sector: was he a peddler, wholesaler, importer, or a manufacturer of Holy Land goods?

Another factor that makes it difficult to generalize about business sectors in the Colony was the tendency of Syrians to be in many sectors simultaneously or to change businesses from year to year. Nineteenth-century Syrians owned cafés that were also boardinghouses that were also dry goods emporia, banks that were also dry goods businesses, grocery stores that sold Oriental trinkets, and barbershops that sold Oriental sweets. This practice sounds odd to us today in an age of extreme specialization and niche selling, but it is still true in the Middle East that diversification usually wins out over specialization: large holding companies can have Chanel perfumes and a major engineering contractor under the same roof.

It should be noted that the merchants themselves provided these

[20] *Al Hoda*, December 20, 1898: 1.

categories of occupation and sector to the census takers, wrote them on naturalization documents, and put them in the business directories. If their businesses seemed to change from year to year (from, say, Oriental goods to dry goods), sometimes it was because they were simply using different terms to describe the same thing, and sometimes it was because they really had changed their product line. If they called themselves merchants, the vagueness of the term gave them leeway in what they sold, which could change depending on the market. Given these caveats it is instructive to look at the relative proportion of different sectors.

By far the most common trade was in dry goods. Dry goods are by definition textiles, ready-to-wear clothing, and notions, as distinct from hardware and groceries. Obviously this category subsumed a huge variety of goods, which were sometimes specified in the data and sometimes not. The largest subcategory of dry goods was "notions": needles and thread, or "small lightweight items for household use." As well as being the peddlers' stock in trade, notions became the most common business for wholesalers and small shop owners in the nineteenth century. It was a natural progression. Although the word has pretty much disappeared from the retail trade today, when I was young every department store still had a notions section, where were sold needles and thread, shoe polish, hangers, seemingly all the small goods related to sewing, as well as household items that didn't fit into other departments. My mother calls her father's peddling "selling shoelaces."

Oriental goods or Turkish goods comprised the next largest category of dry goods. Oriental goods covered a wide range of products, including Oriental textiles; "Jerusalemite goods," such as olive wood boxes, rosaries, and crucifixes; Oriental jewelry; inlaid furniture; brassware; and so forth. Falling within this category, but called out separately, were Oriental antiquities, antiques, carpets, and art. Oriental goods could also sometimes mean Oriental groceries, which wholesalers imported from the Middle East or produced themselves and sold along with other Oriental goods, as Sahadi's does today.

A large number of nineteenth-century merchants were in the "rag trade" or "needle trades," heralding a mass movement of Syrians into textiles in the first decade of the twentieth century. At first, many of the earliest textile dealers were importing ornate Turkish embroideries and fabrics, such as those listed in Rustum's chart of wholesale prices.[21] But in the earliest days of the Colony, Syrian women worked at home to make more homely textiles, such as linen

[21] Rustum 1995 (1895): 37.

towels, handkerchiefs, and lace collars for the peddlers to sell. Although trade in cotton goods was not mentioned in the census or any document, we can infer its importance from the fact that every issue of *Kawkab America* reported on American cotton prices. Many of the early Syrian immigrants to Manchester, England, were involved in this trade, and perhaps the publication of American prices was aimed at them. But it might also be true that Syrians in the United States were dealing in cotton piece goods. Shirtwaists, petticoats, and other underclothes, as well as men's shirts, were made of cotton, and the Syrians may have been wholesaling to American-owned factories.

In the last few years of the nineteenth century, however, Syrian men began to set up small factories of their own to produce silk and cotton goods, and in 1903, dozens of kimono factories sprang up almost instantaneously. Most of the employees in these textile-manufacturing businesses were women. We will encounter more on women's role as factory workers in chapter 10. Businessmen also began to replace the laces and linens that had been made at home with imported goods, contracting with factories abroad. The merchants would then wholesale these goods to trousseau shops around the country, export them to other markets, or sell them in their own retail shops around the United States.

Ship manifests attest to the numerous trips these businessmen took to visit their textile suppliers in Paris, Dublin, Manchester, Madeira, Venice, Florence, Japan, and China. They were also traveling to see customers in these places, as well as in Latin America, Australia, Mexico, and elsewhere. At the height of the Syrians' commercial success, they were importing and selling "French Cluny, Belgian linen, Italian filet and cut-work, Philippine underwear and negligees, Japanese silks, and drawn work."[22]

When a man started a wholesale business, he needed room to store goods as well as a showroom, so he rented part or all of one of the tenements on Washington or Carlisle. An 1892 article in *Kawkab America* mentioned that rent for tenement space (for a store) was about 30¢ per day, and for manufacturing space (presumably a larger unobstructed space), between 50¢ and $1 per day. But according to the newspaper, even at these rents, a man could make a profit of between about $1.25 and $2.00 a day.[23]

The wholesaler or supplier, if he could afford it, would rent the basement for storage and the parlor (which had a window on the street) for his showroom. He often put his family in the rooms above and sometimes, if he were

[22] Ansara 1931: 70.

[23] *Kawkab America*, July 8, 1892.

a real estate entrepreneur as well, sublet rooms to his fellow Syrians. Every reporter commented on the fact that these wholesalers were always willing to sell retail as well, so that one could wander in and out of these "stores" (as the Syrians called them) and buy whatever was on offer.

A reporter who ventured into the Syrian Colony in 1892 described the house of a wholesale merchant and the arrangement of his goods. I quote him at length, because his is one of the few descriptions we have of the incredible variety of goods handled by a single merchant.

> The houses, especially on the Washington-st. side of the block, are old, weather-beaten, dingy and sometimes dirty, the cellars are devoted to trade and packed full of everything which a peddler can carry in his pack or find a market for in his wanderings, and the first or ground floor is generally used as a display-room and office, where goods are sorted out and bargains made....
>
> Go inside one of these stores, where pins by the hundred gross rest against shoe-blacking by the case, and scapulars and rosaries, beads and prayer-books are almost hidden from view by boxes of cheap cologne and ornamental shell-work, and if you can find some one who can translate your English into Arabic and tell the proprietor what you want, with a wave of his hand this latter-day magician will alter the whole scene, and for a brief time you will realize that "things are seldom what they seem...."
>
> Your eyes are dazzled by a great square of yellow satin, covered with delicate tracery of silver wire, fine as a spider's web, and glinting in the sunlight as if of burnished steel.... Silks and satins, lacework, embroideries, follow each other in rapid succession until the eyes are reveling in a bewildering maze of gorgeous, fantastic and beautiful colors, and your fingers begin to itch and your purse strings to loosen, while the alert keen-eyed dealer assures you that all these wonderful combinations of parti-colored threads are the work of hands as brown as his own.... He has some rugs which are a delight to the eye.... And the quaint specimens of Oriental carving, the marquetry work, the little tables in which the wood is lost in the wealth of inlaid pearl with which it is adorned, the long, curved sword of Damascus steel.[24]

[24] "A Picturesque Colony," *New-York Daily Tribune*, October 2, 1892. Nageeb Arbeely, the editor of *Kawkab America,* wrote a letter to the editor of the *Tribune* the following week, complimenting him on this "able and interesting article."

A similar article, written six years later, again describes the merchant's stock: "The bulk of the stock in any given shop is likely, of course, to consist of pins, needles, thread, blacking, collar buttons, shoestrings and other articles that peddlers need, but proper inquiry will always bring forth marvels in eastern silks, satins, lace work and Syrian embroideries which the shopkeeper will offer at prices quite as extraordinary as the goods themselves."[25] We are not told whether the extraordinary prices were extraordinarily high or low.

Thus Syrian stores were often both wholesale and retail businesses under one roof. Note too that they supplied goods to both *kesha* and *jezdan harir* peddlers. No wonder so many of them simply described themselves as merchants; they dealt in everything! In the following sections, we will highlight some of the merchants who specialized in one area or another of the trade.

### *Notions and Dry Goods*

Salim Elias—a Maronite from Baskinta—immigrated in 1885, and, after peddling for a few years, he opened an import/export company in the building where he lived at 59 Washington; in 1888 he was able to send for his family. He partnered with Salim Ganim and then Ganim's son, Beshara, after the father went back to Baskinta. Elias and Ganim sold novelties at 73½ Washington (the basement?), but in an advertisement in the very first issue of *Kawkab America* the company called "Salim Elias" had offices at "59 Washington St., N.Y. & 62, rue de Saintonge, Paris."[26] Elias must have been running two companies simultaneously, one in his old space at 59 Washington (where he lived), and a second at a new venue. Ganim's name was not mentioned in the *Kawkab America* ad, nor was the business at 73½ Washington. The partnership with Ganim moved to 19 Morris Street in 1894, while "Salim Elias" continued at 59 Washington. Since both companies listed their trade as dry goods, it is difficult to know if they were competing against each other, whether they had separate niches that are impossible for us to discern, or whether in fact they were one business. This practice of a man being an owner/partner of more than one company at the same time, while not common, was also not rare. We saw in chapter 3 that Yusef Balesh owned a shop with a partner and had a sole proprietorship at the same time in the same building.

[25] "Our New York Letter," *The Oswego* (NY) *Daily Palladium*, February 10, 1898.
[26] *Kawkab America*, April 15, 1892.

7-6. Advertisement for Salim Elias's store (Maloof 1899) (courtesy of Antiochian Heritage Museum, Ligonier, Penn.).

Elias imported goods from Paris as well as the Middle East and exported other goods to Europe, other parts of the United States (which the Syrian merchants called "inland" or "the states"), Australia, and South America.[27] In 1895, the partnership with Ganim dissolved and Elias went into business with Tanious Abdoo, another Maronite from Baskinta. This partnership lasted many years. They first set up shop at 31 Washington, but in 1898 they took over three floors at 69 Washington (where Elias then lived), importing and selling Oriental, European, and American goods. The sign on the building again referred only to Elias. Perhaps Abdoo too was a silent partner? In 1902, Elias had a dispute with another Syrian, Michael Karin (Karam?), and had him arrested for taking almost $1,500 worth of "fine Mediterranean sponges" on credit and not paying for them. Karin was held in default of $1,800 bail,[28] more than he owed Elias.[29] Elias was the sole plaintiff in the case, a fact that may again imply that Abdoo was a silent partner, or that Elias maintained a sole proprietorship as well.

[27] "Notices," *Kawkab America,* June 17, 1892.

[28] "Syrian Goes to Jail," *BDE,* August 28, 1902.

[29] Mediterranean sponges had a brief popularity at the turn of the century, when every department store was advertising them and many peddlers carried them. The Syrians and the Greeks were the major suppliers.

As seemed to be the pattern throughout the Colony, Elias's store at 69 Washington was at street level (actually three steps above street level), and the two upper floors served as offices and housing for his family: two of his four sons and his unmarried daughter worked in the business. Above the third-floor windows, the sign said "Dry Goods" in English and Arabic; on the second, "Jewelry" in both languages, and above the entrance: "Importers—Salim Elias—Exporters." The middle window on the ground floor had been broken through to give access to the store, while the original door to the building now gave access to the upstairs rooms. The cellar entrance had not been enlarged; it was still a set of slanting wooden doors covering a set of stairs, and may have served as a storeroom for the business. Elias claimed that his company was "the oldest, largest, most famous" Syrian shop in the United States, calling it "Le Grand Magazin syrien."[30]

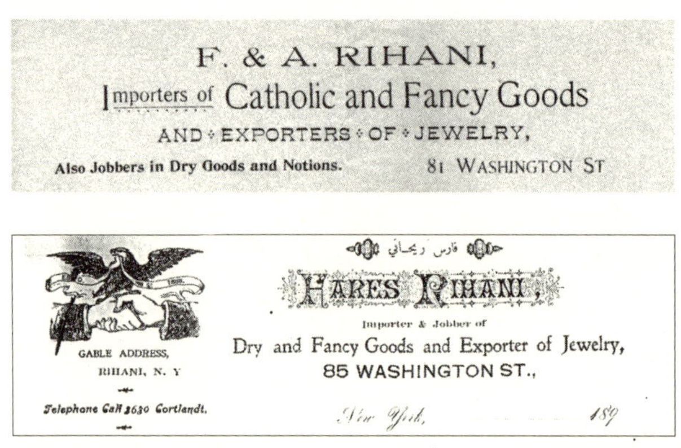

F. & A. RIHANI,
Importers of Catholic and Fancy Goods
AND EXPORTERS OF JEWELRY,
Also Jobbers in Dry Goods and Notions. 81 WASHINGTON ST

فارس ريحاني
FARES RIHANI,
Importer & Jobber of
Dry and Fancy Goods and Exporter of Jewelry,
85 WASHINGTON ST.,
New York, 189
CABLE ADDRESS,
RIHANI, N. Y
Telephone Call 3630 Cortlandt.

7-7. F & A Rihani letterhead, ca. 1895 and Fares Rihani letterhead, ca. 1898 (courtesy of the Ameen Rihani Museum, Freike, Lebanon).

Elias's former partner, Beshara Ganim, went into partnership with his cousin Antoine Sadallah to open an import/export business in "dry and fancy goods, jewelry, notions, etc." under the name of Ganim and Sadallah, first at 19 Morris Street (where Ganim and Elias had been based) and later at 81 Washington.[31] They continued to work together until 1900, when Beshara brought in his younger brother Shakir and opened a wholesale Oriental grocery business called Beshara Ganim and Bro. A.J. Sadallah worked on his own

[30] *Al Hoda*, March 15, 1898.

[31] http://savewashingtonstreet.org/photographs/business-related-artifacts-from-little-syria/?afg7_page_id=3.

for a while and then brought in members of his family to sell and manufacture dry goods at 60–62 Washington, a double building that was home to a large number of Syrian companies, both manufacturers and wholesalers/suppliers. The Faour Brothers, who later became well-known bankers, started out as merchants of dry goods, particularly Oriental trinkets; they had their first store at 19 Morris as well. All of these families, it should be noted, were Maronites.

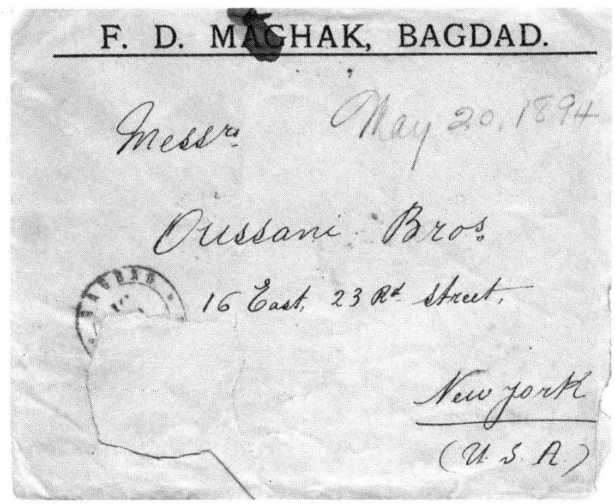


7-8. Envelope from a Baghdad supplier to "Oussani Brothers," 1894 (courtesy Gail O'Keefe Edson).

The brothers Massoud and Joseph Moshy were Maronites from Jezzine who had immigrated in 1890. Together they owned a firm that was quite diversified in its offerings and mainly supplied peddlers. Like others, they probably peddled when they arrived, but eventually set up their supply house at 59 Washington, after Salim Elias had moved to Number 69. They seem to have occupied the entire five-story building. In their ads in *Al Hoda*, their name is emblazoned on the pediment in Arabic and English, and the sun's rays are emanating from the building. A postman walks up to the front door, apparently bringing orders to the firm. On either side of the building are two men. The one on the left is rather scruffy and dejected looking: his head is bowed, his beard is unkempt as are his clothes, and he is carrying a *keshi* slung over his shoulder. He is the sorry peddler who has not been doing business with the Moshy Brothers. The man on the right also has a *keshi*, but looks quite spruce with his bowler hat, handlebar mustache, well-fitting suit, and walking stick. He has bought his goods from the Moshy Brothers and prospered.

7-9. Advertisement for Abd-el-Nour & Maloof (Maloof 1899: 301) (courtesy of Antiochian Heritage Museum, Ligonier, Penn.).

Antoni Tadross came to the United States in 1884; his brother Nami followed in 1889. They were an Orthodox family from Tripoli. Antoni peddled when he first arrived, but settled into the jewelry (trinkets) business at 19 Morris. In 1891, the brothers set up a partnership (Tadross Brothers) selling notions at 77 Washington. Elias el Hajj became the company's agent in New Mexico, spending several years there. The partners rather soon went their separate ways, Antoni staying in the dry goods business and Nami moving into carpets. Antoni continued to live at Number 77, but his business soon occupied all six floors of 79 Washington,[32] with the name "A. Tadross & Co." emblazoned on the pediment and "dry goods, underwear, hosiery, notions, jewelry" on each of the lower floors. His retail store, on the ground floor, had the company name repeated above the door. For a while, he employed his nephew Michael Kaydouh and later, Najeeb and Kareemi Freije, who lived in

[32] Mokarzel and Otash 1909. Originally three and a half stories, Number 79 had three floors added around the turn of the century, perhaps by Tadross himself.

the building. Antoni also sold his own brand of straight razors, as did many of the dry goods dealers, importing them from Germany already engraved with his name. He traveled extensively for the business, and in a 1901 passport application, he stated that since immigrating, he had lived in Philadelphia, New York, Buffalo, Toledo, and Brooklyn. The family moved to the Sunset Park district of Brooklyn at the end of the century, and Antoni joined forces with George Ackary; they continued to sell dry goods from 79 Washington. Antoni died in 1913, leaving an estate of $20,000.

Other Syrians who sold mostly notions and novelties (but who stocked other goods as well) included Petrus Saad & Bros., the brothers Michael and Elias Abousleman, Khalil and Stephen Nicola, Fares Rihani, Nacle Forzly, Maroon Fagher, Salim Mikwee, and many more, some of whom appear in this book in other contexts.

Although many self-employed merchants started out like these men as general dry goods dealers, by the 1890s they were beginning to specialize and find their niche. In many cases, they remained in these specializations until their death.

### *Oriental and Holy Land Goods*

Oriental goods were usually synonymous with Turkish goods, but Syrian merchants sometimes also sold fancy goods from the Far East, both China and Japan. In city directories of the period, the heading "Oriental Goods" included Syrian, Armenian, Chinese, and Japanese merchants. Holy Land goods such as olive wood items, "holy water," and religious jewelry, eventually gave way to more specialized religious items or to the ornate Oriental tapestries that became a hallmark of Syrian merchants.

John Abd-el-Nour emigrated from Damascus in 1880. As described above, Abd-el-Nour had a long succession of partners (one wonders if he was difficult to work with or simply mercurial in his business dealings), but one notices that his name was always listed first. This suggests, perhaps, that he was the majority partner, a surmise that is supported by his having been identified as a merchant on the ship manifest at his arrival, and by the fact that he traveled first class whenever he went to Europe.

Abd-el-Nour's first and primary occupation was as a dealer in Oriental goods; these are what he was showing in Louisville in 1883 and 1885, what he sold in his first store, and later, what he took to the Chicago fair. When in 1894 he was wanted as an accessory to, or as the leader of, a smuggling operation, the contents of his trunks revealed a treasure trove of fine Oriental textiles: "handkerchiefs and numerous embroideries, gold-braided girdles and table scarfs."[33] In 1896, his business was described in the *New York Press* as importing the "highest class of Turkish and Oriental fabrics and embroideries." He reportedly had factories in Constantinople and branches in Damascus and Paris.[34] In these cases, where a man was said to "have" a factory, it is not clear whether he set up and/or owned the factories or whether he simply contracted with existing factories to produce goods to his specifications. His various homes were decorated in the latest Orientalist style, which included Oriental carpets, fine tapestries, and inlaid tables. In the oft-quoted *Tribune* article of 1903, reproduced in Miller's book in 1903, Abd-el-Nour's Staten Island home was used as the illustration for the Syrian as capitalist.[35] That the room was decorated in the Oriental style (surely from his own stock) and accented with French statues shows Abd-el-Nour to have been a man of his time.

Other nineteenth-century Oriental goods establishments included Moussa Zalka & Salim Marrash, the Oussani brothers, Nicola Abo Samra & Shakir Nasser, the Andalaft brothers, Joseph Ayoob, "Mallouk, Balesh & Geha," and "Saba Brothers & Dibs."

Another prominent dealer in embroideries and fancy textiles, and one who exemplifies the transition from peddler to fancy goods merchant to textile manufacturer, was Abdow Lutfy, one of the earliest immigrants and a "big man" in the community. From an Orthodox family, he emigrated with his wife and sons from Zahleh in 1885. We saw him in the 1890 census at 77 Washington. As was usual, he peddled when he first arrived, and perhaps his wife did as well. He formed a company with his sons Deeb, Michel, Antoun, and Ameen ("Abdow Lutfy & Sons") in about 1890 to import fancy goods; it was located at his (or their?) home at 77 Washington. During these early years, his sons also traveled on the lecture circuit around the United States; these trips will be described in chapter 8.

The company got larger and the sons began to take a more active role. Deeb went to the Far East in 1893 with his cousin Abdallah Lutfy to establish business contacts and suppliers there. Ameen left New York to open a store in Montreal, while Deeb, Michel, and Antoun remained in business with their

33 "Smuggler Abd-el-Nour," *The* (NY) *Sun,* December 5, 1894.

34 "Oriental Embroideries: John Abd-el-Nour," *The New York Press.*

35 "Victims of the Turk Finding Homes Here," *New-York Tribune Illustrated Supplement,* October 11, 1903.

father. Antoun then went out to Cleveland, Ohio, to set up a Lutfy shop there, which Abdallah managed.

Each year during the "season," the three sons went to Saratoga Springs, New York, to sell the company's goods in two shops in the Grand Union Hotel; they had formed their own company (Lutfy Bros.) to do so. Abdow went back and forth between there and New York City, checking up on the business and carrying goods with him. Many Syrian dealers did the same, setting up small shops or bazaars in Newport, Rhode Island, or Atlantic City, New Jersey, in the summers, and in Tampa or St. Augustine, Florida, in the winters. Like the "ladies of the road" described below, they followed the "quality," season after season: "Many of these men will sell really fine goods and have regular customers among the fashionables, who buy from them year after year."[36]

Simultaneous with these activities (around 1898), Abdow Lutfy set up a partnership with Elias Macksoud, another Orthodox man from Zahleh. The two families were related by marriage; Abdow's sister Ramza was married to a Macksoud. Joseph Macksoud, Elias's father, who had immigrated alone in 1890 at the age of seventy-three, started a business selling Oriental trinkets. By the time Elias arrived in 1893, Joseph was ready to retire. Elias, after a stint as a laborer in the brickyards of Dutchess Junction, set up a successful business importing embroideries and fancy goods. The two families lived together at 7 Battery Place. In the new partnership, Macksoud was the junior partner. The following year, he became Lutfy's son-in-law.[37]

Lutfy and Macksoud imported "assorted goods: embroideries, Turkish, Syrian, Parisian,"[38] the same goods that the Lutfy sons were selling in Saratoga Springs. The firm of Lutfy and Macksoud shared space with Abdow Lutfy & Sons and Lutfy Bros. at 2 Carlisle Street. Macksoud formed a separate partnership, also based at 2 Carlisle, with Abdallah Lutfy, who sold Lutfy and Macksoud's Oriental goods in The Arcade in Cleveland.

### *The Move toward Specialization: Textiles*

These partnerships between the Lutfys and Macksouds were the first forays into a long and harmonious business and personal relationship. Elias Macksoud's partnership with Abdow Lutfy lasted until the latter's retirement, when

[36] "Oriental Merchants of New York," *Anaconda* (MT) *Standard*, October 23, 1898.
[37] "A Syrian Wedding," *NYT*, February 7, 1899.
[38] Maloof 1899: 304.

Deeb took Abdow's place at Lutfy & Macksoud. The company began to manufacture kimonos and seems to have been the earliest kimono factory in New York, founded in 1903.

Mass kimono manufacturing was strictly a twentieth-century business and exclusively Syrian: of the 457 entries under "kimono" listed in city directories between 1903 and 1920, every entry was Syrian. It was also the most common garment manufactured by the Syrians. Although it is often said it was modeled on the Middle Eastern *abaya*, in fact it had much more in common with its Japanese namesake. The unfitted, pieced design meant the kimonos could be run up easily without a pattern, and there were no issues of fit or size. As early as 1892, New York dressmakers were advertising Japanese kimonos for American women, but it wasn't until the Syrians entered the business that they became ubiquitous in women's closets.

Lutfy & Macksoud's factory was described in an article in the *New-York Tribune*: "Thus on the fourth floor of No. 108 Greenwich-st. nearly a score of women may be found at work any weekday, sewing kimonos from brilliantly colored fabrics. The room is bright, and occasionally the women hum a native song as they work."[39] The accompanying photographs of a kimono workshop, although not identified, were surely taken at Lutfy & Macksoud's. Perhaps the man measuring the sleeves of the kimono is Elias Macksoud and the model his wife, Shafika. The kimonos were made from brightly printed cotton; Lutfy & Macksoud also manufactured cheesecloth and cotton crepe at a factory at 108 Greenwich. Their office was around the corner at 2 Carlisle. Deeb's brother Anthony (Antoun) was a clerk in the business, and Elias's brother Gabriel joined as a partner. The Macksoud brothers came to be known as "The Kimono Kings."

After the dissolution of the partnership (Lutfy and Macksoud filed for bankruptcy in 1911), the Macksouds continued to manufacture kimonos under the name "Mendik Kimonos" until the 1920s. The families remained close.

My maternal grandfather, F.M. Jabara, although not technically a nineteenth-century merchant, serves as a classic example of the trajectory of the early immigrants who resisted the call to continue in a diversified business and moved into specialized fields, fields that grew directly out of their experience as notions salesmen. When he arrived in New York alone in 1902, my grandfather-to-be peddled notions for three years. His letters to my grandmother while she was peddling with her mother in the resorts of upstate New York

[39] "Victims of the Turk Finding Homes Here," *New-York Tribune Illustrated Supplement,* October 11, 1903.

indicate that he had been to many of those same places when he was a peddler. He then formed an importing business with Albert Salamy; the two men had immigrated the same year from the same town (Jdeideh Marjayoun). The company was called "Salamy and Jabara" and was located at 20 Rector Street. Was Salamy listed first because he was older, invested more, or was it just chance? My grandfather called their business "the place," as opposed to "the store," meaning there was no retail component.

Salamy and Jabara moved into the manufacturing of kimonos and dressing sacques in 1908, setting up their facility at 72 Trinity Place, right across the street from Trinity Church. The company dissolved less than a year later, when two of Jabara's brothers joined him in 1909. They formed "F.M. Jabara and Bros., Importers," first continuing at 72 Trinity Place, but soon moving to 85 Washington. Salamy continued on his own, keeping his office at 72 Trinity Place and importing Japanese drawn work and fine Irish linens.[40] In that same year, Jabara made what was the first of many trips to Ireland to purchase Irish linen for hand towels and handkerchiefs, and then went on to Paris to buy French lace, which he shipped back to America. He had arrived in 1902, probably penniless, set up his own partnership in 1905, and already had an international network of textile suppliers by 1909, as did Salamy.

By the 1910s, F.M. Jabara and Bros. had agents and factories under contract in three countries; offices/showrooms in Chicago; Petoskey, Michigan; and St. Augustine, Florida (both of the latter were perhaps seasonal shops), and they sold to retail shops (so-called trousseau shops) all over the United States. Jabara would buy linen in Ireland and lace in Brussels or Paris, ship them to factories in China, Portugal, or Italy (in each place one of his relatives represented the company), and have them made into fancy hand towels, tablecloths, napkins, dresser scarves, or handkerchiefs. Each piece was sewn and then embellished with handwork, using embroidery, drawn work, appliqué, or lace.

Jabara continued to do much of the buying and went abroad twice a year over the next two decades. The company moved out of the neighborhood and uptown to 220 Fifth Avenue (at 26th Street) in 1918. Many Syrian businesses had preceded them, and they in turn were simply following the northward trajectory that the major department stores had pioneered. The company fell apart in acrimony in 1944, each brother founding a competing business. It had lasted more than three decades.

By the early twentieth century, manufacturing, importing, and wholesaling

[40] Abdou 1910: 223.

of textiles had become the Syrians' stock in trade. Like the other sectors, its origins lay in the nineteenth-century Colony's first forays into specialization after the peddling interval.

### *Wholesale Grocers*

One of the largest sectors outside of dry goods that became a magnet for the Syrian immigrant was the grocery business, whether a small corner shop or a large wholesale business. The many retail groceries in the Colony have been described above, but it should be remembered that, like peddlers' suppliers, many grocers were both wholesale and retail merchants.

No book about the Syrian Colony would be complete without (re)telling the story of Sahadi's grocery business, which began in the nineteenth century on Washington Street; a grocery store of that name still exists on Atlantic Avenue, Brooklyn. Abraham Abdullah Sahadi immigrated from Zahleh in 1888 and settled at 57 Washington (he is called Abdallah Saadi in the 1890 Police Census, but I'm quite sure it's our Sahadi). By 1893, he was living at 36 Greenwich and running a store selling Oriental tobacco up the street at 48 Greenwich. In 1895, he opened the "A. Sahadi & Co. Eating House" at 45 Washington; there is no indication to whom the "& Co." referred. It may have just sounded grand. He and Zakia opened their first real grocery store at 92 Washington in 1897. It is this store that is pictured in an 1899 article in the *New York Times* (Figure 7-3).[41] By that time, he was selling *'araq* under his own label, the beginning of a large importing business in Sahadi-brand foodstuffs.

In 1899, Abraham's two brothers, Najeeb and Salim, briefly joined the firm, which became "Abraham Sahadi & Brothers." In 1900, however, the two brothers opened what appears to have been a competing enterprise at 83 Washington, selling *'araq*, Syrian groceries, and *narghiles* and tobacco. Sahadi renamed his business "Abraham Sahadi" and remained at 92 Washington. Sahadi was more peripatetic than many of his countrymen, both in business and in residence. He and Zakia changed houses several times, living at 57 Washington, 36 Greenwich, 1 Carlisle, 87 Washington, and 92 Washington, all before 1900. They finally moved to Clinton, New Jersey, but continued to sell Oriental groceries at various venues on Washington Street until his retirement in 1940, when others took over its management. Abraham Sahadi died in 1952. His nephew, Wade (Wadie?) Sahadi, who had worked with him

[41] Cromwell Childe, "New York's Syrian Quarter," *NYT,* August 20, 1899.

since 1919, established Sahadi Importing Company on Washington Street in 1941, and in 1948 moved the company to its present site at 187 Atlantic Avenue in Brooklyn.[42]

Tamer K. Malouf, another successful wholesale grocer, emigrated from Kafr Agab to Australia in 1889, where he opened a textile business with a relative. He married there and had a daughter, and the three returned to Syria. In 1896, he and his daughter immigrated to the United States; perhaps his wife had died. Even though he had had his own business in Australia, he started out as a peddler in New Brunswick, New Jersey, and then moved to New York to join forces with Salim Zaloom, whose father, Farjallah, had started a wholesale grocery business at 73 Washington. Farjallah sold Syrian food and pastries, pistachios from his native Aleppo, and *narghile*s and *narghile* tobacco. Farjallah claimed that Syrians would remember their beloved country by ordering his products.[43] Malouf and the younger Zaloom soon parted ways. By 1917 Malouf owned two companies: the Grecian Importing & Trading Co. at 70 Washington and "TK Malouf & Co." at 60–62 Washington, as well as a warehouse on Greenwich Street. He owned two residential buildings in Brooklyn as well. Farjallah and Salim Zaloom began to specialize in importing pistachios and other nuts and also continued in business well into the twentieth century.

## *Tobacco*

*Large fortunes have been made by Syrians, especially in New York, by the manufacture of cigarettes.*[44]

Cigarette and cigar manufacturing was another important business for Syrians. They began by importing Turkish and Egyptian tobacco but, like other importers, some found it was cheaper and more convenient to use domestic sources; much of the later "Turkish" tobacco was grown in the United States or elsewhere. This fact did not go unremarked by critics of Syrian business practices.

Yacoub (Yak) Oussani and his brother Joseph came to the United States to attend the 1893 Chicago Fair.[45] Perhaps they even began their tobacco

[42] sahadifinefoods.com/history/.
[43] *Al Hoda,* August 23, 1898.
[44] Houghton 1911: II: 655.
[45] Vandor 1919.

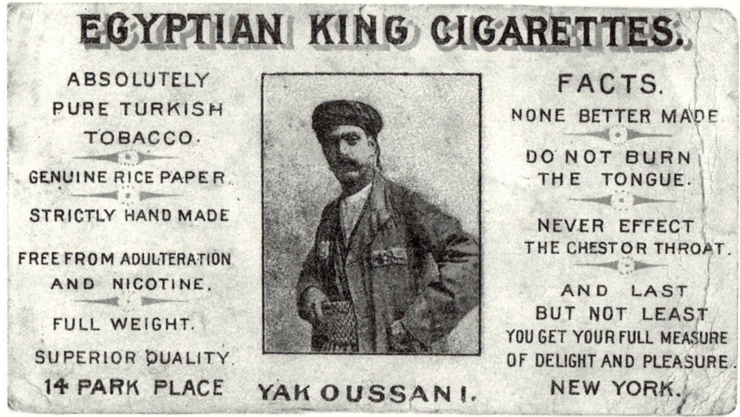


7-10. Advertising card for Egyptian King cigarettes, closed. Card given out by Yak Oussani at the Buffalo fair, 1901. Advertising card, open. Advertising card, back (courtesy of Gail O'Keefe Edson). Note that Oussani used the portrait taken at the Chicago fair on this card.

business at the fair, as on their return to New York, they set up a partnership with Yusef Waked, who had sold cigarettes in Chicago.

The Oussanis actually set up two businesses when they moved to New York: importing Turkish tobacco and manufacturing cigarettes in partnership with Waked ("J. Waked & Oussani Bros."), and importing and selling Oriental goods. Both companies were located at 16 E. 23rd Street. In 1894, they dissolved the partnership with Waked[46] and renamed their business

[46] After he "retired," Waked sold ice cream in Coney Island and then moved back to Chicago and became an underwear manufacturer.

Oussani Brothers. Yak lived on West 29th Street and Joseph on East 31st Street. A third brother, John, arrived in 1895 and joined Oussani Brothers. Their remaining brothers, Peter and Gabriel, sister Teresa, and widowed mother Catherine joined them in 1900.

7-11. Memorial card for Yak Oussani, 1903 (courtesy of Gail O'Keefe Edson).

In 1900, the brothers dissolved their partnership. The Oriental goods were sold at auction ("a most superb collection of Oriental Rugs, Turkish, Persian and Teakwood furniture, Algerian arms, coffee urns, lanterns, hangings, embroideries, enamels, Egyptian dancing girls' costumes, etc."[47]). Yak took over the cigarette business, while Joseph founded "Oussani Construction Co." The cigarette company, "Yak Oussani," made many varieties of cigarettes including the Egyptian King, Egyptian Flower, the Milooki ("The Smoke of Royalty"), and Oussani's Natural. Yak participated in the Pan-American Exposition in Buffalo in 1901, where he built a scale model of his factory in the Manufacturing Building and handed out trade cards bearing the portrait of Sultan Mehmed V, as well as cards with two men standing on the beach chest to chest with their cigarettes touching (Figure 7-10). John Oussani took over the business after Yak's death in 1903 and ran it until the Depression, keeping the name "Yak Oussani."

[47] Advertisement, *NYH,* March 9, 1900.

### *Real Estate*

We don't know how the Oussani brothers' partnership was organized, but Joseph at least must have made a lot of money in the tobacco and smoking parlor businesses because in 1899 he bought a four-story "hotel" on the corner of Lexington Avenue and 29th Street for $24,500 and purchased a large home and fifty-two acres of land in Pocantico Hills, near Tarrytown, New York. Joseph immediately announced plans to build a casino on the property,[48] probably to replicate the success of his New York Turkish smoking parlors. The neighbors, among whom was John D. Rockefeller, objected vigorously, and the plan was dropped. The family summered in Tarrytown for many years. Finally, Joseph put the property up for sale and sold it to Rockefeller in 1912.

In 1902, Oussani Construction Co. built two apartment buildings in New York, both of which still stand: the Semiramis at 137 Central Park North and the Zenobia at 217 West 110th Street, where Joseph and his family lived.[49] He named them after two Middle Eastern queens in honor of his two daughters.[50] He also bought land in Fresno, California, in 1915, where he grew grapes on 320 acres, harking back, perhaps, to an earlier agrarian life in the Middle East. He always kept a foot in the real estate market in New York, with his apartment at the Semiramis, an estate in Hastings-on-Hudson, and the large property in Pocantico Hills. In later censuses, his occupation was always listed as "real estate."

Assad G. Khoury, who also made his money in tobacco, was a real estate investor and developer, as was Assy Shaheen. In contrast to these entrepreneurs, who bought and sold real estate on their own account, several Syrians became real estate brokers after the turn of the century, including Tannous Hayek, Muossa Daoud, and Faris and Joseph Maloof.

### *Straight Razors and Cutlery*

Several Syrians imported cutlery and straight razors under their own trademark, a trade that grew directly out of their notions inventories. Najeeb M. Mallouk emigrated in 1888 to Munich, where he opened a variety store. In 1894, he came to the United States and set up an importing business,

[48] "Casino at Pocantico Hills," *NYT,* December 2, 1899.

[49] "Streetscapes," *NYT*, June 3, 1990.

[50] Gail Edson, p.c., 2013.

"Nageeb Malluk & Co." at 31–33 Broadway, specializing in straight razors using English and German steel and technology. The business contacts he had made in Munich were useful in this enterprise. One of his two trademarks, "The Orient Razor" or "Najeeb Malluk Razor," was engraved in each blade. He claimed that both trademarks had been registered in November 1894, although it seems unlikely that he would have known how to file a trademark so soon after his arrival.

A large, half-column ad in *Kawkab America* in 1895 touted the quality of his cutlery and warned competitors that they should not copy his trademark (the Ottoman seal) or his name, "The Orient Razor."[51] Despite this warning, he sued Said Jureidini in 1898, claiming that Jureidini had imitated his logo on his own inferior razors. He also accused Jureidini of trying to poach Mallouk's suppliers in England. Jureidini had allegedly sold three dozen of these razors to the Faour brothers at 19 Morris Street, who had promptly sold them to customers, so Mallouk filed suit. The Faours had their own brand of razors—with "D.J. Faour & Bros." and the image of Yousef Bey Karam (a Maronite and national hero of the Syrians), the U.S. Seal, and the Ottoman flag engraved in the blade—so one wonders why they were selling Jureidini's razors. Mallouk asked for an injunction against Jureidini's selling any more razors and $5,000 in damages. Mallouk won the suit; Jureidini was forbidden to import razors from Mallouk's supplier, forbidden to use his trademark, and forced to pay Mallouk $590.72 in damages. In 1896, Mallouk added a new brand of razor to his inventory, "The American Home Razor," which he also claimed to have patented.[52]

Mallouk not only wholesaled razors in the United States but also exported them to Colombia, where his brother lived. In 1912, he moved to Cartagena to work with his brother in the company Najeeb Hermanos but in 1917 came back to New York to export goods once again. By then, however, German razors would have been illegal to import, so perhaps they closed the company.

"Richard Korkemas & Co.," a dry goods firm founded in 1897, also imported straight razors. Korekemas, too, had his own brand, "Teddy Bear," which was manufactured from German steel. His razor cases read "Korkemas." When the firm consolidated with M. & A. Michael in 1909, the consolidated company was said to be worth $120,000. Nevertheless, shortly after consolidation they were forced to declare bankruptcy because, although their assets

[51] *Kawkab America,* January 31, 1896.
[52] Advertisement, *Kawkab America,* January 31, 1896.

were twice their liabilities, they were unable to collect outstanding accounts and therefore could not pay their bills.[53]

George Forzly, who ran a combined bank and dry goods store (see chapter 8) also sold razors under his own imprint, as did Antoni Tadross. Forzly registered his trademark for the razors in May 1896. Some of these businessmen ordered razors imprinted with their logo to give away as advertising gimmicks and may not have been strictly speaking in the business of selling razors. Like the linen dealers described above, none of these men actually set up manufacturing facilities abroad, but contracted with existing factories in Germany and England to have razors made to their specifications, had their names engraved in the blades, and imported them to the United States.

My paternal grandfather, Joseph Jacobs, peddled dry goods all over the country in the nineteenth century after landing in New York in 1887 from Beirut. He was mentioned in newspaper articles in Fort Worth, Texas, and Denver, Colorado, in 1890 and in Putnam, Connecticut, in 1894. Although he married in New York in 1897, he, with his wife and children, continued to move from town to town, selling goods. Each of his first five children was born in a different state. He tried his hand at many things: he peddled notions, sold religious goods, ran a fruit stand, and finally began to specialize in selling cutlery and straight razors for the Geneva Cutlery Company in Geneva, New York. In 1910, he applied to be their exclusive agent in New York City, where the family had settled permanently several years before. He did especially well during World War I when the higher-quality German razors were embargoed. He boasted that he had never raised the prices of his razors, even when they were in short supply.[54] But just at this time, King C. Gillette invented the safety razor, and during the First World War the government issued them by the millions to the soldiers; when the war ended, the new invention trickled down to the general public. By the 1920s, anyone unfortunate enough to still be in the straight razor business had to adapt or go under; my grandfather declared bankruptcy.

### *Antiquities and Carpets*

In a category by himself but in a business certainly related to the objects that sold with such success at the 1893 fair, Azeez Khayat was an antiquities dealer.

[53] "Syrian Firms in Trouble," *NYT*, July 22, 1909.

[54] "Yusef Yacoub's Business," *Syrian-American Commercial Magazine*, April 1921: 35.

One imagines that he may have already been an antiquities dealer in Syria since his birthplace, Tyre, was (and is) an attraction for archaeology-minded tourists. He and his wife came to the United States in 1893 with a significant stock of goods and immediately opened a store at 141 Sixth Avenue (at Spring Street); he did not need to peddle. The Schenck Art Gallery held an auction in his name in March of that year advertising his collection of Phoenician glass. "Representatives of Museums, Colleges, Institutes and ART DEALERS and AMATEURS RESPECTFULLY INVITED," the ad read.[55] His store moved uptown to 55 W. 11th (between Fifth and Sixth Avenues) in 1898; he and his wife and five children (they eventually had nine) lived there as well. He was one of the few Syrians who didn't live in the neighborhood, one of the few men who could afford to support such a large family, and one of the few merchants who traveled first class when he went on buying trips to Europe and the Middle East.

Khayat's wares were described in a 1902 advertisement for an auction to be held at the Fifth Avenue Galleries as "the celebrated Azeez Khayat Collection of rare Greek and Roman Glass, Coins, Cylinder Seals, Bronzes and other antiquities."[56] These ads appeared frequently throughout his career. Although he opened a curio shop on Pacific Street in Brooklyn in 1902, and apparently lived there for a few years, he was also listed as living on Rector Street in 1905. In the same year he opened a gallery on 34th Street in Manhattan, which he had until 1930.

Several other antiquities dealers from Tyre came regularly to New York to do business, but did not really settle here; they traveled constantly back and forth between the Middle East, Europe, and the United States. One pair, Nahmy Homsy and Salim Ayoub, were sued for substituting cheap glass replicas for a promised shipment of Phoenician glass. Gibran and Michael Farah—also from Tyre—came in 1892 with antiques to sell in New York. One suspects that all of these dealers had booths at the Columbian fair. Homsy eventually settled in New York.

Two men that we know of who began to deal exclusively in Oriental rugs in the nineteenth century were both mentioned above: Nami Tadross and Elias Saadi. Nami Tadross moved into importing and selling carpets "from all over the world" after he and his brother Antoni split up. In a laudatory article published in 1921 on the occasion of his return to Syria, the *Syrian-American*

[55] Advertisement, *NYH,* March 19, 1894.
[56] Advertisement, *NYH*, February 12, 1902.

*Commercial Magazine* described his shaky beginnings. He first stopped in Cyprus, where he bought liquor and tried to sell it at a profit but he lost his nest egg. When he reached the United States, he lost money on his first venture, which was selling (probably peddling) Oriental goods. Although the article does not mention his brother Antoni in these early ventures, we know that they were in partnership (along with Elias el Hajj). Perhaps their split was a result of Nami's improvidence or incompetence, but it seems more likely that Nami decided to strike out on his own. Apparently it took several years of traveling and learning the business before Nami decided to specialize in rugs. He opened his first solo store in New York in 1898 at 117–119 Broadway and a store in Detroit in 1900 with Kalil Bonahoom (Tadross and Bonahoom), which he left in the care of his (Tadross's) nephews, Saleeba and Nessim Zahloute, when he came back to New York. In 1910 he opened at 39 Broadway, moved uptown to Union Square in 1915, and finally to 225 Fifth Avenue (at 27th Street). He died in 1927.

Elias Saadi, who moonlighted as the Protestant preacher, imported rugs; all three of his sons, John, Nessim, and Nayeff, worked in the business. With Elias's untimely death in 1902 the business seems to have been dissolved and each of his sons went his own way.

In the twentieth century, Syrians, along with Armenians, became known as rug dealers. In 1908 there were nine Syrian rug merchants, among them Nami Tadross, most of them still located on lower Broadway. By 1912, there were twenty-five dealers who had moved to lower Fifth Avenue; they, like many other merchants, were following the general migration northward.

Chapter 8

# The Service Professions

## Bankers

Despite the overwhelming preponderance of Syrians who bought and sold goods, Syrian men and women were also service providers, even in the last decades of the nineteenth century. They often combined their service jobs with commerce as if they didn't trust any work that didn't deal with tangible goods.

George Forzly was a child in 1881 when he accompanied his parents, Selim Forzly and Selma Daoun Forzly, from Damascus to Manchester, England, where his father worked in the cotton shipping business. They were probably shipping cotton cloth to Syria. In 1893, the entire family moved to the United States, apparently because Selim had gone bankrupt. Selim's brother Solomon (my paternal great-grandfather) was already here.

When Selim's family arrived, George started a dry goods business at 302 Church Street (at Walker) and then combined that business with a bank he established at 103 Washington in 1896. Forzly's was thus the first Syrian bank in the United States. His sign, in English and Arabic, read: "George Forzly & Co. Bankers. Money Exchanged and Loans. Foreign Money Bought & Sold. Drafts on All Parts of Europe. Importers, Exporters and General Commission Merchants." The "& Co." referred to his father, Selim, and perhaps to his cousin Kalil. So far, so good.

The company went bankrupt in May 1899, having assets of $12,500 and liabilities of $25,000. Forzly closed up the shop one day and disappeared. Among the 150 creditors were merchants Solomon D. Merhige (who had deposited $1,834) and John Abd-el-Nour ($2,189), Archmandrite Raphael Hawaweeny ($4,000), grocer Alexander Yazaji ($1,711), newspaper editors Joseph N. Maloof and Shibli Dammous, and several women, including Louisa Aramoonie, who had deposited $135, a widow, Jamilie Zainey, who lost $800 she had earned from peddling, and a Marion Hage from Canada, who had deposited $430 in bills and was told to return on Monday to retrieve gold. When she returned as instructed, she found the bank closed and an angry crowd gathered around the padlocked door.[1] Hawaweeny's deposit was made up of contributions from his parishioners, who had donated funds to build a church and buy a plot of land at Mount Olivet Cemetery for burial of the Greek Orthodox faithful. According to one article, the depositors had, within the last six months, been offered "five to twenty-five per cent a month interest on their deposits,"[2] which sounds like the attempt of a desperate banker to save himself. The business of the bank had grown enormously under this stimulus.

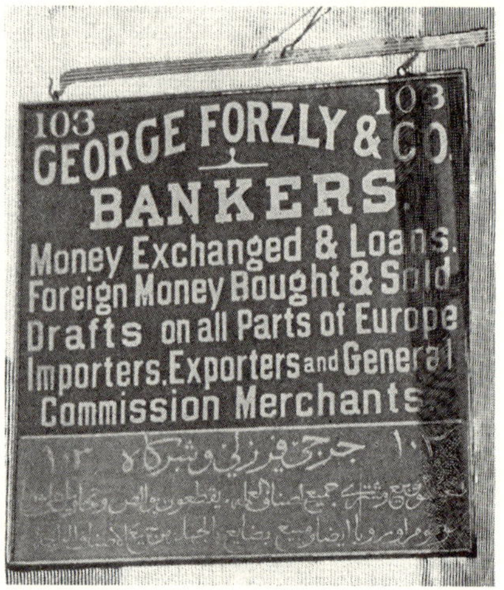


8-1. George Forzly's bank and dry goods store, 103 Washington (Moss 1897).

After getting no satisfaction at the bank, the group of angry depositors went to the Forzly home at 526 Henry Street in Brooklyn and found that all of the Forzlys had apparently pulled up stakes, but this may have been the reporter's assumption rather than the truth. Forzly turned himself in the following week and was charged with larceny on $1,250 bail.[3] Merhige brought suit against him but was prevailed on by the judge to withdraw the suit to give Forzly a chance to make good his debts.

[1] "Petitions in Bankruptcy," *NYH,* May 26, 1899.
[2] "Syrian Bank's Doors Closed," *NYH,* May 23, 1899.
[3] "Syrian Banker Missing," *NYT,* May 25, 1899; "Syrian Banker Surrenders," *NYT,* June 1, 1899.

*Al Hoda* referred to Forzly's as a "shop which was known as a bank" and alluded to questionable dealings behind the bankruptcy, calling it "premeditated" and the result of "[religious] fanaticism." It is true that the depositors (at least as named in the press) did not include a single Maronite or Melkite. The newspaper also implied that the money had been embezzled (by whom it did not say), and Mokarzel stated darkly, "Corruption exists among us."[4]

8-2. Daniel Faour and Brothers' dry goods store, 63 Washington (Moss 1897). The store preceded the founding of the bank.

A meeting of Forzly's creditors was held on June 23, at which time George Saba was named trustee.[5] Although there is no information on whether Forzly did end up paying his creditors, in 1901 Hawaweeny was able to go ahead and purchase the cemetery land, so perhaps he did. If Forzly had embezzled the funds, his subsequent life did not reflect riches; on the contrary, he was reduced to working as a bookkeeper and a cashier for a furniture company in Brooklyn and died in 1905 at the age of 32 of "pericarditis following influenza"—or perhaps a broken heart.

[4] *Al Hoda,* June 6, 1899.
[5] "Banker's Creditors Assemble," *NYH,* June 16, 1899.

Three Maronite brothers, Daniel, George, and Dominic Faour, emigrated to Boston from Kafr Agab in 1884, first peddling Holy Land goods and later opening a dry goods store on Olive Place. The brothers went back and forth to Syria several times, taking the money they had earned back to their hometown. The three finally moved to New York in 1891, opening a dry goods store at 19 Morris and then a larger business at 63 Washington. A handsome sign on that building in English and Arabic read "D.J. Faour & Bros." They supplied peddlers' goods on credit, and it was said that they directed the peddlers whom they supplied to routes that the Faours "owned" in Easton, Scranton, and Philadelphia, Pennsylvania. The peddlers apparently lived in Faour-owned apartments in these towns, and one of the brothers would stop by on a regular basis to collect the rent and resupply the peddlers with goods.[6] They also sometimes loaned the peddlers money or arranged to have money sent to Syria for them, transactions that evolved into more formal banking.

Although they had moved around quite a lot in their early days, in 1900 the brothers signed a five-year lease for 63 Washington and started D.J. Faour & Brothers Bank; they were there to stay. In 1905 they took the plunge and bought 81–85 Washington Street for the business, and in 1914 incorporated as a private bank. At first, they kept the buildings separate, used one for their business and rented out the other two. In the trial of Elias Zreik in 1906, the building and its occupants were well described. The Faours rented all of 81 Washington to Nicola Dibs. He in turn rented out its rooms to others. On the main—or parlor—floor was a barbershop owned by Elias Daher. Across the hall from Daher was a grocery store owned by Makhoul Boutross (he also rented the basement, which served as his storeroom). Up one flight of stairs was Sardi's (Saadi's) restaurant, owned by Sarkis Saadi and Rasheed Assad. Saadi sublet two dark bedrooms behind the kitchen, one of them to Philip Lahood. Up still another flight were more bedrooms, all rented to Syrians. A common sink, no doubt filthy, sat in the hallway.

Later the bank took over all three buildings and joined them together. One article described them thus: "If you pass through Washington Street, you will no doubt notice the large beautiful building at 81, 83 and 85 Washington Street with a marble entrance and modern elevators known as the 'Faour Building.' This is just one of the many buildings belonging to Daniel Joseph Faour and his brothers, owners of a wide range of businesses and the only

[6] Naff (n.d.:15) mentions this practice.

Syrian bank in New York."[7] Since Forzly's bankruptcy, it was indeed the only Syrian bank in New York.

The Faour Bank loaned money to Syrian businesses when they needed it, but they were not do-gooders. They foreclosed on a silk mill in Hoboken, New Jersey, in 1906, which was owned by the Orayeh (Gorayeb) brothers. They then sold it to Joseph Coury, Daniel Faour's brother-in-law. There were some shady dealings, apparently, and the Orayehs felt they had been cheated; they allegedly hired seven men to murder Coury,[8] leaving a young widow and baby son. Five were put on trial; two escaped to the "mountains of Syria." Frustratingly, we do not know whether the men were found guilty.

When Daniel Faour died in 1919, his personal estate was worth $60,000, not much of a fortune compared to industrialists like B.T. Babbitt, but a sizable amount for a Syrian immigrant. One wonders though why some of the bank's assets didn't fall into his estate: in the 1922 annual report of the State Banking Authority, D.J. Faour and Brothers had assets of $694,527 (including real estate worth $278,000) and $100,000 in liabilities. The bank hit rough times during the Depression: the two remaining brothers were said to have settled all the bank's debts with their own money but were forced to close it in 1933.[9]

## Other Professionals: Doctors, Pharmacists, and Lawyers

Among the immigrants were Syrian doctors, pharmacists, and dentists who had earned medical degrees in Syria, some of whom went on to earn second degrees here. Among them were Yusef Arbeely's sons, whom we've described previously. There were several others, including the brothers Ameen and Saleem Haddad. Protestants from the town of Abeih, they both graduated from the Syrian Protestant College (SPC). Ameen received a medical degree in 1888 and immigrated that same year; he earned a second medical degree from New York University in 1889. Saleem earned a degree in pharmacy in 1890 and came in 1891. Ameen not only had a medical practice, he was also an active member of the community: he helped found the Syrian Society and its

[7] *Syrian-American Commercial Magazine*, November/December 1921: n.p.

[8] "Two Shot in Syrian War," *NYT*, January 30, 1907.

[9] "The Superintendent of Banks took possession on February 14th 1933 at the request of the bankers in order to insure the orderly liquidation of the assets, and for the protection of the interests of the depositors" (Peterson 1980: 53).

school in 1892, played a role in the New York Republican Party, and lectured widely. Not content with these accomplishments, he filed two trademarks for a line of perfume, face cream, and toilet cream in 1909, which must have been concocted by Saleem. One of the line's logos depicted Midhat Pasha and the other was trademarked "Young Lady."[10]

8-3. Saleem Haddad's drugstore, 89 Broad Street (Miller 1903).

Like most nineteenth-century druggists, Saleem was also a "soda jerker," proudly mixing up his own fresh fruit syrups and serving sodas at his pharmacy at 89 Broad, on the corner of Stone Street. A photograph of his drugstore, dating from 1903 (Figure 8-3), shows a well-arranged store with plate glass windows on both streets, the window on Broad emblazoned with the word "DRUGS," and "SODA" written on the corner pillar. Two striped awnings shade the windows. Above those, written in large letters, was "HADDAD'S PHARMACY" on the Broad Street side, and "DRUGS" on the Stone Street side. Although Saleem was one of the earliest Syrian residents of Brooklyn (he was in the 1892 census but moved to Manhattan soon after), Saleem and Ameen remained in lower Manhattan for most of their lives: they lived together at 76 Broad, near the drugstore, and Ameen had his medical offices first above the pharmacy and then at 10 Stone Street.

[10] U.S. Patent Office, *Official Gazette,* 1909: 1107.

Three Baddour brothers graduated from Syrian Protestant College before immigrating to the United States: Rasheed (Richard) Baddour earned his medical degree in 1893, and his brothers Joseph and Louis received bachelor's degrees in 1888 and 1891, respectively. Rasheed became an expert in tuberculosis, a disease prevalent in the nineteenth-century New York Syrian community, and he provided half-price consultations to his fellow Syrians. Joseph and Louis set up a drugstore at 1356 Third Avenue (77th Street), a company which survived for at least two decades. A fourth brother, Shikri, was a journalist.

Shukri Bishara Rizkallah received a medical degree from New York University in June 1892. He attended members of the Colony, including Khalil Sawabeeny after his suicide and Arteen Petrakian when he was ill. He returned to Syria permanently in 1894, when he took and passed his medical exams in Constantinople.

A doctor and a polymath, David Hassan Sleem graduated from SPC, earning a BA in 1879 and an MD in 1887. He arrived in New York in 1888 and enrolled in courses at New York University, graduating in 1889. In 1896, he earned an M.S. degree from Columbia University, based on a thesis titled "The Construction of an Electric Railroad."[11] He took out two patents, one for a moisture applicator and another for a surgical device.[12] In all his years in New York, he lived uptown on 97th Street (where he must have had his practice), and he apparently didn't mix much with the Syrian community, save for the fact that Ameen Haddad—another doctor—witnessed Sleem's naturalization in 1897. He was one of two Syrian-American members of the American Oriental Society (Nageeb Arbeely was the other), so he clearly considered himself an intellectual if not a scholar.

In the spirit of the times, one evening Sleem invited a group of scholars (including a man from the Psychical Research Institute) to his home, who among them supposedly spoke fifty languages. They were attempting to determine whether the language claimed by a spiritualist to be a communication from the dead was a genuine one, and if so, to identify it. Nageeb Arbeely attended the session and questioned the spiritualist in "modern and ancient Greek, ancient Coptic, and a choice bit of Nile boatman's patois," but her answer was unintelligible.[13] Ameen Haddad also attended, apparently to test

[11] "Columbian University," *Evening Star* (Washington, DC), June 8, 1896.

[12] Publication number US54545102A, August 27, 1895.

[13] "Spooks No Polyglots," *The New York Press*, November 24, 1892.

her Arabic. The others tried her in French, Greek, and Latin, but they finally came to the conclusion that her gibberish was due to some uncontrollable nervous trouble and was not a language at all.[14] After moving to the Alaska Territory for his health at the turn of the century, Sleem made several groundbreaking maps of parts of the Alaska Territory and died in Valdez, Alaska, in 1913 at the age of 53.

From an Orthodox family in Jdeideh Marjayoun, Rizq G. Haddad received a medical degree from SPC in 1890. He earned a second medical degree from New York University in 1901, commuting from Brooklyn to his classes. He came into his own in the "progressive" Brooklyn community of the early twentieth century, when people first began to eschew midwives and demand that "real" doctors deliver babies. He delivered my mother and all her siblings.

Dr. Abdulmassih G. Mussawir received a BA degree from SPC in 1887 and a medical degree in 1891; he emigrated immediately after graduating. A respected member of the community, his name was often mentioned as a speaker or chair of meetings; he was a keynote speaker at the opening reception for *Kawkab America* in 1892. He lived and worked at 73 Washington Street and dedicated one hour of every working day to providing free health care to needy Syrians. We don't know much about Najib G. Barbour, a doctor who immigrated in 1880, except that he was single all his life and worked out of offices at 75 Washington and 28 Rector until he moved to Brooklyn.

John Saadi, the eldest son of Elias Saadi, the Protestant minister, came to this country in 1891, eight years before his father. On the ship manifest his profession is given as optometrist. He is listed later in Brooklyn as an oculist, but also as a diamond dealer—a not uncommon combination in the nineteenth century. In 1910, he was working as a jeweler in Allentown, Pennsylvania, presumably moving there after his father's death in 1902.

The five Shibley brothers, Maronites from Beirut, and their widowed mother arrived in the 1890s from Middlesex, England (their mother was English). Disentangling them is difficult because each of them had two first names—an English one and a Syrian one. Two of the brothers—probably Ameen and Nassib—published a newspaper at the Columbian fair. Three of them—Anees, Ameen, and Samuel—claimed to be druggists; Anees was the only one who actually earned a pharmacy degree in the United States. Ameen and Anees opened a drugstore at 28 Rector Street, Anees serving as the clerk/

[14] "Her Queer Spirit Talk," *The* (NY*) Sun*, November 24, 1892.

bookkeeper. Throughout the nineteenth and twentieth centuries, the whole Shibley family lived uptown on 106th Street. After he married, Ameen and his wife, Fatneh, moved even farther north to 164th Street, yet they continued to commute all the way to the drugstore on Rector Street until Ameen's death in 1918. Their brother, Wadie, who was a doctor, died in 1901 at the age of 27.

The fifth Shibley brother, Nassib, was a lawyer. When he arrived in New York, he took a job in the law office of Charles Le Barbier, who had been the Queens district attorney. Le Barbier was the lawyer of choice for many of the wealthier Maronites confronted with tax problems in relation to their imported goods. Le Barbier went up against James W. Osborne, the Orthodox congregants' lawyer, in some of the factional battles in the Syrian Colony in 1905 and 1906. Shibley was apparently a successful lawyer (representing both "Americans" and Syrians) and became a prominent Republican speaker and organizer. He was named in a "Who's Who" of Republican leaders. He not only was a political speaker but also gave lectures around New York on the subject of Arabia.

In 1898, Shibley married an American woman named Catherine Harris, and in 1905, presumably widowed, he married again. He met his second wife in court: he defended her sister, who had been accused of killing her husband, and won her acquittal. The newly married couple moved into an apartment on Manhattan Avenue near 110th Street, and they had a son, Leo. In 1908, Nassib killed his young wife with chloroform and slashed his wrists, leaving three suicide notes, one to ask his sister-in-law (the one he had defended) to take care of Leo; a second saying that he wanted to remove his wife from temptation, to wit, her "fondness for the theatre, midnight dinners and automobile parties," and a third, addressed to one of his brothers, apologized with the words, "Oh, my people, I am the first of you—a murderer and a suicide; how the words burn! Forgive me, it was unkind."[15] Friends opined that he was distraught at his inability to support his wife in the manner she seemed to expect.

The large family of Khattar (Charles) Ferris immigrated in 1891 from Beirut. They immediately Anglicized their names, changing Faris to Ferris, and all their first names to American ones. Charles was an educated man and became a clerk in an insurance company; his son George and his grandson Joseph became well-known lawyers. Like the Shibleys, they lived outside the neighborhood, first in Astoria, Queens, and then far uptown on East 121st Street in

[15] "Kills His Wayward Wife and Himself," *NYH*, November 4, 1908.

Manhattan; they were one of the few Syrian families to own their own home at this time (1900). Despite the fact that the family seemed eager to assimilate, Joseph Ferris was deeply involved in the legal battles surrounding the question of whether Syrians were white[16] and wrote several articles for the magazine *The Syrian World* regarding this question.[17] His sister Emma, born in 1886, became a legal secretary, working first for George and then for Joseph.[18]

The priests of the Syrian Colony were all professional men, as well, but they have been described elsewhere. A number of other men took theological degrees in the United States.

## Syrian-Owned Restaurants, Boardinghouses, and Smoking Parlors

*In a number of cities, notably New York, there are Syrian restaurants which, though often apparently squalid and with very primitive service, are highly respectable.*[19]

There were twelve Syrian restaurants in lower Manhattan in the nineteenth-century Syrian Colony. The restaurants were a constant source of fascination to the American press, not just because of the men smoking *narghiles*, which were repeatedly commented on and described, but also because of the strange food. The Syrians "drop into the simple restaurant to eat dishes cooked in Oriental style and to exchange news, sip Turkish coffee, and smoke the narghile or Oriental water-pipe."[20]

The best-known Syrian-owned restaurants were Kalil's, which expanded from Cortlandt Street to Park Place in 1904; Lotfallah Atta's Turkish Coffee Room at 71 Washington; Tannous Shishim's place at 91 Washington; and Habib Hassey's restaurant at 30 Rector Street. Kalil's catered mostly to Americans while the others had mainly Syrian customers. The eldest of four brothers from Mashgara, Alexander Abukalil came to the United States in 1889. In 1891, he opened a restaurant in Ibrahim Khairallah's boardinghouse at 75 Washington. He sent for his brother Gabriel in 1892; they sold Oriental goods at the Columbia fair and continued to sell trinkets in Chicago until 1899, when Gabriel met the wealthy Buffalo "spinster" Margaretta F. Johnson. They

[16] See Gualtieri 2009 for a complete analysis of this issue.

[17] "Syrian Naturalization Question in the United States," *The Syrian World*, February 1928: 3.

[18] Arida & Andria 1930: 63.

[19] Houghton 1911: II: 654.

[20] "Poor Mustapha Arjawalli," *NYT*, July 22, 1894.

married in New York in 1904; he was twenty-nine and she was seventy-five. Her "ante-nuptial gifts" to him were valued at $90,000. "Suggestions of the employment of hypnotic or other undue influences are indignantly repelled, though it is reported that Abukalil is and has been a student of mysticism as understood in Syria."[21]

8-4. Kalil's Restaurant, 61 Cortlandt Street (Miller 1903).

Margaretta's money allowed the four Kalil brothers (two younger brothers had immigrated in 1894) to open a modest little restaurant at 61 Cortlandt Street called simply Kalil's. It was on the ground floor of a five-story tenement near the corner of Greenwich, quite removed from the Syrian neighborhood, an attempt no doubt to appeal to an American clientele. The brash lettering "RESTAURANT" takes up three-quarters of the building's front, and "Kalil's" appears in bold script on the plate-glass window. Café curtains hide the tables inside. Just down the street from their restaurant, at the southeast corner of Washington and Cortlandt, was Lipton's Hotel, where the Kalils perhaps had a second restaurant. Alexander committed sucide there in 1903.

[21] "Wealthy, She Weds Peddler," *The Syracuse Journal,* April 7, 1904.

The three remaining brothers then built a third and much larger restaurant inside an existing six-story building at 14, 16, and 18 Park Place near City Hall. Advertising postcards of Kalil's "Café and Oriental Dens," which were produced in the first decade of the century, show a cavernous dining room ("capacity 1,000") with ornate coffered ceilings, huge chandeliers, live palm trees, and Oriental décor. It was open from seven-thirty in the morning to midnight. The basement served as a lounge, off of which were four Oriental smoking dens, each decorated in its own style (Egyptian, Greek, Roman, and Moorish) and a German Rathskeller. Apparently, one could choose, too, among American, Oriental, or European cuisines.[22] One of the advertisements boasted that Kalil's was "famous for its beefsteak," and a 1906 menu from the Cortlandt Street location is strictly American.[23] The place aspired to be an upper-class establishment: Kalil's own orchestra accompanied the recorded voice of Enrico Caruso, amplified on something called the Auxetophone; concerts were presented at noon and in the evenings. Many famous people dined there over the years, both Syrians and Americans, and the Socialist Club of New York met there regularly.

Two years after their marriage, Margaretta sued Gabriel for divorce, claiming abandonment and accusing him of cheating her out of her whole fortune, $417,000 to be exact, leaving her penniless. Four full columns on the front page of the *Buffalo Courier* detailed the dastardly behavior of Abukalil: "That with persistent and continued coaxing and flattery and cajolery and with hypocrisy and trickery, said defendant deceived this plaintiff." Photographs of the two of them show a dashing young man with an extravagant pompadour and a mustache to match. She, on the other hand, is a rather handsome older woman looking decidedly unhappy. She demanded an accounting of everything he had spent and tried to put a lien on all of his property.[24] He hired James W. Osborne as his defense attorney. They finally settled the case in 1907, Gabriel returning about $150,000 to his wife but succeeding in keeping the restaurants on Park Place and Cortlandt Street. The marriage was annulled, and it was rumored that Gabriel was already engaged to a pretty blonde woman living in Philadelphia. He indeed married her, and they had a son.

The Kalils (as they now called themselves) scattered in the first decade of

[22] "An Elegant Restaurant," *Wall Street Daily News,* June 8, 1905.

[23] http://menus.nypl.org/menu_pages/40324.

[24] "Young Husband Stole Fortune," *Buffalo* (NY) *Courier,* January 20, 1906.

the twentieth century: Gabriel to Philadelphia, Shikri to Brooklyn, and Said to Cranford, New Jersey. They continued to run their restaurants in Manhattan, however. Said opened another Kalil's at 558 Broadway in 1908; now each of the brothers had his own restaurant. The place on Broadway closed sometime in the twenties, while the restaurant on Park Place lasted well into the forties.

Another well-known restaurateur was Lotfallah Atta. Atta had spent his first half-dozen years in the United States based in Nashville, Tennessee, performing all over the United States with Buffalo Bill's Wild West show as a wrestler and strong man. He moved to New York in about 1894 and first opened a restaurant/boardinghouse with Elias Zreik and George Shawi at 57 Washington Street. He then took over an already existing restaurant/boardinghouse at Number 71, belonging to Rasheed Safi, leaving Shawi to run the restaurant at 57. He went on to open a restaurant at 89 Washington; his partner, unusually enough, was a woman, Rufika Jabaly, who may have also been his wife. She must have done thc cooking while Shawi ran the front of the house. This partnership lasted until at least 1910.[25]

Safi, who sold Atta the restaurant at Number 71, had had an earlier restaurant at 75 Washington. Paul Hakim took over the restaurant at 75 in 1894. We know very little about Hakim, but presumably he was an early-arriving member of a family that immigrated from Aleppo in 1898 and 1899. A sketch of the restaurant in an 1894 article shows a Syrian waiter—or Hakim himself—at the arched doorway watching a young man in a fez and smart overcoat leaving,[26] and a famous illustration in *Harper's Weekly* shows it as well.[27]

At Number 71, Atta went into partnership with Wadie Mejdelani, but Mejdelani may have been a silent partner, as he was not often mentioned in newspaper articles. Like many of the Syrian restaurants, Atta's was part of a boardinghouse. Atta was apparently a constant presence at the restaurant and an impressive one: he was over six feet tall and weighed 200 pounds; his head, it was said, nearly brushed the low ceiling of his restaurant. A reporter who wrote about him said, "When a Syrian of any class is handsome he is apt to be exceedingly handsome." The same reporter claimed that Atta spoke no English and didn't need to, as only Syrians frequented his restaurant.[28]

[25] Her name, however, is not in the *Syrian Business Directory* of 1908–1909; only Shawi is listed.
[26] "Red Fezzed Heads; Languorous Eyes," *NYH,* November 11, 1894.
[27] "The Foreign Element in New York, " *Harper's Weekly,* August 10, 1895.
[28] Cromwell Childe, "New York's Syrian Quarter," *NYT,* August 20, 1899.

8-5. Interior, Lotfalla Atta's restaurant, 71 Washington Street (Childe, *NYT*, 1899).

The restaurant was on the parlor floor a half-story above the street. The former gracefully arched entrance of the Federal townhouse had been converted to a dark rectangular entrance that gave onto a foyer, with the stairway straight ahead and the door to the restaurant on the right. The entrance to a basement store had been carved out of the facade under the restaurant. The two original windows on the main floor had been enlarged to allow more light into the restaurant; the former front parlor was the restaurant, and the back room had been turned into the kitchen.

The walls of Atta's restaurant, according to one reporter, were decorated with gaudy wallpaper, a lithograph of the sultan, and displays of guns, pistols, swords, and daggers. At a counter near the door, Atta sold pipes, tobacco, and cigarettes and kept his *narghile*s there when they were not in use. He supposedly imported his own coffee and roasted and ground it himself to make sure it was right; his waiter, Yusef, made each pot under Atta's watchful eye.[29] The reporter indicated that the décor and menu were designed to appeal to members of the Colony. It is true that the menu was strictly Syrian, featuring stuffed squash, grape leaves, okra, mutton, fried eggplant, yogurt, and *kibbeh*

[29] "In a Syrian Coffee House," *Dallas Morning News,* January 22, 1899.

(ground lamb with cracked wheat); each dish cost ten cents.[30] A reporter in 1896 claimed that Atta had a small fountain in the center of the restaurant to "remind his countrymen somewhat of home." A sketch of the restaurant accompanying the article shows a cheerful man in a fez smoking a *narghile* that sits on the rim of the fountain, and standing next to him is a man—presumably Atta—in a Turkish robe. Another man relaxes by the pot-bellied stove reading *Kawkab America* (the Arabic of the title is well-reproduced in the sketch).[31] If there had been a fountain, nothing remained of it in 1899, when the *New York Times* article appeared.

8-6. Men smoking *narghile*s and drinking *'araq* at Atta's restaurant (Childe, *NYT,* 1899).

The photograph in the article shows nothing in the way of Oriental décor except for a man in shirtsleeves and fez sitting with two other men, all seriously addressing their food. The waiter (Yusef?), who is in shirtsleeves and wearing a long apron, brings a plate of food, topped with a Syrian loaf, to the table. Syrian bread was much commented on, reporters likening it to a huge piecrust. At a table in the back, next to the curtained kitchen entrance, are two other men, one sporting a luxuriant mustache and a straw boater.[32]

---

[30] Cromwell Childe, "New York's Syrian Quarter," *NYT,* August 20, 1899.
[31] "Thousands Inhabit the Turkish Quarter, but Not a Single Turk," *New York Press*, December 27, 1896.
[32] Cromwell Childe, "New York's Syrian Quarter," *NYT,* August 20, 1899.

Habib Hassey immigrated from Zahleh in 1893 with his young son Farid. On a trip back from Syria two years later, the ship manifest lists his profession as "saloon keeper," because he had already opened his restaurant in a small three-story building at 30 Rector Street, which was squeezed between two large buildings facing, respectively, Washington and West streets. Like Kalil's, it was a street-level storefront with a tenement above, but much more modest than Kalil's. "H. Hassey's—30—Restaurant" is printed on the plate glass window. The entrance appears as a black hole and is completely unadorned. One reporter called this restaurant the principal Arab café of the quarter,[33] and Miller called it "The Best Native Restaurant of the Syrian Quarter."[34] Ameen Shibley's Soda Fountain/Drug Store is visible next door at Number 28, complete with extravagant awning.

8-7. Hassey's Restaurant, 30 Rector Street (Miller 1903).

In the 1900 census, Nicholas and Maria Fayad (father and daughter) lived with Hassey upstairs at 30 Rector and were, respectively, cook and dishwasher in the restaurant. Under the column heading, "relationship to head of the family" (i.e., Habib Hassey), they are listed as servants, but they may also have

[33] "Syrian Slums Are Interesting," *The* (NY) *Sunday Telegraph,* May 21, 1899.
[34] Miller 1903: 32.

been relatives. In that same year, *Harper's Weekly* showed "Habib Assi, the Syrian Chef" in an illustration for an article about foreign food in New York. He is shown in a white apron and chef's hat, looking quite proud and jolly, standing next to a man in a bowler hat smoking a *narghile*.[35]

8-8. Restaurant owner, Habib Hassey, with a customer smoking *narghile* (*Harper's Weekly*, 1900).

Hassey's wife, Rosa, arrived in 1903 and bore him a daughter in 1904, but none of the family appears with him in the 1910 census, where he was still listed as restaurateur; did the wife and children return to Syria? As Habib was only 42 years old at the time, he must have had many more years of life and work ahead of him, but our knowledge of him ends there. Did he return to Zahleh and rejoin his family, his fortune made?

As noted, many of these restaurants were also boardinghouses: food downstairs, rooms upstairs. The boarders ate alongside the public. One man who lived behind Saadi's restaurant at 81 Washington said it best, "Because I used to sleep there of course I had to eat there."[36] Sometimes the hotel and restaurant belonged to one person (or partnership), and sometimes they were under separate management.

Habeeb Daoud, his daughter Sophie, and his son-in-law Tannous Shishim immigrated from Zahleh in 1889. They first lived together at 71 Washington (all three were presumably peddling), but the two men opened a boardinghouse at 91 Washington in 1893. They claimed it was the oldest boardinghouse in the Colony. Shishim was at first the junior partner, but when Daoud left New York and went to Texas (perhaps when his daughter and Shishim

[35] http://exhibitions.nypl.org/immigrantcity/node/2.
[36] *Trials,* People v. Zreik, 1906: #599, 564.

separated), he left Shishim as sole proprietor. In Moss's 1897 photo, Shishim's has a rather Oriental look to it, with a square bay protruding over the cellar entrance, covered with some kind of a metal grill, which resembles the wooden *mashrabieh* on Egyptian houses. Through the grill you can just make out the tables and chairs in the former parlor. Shishim eventually began to call himself a restaurant keeper rather than a boardinghouse owner, and he may have turned over the running of the hotel to a relative, Assad Shishim. Sometime after 1905, he bought a restaurant on Coney Island, leaving Manhattan—and the life of a hotelier—behind.

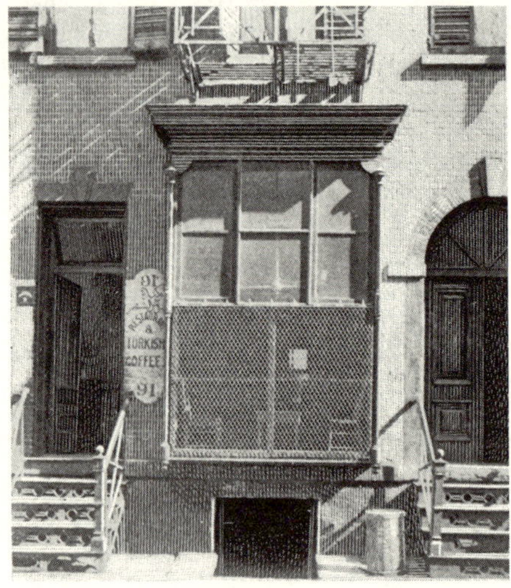


8-9. Tannous Shishim's restaurant, coffee house, and boarding house, 91 Washington Street (Moss 1897).

After arriving in 1889 from Zahleh, the same year as Habeeb Daoud,[37] Muossa Daoud lodged at 122 Washington while he apparently peddled, although Younis suggests that he was working in the brickyards of Dutchess Junction.[38] In 1892, he opened a variety store at 111½ Washington. He established his first boardinghouse and dry goods supply at 17 Rector Street in 1895; he found it advantageous to meet people at the Barge Office or Ellis

[37] Were they relatives or even brothers? It is not clear. They never lived together nor were they associated in any business.

[38] The brickyards in Dutchess County, New York, had a significant Syrian workforce. H.H. Jessup wrote that Daoud was "in the brickyards," and Daoud spoke authoritatively about them.

Island, help them through immigration, and encourage them to stay at his place. He also bragged that it was these same people to whom he gave dry goods on "credit of three, four, five, and six years."[39] His name was one of those that immigrants used as a reference when coming to New York, whether they knew him or not. In the 1900 census, after he started renting out rooms at 96 Greenwich, he was listed as a "dealer in shells," shorthand perhaps for the notions business to which the peddlers boarding at his place were no doubt tied. In 1903, Daoud moved to 67 Washington; he continued to rent out rooms but apparently gave up dry goods and became a real estate and steamship ticket agent. In the 1910 census, there were thirteen boarders at Number 67, but only five of them were Syrians, including Daoud and his sister Heilani. Two of the boarders were Oriental goods peddlers, so perhaps he was still a supplier despite his work in real estate and ticketing. He lived there until 1932, when he moved to 30 Greenwich, where he rented a room for twenty dollars a month; in 1940, he was working as a "helper" in a cotton house. He was seventy-two.[40]

Any moderately ambitious merchant could rent a floor or two of a tenement and re-rent to his fellow citizens, so there were several other boardinghouses in the Colony. One, Abdallah Hamati's at 71 Washington, was the site of Lotfallah Atta's restaurant. Abraham Rihbany mentions staying at a place belonging to Ibrahim Khairallah at 75 Washington in 1891.[41] Maroon Fagher, who was a notions dealer, also took in boarders at 5 Carlisle Street, but we don't know if there was an in-house restaurant. Moses Abboud's boardinghouse at 96 Washington had, in the 1900 and 1905 censuses, over 60 boarders, of whom only a few were Syrian, which makes one wonder whether he actually ran the house or only sublet one floor or even one room. As at other boardinghouses, the professions of the residents were of the simplest kind: washerwoman, peddler, longshoreman, and the like; they were housing for the poor. Even Fares and Abdow Rihani, dry goods merchants, rented out rooms to other Syrians at 81 Washington Street. In October 1897, Fares sued Boutros Oraya (Gorayeb) for nonpayment of $63 in rent.[42]

---

[39] "Moussa *[sic]* Daoud Their Leader," *NYT,* June 4, 1894.

[40] Younis (1995:136) asserted that he was Jewish ("Moses David"). He claimed, however, to have attended a Catholic high school in Syria, and if he was related to Habeeb Daoud, he was certainly Maronite. Younis (*ibid.*) also has him moving to Staten Island, but the censuses are clear: he lived in Manhattan all his life.

[41] Rihbany 1914: 194.

[42] *Trials,* Fares Rihani v. Boutros Oraya, 1897: O-61.

Although boardinghouses often doubled as brothels in nineteenth-century New York, there is no evidence that this was the case in the Colony. In fact, the very crowded conditions of these houses, the fact that Syrian women and men lived at close quarters, and their placement right in the middle of a conservative Syrian community, probably militated against any such use. They were certainly insalubrious, as described above. The Syrian entrepreneurs benefited from fitting as many people as possible into those tight spaces.

There were several Syrian-owned café/pool halls in the community, one at 57 Washington Street, whose owner we don't know, one at 63 Washington, owned by Aziello(?) Shohfi, and a third at an unknown address (2½ Carlisle?). There is a photograph of the last in an 1899 *New York Times* article: "Pool Room" is written above the doorway, which is a few steps below street level, and "Coffee" is written above the street level entrance, but we don't know if these were separate establishments or who owned them.[43] In the 1899 article, children are gathered in front of the pool hall to take advantage of an ice cream pushcart, and a fruit vender has his stand to the right of the door. In 1903 the spot was again chosen for a photograph of Syrian children,[44] so perhaps the connotation of a pool hall as slightly disreputable was not shared by the community.

There were a number of Syrian-owned "Turkish Smoking Parlors" aimed at American customers, in contrast to the Syrian cafés, where Syrian men gathered to smoke, play backgammon, chat, or have a meal, and which were not called smoking parlors. These smoking parlors were first seen at the 1876 Centennial Exposition in Philadelphia, where the American public was reportedly introduced to hashish.[45] The same was true at the Columbian Exposition of 1893, and reporters commented on the long lines waiting to get into these parlors. Turkish smoking parlors became a craze in the nineteenth century; it is said there were 500 in New York City alone. If true, they were more ubiquitous than Starbucks. Many of them opened in the Tenderloin—on the west side around 29th Street—in 1895.

---

[43] Cromwell Childe, "New York's Syrian Quarter," *NYT,* August 20, 1899.

[44] "Children of Lebanon in Gotham," *NYH,* March 29, 1903.

[45] In an 1895 article, a New York City reporter claimed that in the Syrian Quarter, hashish was taken as a paste: "In the Syrian and Turkish colonies of the city hasheesh is prepared in the form of a confection by working the pure extract into fig paste or nougat. The resulting mixture is almost black in color, of a strong narcotic odor and of a peculiar, yet, in small quantities not altogether disagreeable taste. This paste, or one similarly made with equal parts of opium and hemp, is the hasheesh of the east. In Turkey it is frequently served as the closing course of a repast." "Hasheesh," *Plain Dealer* (Cleveland, OH), March 24, 1895.

8-10. Portrait of Joseph Oussani, 1896, when he was the proprietor of the Cairo Café (courtesy of Gail O'Keefe Edson).

The first of these parlors was Joseph and Yak Oussani's "Oriental Hall" at 29th and Broadway, opened in late 1894. The Oussanis had been at the Columbia fair and must have taken the idea of the smoking parlor from its success there, and if, as I've surmised, they were involved in selling Turkish tobacco at the fair, it is likely that they did business with the smoking parlors. They were astute marketers. The press at first called the Oussanis's place a "Ladies' Smoke Room," because the brothers opened it with the express intention of accustoming Americans (both men and women) to women smoking in public. As one of the brothers said, "Why should they be ashamed?"[46] Reporters described the parlor as being furnished with divans, inlaid tables, and Oriental draperies, with scimitars adorning the walls. It soon began attracting the after-theater crowd, who all came to smoke and drink Turkish coffee or Persian tea until the early hours of the morning. An illustration shows two well-dressed women lounging on a divan smoking cigarettes. If the sketch is an accurate portrayal, it must have been amazing for these Victorian women to lounge in public, much less smoke.[47]

[46] "The Ladies' Smoke Room: Where Up to Date Women Enjoy the Delights of Tobacco," *The* (NY) *World,* December 16, 1894.
[47] Ike Swift, "Sketches of Gay New York, No. 10: In the Tenderloin," *National Police Gazette,* May 20, 1899.

The Cairo Café as it was called (capitalizing on the attraction of the same name at the Columbia fair) was a success from the first day, attracting the "swells" of New York, and dozens of similar establishments opened up over the next six months. The Oussani brothers themselves immediately opened a second place around the corner from the first called the Chibouk.[48]

The backlash to the Café's sudden popularity was intense and vitriolic. One writer reported gleefully on the tendency for young drunken louts to come into the Cairo Café, abuse the "Turcos" who ran the place, and try to start fights with the "Bedouin" bouncer.[49] The six sub-headlines describe his overwrought view of the place:

Picturesque Groups and Fighting Talk in the Rooms of the Men from Bagdad
Many Dainty Smokers Seen
A Fashionable Crush Early, and Later Young Men Who Talk Defiance
Gamblers Also Numerous
Turks Have a King of Clubs of Their Own Now and Breathe Slaughter

Although the reporter explicitly said that the men were drunk when they arrived, others accused the Oussanis of selling liquor illegally. "The so-called Turkish smoking parlors that now cast their seductive influences around the gay amusement seekers of the city are merely new covers for old vices," one reporter declared.[50] He decried the effort to make them respectable places for women. Instead, he wrote, "Men without character or reputation and women without continence or shame occupy the lounges, smoke the hubble-bubble and sip the black coffee, with half an inch of sediment in the bottom of each small cup,"[51] as if the sediment itself were a sin.

Stories of fights, drunkenness, and questionable women sullied the establishment's reputation. The brothers, in a paid article in *Kawkab America*, tried to deflect their critics by describing their clientele as "people of good taste who enjoy our Oriental customs and entertainment." They claimed that newspaper editors, actors, actresses, lawyers, and other important people frequented their cafés. They suggested that the "Orientals" of the city, rather than being ashamed, should be proud of the places and talk them

[48] A *chibouk* is a long-stemmed Oriental pipe.
[49] "New York's New Smoking Fad," *NYH,* April 28, 1895.
[50] "Only a Cover for Vice," *The* (NY) *Press,* April 13, 1895.
[51] "Only a Cover for Vice," *The* (NY) *Press,* April 13, 1895.

up to all and sundry.[52] And certainly the sketch of the café in the 1895 article cited above shows a rather conventional Victorian interior, with men in top hats and women in evening gowns sitting upright, enjoying their *narghiles*, *chibouks*, and cigarettes.[53] But Turkish smoking parlors quickly became equated with vice, if only because women first learned to smoke in public in them.

By 1899, the Cairo Café had acquired an even more questionable reputation. Here are excerpts from a national newspaper's full-page article about the Tenderloin district of New York:

> It is in the Tenderloin where the Turkish smoking parlor flourishes; where the Cairo café does a big business after midnight and where a hundred and one attractions from the Orient may be seen without the aid of a man with a lantern....
> To his ["the big Persian who runs the place"] keen eye, woman, radiant with diamonds, sheathed in silk of the latest style, is queen of the universe. He knows these Tenderloin women. He knows they are extravagant and whimsical. He knows they must spend money—when they have it, and he knows they are always with the kind of men who have money.
> So you see, he smiles.
> He sells them imported cigarettes with gold tips and charges them ten times what they are worth, and he serves them with a black liquid he calls café noir, and which he swears by all the gods he ever knew came direct from the private plantation of the Sultan of Turkey.
> He sells them gilt trinkets of Oriental design, and he conducts them to cosy nooks where they may talk away to their hearts content.
> In the language of the Tenderloin he is a "wise guy" and he gets the money.[54]

The Oussanis had a man and woman in the front window of the Chibouk rolling cigarettes to bring in the crowds, and bring in the crowds they did. One can see how the two Oussani businesses—tobacco and the smoking parlors—supported each other. A half-column article describing the pleasures of the Chibouk noted: "To visit the 'Chibouk' is the latest fad of men about town and women of the 'half world.'... Several young women were sitting about the room on the heavy plush couches. Boyish looking gentlemen" were playing the nickel slots. When Oussani tried to close the place at 2 A.M. the

[52] *Kawkab America,* October 4, 1895.
[53] "New York's New Smoking Fad," *NYH,* April 28, 1895.
[54] Ike Swift, "Sketches of Gay New York, No 10: In the Tenderloin," *National Police Gazette* 74: May 24, 1899.

gamblers rebelled (having steadily lost their nickels) and proceeded to wreck the place.[55]

Four months later, Joseph Oussani was arrested. A number of American women and men and three Syrians were arrested with him. At first the charge was selling hashish. According to news accounts, one of the Americans arrested claimed to have bought hashish at a restaurant at 45 Washington Street and brought it up to Joseph.[56] All were discharged except for Joseph and the three Syrian men, who were released on bail. A seventeen-year-old boy who had gone there frequently testified that he had seen "lewd women and effeminate young men" in the place, as well as women dancing on the tables. He averred that women "whom he knew to be prostitutes" had spoken to him.[57] The makeup of the people arrested does suggest that it was a brothel as well as a smoking parlor. Only Oussani and the Syrian men were held for trial. The hashish charge was dismissed, but they went on trial for running a disorderly house (a brothel). An employee, Maggie Shay (Shea) testified she had never seen any disorderly acts or people in the place.[58] Joseph was acquitted and married Maggie Shay the following year.

The Cairo Café was raided again in 1900 and Joseph Oussani's now-wife, Margaret (no longer referred to as Maggie), was fined $1,670 for serving liquor without a license. Why she was arrested rather than Joseph is not clear. This raid was part of a larger operation that aimed to expose the corruption of the New York police department. Many cafés, smoking parlors, and brothels were caught up in the sweep, but nothing seems to have changed, either in the nightlife of the Tenderloin or the ease with which the proprietors got away with breaking the law.

The Oussanis' original goal—to make it acceptable for women to smoke in public—was quickly overtaken by the proliferation of "Turkish smoking parlors" providing hashish and/or opium,[59] liquor, and prostitutes. Most were probably owned by "Americans," as alluded to in the article which stated, "As for the Turks, most of them are as English as can be,"[60] but the Cairo Café remained the best known, for good or ill. In 1896, Stephen Crane wrote a

[55] "They Wrecked the 'Chibouk,'" *NYH,* March 22, 1895.
[56] We know of no Syrians living or working at Number 45 in 1895.
[57] "Scenes at the 'Chibouk,'" *Evening Telegram* (NY), July 10, 1895.
[58] "Scenes at the 'Chibouk,'" *Evening Telegram* (NY), July 10, 1895.
[59] "Were these [cigarettes] analyzed more opium than tobacco would be found in them." *Omaha World Herald,* July 3, 1895.
[60] "Only a Cover for Vice," *The* (NY) *Press,* April 13, 1895.

6 THE NATIONAL POLICE GAZETTE: NEW YORK.

SKETCHES OF GAY NEW YORK

WRITTEN SPECIALLY FOR THE POLICE GAZETTE.

No. 10. IN THE TENDERLOIN.

There will be more about the New York Tenderloin next week. It is one of the greatest places in the world, and Ike Swift writes from personal observation.

"JOE" OTT.

[WITH PORTRAIT.]

Do you want a sporting gallery absolutely free of cost? Then take the POLICE GAZETTE regularly, and have the supplements which are the most valuable ever published.

HORSES PLUNGE INTO OLD OCEAN.

JOHN J. GABAY.

TEMPTER OF EVE IN THE FLOWERS.

WOMAN AND HER LOVERS

AMATEUR AND PROFESSIONAL

TENDERLOIN STORIES WILL BE CONTINUED NEXT WEEK...DON'T FAIL TO READ THEM

8-11. "Sketches of Gay New York," about the Cairo Café, 1899.

series of articles for William Randolph Hearst's *Journal* called "The Tenderloin as It Really Is." His "research" began at the Cairo Café, where he "met with two chorus girls…and the three of them headed for another brothel on Thirty-first Street."[61]

A few other smoking parlors were owned by Syrians, including some (described in chapter 10) that were owned by women. Theodore Roosevelt had just taken over as New York City chief of police and was beginning to make his mark on the "Island of Vice"[62] when the police raided a Turkish smoking parlor run by Abraham Ashe, located at 86 Fourth Avenue (at 11th Street). "The parlor was fitted up like a Turkish resort, with hanging rugs, divans,

[61] Pizzitola 2002: 21; "Defended by Novelist Crane," *The* (NY) *Evening Telegraph,* October 16, 1896.

[62] Zacks 2012.

and Oriental tables." The police told the magistrate that women and men frequented the parlor, implying that it too was a brothel. The police arrested five women and three men, along with the proprietor and his helper Charlie Feurres. Abraham Ashie was a respectable Maronite family man from Baabda, living with a wife and three children on Morris Street, and Charles Ferris—could it really be the same man?—was a clerk and the father of the lawyer-to-be George W. Ferris. Ashie and Feurres were each held on $1,000 bail. One woman and two men were discharged, and the others were fined ten dollars each.[63] This is what Houghton meant when she stated that most of the less respectable establishments catered not to Syrians, but to Americans, as they were located not in the Syrian neighborhood but "on the east side."[64] The only other smoking parlor that may have been owned by a Syrian was the "El Mansoura" on 29th Street. The owner claimed that it was the "only true Oriental smoking parlor in America," whatever that may have meant.

Coney Island, like the Tenderloin, had a salacious reputation, and the Syrians seemed to be enthusiastic participants, as proprietors, employees, and customers. Several Syrian families lived in Coney Island and worked at the Syrian-owned Turkish smoking parlors and other enterprises there. George Jabour's Turkish theater and his Turkish smoking parlor were two of the most notorious. His establishment figured in numerous lawsuits, police raids, and scandals.

In an article about Coney Island, with the sub-headline "Expect to Be Cheated," a reporter asserts,

> The Turkish smoking parlors are misnamed with respect to every word that their name contains. They are not conducted by Turks at all, but by Syrians. The proportion of smoking to drinking that is carried on in them is precious small, and no place could look more like a dive and less like a parlor. The little tobacco that is consumed in them is grown anywhere but in Turkey, and usually in Connecticut. However, it is rolled into cigarettes that are manufactured by a firm which proclaims itself to be purveyors to the Sultan, and this is enough to make it of a delicious flavor. The women who frequent them have a smack of the Bowery rather than of Constantinople, and nearly all of them are disarmingly free of any foreign accent.[65]

[63] "Turkish Parlor Raided," *The* (NY) *Evening World,* July 12, 1895.

[64] Houghton 1911: II: 654.

[65] *BDE,* August 5, 1900: 15.

Again, the presence of women who "smack of the Bowery" suggests that these were brothels as well.

Another article reported, "Three men, representing the Law Enforcement Society, called upon the Mayor to address the alleged wickedness prevailing at Coney Island." One of the men described "several extremely noxious spots at the beach, among them the Turkish smoking parlors, where from the outside men can be seen sitting on the divans hugging the women in full view of the public."[66] Whatever the euphemism "hugging" conveyed, it was not good. Reporting on the same case before the district attorney, the *Brooklyn Daily Eagle* said, "The beach could be relied upon to provoke nothing but an exceedingly bad attack of nausea. It was degraded by the coochee coochee [dance] and demoralized by the Turkish smoking parlor." The editorial suggested there was a difference between liberty and license, and that Coney Island had "become rank and smell[s] to heaven."[67] Later that year, the police acted. They arrested forty fortune tellers and two "coochee-coochee" dancers, one of whom was Fatima, the supposed wife of George Jabour, who was performing at his Turkish theater on Tilyou's Walk. When Jabour, Fatima, and the other dancer, "La Belle Rosa," pleaded with the judge to allow the Turkish theater to remain open for the rest of the season, the judge agreed, stipulating, however, that no further dancing should be performed.[68] When Jabour asked if he could present "living pictures" (scantily dressed women or women wearing flesh-colored body stockings posing as statues), the judge replied, "If you attempt to put on any living pictures or allow any dancing whatever to take place, I will close your show without a moment's notice."[69]

Other crimes that occurred in Syrian-owned establishments on Coney Island were perpetrated against other Syrians and brought to the attention of the authorities. The proprietor of a Turkish café on Sea Beach Walk stabbed a young Syrian woman who worked for him as a waitress. The man, whose name was variously given as Nazaab Farino and Nazaad Sarisa, and the waitress, Nazira Joseph, apparently quarreled over fifty cents.[70] The girl ran out and fainted on the street, and he ran after her. A crowd gathered, and several

[66] "Coney Island Wickedness," *The* (NY) *Sun*, June 22, 1897.
[67] "The Coney Island Crusade," *BDE,* July 1, 1897.
[68] "Purging Coney Island," *BDE,* August 18, 1897. The numerous controversies about belly dancing are discussed in more detail in chapter 10.
[69] "Purging Coney Island," *BDE,* August 18, 1897.
[70] "Stabbed for Fifty Cents," *BDE,* July 2, 1899.

people called for him to be lynched. He was saved by a group of Syrians, but taken by the police to the Coney Island jail.[71]

A Syrian man from Montreal was drugged and robbed in the Cairo Café in Coney Island in 1900.[72] An 1898 story told about a certain Syrian named David Bacalamie (Bellamah?) who robbed Fatima Ben Solomon of $135; she was a belly dancer in a show at Coney Island. Bacalamie was caught trying to escape on the steamer *Bretagne*.[73]

In 1899, George Jabour opened a third establishment, a Turkish smoking parlor called the Kairo Café, at 9–11 Myrtle Avenue, Brooklyn. His flyer announced that there would be Oriental beauties present, which acted as a red flag to the police. When a policeman looked in the window just before it opened, he found the furniture to be similar to that of "Raines law hotels" (i.e., bars and brothels).[74] What could such furniture look like? Were there beds? In any case, the police let the place open but warned Jabour that they would be watching him, both for the illegal sale of liquor and for the Oriental beauties. Jabour, who owned the place on Coney Island and this new establishment, went on to found a traveling circus. He was also the publisher of *Al Alam*, the pro-Turkish newspaper. He was certainly a man of parts.

Once again, in 1900, this time in the name of health reform, the sanitary inspector closed down several resorts on Coney Island, including George Jabour's two venues.[75] When nothing changed, the police closed down all the Coney Island establishments at midnight on a Saturday night and then forced the people in the streets to go home. There was "considerable grumbling among the keepers of the places of amusement"; one of whom was heard to say, "We will have to get a license to live, next."[76]

---

[71] "Crowd Saw Girl Stabbed 11 Times," *The New York Press*, July 2, 1899.

[72] "Syrian Drugged and Robbed," *NYT*, September 16, 1900.

[73] "Steamer Searched for Syrian Thief," (NY) *Evening Telegram*, August 13, 1898.

[74] "Jabour's Smoking Parlor," *BDE*, November 13, 1899.

[75] "Reform at Coney Island," *NYT*, August 4, 1900.

[76] "Quiet at Coney Island," *New-York Tribune*, May 26, 1902.

## Entertainers and Lecturers

*All you have to say is that you are a poor persecuted Christian from the Holy Land and the gold will flow in a rapid stream into both your hands.*[77]

One of the most interesting professions taken up by Arabic-speaking immigrants—both men and women—was that of entertainer. Women entertainers will be described fully in chapter 10. Arab entertainers had been touring the United States since at least the early 1850s, most of them North African. In 1863, the Ali Ben Abdallah troupe landed in New York and performed in a tent set up in Brooklyn. The troupe exhibited feats of strength, swordplay, gymnastics, and equestrian stunts.[78]

Directly after the Philadelphia fair of 1876, a certain Professor James Rosedale of Jerusalem began to bring over groups of performers from the Holy Land, including Selim Hashmi, the "first discoverer of Livingstone, a Reed Player and Bedouin Dancer, Khawadja Yakoob [El Bahzoozie], Sword Dancer, a Whirling Dervish of Baghdad, and Rebeca Bendevi, Native of Jerusalem," who was a dancer. The show offered the public "living illustrations of life in the Orient."[79] They performed a Bedouin wedding ceremony, complete with a feast of chicken, bread, and other "substantial things," and reenacted a Bedouin highway robbery and a Mohammedan at prayer. The players showed a Turkish court in Palestine in which the judges were both bribed. The reporter did not believe that these people were chiefs or Bedouins, but was convinced that they were genuine Arabs and that "they portray truthfully the remarkable customs of their country."[80] They were in fact "genuine" Arabs, but this kind of pseudo-ethnographic mumbo jumbo, combined with blatant exoticism, was a direct offshoot of the way the world's fairs approached the display of the "other." In 1883, two members of his troupe sued Rosedale for cheating them each out of $100.[81]

P.T. Barnum was advertising Arab performers in New York as early as 1884, in "the greatest assembly of curious human beings ever seen together on earth"; in 1885, they appeared again in a "Vast Ethnological Congress of

[77] *Presbyterian Letters*, Harris, August 1893.
[78] Advertisement, *New-York Tribune,* August 28, 1863.
[79] Advertisement, *Repository (*Canton, OH), January 6, 1881.
[80] "Odd Sights in Brooklyn, A Howling Dervish in Mr. Beecher's Pulpit," *NYT,* December 11, 1880.
[81] "Defrauding Arabs," *Truth* (NY), April 20, 1883.

Strange and Heathen Tribes."[82] The Moroccan troupe was under the management of Abdallah Ben Said; when they performed at Madison Square Garden, their athletic achievements "evoked much applause."[83] The troupe's leader was accidentally shot by one of his co-performers a couple of months later when they were practicing sharp shooting for the Buffalo Bill show.

Tony Pastor's Theater on 14th Street advertised "The Whirlwinds of the Desert, just arrived from Cairo, Egypt. Hadj Tahar and Hassin Ben Ali with their troupe of 20 genuine Moorish and Bedouin Arabs in a realistic picture of the East: A Moorish School in Suez, Africa, introducing Moorish Customs, Sports, Games, Dances and Wonderful Tumbling, Leaps, Vaulting, Musket Drill."[84] Hassan Ben Ali and a group of Moroccan entertainers performed a Moroccan wedding at New York's Park Theater in 1893. The groom was called "Abd-el Hassan" and the bride was "Lala Ro-Kia," a name borrowed from Thomas Moore's Orientalist fantasy of 1817. Ben Ali "officiated." There were fifty "Moors" in attendance, an impressively large company.

Elias M. Malluk, a Syrian, brought over a troupe of thirteen Turkish "howling dervishes"[85] and thirteen Egyptian jugglers in 1892, anticipating the Chicago fair by a year. They performed for 500 people at Madison Square Garden, and at one point one of them supposedly bit off the head of a snake.[86] They were apparently not a success, and shortly after, they began to complain that Malluk had not paid them. They were living ten to a room in lodgings on East 26th Street and had no money and no way to get home. They processed in full costume to the office of the mayor to ask for help and then appealed to the superintendent of immigration. Both refused them, the superintendent saying they were able-bodied men and should work for their passage home.[87] We do not know their fate. Malluk had by this time already settled down in New York, filed his first naturalization papers, and become an importer, apparently washing his hands of his poor charges.

Then the Columbian fair happened. Hundreds of Middle Easterners trekked to Chicago. Every one of them could be called an entertainer, whether they were serving Turkish coffee, appearing in native costume, acting as

[82] Advertisement, *NYH,* March 29, 1885.
[83] "Barnum Overjoyed," *NYT,* April 2, 1886.
[84] Advertisement, *NYH,* October 5, 1890.
[85] Perhaps the reporter meant whirling dervishes, or perhaps these men performed some more exotic act.
[86] "Dervishes Dine on Snakes," *NYH,* August 6, 1892.
[87] "Dervishes Seek Succor," *NYH,* September 10, 1892.

donkey boys or camel drivers on the Street of Cairo, or actually performing in the pageants and theaters.

A photographic essay of the ethnic types appearing at the fair included, and made a clear distinction between, "Arabs" (Bedouins), "Turks," Moorish people, Persians, and Egyptians. But one occasionally sees the same individual dressed in different costumes, so these distinctions were slippery, if not meaningless. The only Middle Easterners not often pictured were Syrians; they were simply not exotic enough, and mostly they were managers, not participants. If we can believe *Kawkab America*'s assertion, many of the Syrians at the fair were already living here, and thus too westernized to be pictured as the exotic "other." The only obvious Syrians in the photographs were the "Europeanized Turks" who are pictured lounging on a stack of carpets looking quite dapper in their robes, European suit jackets, and *fezzes*. They are shown with three "Asiatic Turks" to contrast these "two closely associated people," but probably all were Syrian (Figure 5-6). The Syrians at the fair were running the concessions, not performing in them. They knew how lucrative it was to dress up for the American public, but they usually dressed others, not themselves.

Those men and women who came specifically for the fair went on to dominate the world of Arab entertainment in the United States and Europe; others continued a career that had only been enhanced by their appearance at the fair. The demand for these entertainers was almost continuous over the final decade of the nineteenth century; they performed in numerous traveling shows (such as Wild Bill Hickok's), circuses, minstrel shows, vaudeville acts, world's fairs, and finally the amusement parks that sprang up all over the country. They fanned out across the United States, and many came to New York under the aegis of their Syrian or North African managers, or were taken up by American impresarios.

Almost two dozen Moroccans (or North Africans) had been and continued to be the most prominent performers. Many of them listed their profession as "acrobat," "showman," "performer," "actor," and "camel rider" on various documents.[88] The nature of their work demanded that they be on the road constantly, but New York, as it does today, boasted a huge number of theaters, which were an attraction. Judging by the names of the troupes, it seems that even as early as 1860, these North African troupes were put together and managed by North African impresarios. They would hire an American agent to book the theaters or the show, but it seems that the North Africans

[88] "An Arab Troupe in Town," *BDE*, April 27, 1893.

were in charge. Of these managers, three lived more or less permanently in New York: Hajji Tahar, Abdullah Ben Said, and Hassan Ben Ali.

Tahar was the manager of a troupe that performed all over the United States; a criminal trial described more fully below gives us some insight into the inner workings of the troupe. At the time of the trial (1900), the troupe was performing at Koster & Bial's theater in New York and living in Tahar's quarters at 108 Eighth Avenue (at 15th Street). Whether they were paying Tahar for their beds was not stated. None of those living with him were Arabs (they were Filipino, American, and English), but all had what Tahar must have thought the Americans would think were Arabic-sounding (or at least exotic) stage names: the two English acrobats, for example, were called "Barodi" and "Targula." Other members of the troupe (who were not living with Tahar at the time) seemed to be a mixture of North Africans and Americans.

Tahar had three rooms: two sleeping rooms and a kitchen. He kept the trunks of costumes in the kitchen, and the trunks doubled as beds for the Filipino performers. The two English boys slept in one room (in one bed), and Tahar slept in the other room, apparently with one or another of the female members of the troupe (never mind that Tahar had a wife and new baby living nearby). Another Filipino actor and a North African performer named Hajji Hammed lived in another part of the same building, obviously part of Tahar's troupe. Tahar employed an agent named Howard F. Jones, who booked their act around New York and elsewhere. It seems that the composition of the troupe was quite fluid; people came and went as Tahar or they saw fit; and each new booking demanded novelties that Tahar had to provide by hiring new performers, if necessary, or retraining the ones already with him.

Another entertainer from Morocco, Hassan Ben Ali, who had been performing around the United States in the 1880s, went back to Morocco to prepare for the Columbian Exposition and took with him a telephone, a battery, and a phonograph, all of which he reportedly demonstrated to the sultan of Morocco.[89] He had gone, he said, to collect Moroccan dwarfs for the fair and was determined to bring back a complete village to reconstruct in Chicago. While there, the sultan awarded him a horse and a title, which he boasted of in a letter to Nageeb Arbeely, the editor of *Kawkab America*. Arbeely duly re-

[89] "A Telephone and a Phonograph for Suz," *New-York Tribune*, November 22, 1891; *Kawkab America*, April 29, 1892.

ported it.[90] Arbeely was apparently partners with Ben Ali in his Columbia fair venture because it was Arbeely who went to Chicago in 1892 trying to obtain permission to show these North African wonders to the American public. Ben Ali was even planning a reenactment of the violent capture of Africans by Arab slavers. When he and his retinue met President Harrison in 1892 on their return from Morocco, "the whole party threw themselves prostrate on the floor and remained there, refusing to be seated."[91]

Both before and after the Columbian fair, Ben Ali traveled widely with his troupe but was often performing in New York. In 1893, his twelve-member Royal Moorish Troupe was at Proctor's with their acrobats, contortionists, and gun spinners,[92] and in 1894, they were performing at Koster & Bial's.[93] Ben Ali's advertisements always trumpeted the fact that he worked with no agents or managers, and that theaters should deal directly with him. In 1899, he brought over a group of Moroccan immigrants to join his company and brought them before a New York judge to be naturalized. Ben Ali was later sued by two of these performers for back pay and was forced to pay them each $260.[94] The "Hassan Ben Ali Arabs Co." moved to Coney Island around the turn of the century but continued to play on vaudeville stages well into the twentieth century, even after Ben Ali's death in 1914.

These troupes were also hired by the new amusement park at Coney Island, particularly the Streets of Cairo, modeled directly on the similarly-named attraction in Chicago. Victor Roditti employed seventy-eight people in the summer at the Streets of Cairo concession. Some of them he brought from North Africa, while others he "picked up here and there." They were musicians, dancers, camel drivers, and "Nubian giants." Abdallah Ben Said and Hassan Ben Ali were leaders of the troupe. One of the camel drivers, Salam Ben Salah, was charged with grand larceny for the theft of some of the attraction's costumes, including embroidered vests. The owner of the vests, Murdoch Zletoors (Srour?) swore out the complaint.[95] The Syrian Elias Zreik, of whom we will hear more below, was also a camel driver at Coney Island, as was Elias Trad, who worked in George Jabour's establishment there. The famous camel, Holy Moses, who had performed at the Columbian fair,

---

[90] *Kawkab America,* March 5, 1892.
[91] *NYH,* May 12, 1892.
[92] Advertisement, *NYH,* April 16, 1893.
[93] "Variety, Music and Beasts," *New-York Tribune,* October 17, 1894.
[94] "Arab Whirlers in Court," *NYH,* March 25, 1899.
[95] "A Former Coney Island Employee in Trouble," *BDE,* November 29, 1896.

unfortunately had to be shot at the end of one summer because of some skin disease; his loss, it was said, left the camel drivers bereft.[96]

Though Arabic speaking, the Moroccans didn't live in the Syrian Colony, but were scattered from 30th Street to Greenwich Village—or lived in the Coney Island concession. Abdullah Ben Said, although at first on 29th Street, by 1900 had settled down among the Syrians in South Ferry, Brooklyn, and become a theatrical manager. They were probably the only Arabic-speaking Muslims in New York at this time. Several of these showmen married "American" women, became citizens, and settled down in the United States.

Some of the Moroccans, rather than manage their own troupes, joined Al G. Field's minstrel show. Field was a well-known producer of black minstrel shows, but he would occasionally build shows around exotic themes. The poster for the show (dated about 1900) depicts acrobats making a human pyramid, sheikhs in turbans with daggers tucked into their belts, and a background image of the Great Sphinx. Their names as listed on the poster were Sheik Hadji, Turan-Sha, Sheger-ed-Durr, and the like.

The editor of *Kawkab America* had this to say about these Arab troupes: "There are several supposed, or so called Arab troupes travelling in this country; but, we know only of two who could lay claim to being genuine, Sie Hassan Ben Ali's and that of Hajji Tahar Ben Mohammed."[97] It is unclear what was genuine about these performances since acrobatics, pyramids, and displays of strength were certainly not limited to Arab performers. It may simply have been their origins that made them genuine. A North African performer and impresario named Hadji Cheriff, who settled in New York and plays a part in this narrative, is shown in a short Edison film. Dressed in exotic costume, he cartwheels and jumps and whirls in Edison's Black Mariah studio.[98] Except for the clothes, nothing he is doing is particularly "Arab."

Although North Africans dominated this field, some Syrians also performed in these spectacles. Elias Zreik, who lived in New York, was said to have been a "strong man" in Buffalo Bill's Wild West Show—he was allegedly almost seven feet tall and was called "Big Mike" by some of the other Syrians of the Colony—but by the time he got to Coney Island, he was simply a camel driver. He had begun to build his image as soon as he arrived in New York. A full-page illustrated article, titled "NEW YORK SYRIAN WHO

[96] "Coney Island Turks," *BDE,* January 24, 1897.

[97] "Sie Hassan Ben Ali," *Kawkab America* (English), November 4, 1892.

[98] http://www.criticalcommons.org/Members/kfortmueller/clips/hadj-cheriff-18943 . Accessed February 16, 2015.

THE WORLD: SUNDAY, OCTOBER 16, 1898.

NEW YORK SYRIAN WHO KILLED 200 TURKS TO SAVE HIS FAMILY FROM MASSACRE.

ZRIEK, GIANT OF LEBANON, TELLS HIS THRILLING STORY OF TURKISH HORRORS—FOUGHT THE SULTAN'S SOLDIERS FROM HIS BOYHOOD.

ELIAS ZREIK

SAW FOUR SUNS IN THE SKY.

8-12. Illustrated article about Elias Zreik, 1898.

KILLED 200 TURKS," detailed his heroic exploits, calling him the "Giant of Lebanon." It seems he defended his village single-handedly from a horde of well-armed Turks. A portrait of Zreik in an oval frame in the article shows him in a Greek-style cap, sporting a very large bushy moustache, and holding a rifle. He was billed as a speaker, along with Nageeb Arbeely, at the Syrian-American Club's meeting at the Hotel Grutil on Greenwich Street, where he talked about his victories over the Turks (one wonders if the Syrians were as gullible as the American reporter).[99] Five years later another long article appeared, relating once again his exploits in breathless prose and including a photograph of him sitting in a chair staring defiantly at the camera, with his legs arrogantly thrown open, two swords tucked into his sash, and a third held like a walking stick in his left hand.[100] He looked formidable.

[99] *The World* (NY), October 16, 1898.
[100] "Last of the Zoreiks," *The* (NY) *Sun,* October 18, 1903.

Lotfallah Atta, the owner of a restaurant at 71 Washington, had achieved notoriety by holding twelve men aloft in the Buffalo Bill show.[101] Isaac Monyaco (Munyer), an Egyptian (but possibly of Syrian descent) was in "show business" in Coney Island. George Jabour, a merchant, owner of a newspaper, and entrepreneur, ran an establishment at Coney Island and another in Brooklyn that featured belly dancers, one of whom was said to be his wife. An article on the first page of an 1894 issue of *Kawkab America* featured a certain Salim Nasser from Shweir, who was a strong man in Buffalo Bill's Wild West Show. He could carry fifteen people on his shoulders in a human pyramid; there was a sketch of him in the newspaper, a very handsome man in Oriental garb.[102]

One didn't necessarily have to have experience to get work as a performer. A classified ad in the *New York Herald* in 1893 advertised, "WANTED—15 Syrian boys. Apply at stage door. Casino, Broadway and 39th st. 10 a.m. today."[103] The Syrian boys were perhaps being recruited for the comic opera "The Rainmaker of Syria," which opened on September 25, 1893. None of the main actors were Syrian, of course, but it did have a chorus of sixty. It was not a hit.

In 1897, in a typical example of Middle Easterners exploiting their successes at the fair, another "Moslem" wedding took place in Joseph Oussani's Cairo Café on West Twenty-ninth Street; it was either a put-up job to get free publicity for the café or a bit of theater designed to bring in tourists—or both. It was of a piece with the Oriental entertainments popular at the fair and was similar to the wedding performed by Ben Ali's troupe at a New York theater in 1893. One "Moulla Hashem," who was also a member of the orchestra, united "Ayesha" and "Mohammet Ali" in matrimony. "When Oussani was asked whether it was a genuine [wedding], he swore by the beard of the Prophet that it was as genuine as they have anywhere."[104] Of course, Oussani was a Christian, so swearing by the beard of the Prophet probably did not mean much to him.

The flamboyant "Arabian" entertainments in the circuses, theaters, and vaudeville houses give off a whiff of farce, not just in the blatant hucksterism of owners like P.T. Barnum, but also from the point of view of the performers

---

101 "Fought in a Tenement," *NYH,* May 1, 1897.

102 *Kawkab America,* September 21, 1894.

103 Advertisement, *NYH,* September 21, 1893.

104 "Wedding by Moslem Rites," *NYT,* March 24, 1897.

themselves. One cannot help but think how often and how much they must have laughed at their own bogus depictions of the exotic east, the look of wonder on the faces of the audience, and the money that these suckers were willing to spend to see them.

In more refined venues, Oriental entertainers performed at charity events, providing employment for professionals or amateurs who were willing to dress up. Sometimes the American women sponsoring the event would dress up as Arabs themselves and serve Oriental pastries, but often they would hire Syrians for authenticity. A charity tea given by society ladies in 1897 for the benefit of a tenement house had an Egyptian theme. Two performers, Ben Shawy and Abdo Himmam, who had appeared at the Columbian fair, sang Egyptian songs in their native costumes "with sword accompaniments."[105] Nadjim Merhige and his wife put on "A Syrian Wedding" at the First Presbyterian Church to raise money for the *New-York Tribune*'s Fresh Air Fund.[106] American commercial establishments also used Orientalism to sell goods: the New York department store John Wanamaker opened "A Corner from the Purple East" in 1899 and hired a Syrian band (a real one), craftsmen working in silver filigree and making slippers, and someone to serve Turkish coffee at all hours.[107]

Even more refined than these entertainments were the lectures about the Holy Land or the Arab East given by Syrian men and women who traveled the country. This followed a long tradition of American missionaries who would come back from their time abroad and give lectures about life in the Holy Land. But now the Syrians themselves were doing it, and it seemed that almost everyone did it at one time or another, even those who were already merchants in New York. Some of the Syrians used the church as their entrée, some used prominent residents of a town, but all sought to project the highest respectability and refinement. To bring in funds they either charged admission or brought along Oriental goods to sell at the end of the lecture or performance.

Yusef Arbeely traveled around with his sons giving talks on the customs of the Orient beginning as early as 1881, less than three years after arriving. At first the lectures were similar to those lectures given by returning missionaries: they were serious and earnest, aimed at educating the audience about the

---

105 "Twinkles," *New-York Daily Tribune*, April 18, 1897.

106 *New-York Daily Tribune*, February 1, 1898.

107 Advertisement, *NYH,* January 12, 1899.

Middle East. "Nayeeb *[sic]*, Yusif and Habeeb Arbeely, members of the only Syrian family in America, will by request appear in their native costumes to address the people of Washington on the mission work and religions of Palestine."[108] Nageeb was twenty-two and Habeeb was nineteen. Soon the presentations became more dramatic than educational, although they were still expected to have a gloss of ethnographic authenticity, which was later exploited to such marvelous effect at the Chicago World's Fair. The thrill of the exotic was something the Syrians cultivated much like their vaudeville brothers.

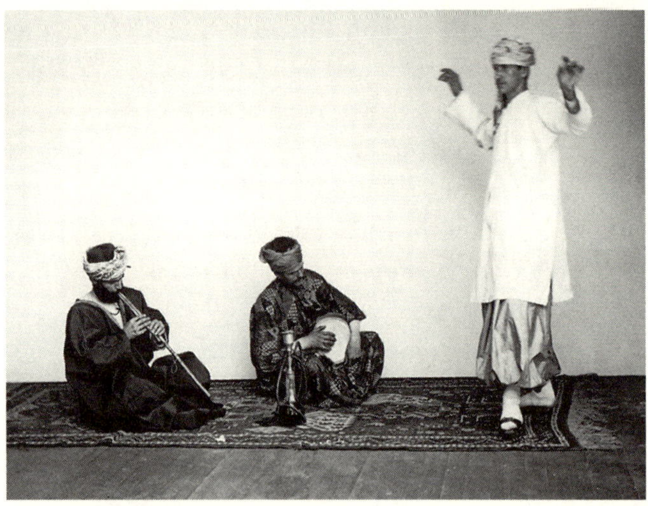

8-13. Three Arbeely brothers (from left, Nageeb, Habeeb(?), and Fadlallah(?)) demonstrating Arab dance, ca. 1885 (National Anthropological Archives of the Smithsonian Institution).

At an event in Washington, DC, put on by the Woman's Foreign Missionary Society, the Arbeely family presented "An Evening in the Holy Land." They were dressed in native costumes, performed the Mohammedan sword dance, and reenacted a Muslim marriage ceremony (Figure 8-14). Admission was twenty-five cents. Arbeely established his bona fides by carrying with him references from the well-known missionaries H.H. Jessup and C.C. Van Dyke, and from Horace Maynard, the U.S. minister to Turkey.[109] Given Yusef's position of responsibility at the Patriarchal College in Beirut, there is little doubt that he knew these men.

[108] Classified Advertisement, *Evening Star* (Washington, DC), July 7; 1883; July 14, 1883.

[109] Advertisement, *Evening Star* (Washington, DC), March 25, 1885.

A Syrian from Antioch, Ezekiel Taminosian, traveled around with a troupe of performers demonstrating Syrian nuptials, sword fighting, native songs and dances, and juggling.[110] A sketch of him shows a picturesquely attired Eastern grandee with a beautiful mustache, deep-set eyes, and a faraway gaze. His story, as told to a reporter, sounds unlikely in the extreme—travel from his native Antioch to Jerusalem, Constantinople, Smyrna, "darkest Africa," and Malta, where he caught ship to Liverpool and, finally, got himself on a ship going to New York. He earned enough money to enroll at Northwestern University in 1882 or 1883.[111]

Ameen Rihani and Ameen Haddad both lectured in New York and elsewhere on various topics related to the Middle East. Abraham Rihbany also went on the lecture circuit throughout the Midwest in the 1890s. When he left New York to begin his tour in 1893, he says, he was given a supply of silk goods on credit to sell on his travels. He is one of the few Syrians to admit to having absolutely no head for business and hating the idea of buying and selling.[112] It is a tribute to his skills as a lecturer and sermonizer and to the incredible generosity of the people he encountered in the Midwest, then, that he was able to become, with no college degree, no theological training, and imperfect English, a full-time minister in America. In 1900, he shocked his followers by withdrawing from his position as minister of a Congregational Church in Michigan, giving as his reason that he no longer believed in the divinity of Christ.[113]

Another nationwide lecturer was Asad Rustum, the son of Mikhail Rustum, who authored the 1895 book *Stranger in the West.* Asad was called the "Syrian boy preacher" because he began traveling the church circuit at the age of seventeen along with his sister Effie, who was thirteen; he preached and she sang. Like the others, he also lectured on the customs of the Orient, dressed up in costume, and performed "wedding and funeral ceremonies of the natives."[114] He later became an author like his father and settled down in New Jersey.

Several members of the Presbyterian Moghabghab family from Ain Zehalta joined the lecture circuit in the nineteenth century. Presenting themselves

[110] "Oriental Entertainment," *St. Louis Republic,* December 9, 1888; "A Syrian Visitor," *St. Louis Republic,* December 11, 1888.

[111] "He Is a Christian Dervish," *The* (NY) *Sun,* April 22, 1894.

[112] Rihbany 1914: 248.

[113] "A Syrian Is to Rewrite Bible," *Buffalo Evening News,* September 14, 1900.

[114] "Returns from the Holy Land," *Daily Telegram* (Adrian, MI), April 6, 1893.

as "native missionaries," Saleem and Kaleel Moghabghab and their wives, Najla and Nabeeha Moutran, traveled the country appearing in the "costumes of the Druses and Mohammedans."[115] Since admission was free they must have been selling Oriental goods after the lecture or collecting donations. They made several countrywide circuits, lecturing wherever they found a suitable venue. Kaleel died in Colorado in 1892; we don't know what happened to his wife. Saleem and Najla eventually returned to New York; he opened a dry goods business and she became the well-known women's fashion retailer, "Mme. S. Moghabghab," with stores in Miami, Atlantic City, and New Hampshire, as well as a pillar of the New York Syrian Colony.

Two other Moghabghab brothers, Faddoul and Naoum, came to the United States in 1892 to attend the Columbian fair. Naoum graduated in the first class of the Syrian Protestant College in 1870, Faddoul in 1886. Because of his apparently excellent English, Naoum served as a guide and translator for tourists at the fair. After the fair, both began traveling around the country, Faddoul in the northeast and Naoum in the south. Styling himself "reverend," Faddoul was known for his interpretation of the Twenty-third Psalm, which he based on his supposed experience as a shepherd in the Holy Land. According to his own reckoning, by 1907 he had given more than five hundred lectures on the subject.[116] William Allen Knight immortalized his message in the book, *The Song of Our Syrian Guest.*[117]

Another well-known itinerant preacher and lecturer was Anton Fares Behannesey, who wrote and put on Oriental plays, which were performed by local residents. The players got to wear the costumes he brought with him, and he attracted a wide audience. One day, Behannesey disappeared; people feared him kidnapped. Because he was so well known, the story appeared in dozens of newspapers throughout the country. A year later, when he returned to the United States, he claimed he had indeed been abducted and taken by force to Beirut by his uncle, who was angry at Behannesey's conversion to Protestantism. He announced to his fans that he had escaped and was on his way back to Chicago.[118]

Nageeb Arbeely—editor of *Kawkab America*, immigration official and interpreter at Ellis Island, ex-consul general to Jerusalem, and son of the

[115] "Day's Diary," *Aspen* (CO) *Daily Chronicle*, October 13, 1891.

[116] Moghabghab 1907: 7.

[117] Knight 1904. Moghabghab sued Knight for using his name and his stories without permission but lost the case.

[118] "The Abduction of a Syrian," *BDE,* August 11, 1892.

8-14. Faddoul Moghabghab as a Syrian shepherd and an American citizen, ca. 1906 (Moghabghab 1907).

illustrious first immigrant—was much in demand, both by reporters who sought his opinion on many topics related to the Syrians, as well as by audiences in New York. He also gave talks illustrating the customs of the Holy Land. At an anniversary affair for the New York Shriners, Mecca Temple, in Madison Square, Arbeely reported that one hundred New York Syrians performed for an audience of 15,000. He first gave a lecture, and then his troupe performed a Muslim's preparation for prayer, a Bedouin marriage, a sword fight, and concluded with a performance of howling dervishes.[119] Who in the Syrian community consented to play a howling dervish? One Syrian man who wore the "short skirt dress of his country *[sic]*, gave a short impromptu skirt dance [?] and was recalled three times."[120] Were these performers paid? Did they sell goods? Coudsy and Andalaft set up a display of Oriental goods at this event, and perhaps they gave a cut to the troupe. Arbeely did make gentle fun of the Shriners for whom they performed by observing that the "red fezzes [worn by the Shriners] were as perplexing to the Orientals on the platform as the costumes of these were interesting and novel to those whom they faced."[121] But the Shriners bought many column inches of advertising in *Kawkab America*, so, if for no other reason, Arbeely

[119] "Entertained by Arabs," *NYH,* January 14, 1893; *Kawkab America,* January 19, 1894.
[120] "Entertained by Arabs," *NYH,* January 14, 1893.
[121] "An Oriental Entertainment for the Mystic Shriners," *Kawkab America* (English), January 20, 1893.

had an obligation to entertain them. Arbeely's tone in reporting this event in the newspaper seems to be one of pride: that the Syrians' performance was attended by so many people and that there were important people in the audience ("mayors, judges, government officials"), all of whom came to see Nageeb and his fellow Syrians perform.[122]

What were the feelings of these performers toward their audiences and toward themselves dressed up in these "Mohammedan" costumes? As with the previously mentioned Moroccan circus acts, one wonders how seriously these Syrians took the work. The fact that these Christians (Protestants and Orthodox for the most part) could, with straight faces, depict "a Moslem's preparation for prayer" taxes the imagination. Did they really have in mind educating the American people? Was it pure showmanship? Or was it simply a relatively painless way of earning a living? One can only imagine that it was a complicated convergence of all these motives and feelings residing in the breasts of the men and women performers.

To end this section on "Oriental" entertainers, I must report the sad story of a group of poor Syrians who ended up as a kind of freak show in Bunnell's Dime Museum in the Bowery. Some seventy-five performers came as a group. According to Jessup,[123] most were Maronites who arrived with the intention of begging, a rather blatant case of religious stereotyping. One Elias Nicola, who was a Protestant from Hesbaya, had been "imposed on and fleeced everywhere," and thus worthy of Jessup's sympathy. In the American newspaper accounts the troupe's story was embellished by their daring escape from Alexandria during the massacres of 1882. They had ostensibly supplied themselves with a stock of goods from relatives in Jerusalem, but they were robbed on the way and landed at Castle Garden penniless,[124] a story that has the whiff of fable about it. Nicola (and the others) ended up at Bunnell's pretending to be "wily Arab[s] or cannibal[s]." They were paid a few cents a day and given only enough food to keep them alive. Jessup thought the whole group, save Nicola, should be sent back for being paupers.[125] The group's fate is unknown.

[122] *Kawkab America,* January 19, 1894.

[123] *Presbyterian Letters,* H.H. Jessup to Ellinwood, February 11, 1884.

[124] "Refugee Arabs," *Truth* (NY), February 8, 1884.

[125] *Presbyterian Letters,* H.H. Jessup to Ellinwood, February 6, 1884.

## Leisure: The Syrians Entertain One Another

We do not know very much about how the nineteenth-century Colonists spent their leisure time. American newspapers reported endlessly on Syrians sitting in cafés drinking coffee, playing backgammon, or chatting. The Arabic papers took leisure-time behavior for granted and didn't write about it. Sundays, especially, were no doubt a time when they rested, either sitting under Babbitt's awning, strolling in Battery Park, or visiting one another.

On the opposite end of the entertainment spectrum from the "playing east" described above was a performance of Euripides' *Andromache*, given in Arabic by members of the Syrian Young Men's Association and open to the public. The performance was given at the Chickering Theater at 5th Avenue and 18th Street, which seated 1,247 people; we don't know how many actually attended. The proceeds were to benefit the poor of the Syrian Colony. Ameen Rihani played Orestes; George Jabour was Pylades, N. Kazma took the role of Pyrrhus, T. Farah played Hermione, and Elias el Hajj played Andromache.[126] Men played all of the roles, a fact archly commented on by American newspaper reporters. Ameen Rihani had been a member of a traveling theater company in his youth and had played in *Hamlet* and other plays before the company went bankrupt, forcing him to return home. One imagines that the impetus for this performance came from him, and it seems likely that he did the translation into Arabic. The company planned to present *Hamlet* in English in the future, and it was reported that el Hajj had written a play titled *Princess Najla*, which he hoped would be performed by men *and* women.[127] Although American reporters attended the performance, the fact that it was in Arabic is a clear sign that it was aimed at Syrians.

A few other examples of Syrians entertaining their own (as opposed to performing for Americans) were reported in *Kawkab America*; one article described a musical entertainment evening held at Rasheed Safi's boardinghouse at 75 Washington Street. Two Syrian musicians (Daoud Geagea and Namer Abu Saleh) played music while four other men performed sword dances, acrobatics, and stick dancing. Although this troupe was apparently professional (it appeared regularly in American theaters), the fact that they performed in a local boardinghouse implies that this time their performance was meant for

[126] "Andromache in Arabic," *The* (NY) *Sun,* March 15, 1896.
[127] "Shy Syrian Women," *The New Haven* (CT) *Evening Register,* April 23, 1896.

other members of the Colony.[128] The newspaper noted that Americans did attend. *Kawkab America* mentions several other musical evenings as well, at the homes of the Tadross Brothers, Abdow Lutfy, and others, giving the impression of a community that took some pleasure in its leisure time. One week, *Kawkab America* reported, there were four such parties; at one of them, women were present "in the American fashion."[129] Community members played the 'oud, there was dancing, and men recited poetry, either their own or that of others. These parties were informal events and differed from the meetings and commemorative gatherings already described, which inevitably featured speeches by prominent (male) members of the community.

Not to be forgotten was the poetry composed and publicly performed (or printed) for every occasion: weddings, birthdays, baptisms, and public holidays. The Syrians recited poems extemporaneously at weddings or printed celebratory or laudatory poems in the newspapers. Everyone, it seems, was a poet—or at least every male. Asad Rustum, a poet himself, listed eight men who wrote poetic eulogies when Yusef Arbeely died.[130]

We know too that Battery Park was a place where adults and children spent much leisure time. The Trinity Church assessment of 1913 noted that Syrian children regularly used Battery Park as a playground,[131] and we have cited examples of men who would become lyrical when describing the Park. We have almost no information on whether the youngsters played sports or entertained themselves the way most slum kids did, with stickball and other games. There is a photograph in the Library of Congress of Syrian boys on Washington Street playing marbles, with a young girl who has charge of her little sister and brother in their stroller, looking on.[132]

Two Mallouf brothers—Nasseem and Najeeb—present a striking anomaly; they are the only nineteenth-century Syrians who were serious sports figures. Most new immigrants were too busy striving to "play" at sports. Their mother, Hannah, was probably Selma Gobreen's sister, whom Jessup described scathingly as a woman who left Syria in 1887 with "men of disreputable character," and who was raising money under "false pretenses." Like so many others, she was selling goods under the guise of missionary work in Boston and New York. In the 1890's Hannah traveled from resort hotel to resort

[128] *Kawkab America*, July 22, 1892.
[129] *Kawkab America,* November 25, 1892.
[130] Rustum 1895: 167.
[131] Trinity Church Men's Committee 1914: 30.
[132] Library of Congress, Bain Collection, LOT 10832-3.

hotel, often being listed as a guest, even though she must have been a "lady of the road," selling goods to other guests. Her husband, as we know from Jessup's letter, she had left at home.[133]

Both boys were accomplished athletes at the boarding schools they attended, particularly the elder brother, Nasseem. He won his first medal for field sports in 1897 at the Rugby Academy in Manhattan. He went on to St. Paul's School in Garden City, Long Island, where he became a serious golfer. Najeeb followed suit. They both won dozens of tournaments while at St. Paul's; Nasseem, however, was much the better player. Najeeb, for his part, won highest honors at St. Paul's for overall achievement. For a woman alone to be able to pay tuition for two boys at two private schools, as well as their travel expenses and entry fees to dozens of golf tournaments, means she either made a substantial living selling at the resort watering holes, or she came to the United States with a fortune. Nasseem went on to play golf for Cornell (newspapers referred to him as "the well known Cornell crack"), but he dropped out before graduation to marry a local girl. The brothers' athletic careers seemed to fade at about the same time, 1905, and they went on to rather lackluster careers in New York City: Nat, as Nasseem called himself, eventually worked his way up to become the owner of a small trucking company, while Najeeb, who changed his name to Edward, worked as a salesman in a movie distribution company.

[133] *Presbyterian Letters*, HH Jessup to Mitchell, September 25, 1887.

# Chapter 9

## The Arabic Press in New York

*It* [the Arabic press in New York] *has helped plant the love of America in the hearts of millions of peoples speaking the common Arabic language....*[1]

*Journalists found no better way to make a living, sell, and prosper than to air sectarian feelings among their readers and pose as champions of religious solidarities in their own sects.*[2]

Those Syrians who were literate when they arrived but unable or unwilling to go into trade sometimes had a hard time of it. A rather moving work-wanted advertisement published in 1891 encapsulates for me the difficulties that educated Syrians encountered in trying to find work if they could not or chose not to peddle or start their own businesses: "A Syrian graduate of an American college at home, 27 years old, speaking Arabic, English and a little French, desires a position as clerk, or as assistant bookkeeper, in any store anywhere; best of reference as to honesty. 27 Washington st."[3] This unidentified man was living in one of the most crowded, insalubrious tenements in the Colony. Abraham Rihbany, whose autobiography describes his desperation in trying to find work when he landed in New York with nine cents in his pocket, could easily have inserted this ad. He thought he would rather die than peddle. He became a bookkeeper (and was paid twenty dollars per month, less than a quarter of what a peddler could make in those days, and about the same as a silk worker) and then was hired as the second Arabic editor of *Kawkab America* (at $40 per month plus a bed at the newspaper's office) before leaving on his travels around America finally to become a minister.[4] When Michael Shadid first arrived in New York, he too tried to turn his literacy and knowledge of English into work, applying for jobs as a clerk

[1] Mokarzel 1927: 6.
[2] Naimy 1985: 15.
[3] *NYH,* April 1, 1891.
[4] Rihbany 1914.

or bookkeeper. But he was unsuccessful, he says, because there was so much competition, and he finally fell back on peddling, as did so many others.[5]

Many of these educated Syrians cobbled together a living by having many lines of work. Nageeb Arbeely, who had served as U.S. consul in Jerusalem, was an interpreter at Ellis Island, newspaper editor/publisher, notary public, print shop owner, lecturer, broker for concessions at the world's fairs, and dry goods merchant. My great-uncle Asad Milkie emigrated in 1888 from Bishmezzine and must have had a missionary education, as did his sisters, my grandmother and great-aunts; all could read and write at least some English and Arabic when they arrived. He had literary aspirations, however, as his sisters did not (or if they did, how would we know?). He was listed in the 1890 Police Census at 95 Washington. In his 1895 naturalization papers he called himself a clerk, but in the same year he is listed as a printer in a city directory. He cobbled together a living writing for a number of Arabic newspapers both here and abroad. He made several submissions to *Kawkab America* as well as to *Al Hoda* (being Orthodox did not prevent him from being a regular contributor). Was he or any writer paid for these essays? Both *Kawkab America* and *Al Hoda* referred to their correspondents as journalists, but whether these men were employed or paid at all for their work is unclear. Milkie also wrote regularly for the Egyptian daily *Al Ahram.* In 1904, he founded and edited a newspaper with Najeeb Badran, called *Ad Daleel* (The Directory), which lasted for about five years. Milkie must have been the compositor/printer as well.

Despite this rather checkered career, Milkie was apparently respected in the community, as every "literary" man was; when *Al Hoda* celebrated its twenty-fifth anniversary in 1923, he was one of the speakers at the event. Being respected, however, did not translate into wealth. To supplement his income, he sold eczema ointment, which he advertised in *Al Hoda*; it wouldn't be surprising if he were an agent for other products as well. The women in his family seem to have been the breadwinners; his daughters, sisters, and probably his wife and mother all worked, while he wrote and his only son invented things.

Syrian printing shops were mostly adjuncts of the newspapers; they produced posters, handbills, books, cartes de visite, and anything else that was wanted. The Oriental Press was advertised in every single issue of *Kawkab America*. *Al Hoda* also had its own printing arm. Both the el Hajj brothers—

[5] Shadid 1939.

Yusef and Elias—were printers, compositors, and writers. Two Syrian brothers, Nicola and Abraham Macksoud, set up a printer's shop with an American partner at 30 Sullivan Street in 1902.

The Arabic-language press played a vital part in the early Syrian community, serving as a literary outlet for educated men (and a few women), mouthpieces for different political factions, and unifier of the Arabic-speaking diaspora, and not just in New York. American Arabic newspapers were sent abroad—to Europe, South America, Australia, and the Ottoman Empire—and Arabic newspapers from the Middle East came to the United States. Those printed here served to inform other Syrians of the great attractions of the United States, because every newspaper was pro-American. Dissenting voices were sometimes given space in the papers, and occasionally the editors themselves were these voices, but in the main, the newspapers (and other printed material) showered unstinting praise on America and Americans.

There were an astonishing forty-four Arabic-language publications conceived in New York during the period 1892–1930, eleven in the nineteenth century. Some were nonstarters or very short lived, but some survived well into the twentieth century. This number does not compare to the one hundred Yiddish newspapers published in New York between 1885 and 1900,[6] but for the much newer and smaller Syrian community, it was an achievement. As Melki (1972) and others have pointed out, putting out an Arabic newspaper in the United States was a laborious process: Arabic type had to be imported, there were more than 100 forms of the letters that had to be set by hand, and compositors were difficult to find. Occasionally one sees in the early issues paragraphs printed backward or upside down, letters missing or wrongly written, and misspellings. It is surprising that these errors did not occur more often. Reports that Arabic type had to be smuggled in when the Ottoman government put restrictions on its export may also have been true, making the appearance of new Arabic-language newspapers at this time even more remarkable.[7] The linotype machine was not used until 1912, when Salloum Mokarzel adapted it for Arabic.[8]

Most of the newspapers assumed the confessional stance of their owners: *Kawkab America*, for example, was Greek Orthodox, as was *Mira'at al-Gharb*

[6] Epstein 2007: 222.

[7] "Syrian Clamor for Arabic Type," *The Sunday Telegraph* (NY), July 2, 1899.

[8] Mokarzel 1927: 11.

(Mirror of the West); *Al Hoda* was Maronite. The quotation at the beginning of this chapter expresses a narrow, if common, view of the newspapers of the period. The newspapers also reflected their owners' attitudes toward social and political issues in the Ottoman Empire, attitudes that were only roughly aligned with their religious affiliation. They also were uniformly pro-business and pro-American, regardless of their religious or political views, albeit with some misgivings about the American way of life. To their own question, "Did Emigration Benefit the Syrians?" the editors of *Kawkab America* responded with a resounding "Yes."[9]

Issues of only two nineteenth-century Arabic-language newspapers—*Kawkab America* and *Al Hoda*—are extant; early issues of the other papers have disappeared. Information about the others comes mostly from contemporary news articles in the American press.[10]

## Kawkab America

Founded by Abraham and Nageeb Arbeely, two of Yusef's six sons, and Arteen Petrakian in March 1892, the first issue of *Kawkab America* appeared on April 15. Petrakian and Nageeb had met at the Barge Office on the day Petrakian arrived. Abraham was the senior editor, but Nageeb and Petrakian did the work of putting out the paper. It had the distinction of being the first Arabic-language newspaper in the United States, with headquarters on the fourth (and top) floor of 45 Pearl Street (near Broad), quite removed from the neighborhood. Its mission statement, printed in English in the inaugural issue, was stated as: "An Oriental Weekly devoted to the development of direct helpful relations and good understanding between the East and the West."[11] Its mission in Arabic was quite different: to connect the Ottoman diaspora around the world, and to publish literary essays, news, and advice, as well as to develop good relationships with businessmen, in order to raise the status of Syrians among foreigners.[12] The Arabic description of the paper, "a political, scientific, and literary newspaper," appeared on the masthead in every issue. The English page of the second issue featured a story about "KawKab

[9] *Kawkab America*, June 17, 1892.

[10] For this reason, Melki's 1972 dissertation on the Arab-American press treats mainly the twentieth century.

[11] *Kawkab America* (English), April 15, 1892.

[12] *Kawkab America*, April 15, 1892.

America's Oriental House Warming," regaling its American readers with scenes of Oriental splendor: picturesque costumes, sips of Arabic coffee, and a "profusion of silk draperies, portieres and keffiehs, fresh from the looms and Bazaars of Damscus, Busrah, and Aleppo…."[13]

KAWKAB AMERICA

Vol. 1. No. 3, New York, Friday, April 29, 1892.

"Kawkab America"

OFFICE, 45 PEARL STREET.

An Oriental Weekly devoted to the development of direct helpful relations and good understanding between the East and the West.

The Month of Ramadan.

Syrians in America.

In the Court of Morocco's Sultan.

The Iron Horse and the Ship of the Desert.

Some Points in Syrian Etiquette.

The Apostles' Statues in Dark Africa.

An Oriental Soldier's Fidelity.

The Kawkab's Reception.

NOTICE.

The Balkan States.

LOCAL NEWS.

The Secretary of State Hon. James G. Blaine.

SCHOOLS OF NEWSPAPERS.

9.1. *Kawkab America,* 1892.

Petrakian and Nageeb Arbeely soon fell out; Petrakian left the newspaper less than six months after its first appearance. In May 1893, he sued Arbeely, claiming he (Petrakian) owned one-quarter of the newspaper as well as one-quarter of its publishing and printing arm, the Oriental Press. The original contract, which would prove his claim, had been stolen from him so the judge would have to take his word for its contents. This did not sit well with the judge. Not only did Arbeely claim that Petrakian had failed to pay his share of the initial investment ($250 for one-quarter of the companies), but he also complained that Petrakian was unskilled at setting Arabic type, the job for which he had been hired. Arbeely won the case resoundingly. Not only was Petrakian forced to give up all claim to ownership of the companies,

[13] *Kawkab America* (English), April 22, 1892.

but Arbeely countersued, and Petrakian had to pay Arbeely $435 that he owed him.[14] As a result, all Petrakian's ties with the paper were severed; his brother Ohanes lost his job as *Kawkab America*'s agent in Beirut, and Arteen and another brother, Habeeb, had to move their residence and company out of the newspaper's premises at 45 Pearl.[15]

Abraham Rihbany took Petrakian's place as the Arabic editor. Presumably Nageeb continued as the English editor since Rihbany's English was rudimentary when he arrived. Rihbany was paid forty dollars a month (twice what he had been paid as a bookkeeper, the first job he got when he came to New York) and given accommodations at 45 Pearl. In his autobiography, he described the office as consisting of three rooms and a kitchenette. "The proprietor and the publisher slept in the main office, in folding beds which were disguised in the daytime to appear as something else. The compositor [Yusef el Hajj] slept among his type-cases, Mr. Arbeely's brother [Nasseem] in the kitchenette, and I in my 'editor's room.'"[16] The cofounder, Abraham Arbeely, who was a practicing physician in Washington, DC, slept in the editor's room when he was in town and saw patients in the back room. Apparently the dormitory was well disguised during the day, since an American reporter described the offices as being decorated in Oriental splendor, with two "divans" (obviously the beds), Persian rugs on the floor, crossed daggers on the wall, and inlaid tables. A sketch of the office appearing in a Colorado newspaper shows a man in a frock coat seated at a roll-top desk, with a divan decorated with Oriental cushions, a *narghile* on the tile floor, and musical instruments hanging on the walls.[17]

The appearance of the paper's first issue was celebrated in many New York newspapers,[18] and the story was picked up around the United States. One article claimed that the paper already had correspondents in "India, Egypt, Zanzibar, Morocco, Syria, Palestine, Tunis, and Algiers, where the subscription lists are already large."[19] This sounds like the Arbeelys hyping their paper, as they were wont to do, but each issue did announce the addition of a *Kawkab America* agent in some far-flung land.

[14] *Trials,* Arteen Petrakian v. Najeeb Arbeely, February 1, 1894.

[15] They eventually went into the wholesale liquor business, and in 1910 Arteen began manufacturing embroidered goods.

[16] Rihbany 1914: 232–233.

[17] "Printed in Arabic," *Rocky Mountain News* (Denver), June 4, 1892.

[18] For example, "A Newspaper in Arabic," *NYT,* April 13, 1892; "Kawkab America in Arabic and English," *NYH,* April 24, 1892.

[19] "Gotham Gossip," *Times-Picayune* (New Orleans, LA), April 21, 1892.

In its first Arabic issues, the paper published essays on everything from the advantages of yawning to the great inventor Thomas Edison. It had two main audiences, diasporic Syrians and Syrians at home in the Ottoman Empire. For the latter, it published articles about the advantages of immigration and the opportunities of doing business in America. The editors reported on the cost of living in America (i.e., New York), which they admitted was much higher than in their native Syria, yet they claimed that anyone could make money if they worked hard. For the former, the paper gave advice ranging from the moralistic ("Don't chase after the almighty dollar at the expense of your honor") to the practical—letters from readers alerting others about license fees, tax liabilities, swindlers to watch out for, or shakedowns by the local police they were likely to encounter in various states.

One article serialized in three early issues, titled "Syrian Immigration or, A Dialogue between Malek & Zuheyr," gave a step-by-step account of a trip from Syria to New York. Malek was the innocent, Zuheyr the experienced traveler. Zuheyr explained to Malek the process of getting from Syria to Port Said, then to Alexandria, on to Marseilles, and finally to Le Havre, where he would ship to New York. He advised Malek not to eat the food provided by the shipping company as it was "disgusting," but to bring his own or buy from a private company on board, despite the cost. He described the customs examination on arrival, including a list of objects that were permitted and those that were not, and described the medical examination, as well. Finally, he listed all the questions that the immigration official would ask.[20] Since the publisher of the newspaper, Nageeb Arbeely, also worked as an interpreter at the Barge Office, the questions were no doubt accurate. As the first immigrant family, the Arbeelys had felt an obligation to their fellow countrymen to let them know what America was like and encourage them to come. They fulfilled that obligation in the pages of their newspaper.

The paper also served as a clearinghouse for people whose loved ones had disappeared after leaving Syria. Every issue contained several of these poignant announcements: "so and so, from the village of such and such, left 5 years ago and we haven't heard anything from him since." Sometimes someone from Middle America would post an announcement in a subsequent issue saying he had information about the person, and presumably this would lead to a reunion of the parties (or else to the "lost" one fleeing deeper into American obscurity).

[20] *Kawkab America,* July 1, July 15, and July 22, 1892.

For much of 1892 and 1893 there was extensive coverage of the Chicago fair, some from the pen of Nageeb Arbeely, who chronicled all the odd specimens landing at the Port of New York that were headed to Chicago, and some from the newspaper's special correspondent(s) in Chicago (unnamed, but possibly Yusef Balesh or Abdallah Jabbour, or both men). Taking up many column inches in 1893 were paid advertisements listing the new officers and members of local Shriners groups, each with a star and crescent above the text.[21] World news, particularly that from the Ottoman Empire, made up an increasing majority of the articles; as the years went by (at least in the four years of issues that exist), mentions of Syrians shrank to marriages, deaths, and their comings and goings, and advertisements made up the last of the four pages.

Starting out as a five-column, four-page weekly (appearing on Fridays), and measuring sixteen by twenty-two inches, the newspaper at first consisted of three pages in Arabic and one in English. An annual subscription cost three American *rials*. The Arabic pages had headlines in English, and the English page had headlines in Arabic. After only a year the paper dropped its English page and became exclusively Arabic, and eventually the English headlines vanished as well. Perhaps the editors realized that very few Americans were actually interested in the doings and opinions of the tiny Syrian Colony on the Lower West Side.

In its early years, the paper was characterized by a servile loyalty to the Ottoman regime and an assumption that all of its readers (whether in the Ottoman Empire or the diaspora) were Ottoman subjects. A star and crescent were printed at the top of page one. A special gilt edition printed on parchment was supposedly sent to the sultan in Constantinople so he could keep up with the activities of his subjects overseas.[22] It was assumed that all Syrians in foreign countries would return to Syria one day, albeit improved in mind, values, and business acumen by their exposure to other cultures.[23] The return of these immigrants to the land of their birth, the editors asserted, would no doubt positively affect the indolent attitudes of their countrymen who had stayed at home.

The newspaper lost its second editor, Rihbany, after about a year. We don't know who took Rihbany's place, but perhaps it was Yusef el Hajj or his

[21] Nance (2009: 98–110) gives an appropriately skeptical history of the New York Shriners.
[22] Dexter Marshall, "New York Letter," *Oswego* (NY) *Daily Palladium,* February 10, 1898.
[23] *Kawkab America,* April 15, 1892.

brother Elias. Both Yusef and Elias were compositors, printers, clerks, writers, and poets, so either one of them may have served as editor. While Yusef had worked for the Arbeelys from the very beginning, Elias (after having served as the Tadross Brothers' agent in New Mexico) was working as a printer at 225 William Street; whether this print shop had any relationship to the Oriental Press owned by the Arbeelys is unclear. Said Shoucair, who arrived in 1893, was also a compositor, and certainly worked for *Kawkab America* by 1898; it was he who took over the day-to-day running of the newspaper after Arbeely died. Any of these men might have taken over from Rihbany. In any event, sometime in 1895 or 1896, the newspaper hired Najeeb Diab, a young man from Rumieh. He had written a few articles for the newspaper in 1894 and must have impressed the publishers. He served as editor until 1898, when he left to start his own newspaper, *Mira'at al-Gharb*, which appeared in 1899.

From the beginning, *Kawkab America* claimed to have a circulation of 150,000, which was certainly hyperbole. An 1894 directory of newspapers in New York gives its circulation as somewhere between 400 and 800 copies.[24] That may have been only its New York City readership, but in any case it does not support the paper's claim to 150,000 readers, which probably was wishful thinking. In September 1893, seventeen months after its founding, the publishers offered to sell shares in the paper in order to expand.[25] They did not report the results of this offering or whether the paper "expanded," but at least it survived.

In the beginning, Syrian firms in New York had been the sole advertisers, but soon firms from other cities and countries—Boston, Connecticut, Marseille, and Yokohama—began advertising. After only a few more months, ads for Jewish and other non-Syrian firms began to appear, nearly supplanting the Syrian ads. Dry goods wholesalers such as Leopold S. Friedberger at 369 Broadway ("the largest salesroom in the city") and H. Finkelstein (9 E. Broadway) appeared in every issue; these were the wholesalers from whom Syrian suppliers bought their goods. Foreign steamship lines and American banks advertised in every issue as well. All of these ads were in Arabic; the newspaper must have provided translation services for its advertisers.

Articles in the newspaper were usually unsigned; whether this means that the editors wrote them, they were lifted from other newspapers, or they were

[24] Anonymous 1894, *American Newspaper Directory:* 541.

[25] *Kawkab America,* September 8, 1893.

written by members of the community who preferred to remain anonymous we don't know. The newspaper had a number of regular contributors who signed their articles with ciphers such as "an Ottoman," "Tarek," or "A.N." The same A.N. wrote letters to *Al Hoda* as well. Perhaps contemporary Syrians could identify these men; we cannot. Others were proud to sign their names: Daoud Nakkhash, Yusef el Hajj, Sheikh Abi Nazera, Abdallah Jabbour, and Iskandar Debbek all wrote more than a few articles for the newspaper, but each wrote for only a short time and was replaced by someone else.

The paper also encouraged readers to contribute opinions: for example, Syrians were asked to name their choice of the ten most influential Syrians, and responses came from all over. Somewhat more controversially, the paper asked readers to answer the question, "Do American missionaries play a positive or negative role in Syria?" There were a number of spirited responses on both sides of the question, several writers impugning the honesty and probity of the missionaries. Not surprisingly, the Presbyterian Mission in Syria took offense:

> The report is that the Syrian Mission is being most abominably slandered in the new paper the "Kawkab America" of New York. We sincerely hope that no one will pay any attention to such talk unless they go too far, when it would be advisable to squelch the whole paper by a suit for abominable lying. Of this I am assured they have done enough already but I feel almost sure that all they do it for is to throw forth a reply & bring on controversy, both of which it would be below the dignity of any missionary to engage in.[26]

The paper had a regular section called "Correspondence" and another called "Telegrams," both of which printed messages from Syrians around the country and the world. Sometimes the letters were actually long opinion pieces or poems by Syrians with literary credentials, among them Asad Milkie, Najeeb Diab, and Mikhail Rustum. Many men contributed original poems celebrating events in the community here or at home. The only thing that separated these amateur writers from those listed above was the relative infrequency of their contributions. We don't know if any of these men were paid.

In 1898 the paper became a daily. It was said by then to have a circulation of 10,000 in the United States and 5,000 in Latin America, but these figures

[26] *Presbyterian Letters,* William Jessup to Mitchell, September 23, 1892.

still seem exaggerated. Certainly by this time the paper had become more anti-Turkish,[27] and its circulation in the Ottoman lands must have drastically decreased. In the same year, Najeeb Diab left the paper and Khalil M. Asswad took his place as editor.

Both Abraham and Nageeb Arbeely had other full-time jobs. Abraham had a flourishing medical practice in Washington, DC, and as the years went by he was seen less and less in New York, leaving Nageeb to manage the paper. Nageeb's day job was as an interpreter (and/or an immigration official) at Ellis Island. In both capacities—publisher and immigration official—he became a spokesman for the Colony, at least as far as other American newspapers were concerned: he was asked to opine on happenings in the Ottoman Empire or interpret the doings of the Colony to the American press. He was an assiduous reader of the New York newspapers as well, combing them for articles about the Syrian Colony. He often reported on these articles in his own paper, praising or criticizing the American press depending on whether their coverage was complimentary or disparaging to the Syrians, and writing letters to the editors praising or criticizing their coverage of the Syrian Colony. He was a member of the American Oriental Society and served as president of the Syrian Orthodox Benevolent Society. In 1892, he became licensed as a notary public and advertised his services in *Kawkab America*, noting that he could serve clients in "French, German, Italian, Syrian and other languages," and that he would be available after 5 P.M., when his job at Ellis Island ended, any day of the week.[28] He was also a merchant, trading in Syrian goods (such as cracked wheat or tobacco), which he advertised in the newspaper. He represented a Syrian inventor of artificial silk, and he bought the master concession for the Oriental section of the Cotton States Exposition in 1894. He was a polymath and a very busy man.

Nageeb Arbeely died in 1904 at the age of forty-three (all of his brothers also died in middle age), but the newspaper continued under the leadership of his brother Abraham and Said Shoucair until 1910.[29]

[27] Editor Diab was quoted in 1898 as saying, "We are not friendly to the Constantinople Government as it is now carried on and we are decidedly against the present Turkish Consul in New York," a political stance that he carried over to his own newspaper, *Mira'at al-Gharb*, which he founded that year. Perhaps this open statement of hostility precipitated his departure from *Kawkab*. Hatred of the consul was about the only opinion on which he and Naoum Mokarzel, the editor of the rival newspaper *Al Hoda,* were in agreement. A few years later, several members of the Syrian Colony tried to have the consul removed.

[28] *Kawkab America,* September 30, 1892.

[29] Melki 1972: 6; Abdou 1910: 328.

## Al Hoda

*Al Hoda* was the longest-lived and therefore most influential of the Arabic publications. It began life in Philadelphia in 1898. Its founder, Naoum Mokarzel, had had a variety of jobs in New York before moving to Philadelphia, among them as publisher of a short-lived paper called *Al Asr* (The Epic), in partnership with Najeeb N. Maloof, but it wasn't until he began publishing *Al Hoda* that he found his métier and his voice. For the purposes of this study, I have considered *Al Hoda* a New York newspaper from its inception since most of its early articles dealt with the New York Colony. Naoum's true home and base of support were in New York (he had spent almost a decade there before moving to Philadelphia), and his eyes were always focused north. His brother Salloum joined the paper in 1899, and together they moved it to New York in 1903. Salloum continued to publish it after Naoum's death in 1933, giving up his own publishing ventures to do so. When Salloum himself died in 1952, his daughter Mary took on the task, and although she knew no Arabic, she was able to keep it going until 1971.

The first issue of *Al Hoda* appeared on February 22, 1898, a Tuesday, and it appeared every Tuesday thereafter. It consisted of eighteen pages of three columns each, quite a tome compared to the four pages of the first issue of *Kawkab America*. It had dark paper covers, making it almost like a magazine. William McKinley's portrait took pride of place on the first cover. A yearly subscription cost four *rials*. One wonders where Naoum found the money to launch such an ambitious project after having failed at his first two ventures. He must have had a substantial nest egg despite these failures. Mokarzel hired Ameen Gorayeb as the paper's first editor. From the very start Mokarzel claimed, as had the Arbeelys about their venture, that he had agents in forty countries distributing *Al Hoda*.[30]

The first issues contained no news at all, but rather essays on political philosophy, natural science, and the Syrian diaspora. One anonymous letter writer (perhaps Najeeb Diab?) criticized Mokarzel for putting the title *ostad* (professor) in front of his name; he filled two pages defending himself. The famous "A.N." wanted to know the number of Maronites, Melkites, and Orthodox in New York, to which Mokarzel promised to find the answer.

Editor Gorayeb wrote an article in which he contended that the Syrian immigrants were not as advanced as other immigrant groups because they

[30] *Al Hoda,* September 13, 1898.

were divided among themselves.[31] He admitted, however, that things had improved since the first arrivals. Mokarzel wrote an article urging Syrian businessmen to come together and help one another by forming trade associations or simply by cooperating. "If you improve the situation of the Syrians in New York," he wrote, "you improve the situation in every city in the United States."[32] In 1928, Naoum's brother Salloum was still trying to unite the Syrians in America.[33]

Ameen Rihani contributed several essays, one about the use of the Arabic language in the Ottoman Empire[34] and another exhorting the Syrian community to subscribe to *Al Hoda* and support Syrian journalism in the United States.[35] The only female journalist at this period was Marie T. Azeez, who wrote a two-part essay on the state of Syrians in America today.[36] There were unsigned laudatory essays about Anatole France, Napoleon, and a number of U.S. presidents, presumably taken from English or French-language publications and translated by Mokarzel or Gorayeb. Shibli Dammous, who was to found his own New York newspaper in 1899, contributed a poem on the Spanish-American War, and there were several articles in support of that war. We don't know whether any of these contributors were paid, but in one article, Mokarzel defended "my journalists," so perhaps they were. Advertisements by Syrian firms (most based in New York) filled the last few pages.

Mokarzel also apparently published a monthly newspaper that appeared alongside the weekly, but it ceased soon after because of money constraints. Several enigmatic references to a second newspaper published by Mokarzel, *Al Watanieh* (Patriotism), may refer to this monthly whose publication had been suspended for lack of funds in 1898, but nothing more is known about it. In September, Mokarzel advertised for a writer who knew Arabic and English, as well as a typesetter—perhaps an indication that the paper was expanding.

By November 1898, only six months after it began, *Al Hoda* had grown to twenty-four pages, of which six full pages were advertisements, including ads from Syrian firms in Colombia, South Africa, and Brazil, giving credence to Mokarzel's claim that his paper was distributed in forty countries. In early 1899, he bragged that *Al Hoda*'s circulation had surpassed that of *Kawkab America*.

[31] *Al Hoda,* May 17, 1898.

[32] *Al Hoda,* September 27, 1898.

[33] W.A. Mansur, "A Federation of Syrian Societies," *The Syrian World* III.6 (December, 1928): 3-9.

[34] *Al Hoda*, April 5 1898.

[35] *Al Hoda,* August 29, 1900.

[36] *Al Hoda*, February 14, 1899; February 28, 1899.

9-2. Studio portrait of Naoum (seated) and Salloum Mokarzel, taken in Brooklyn ca. 1903 after they moved *Al Hoda* to New York (Faris and Yamna Naff Collection, National Museum of American History).

From the beginning Mokarzel took a belligerent tone, challenging the veracity and ethics of other newspapers. He wrote several articles accusing them (especially *Kawkab America* and *Al Islah*) of perpetrating falsehoods, spreading misinformation, and expressing disloyalty to the Ottoman regime. He reacted to criticism with personal attacks and sarcasm, and this tone carried over into the letters from readers who wrote their own attacks on these rival newspapers. In a ludicrous contest of his own devising, Mokarzel compared the number of words in a single issue of each of the three leading newspapers: *Kawkab America*, *Al Hoda*, and *Al Ayyam*. Not surprisingly, *Al Hoda* won with the most words. The content of those words was of no importance.

Although *Kawkab America* had reported on events of interest to and about all Syrians when it was the only Arabic newspaper, by the time *Al Hoda* was founded, each paper had taken up its sectarian cudgels and pointedly ignored news about Syrians of other religions. Certainly as the century turned, the newspapers became more and more virulently sectarian, and their role in the internecine battles that took place during the first five years of the twentieth century was seminal. Even within the Maronite community there were feuds. Yusef Yazbek, a Maronite priest, accused *Al Hoda* of being a mouthpiece of the Maronite priest Khairallah Stefan.[37]

Around the turn of the century (unfortunately, one year of the newspaper is missing from the archive: July 1, 1899–July 1, 1900), the paper again radically changed its format, from a twenty-four page weekly to an eight-page semiweekly appearing on Wednesdays and Saturdays. At the same time, the content was significantly reduced; it now consisted of only one long article—usually a serial biography of one of the American presidents, presumably taken from another publication and translated into Arabic—a short philosophical or political tract, and the rest paid ads. None of the articles had news value; they were all fillers. The same long list of books, for example, appeared in several issues under the headline, "What Books Do We Need?"[38]

Mokarzel announced that any article submitted by his readers which was not a political article would be considered a "vanity" ad and had to be paid for: five *rials* for ten lines or less, ten *rials* for one full column, and five *rials* for every additional column—a very expensive proposition for individuals who might want to publish their literary musings. The change in format and apparent hardening of publication policy may have been matters of pure economics: two issues a week, with fewer total pages, meant more space for paid advertisements and less newsprint cost. It also may have been a result of Salloum's joining the paper at this time, although his role at *Al Hoda* is usually characterized as subservient to Naoum's, only coming to the fore after Naoum's death.

## Other Nineteenth-Century New York Newspapers

The only early Arabic newspaper besides *Kawkab America* was *Al Asr* (The Epoch), founded by Naoum Mokarzel and Najeeb N. Malouf in late 1893; it lasted less than a year. Other Arabic newspapers, all founded at the end of the century, included *Al Mushir* (The Guide), an anti-Ottoman paper founded by Salim S. Sarkis in Egypt in 1894 and brought to New York in 1899; the

[37] *Archdiocese Letters,* Yazbek to Corrigan, March 18, 1902.

[38] In *Al Hoda,* August 8, 1900, for example.

previously mentioned *Mira'at al-Gharb*; *Al Ayyam* (The Days), another anti-Turkish publication founded by Joseph N. Maloof in 1897; *Al Alam* (The World), a pro-Turkish newspaper supposedly funded by the Turkish legation and published by George Jabour in late 1898; *Al Islah* (The Reform), founded by Shibli N. Dammous in 1899;[39] and *Al Da'ira al Adabiya* (The Literary Circle), founded by Esau (Eissa) el-Khoury in 1900. A publication which must have been revolutionary for its time, but about which we know nothing, was a magazine founded by Marie T. Azeez (later to be Esau el-Khoury's wife) called *Al Mustahsan* (The Commendable?). In the sole mention of the magazine, which appeared in *Al Hoda*, *Al Mustahsan* was referred to as an English-language magazine for women.[40] This seems unlikely given its Arabic name, but if true, it would have been the only wholly English-language publication until Rihani's *The Book of Khalid* in 1911. It must have been short lived; one imagines that it folded at the same time as *Al Da'ira*, that is, with the death of Esau el-Khoury in 1904. All of the Arabic papers were apparently sold by subscription only, not on newsstands.

According to Mary Mokarzel, Naoum's niece, *Al Asr* was printed with gelatin mats, which must have been a laborious process and may have contributed to its early demise, or perhaps it could not compete with *Kawkab America*. Although copies of *Al Asr* have not survived, there were several semi-oblique references to it in the pages of *Kawkab America* in 1894. Neither its name nor the names of its editors was ever mentioned, but it must be the referent, as there was no other Arabic-language paper in New York at that time. Every Syrian reader would have known the identity of the two men who were pilloried in the pages of *Kawkab America*: Najeeb N. Maloof and Naoum Mokarzel. The editors of *Kawkab America* accused the editors of *Al Asr* of being "jealous and envious of the success of their countrymen," "countrymen" referring of course to themselves and their newspaper. They accused "a person" (either Maloof or Mokarzel) of not paying for his *Kawkab America* subscription. And they defended their coverage of a fistfight between Najeeb Maloof and Habeeb Petrakian as factually correct and courageously forthright: "We published it regardless of how it would affect them, even though we have friends in the Maloof family." They went on to accuse the *Al Asr* editors of trying to increase circulation by insulting other papers, and then proceeded

[39] A thorough study of the literary contributions of the Arab-American press in the twentieth century appears in Henry Melki's 1972 dissertation.

[40] *Al Hoda*, August 25, 1900.

to call the editors' opinions "stupid" and the editors themselves "liars."[41] No wonder there were suits and countersuits for slander between the two papers. *Kawkab America* made a rather left-handed attempt at reconciliation when it reported on the baptism party of Antoni Tadross's son, where the two men in conflict, Maloof (Maronite) and Tadross (Orthodox), supposedly reconciled. Although *Al Asr* closed quickly (an occasion that I'm sure was greeted with glee by the editors of *Kawkab America*), Mokarzel carried on the battle when he began to publish *Al Hoda* in 1898.

Joseph N. Maloof's *Al Ayyam* was a semiweekly paper of eight four-column pages printed on pink paper and carrying several illustrations in each issue.[42] It declared itself the organ of the Young Syria Party and advocated for reform of the Turkish government. Its first editor/printer was Esau el-Khoury; upon his death, Mansour J. Haddad took the position. George Jabour's *Al Alam* was a mimeographed weekly, reportedly completely free of advertising, which must have reflected the deep pockets of the Turkish legation.[43] A nasty dispute over "coochee-coochee" dancing between the two papers, which ended up in court, will be described in chapter 12. *Al Alam* closed in 1900 after appearing for only two years, supposedly because "many people were against it,"[44] but it is curious that the Ottoman government could not or would not save it. *Al Hoda* was supportive of the paper's position and lamented its demise. *Al Ayyam* survived until 1905.

Najeeb Diab was strongly anti-Turkish, both when he was editor of *Kawkab America* and in his own paper, *Mira'at al-Gharb*, so much so that the Turkish government confiscated his land in Syria and issued a warrant for his arrest. He reported this threat to the U.S. State Department, which assured him the matter would receive attention.[45] Because of the threat, he could not travel to Turkey had he wanted to, and he later claimed that the government had put a price on his head. When an amnesty was declared for all political exiles in 1908 under the constitutional reform, with the aim of encouraging them to return to Syria, Diab and other members of the Syrian Colony were "unmoved."[46] Diab's son-in-law, the writer and poet Elia Abu-Madi, edited the newspaper for a decade, during which he produced many of his famous

[41] *Kawkab America*, July 20, 1894.
[42] "Copy of This Paper Goes to the Sultan," *The New York Press,* February 13, 1898.
[43] "Champions the Sultan," *NYH,* January 1, 1899.
[44] *Al Hoda,* November 24, 1900.
[45] "Grand Turk Wants Diab," *New York Sun,* April 2, 1902.
[46] "New York Turks Unmoved," *The Evening Post,* July 25, 1908.

poems and essays, before founding his own newspaper in 1929, called *As Sameer*. After Diab's death in 1936, *Mira'at al-Gharb* continued under the management of his widow, Angelina, and the editor Farid Ghosn, who had worked for Diab for many years.

*Al Islah,* founded by Shibli N. Dammous in February 1899, was an active agitator for Turkish reforms. The first issue contained a poem exhorting Syrians abroad to think of themselves as free and to become citizens of their new country. He was quoted as saying, "There is an Arabic periodical in this city and another in Philadelphia [referring of course to *Al Alam* and *Al Hoda*], which are avowedly in the hire and pay of the Turkish government."[47] One notes the adverb "avowedly." One article suggested that the grave shortage of Arabic type in this country was due to a prohibition the Ottoman government put on its export in an effort to stem the tide of anti-Turkish press in America.[48] Dammous moved to Fort Wayne, Indiana, the following year, married there, became a dry goods merchant and returned to Syria in about 1910.

From an illustrious Armenian publishing family in Beirut, Salim S. Sarkis worked at his uncle Khalil Sarkis's newspaper, *Lisan al Hal,* when he was young. Salim was often in trouble with the Ottoman authorities and published newspapers in exile in England and France before starting *Al Mushir* in Cairo in 1894. It was an eight-page journal in Arabic and English, but we don't know if it had the same format when he brought it to New York in 1899. When asked by a reporter to send a message to the American people, Sarkis wrote, "As America extended her hand to Cuba, so shall she some day offer her help to down-trodden Syria."[49]

A reporter described three of the editors—Maloof, Dammous, and Diab—as "delicately nurtured gentlemen, of the highest mercantile order." Maloof was, in addition, a man of "extraordinary personal attractions, a romantic figure who, it would seem, had stepped out of the pages of a Syrian novel," and Dammous was described "pen in hand, correcting the quaint proofs, rolling countless cigarettes of Syrian tobacco."[50] This article captured the literary nature of these early newspapers in which more essays and poems than news appeared, but also alluded to the fact that all the editors were merchants as well as literary men.

---

[47] "Turks Menace Syrians in New York," *NYH,* March 12, 1899.
[48] "Syrian Clamor for Arabic Type," *The Sunday Telegraph* (NY), July 2, 1899.
[49] "The Lafayette of the Syrians Has Arrived," *Philadelphia Inquirer,* September 17, 1899.
[50] "New York's Syrian Quarter," *NYT,* August 20, 1899.

From the very beginning, the editors of the newspapers attacked one another in their respective pages, often anonymously. Not all of these articles were written by the publishers/editors, either; sometimes people paid to insert their own (unsigned) articles; others hurled insults in the (anonymous) classified section. All of the inflammatory words, however, were laid at the feet of the publishers, and it was they who were sued. In addition to those first salvos between *Kawkab America* and *Al Asr* described already, *Al Hoda* attacked *Kawkab America* mercilessly, accusing it of printing falsehoods, being ignorant, slandering others, and being fanatically Orthodox. These articles were unsigned, presumably written by Mokarzel himself. We don't know whether Nageeb Arbeely or Najeeb Diab wrote the similarly slanderous accusations in *Kawkab America*; one suspects Diab. *Al Ayyam* and *Al Alam* fought one another in the courts. The editors of *Mira'at al-Gharb* and *Al Hoda* insulted each other. Though the language of the attacks was personal, they exposed serious sectarian and political fault lines within the Colony. The founding in 1899 of the New York branch of the Young Syria Party, which called for the overthrow of the Ottoman regime, exacerbated these differences as the newspapers took a pro- or anti-revolutionary stance. The Orthodox bishop Hawaweeny was deeply involved in these battles; instead of tamping down the violence, he often added more fuel to the fire. He sued Joseph Maloof after *Al Ayyam* accused him of being a stooge of the Ottoman government. Lasting more than a decade, these newspaper battles became a real war in the Syrian Colony, culminating in 1905 when one of its members was killed; this war is described in chapter 11. This did not deter the literary-minded men: eighteen new Arabic newspapers were founded in the first decade of the twentieth century.

## Arabic-Language Books

Other literary efforts by members of the Syrian Colony in the nineteenth century were heartfelt, if sporadic. The newspapers were the main outlet in which men and women would publish essays, poems, and stories; they also, however, produced a number of books in Arabic that were printed by the presses attached to the Arabic newspapers, which were the only presses capable of printing Arabic in New York. These were all nonfiction, and most were "how-to" books, produced for the betterment of the Syrian immigrant. In 1895, Abraham J. Arbeely, a founding editor of *Kawkab America*, published

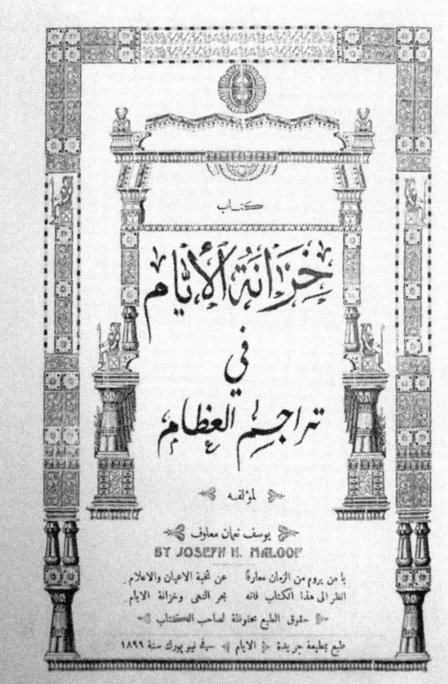

كتاب

خزانة الأيام

في

تراجم العظام

لمؤلفه

يوسف نعمان معلوف

BY JOSEPH N. MALOOF

يا من يروم من الزمان معارفة عن نخبة الاعيان والاعلام

انظر الى هذا الكتاب فانه بحر النهى وخزانة الايام

حقوق الطبع محفوظة لصاحب الكتاب

طبع بمطبعة جريدة الايام في نيو يورك سنة ١٨٩٩

9-3. Portrait of Joseph N. Maloof and title page from Maloof 1899 (courtesy of Antiochian Heritage Museum, Ligonier, PA).

a book at the Oriental Press called *Al Bakoora al Gharbia*, which was later expanded to *Al Bakoorat Al-Gharbeeyat fi Taleem Al-Lughat Al Englezeyat.*[51] It presented, he said, a clear and simple way to learn English, and included useful vocabulary, English translations of Arabic aphorisms, and instruction in such niceties as how to write a letter proposing marriage, read a menu, or announce the opening of a business in English. He divided the vocabulary into categories such as games, science, war and politics, weights and measures, plants and animals, nationalities, illnesses, and even gave conversion rates for a dozen currencies. Five pages of word-lists are devoted to "Wearing Apparel, Dry Goods and Notions." It appeared in weekly sixteen-page fascicles, each of which included a workbook; a subscription cost one American *rial*, and a bound copy of all of the fascicles was available through the newspaper for 1½ *rials*.[52] The bound volume was a hefty 630 pages, and in 1896 he added a forty-page supplement aimed at English speakers who wanted to learn Arabic. The price increased to $2.95. One American reporter said hyperbolically,

[51] Arbeely translated this difficult title himself as *The First Occidental Fruit for the Teaching of the English (and Arabic) Languages*. It might simply be called *An Arabic-English Primer.*

[52] *Kawkab America,* November 1, 1895.

"Few popular novels have had a larger circulation."[53] A more learned reviewer found the book useful for Arabic speakers but less so for those hoping to learn Arabic.[54] He added, "The printing is not very careful, but the binding, green cloth stamped in gold on back and side with the Arabic title in an ornamental hand, is most effective."[55] It must have sold well, because a third edition appeared in 1911, with added vowel marks and illustrations.[56]

*Kawkab America*'s Oriental Publishing House was the only Arabic press in existence at the time, and Mikhail Rustum published his book of rhyming essays and helpful hints, *The Stranger in the West*, with the company in 1895. Rustum later became the editor of the newspaper *Al Muhajer*, and he published at least two subsequent volumes or editions of *Stranger in the West*, the second in about 1904 and the third in 1909. The book was a compilation of essays, some of practical value (such as his price list for peddlers), some opinion pieces (such as his summary of the successes and failures of the Columbian fair), and some simply poems about living in America.

In 1898, Archmandrite Raphael Hawaweeny published a book of Orthodox liturgy (perhaps not a literary effort as such) titled *The Book of True Consolation in the Divine Prayers*. Bishop Nicholas of the Russian Synod recommended it be used in all parishes.[57] The Oriental Publishing House also printed it. Not to be outdone, Gabriel Korkemas, the Maronite bishop, wrote a book on Christian living. Published by *Al Hoda* in 1899, the book was available through the newspaper (in Philadelphia) or directly from Father Korkemas at 27 Rector Street. Joseph N. Maloof published his *Kizanat Al Ayyam* in 1899. Like many of its contemporaries, the book was a compilation of essays that had appeared in the pages of *Al Ayyam* about great men. It was sold by subscription (the subscribers' names are printed in the back of the book) and available from the newspaper's office at 60 Washington Street. *Al Hoda* published a biography (perhaps written by Mokarzel) of Yusef bey Karam, a Maronite hero, in 1900, which cost fifty-five cents. A book about the 1860 massacres in Lebanon and Damascus also appeared in 1900. Apparently authored by Elias A. Khoury, the book was available by subscription for one-half *rial*, or one *rial* after publication from the offices of *Mira'at al Gharb*. *Al Hoda* advertised a book titled *A History of Four Sultans* in 1900; we don't

[53] "Congress to Tackle Immigration Problem," *Rocky Mountain News (*Denver) January 9, 1898.
[54] Macdonald 1899: 181.
[55] Macdonald 1899: 182.
[56] Anonymous 1912: 1137.
[57] Issa 1991: 22.

know who wrote it or even if it was written by a Syrian in America. One could purchase the regular edition for one and one half *rials* or the deluxe edition for two *rials* at the *Al Hoda* office. All of these books were paid for by the authors and sold by subscription before publication as well as after.

Apparently several of the merchants in the Syrian Colony sold books along with notions and dry goods: David Biskinty sold Presbyterian tracts at his store, D.J. Faour and Bros. sold French and English books, as well as literary and religious (presumably Maronite) books. Several squibs in *Kawkab America* answered inquiries as to the availability of Arabic books in New York, and *Al Hoda*'s long list of "Books You Need" must have been available in the Colony. These books were imported from Egypt or Syria. The Syrians of the diaspora were clearly hungry for reading material, which merchants as well as writers were eager to provide.

## Chapter 10

# Women and Work

*The women who must become wage earners go out to peddle lace or Oriental goods, enter factories, or take in sewing at home. At such work they remain unless a fortunate marriage releases them.*[1]

In her study of Italian and European Jewish women migrants in the nineteenth century, Kathie Friedman Kasaba castigates earlier researchers for neglecting women's important economic role in immigrant communities. She notes that their reliance on U.S. immigration and census data skewed the record because these sources excluded women's paid work at home.[2] This absence certainly affects the data relating to women's work in the Syrian Colony.

The number of women reporting a profession in the 1900 census (141) represents only 43 percent of the total number of women (over fifteen years old) in the census. We can assume that many more than that were working, since many of the jobs that we know were filled by women were not reported on the census. Workingwomen were perhaps reluctant to report their occupations, either because they were paid under the table or for some cultural reason, internal to the Colony or external. If there were some embarrassment associated with women admitting to being breadwinners in front of male relatives or the census-taker, they may have remained silent. As the following sections make clear, women worked in a variety of jobs, but they were first and foremost peddlers.

[1] Miller 1903: 32.
[2] Kasaba 1992: 17.

## Peddlers and "Ladies of the Road"

A traditional description of the Syrian migration holds that single men came over first, made their fortune, and then brought their women over to establish families. These women often became their husbands' "helpmeets." A contrasting and slightly more cynical view holds that single men came over first, realized that their women could be effective peddlers and earn a living, and sent for more women to join them. A third view, and one only recently aired, was that women sometimes came first, made their nest egg, and brought their families over.[3]

A woman who arrived in the United States unaccompanied by a man must have started her career in peddling, unless she were joining a male family member here who had the wherewithal to support her. But certainly hundreds of stories attest to women beginning peddling quite early. One article, for example, describes the arrival of four Syrian women peddlers in Denver, Colorado, in 1890. They were gaunt, and three of them carried babies. Their trinkets, although said to be from the Holy Land, were, according to the reporter, "manufactured in Greenwich Street, New York, where the men who control most of the Syrians in America reside."[4] The reader will recall the article about women being called "chattels," controlled and exploited by the Syrian "padrones" in New York.

The women in Colorado belonged to a colony of a dozen Syrians who "squatted in the bottoms," a swampy piece of land on the Platte River. Did the women peddlers pick up their goods in New York and take the train west? Probably not. There were already dependable supply depots for Syrians in remote parts of the country, and any Syrian community, no matter how small, had at least one supplier in its midst. Certainly by 1894, *Kawkab America* noted at least one New York businessman, Assaf Abalan, regularly going to Denver "to do business."[5]

Is the fact that these women were gaunt indicative of the hardships of this existence, trudging from place to place in the no-(wo)man's-land of the West? And were they in fact controlled by men in New York, or were they entrepreneurs? Probably both: the wholesalers/suppliers in New York, already well established in 1890, no doubt had some control over the inventory all peddlers carried. They also controlled the terms of credit, and would in some

[3] Gualtieri 2004.
[4] "Only a Lemon Skin," *Rocky Mountain News* (Denver), July 7, 1890.
[5] "Coming and Going," *Kawkab America,* January 12, 1894; April 13, 1894.

way enforce their repayment. Yet almost every peddler described this relationship not as one of master and indentured servant, but as one of beneficent merchant helping the newcomer start out.

It should be remembered that it was not unheard of for Syrian women to work outside the home in their native country; many of the silk mills in Mount Lebanon exclusively employed girls and women, except for the foremen and machine technicians. When the mills were first built the owners usually hired relatives, which made it more acceptable to the girls' families. When needed, the owners brought in women from France (where silk production had been a traditional skill for many generations) to teach the girls how to operate the equipment. Once the girl or woman got used to working outside the home, she began to feel free to change to another mill not owned by a family member if the pay or conditions were better. She gained an appreciation for earning money and became aware of a certain freedom in a capitalist society, where one can change jobs at will. Her pay was abysmal (estimated at just enough to buy her own bread) but was still seen as a contribution to the family's welfare. Since the mills did not operate year-round (there were so many built in a short span of time that they were consistently underutilized), the family was able to tell itself that the women weren't really breadwinners, but simply using their spare time to supplement the household earnings.[6] There was the whiff of scandal attached to the girls working in the mills; the Ottoman/Persian term *karkhaneh* (factory or workplace) came to refer to a brothel.

As mentioned above, these businesses in Mount Lebanon lasted at the most two generations, when the price of silk plummeted as customers turned to other, cheaper suppliers. But our generation of female immigrants included those who had been in the mills or had seen their mothers and sisters go out to work. My grandmother, who came from Bishmezzine in 1897, was too young to have worked in the mills, but it is possible that other members of her family did; a member or members of her extended family, the Milkies, owned one of the mills in the village. We will look at women in the textile industry later in this chapter, but suffice it to say that the idea of working, earning a living, and going out every day was well established in the minds of at least some of the young women who came to New York, many of whom started out as peddlers. As far as we know, women were not in trade, either in Syria or at the world's fairs, but they took readily to the idea and proved themselves skillful—more than skillful—at it.

[6] Quataert 2004 (1991): 259.

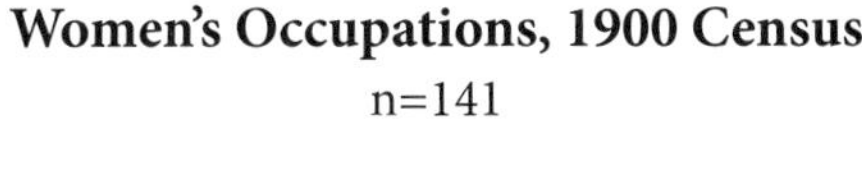
**Women's Occupations, 1900 Census**
n=141

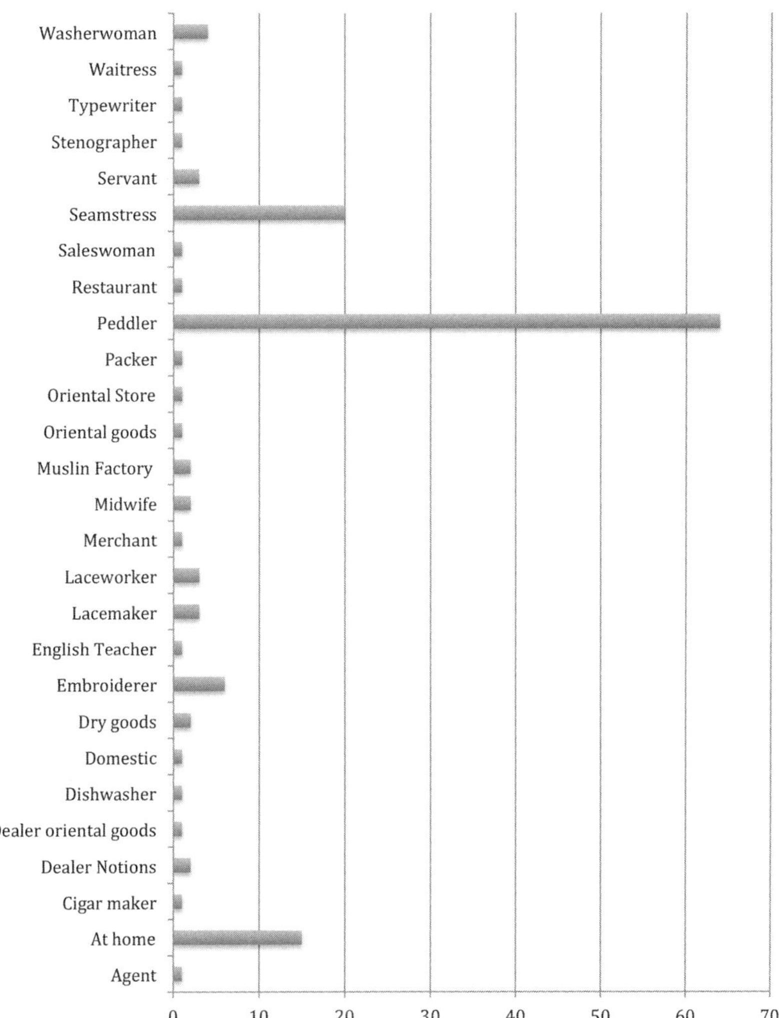


Of the 141 women whose professions were given in the 1900 census, sixty-six were peddlers (46.8%). Just as in the case of the men, the census may have undercounted peddlers because the summer, when the census was taken, was when they were out on the road. Possibly more daunting was that many Americans held women peddlers in contempt, a fact that may have prevented women from telling the truth about their work. Of the sixty-six women peddlers, twenty-two were single, twelve were widowed, and thirty-two were married. Among the single peddlers were two girls of fourteen and one girl of thirteen. Twenty-three women who peddled were boarders and thirteen were heads of households, while the rest were relatives of the household head. Most lived with relatives or husbands who were also peddling, some were supporting children who were at school, and seventeen women seemed to be on their own. There were no women peddlers in Brooklyn.

Women peddlers, like the men, started out selling trinkets and Jerusalemite goods and then added notions, which appealed to housewives, especially those in the countryside who had no ready access to general stores. At the same time, some women peddlers took up the "silk bag" trade and sold fancy goods door-to-door, appealing to a wealthier class of women. The customers for peddlers were most often women, as women stayed home during the day—whether in the country or the cities. Women peddlers could more easily approach women customers, and so they began to contribute substantially to the family income. We do not know how many of the New York peddlers—men or women—went on long peddling journeys, leaving town for weeks at a time, how many left town each day and returned, or how many of them peddled right in New York City.

One reporter described a Syrian girl's method of selling: she traveled as a "peddler drummer" around New York and nearby cities and towns, and her profits sometimes reached fifty dollars a day. She sold "Oriental jewelry, silver filigree and embroideries," carrying her wares about with her in a dress suitcase (as opposed to a *keshi* or *shenta*). Instead of going aimlessly from house to house, she interested local clergymen in her cause and obtained lists of potential customers. "The plan has worked, and brilliantly."[7]

We know about a New York peddler called "Margery the Syrian," whose story appeared in a St. Louis newspaper. Her beauty was her sales pitch. She worked in the Tenderloin, walking into men's domains (barbershops, cafés, office buildings) without a qualm and selling her trinkets to the willing customers inside. It was only after she left that the men realized they had been hypnotized. "At her humble home in Rector Street [Muossa Daoud's boardinghouse] they never tire of telling what a wonderful saleswoman she is."[8] Who this marvelous woman was is anyone's guess.

Like the men, the women were not above exploiting their exotic aura to sell goods. "'I wear my kerchief because it is good for business,' said one swarthy matron as she came out of a grocery store with a huge plate of a peculiar

[7] "Syrians Settling Here Make Asiatic Quarter," *BDE,* November 2, 1902.

[8] "Margery, the Syrian," *St. Louis Republic,* January 21, 1895.

kind of macaroni her hands. 'If I dressed like an American lady nobody would notice me.'"[9]

Alixa Naff was so taken with the stories that people told about their peddler ancestors that she collected them on three-by-five cards; they are part of her archive at the Smithsonian Museum. One of the funniest stories involved two Syrian women peddling in upstate New York. One of the women farts. The other turns to her and says, "What will this lady [customer] think of your manners when you do that in public?" The first one replies, "Don't worry about it, she doesn't understand Arabic." Just like the men, the women took great delight in their gaffes as they learned the language and customs of the Americans, and they also liked to tell stories about the gullibility of their customers.

The reaction of Americans to Syrian women peddling in New York or in the countryside ran the gamut from horror to disapproval to grudging admiration. The Immigration Commission *Report* of 1901 was scathing in its criticism of men who "allowed" or "forced" their wives to peddle. The anonymous writer explained that since the Syrian is indolent and ill-suited to hard work, he used women's labor to compete with the hard-working American: "This consists in sending his wife and daughters, or the wives and daughters of his countrymen, out to peddle door to door the silks, rugs, bijouteries, and antiques in which he traffics."[10] The early women peddlers rarely sold such elegant objects, but by 1901, when this report was written, many women peddlers had moved into fancy goods. "The real offenders are the merchants, so-called, whose cupidity and indolence, reinforced by exaggerated patriarchal authority, enables them to make use of the pleasing appearance, glib tongues, and insinuating manner of their women."[11] It does sound like the description of a pimp with his girls, and recalls the article cited above in which it was alleged that Syrian padrones preferred to import women to peddle for them, as they were more malleable, less likely to stray, and worked harder than men.[12]

The New York merchants were described as "start[ing] the peddlers out with goods on consignment, and map[ping] out their journey over the country,"[13] implying of course that the woman peddlers were under the sway of the merchants and had no freedom of their own; like some of the male peddlers

[9] "The Asia Minor of New York," *Kansas City Star,* November 21, 1898.

[10] Industrial Committee on Immigration 1901: XV: 443.

[11] Industrial Committee on Immigration 1901: XV: 443.

[12] "Syrian Immigrants," *Omaha World Herald,* October 7, 1897.

[13] "They Pose as Armenians," *Boston Herald,* December 2, 1897.

described above, they were seen as indentured to the so-called padrones. No one seemed to believe that the women were working for themselves. We know from many examples, however, that these women often worked on their own account, kept their money, and used it as men did, to buy more goods, contribute to household expenses, and, possibly, occasionally enjoy themselves.

Both men and women peddlers have said that sometimes a merchant would direct them to a route or a certain place to take up their peddling, for which many of the newly arrived immigrants were grateful. If the route were "owned" by the merchant, how did this hurt the peddler? Of course if the merchant had paid the peddler's transportation, as well as given her first consignment on credit, she started out heavily in debt to him, but that was true of the men as well. Part of the challenge to the peddlers, and something they bragged about, was how fast they could pay back their debt to someone whom many saw as their benefactor. One should not dismiss, however, the notion that some of these people were indentured in some way, and the many court cases where a wholesale merchant sued a peddler (sometimes a woman) may indicate that there was little forgiveness where debts were concerned, no matter the "family feeling" or supposed generosity of these suppliers. In at least one case, a woman peddler sued her supplier—and won.

The flip side of the American view of the woman peddler as victim was the woman peddler as a cheat. An article in 1897 described duplicitous Syrian women peddlers who had been brought over by New York merchants and pretended to be Armenians, or were wont to show letters of reference from prominent people, or carried babies not their own. And, even worse, it was discovered that some of these peddlers had money! These accusations, though presented as horrible sins, probably had a kernel of truth. One can easily imagine Syrian women calling themselves Armenians to make it clear to an American housewife that they were Christians—and respectable. Armenians had come to the United States earlier and in greater numbers than Syrian Christians, and Americans were more familiar with them than with Syrians. We have seen several examples of men and women who possessed and proudly displayed letters of reference either from prominent socialites or from ministers of the church, some of which were forged. That women, like men, told lies to induce Americans to buy from them is probable. If they did not know how to take advantage of the gullibility of the American consumer when they arrived, they certainly learned at the Columbian fair.

The Americans were offended by two things: that women were working in a profession that was often taken for begging, and that they were breadwinners in a household that sometimes included a husband or at least an adult male—both anathema to nineteenth-century sensibilities. An article in the *Brooklyn Daily Eagle* of 1902 describes a certain young Syrian woman living in Brooklyn who is about to get married. She has been in this country for six or seven years, and has been a peddler in New York and nearby towns. After her marriage, she will resume peddling and be the "breadwinner of her new home."[14] The reporter had nothing but admiration for her, yet nothing but contempt for the Syrian man who would allow, encourage, or force his wife to work for him.[15]

My great aunt, Jamilie Milkie, felt compelled to answer the charge leveled by the reporter. Jamilie was a peddler from the time she immigrated in 1897 until she died in a boardinghouse fire in 1921 in North Carolina, where she was finally about to open her first shop. She never married, living with her married brother's family in New York when she wasn't on the road. She wrote a letter to the editor of the *Brooklyn Daily Eagle* (she sent the letter from Amesbury, Massachusetts, where she was peddling) in response to the article just cited. She defended Syrian men as "industrious and noble, fond of labor and activity" and characterized her profession as one of liberation and emulation: women peddlers, she said, often supported no one but themselves, and in this, as in other things, followed their American sisters' example. "When we come to this country we learn the ambition from our American sisters to be self-supporting and independent."[16] The appeal to her "American sisters" is admittedly a bit fawning, but her general point—that earning one's own living is liberating—seems heartfelt, and was a sentiment echoed by women throughout the twentieth century.

Louise Houghton, in her 1911 description of the Syrians in the United States, tells of meeting a refined, "beautifully dressed" young Syrian woman at a dinner party. The woman left the party early because "she was to start early next morning on a peddling tour." Then, "two or three years later, meeting her again, she asked me why it was that American ladies took it for granted that women peddlers were of low class."[17]

The question was rhetorical, but a letter in response to Houghton's article

[14] "Syrians Settling Here Make Asiatic Quarter," *BDE*, November 2, 1902.

[15] It should be noted that in the 1900 census, the husbands of the women peddlers were also peddlers; they presumably went out on the road together. The reverse was not true; the wives of male peddlers were not necessarily peddlers themselves.

[16] "Men Not Shirkers," *BDE*, November 23, 1902; see also Bier 2009 for a discussion of this letter.

[17] Houghton 1911: II: 648.

came from an anonymous charity worker in Boston. "We have had many married women who peddle. Some of them have left their husbands in Syria, and some of them, in the testimony of their own educated countrymen, are of immoral character."[18] It is hard to believe that Syrian men would think or say such a thing about woman peddlers, as so many of them plied the trade and contributed to the family income. On the other hand, the women's release from the strictures of a closed Syrian society may have given a few of them license to behave in ways that were seen as immoral. More likely, it was American men who saw the trade as immoral, and perhaps this American view was being refracted through Syrian men's eyes.

This debate—whether the practice of women working outside the home, primarily as peddlers, was bad—was also carried on within the Syrian community itself. The four intertwined issues were: (1) the fact of women working at all was a stain on the honor of Syrian men, (2) peddling exposed them to dangers, both moral and physical, in which their honor might be compromised, (3) being out on the road provided temptations for immoral behavior, and (4) women peddling were subject to American condemnation, which was also an insult to the Syrians as a whole. Yousef Mandour, a tobacconist from Shenandoah, Pennsylvania, wrote an impassioned letter to *Kawkab America* pleading with Syrian men to forbid their women to peddle because doing so damaged the reputation of Syrians as a group. Peddling, he said, subjected women to attack and abuse by Americans, and it also meant that they could be harassed or arrested by the police, which reflected badly on the Syrians, adding that Syrian men should take better care of the gentler sex and not allow them to be subject to talk among Americans.[19]

Khater presents some evidence of the Syrians' dilemma in regard to their women working, citing articles from the early twentieth century in which the propriety of women going out to work was debated in the Arabic press.[20] The debates remained essentially the same. On the one hand, some Syrians believed that it was wrong to subject their women to the insults of strangers, endangering their honor (and therefore that of their husbands, brothers, or sons), whereas others, like my great-aunt, felt it was liberating and an emulation of American values. In addition, everyone knew that without women's work, the Syrians' goal to join the American middle class might be unattainable.

[18] Houghton 1911: III: 1088.

[19] *Kawkab America,* July 5, 1895.

[20] Khater 2006: 94.

Afifa Karam, a pioneering Syrian-American journalist in the second decade of the twentieth century, believed that working women, although not immoral, were exposed to dangers which could compromise their honor, and that the best situation for a woman was as a helpmate in a loving family.[21] Of course, such a debate could be taken seriously only when the community had reached a stage where families were less dependent on wives, sisters, and mothers for economic help than in the nineteenth century.

One assumes that the women peddlers were weighed down almost as heavily as the men and weathered the same hardships they recounted: exposure to extremes of cold and heat, lack of shelter, the difficulty of finding a place to bathe, and the fatigue of carrying a heavy case over miles of road. But there were also dangers particular to being a woman on the road that were the flip side of women peddlers having freedom and self-sufficiency. Notions peddler Sagheera Suleiman was attacked in Vermont while she was peddling alone; she apparently fought the perpetrator off valiantly and brought him to justice. He was sentenced to eight years in prison.[22] The fact that it was reported in the Arabic press meant that it was not seen as shameful for Sagheera to have been assaulted, and that the editors felt it important to report that the would-be rapist had been caught and punished. That he was an American served as both a cautionary tale and a dig at American morals. The owner of a New York store—again an American—assaulted a young peddler by the name of Nazery Izem, who escaped unharmed.[23] Actual rapes, although they must have occurred, were not reported. The danger was mitigated somewhat by women traveling in pairs or with their husbands, and we know, anecdotally at least, that this was common.

An unusual case, but perhaps not unique, was that of Esther Hleis (Elias?), a middle-aged Syrian woman who began peddling on the streets of New York soon after she arrived in 1890. She got lost and could not find her way home. Since she spoke no English, she could not make herself understood, and she began to cry. A policeman took her to the Tombs, where of course no one could understand her, so they sent her to the hospital for the insane at Bellevue. There the doctors wrote of her being depressed and crying for no reason and subsequently sent her on to Blackwell's Island, the hospital for the insane, convinced she was an unbalanced Italian. Only by pure chance did

[21] Cited in Khater 2006: 95.

[22] *Kawkab America*, December 21, 1894. The fact that he received an eight-year sentence would imply that she was actually raped, but that is not how it was reported.

[23] "Syrian Girl Ill Treated," *Trenton Evening Times*, April 26, 1896.

Dr. David Hassan Sleem hear her speak and realize she was not Italian. Thanks to Sleem, she was released a short time later, but she had spent many weeks imprisoned in the asylum. It's not hard to imagine the panic that her family must have felt, wondering what had happened to her. The *Herald* reporter was scathing in his assessment of the doctors in this case, and the system under which people were committed with apparently no oversight.[24] After the article appeared there was a hearing before the Lunacy Commission, but all that apparently resulted was the firing of the one honest doctor who had tried to free her.[25] One wonders if a man who found himself lost would have ended up on Blackwell's Island.

Maggie Coury, a Syrian girl of fifteen (who, the reporter noticed, had the body of a twenty-five-year-old) accused an "American" woman of stealing a fifteen-yard length of lace.[26] That she had the temerity to accuse an American speaks eloquently of the pride and independence of these peddlers, but also points up another danger that peddlers encountered on the road.

Another notorious case was that of Nellie Davids, who was said to have swindled a number of "colored" women in Jersey City by selling them face powder that was supposed to bleach their skin from "sable to white." Two white women claimed she had also duped them by pretending to be a medium and "magnetic healer" and then stealing from them. The reporter described her as "tall, shapely and comely," which made it no surprise, in his view, that she was able to swindle others. Nellie and her husband, Clarence, (and their child) were captured in Buffalo and brought back to stand trial in Jersey City; the police claimed that her trunks were full of goods that did not belong to her. She was convicted and shockingly sentenced to eighteen months in prison; he was released on costs,[27] partly because the judge believed Clarence had been misled by his wife, and partly in order that their two-year-old daughter should not be orphaned. Nellie "fainted" when the sentence was pronounced, and the reporter gleefully described her transparent attempt at suicide with a hatpin.[28] The particular vitriol that reporters reserved for women malefactors was striking. Davids was the same woman who was sued by Joseph N. Maloof for $350 for nonpayment for goods given by him to her on credit, which she was compelled to pay back.

---

[24] "Sane in a City Asylum," *NYH,* October 14, 1894.

[25] "Dr. Dent Has His Revenge," *NYH,* November 12, 1894.

[26] "Says Her Lace Was Stolen," *BDE,* August 17, 1899.

[27] "Stole All She Could," *Jersey Journal* (Jersey City, NJ), June 1, 1897.

[28] "Mrs. Davids' Charm Did Not Work," *The* (NY) *Sun,* June 25, 1897.

As women peddlers became more ambitious they moved to selling the imported Oriental textiles and jewelry that their male counterparts were selling, or began slowly incorporating white goods or fancy goods, such as hand-embroidered handkerchiefs, towels, and napkins, into their wares. Other Colony women may have initially made these latter items at home, but they soon came from abroad or from workshop-factories run by Syrians in New York.

According to a reporter in the *New York Times*, a "new" kind of Syrian woman peddler emerged around 1894: "The Lady of the Road." Each summer, this lady followed the money from one watering hole to the next, selling whatever would appeal to the upper classes. She sold "curious laces, Oriental embroideries, and old brass and silver often beaten into ancient arabesque designs."[29] My maternal grandmother traveled with her mother and her sister Jamilie to the middle-class resorts of upstate New York (Clifton Springs, Niagara Falls) in the summers leading up to her marriage in 1907, presumably selling these curious laces. They would put up in a boardinghouse and go door-to-door, selling to women whose families had rented homes for the summer or were staying in the fancy hotels. In 1899 the *Times* reported that the Syrian quarter of New York was nearly depopulated of the better class of its inhabitants in summer, which is one of the reasons why peddling in the 1900 census is so underrepresented.[30] But one also imagines that these women would no longer call themselves peddlers, in any case. In the census, we have three women who call themselves "dealers" of Oriental goods or notions, a woman who calls herself a "merchant," and another woman who is called a "saleswoman." Another woman's profession is given as "oriental goods" and a sixth as having an "oriental store." All of the first five could be peddlers, or something more sophisticated, but the last sounds distinctly like a supplier. Unfortunately, we have no further information about any of these women.

"The dark-haired Syrian women have their vacations in the Winter, but in the Summer they are scattered about the country at the most fashionable Summer resorts selling the goods of their husbands, fathers and brothers, who have shops on Fifth Avenue in New York as well as in less fashionable districts."[31] Jamilie Milkie in her 1902 letter asks, "What is better than to be among the nicest class of American ladies, boarding at either the Young Women's Christian Association or at a respectable boardinghouse, trading

[29] "Camp Followers of Vanity Fair," *NYT*, July 31, 1903.
[30] Cromwell Childe, "New York's Syrian Quarter," *NYT*, August 20, 1899.
[31] "How the Summer Woman Shops," *NYT*, July 30, 1899.

with the most refined ladies of the town, learning their artistic taste, listening to their sweet conversation and copying their beautiful manners?"[32]

These forays to the summer resorts ranged from classic peddling door-to-door and moving from town to town (as my grandmother did), to actual shops set up in one of the fashionable hotels, like those of the men. These shops were rented every season and became a permanent part of the resort, such as the four "Madam S. Moghabghab's French Parlors," which were located at the Mt. Washington Hotel, in Bretton Woods, New Hampshire; the Hotel Ormond, in Ormond, Florida; the New Clarendon in Seabreeze, Florida; and a stand-alone shop in Atlantic City, New Jersey.[33] There is no way of knowing whether these shops were actually under the control of their namesake or if the shopkeepers' husbands, fathers, brothers, or other men owned them.

It must have also been true that the line dividing these ladies of the road from their customers was blurry: sometimes one finds them listed in the society columns of newspapers as guests in the upper-class hotels, when in fact they were saleswomen. The confusion must have been gratifying to them if not to their customers. Mrs. Hannah Mallouf, whose golfing sons were described in chapter 8, appeared every summer at posh hotels in Richmond Springs, New York, and every winter at a resort in Lakewood, New Jersey. She did not advertise but must have had a way to get the word out that she had fancy goods for sale. The Immigration Commission, as always, put the worst possible light on the lady of the road: "Particularly does this class of Syrian [the peddler] realize the worst attributes of the parasite…the women mendacious and intriguing, flitting from the White Mountains to Palm Beach, from Mackinac Island to Hot Springs, as the season varies, following as closely as possible the wake of the wealthy."[34]

Thus, the many permutations of peddling included peddling door-to-door; going from resort to resort selling to vacationing women; setting up little booths or shops in these resorts; going back year after year and becoming fixtures in the resorts; attracting upper-class customers in New York City or elsewhere to whom they catered; and opening permanent shops in New York or elsewhere. Like the men, they must have varied their goods according to the market, changing stock from year to year and customer to customer. But

[32] "Syrian Men Not Shirkers," *BDE*, November 2, 1902.

[33] Advertisements, *Miami Herald*, 1910.

[34] Industrial Commission on Immigration 1901: XV: 443.

certainly what distinguished many of the women, as it did the men, was their stock of Oriental goods and their specialization in textiles. It was not until the twentieth century that Syrian women began to design for the American market and make their mark in strictly American commerce.

Once they had children, life for women peddlers became more complicated. Some women took their children on the road; others left them in the crèche founded for that purpose by the Syrian Women's Union or, if they were old enough, in school. Many women needed or wanted to stay home and still contribute to the family purse. They accomplished this in a variety of ways, which are described in the following sections.

## Women Trading on Their Own Account

The most enterprising of the nineteenth-century peddlers or ladies of the road set up in their own businesses, sometimes with their husbands, sometimes on their own. They opened small retail shops selling dry goods, cigars, or groceries. Some women may also have set up a network of home sewers to make kimonos, laces, tablecloths, or napkins, but we have no firm evidence of this. We know of no women who were importers or owners of factories in the nineteenth century.

As I mentioned, even as late as 1909, the *Syrian Business Directory* listed only seven women in business for themselves (out of a total of 408 businesses listed). Only two were "in trade": a manufacturer of pillow shams who had taken over the business from her recently deceased husband (Mary Ashkar), and a grocer (Mary John Arbeely).

In the 1900 census, several women called themselves "dealers" of Oriental goods or dry goods. We don't know what this means. Were they simply peddlers who wanted to give a good impression, or did they have a fixed place of business and sell to peddlers like their male counterparts? The little information we have for women who imported, manufactured, or wholesaled goods on their own account comes from American newspapers.

One notorious case in 1894 involved the arrest of Selma Gobreen, a Syrian woman married to the prominent New York merchant John Abd-el-Nour. Before her arrest, and even before her marriage, Gobreen lectured widely at religious gatherings and in the homes of upper-class American women, trying to raise money for the "advancement of religion in Syria." H. H. Jessup, a Presbyterian missionary in Syria, had warned his colleagues in New York against Gobreen. She was traveling with her sister Hannah Maloof, who "left her husband and three children and went off with men of disreputable character." The two of them were raising money under false pretenses, he said. He doubted that even "one cent which they receive will ever reach the Syrian poor." They were calling themselves Protestants when, in truth, "They are not Protestants & never have been. They appear to be adept in pious language, but do not be deceived by them."[35] This letter apparently did not materially affect her status with the Church since she continued to serve as an interpreter at Castle Garden on behalf of the Presbyterian Mission in New York. When she was arrested in Detroit, she had letters of reference from many prominent women, including Mrs. Russell Sage. Gobreen's apparent duplicity and hypocrisy outraged the press (as it had Mr. Jessup), and her downfall was greeted with glee: "She and Abd-el-Nour have been posing as Christianized Syrians, and she has done a thriving business selling Oriental goods at church fairs and lectured in Oriental costume at charitable entertainments."[36]

Gobreen was accused of smuggling goods across the Canadian border without paying import duty. Arrested along with her were her brother Assad and two American women. Two people on the Canadian side were also arrested. The police were also looking for Abd-el-Nour in New York, but he slipped through their fingers. The crime was described on the front page of the *San Francisco Chronicle*: "The officers know for a fact that the women have been crossing daily on the ferry [from Detroit to Canada] and that they never made a return trip without at least $500 worth of the finest handkerchiefs, filmy coverlets, table scarfs, and other exquisite productions wrapped around their bodies."[37] Did the Treasury agents undress them? The story was front-page news in Detroit, Chicago, and many other cities, and the *National Police Gazette* wrote a full page about her, which included a sketch of an odalisque in harem pants and beads reclining on a divan smoking a hookah.[38] The headlines of these articles are amusing and crudely alliterative—"Selma the Syrian Siren"—but for Selma it must have been anything but amusing. How was Gobreen caught? It seems that the scheme had been suspected by the police for more than a year, because rival (Syrian?) dealers in New York, whose prices were being undercut by Abd-el-Nour's, had denounced the couple.

[35] *Presbyterian Letters*, HH Jessup to Mitchell, September 25, 1887.

[36] "Abd-el-Nour and His Smuggling Wife," *New York Herald-Tribune,* December 5, 1894.

[37] "Cheated Uncle Sam," *San Francisco Chronicle*, December 3, 1894.

[38] "A Fair Syrian Siren," *National Police Gazette,* December 29, 1894; "Selma, the Syrian Siren. Uncle Sam Says She's a Very Smart Smuggler," *Wheeling* (WV) *Register*, December 23, 1894.

Only one article painted a sympathetic portrait of her—an article written by a woman—the writer's view being that "someone who had influence over her" was using Selma as a tool—namely, her husband, John Abd-el-Nour.[39] It is not clear from the articles whether Gobreen was working on her own account; it could easily be that Abd-el-Nour was in charge. It seems unlikely that he would have let her take those kinds of risks, although he may have thought that, being a woman, she would be above suspicion. However, she seems to have had money of her own, which suggests that she was working for herself, and indeed most of the newspaper articles considered her the malefactor.

Whether this attitude was prompted by the entertainment value of a woman smuggler or because she truly was in charge, she seems to have taken the rap for the crime. A few weeks after her arrest she went on the offensive, accusing Detroit police of stealing $6,000 worth of diamonds that belonged to her. The Treasury agent laughed at her,[40] and indeed it seems unlikely that she was carrying $6,000 worth of diamonds on her person when arrested. Abd-el-Nour was never charged; he hired an Ontario lawyer named Ward Stanworth to defend Selma, and the defendants apparently reached a monetary settlement with the government. Houghton alludes to her in her 1911 essay: "a very beautiful woman of high social standing who has been convicted of smuggling in collaboration with her husband, and who has suffered the legal penalty,"[41] the legal penalty being paying what she owed to the government. Like the other tax evaders, she did not go to jail.[42]

There were many stories of police harassment of peddlers, and some of it must have fallen on women. Perhaps this case was an example, or perhaps she (along with her husband?) really was a smuggler. It is interesting that in the two swindling cases we know of involving women—Nellie Davids' and Selma Gobreen's—the women were indicted while their husbands were not, which attests either to the independence of these working women from their husbands or to the eagerness of American judges to make an example of women who dared to work.

Another tantalizing hint of a woman who may have been working for herself is just that, a hint. Fareeda Flutie came to the United States in 1892 with her brother Elias to work at the Columbia fair; she was eighteen. When

39 "Selma the Syrian Siren," *Wheeling* (WV) *Register*, December 23, 1894.
40 "Says They Stole Her Diamonds," *Daily Inter Ocean* (Chicago, IL), January 3, 1895.
41 Houghton, 1911: III: 799–780.
42 "Wholesale Smuggling," *The* (NY) *World*, December 4, 1894.

they settled in New York after the fair, they lived together and apparently went into business together, as her profession is given as "importer" in her naturalization papers. As she was unmarried and remained so, she was one of the few women who applied for naturalization on her own. She had some social standing in the community, having been chosen to present a gift of a fine Oriental tapestry to President Cleveland, which he received from her hands.[43] She was also one of the founders of the Daughters of Syria. She spent the majority of her life in an insane asylum in Northfield, New Jersey. Elias married and had a family, and they lived just down the road from where Fareeda was confined.

A long, dramatic letter was published in *Kawkab America* in early 1895, outlining the troubles of a certain Umm Ibrahim Faris, who lived in Texas. It was clear that Umm Ibrahim owned a store that supplied peddlers, and that her partner was another woman. At the end of a sad story of her son's betrayal (he was allegedly "seduced" by her partner) and her loss of the store, she emerged triumphant, regaining her store through the good offices of the rest of the Syrian community. The writer credited her with great business savvy.[44] The story made it into print only because it was so dramatic, but women owning their own (wholesale) stores must have been, if not common, at least possible.

The only other Syrian woman from the nineteenth-century Colony who made a significant career in trade was Marie el-Khoury. She emigrated from Beirut in 1891, at the age of nine, with her sister Alice and parents, Julia and Tannous Azeez. Her father was one of the few early immigrants whose profession was given on the ship manifest as "merchant," implying that he was already well off and perhaps carried substantial goods with him. He began as a jeweler at 37 Washington Street, and then set up an Oriental jewelry store selling pearls and Persian stones on the boardwalk in Atlantic City. It was called "The Little Shop of T. Azeez." His store did not apparently sell the cheap Oriental jewelry that other Syrian shops offered, but jewelry made from genuine precious stones. Marie worked in the shop as a young girl, learning the trade. After she finished school, she had literary aspirations and wrote for English and Arabic newspapers including *Kawkab America* (the then editor of the paper, Najeeb Diab, was the witness for her naturalization) and *Al Hoda*. She was said to be the publisher of a woman's magazine in English,[45]

[43] *Kawkab America,* November 24, 1893.

[44] *Kawkab America,* February 1, 1895.

[45] *Al Hoda,* August 25, 1900.

but I have found no other references to it. In 1901 she married Esau (Issa) el-Khoury, the compositor for *Al Ayyam* newspaper and founder of his own newspaper, *Al Dai'ra.* He was also a writer and editor and a revolutionary, one of the founders of the Young Syria Party described below.

With the untimely deaths of her husband in 1902 and her father in 1905, Marie took over the latter's business and, in the 1910s, moved it back to Manhattan, keeping its original name in honor of her father. She found investors for the shop among the wholesale dealers who knew her father and opened her first location on Fifth Avenue at 46th Street, a rather daring foray for a Syrian merchant (and a woman) in the second decade of the twentieth century, but she knew to whom she wanted to sell. She lived around the corner from the store, in a townhouse on West 44th Street, with her mother and sister. The shop moved twice more, each time a little bit farther north. As "Mme. el-Khoury," she dictated jewelry fashion ("If you are wearing pearls, wear nothing but pearls"[46]), and she used "Hindu philosophy" in her designs. As her obituary stated, "The shop became a rendezvous for New York society women seeking jewelry of the finest design." She was also famous as an epicure and used to plan menus inspired by her gems.[47] A newspaper photograph shows an elegantly coiffed black-haired woman with dramatic makeup wearing a spectacular necklace. She is holding a pair of jeweler's tweezers, contemplating a necklace design.[48]

## Textile Workers: Home Work, Piecework, and Factory Work

Many Syrian women and girls had worked in the silk mills in Mount Lebanon before coming to the United States. In a series of stereographic photographs housed at the Library of Congress we see perhaps two dozen young girls around twelve years of age; they are at the "largest silk mill in Mt. Lebanon," standing over the vats in which cocoons are being boiled, while nearby older women are sorting the silk by quality. The male supervisor stands and supervises.

In New York, women who were unwilling or unable to go out and peddle did piecework at home, providing the lacework, fine embroidery, and drawn

[46] "Art of Wearing Splendid Jewels Rare in America," *New York Evening Post,* December 8, 1931.
[47] "Marie el-Khoury, Designer, Was 74," *NYT*, September 28, 1957.
[48] Kathleen MacLaughlin "Success as a Jeweler Crowns a Vocational Detour," *NYT,* February 18, 1940.

10-1. 60–62 Washington Street, where a number of Syrian businesses employed women in factory work (Miller 1903).

work that the peddlers were beginning to sell along with Holy Land goods and notions. The Immigration Commission reported that it took six hours for a Syrian woman to make twenty-five cents' worth of lace to sell,[49] although this is hard to believe. A reporter in 1895 asserted that "one seldom sees a Syrian girl or woman sitting in the doorways or windows of their quarters without a bit of lace work in hand, their necks decorated with great quantities of coarse lace work and their hands still adding to the string."[50] In 1899, several Syrian women who were selling laces on the street—laces made by their countrywomen—were arrested for peddling without a license. According to the article, the laces were knotted laces, actually macramé, rather than lace fabric.[51] According to the reporter, both the lacemakers and the lace sellers worked for a hairpin manufacturer named "Slimen-el-Karaeb," a name we do not recognize. Fares Rihani must have been referring to finer laces when he stated categorically in 1903, "No, we don't make lace by hand in this coun-

[49] Industrial Commission on Immigration 1901: 443.

[50] "Busy with Their Knitting," *Aspen* (CO) *Daily Times,* September 26, 1894.

[51] "Distress in Syrian Colony," *NYH,* October 29, 1899.

try.... [I]t would cost too much."[52] In a 1906 customs case, Michael Klele was arrested for smuggling Syrian lace into this country in a bag of dried peas.[53]

Out of 514 women and girls in the 1900 census, only 34 named occupations associated with textiles. They were lacemakers and seamstresses, makers of art needlework, fancy work, or embroideries, and two "muslin factory operators." Of course those who are listed as "at home" on the census may have been textile workers, as may any number of those for whom no occupation was listed.

We know that far more than thirty-four women must have worked in textiles, either at home or in factories. Miller reports, for example, that in 1903, 12.9 percent of the residents sewed kimonos at home; 98 percent of these sewers were women.[54] The kimono business did not take off until about 1903, but the proportion of women working at home sewing other textile items may have been similar in 1900; this would imply that about sixty-five women were sewing at home, opposed to the thirty-four recorded in the census. We are not even sure that all thirty-four were at home; certainly the muslin factory operators were not. Perhaps the dramatic disparity between what we suspect (sixty women sewing at home) and what we know (thirty-two women or fewer sewing at home) was due to home piecework being done under the table, and being told not to talk about it to the census taker. The reporter at the *Tribune* attests to the ubiquity of Syrian women sewing at home:

> Throughout the Syrian quarter most of the olive skinned women are always sewing. Instead of going to a matinee, they sew; instead of reading the papers and magazines in the evening, they sew; instead of playing bridge, whist or giving receptions, they sew. Some of the women sit on the bare floors of their tenement homes and sew with needle and thread. Others, who have learned of the wonders of the sewing machine, save up their earnings and sew with a machine. When a peddler has earned enough to bring his wife or his mother or his sister from the home land, he puts her to work sewing.[55]

"Far better and healthier for these working Syrian women are the kimono factories," he goes on,[56] and by 1903, when this article was published, there were numerous Syrian-run kimono factories in New York. But there were

[52] "Victims of the Turk Finding Homes Here," *New-York Tribune Illustrated Supplement,* October 11, 1903.
[53] "Found Lace in Bag of Peas," *NYT,* August 15 1906.
[54] Miller 1903: 11.
[55] "Victims of the Turk Finding Homes Here," *New-York Tribune Illustrated Supplement,* October 11, 1903.
[56] "Victims of the Turk Finding Homes Here," *New-York Tribune Illustrated Supplement,* October 11, 1903.

factories (or workshops) much earlier as well, at which Syrian women worked. Miller counted 26.8 percent of the residents working in factories, of whom 42 percent were women, from which we may extrapolate that about sixty women were working in factories in 1900. But only two women in the 1900 census admitted to being factory workers.

We do not know if there was any meaningful difference between the pieceworker working at home and the factory worker, other than the fact that the latter left the house in the morning. Was the factory worker paid a salary or by the piece? Was there a difference between what was produced in the factories and homes? The only thing we do know for certain is that some women went out to work in Syrian-owned factories in the neighborhood, and others continued to do piecework at home.

What is the evidence for nineteenth-century women's textile factory work? The building at 60–62 Washington housed a number of Syrian wholesale and manufacturing companies that must have employed Syrian women. Number 60–62 was, as the address implies, two buildings joined together, situated right next to Babbitt's Soap Factory (Number 64 was the Babbitt Company stable). Number 62 was 25 feet wide by 90 feet deep, while Number 60 was 50 feet by 180 feet, apparently reaching all the way to West Street. A 1903 photograph shows Number 62 (Figure 10-1) as having five stories; the top floor was added around the turn of the century. A street-level entrance at the north end of Number 62, above which is written the numbers 60 and 62, gave access to the upper floors. There is a second entrance at Number 60, with a rickety-looking stair going up to the store or stores that were a half-story above street level, and a third entrance into a half-basement store, in which a man stands, only his head and torso visible above the sidewalk. A fire escape covers the facade of Number 62 and half of Number 60. It is an awkward joining of two buildings of different size, age, and configuration. Miller captions his photo, "A Five Story Business House on Washington Street, Occupied by Syrian Firms."[57]

The businesses housed at 60–62 Washington included Abdallah Daas & Co. (cotton goods); Simon, Barson & Co. (suspenders, aprons); Elias and Michael Abousleman (apparel, sleeve garters, and notions); A.J. Sadallah (import/export, commission merchant, men's shirts); Shohfi Bros. (embroideries), Peter Khoury (dry goods and cutlery), Salim Milan (brushes); and Constantine Biskinty & Co. (dry goods). Ezra Sitt, an Aleppan Jew, also had

[57] Miller 1903: 10.

a suspender factory in the building. He was one of a handful of Jews whose companies were in the Syrian Quarter and whose dealings with Syrians transcended the simple buying and selling of goods.

In a short item in a 1900 newspaper it was reported that a fire broke out at 60–62 Washington Street, causing a panic among "200 Syrian girls and boys employed by the exporting company A.S. Daas & Co."[58] The fire, which had started in the offices of the newspaper *Al Ayyam* on the second floor, was sending smoke up the elevator shaft to the fourth floor, where Daas's factory was located. Although 200 employees sounds like an exaggerated number, if it were true, it would imply a very large workforce of Syrians by 1900, and A.S. Daas & Co. was only one of many workshops in the building.

Certainly any single floor of the conjoined building was large enough to house 200 employees, but whether this number was accurate is difficult to know; if it was accurate, perhaps they were the employees of several of the firms in the building. How many of these 200 were women?

Other references to women working in factories are elusive. You will recall the 1897 citation from Moss: "fifty Syrians [worked] on coats and vests in a room on the top floor [of 81 or 83 Washington Street.]"[59] Moss was made aware of this factory because a Department of Labor inspector (Mrs. Nagle) had gone to investigate the working conditions there. The majority of the employees must have been women or the state would not have sent a woman inspector, but we don't know whether the number of employees is accurate or who owned the factory. We do know that Fares & Abdow Rihani had their fancy goods business there, and Najeeb Naja manufactured tablecloths, aprons, and other articles from 1898 to at least 1901, so it may have been his. None of these products, however, could be mistaken for coats and vests. Another article refers to a "score" of workers in an unidentified kimono factory. Only instinct tells us that the majority of these were probably women.

Two photographs of the "Lutfy and Macksoud," kimono factory appeared in 1903.[60] In one, three women are doing hand sewing, a man works at a sewing machine, and the proprietor or foreman (Elias Macksoud?) stands next to shelves of fabric or finished kimonos. Another photo captioned, "His Wife a Breadwinner," shows the same proprietor measuring the sleeve of a kimono being modeled by one of his employees (his wife, Shafika?). The sub-caption

[58] "Fire Startled Employees," *BDE*, August 10, 1900.

[59] Moss 1897: 272.

[60] "Victims of the Turk Finding Homes Here," *New-York Tribune Illustrated Supplement,* October 11, 1903.

reads, "Some of the Syrian women are beautiful in face and figure and get good pay as models." Houghton[61] also includes a photograph of the Merhige Brothers and Shohfi kimono factory at 85 Washington. This photograph was taken in 1911, after the Faour Brothers had bought the three buildings, 81–85, but before their bank had expanded to all three addresses. Solomon Merhige and John Shohfi (one assumes) are standing in the back of a room where nine women are sewing at a long table. A mannequin wearing one of their kimonos stands watch. There is nothing of the sweatshop evident in the photo, although no doubt the work was taxing, poorly paid, and boring. But for women who wanted to remain close to their homes, perhaps after several years of peddling, this work was one of the few alternatives available to them.

These few examples give a possible range of size of the workforce in these factories: from five to two hundred, an unhelpfully large range. Not many more than a dozen employees would fit into most of the tenement rooms available on Washington Street. The fact that churches and factories coexisted in some buildings with residences means that large unobstructed spaces did exist in the neighborhood but were rare. It was only later that some of these factories, as they expanded, moved to other parts of the city, to the suburbs, or offshore.

The best source for details about women's work in textile factories is the 1905 arson trial mentioned in chapter 7. Although the trial took place five years after our upper date limit, it seems reasonable to assume that the conditions described were similar to those of the Syrian manufacturers of the late nineteenth century. Kalil Matta and Elias Karam's petticoat workshop was small, similar in size to the factories pictured in Miller and Houghton. Located at 157 Cedar, where the Orthodox and Maronite churches had been temporarily located, it employed at least ten people, seven of whom were girls and women. Number 157 was a wholly commercial/manufacturing building having large expanses of floor space on its upper levels. Elias Karam's three sisters, Katie, Kamala, and Mary, all worked at the factory, along with Victoria al Kazem and Freda Galab. There were at least two other (probably American) employees who were not called as witnesses: Ethel and Jasmine. We don't know the total number of workers.

Katie Karam's story stands in for all of them. She had come to the United States in 1896 with her siblings, all heading for Boston. They lived together and worked in a textile mill there until five months before the trial; Elias was a

[61] Houghton 1911: II: 659.

cutter, the sisters were sewers. When the family moved to New York with Matta in order to set up their factory, there was some down time while Karam and Matta organized everything, so Katie went to work for Lutfy and Macksoud (kimono makers) for a few months until it was time to start in Matta's factory. At Matta's, she worked on the double needle machine, the hemstitching machine, and sometimes on the plain sewing machine. The machines were run by electricity that was generated by a motor that had to be turned on every morning; it was Katie's job to do this. The other floors of the building had no electricity, so the employees needed a lamp to go from the fourth-floor factory to the water closet on the fifth floor. Katie took the ferry every morning from Brooklyn with her sisters, her brother, and Matta, who was their cousin, and they returned home together every evening; they all lived on Emmett Street. She worked a nine-hour day with a half hour for lunch. Neither she nor her sisters were paid a salary, presumably because her brother had been given a piece of the business in lieu of salary. They must have saved money from their previous jobs to pay for necessities. Victoria al Kazem lived at 43 Washington Street and had begun working for Matta and Karam in October, when the factory opened. In November she moved to Simon, Barson & Co., making suspenders at 60–62 Washington, and in December she went back to Matta and Karam. This fluidity of employment among young women echoed that of the men in the early years of the Colony and perhaps reflected the fluidity of employment in the silk mills in Mount Lebanon.

## Other Factory Work

An 1894 article in the *New York Herald* described the beautiful Narfetta Zaleel (Kalil?), who was displayed in the window of her boss's cigarette factory rolling cigarettes. "With the thin spangled burnoose dangling about her brow she looks like a study in bronze. The swarthy proprietor of the store knows it, and this is why Narfetta sits in the window." The writer added that she rolls two cigarettes for every one by her male coworkers.[62]

Similarly, an 1898 article says, "He ['the Turk'] is somewhat of a genius as an advertiser, and about the first thing he does, when he gets a plate glass window between himself and the public, is to put a woman behind the plate

[62] 'Red Fezzed Heads; Languorous Eyes," *NYH,* November 18, 1894.

glass rolling cigarettes."[63] Then the reporter goes on to say that the woman is probably his wife, and he will often put his children in the window too. Perhaps her boss, knowing that this would sell Turkish cigarettes, had imposed the "spangled burnoose" on Narfetta. Yak Oussani put a man and a woman in the window of his cigarette factory to draw visitors, and sometimes the Turkish smoking parlors would do the same, even though they weren't, strictly speaking, making cigarettes there.

A photograph in Houghton shows the workroom of Abdullah N. Barson's cigarette factory at 40 West Street. A man, presumably Barson, dressed in a jacket, stiff collar, and tie, is standing behind five women working at a long table rolling cigarettes. None of the women in Houghton's photograph are wearing a "thin spangled burnoose": they look thoroughly Western. None of them, for that matter, is sitting in a window open to the public eye. My maternal grandmother worked in a cigarette factory in the early years of the twentieth century. She commuted every day on the ferry from Brooklyn to Manhattan, along with many of her fellow Syrians.

The Hawie Brothers' mirror factory (Figure 10-2) was larger than the factories described earlier (which is probably why the Hawies set up on Canal Street rather than in the neighborhood), employing, according to Miller, thirty to forty Syrians and Americans. Twenty-one of them—sixteen men, four women, and a boy—are visible in the photograph. The women are sitting together at two tables, perhaps making frames for the mirrors, the men at several other tables. The glasscutters are wearing leather aprons. Three or four men in shirtsleeves are each standing at an unidentifiable machine (perhaps a silvering machine?). The lamps are gas, but the machinery looks electric. Miller noted that the Hawie Brothers, who were ironworkers in Syria, had invented most of the tools and machinery used in their factory.[64]

These factory jobs were hard and low-paying. If the Syrian-run workshops only had to compete with the textile mills in the New York area that paid around four dollars per week to their workers, then the bar was set very low. Miller claims that in 1903 Syrian factory owners paid between seven and nine dollars a week,[65] which he said was low, but which from my research seems comparable to other factories at the time.

The Syrian-owned factories were not sweatshops as defined in the

[63] "Oriental Merchants of New York," *Anaconda* (MT) *Standard,* October 23, 1898.
[64] Miller 1903: 30.
[65] Miller 1903: 30.

nineteenth century. Sweatshops were small factories set up in tenements (as these were), but the term "sweatshop" applied only to factories run by contractors or subcontractors who were working for large commercial firms. The subcontractors who ran these sweatshops were under extreme pressure to cut costs; hence the inhumane treatment meted out to the employees and the opprobrium that still attaches to the word. The term soon came to be applied to any factory where the work was hard and poorly paid and the treatment inhumane. The move toward unionization originated among textile workers in New York.

10-2. Hawie Brothers' mirror factory, 275 Canal Street (Miller 1903).

Syrian factory owners, however, generally worked for themselves, no one else. The fact that most of them called themselves merchants rather than factory owners or manufacturers implies that they themselves wholesaled the goods made in their factories; they may have even sold their products retail as well, if they followed the trade practices laid down earlier in the Colony. They seem to have had a monopoly, at least in kimono manufacturing, which also meant that they weren't forced to cut wages to the bone. They worked and lived in the same (small) community as their workers and had to answer to their neighbors; anonymity was not possible. And although there was a never-ending stream of new immigrants and a desire on the part of Syrians to work for other Syrians rather than Americans, the strong ambition to work for oneself limited the number of available employees. The owners had to keep the ones they had, and they couldn't have done so if they had treated them badly. Miller says the Syrian factory hand found the "return regular, the work not too hard, and the conditions under which he works not unhealthful."[66] But the absence of damning evidence does not prove that the employees of these Syrian-owned factories were treated well. A labor spokesman, Edward McSweeney, who obviously was worried about jobs being taken away from his Irish workers by lower-paid immigrants, asserted, "They [the Syrians] are more of a living danger than all the other races in the United States. They are now the controlling factors in the sweating trades, which were formerly controlled by Jews and Italians."[67]

## Midwives

In the nineteenth century, there were two, or possibly three, midwives in the community, Mannie K. Shahdan, Malake Nafash, and Barbara G. Sirgany. Shahdan and Nafash delivered almost all the babies in the Colony for whom we have birth certificates. Nafash delivered most of the Orthodox children; Shahdan delivered the Maronite babies.

As described earlier, Nafash emigrated from Damascus without her husband and children in 1896 but brought her two daughters over as soon as she could. Her husband stayed behind. She first lived at 17 West Street, but of course she delivered babies at her patients' homes; there was no need for an office as such. The family moved to the South Ferry area of Brooklyn in the late nineteenth century, but she continued to keep a business address at 18 Morris Street. My maternal grandmother went to her or to Mannie Shahdan for an abortion in about 1913. She described taking the ferry to lower Manhattan and being "operated on" on a kitchen table. Nafash worked as a midwife until her death in 1939.

Mannie Shahdan, also known as Umm Elias, must have had a similar experience to Nafash's. She had had nine children, of whom six survived. A Melkite, she was from Beirut, but had lived in Egypt before coming alone to the United States in 1887. Three of her children joined her in 1895, although her husband, if he was still living, never made the trip. The family boarded

[66] Miller 1903: 30.

[67] "Our Many New Races," *Boston Herald*, March 20, 1902.

with a dozen other Syrians at 3 Carlisle Street, which served as Shahdan's business address as well. Shahdan remained in business in Manhattan (always at 3 Carlisle Street) until at least 1908. In 1915, she was lodging alone in Brooklyn and her profession was listed as "Registered Nurse." Interestingly enough, an American doctor, Elizabeth Cameron, who had an office at 51 Washington Street, advertised (in Arabic) in *Kawkab America* that Umm Elias worked for her or with her. As a further inducement for Syrians to come to her, Dr. Cameron bragged that she had cured the barber Beshara Daher's daughter of a muscle disease that had resisted all other treatments.[68]

10-3. Midwife Malake Nafash, ca. 1908 (courtesy of Renee Hoenig).

The Shahdans and the Sirganys were related by marriage. Two of Barbara Sirgany's sons, Ameen and Michael, came to New York from Zahleh in 1893, and were both listed in the 1900 census as painter and carpenter, respectively. Their siblings and future wives came in 1898 and 1899. Barbara Sirgany may have come with her sons and practiced midwifery in the nineteenth century, but we have no record of her on any birth certificate. It is more likely that she arrived around 1900. According to the 1910 census, she had seven living children (out of eighteen pregnancies), but as far as we know, only four of her children ever came to the United States. She was listed as a nurse in 1903 and

[68] Advertisement, *Kawkab America,* October 27, 1893.

as a midwife in the 1909 *Syrian Business Directory* at 59 Washington, but by 1910, although the whole extended family (of fourteen) was still living at 59 Washington, she had retired; she was 65.

## Women-Run Restaurants, Smoking Parlors, Bars, and Brothels

There were dozens of references in American newspapers to women who were the apparent owners of establishments serving the public. Usually these articles were about crimes the women had committed or which had been committed on their property. We have one tantalizing reference to a women-run restaurant that appeared in 1893. Two young Syrian girls apparently ran a restaurant in Whitehall Street; their specialty was the twenty-five-cent dinner. One of the girls was Sarah David, 22 years old, who sued Kaisar Yamin for breach of promise.[69]

Of the numerous Turkish smoking parlors that opened in New York in 1895, some were run by Syrian women. Just as in the male-owned establishments, these parlors sometimes served as fronts for bars and/or brothels and were constantly being raided by the police, sometimes closed down and the owners arrested. In 1895, a woman named Selima Ellis (Elias) opened the Oriental Smoking Parlor at 225 West 25th Street and advertised it by putting out a notice touting the advantages of smoking Turkish tobacco in a Turkish parlor. She was arrested that same year with a man and five women (dressed in "full Oriental costume") on charges of maintaining a disorderly house. Ellis claimed to be Egyptian and the man called himself "Mahamet Ben Hassin of Cairo,"[70] but we know no more about them.

On May 18, 1897, a Syrian woman of nineteen, Lulu Yamelan (Yamin?), who resided in a smoking parlor on Henderson's Walk, Coney Island, was arrested for allegedly stealing twenty-three dollars from a client, Jacob Izenberg. The case was dismissed when it was found that the alleged larceny was not committed in the presence of the arresting policeman. Small wonder there were no witnesses if Izenberg was patronizing a prostitute! The owner of the smoking parlor, Margues Hocho (?), had been caught selling beer without a license only a few days before.[71] There is a Lulu Yamin who is mentioned as

69 "Yamin Says His Sister Objected," *The* (NY) *Sun,* July 15, 1893.

70 "Raid on a Turkish Smoking Parlor," *NYT,* June 21, 1895; "'Smoking Parlor' Raided," *NYH,* June 21, 1895.

71 "Arrested without a Warrant," *BDE,* May 18, 1897.

a donor to a Maronite cause in an early edition of *Al Hoda*. Could a prostitute be accepted in the Maronite confraternity? If so, it shows great liberality on the part of the Syrians, or perhaps the fiction of the smoking parlor was carefully maintained. It is also possible of course that the police and the newspapers got the name wrong. The outcomes of these cases are almost never reported.

A month later, Lillie Aymar, proprietress of the Turkish Smoking Resort, also on Henderson's Walk, had a former employee, Farjallah Sarphone, arrested for grand larceny for stealing $56.75 from her.[72]

A 1902 headline, "Raid at Coney Island: Roundsman Clark Swoops Down on a Turkish Smoking Parlor," concerned a nineteen-year-old Syrian woman Marion Duraney (Deratany?), who was the alleged proprietress of a brothel. She was arrested with seven "inmates" for violating the liquor tax law, vagrancy, and keeping a disorderly house. Officer Clark claimed that he had been "accosted" on the street by one May Graner, 21 years old, who invited him into the smoking parlor on Henderson's Walk in Coney Island. "The place is directly in the rear of the loop-the-loop and consists of only two rooms." He ordered a drink and was served from a "hole in the wall." There was, he testified, no sign of a liquor license in the place. Clark called it "one of the most disreputable houses on Coney Island." The "girls" in this house were certainly not Syrian. It would not be surprising if such a pattern were usual for these houses: a Syrian madam and American girls. Two of the girls were sent to the House of the Good Shepherd for six months, but the fate of the Syrian proprietress was not reported.[73] The place itself sounds unprepossessing at best, a two-room hovel with the smoking parlor/bar in the front and a bedroom in the back.

Except for Lulu, none of the other Syrian women mentioned above appear elsewhere in our database, because their names were inaccurate, they were marginal figures in the community who did not appear in other sources, or they were not Syrian at all.

That some Syrian women were madams and prostitutes seems clear: in a letter to the editors of *Kawkab America*, Yussef el Hajj, the newspaper's compositor, complained bitterly about the Syrian prostitutes who were ruining their countrymen's reputation (like the belly dancers). They were found, he said, at different houses (brothels?) and showed themselves openly at the

[72] "Held for Grand Larceny," *BDE*, June 22, 1897.

[73] *BDE*, August 30, 1902; September 6, 1902.

market (Washington Market?).[74] Did these women work for themselves, or were they managed or controlled by (Syrian) men? Were the madams owners, or did they serve a male master? Without further information, it's impossible to answer these questions.

### Dancers and Entertainers

When Syrian women appeared as individuals in the American newspapers (rather than as an example of an exotic type) it was usually because they had done something wrong. They were madams, prostitutes, peddlers (mendicants), smugglers, swindlers, and, most frequently, belly dancers. All of these "sinners," it should be noted, were workingwomen. Belly dancers were the perfect symbol of the Orientalist fantasies of American men: lust for the exotic and erotic alternated with contempt and rage at the "immorality" of the dancers. The history of belly dancing in the United States is a vexing one, because the women were treated as tropes or types, not as individuals, and it is difficult (no, impossible) to trace the careers of Middle Eastern dancers.

In January 1897, "Little Egypt" was in the headlines of all the New York papers. She had been entertaining a group of wealthy men at the elegant Sherry's Restaurant at 37th Street and Fifth Avenue when a zealous policeman named Chapman raided the place without a warrant. The affair became known as "The Awful Seeley Dinner" after the man who hosted the party, Herbert Barnum Seeley, a grandson of P.T. Barnum. Chapman tried to arrest Little Egypt for improper behavior, but he himself was instead put on trial for exceeding his authority (not with her, but in breaking up a wealthy men's dinner). Although it was Officer Chapman who was put on trial,[75] it was Little Egypt who made headlines.

The woman known as Little Egypt was Ashea Waba (Assea Wahby), and she danced the "coochee coochee" on vaudeville stages as well as in men's clubs around New York. She was famous, although we don't know much about her past. Carlton claims she was Algerian and perhaps danced at the Chicago fair.[76]

[74] *Kawkab America*, September 1, 1893.
[75] Zacks (2012: ch. 22) gives a wonderful summary of the trial.
[76] Carlton 1994: 76.

10-4. Three Egyptian dancers, Chicago fair (Buel 1894). Note the netting covering their torsos, unlike the more modest Algerian dance costumes in the following photographs.

Even though she was a witness rather than the defendant in the case, she met hostile questioning from the defense attorney trying to justify Chapman's behavior. She reportedly met this hostility with dignity, insisting that what she did was not wrong. Her theatrical agent testified in support of her statement. He stated that she had been asked to do two turns at the dinner: an Oriental dance and a pose. When asked if he had agreed that Little Egypt would dance in the nude, he said that he "never got involved with that kind of thing."

In published transcripts of the trial there was a recurring question about what she wore, whether she danced in the nude, or whether any part of her body was bare. There were conflicting responses, not least from Wahby herself, whose speech, if one can believe the newspaper transcripts, was a very broken mixture of French and English. She herself claimed she danced in the "altogether" (the meaning of which was never clarified) while others swore she was completely covered. The lawyers asked probing and prurient questions about the kind of fabric that covered her torso: was it a closely-knit mesh or could you see through it? One of the other entertainers described it as "mosquito netting." Little Egypt herself said, "The gauze was very thin where me leeta leg was."[77] The reader cannot help but think she is mocking everyone in the courtroom: the lawyer, the judge, Officer Chapman, and the reporters.

The trial occupied the papers for weeks, but finally Chapman was acquitted,[78] and the men who attended the dinner were not even called to the witness stand. Even before the end of the trial, the event was being parodied in music halls in New York; the publicity did wonders for Little Egypt's career. Oscar Hammerstein put on a burlesque of the case called *Silly's Dinner,* which starred Little Egypt herself. The police tried to shut the show down because of the dancing, but Hammerstein prevailed. It was rumored that Little Egypt earned $1,000 a week for that performance.[79] Herbert Seeley never lived the scandal down and was ever after known as "Little Egypt Seeley."

In 1908 Wahby died of gas asphyxiation, leaving an estate, the size of which ranged in various reports from $30,000 to $200,000. In the lawsuit that followed, her (American) husband claimed that her real name was Catherine Divine.[80] She did not live in the Syrian Colony but in the Tenderloin, close to her work. Certainly if she was an American, there would be no reason for her to live in the Colony. If she was, however, Arab (whether Syrian, Algerian, or Egyptian), the distance from the Colony probably provided her with a measure of freedom unattainable in the conservative Syrian society of Washington Street. She was the most famous belly dancer of the age, but not by any means the only one.

Belly dancing was possibly first seen in the United States at the 1876 Centennial Exposition in Philadelphia when a Tunisian merchant, M. Valenti, set up a Tunisian café in which there was entertainment. Whether this included belly dancing is unclear. A reporter described a group of musicians, which included two young women playing the drums, one of whom rose and danced in a manner that he described as "the swaying to and fro of her body, keeping time to the music by moving backward and forward and dexterously waving a couple of handkerchiefs."[81] No one seemed to be shocked, and she was roundly applauded. At the Paris fair of 1889, belly dancing

[77] "Chapman and Egypt Tell," *The* (NY) *Sun,* January 13, 1897.

[78] Bier 2009 discusses this case at length.

[79] Carlton 1994: 76.

[80] "Banker Hamlin Claims 'Little Egypt's' Estate," *Idaho Statesman,* January 21, 1908.

[81] "Features of the Exposition," *The Daily Graphic* (NY), June 8, 1876.

10-5. "Jamelee," Syrian dancer at the Chicago fair (*Portrait Types,* 1894).

(*la danse du ventre*) was a major attraction, and by the time of the Chicago fair in 1893, the entrepreneurs (many of whom were Syrians) knew this would be a goldmine.

One hundred and seventy-five Egyptians landed at Ellis Island on April 11, 1893, on the *Guildhall,* bound for Chicago, including eleven "dancing girls," two female flower sellers, two "Egyptian ladies," and a "girl." Several disembarking acrobats performed for those gathered on shore, and then the audience begged for the belly dancers to show what they could do. The editor of *Kawkab America* described the spectacle:

> At the word, go! A beautiful Egyptian damsel dressed with the gaudy colors of her native country and decorated from head to foot with many of its fineries, took away the veil which had heretofore hidden her lovely face, and with a graceful jesture *[sic]* with her hand, beckoned to the musicians to play for her.... Her 'Danse Du Ventre,' as the name implies, consisted in the measured movements of the stomach, shoulders and loins in accompaniment with the music, with hardly any noticeable movements of the feet. The body swayed gently to and fro, the eyes changed their expressions with almost each movement, the dancer advanced in measured steps while various parts of her body were kept in shivering-like motions

> independent from each other. She held two handkerchiefs which she used to emphasize the harmonious and undulating movements of her body.[82]

It was the first and last time that the word "measured" was used to describe belly dancing.

Two weeks later, the Syrians bound for the fair arrived on the *Cynthiana.* Twenty-three out of a total of 274 immigrants were female; all were listed as "performers," and most of them were probably dancers.

10-6. "Salina," Algerian dancer at the Chicago fair (*Portrait Types,* 1894).

At the fair itself, lines formed to get into the Turkish Theater and all the other venues where belly dancing was offered, despite admission charges of twenty-five or fifty cents. It may be, in fact, that belly dancing saved the Columbian fair from bankruptcy; certainly Cairo Street was the biggest moneymaker in the fair, and the dancing was a huge part of its success. Everyone knew that "people were not interested in watching anything except the

[82] "The Egyptians at the Immigration Bureau," *Kawkab America* (English), April 7, 1893.

Egyptian girls dancing."[83] An ethnologist, in an introduction to one of the books about the fair, wrote, "Here in the playhouse of the [Cairo] street were gathered the dancing women, and here was to be witnessed the national dans [sic] du ventre which not being understood was by many regarded as low and repulsive."[84] Carlton speculates that the fair promoters were very canny in encouraging the press, several respectable society women, and Anthony Comstock (the founder and head of the New York Committee for the Suppression of Vice) to fulminate against the immorality of these performances. As described above, the managers of the fair frequently tried to shut down these venues, thus guaranteeing their success.

A full-page photograph of three belly dancers at the Chicago fair captures the mix of revulsion and sexual thrill that these dancers evoked. Captioned "Three Dancing Girls from Egypt," the description reads:

> Visitors to the Midway Plaisance theatres will recognize at once in the photograph herewith the girls who delighted spectators by their contortion dances in the Egyptian theatre. While their exhibitions were sensationally, if not sensually, amusing, the girls were not otherwise calculated to attract attention save it be by their immodest costumes. Writers of Oriental stories have created the impression among the uninformed that houris of the East are sylph-like and beautiful; but close contact reveals them as we behold them here, destitute of animation, formless as badly-stuffed animals, as homely as owls, and graceless as stall-fed bovines. But truth compels us to add that the dancing girls in the Midway were not the best types of their race either in form or character, and that their abdominal muscles were the only portions of anatomy or mind which showed any cultivation, while these, to their shame, were displayed to serve the basest uses.[85]

Sol Bloom, the man who developed and promoted the Midway Plaisance, is credited with composing (or publishing) the song that was ever after associated with Orientalist performance: "The Streets of Cairo, or the Poor Little Country Maid." We learned it as children: "There's a place in France/where the women wear no pants."[86] It is also the universal tune of snake charmers.

Many Syrians were offended by the dancing as well, feeling that it sullied

---

[83] *Kawkab America*, June 30, 1893.

[84] Anonymous, *Portrait Types* 1894. "Introduction" by F.W. Putnam.

[85] Buel 1894: n.p.

[86] http://en.wikipedia.org/wiki/Sol_Bloom.

the Syrians' reputation, and they frequently protested that the dancers were not Syrian at all. Buonaventura, however, says that the main attraction at the Midway was indeed a Syrian, Fahreda Mazhar.[87] There is no way to know whether she was indeed Syrian, North African or Egyptian. The sheer number of dancers and the prevalence of Syrian entertainers at the fair would argue for the presence of Egyptian, Syrian, *and* North African dancers.

When asked his opinion about the propriety of the *danse du ventre,* Nageeb Arbeely, the probable author of the description of the dancers at New York harbor, replied that he thought the dance as presented at the fair was much exaggerated; that the women were showing more of their bodies than the women do in the Middle East; and that women should be barred from the audience.[88] He refused to condemn it outright, however, and in that, I think, he was being a smart businessman, knowing that the huge audiences were very profitable for Syrians at the fair and a good foundation for future business for Syrian traders.

One article cites a "dignified and cultivated Syrian" who wrote a letter to the fair authorities "explaining the viciousness of what is shown there, and protesting against it in the name of decency."[89] One wonders who this Syrian was. It must have been one who had no investment in the entertainment venues. One also wonders whether the women were encouraged or coerced into showing more of their bodies by their managers, once it was clear that the audience was more interested in the eroticism than in any authentic performance. Finally, the same reporter spelled out the problem: "How are the distracted and badgered managerial gentlemen to decide just at what point the rights of concessionaires and ethnologists end and covert vice and unpleasant nudity begin?"[90]

The dancers earned $500 for their six-month stint in Chicago, and some of them used the money to form their own dance troupes and travel around the country, or else they went home and lived very well for a while. In 1894—less than a year after the fair closed—the newly minted concept of the amusement park, including belly dancing, moved first to Coney Island and then spread around the United States. Oriental entertainments sprang up all over the country, from Omaha to San Jose. Bostock's Midway Carnival, for example, set up

[87] Buonaventura 1998: 101–102.
[88] "Those Wicked Dances," *Tacoma Daily News,* August 15, 1893.
[89] "La Danse du Ventre," *The* (NY) *Sun,* August 20, 1893.
[90] "La Danse du Ventre," *The* (NY) *Sun,* August 20, 1893.

in Brooklyn in 1900. The show had "Oriental dancers who had been with Mr. Bostock since the close of the great fair."[91] Nicola D. Abdelnour was in charge of the "Oriental Department" at Bostock's. There was no possibility that these troupes could all have had authentic North African or Egyptian dancers; there just weren't that many at the fair. American imitators were required, and appeared almost immediately. "Little Egypts" popped up everywhere.

A twelve-second film of a dancer who supposedly performed at the Columbian fair ("Princess Ali") was made by Thomas Edison two years after the close of the fair. It shows a graceful, slender, serious young woman accompanied by two musicians.[92] Judging by their clothes, they were North Africans. To our eyes, there is nothing in the least erotic about the woman's dress or her movements, but she is beautiful. In contrast, Edison made several other motion pictures, which were meant to be titillating. Carlton[93] identifies the dancer in one of the films as someone called Madame Ruth, also supposedly a performer at the Chicago fair. Another film, made perhaps at the turn of the century and called "Fatima's Dance," is supposedly a film of Fatima Djemille (c. 1890–1921),[94] another dancer known as Little Egypt. Buonaventura is convinced that this woman too was Middle Eastern, both because of her clothing and because the style of her dancing was authentic.[95] One of these early films was censored by having a kind of "white picket fence" painted across the lower half of the dancer, probably the earliest instance of film censorship in the world.

Another Edison film, titled *Passion Dance*, was shown in hand-cranked Edison kinetoscopes at Coney Island. Shots of men looking into the machines are intercut with the dance in the YouTube version. The movie is remarkable not only for the liveliness and sensuousness of the dancer's thrusting hips, but also for the smile on her face.[96] The film held the record in peep-show attendance until it was banned.[97] One wonders why the men preferred to see the kinetoscope version, when live dancers were performing just a few steps away. Perhaps the novelty of the moving picture was as much of an attraction as the subject matter.

---

91 "Bostock's Midway Carnival," *BDE*, April 8, 1900.
92 www.youtube.com/watch?v=7sUhmmoiNxc.
93 Carlton 1994: 78.
94 http://www.youtube.com/watch?v=sj4aABDTjos. The birthdate assigned to her cannot be accurate.
95 Buonaventura 1998: 105.
96 http://www.youtube.com/watch?v=KVGdP7oI1Ec.
97 Buonaventura 1998: 104.

The real names of the dancers are elusive, which is why it is so difficult to know how many of them were actually Middle Eastern. Little Egypt, Fatima, Sayeda, Millie (a corruption of Mademoiselle) and other names became generic for all belly dancers, making it impossible to identify, let alone follow the career of, an individual dancer. Attempts to distinguish one Fatima from another, to assign an identity to each dancer, have proved futile. There are more than a thousand newspaper articles and advertisements mentioning Little Egypt between 1890 and 1910, and it is clear that at least a score of women used the name, including many Americans.[98] The women were advertised as "Little Egypt," "the original Little Egypt," or, even more specifically, "the Seeley Dinner Little Egypt." One of the few Syrian claimants to the throne whose name we know was Zarapha Scharba, who was arrested in Omaha along with five or six other vagrants. She was "on the tramp" and disguised as a man, supposedly to escape an abusive stepfather. She claimed she was the original Little Egypt, and the reporter asserted that she was indeed "the living image of the newspaper portraits of the famous Little Egypt." Several men who had seen Little Egypt at the fair were ready to testify that Zarapha was she. She gave her English name as Cora Rout.[99] When she died two years later, the paper said, "She was not the Little Egypt who created the sensation at the Seeley dinner in New York, but she is the Little Egypt of World's fair fame, and in her line she was considered a prodigy."[100] Was she even Syrian? Not if Cora Rout was her real name.

One newspaper reporter at least recognized the paradox of the scores of Little Egypts: "If the New York girl is Little Egypt, who the dickens is the little woman who has been drinking wine in Butte?"[101] A few months later, an advertisement responded to the obvious skepticism members of the public were feeling about the proliferation of Little Egypts. The program of an "Oriental Theatre" included:

> La Nina Pare, the Queen of the Orient, the Sword Dancer of Algiers; La Belle Fatima, The Sultan's Favorite in Turkish Dance; and Little Egypt, The Egyptian Marvel of Eastern Terpsichorean Art, whose sensation, created at the Seeley dinner in New York City recently is still fresh in the minds of all." The ad then ends with the following challenge: "(N.B. The management will forfeit $1000 to anyone who can prove that this is not the original 'Little Egypt.')[102]

[98] Here as elsewhere, I use the term "American" as the Syrians did: as a synonym for non-Syrian or non-Arab.

[99] "Is Little Egypt in Omaha?" *Omaha World Herald,* August 21, 1897.

[100] "Little Egypt," *Omaha World Herald,* August 7, 1899.

[101] "Now Which 'Tis, Anyway?" *Anaconda* (MT) *Standard,* January 10, 1898.

[102] Advertisement, *Repository* (Canton, OH), August 28, 1898.

The management's money was perfectly safe.

A reporter who wrote with fascination about the performers from the Street of Cairo at Coney Island noted the presence of "one of the score or more 'original Fatimas.' She is said to be the original Turkish Fatima who gained fame at the world fair, and is one of the cleverest muscle dancers in the country."[103]

Farida Mazhar, a dancer at the Chicago fair, whom most agree was truly Syrian, was pictured in a sketch accompanying a disapproving article about the *danse du ventre* at the fair. Despite the vitriol of the text, she is portrayed as a dignified presence, with well-coiffed hair, eyebrows that join above her nose, and a seemingly authentic dancer's costume. However, the caption admits, "in compliance with the scruples of the managers of the fair, a thin woolen undershirt has been substituted for the ordinary gauze shirt, which fully reveals the color and the muscular variations of the surface beneath."[104] Farida went on to perform in traveling shows that toured the United States, sometimes billed as Little Egypt, sometimes as Fatima, and sometimes by her real (married) name, Farida Mazhar Spyropolous. Her husband apparently managed her act. She brought several lawsuits against other women who were using the name Little Egypt. She performed for perhaps the last time in 1933, exactly forty years after her American debut, at Chicago's Century of Progress, under the name "Little Egypt."[105]

I think we can assume that many of the dancers at the fairs were Middle Eastern; the attempt to present exhibits that showed the Oriental way of life would have demanded, at least at first, that real belly dancers be brought to the fairs, and we have seen the presence of a number of dancers on the ships coming from the Middle East. We know that many of them did go on to perform in traveling shows around America. But if the Seeley's Dinner Little Egypt, aka Ashea Wahby, was actually Catherine Divine, Zarapha Scharba was really Cora Rout, and Zuleika was Grace Williams, then American women began performing "Middle Eastern" dances as early as 1893 and were ubiquitous by 1897. It is probable that what these women did on stage had no resemblance to belly dancing or any kind of Middle Eastern dancing. The exotic trappings were a thin cover for the beginnings of burlesque.

In the world of carnivals, amusement parks, vaudeville, and burlesque the

[103] "Coney Island Turks," *BDE,* January 24, 1897.

[104] "La Danse du Ventre," *The* (NY) *Sun,* August 20, 1893.

[105] http://www.columbiaspectator.com/2009/04/14/little-scandal-goes-long-way.

name assigned to the dance degenerated from its first exalted French name, la *danse du ventre*, to "contortion dancing," "muscle dancing," "belly dancing," "the Nautch dance" (after an Indian traditional dance), "coochee-coochee,"[106] the "hootchie-cootchie," and finally to "cooch." Like the names, the dance itself degenerated from the refined ethnologically authentic to the frankly sexual.

Two separate aspects of belly dancing—the "erotic" movements and scanty clothing—became targets for police intervention. The New York police were especially zealous in trying to enforce morality around these performances, for which the condemnation was as universal as the attendance was large. At one of the performances at the 1893 New York expo at the Grand Central Palace, Police Inspector Williams was in the audience. After witnessing the dancing, he stood up and yelled, "Stop that!," then shut the show down.[107] One wonders how much and what he saw. The four dancers at the Palace (Algerians, according to Nance[108])—Farida (was this Farida Mazhar?), sisters Zora and Zulika Zimman (was the latter Grace Williams?), and Fatima Mesgish—were arrested for indecency. All the dancers said that nothing they did was indecent. Farida, in testimony, averred that the high kicking that American dancers did was truly indecent, and she also objected to the evening dress of American women as improper; her dancing, she said, was perfectly respectable.[109] In fact, the *Times* reported that the women seemed to treat the whole thing as a joke: "they laughed and chatted gaily and took a great interest in what was going on."[110] Their lawyer reiterated their contention that their dancing was art, not obscenity. The judge allowed the dancing to continue (he had attended their performance at the Chicago fair) and set bail for the women at $300, which their manager M. Delacroix promptly paid. They continued to perform at the Palace, albeit in a "toned-down" version, with "smiles of triumph."[111] One doesn't know whether the movements or the clothing prompted the arrest; both seemed to be at issue.

Shafika Lutfy, the daughter of Abdow Lutfy, was deeply offended by the signs advertising these belly dancers at the New York expo, implying, as she thought, that the dancers were Syrians. After she unsuccessfully tried to

[106] In the press, the dance is sometimes spelled "couchee-couchee," perhaps alluding to the French verb *coucher*. I have used that spelling only in quotations from the press; otherwise I use the more vernacular spelling.

[107] "Too Oriental for Williams," *NYT,* December 3, 1893.

[108] Nance 2009: 185.

[109] "Worst Williams Ever Saw," *The* (NY) *Sun*, December 4, 1893.

[110] "Police and Law Defied," *NYT,* December 5, 1893.

[111] "Police and Law Defied," *NYT*, December 5, 1893.

persuade the manager to take down the signs she tore them down herself, to the approbation of other Syrians who refused to be associated with indecent Egyptian belly dancing.[112] The editors of *Kawkab America* equated belly dancing with prostitution,[113] only six months after Arbeely had admiringly described the arriving belly dancers on their way to the fair. Had the quality of the dancing changed that much? Or were the Syrians simply frightened of being associated with any kind of scandal? Notwithstanding the distaste with which the Syrians professed to view this dancing, *Kawkab America* allowed a classified ad to be inserted in its pages searching for a beautiful Oriental dancer to perform in a New York theater. Applicants were to contact the paper's management.[114]

As Nance points out, one of the many striking things about these performances was the number of women in the audience. Even at the Chicago fair, despite the hot debate about its immorality, a goodly number of women attended these dances.[115] M. Delacroix proclaimed to all and sundry that even Mrs. Parker Palmer (the very proper Head of the Women's Committee at the fair) had seen them. Mrs. Palmer sometimes denied having seen the dancers at all, and at other times said she went only in order to decide whether to condemn them. Reporters claimed to be shocked at the fact that women attended and even more shocked that they sometimes brought their children, but apparently women made up an important part of the audience, including at Coney Island.[116]

The *danse du ventre* was banned in New York in 1894 (less than six months after the close of the Columbian fair). Then, in 1897, the Stage Regulation Bill was passed. Spearheaded by Anthony Comstock, it proscribed the wearing of tights and see-through clothing in a public theater or resort in the presence of the opposite sex.[117] Theater impresarios got around both these proscriptions very cleverly. In terms of the ban against the erotic movement of the belly dance, they began using ethnographic-sounding names. A "Hawaiian traditional dance" by one Mlle. Zara and the Moroccan impresario Hadji Cheriff attracted the attention of the police but was allowed to continue. A dancer at Coney Island, who was arrested for dancing the coochee-coochee,

[112] *Kawkab America*, December 15, 1893.
[113] *Kawkab America,* December 8, 1893.
[114] Advertisement, *Kawkab America,* December 15, 1893.
[115] "La Danse du Ventre," *The* (NY) *Sun,* August 20, 1893.
[116] Nance 2009: 189.
[117] Bier 2009: n.p.

claimed she was a Mexican, dancing a purely Spanish dance."[118] Another troupe of performers on the Lower East Side were given rules to which they had to conform: "They may kick as high as they please but I won't have any contortions of either end or in the middle."[119]

The contortions were one thing; nudity was another. As we saw in the trial of Ashea Wahby, the court was fixated on her clothes: how much of her skin was allowed to show? Did she wear flesh-colored tights or not? Was her torso covered, and if so, with what? Was the fabric transparent? Had she really signed a contract agreeing to drop her gauze draperies? In a time when the sight of a woman's ankle could arouse men, the suggestion of nakedness—let alone nakedness itself—was shocking to the general public. At the same time, the fact that Little Egypt or some of the others might have been dancing nude or partially nude contributed to the increasing popularity of the Oriental "strip-tease," the rise of burlesque, and the concomitant increase in police raids.

Two illustrations in the *National Police Gazette* pandered to the prurient crowds. One front-page illustration showed "Little Egypt" with her draperies alluringly pulled away, wearing black fishnet stockings, the very briefest of shorts, and only fishnet over her midriff.[120] Another article about a show in Coney Island showed "Fatima" bent over backwards and thrusting her hips toward a "crowd of sports," who grinned lasciviously at the dancer. She was modestly dressed, but as the article noted, this only showed "that clothes can be used to display as well as conceal." At the end, she supposedly performed in nothing but a "pair of black stockings." The audience in the sketch was exclusively male,[121] as must have been the readership of the newspaper.

In 1897, a woman known as "Garmenia," was arrested for dancing nude at August Hoffman's Theater in Brooklyn. Formerly a dancer at the Street of Cairo in Coney Island, Garmenia was said to be Little Egypt in disguise,[122] although how one can be in disguise while dancing nude is puzzling. "Even after three-quarters of her dance had been cut out at the streets of Cairo last summer the police saw enough of what remained to call [it] immodest and warrant her arrest."[123] In the raid of Turkish establishments in Coney Island in 1897, four women were arrested for doing the coochee-coochee dance:

[118] "Adjie to Dance for the Jury," *BDE,* July 10, 1896.

[119] "Danse du Ventre Must Stop," *The* (NY) *Evening World,* April 13, 1894.

[120] "Little Egypt and Anita," *National Police Gazette,* December 28, 1895.

[121] "Danse du Ventre in Brooklyn, NY," *National Police Gazette,* March 31, 1894.

[122] "Another 'Seeley Dinner,'" *St. Albans* (VT) *Daily Messenger,* February 4, 1897.

[123] "Coney Island Turks," *BDE,* January 27, 1897.

Fatima, La Belle Rosa, Zuleika, and La Belle Saida. Fatima was supposedly the wife of George Jabour, the owner of the Turkish Theater. If she was indeed his wife, it's possible that she was Syrian. We know that at least one of the dancers was an American (Zuleika was Grace Williams), but what about the other two? Both Zuleika and La Belle Saida worked for American impresarios. On promising the judge that Saida would no longer perform, her boss was able to keep his show open.[124] After the summer season, many of these performers were stuck in Coney Island, living in unheated rooms that had once served as theaters or coffeehouses. These rooms, according to the reporter, were furnished in the Oriental style, the divan belonging to "Fatima and usually occupied by her and four or five others."[125]

Like the dancers at the Grand Central Palace, belly dancers began to tone down their dancing or drape themselves in robes, at least when the police were likely to be present. When the Hadji Cheriff Troupe played at Miner's Bowery Theatre, "the women were clad in loose fitting varicolored garments that covered their forms entirely from their ankles to their necks. The old blue laws of Connecticut could not have demanded more. Their costumes reminded one in the makeup, if not in color, of the regulation Asbury Park bathing suit."[126] There was not a single contortion. The (male) audience members were not happy; they started yelling, "Get a move on, you!" and finally left the theater in disgust.

Most of these "Arabian" performances took place in American-owned venues: Koster & Bial's Theater, Proctor's, the Casino, and Hammerstein's. But it seems likely that some of the smaller venues owned by Syrians—Turkish theaters, restaurants, or smoking parlors—also featured belly dancers as part of the entertainment. Whether owned by Syrians or Americans, the audiences were not Arabs, but Americans—and usually, but not exclusively, men.

George Jabour, who hailed from Constantinople, owned the Turkish Theater on Tilyou's Walk, Coney Island. He sued a *New York World* reporter for extortion in 1897, and in the course of the trial it came out that Jabour's wife, Fatima, danced the coochee-coochee dance in his theater. Jabour replied that she did not dance the coochee-coochee, merely "executed the muscle dance, but did it properly."[127] The distinction between muscle dancing and

[124] "Good-Bye to Wriggle Dances," *The* (NY*) Sun,* August 11, 1897.

[125] "Coney Island Turks," *BDE,* January 24, 1897.

[126] "New Danse du Ventre: How the Oriental Dance Should Be Performed to Avoid Police Interference," *NYH,* April 14, 1894.

[127] "Murray Was Acquitted," *BDE,* August 13, 1897.

the coochee-coochee is now lost to us, and was certainly lost on the judge. The trial lasted only two hours, and the judge dismissed the case as entirely uncorroborated, acquitting the reporter. He did not even have to mount a defense. The judge's last words to the court were, "I think he (Jabour) has been running an indecent and immoral show and I believe the defendant innocent. Complaint dismissed. Defendant discharged."[128] Was Fatima really Jabour's wife? Was this the same Fatima Djemille that Carlton reckoned was truly Middle Eastern?

In 1898, a fight broke out between the editors of *Al Ayyam* and *Al Alam* newspapers over "couchee-couchee" dancing. The compositor of *Al Ayyam*, Esau el-Khoury (the future husband of Marie T. Azeez), claimed that Elias Trad, a henchman of George Jabour, the editor of *Al Alam*, had stabbed him. Khoury said that his newspaper had published an editorial threatening to go to the Board of Public Morals to demand the prohibition of belly dancing, "which has worked great harm to the Syrians and their reputation in this country" (as it was translated for the judge). The compositor also claimed that a bribe had been offered him by "those that hold and trade in this abusive dance" if he would refuse to compose these critical articles. "Those" clearly referred to Jabour, who owned such a place on Coney Island. Trad was "nothing but a camel driver," averred el-Khoury.[129]

It must be said that the fights probably had less to do with belly dancing than with the factional battles that were already swirling around the Syrian newspapers at this time. A sub-headline of the article in the *Sun* stated, "Denunciatory Article [in *Al Ayyam*] Declared to Preach Anarchy," so there may have also been a political motive behind the attacks. Other newspapers treated it as a plagiarism case or a case of censorship of one newspaper by another. The real motive behind the stabbing was never made clear. Trad was at first let free, which enraged the editor of *Al Ayyam,* but a coochee-coochee dancer named Caroline Dibs testified that Trad had attacked el-Khoury, and based on her testimony the judge held Trad on $1,000 bail, although he was finally acquitted.[130] The judge declared it was all a "tempest in a teapot."

After yet another raid on his Turkish theater, specifically aimed at the coochee-coochee dancers, Jabour seemed about ready to pack it in. He reportedly talked to the manager of Street of Cairo about selling, but apparently

[128] "Murray Was Acquitted," *BDE,* August 13, 1897.

[129] "Syrian Couchee-Couchee," *The* (NY) *Sun,* March 23, 1898.

[130] *The* (NY) *Sun,* March 23, 1898.

they could not come to an agreement.[131] Notwithstanding these setbacks, the variety show that Jabour built at Coney Island soon morphed into the Jabour Carnival and Circus Company, featuring a Ferris wheel, a loop-the-loop, and its most popular attraction: "Moorish dancing girls." After the dancing girls, Fatima, the trained bear, did her turn.[132] The circus traveled all over the United States from 1901 to at least 1904, but Jabour declared personal bankruptcy in 1903, with liabilities of $87,000 and no assets.[133]

As late as 1911, Houghton reported that there were several Syrian-owned Turkish theaters still running in New York, "with Turkish dances and fortune-telling. But they are on the East Side and are not patronized by Syrians."[134] Certainly by this time, most of the dancers were American women who were paid to dress up in Oriental garb (like Mae West) and imitate belly dancers on the burlesque stage. Genuine Middle Eastern dancers became redundant because it's doubtful that the audience cared who was taking her clothes off for them. It's probable that American women were dancing these erotic Orientalist fantasies very early (if not actually at the Chicago fair, certainly immediately afterward); the number of genuine Middle Eastern dancers was always tiny. In fact, it is hard to imagine nineteenth-century Middle Eastern women performing nude or seminude on stage. But just because it's hard to imagine doesn't mean it didn't happen. Women, like men, will do many things if their livelihood depends on it. By the end of the century, the Syrian population was moving out of the scrabbling new immigrant stage into the middle class, and belly dancers had no place in that upwardly mobile society. No woman, it should be noted, claimed to be a dancer or an entertainer in the 1900 census. The intra- and internecine strife in the Syrian Colony over coochee-coochee dancing showed that some members saw it as a threat to the community's reputation, while others profited from it.

There were other kinds of work open to women entertainers, and a number of Arab women performed in vaudeville and circus acts, not as belly dancers but as acrobats or ethnic types. We know that Middle Eastern women were part of all of the "Arabian" troupes: Hajji Tahar's, Ben Said's, Ben Ali's, and Hadji Cheriff's. There was an Arab woman scheduled to perform for Barnum and Bailey's circus in 1897. She was probably an acrobat. The

[131] "Coney Island Crusade Goes On," *NYH,* August 12, 1897.
[132] "Pictures of Fair," *Watertown* (NY) *Daily Times,* May 27, 1903.
[133] *The Billboard,* 1902–1903: 7.
[134] Houghton 1911: II: 654.

woman, Fadilla Mohamed, was the daughter of Sheik Elias Mohamed, himself a performer at Wild Bill Hickok's Wild West Show in New York. According to the story, her father had contracted with the well-known Moroccan impresario Hajji Tahar to put her in the circus. She rebelled by disappearing before the Barnum and Bailey ship sailed for England.[135] Whether Fadilla and her father were North African, or even really Arab, is impossible to ascertain, but the fact that Sheik Elias did business with Hajji Tahar—given the insular quality of the Moroccan community here—suggests that father and daughter were Moroccan.

We also have documentation of two American women, disguised as Arabs, who performed in these shows; so just as belly dancing was immediately coopted by American women, so was circus entertainment. In an article titled "Alice Noonan, Mohammedan," the *Times* told the unlikely story of an Irish girl who had married the Algerian Hadji Bendib, converted to Islam, and made the pilgrimage to Mecca with her husband. They performed together in Mr. Bailey's circus at Madison Square Garden.[136] Another performer, Mrs. Massoud Ben Hadji, was an acrobat with Hassan Ben Ali's troupe; a reporter said, "Her face betokened Hibernian rather than Oriental origin."[137] She was simply an American woman married to a Moroccan who was passing herself off as an Arab entertainer.

Just as Fadilla rebelled against her father's effort to place her in Hajji Tahar's troupe, two court cases, discussed in chapter 14, forcefully bring up the idea that some young and/or female performers were apprenticed, indentured, or sold by their parents to the leaders of the troupes. It is difficult to tease out the degree of coercion involved in these arrangements. These practices of course were not limited to Arab troupes, nor were the victims necessarily Arabs, but certainly there were some Arab perpetrators and some Arab victims.

## Women on the Lecture Circuit

In the same way that some of the male Syrian "intellectuals" made their living by lecturing about the Holy Land, women traveled around the country giving talks and presentations. In 1890, Ramza Macksoud, her fifteen-year

[135] "Achou Schamdjain's Quest," *BDE,* December 1, 1897.

[136] "Alice Noonan, Mohammedan," *NYT,* March 31, 1895.

[137] "Arab Whirlers in Court," *New-York Tribune,* March 25, 1899.

old niece Shafika Lutfy (who later tore down the belly dancing sign at the New York expo), and Shafika's brothers, Deeb and Ameen, traveled around the country giving demonstrations of Oriental customs. Mrs. Macksoud took top billing in all the announcements. All three Lutfys were the children of the merchant Abdow Lutfy of New York; Ramza was his widowed sister. An "Oriental Reception" was usually given at the home of a prominent socialite and then repeated at a local church. The Lutfys were described as "native Syrians and representatives of one of the oldest and most aristocratic families of Damascus."[138] They reenacted a Syrian wedding, complete with five bridesmaids, chanted wedding songs, and served a "wedding feast" of Turkish sweets. They even gave a demonstration of Muslims praying. In the announcement before one of the shows it was stressed that they "are not objects of charity, and no collection will be taken, but if any wish to buy any of their goods they will have the opportunity of doing so."[139] "The ladies who are right good looking for Syrians didn't charge anything for the broken and otherwise mutilated English they distributed, but when their vocabulary gave out they offered for sale some articles they had with them, and quite a number of purchasers paid four prices *[sic]* for several things and went home glad of the opportunity to do something for the far-off mission fields of Syria."[140] Did the reporter mean the audience paid four times what the articles were worth?

Collecting money for mission work in Syria is only one one of the pitches they used. In other venues, the Lutfys claimed to be earning money for college: Shafika "hoped to enter Wellesley," Deeb planned to attend Union Theological Seminary, and other members of the family were allegedly studying at Columbia.[141] As far as I can tell, none of the Lutfys ever went to college; all were too busy making a living or, in Shafika's case, marrying and raising a family. Sometimes they claimed they were raising money for the Syrian poor, but of course they were simply making a living. At one of these events, Ramza claimed she was accumulating funds for her children, "for she is a widow,"[142] which was true, but we don't know whether she had children or whether they needed to be supported.

---

138 "Oriental Reception," *Rocky Mountain News* (Denver),January 21, 1891.

139 "Real Syrian Women Will Talk," *Daily Register* (Rockford, IL), June 4, 1890.

140 "The Syrian Ladies' Show," *Daily Register* (Rockford, IL), June 5, 1890.

141 "At the Churches," *Rocky Mountain News* (Denver), January 11, 1891.

142 "From Far Off Syria," *Omaha World Herald,* June 15, 1890.

The family appeared again in a newspaper in Worcester, Massachusetts, in June 1892, when Shafika lost a watch. When it was returned to her, she was quick to tell the reporter about the Syrian handiwork she and her aunt had for sale.[143] Ramza Macksoud claimed that the students at the Damascus school where she taught had made these goods, but they were probably imported in bulk by her brother Abdow and supplied to her, just as he supplied other *jezdan harir* peddlers. Although we might regard these people as hucksters, they were simply peddlers dressed up in intellectual garb, using Orientalism to sell themselves and their goods. There seemed to be no shame attached to the practice in the Syrian community. Ramza became a respected member of the New York Colony, serving several terms as an officer of the Syrian Women's Union, as did Shafika, who went on to marry a prominent New York merchant, Elias Macksoud. The Lutfy brothers became successful merchants, first working with their father and then on their own.

Other woman lecturers in the 1890s took a different path, foreswearing costumes and reenactments and concentrating on delivering high-minded lectures on conditions in Syria or other topics. Hanna Korany had been a journalist in Syria and came to the United States with her husband to attend the Chicago fair as the "representative of Syrian womanhood," whatever that meant. She traveled around the country giving lectures, but she died in 1898 at the age of twenty-seven.

Layyah Barakat had a harrowing story to tell about her persecution by the Turks. She was a Presbyterian convert from Abeih who married the Presbyterian minister Elias Barakat; they narrowly escaped with their lives in the Alexandrian massacres of 1882 and came to America. Supported by the Presbyterian Mission, they traveled and lectured around the United States, sometimes separately and sometimes together. The Protestant missionary Henry Jessup was a great fan of Mme. Barakat's, feeling that she was an ideal spokesperson for the Presbyterians' efforts in Syria,[144] but others were not as taken with her. A bitter letter from another Presbyterian missionary reads, "Layeh Barakat, one of the most earnest advocates of 'doing something' for Syrian woman and who showed considerable ability to interest people to give for missionary labor by a native of Syria, has not stepped foot on

[143] "Her Watch Returned," *Worcester* (MA) *Daily Spy,* June 2, 1892.

[144] *Presbyterian Letters,* H.H. Jessup to Ellinwood, July 8 1884. "I little thought when she sat on a mat in my house in Mt. Lebanon in 1872, that in twelve years that Syrian girl would be melting great congregations to tears by her pathetic story far beyond the seas!"

Syrian soil since she left it eleven years ago. All the money she has collected for missionary work is still in her possession, for nothing is being done, or has been done, unless an occasional dollar to her poor old mother is called missionary work."[145]

In a class all her own, Alice Azeez began lecturing on the "manners and customs of Arabs and Mohammedans of the Syrian desert" in New York churches in 1892.[146] Her English was apparently fluent, learned in British schools in Syria. She would appear in native costume and play "Syrian airs" on the piano.[147] She was only sixteen. In 1894, she went back out on the road, claiming to be a Syrian princess by the name of "Fannitza Abdul Sultana Nalide," which sounds nothing like Alice Azeez. To add to her air of mystery, she said she had been living "in seclusion" in Brooklyn, although the number of interviews she gave in the many cities she visited during 1894 make it difficult to see how this could be true. She had mastered, she said, the "Arabian, Assyrian, Grecian, Latin, French, German, and English languages," and her needlework was collected by the Metropolitan Museum.[148] She also took out a patent for a fabric design in 1898; the fact that she was able to take out a patent at her relatively young age is rather remarkable.[149]

Like many of the other Syrian lecturers, Azeez claimed she wanted to give her life to "the amelioration of the women of her race"[150] and to build a monument to her father,[151] although in 1894 her father was still alive and the proprietor of a successful jewelry store in Atlantic City. The occasion for the article was her enrollment in the Harvard Annex (which later became Radcliffe College) to learn the ways of the West so that she could bring them home to her benighted sisters. There is no evidence that she actually enrolled. Did all this treacle come from her, or did the reporter invent it? One imagines she fed it to him by the spoonful.

In 1903, Alice was still actively promoting herself. A reporter accurately noted, "There are very few women of her age that can do more things to make money, or [do] them better." He reported that she had recently written a book about a Syrian girl's life in America, imported hundreds of Syrian

[145] *Presbyterian Letters,* Harris to Ellinwood, September 25, 1893.

[146] "Our New York Letter," *St. Louis Republic,* November 29, 1891.

[147] "In Her Native Garb," *The* (NY) *Press,* March 6, 1892.

[148] "In Her Native Garb," *The* (NY) *Press,* March 6, 1892.

[149] Publication number USD29351 S, published September 13, 1898.

[150] "Talented and a Princess," *Cleveland Plain Dealer*, September 23, 1894.

[151] "Fannitza Abdul Sultana Nalide," *Chicago Tribune,* October 6, 1894.

plants to grow in the New York Botanical Garden, given talks about Oriental life out west, and invented a shower nozzle that sprayed water in the shape of a flower.[152] She was no longer using her princess moniker, nor did she mention her cousin—"the richest man in Beirut"—again; but she did admit that her father's economic reversals in Syria had forced them to come to the United States. Alice's new project was to start a women's magazine. "Yes," she said, "I suppose it does take a lot of money to start any sort of periodical in New York, but that doesn't frighten me. I shall soon earn money enough."[153] One has the feeling this was not an idle boast. We do not know if anything came of it. She finally settled down and became a landscape painter living in New York City with her widowed mother and sister, the jeweler Marie el-Khoury.

Sometimes these ladies did not even bother to give lectures. There were many articles in the society columns of newspapers describing visiting Syrian women being hosted by local matrons. The host guaranteed the guest's respectability and authenticity. The article would specify the hours at which the guest would be "at home," ready to receive women callers. She would always have things to sell. There was very little difference between these women and the "ladies of the road" described above, the latter perhaps being slightly more open about being primarily saleswomen. Again, these women who sold goods at the homes of the wealthy were regarded as perfectly respectable, both by the women in the local community who bought their goods and by the sellers' Syrian compatriots at home. When my mother went off to college in Lexington, Kentucky, in 1932, her father sent with her several dozen fine linen handkerchiefs from his stock, along with an invoice, and my mother sold these to her classmates (at retail), providing her with spending money.

It is also noteworthy that many of these speakers were described as new converts from Mohammedism to Christianity, but of course they were all Christians to begin with. It is well known that the number of converts from Islam to Christianity in Syria in the nineteenth century could be counted on the fingers of one hand. If these ladies were indeed recent converts, it was from one of the other Christian sects, but admitting this would spoil both the aura of sanctity around the new convert, as well as diminish the thrill of the conquest over Muslim "heresy."

---

152 "Miss Azeez from Syria," *The* (NY) *Sun*, September 27, 1903.
153 "Miss Azeez from Syria," *The* (NY) *Sun*, September 27, 1903.

All of these rather low-key, high-toned events, which began with a presentation of some aspect of the "Oriental" way of life and ended with a sale of Syrian tapestries and objects, both benefitted from and fuelled the Orientalist craze sweeping the country.

## Chapter 11

### Syrian Brooklyn in the Nineteenth Century: "Dainty Homes in Tenements"

*The very best and most prosperous class of Orientals, it should be said, do not live here [in Manhattan] at all. Their men come to Washington Street to [do] business during the day, but their homes are in Brooklyn or on Staten Island.*[1]

Although most people think of the Syrian enclave of Brooklyn as a twentieth-century phenomenon, in fact the movement to Brooklyn began in the early 1890s.[2] While the majority of these early settlers lived in the South Ferry section around Atlantic Avenue, which would become the heart of "Little Syria," others lived farther afield, most notably in the neighborhood that Miller called "South Brooklyn," but which was referred to as West Brooklyn on late nineteenth-century maps, and is today known as Sunset Park.[3]

One of the first Syrians to settle in Brooklyn was Thomas Rahaim, a Maronite from Jezzine, who lived at 32 Willow Place in 1890, in the heart of South Ferry. He moved to Manhattan a few years later but returned to Brooklyn in 1898. Albert Tueni, about whom we know nothing except that he was a grocer, lived at 30 President Street that same year. The boardinghouse on Willow Place became a stopping place for Syrians for many decades.

- Saleem F. Haddad (Ameen's brother) is listed in the 1892 census as living near Dean and Bergen streets in Brooklyn. He moved to this odd neighborhood from another equally odd neighborhood (West 131st Street in Manhattan), but what he was doing at that address and how he found his way there are mysteries. No other Syrians lived in the

[1] "New York's Syrian Quarter," *NYT,* August 20, 1899.
[2] *Harper's Weekly* counted thirty families in Brooklyn in 1895. "The Foreign Element in New York: The Syrian Colony," *Harper's Weekly,* August 10, 1895.
[3] The names and boundaries of these neighborhoods changed constantly in the nineteenth century, but the South Ferry neighborhood generally encompassed Brooklyn Wards 1 and 6, while the South Brooklyn neighborhood was made up of parts of Wards 8 and 30.

neighborhood. Less than a year later, Saleem and Ameen moved in together at 76 Broad in Manhattan, near Saleem's drugstore, where they remained.

- The most unusual of the early Brooklyn residents, and one we know little about, was Khalil O. Hammwy. In 1892, he and Elias M. Abousleman opened a fan workshop, one branch of which was located at 3 Carlisle Street and the other at 125 Court Street in South Ferry—the first and only Syrian business in Brooklyn at that time. Abousleman ran the Manhattan business and Hammwy the Brooklyn workshop, where he lived. They produced novelty fans (called Zahra fans) for the Chicago fair.
- In 1892, four Syrian children were inmates at St. John's Home for Boys, an orphan asylum of forbidding aspect in the Crown Heights section of Brooklyn. One of them, Solomon Herro, died of pneumonia the following year at his parents' home at 71 Washington; he was twelve. The presence of these boys in a Brooklyn asylum may indicate that their parents were living in Brooklyn at that time.
- Abdow Lutfy apparently moved his family to Brooklyn sometime in the first five years of the 1890s, because in 1895, he moved them back to Manhattan, taking the middle and top floors of 7 Battery Place,[4] next door to Michael Kaydouh's family.
- Shaheen J. Dowaliby, an importer who had a business on Rector Street in Manhattan moved to South Ferry in 1893, as did Michael Karam, a peddler, who lived at 70 Court Street. Moussa Zalka, an Oriental goods merchant whose store was at 29 Broadway, lived at 42 Joralemon Street in 1893. Nageeb Arbeely bought a house in Sheepshead Bay—remote from the growing Syrian community in South Ferry—and moved there in 1893.
- Antoine L. Khoury and his business partner Adeeb Haddad lived at 289 Hicks, a narrow four-story brownstone, beginning in 1894; they had their importing business at 2 Carlisle Street. Antoine's brother Habeeb moved in in 1898.
- The John Saadis, the family of the Presbyterian minister Elias Saadi, settled in Boerum Hill in 1896.
- My grandfather gave his address as 24 Hamilton Avenue, near the embarkation point of the Hamilton Ferry, in 1897. As he moved

[4] *Kawkab America,* October 11, 1895.

constantly in the 1890s, this may have been a temporary address or an address of convenience. Elias Kirdahy and George Sadallah also lived on Hamilton Avenue in that year.

- John Abd-el-Nour and his wife, Selma, lived at 31 Truxton Street in 1897. Like all of his residences, it was far outside the Syrian community that was beginning to be built in South Ferry. Their son Hector was born there in 1898, but the family soon moved to Staten Island.[5]
- Najeeb M. Mallouk was one of the earliest Syrians to live in South Brooklyn, at 309 49th Street, where he moved in 1897. Elias and Michael Abousleman followed in 1898 but moved to South Ferry a year later.
- In 1897, the family of George Forzly moved to President Street, and his cousin Kalil, who worked for him at the bank, lived on Sackett Street. Nacle Forzly and his family moved to 547 Henry Street, a handsome four-story brownstone in South Ferry, that same year. Selim Kisbany and George Abdallah moved to South Ferry the following year, as did Selim Marrash, who partnered with Moussa Zalka (also living in South Ferry) to import Oriental goods from their office at 29 Broadway in Manhattan.
- Tannous Azeez, the jeweler, and his family lived at 41 Joralemon Street in 1898 but moved to Atlantic City in 1900.

By 1900, one-quarter of the Syrians lived in Brooklyn, although all businesses and the majority of residences were still in Manhattan. In Miller's 1903 survey that proportion had increased to one-third. They were not yet ready to buy houses, but they were able to rent more spacious quarters in Brooklyn than were available in lower Manhattan. The number had reached a critical mass just after 1900, and many Syrian businesses sprang up in Brooklyn, mostly serving the Syrian community itself. The 1909 *Syrian Business Directory* lists forty-eight Syrian businesses in South Ferry: doctors' offices, groceries, butcher shops, ice cream stores, shoemakers, bicycle shops, music stores, bakeries, and restaurants. There were even a few companies making shirtwaists and embroideries, but the vast majority of businesses—wholesalers, manufacturers, and import/export businesses—were still in Manhattan.[6] Miller has a photograph of a grocery shop in South Brooklyn, but its name

[5] It is to Abd-el-Nour's move to Staten Island in 1899 that the epigraph of this chapter refers.

[6] DiNapoli's thesis (1977) and her essay in Benson (2002) describe the South Ferry community of this period well.

is impossible to read. Only one shop—Khalil Beshewate's confectionery on 5th Avenue—was listed in South Brooklyn in the 1909 *Directory*. Two other businesses, perhaps run out of their homes, were those of the lace dealer, Shaheen Dowaliby, on 56th Street, and the real estate agent, Elias Moussi, on 5th Avenue.

## South Ferry

South Ferry, which many of us still call "Little Syria," was bounded by the East River on the west, Joralemon Street on the north, Boerum Place on the east, and Congress Street on the south, with the spine of Atlantic Avenue running east-west through it, ending at the ferry. Those living there could walk to the ferry that took them to lower Manhattan, a distance of five or six blocks at the most. The ferry cost one cent between seven and nine in the morning, two cents thereafter. To take a pushcart on the ferry cost one and a half cents.[7] It is estimated that the Brooklyn Ferry Company, which ran routes across the East River, carried 125,000 foot-passengers a day. We know of no Syrian businesses in South Ferry in 1900, but given the number of Syrians living there, it would seem likely that some small shops had already sprung up; still, nearly everyone in the community took the ferry every morning.

One of the early residents of South Ferry, and one whose living situation was described admiringly by a reporter, was Michael Deeb Kaydouh. He came from Tripoli in 1885 with his widowed mother and sisters. The family settled at 8 Battery Place. He worked for his maternal uncle, Antoni Tadross, when he first arrived and then went into the dry goods business himself, first with Nahoum Merhige, who later married Kaydouh's sister Minnie, and then on his own. He had a checkered career until 1903, when he opened a cigar store and soda fountain/restaurant in the Whitehall Building on the Battery; a photograph of the shop is in Miller's book. "Kaydouh's" is written above a large sign reading "SODA." He opened the Annex Café and Restaurant at 3 Rector Street, catering to the bankers and government officials from the surrounding office buildings, and eventually bought the building. A 1915 photograph of a banquet of the Syrian Merchants' Association shows more than one hundred men seated at long tables in the main dining room

[7] Felton 1912: 12.

of the Annex.[8] He kept his shop in the Whitehall Building as well, letting an "American" partner run it.

The Kaydouhs moved to Brooklyn in 1898 or 1899, settling at 311 Henry Street, a four-story tenement on the corner of Atlantic Avenue (like many corner buildings in Brooklyn, it also had an Atlantic Avenue address: 121). A reporter from the *Brooklyn Daily Eagle* visited his apartment one day in 1902: "Only one short block from Brooklyn's 'Block Beautiful' [Henry Street between State and Joralemon], was to be found Miss Hannie Kaydouh [Michael's sister] and her family. For such scenes of comfort, and even luxurious, fitting up he [the reporter] had never before come across in his tenement travels."[9] Despite this glowing report, a longtime resident of the neighborhood expressed her distaste at the influx of foreigners and feared she and her family would have to move.[10]

In 1912, Felton (who echoed Miller in every aspect of his study, and who actually did very little original research) found the Syrian families living in an average of five rooms, for which they paid twenty dollars per month, compared to the four or five dollars per month that single men and women paid for a bed in a Washington Street tenement. The rents in the South Ferry neighborhood had risen 66 percent between 1903 and 1912 as a result of the influx of prosperous Syrians. "The houses are all clean and artistically furnished…and the young women often finish high school and many are first-class musicians."[11] The twenty-five residents who lived in a four-story brownstone in South Ferry, however, might not feel that their quarters were especially spacious.

Quite soon the neighborhoods that had so attracted the upper echelon of the Colony began to house more and more poor newcomers, resulting in the deterioration of average living conditions, although they were never as bad as those on Washington Street. My maternal grandfather arrived in New York in 1902 and went directly to South Ferry, bypassing Washington Street completely. He settled in a boardinghouse at 84 State Street. Of the eighteen people living in the house, seven were Syrians, five of whom were peddlers of Oriental goods (my grandfather among them). All the Syrians had been in the United States five years or less. He and others like him definitely brought down the tone of the neighborhood.

[8] *Syrian-American Commercial Magazine,* April 1921: n.p.

[9] "Dainty Homes in Tenements," *BDE*, November 2, 1902.

[10] "Dainty Homes in Tenements," *BDE*, November 2, 1902.

[11] Felton 1912: 12–13.

In 1915, Louise Ensign Catlin made a study of the South Ferry community, for which she received an MA in political science from Columbia. About the conditions in South Ferry in that year she remarks: "Here the congestive conditions are deplorable and the landlord cannot guard against them. He would have to hire a night watchman to club down the lodgers who slink up at night and whose numbers are unavowed by his proverbially deceitful Syrian tenants."[12] Although racist and hyperbolic, the observation is indicative of the fact that things even in bucolic Brooklyn had become crowded, and Brooklyn South Ferry was beginning to resemble a Syrian ethnic enclave, with lots of street activity, small shops, and most likely the chaos and dirt that go with such an increase in density.

The boardinghouse at 32 Willow Place, where Thomas Rahaim lived in 1890, is in South Ferry. It is a large, handsome building of five stories, with windows and doorways trimmed out in alternating bands of red and white brick. Today it is an apartment building, but in 1900 it sheltered thirty-five boarders, of whom fourteen were Syrians: the Moshys, the Mouakads, and the Sarkises, as well as four single roomers. Two large extended families, the Mallouks (headed by Mary Mallouk) and the Abo Samras (headed by Nicola Abo Samra), lived at 84 Pacific Street—seventeen Syrians in all. The Abukalils and Salims lived at 41 Willow, a classic four-story brownstone. The east side of Hicks Street from Joralemon to Pacific Street was dotted with Syrians: one Syrian roomer at Number 285, five at 289, some of the Rahaim family at 305 (two of the brothers were rooming around the corner on Garden Place), Nami Tadross and his wife at 313, Shamis Abraham and his family at 315, the Naufal family at 353, and the Srauges at 357. Some of these buildings were large custom-built boardinghouses and some were single-family dwellings converted to boardinghouses or tenements. 289 and 315 Hicks, for example, were rather small four-story brick townhouses that held twenty-five tenants each, some of them Syrian. The number of Syrians who were in Brooklyn without their families was relatively small: only about 10 percent of the Syrians were roomers or boarders. Some of these men and women were living in the households of other Syrians (and may have been related), and others were not. The successful men and women of the Manhattan Colony were bringing over spouses and children from Syria or building families here and moving them to Brooklyn. For many of these families, South Ferry was a way-station until they could move to South Brooklyn or further afield. For others,

[12] Catlin 1915: 29.

the boarding house life (still crowded, but an improvement on Washington Street) gave way to home-ownership, when they bought single-family homes in the neighborhood, making every block a "block beautiful."

## South Brooklyn

The second cluster, comprising about half the Brooklyn Syrian population, lived in what Miller called "South Brooklyn" in the neighborhood that we now call Sunset Park. The majority of the Syrians lived in a rectangle bordered by 39th and 60th streets and 2nd and 5th avenues. There were no Syrian businesses in this community in the nineteenth century and none were listed in the 1909 *Business Directory;* all the residents commuted to Manhattan for work as well as leisure. Most took their meals in Manhattan, as there were no Syrian restaurants in Brooklyn in 1900. Residents took a trolley along Third Avenue to reach the Hamilton Ferry, which docked at the southeastern corner of Battery Park.

South Brooklyn was a neighborhood of single-family homes, but some of these housed more than one Syrian family. One house at 363 52nd Street—a two-story brick with a basement—sheltered eleven Syrians, including Salim Elias's family and several Syrian boarders. It may be that Elias had rented the whole house and was subletting to others, or that these boarders were relatives. Like the South Ferry neighborhood, most of the buildings inhabited by Syrians in South Brooklyn housed families rather than single men or women, an indication of the changing character of the Syrian population by 1900, and of the immigrants who first moved to Brooklyn. Fares Rihani's family lived at 1089 Fifth Avenue. Antoni Tadross's extended family lived at 256 60th Street (he was one of the few Syrians to own his own home). The Forzlys (including George, the man whose bank went under in 1899), had moved from President Street to 255 10th Street. The Moussis lived at 276 52nd Street, the Birdsall/Axem/Mokarzel extended family at 1055 50th Street, the Munyers at 261 45th Street, the Gabriel Awads and the Alfred Khourys at 1153 Fifth Avenue, and Maroon Fagher's family at 1140 Fifth. Although they were not listed in the census, Nayef and Selma Haddad (he was a silk worker) lived at 560 48th Street with their children and Nayef's widowed mother. Najeeb Mallouk and the brothers Michael and Elias Abousleman had settled in the neighborhood before the turn of the century.

Miller found the same high standard of living in both Brooklyn communities in 1903. He was unstinting in his approbation of them: "Judged by the standard of excellence they should be placed in the following order: First, South Brooklyn; second, South Ferry; third, Manhattan."[13] The Brooklyn residents had more space and light and they were able to keep their houses cleaner than in Manhattan. Many had private baths. They also had higher literacy rates, more children in school, fewer women working, and longer tenancies than those in Manhattan. The living conditions were not ideal: it was still relatively crowded in the Brooklyn tenements; a major difference was that instead of living cheek by jowl with strangers, the Syrians were now living "cozily" together as families.

## Other Brooklyn Neighborhoods

As mentioned previously, a small group of Syrians lived in Coney Island where they had businesses, including Frida and George Shishim, George and Emma Habeeb, Kalil Forzly (who had moved from Sackett Street), and Yusef Waked. Nageeb Arbeely lived with his wife and five children on Ocean Avenue and V Street, in Sheepshead Bay. He had retired from his Ellis Island job following a stroke and contented himself raising chickens and pigeons in his "handsome home."[14] Shakir Nasser lived close to Arbeely. They must have chosen to live that far out because the neighborhood was cheaper than either Atlantic Avenue or South Brooklyn; they were among the few Syrians in the 1900 census who owned their own homes. Syrians were scattered in other parts of Brooklyn, including the neighborhoods of Prospect Park and Boerum Hill.

By the 1920s upper-class Syrians began to feel the pressure of the less well-off moving into these neighborhoods. They moved once again, this time to the new housing developments in Bay Ridge or to the suburbs of Staten Island, Long Island, New Jersey, or Connecticut, where they could own large single-family homes with gardens and backyards. The old Manhattan neighborhood was never completely abandoned by the Syrians—until it was razed in the 1940s—but fewer and fewer chose to live there. By the time it was destroyed most had already moved out, and their businesses had long ago moved uptown to Fifth Avenue, Brooklyn, or the suburbs.

[13] Miller 1903: 18.
[14] "'Teddy' Too Fond of Chicken Fare," *NYH,* June 28, 1902.

# Brooklyn residences, 1900.

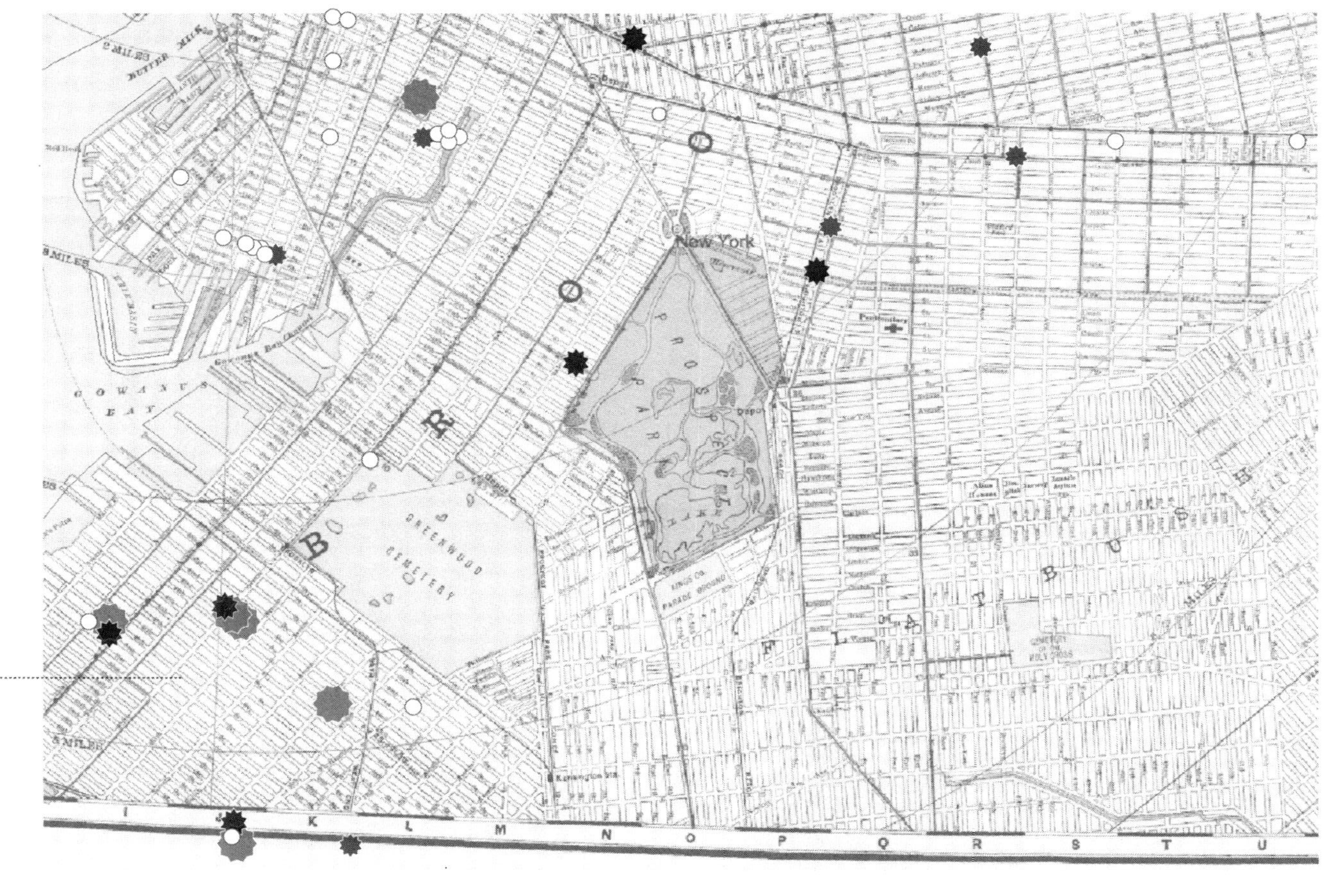


Basemap: Ullits, Hugo, Part of Wards 1, 3, 4, 6 & 10.
Land Map Sections, Nº 1 & 2, Volume 1,
Brooklyn Borough, New York City, 1898 - 99
New York Public Library Digital Gallery.

## Brooklyn South Ferry residences, 1900.

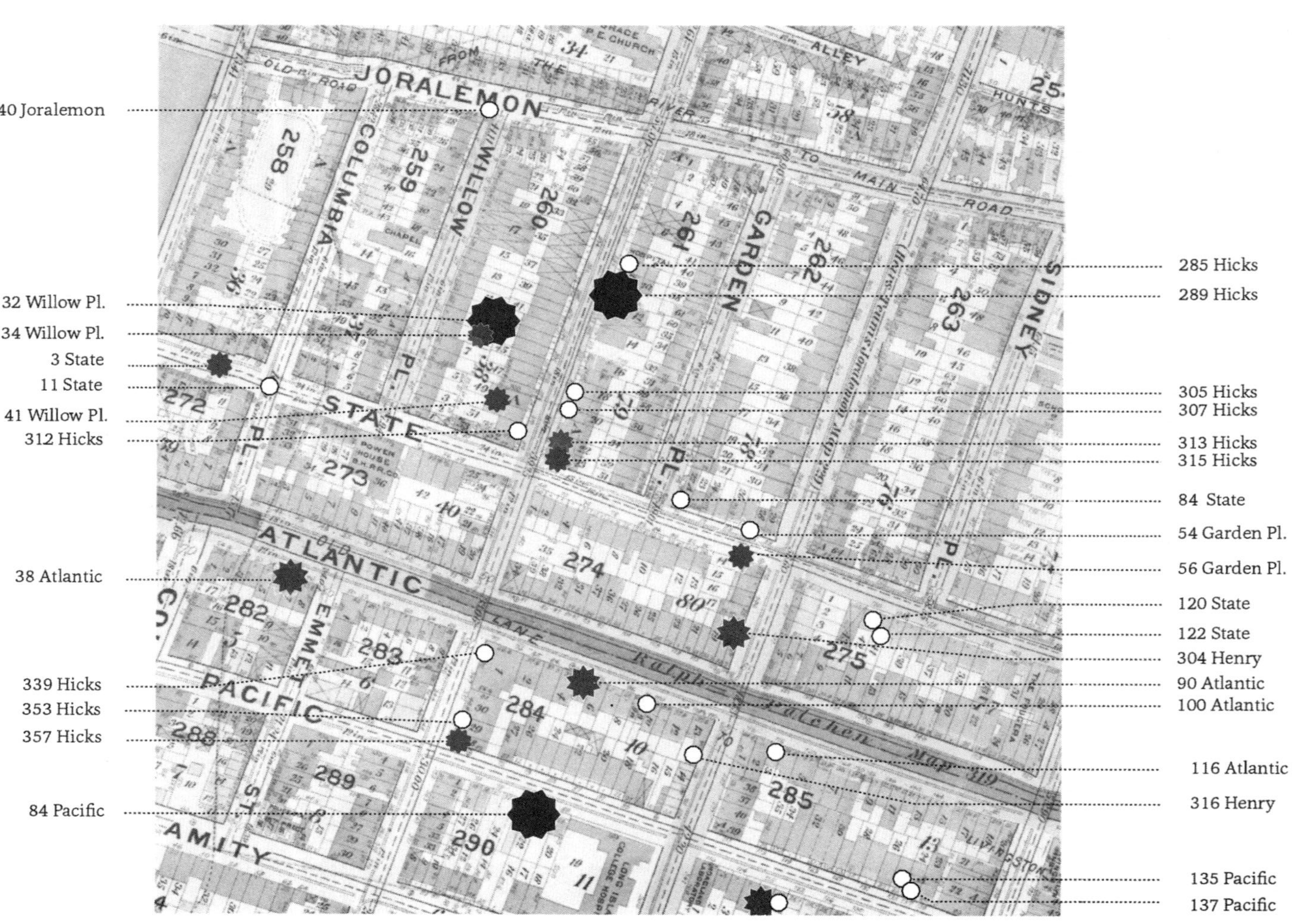

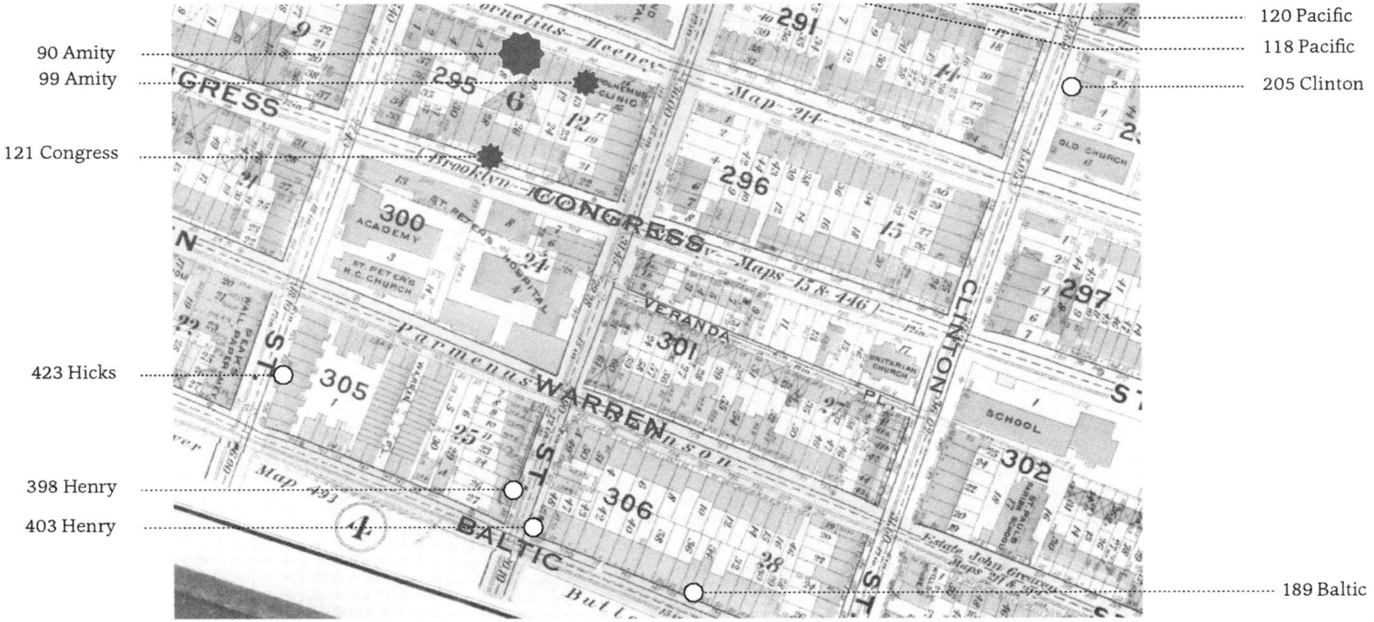

90 Amity
99 Amity
121 Congress
423 Hicks
398 Henry
403 Henry
120 Pacific
118 Pacific
205 Clinton
189 Baltic
CONGRESS
WARREN
BALTIC
CLINTON
VERANDA
ACADEMY
SCHOOL
OLD CHURCH
UNITARIAN CHURCH
ST. PETER'S R.C. CHURCH


N°. PEOPLE
1 to 5
6 to 10
5 7
8 11
21 to 27


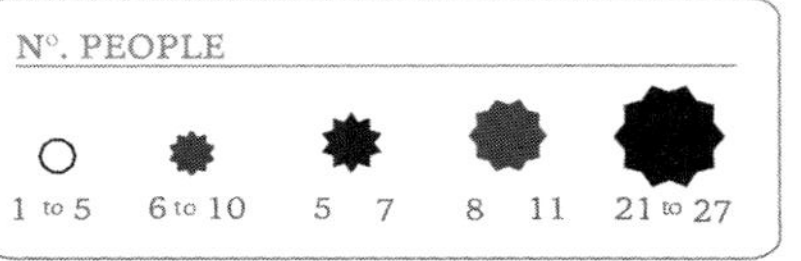

Basemap: Ullits, Hugo, Part of Wards 1, 3, 4, 6 & 10.
Land Map Sections, N° 1 & 2, Volume 1,
Brooklyn Borough, New York City, 1898 - 99
New York Public Library Digital Gallery.

## Chapter 12

## Law and Order

*The almost universal testimony is that our Syrian citizens are quiet, peaceable, and law-abiding, and considering their antecedents, remarkably able morally to stand alone.*[1]

Every researcher asserted that Syrians were law-abiding citizens. This chapter looks at the accuracy of that belief. Miller, for example, interviewed policemen and searched the reports of the Commission of Charities and Correction, and this search "failed to bring out the slightest flaw."[2] Even a reporter for the *New York Herald* reported that "admirers of the Syrians [assert that] no Syrian or Armenian who has ever come to America has ever been found guilty of any grave crime. On the contrary, history, it is claimed, proves that no men are more peace loving than they are."[3]

The most eloquent—and elegant—of these paeans was published in 1892 in the *New York Herald*. It is a long piece of two and one-half columns, including sketched illustrations, titled "A Picturesque Colony." Here is the final paragraph in its entirety:

> With reference to this Colony, these points should be remembered—that the Colony is growing in numbers and wealth constantly; that its members are anxious to learn American ways and manners, and to become citizens as soon as the law will permit; that they are, as a rule, quiet, orderly, sober and industrious people, who are beginning to see the benefits to be derived from united effort, and who are destined to become in the near future, under the leadership of men who are thoroughly acquainted with their capabilities and needs, a factor in the body politic which will make itself felt for good.[4]

[1] Houghton 1911: III: 796.
[2] Miller 1903: 41.
[3] "Skillful Syrian Immigrants," *NYH*, September 29, 1889.
[4] "A Picturesque Colony," *NYH*, October 2, 1892.

When a reporter interviewed a policeman in the Syrian Quarter in 1900, the cop replied (in a strong Irish brogue) that "they keep clear of the strong arm of the law," and "there are no crooks among them."[5] These outsiders also acclaimed their probity in business: William Cole calls Syrian businessmen "naturally conservative," and adds, "Allowing for their Oriental cunning... they are thoroughly honest."[6] Houghton and Miller agreed with this assessment, including the caveat that the Syrian can be "tricky" in business. Miller believed that the adverse conditions in which the Syrian was brought up in his own land, made "lie or die" his only alternatives. This the Syrian had in common with every other downtrodden group and it explained the sometimes-deceitful way in which he sold his merchandise, but according to Miller, continued residence in the United States would ameliorate these tendencies.[7] Thus, this sharpness in business was a product of his background, not part of his character.

The editor of *Kawkab America* asserted that two New York wholesalers who regularly did business with the Syrians had "not lost any money through them, except a small amount due Mr. Friedberger from a Syrian who died in South America. All American dealers give our people an excellent reputation as close buyers and honest people."[8]

The Syrians themselves were ambivalent about the probity of their race. To the outside world, they bragged, "During ten years of immigration, the number of the Syrians have reached 150,000 in North and South America. They all seem to be getting along well in business, and to have added less to the annuals *[sic]* of crime than any other nationality."[9] The opinions expressed in the Arabic pages were somewhat different, chastising Syrian peddlers who lied to their customers or cursed them when they didn't buy anything, the women and men who presented immoral entertainments to the Americans, and the Syrians who fought among themselves. They hastily added that these bad apples were not representative of the whole or even the majority of their fellow countrymen, but the laments appeared often enough to prove that these behaviors were of some concern to the Syrians themselves.

Notwithstanding the almost universal assessment of Syrians as peaceable, absent from police blotters, and possessing souls of probity, New York

[5] "The Syrian Colony," *Bay City* (MI) *Times*, June 22, 1900.
[6] Cole 1922: n.p.
[7] Miller 1903: 41.
[8] "Oriental Items," *Kawkab America* (English), February 17, 1893.
[9] "Oriental Items of Interest," *Kawkab America* (English), August 12, 1892.

newspapers paid interminable—and gleeful—attention to the violence that cropped up on Washington Street and to the chicanery of the few Syrians who broke the law. The fights among Syrians were particularly notorious, and several of them occurred between the followers of the various newspapers and, hence, religions. The reports in the American press were usually livened up with references to swarthy Arabs wielding knives or scimitars.

### Fighting among Themselves

A notorious "war" among the Syrians, which reached the boiling point in 1905–1906, had its roots in nineteenth-century disputes, which were manifested in both words and deeds. There were skirmishes between the followers of the two major papers, *Al Hoda* and *Kawkab America*, and more personally between the two papers' founders even before the founding of *Al Hoda* in 1898. Although these battles have usually been characterized as religious (and certainly were seen that way by most of the American reporters), in fact they seem to have begun as personal disputes and then become mixed up with religion and politics. Although we do not know the religion of all those involved, there was certainly a division based on religious affiliation, but the battle lines constantly shifted and were sometimes based solely on the premise of "the enemy of my enemy is my friend."

The first documented case of intra-Syrian battle was reported in *Kawkab America* in early 1893, when a fight broke out at Rasheed Safi's boardinghouse at 75 Washington Street.[10] The police were sent for, but as far as we know no arrests were made. In 1894 the battle began in earnest when Najeeb Naaman Maloof (a friend of Naoum Mokarzel, with whom he founded the newspaper *Al Asr*) got into an altercation with Habeeb Petrakian. Petrakian, who had a silk business at 61 West Street, was the brother of Arteen Petrakian, the former managing agent of *Kawkab America*.

On the day of the fight, Maloof, also a silk dealer, accosted Petrakian in the street, claiming that Petrakian owed him money, which he denied. The argument between the two men turned into a fistfight and Petrakian had Maloof arrested for assault. *Kawkab America* reported the incident and Maloof turned around and sued the editors for $10,000 in damages, charging that their paper's characterization of him as a "degraded vagabond, rogue and

[10] *Kawkab America*, January 20, 1893.

disturber of the peace" was slander. Maloof's story was related in a *Herald* article in which he claimed that the Arbeelys had asked him to use his influence to persuade immigrants to subscribe to *Kawkab America*. When he refused to do this, the Arbeelys launched their attack.[11] Interestingly enough, at least according to Maloof, an Egyptian newspaper entered the fray and accused the Arbeelys of maligning him.[12]

The Arbeelys, for their part, asserted that they reported the facts as they saw them, even though they had friends in the Maloof family. There was also no love lost between the Arbeelys and the Petrakian family, and therefore no reason for the Arbeelys to take their side. Arteen Petrakian had just brought a lawsuit against Nageeb Arbeely seeking to take over the newspaper. Habeeb had been forced to move his store out of 45 Pearl Street (the newspaper's headquarters) when Arteen and the Arbeelys fell out. In light of these circumstances, the coverage was very balanced: the newspaper was more worried about the impression made on American observers than about the facts of the case itself. They urged Syrians to work out their disputes peacefully, regardless of their political or religious affiliations.[13] The case against the Arbeelys was dismissed.

The following week, the Arbeelys had Mokarzel and Maloof arrested for publishing scandalous stories about them in *Al Asr*, Maloof and Mokarzel's short-lived newspaper. The Arbeelys accused Mokarzel and Maloof of calling Yusef Arbeely, their father, "vile names." Mokarzel and Maloof were each held on $500 bail, but freed the next day.[14] Unfortunately, no copies of *Al Asr* survive so we do not know what the stories involved. One American reporter noted sarcastically, "These Syrian gentlemen appear to have been quick in acquiring the amenities of New York journalism."[15]

In 1896, another fistfight broke out in the Colony between a recent immigrant, Salim Farra (Farah), and Michael Salloum and Costa Saadi. Heads were bashed, a doctor treated scalp wounds, and all three men were arrested. The two accused Farra of belonging to a secret society.[16] What this secret society might have been is a mystery, unless it was a nascent version of the Syrian Revolutionary Party founded in 1899 and described below. Naoum Mokarzel and "Habeeb Basha" (presumably Habeeb Petrakian) also fell out, and

[11] "Syrian Editors Sued for Libel," *NYH*, August 9, 1894.
[12] "Syrian Colony Interested," *The* (NY) *Sun*, July 29, 1894.
[13] "Libelled in Hieroglyphics," *The* (NY) *Evening World*, July 28, 1894.
[14] "Syrians against Syrians," *NYT*, August 5, 1894.
[15] *Philadelphia Inquirer*, August 6, 1894.
[16] "Was a Mixed Up Fight," *NYH*, January 2, 1896.

Habeeb was arraigned on a charge of felonious assault for attacking Mokarzel with an iron bar. Mokarzel told an American reporter that Habeeb's attack was prompted by Mokarzel's "courageous" muckraking stance in *Al Asr*. His paper, he said, brought to light the tyranny of a few of the prominent men of the Colony who wished to keep the rest "as ignorant and dependent upon the intelligent Syrians as possible."[17] The case was apparently dismissed.

In 1897, Ameen Rihani (a Maronite) gave a speech to the Syrian Women's Union in which he described the factional battles taking place in the Colony and laid much of the blame on the Orthodox bishop Hawaweeny. Alexander Yazaji responded with a letter to the editor of *The Press* asserting that no such dissension existed and defending Hawaweeny as a man of peace.[18]

When Mokarzel began publishing *Al Hoda* in 1898, he used it as a vehicle to insult *Kawkab America* to an extent not much seen today. When, for example, Mokarzel published an article in which he alluded to editor Najeeb Diab's leaving *Kawkab America* under murky circumstances (Diab worked for the Arbeelys before starting his own newspaper in 1898), Diab published a letter in *Al Hoda* assuring its readers that he had left *Kawkab America* for purely personal reasons. Several articles in *Al Hoda* accused *Kawkab America* of errors, falsification, and misleading the public. Even more lurid was the four-page supplement published by Mokarzel and his wife, Sophie, accusing *Kawkab America* of lying and slandering them, which will be described further in chapter 13.

According to the *New York Times*, "Each faction has its leaders and newspaper. Once in a while the chronic feud breaks into open war, and then there are brawls and killings down on Washington Street."[19] In fact there were no killings until 1905, but there certainly were brawls, some of which played out in the pages of the Syrian newspapers and some in the street. Apparently many of the battle lines were drawn in articles that anonymous writers paid to have published in the newspapers. One would think this would protect the editors from accusations of slander, but inasmuch as the editors accepted the articles and the fees, apparently without demur, the victims sued them. And the vitriol spilled over into the editorial pages as well. "A thousand private grievances were aired this way. A thousand petty quarrels were fanned into bitter feuds with the promise of a bloody outcome."[20]

[17] "Woes of a Syrian Poet," *NYH,* January 3, 1897.
[18] "Syrian Colony at Peace," *The* (NY) *Press,* February 15, 1897.
[19] "The Syrian Colony of New York and Its Characteristics," *NYT,* May 25, 1902.
[20] "Bitter Syrian Feuds Caused by Church War," *BDE,* February 4, 1906.

Joseph N. Maloof, the brother of Najeeb Maloof, edited the newspaper *Al Ayyam*, which began publication in 1898. He published articles critical of the Ottoman Empire and urged his fellow Syrians to become American citizens. He also published a book in 1899 that was a compendium of the lives of great men, including President McKinley, to whom it was dedicated. It also included a translation of the United States Constitution. A handsomely bound copy was sent to the White House. Maloof stated to a reporter, "If it shall have brought a goodly handful of my compatriots into the confines of a free government, causing them to forswear forever the star and crescent in favor of Old Glory, I shall have achieved a great end."[21]

This did not sit well with George Jabour's newly founded *Al Alam*, which, in response, reminded Syrians that they were Ottoman subjects who would want to return to their homeland someday. Bishop Hawaweeny wrote to *Al Alam*, praising it for its loyalty to the sultan. Maloof then accused Hawaweeny in *Al Ayyam* of being a tool of the Ottoman rulers, taking money from their agents, and using his influence as a religious leader to prevent any reformist or revolutionary propaganda from being promulgated in the community. Hawaweeny admitted that he had indeed met with the sultan's representatives, but claimed that he was only interested in maintaining peace in the Colony, which was why he tried to suppress the revolutionaries. Hawaweeny brought a slander suit against *Al Ayyam*.[22]

At the same time, and probably in response to the same article, Nami Tadross, a prominent rug dealer, sued George Jabour for libel and asked for $2,000 in damages. He alleged that *Al Alam* had called him "a donkey and a jackass and compared him to a decayed clam[?]."[23] Jabour was arrested but released on $250 bail. In one article about this incident, Jabour was styled as a defender of young Syrian womanhood, having taken Syrians and Turks of New York to task for "teaching the girls movements in the dances that would cause them to be beheaded if they gave such an exhibition in Turkey or Syria."[24] This is rich, coming from the proprietor of the Turkish Theater in Coney Island that featured two coochee-coochee dancers. A day after this article appeared, he claimed that someone tried to assassinate him, and after writing a second "brave" editorial, "he escaped from being stabbed in his room only

[21] "Syrian Compliment to the President," *NYH,* May 7, 1899.
[22] "Lively War between Syrians," *NYT,* January 13, 1899.
[23] "War in Little Syria," *Sun* (Baltimore, MD), January 20, 1899.
[24] "Sues a Turkish Yellow Journalist," *BDE,* January 19, 1899.

by stabbing the other fellow first."[25] His alleged would-be assassin was not identified, and nothing more of the incident came to light.

Norman Duncan's collection of stories about the Syrian Colony, *Soul of the Street* (1900), satirized the propensity of Syrian publishers to take money from the Ottoman authorities in return for their wholehearted support. The venal publisher "Salim Shofi" is bribed by the Ottoman Consul to refrain from publishing an article critical of the sultan, which had been written by the idealistic, much-abused editor, "Khalil Khayat." The real Khalil Khayat was an editor of *Kawkab America* at the time the book was published, but whether Duncan's story represented *Kawkab America* or *Al Alam*, the practice must have been well known.

As was not unexpected, given his loyalty to the Turkish sultan, George Jabour was accused by Maloof's followers of being un-American, which led him to publish the following unusual defense in the *New York Times*:

> George Jabour...desires it to be known that although his paper is published in the Syrian language, neither he nor the Al Alam are un-American. He declares that he is in no way interested in preventing Syrians, or other foreigners, from becoming American citizens. Mr. Jabour is a naturalized citizen of this country. He is also one of the founders of the Syrian-American Club at 63 Greenwich Street, this city. A cardinal principle of this club is the promotion of the naturalization of Syrians, and Mr. Jabour is a member of the Committee on Naturalization.[26]

This long-simmering dispute soon broke out into open warfare. First, Naoum Mokarzel was arrested near his home in Camden, New Jersey, apparently at the "instigation of rival newspaper people" for sending obscene matter through the mail. He was released for lack of evidence.[27] Three unnamed Syrians were wounded in a battle on Washington Street—two were shot, and one had his throat gashed.[28] Later the same year, "about twenty Syrians" in front of 81 Washington Street attacked Salim S. Sarkis, editor of *Al Mushir*, and his friend Kalil Freije on the street. Sarkis, from an illustrious Armenian newspaper family, had founded *Al Mushir* in Alexandria in 1894 and brought it to New York in 1899, apparently because his life had been threatened by the Ottoman regime

[25] "Sues a Turkish Yellow Journalist," *BDE*, January 19, 1899.

[26] "Syrian Editor Not Un-American," *NYT*, January 19, 1899.

[27] "Syrian Editor Declared Not Guilty," *Philadelphia Inquirer*, April 21, 1901.

[28] "Three Syrians Found Wounded in the Street," *Syracuse* (NY) *Evening Herald*, March 3, 1901.

in response to his virulent anti-Ottoman sentiments.[29] Those same sentiments, he claimed, incited the attack by his countrymen. Sarkis charged two men with assault, David Madower and Anthony Faour, but he also let it be known that "Syrian priests" whom he had offended in his newspaper were manipulating them.[30] Since Madower and Faour were Maronites, the priests he alluded to were probably Korkemas and Stefan, but in fact he may have been referring to Hawaweeny, who, as we have seen, seemed to be in the pay of the sultan.

A series of articles in the *New York Times* chronicled the ever more serious battles between the followers of Hawaweeny (Orthodox) and Naoum Mokarzel (Maronite) in the fall of 1905. In August, Mokarzel claimed that the bishop had called upon his congregants to "crush" Mokarzel, while Hawaweeny asserted he had urged his followers to "forgive." Yet he also said, "Mr. Mokarzel respects nobody," a statement sure to enrage Mokarzel. [31] A supposedly non-partisan Syrian declared that the danger lay with the ruffians who were protecting the bishop, one of whom had killed someone in Syria. He may have been referring to Elias Zreik. Hawaweeny was under armed guard because he claimed his life had been threatened. A newspaper reported that in the course of these battles, fourteen warrants had been issued and twenty-nine people injured.[32] In September, Hawaweeny himself was arrested, together with Najeeb Diab, who was the editor of *Mira'at al-Gharb*, both of them accused of leading the "factional fight that for many months has been waged between the Brooklyn Syrians of the Greek Orthodox and the Roman Catholic faith."[33] Hawaweeny was accused of firing a revolver in the street and conspiring to "do bodily harm" to his opponents.

The riots lasted from September to December 1905; each time violence broke out, the participants were hauled into court, and even as they were being tried, their friends would be fighting in the street. In one incident—the bishop was not even present—the rioters included two Shibley brothers (Anees and Ameen), Tony Saba, Hafez Abdulmadi, Moussa Abalan, George and Henry Boutross, Nicola Dibs, Michael (Mansour?) Sharbel, and Joseph N. Maloof.[34] Hawaweeny's trial took place in November, and both factions

---

[29] Sarkis was one of the keynote speakers at the first meeting of the Syrian Revolutionary Party in Madison Square in 1899.

[30] "Syrian Editor Attacked," *NYT,* November 10, 1901.

[31] "Champagne Glass Club and a Bishop at War," *NYT,* August 28, 1905.

[32] "War to the Knife on Syrian Bishop," *New York Evening Telegram,* September 22, 1905.

[33] "The Bishop Is Arrested," *NYT,* September 19, 1905.

[34] "Syrian Factions in a Riot," *The* (NY*) Sun,* October 24, 1905.

were heavily represented in court; a dozen policemen were on hand to prevent any violence.[35] Hawaweeny and Diab were cleared in December, but not before several more fights broke out, in one of which shots were fired.

After his acquittal, Najeeb Diab brought a suit for $50,000 against the six men—all Maronites—who had instigated his arrest. They were Naoum Mokarzel, Anees Shibley, Antoun Lutfy, Nasri Hatin (Hatem?), Najeeb N. Maloof, and Joseph Macksoud. The six were released on bail of $1,500.[36]

Probably related to this affray was the suit for defamation brought by Najeeb N. Maloof (the same man who sued the Arbeelys in 1894) against Najeeb Diab, the publisher of *Mira'at al- Gharb*, in 1910. He demanded $25,000 in damages. Diab had allegedly published an article in 1905 in which he accused Maloof of "roaring, shouting, and cursing from his mouth, using abusive language," and then physically attacking Essa Awad on the street. The case was dismissed.[37] Not coincidentally, Maloof & Co. at 17 Broadway was raided in January 1906, and the customs inspector seized a trunk of laces.[38] Someone had denounced him.

When fights erupted, the police were called, the perpetrators taken to jail, and then apparently released. Most of the lawsuits were for slander, not for assault. Inasmuch as none of these arrests, suits, and countersuits are represented in the court records of the city, and as we are never told the outcome, we can only assume that they were dismissed before they went to trial, and perhaps were less serious than they seemed. Certainly the American newspaper accounts are tinged with humor and condescension, as if the Syrians were children fighting in the schoolyard. The injuries, I imagine, were real enough, as were the raw emotions, but from the distance of a century, much of it does seem to have been, as one judge put it, "a tempest in a teapot."

The conflict reached a climax in 1906 with the murder of John Stefan, brother of the Maronite priest Rizkallah Stefan.[39] John Stefan had just arrived in New York and was eating dinner with several others in a restaurant owned by Sarkis Saadi, on the second floor of 81 Washington. According to prosecution witnesses at the murder trial, the cousins Elias and George Zreik, members of the Orthodox Church, had been to the editorial offices of *Al Hoda* searching for Naoum Mokarzel. When they couldn't find him, they went to

[35] "Sentiments by J.W. Osborne," *The* (NY) *Sun,* November 17, 1905.

[36] "Syrian Editor Retaliates," *NYT,* January 18, 1906.

[37] *Trials,* Najeeb N. Maloof v. Najeeb M. Diab, 1910: M-240.

[38] "$10,000 Lace Seizure Bit of Revenge, Maybe," *New York Press,* January 6, 1906.

[39] "Syrian Factions Fight; 1 Dead, Another Dying," *NYT,* February 1, 1906.

Saadi's restaurant asking for George Khoury and John Stefan, who were there eating dinner. The four began yelling epithets at each other, and then they and the others at Stefan's table got up and began fighting. In the ensuing melee, Elias Zreik was shot and John Stefan was stabbed. Although it seemed at first as though Stefan had been killed accidentally in the confusion of the battle, the coroner discovered he had been murdered—stabbed and garroted.[40] Elias ran to Springarn's Drugstore on the corner of Rector and Washington to have Louis Springarn treat his bullet wound, George Zreik ran upstairs, and John Stefan lay dead on the floor of Saadi's restaurant.

To add to the confusion, Raphael Salish of 26 Rector Street accused Naoum Mokarzel of shooting him in the back on the corner of West and Rector streets that same night. The police jumped to the conclusion that the assault was related to what had happened in the restaurant. When Mokarzel's trial for this supposed assault came up in May 1907, however, Salish did not appear and the case was dismissed, so the Salish/Mokarzel involvement in the Stefan murder remains cloudy.

Ten Syrians were arrested in connection with the murder of Stefan (including Naoum Mokarzel); only two were held for trial: Elias and George Zreik. Elias Zreik was said to be a giant—almost seven feet tall and inhumanly strong. His countrymen called him "Big Mike." He had been in trouble with the law before; he was an enthusiastic brawler who'd been arrested several times. Both Zreiks had been performers, camel drivers, and strong men at various entertainment venues in New York, and Elias had performed at the Chicago fair. He had been adulated in the American press as a hero after supposedly defending his village in Lebanon single-handedly against the Turks. In 1900, Elias worked in a Turkish smoking parlor on Bushman's Walk in Coney Island and seemed to have also been a butcher on Washington Street. In 1905, just before the events leading up to the trial, he was living at 8 Carlisle and listed as a laborer. He was also an active member of the Orthodox Church at 77 Washington.

The two men (sometimes they are referred to as brothers, sometimes as cousins) were remanded to the Tombs and held awaiting the grand jury's verdict, which decided that the case should go to trial.[41] The trial took place

[40] "Syrian Garroted and Stabbed," *New-York Tribune*, February 2, 1906.

[41] "Syrians Held in Feud Murder Case," *New-York Tribune,* March 10, 1906; "Held for Syrian Murder, *The* (NY) *Sun*, March 10, 1906.

in October 1906. The transcript runs to 610 pages.[42] Although George was inpleaded with Elias, Elias demanded and was given a separate trial, and he was tried first. Dozens of witnesses from the Syrian Colony were subpoenaed: those who were in the restaurant of 81 Washington that evening, those who had been in the barbershop on the first floor, those who lived in the upstairs rooms, and many others. The court had to find two Arabic interpreters for each witness whose English was not up to the task, and it is not always clear when the witness is speaking and when the interpreter is speaking. There was much mutual misunderstanding at every stage of the proceedings and endless repetitions of the same questions and same answers, leading to frayed tempers on the part of the attorneys, the judge, and the witnesses themselves. It must be said that despite the seriousness of the case, the trial had its moments of farce.

The prosecution presented its case, essentially the same as that outlined in the newspapers and given above: that is, that these two men—Elias and George Zreik—set out to kill their enemy, Naoum Mokarzel, and when they couldn't find him at his office, they went to the café where Maronites were known to hang out and picked a fight with two of the men having dinner. They murdered Stefan, and Elias Zreik was wounded in the scuffle.

The story was murky to say the least. That it was a factional fight no one doubted. That there had been anger on both sides was clear. But no one could explain how Stefan could have been strangled *and* stabbed, or who had done it. No one knew what role George Zreik had played. No one could say who shot Elias. The defense, just to confuse the record further, accused David Madower, one of the Maronites who was eating dinner with Stefan, of accidentally killing Stefan—strangling him in his attempt to loose his hold on him after he had been stabbed. None of it made much sense, and in the end the jury could not reach a conclusion on Elias; he was set free. Once Elias's trial fell apart, no one felt there was enough evidence to try George, and he was released as well. Stefan's murder was never solved. The funeral cortège consisted of seventy-four carriages; the undertaker, Mooney of Greenwich Street, said it was the largest funeral since the death of Police Chief Murphy. The road to the cemetery was lined with police to prevent further violence, but everyone remained calm.[43]

Elias went on to a checkered career as a candy store proprietor and a coffee importer, dying in Brooklyn in 1933. We know nothing more about George.

[42] *Trials,* People v. Zreik, 1906: #599.

[43] "Murdered Syrian Buried," *The* (NY) *Sun*, February 4, 1906.

There was never again that level of violence within the community; it must have been a sobering experience for both sides of the factional divide, and one that did not bear repeating.

It should be mentioned that these battles were not unique to New York. There were (apparently) factional fights being waged among the Syrians in Cleveland, Chicago, Denver, Omaha, Springfield, Massachusetts, and other places, many beginning in the 1890s and becoming acute around 1905. Whether the New York occurrences sparked these flames or they were homegrown is impossible to say.

## Violence between Syrians and Non-Syrians

The fighting among the Syrians seems to have been a match of equals, whereas in the fights with their Irish neighbors, the Syrians were usually the losers. Several New York newspaper articles attested to gangs of "American" (mostly Irish) toughs beating up Syrian residents on Washington Street. Moss describes several of the neighborhood gangs that hung out on Washington Street in the 1890s: the Stable Gang at Clancy's Stable, located at 14 Washington, "which devoted its attentions principally to immigrants"; the Silver Gang nearby, which "relied on the more fashionable calling of burglary"; and the Potashes, who hung around the Babbitt Soap Factory. These gangs had a sense of humor, anyway. The Potashes were a collection of Irish toughs, headed by Red Shay Meehan, who terrorized the whole neighborhood. The editors of *Kawkab America* and several letter writers noted the presence of these gangs of kids hanging out on Washington Street, throwing rocks, and using bad language.

In January 1892, the Syrians—under the rubric of the Syrian Union of America, perhaps invented for the benefit of the American reporters—held a meeting at the Daoud/Shishim boardinghouse at 91 Washington Street to discuss how to deal with the aggression of the Irish toughs who were repeatedly attacking their children and insulting their women. Fully 200 Syrians were present, including "fifty delegates from the various Syrian business firms in this city and vicinity." The reporter astutely observed, "Syrians do not drink intoxicating liquors and few of them are voters, so the [Irish] politicians and saloon keepers do not like them."[44] Salim Elias had been beaten up a week

[44] "Syrians Ask for Protection," *NYH*, January 21, 1892; "Persecutions of Syrians, *NYT*, January 22, 1892.

previously, and the Syrians claimed a policeman had simply watched. The leaders of the meeting, Nageeb Arbeely and Dr. Abdulmassih Mussawir, declared themselves ready to move the whole Colony to some other place where they would be protected. They adopted a resolution asking protection from the police superintendent and another appealing to the New York newspapers to "bring their wrongs before the public." Xenophon Baltazzi, the Ottoman consul-general, attended the meeting and urged the Syrians to report all attacks to him so that he could refer them to the police. There is no evidence that they did so. Instead, they continued to report these incidents to the police themselves and hope for redress.

Three months after the meeting, in an article titled "Rage among the Syrians," a *New York Herald* reporter described a riot at the corner of Rector and Washington streets, in which two members of the Colony were set upon by their Irish neighbors and beaten. The Syrians claimed that "three or four hundred persons" participated in the row, and that the police did nothing to stop it. A woman named Nellie Whalen, who lived at 15 Rector, felled Bader Halaby, of 21 Rector, with a cobblestone, fracturing her skull. The Syrians complained that the policemen laughed while they watched the Syrians being beaten, and that one of them even yelled, "Go for them. Kill the things!" The policeman denied the charge.[45] Two Irishmen were arrested and released on $300 bail; Whalen was arrested but released a few days later for lack of evidence. Sixty Syrians, led by Nageeb and Abraham Arbeely, went to the police to protest their inaction and ask for permission to carry revolvers; permission was refused. The reporter asserted that the attacks were motivated by the fact that the Irish were angry with the Syrians for driving up rents in the neighborhood;[46] no other reference to such a motive appeared. Most of the policemen in this era were Irish and would have had a natural sympathy for the "Irish aggressors" on Washington Street. Perhaps paying for protection was the only way to get it. The editors of *Kawkab America* looked forward to the day when there would be Syrian policemen who would be assigned to Washington Street.[47]

In response to this attack, a front-page editorial in the English section of the inaugural issue of *Kawkab America* was headlined "The Outrages on the Syrian Colony." After haranguing the police and the public for allowing such attacks to happen, the editor addressed the perpetrators:

[45] "Rage among the Syrians," *NYH*, April 5, 1892.

[46] "Rage among the Syrians," *NYH*, April 5, 1892.

[47] *Kawkab America*, June 9, 1893.

> Young men of Greenwich and Washington Sts.! Do you know that it is not manly nor brave to insult helpless women and maltreat poor and inoffensive people? Nor is it fair for Five or Six people, to assault, like you have often done, one single person, and a stranger that does not bother you, whose only fault is his difference from you in language and mode of dress. Remember! There is a time when patience ceases to be a virtue, and if some of you have escaped the Penitentiary for some offenses, you are known to have committed against them, you will not escape one of these days such a punishment as you deserve, and as they would be apt and able to give you, should you persist in your outrageous conduct and high-handed lawlessness.[48]

The plea, ending with a threat, seems to have been ineffectual.

The next year, Robert Cleary, a fifteen-year-old boy living at 51 Washington, attacked three Syrian peddlers who were selling candy on the corner of Morris and Washington.[49] On the one hand, this seems like simply a kid being a hoodlum, but there did seem to be continuing enmity between the Irish and the Syrians. Only a couple of weeks later, three Syrians were reportedly beaten and kicked by a gang of thugs. Salim Elias ended up in the hospital once again, with two broken ribs, his second beating at the hands of the Irish. An editorial in *Kawkab America* after this "near-fatal injury" (a bit of hyperbole to encourage action) urged the Syrians to form an association to stand up to these outrages. The membership fee would go toward legal fees for the victims.[50] Later in the year, Shamooney Elias, wife of Salim, was attacked; no one was arrested for the crime. *Kawkab America* asked anyone who had seen the incident to report it to the police.[51]

Habib Wahby, a truckman, was attacked twice in 1894. The first incident involved a fight with a German employee of the soap factory who threw a nail at Wahby and supposedly blinded him in one eye.[52] Later that same year, he again ended up in the hospital when Joseph Cunningham beat him with a cart rung.[53] Karl Hill, proprietor of a saloon at 43 Washington Street, where the attack occurred, was also arrested.[54] Wahby was either incredibly unlucky or provoked these attacks. Whether the "Americans" were always the

[48] *Kawkab America* (English), April 15, 1892.
[49] "Syrians Badly Beaten," *The* (NY) *Evening Telegram*, June 12, 1893.
[50] *Kawkab America*, June 23, 1893.
[51] *Kawkab America,* December 8, 1893.
[52] *Kawkab America*, June 8, 1894.
[53] "Felled with a Cart Rung," *NYH,* October 24, 1894.
[54] "Syrians Demand Protection," *The* (NY*) Sun,* January 23, 1892.

aggressors, as the Syrians claimed, is not clear, although all of the American newspapers blamed the Irish.

A policeman raided Aziello Shohfi's pool hall at 63 Washington Street after he noticed Shohfi looking furtively out the door. Thinking Shohfi was acting as a lookout, he rushed in, wielding his club, and found a couple of dozen men, who immediately ran out the back door. Eight were arrested. For what? This story is completely nonsensical and yet it found its way into several newspapers, which means, I suppose, that the raid did occur. But what the men were doing there, and whether what they were doing invited the intervention of the police, remained unaddressed; was it simply because they were playing pool?[55] Muossa Daoud also came in for some punishment when his ear was split open by a policeman who was trying to clear a group of Syrians off the sidewalk. Daoud, the injured party, spent a night in jail.

Even the Immigration Commission, generally virulently racist when describing the Syrians, stated, "The Syrian in New York has housed himself in the tenements of the old First Ward, from which he has dispossessed an undesirable Irish population, the remnant of which torments him."[56] *The Sun* advised the Syrians to remain patient and not to engage in strife with the "Washington street rowdies." They should seek police protection instead.[57] That the police seemed unable or unwilling to stop these attacks, and sometimes precipitated them, meant that the Syrians must have felt that they had to protect themselves. The editors of *Kawkab America* urged the Syrians to learn how to defend themselves against these Irish thugs. Moss claimed that these gangs had "passed out of existence," by the time of his writing (1897),[58] but certainly the attacks on the Syrians continued.

The Syrians sometimes gave as good as they got. In 1893, a fight broke out between a bunch of Irish thugs and a couple of "Bedouins" who were passing through on the way to the Chicago fair. The gang threw rocks, but when one of the Bedouin took out a sword, the Irish fled.[59] If this episode had not been reported in *Kawkab America*, I would take it as simply another Orientalist fantasy, but perhaps these Bedouin really did have swords and really did draw them.

In 1897 a fight broke out between the Syrians and Greeks living at 105

[55] "Twenty-one of Them Escaped," *NYH,* March 16, 1896.

[56] Industrial Commission on Immigration 1901: 444.

[57] *The* (NY*) Sun,* February 2, 1892.

[58] Moss 1897: 275.

[59] *Kawkab America,* May 12, 1893.

Washington Street. In some versions, Lotfallah Atta and his brother George, restaurant keepers at 71 Washington, ran up there to try to restore peace; in others, Lotfallah Atta was found beating up a Greek woman. In any case, Lotfallah and a Greek man were wounded and taken to Hudson Street Hospital.[60] It was said to be a fight between the pro-Turkish (Syrian) and anti-Turkish (Greek) residents, and was sparked by the sight of the Syrians wearing fezzes. The Ottoman consul, Baltazzi Bey, alerted the U.S. government that every effort should be made to protect the Syrians from the Greek aggressors.[61]

Policeman Bernard F. McKeever, with his head completely bandaged and his jaw wired shut, appeared in court to testify against two Syrians, neither of whose names is recognizable, but who may be George and Elias Zreik. McKeever testified that a group of "Assyrians" had been walking up Washington Street carrying clubs and creating a disturbance. He ordered them away and they set upon him with the clubs. It turned out that one of the Syrians was also injured and had to go to the hospital. The Syrians were each held on $1,000 bond.[62] What were these clubs that the Syrians were supposedly carrying? And why would they be walking up the street with them? Was it perhaps the way they had decided to defend themselves against the Irish gangs, or was it a figment of the policeman's imagination?

A small riot broke out on Greek Easter Sunday, 1902, involving Tony (Tannous) Saba, a "banker and man of influence," of 73 Washington, John (Abdallah) Hamati, the owner of the boardinghouse at 71 Washington, and a group of Irish residents—men and women—who streamed out of the "groggeries" lining Washington Street. Most of the American accounts blamed the Syrians: the fight was due either to the Syrians' "traditional dislike for their fellow-workmen and competitors, the Irish," or to "men maddened by copious imbibing of arrack,"[63] or to Tony Saba having pushed an Irishwoman who was standing in front of 15 Washington.[64] Saba and Hamati were arrested, and at the station "a large Syrian carving knife, double-edged, about fourteen inches long, was found on Hamati."[65] The injured were Hamati himself, Thomas Connolly, James Harron, and George Kahsos. Although this was clearly a fight between the Syrians and their Irish neighbors, the *Times* and the

[60] "Fought in a Tenement," *NYH,* May 1, 1897.

[61] "Mustapha Bey's Warning," *NYT,* May 9, 1897.

[62] "Policeman vs. Assyrians," *Daily People* (NY), November 6, 1901.

[63] "Rioting in New York," *Boston Herald,* April 28, 1902.

[64] "Syrians in Small Riot," *New-York Daily Tribune,* April 28, 1902.

[65] "Riot in Syrian Quarter," *NYT,* April 28, 1902.

*Tribune* averred that the fight was really just an excuse for the Syrians to break into another factional dispute.

A month later, policeman John J. Keenan was attacked by a group of four Syrians when he raided 71 Washington Street after hearing gunshots coming from within. Apparently Michael Gorra, who was about to join a Wild West show, was demonstrating his trick shooting. When Keenan barged in, he was set upon by the Syrians and supposedly seriously injured. He called for reinforcements and a squad of police arrived. "The fight continued at red hot pitch, and the Syrians had to be clubbed into submission."[66] Four Syrians were arrested; when they appeared before the magistrate, they "presented a sorry appearance." One of them was unable to rise at the end of the arraignment. The fact that Lotfallah Atta's place was the scene of so many of these fights implies that Atta himself was, if not an instigator, at least an enthusiastic participant. Being one of the "strong men" of the Colony probably made his participation mandatory. An Irish policeman is quoted as saying that he'd had to arrest Atta numerous times—"he's a reg'lar divil w'en he's dr'runk"—and that once Atta had nearly killed him with a bit of gas pipe.[67]

Five men attacked George Faour, one of the banking Faours, in front of a Syrian restaurant as he was on his way to the Western National Bank; Faour was badly injured. His brother Fanuls (Daniel) came to the rescue and both were arrested, along with one of the would-be robbers, Joseph Hey. Hey was let go, whereas the Faour Brothers each had to pay a five-dollar fine. Not surprisingly, George found this decision outrageous since he was the one who had been attacked and said so in no uncertain terms to the judge. The judge agreed to have Hey rearrested and this time held for "highway robbery." Meanwhile, the money that George was taking to the bank—thirty-one checks amounting to $3,139 and a draft on a French bank for 3,600 francs—were found on the street and returned to the Faours. "The Faour Brothers are going to court this morning to claim the ten dollars they paid in fines."[68] Again, this incident sounds like a simple robbery, where the victim happened to be Syrian. The number of attackers and the injury Faour sustained, however, might indicate a special viciousness shown by the Irish when it came to Syrian marks.

Although reporters attributed these attacks to disgruntlement on the part of the Irish for various offenses committed by the Syrians (they did not

[66] "Syrians Attack Policeman," *New-York Tribune*, May 26, 1902.
[67] "In a Syrian Coffee House," *Dallas Morning News*, January 22, 1899.
[68] "Syrian Banker Robbed," *NYT*, May 8, 1901.

patronize Irish businesses, they were not voters[69], or they were driving up rents[70]), they were probably really motivated by some combination of race hatred, fear of competition, and the violence which is often a feature of the crowded conditions of the slums. And of course, we cannot absolve the Syrians of their part in these battles; they may have provoked some of the enmity. As we have seen, they were not entirely peace-loving themselves.

### Smuggling, Tax Evasion, and Forgeries

Violence in the streets was only the most obvious way that Syrians came to the attention of the police. The smuggling scandal involving John Abd-el-Nour and Selma Gobreen Abd-el-Nour (described in chapter 10) was only the most spectacular of the tax-evasion schemes perpetrated by Syrian merchants, but there were others. The ones who were caught probably represented only a small percentage of the actual malefactors. All of the schemes were of the same ilk: Syrian merchants trying to pay less duty on goods than was due, either by smuggling them across borders, falsifying paperwork, or covering expensive goods with cheap goods when the customs inspectors came around.

Gobreen and her accomplices were arrested with smuggled goods worth $30,000; she and her partners had wrapped the goods around themselves under their clothes when they crossed the Canadian border. Abd-el-Nour, when his trunks of goods were opened in the wake of his wife's arrest, was found to have concealed the richest textile objects from the customs inspectors by covering them with cheap goods. It was said that Gobreen had been arrested in Boston the previous year for a similar offense. Abd-el-Nour escaped the authorities' clutches.

George Shawi, Kalil Freije, and Charles Eshau, who had cigarette factories at 57 and 109 Washington Street, were arrested in a raid for neglecting to pay taxes on some 2,000 packages of cigarettes. They were held on $500 bail each.[71] The city filed eleven suits against Thomas and Joseph Rahaim, dealers in religious goods, between 1903 and 1907, for unpaid taxes—all of which the brothers lost.

Joseph Ayoob, a Syrian merchant living at 81 Washington and one of John

[69] "Syrians Ask for Protection," *NYH*, January 21, 1892; "Persecutions of Syrians, *NYT*, January 22, 1892.
[70] "Rage among the Syrians," *NYH*, April 5, 1892.
[71] "Notes from the Courts," *NYT*, August 21, 1894.

Abd-el-Nour's early partners, had also been arrested for undervaluing goods in his possession (rich silks), so as to pay less in customs duties.[72] The goods were worth about $3,000, but Ayoob had listed their value at 40 percent of that, according to the customs officials. He had set up an office in New Haven, complete with an alias, in order to take advantage of the less stringent customs enforcement there.[73] A year after he settled the case, he described what had happened and why, as a result, he had stopped importing Oriental goods:

> A Syrian cannot fight the customs officers. He may be innocent, but they will convict him. You see it is like this: At home not many people speak English, just as here you find few speak Arabic. I want to import some goods. My friends there find one who speaks the English and he makes out the invoice. He does not know well how and he makes a mistake. Then the customs men call it lying.... When Americans have these mistakes they are corrected and the Americans get off; the Syrians never. I have done $100,000, $200,000 business in importing, but I no longer do so. I cannot fight the customs men. Now I manufacture in Astoria and here these goods, which look like Syrian goods, sell well, and I can do a good business.[74]

In Ayoob's case, this may indeed have been the reason why he switched from importing to manufacturing the same goods. But with or without overzealous customs officers, it must have been much more profitable to manufacture these goods close to home and still sell them as Holy Land goods. This practice enraged some people.

An article titled "Fakir's fairyland" described the culture of fakery in New York City, where "faking has become one of the finest of fine arts." After lambasting the New York Italians who made "Benedictine and Chartreuse" liqueurs, and the fake gems coming out of John Street, the reporter moved on to the Syrians. "Syrian relic-makers may be found in a cheerless back attic in a house on Stone Street," he says. (I have found no evidence for Syrians living or working that far to the east, but let us take him at his word.) The relic-makers were from Palestine; they were carving relics from sandalwood and olive wood. The reporter admitted that the wood was identical to that used in the Middle East, and so was the workmanship.

[72] "Only One Out of Many," *NYT,* June 18, 1893.
[73] "New Method of Smuggling," *NYH,* June 18, 1893.
[74] "Smuggler Abd-el-Nour," *The* (NY*) Sun*, December 5, 1894.

He maintained, however, that they were not authentic Holy Land goods. "Each is marked with 'sacred symbols' and the word 'Jerusalem' in Arabic. Now the Garden of Gethsemane and Bethlehem are in Stone street." The reporter showed special contempt for a "stone jug of Oriental design, filled with Croton [Reservoir] water and marked 'Jordan water' [and] sealed with the Greek Church seal." This so-called holy water, he said, was used for baptisms and christenings.[75] And thus the pun "fakir/faker" came into the mainstream press.

A similar indictment of the Oriental goods business was published in the *Daily People* three years later: "So the slave…sets out with his pushcart, his 'Smyrna' rugs, made in Yonkers; his 'curios' made here in New York with the aid of improved machinery; his 'Oriental' fabrics, made in Providence, Patterson, or some other nearby place; or his 'relics' of Mohammedan 'atrocities,' which are also made on the premises."[76] What could relics of Mohammedan atrocities have been? The same accusation of fakery was lodged against cigarette makers who bought their "Turkish" tobacco in Connecticut, and belly dancers who probably came from the Bowery. Even Jacob Riis's glancing notice of the Arabs made this point, "Even the Arab, who peddles 'holy earth' from the Battery as a direct importation from Jerusalem, has his exclusive preserves at the lower end of Washington Street."[77]

Ayoob's feeling that Syrians were especially picked on by customs inspectors, if widespread, must have made chicanery like this acceptable to other Syrians, if not their customers. In any case, no one actually went to jail for tax evasion, smuggling, or claiming a false origin for the goods they were selling; if convicted, they paid what they owed, along with their legal fees, and went on their way.

The violence among Syrians, fights between the Syrians and outsiders, smuggling, numerous arrests at Turkish smoking parlors—all of these run-ins with the law seem to belie the characterization of the Syrians as souls of probity. Yet we have to remember that newspapers' coverage surely exaggerated the frequency as well as the seriousness of these infractions.

75 "Fakir's Fairyland," *Daily Advocate* (Baton Rouge, LA), March 25, 1899.
76 "The Prey of Sharks," *Daily People* (NY), April 30, 1902.
77 http://www.bartleby.com/208/3.html.

## Civil Suits

The civil suits involving Syrians consisted, for the most part, of merchants suing to recover money owed them by retailers or peddlers. The majority (28 out of 32) of these cases involved Syrian against Syrian. Najeeb N. Maloof (the same man who sued the editors of *Kawkab America* and *Mira'at al-Gharb* for slander), for example, sued Charles Safi for $66.50 for "certain gifts and merchandise, to wit Oriental Goods and Novelties."[78] Maloof won the suit. In the same year, Joseph N. Maloof (Najeeb's brother) accused Mr. and Mrs. C.H. Davids of taking $300 worth of Oriental goods on credit and not paying him. According to him, the couple took goods on credit, claiming that Mrs. Davids had a friend who would buy them and they would return to pay for what had been selected. They did not return. She was arrested on $1,000 bail,[79] more than what she owed Maloof. This is the same woman who was arrested the following year in Jersey City for stealing from houses where she was selling goods. Her husband was implicated in both cases, but she seems to have been blamed. Were they confidence tricksters or innocent peddlers who were unlucky?

The company, "F. & A. Rihani," was the plaintiff in six court cases in which the partners sued to recover money from peddlers who had not paid them for their goods. Four of the cases were for amounts ranging from sixty to ninety dollars. The fifth, however, against Siman A. Mansour, was for $251, and the sixth, against not an individual but a company, "Bouhyder, Sadallah & Abouhyder," involved $208 worth of goods. The Rihanis won all six suits. In another such case reported in *Al Hoda*, Fares Rihani accused George Rizk of leaving town without having paid $115 owed to Rihani. He was caught on the boat, tearfully returned the money, and then begged Rihani to loan him eight dollars so he could continue his journey. Rihani did so.[80]

Salim Elias, a merchant from Baskinta who owned a store at 69 Washington Street, filed suit against one Amin Zalloum in Philadelphia for $500 owed him. When Zalloum got wind of the suit he closed his store and fled.[81] Elias also had Michael Karam arrested for failure to pay $1,479.99 owed him for a shipment of Syrian sponges given on credit. As Karam was unable to

[78] *Trials,* Nageeb N. Maloof v. Charles Saffy, Feb. 18, 1896: S-189.

[79] "Husband and Wife Held," *NYH,* November 29, 1896.

[80] *Al Hoda* June 21, 1898.

[81] *Kawkab America,* May 20, 1892.

post the $1,800 bail (more than what he owed Elias), he was remanded to the Raymond Street jail.[82] Beshara Ganim and Antoine Sadallah, importers, sued Zayen D. Sfeir for $223.77 for non-payment for goods in 1898 and won the case. The plaintiffs, in fact, won in every recorded case, making it pretty clear that peddlers did indeed default on their payments, contrary to the myth of every Syrian family working themselves to the bone to pay back debts, sometimes not their own. With thousands of these transactions taking place every month, however, fewer than forty reported cases is a small percentage of defaults.

In a unique example of a peddler—and a woman—suing her supplier, Jamilie Zainey sued Najeeb N. Maloof, describing a complicated set of transactions and loans, in which he owed her money.[83] Zainey was a recent widow who came to this country with her two sons in 1897 and earned enough to send them to college and deposit $800 in George Forzly's bank (she lost that money when the bank folded in 1899). Najeeb claimed he owed her no money; on the contrary, she owed him money for goods not paid for. Amazingly, Zainey won the suit, and Najeeb was forced to pay her $2,200, a huge sum.

My paternal grandfather chastised his fellow Syrians for their tendency to sue each other in a letter to the editor of *Kawkab America*.[84] In it he expressed disapproval over the discord that was so manifest in the Syrian community of Denver, not only by the public fighting that went on but by the number of lawsuits being filed by Syrians against other Syrians. He cited one case in which a single Syrian had filed eight lawsuits against another Syrian. He lamented that these practices had made laughingstocks of the Syrians. The number of lawsuits involving the New York Colony was small and would not have caused a ripple of attention in American observers.

Two personal injury cases were also adjudicated and are instructive only because in these cases the Syrian plaintiff took on the outside world. Abraham Maloof sued the Metropolitan Street Railway Company for $3,000 (for medical expenses and lost wages) for an injury sustained when a car began to move while he was trying to board. The suit sounded fraudulent as he argued it; it looked and felt as if he were trying to cheat the company, and indeed he lost the suit and was forced to pay the defendant $108 in court costs. The second involved an accident in which Salim Maloof sustained injuries when

[82] "Syrian Goes to Jail," *BDE*, August 28, 1902.
[83] *Trials*, Jamelia Zainey v. Najeeb N. Maloof, 1903: M-487.
[84] *Kawkab America*, December 7, 1894.

he was knocked down by a wagon belonging to an American company, Century Express. This Maloof was awarded $119.15 in damages. Century Express appealed, but lost the appeal.

In a case that found its way into the newspapers, Joseph Oussani sued one of his tenants at 32 West 29th Street for a year's rent when she did not vacate her rooms in a timely fashion. She won the case but was reversed on appeal, and Oussani was awarded the rent plus court costs ($32.50).[85]

In all of these cases, non-Syrian lawyers represented the plaintiffs and defendants; S. Victor Constant, Adolphus Pape, and George Coffin prosecuted most of these claims. These civil cases represent the internecine stresses of any immigrant community trying to adapt to a new culture, new business practices, and a new legal system.

## Criminal Cases

What about the few serious crimes involving Syrians? We have looked at the murder of John Stefan and the resulting charges against George Zreik and trial of Elias Zreik, as well as at the attempted arson trial of Elias Karam and Kalil Matta. All four men were acquitted. A murder trial took place in 1898 in Boston involving a Syrian defendant named Elias Farhat Kfoury, who was supposed to have murdered another Syrian named Kenaan Shibley. I have not been able to uncover any other details of the crime. *Al Hoda* accused *Kawkab America* of promoting sectarianism and trying Kfoury in the press by writing a headline in which Kfoury was described as a murderer.[86] The Syrian Maronite Charitable Organization of New York City organized a fund-raising effort for his defense; $12,500 came in from (presumably Maronite) Syrian merchants in New York alone, and another $14,590 came in from Syrian communities in other parts of the United States and Canada. They were apparently able to hire a prestigious law firm, and Kfoury was acquitted. He and his brothers ran a grocery store in Lawrence, Massachusetts, until at least 1908.

The banding together of supporters for Syrians put on trial was an important aspect of the Syrian community's response to the American legal system. This was what an anonymous writer in *Kawkab America* had advocated in

[85] *Trials,* Joseph Oussani v. Sadie L. Thompson, 1897: T-48; "New York Letter," *Rome* (NY) *Semi-Weekly Citizen,* June 1, 1897.

[86] *Al Hoda,* October 18, 1898.

1893. The prosecuting attorney in the Zreik trial kept asking the witnesses whether "the committee" had had any influence on them. According to the prosecution, the committee consisted of Nicola Dibs, George Saba, and several other Orthodox men who were interested in securing Elias Zreik's release. All the witnesses denied the existence of any committee, yet it would not be unheard of for a group of Greek Orthodox men to band together to try to get one of their own acquitted, just as the Maronites did in the Kfoury case. I have not been able to determine whether in fact there was a committee, and if so, whether it had any influence on the trial. Zreik was, however, represented by a prominent New York lawyer named James W. Osborne (a former assistant district attorney), who must have charged a hefty fee; perhaps the alleged committee paid that fee.[87] It seems unlikely that Zreik, a camel driver, would have had the wherewithal to do so. Like Kfoury, he was acquitted.

Another murder, that of Joseph Coury, was supposed to have been the work of a gang of men paid by three Orayeh brothers in retaliation for Coury having taken over their foreclosed silk mill in Hoboken. Four men were arrested. I do not know the outcome of the trial. A third murderer, Habib Saad, was convicted of killing his cousin Catherine in Lockport, New York, and sentenced to life imprisonment. The judge, however, was sympathetic and told Saad that if he could provide an alibi, the judge would reconsider the conviction.[88] The murder of a Syrian peddler in Pennsylvania by two other peddlers was apparently never solved. An Algerian by the name of Ameer ben Ali was sentenced to life imprisonment for the murder of a woman named Carrie Brown in 1891. He was pardoned in 1902.

According to an article in the *Baltimore American*, "Well-informed Syrians in this city [Jersey City, N.J.] assert openly that conviction of Syrians on the charge of murder has been so difficult to obtain that an impression has been created that ends of justice are often defeated by the extreme clannishness of the Syrians making their home in this country. As soon as one of their number is charged with a serious, or even a minor offense, the raising of money for his defense is accomplished with such ease as to point to a compact among the Syrians of this country to maintain the cleanest record in the matter of convictions for criminal offenses."[89] Although this reportage is couched in

[87] A Syrian was quoted as saying, "To [heck] with American law so long as we have Jim Osborne as our lawyer." "Bitter Syrian Feuds Caused by Church War," *BDE,* February 4, 1906.

[88] "Sentenced to Life Imprisonment," *BDE,* November 19, 1891.

[89] "Syrians Clannish," *Baltimore American,* July 1, 1907.

the language of conspiracy, what was the harm of such a system? In fact, how much more vitriol would the newspapers have spilled if one of the Syrians had been convicted of murder? It seems positively humanitarian for the Syrians, if they did so, to band together to help their fellow countrymen.

It was certainly true that in every case of a Syrian being arrested, as reported in *Kawkab America* and *Al Hoda*, a fellow Syrian rushed to his aid. Although never stated explicitly, it seems clear that the rescuer was encouraged by, and perhaps funded by, other members of the community.

These ad hoc committees, along with the more formal associations described below, marked the development of what we now call "civil society" among a new immigrant group. The effectiveness of these committees could be the reason that Miller and Houghton found no Syrian to have been convicted of a serious crime or had recourse to government help in times of crisis, although we have seen, of course, that Syrian families did put their children in care and did sometimes depend on outside charity for help.

Even if a case did not warrant such a well-organized response, it is clear that a crowd of Syrian onlookers, supporters and opponents accompanied every Syrian who appeared in court. It seems that the crowds, just like these defense committees, were often made up along sectarian lines, depending on the religion of the accused, and that they lent moral, if not material, support to him or her.

In at least two cases that we are aware of the verdict was altered by the presence of a priest. In one case, the Maronite priest, Father Stefan, appeared in the courtroom and said he could decide the case himself. The judge dismissed the case (with a sigh of relief, it was claimed).[90] Gabriel Korkemas was asked by the Syrian community in Boston to attend a trial that was not going well for the defendant, Faris Shamoun. Korkemas was credited with "making a deal" with the judge, and the defendant was acquitted.[91]

Despite one reporter's view that the Syrians "adjudicate their own troubles without reference to the venal courts,"[92] the Syrians were familiar with and used the American legal system and believed in its ability to render justice. In every reported case of violence (verbal or physical), whether with other Syrians or outsiders, the victims appealed to a policeman or judge for protection or redress. When they couldn't get satisfaction, they brought lawsuits against

[90] "Syrian Primate Turns Magistrate," *The* (NY) *Evening Telegram,* April 12, 1901.

[91] *Kawkab America,* November 1, 1895.

[92] "Red Fezzed Heads; Languorous Eyes," *NYH,* November 18, 1894.

their countrymen. Even if the Syrians ended up complaining that the authorities did nothing, the complaint contains in it the expectation that they should have done something.

George Faour reversed a judge's decision by protesting its injustice, as did Joseph Maloof in the "coochee-coochee" case described above. Several divorces were taken to the courts despite the public nature of this path. The nineteenth-century Syrians registered thirty-six marriages, seventy-two births, and twenty-five deaths with the city—certainly not all the marriages, births, and deaths that occurred, but a significant number nonetheless—when there was no legal compulsion to do so. One hundred and sixty-three Syrian men took out their naturalization papers in the nineteenth century. They had to be naturalized in order to apply for and receive a passport and they needed a passport if they wanted to do business abroad or return home for a visit, but it is touching nonetheless that these earliest immigrants aspired to citizenship in their adopted country. As previously noted, the Arbeelys, the "first Syrian family," filed their declaration of intent to become naturalized two days after they arrived.

Chapter 13

# Civil Society

*It is never an easy task to bind a large number of Syrians together in any enterprise.*[1]

## Associations

Syrian men repeatedly lamented the factionalism of the community in editorials and letters to the editor. People pointed to the disputes and lack of cooperation among businessmen, seeing this as evidence of the general underdevelopment of Syrian society in the United States. The bankruptcy of the Hamidie Company at the Chicago fair was even said to be a result of these failings. Both Ameen Gorayeb, the editor of *Al Hoda*, and Yusef Balesh, who wrote for *Al Hoda* and *Kawkab America*, pled with the Syrian community to come together.[2] In response, a number of Syrian associations were formed in the nineteenth century, most with a philanthropic purpose, but others were for self-improvement, and one was a political organization.

We have seen that ad hoc committees for the purpose of defending those who had been arrested were a relatively common feature of Syrian society in the nineteenth century. Another informal association, which was mentioned only once and perhaps was short lived, was formed to lower the price of Arabic bread for the residents of the Colony. Announced in an 1895 issue of *Kawkab America*, the committee was formed when the "Turkish" baker at 91 Washington Street (Tannous Shishim?) began charging "outrageous" prices for bread.[3]

Abraham Rihbany and Nageeb Arbeely organized a club in 1891 or early 1892 that they called the *Syrian Scientific and Ethical Society*—a rather

[1] Rihbany 1914: 219.
[2] *Al Hoda,* May 17, 1898.
[3] *Kawkab America,* August 23, 1895.

grand name for what was probably an informal gathering of educated men of the Colony. Arbeely was named president, and Rihbany vice president. Alexander Abukalil offered his restaurant at 75 Washington, on condition that they would purchase food while there. One of the Society's members would give a speech on some lofty topic—the greatness of ancient Syria, say, or the wonders of New York—and then they would discuss it. The members (or at least Rihbany) felt, however, that the restaurant workers did not show sufficient respect for their activities, with dishes clanking and people shouting orders to the cook. When the members (or Rihbany) asked them to stop making noise while the Society met, Abukalil was not about to give up his custom in order to accommodate them; they were evicted and the Society fell apart.[4]

The earliest real association was the *Syrian Society of the City of New York*, which was founded by a group of Presbyterians in mid-1892. A planning meeting was held in January, and then a notice was posted in the *New York Herald* announcing that "a meeting of those interested in the welfare of the Syrian Colony in this city will be held this evening at the residence of Dr. McLaury, No. 244 West Forty-Second Street."[5] No notice was given in Arabic in *Kawkab America*, which had just begun publication. All who attended the first meeting and became members of the board were Americans, the only exception being Dr. Ameen F. Haddad, himself a Presbyterian, who was elected secretary. He seemed to take the lead immediately and became the Society's chief organizer, spokesman, and fund-raiser. We don't know whether the Society was his idea, but in a report at the end of its first year the Society's president, Frederick W. Perry, called him "the father of the Society."[6] At its second meeting, which took place in Brooklyn, Haddad gave a speech in which he outlined the purpose of the Society: "It is estimated that there are not less than 25,000 Syrians in the United States; 1,000 of them permanent residents of the city of New York. Is it not wise, or allow me to say, is it not our duty to devise some means to make these Syrians good Christian American citizens and to educate them, so that when they vote they will do it intelligently and in time become self supporting instead of a burden on the community?"[7] Inasmuch as the members of the Colony were completely self-supporting and

[4] Rihbany 1914: 219–225.
[5] "City Jottings," *NYH,* April 26, 1892; "Care for Syrians," *NYT,* April 27, 1892.
[6] Syrian Society of New York 1893: 4.
[7] "The New Syrian Society Has a School," *BDE,* May 3, 1892.

had never been a burden on the community, many were educated, and all were Christians, it seems that Haddad was pandering a bit to his American patrons.

13-1. Cover of the Syrian Society *Annual Report*, 1893 (New York Public Library).

Nageeb Arbeely claimed he heard about the Society only three months later, when Dr. McLaury asked him to run the organization and join the board, which Arbeely agreed to do.[8] On arriving at a meeting, he was surprised to discover that Haddad was the only Syrian involved and that all board seats were filled. Arbeely, in the English page of *Kawkab America*, claimed that he confronted the group, asking why no Syrians had been invited to the first meetings. Haddad replied, according to Arbeely, that he thought it would be "inadvisable" as Syrians were not accustomed to joining such societies and would not be fit for membership. Arbeely argued the case for a strong representation of Syrians in the Society, inasmuch as its headquarters were in the midst of the Syrian settlement and its purpose was to benefit Syrians. He concluded his editorial by expressing his continued willingness to join "any

[8] "The New York Syrian Society," *Kawkab America*, August 5, 1892.

movement for the help and elevation of our countrymen."[9] Notwithstanding his disgruntled tone, Arbeely and several other Syrians contributed funds to the Society during its first year, and three (Ameen Haddad, David Sleem, and Constantine Biskinty, all Protestants) became life members by contributing twenty-five dollars each. Despite this Syrian participation, it is evident that this was not a homegrown association but one founded by American Presbyterians for the betterment of the Syrian Colony. That its stated purpose was to help Syrian youths assimilate and to make them good American citizens was testimony to its American patronage.

Ameen and his pharmacist brother, Saleem, opened the Society's school soon after the first meeting, setting it up on the second floor of 95 Washington Street. A grocery store took up the ground floor. The first course offered was English; there were two enrollees on the first day. The school curriculum was aimed mainly at boys—the Society hoped to add industrial training and a basic curriculum in order to prepare the students to go on to other schools or enter business—but girls were enrolled as well. Saleem taught the night class, and an American woman, Helen M. Fisher, volunteered to teach the children until a permanent teacher could be found. Several members of the Ladies' Auxiliary contributed time in teaching the children to read or sew; they also contributed needed materials such as chalk, slates, and piece goods. Twelve weeks after the school opened, Miss Alice Frinch arrived from Syria to teach the students. After Alice's marriage to George Uniss in 1900, Martha Haddad took over. Her salary was $871 a year; rent for the space was $731. Every Sunday and Thursday evening there were sermons delivered in Arabic and English, presumably Presbyterian sermons, by a preacher whose salary was paid by the Board of Foreign Missions.[10]

In May the Society announced it was planning to open a home for children whose parents "are now in or going to Chicago,"[11] and Ameen spoke with great optimism about this plan, but at the same time he announced that they were out of funds. They were somehow rescued. Two months after the school's founding, Ameen took a number of students to a "fresh air day" sponsored by the *New York Herald*.[12] Six months later, the school reported having thirty students and looking for a public school in which to give evening classes.

[9] "The New York Syrian Society," *Kawkab America*, August 5, 1892.
[10] When Elias Saadi arrived in 1899 he stepped into this role.
[11] "To Found a Home for Syrian Children," *NYT*, May 5, 1893.
[12] Letter to the Editor, *NYH*, September 12, 1892.

A *New York Herald* reporter visited the school a year after its founding. "The Syrian kindergarten is on the first floor of a crazy old hotel near Rector Street. On entering I found myself in a small room filled with odd desks and benches occupied by bright eyed little tots, girls and boys together....They have an evening school for adults, but Ameen F. Haddad said, 'Our main hope is in the children.'"[13] Eighteen children were enrolled. In addition to lessons in English, geography, and government, the girls learned lacemaking, the equivalent to the industrial training offered to boys. The reporter quoted Dr. Haddad, who complained that as soon as the children began to learn, they were taken out of school by their parents to peddle. He made a plea for support from the public, saying that the school was living hand to mouth: "The Christian world owes much to Syria and we must not let these people go astray." President Perry said, "We don't want the Arabic tongue to cling to these unfortunate people."[14]

In the article, the reporter took it upon himself to "warn" immigration officials about Syrians who arrive in New York ("many of them steal aboard vessels and hide themselves until the voyage begins"), speak only Arabic, and are able to engage in no business but peddling. Nageeb Arbeely took strong exception to this article and its negative portrayal of Syrian immigrants, accusing Ameen Haddad of encouraging this negative reporting.[15] Ameen, however, was only doing what every fund-raiser does: giving the worst possible picture of a situation in order that potential donors will pity the children and give. Through the years, he was regularly forced to make appeals to the people of New York through the newspapers. The *New York Herald* and *Daily Tribune* were particularly supportive in this effort, regularly publishing his pleas and reporting on the school's progress. Haddad would ask each reader to send fifty dollars, which is what he said it cost to operate the school for a month,[16] although the rent and salary amounted to more than that.

Donations allowed him to keep the school going, albeit precariously. The school held an annual Christmas festival to raise money; the YWCA of East 15th Street sponsored a fund-raising soirée for the Society in 1893; and one of the members of the Ladies' Auxiliary, Mrs. Brown, gave a reading at her

[13] "Training Syrians to Be Americans,"*NYH*, May 14, 1893.

[14] "Training Syrians to Be Americans,"*NYH*, May 14, 1893.

[15] *Kawkab America,* May 19, 1893.

[16] "Help Asked for a Syrian School," *New-York Daily Tribune,* February 14, 1895.

home to one hundred people in the same year. All the guests whose names were mentioned were Americans.[17]

These efforts notwithstanding, the summary of four years' work published by the Society in 1898 was gloomy. The school was still functioning, but the home for children had not been built for lack of funds. The Society reported receipts for 1897 of $310.30 and expenditures of $534.90;[18] for the full four years, receipts were $2,310.72 and expenditures amounted to $2,416.96. This deficit did not bode well: in the same year, an article about the school in the *New-York Daily Tribune* reported that it had closed in May again for lack of funds, but was able to reopen in October.[19] When the reporter visited the school he found thirty-four children enrolled, but a list of the scholars in the 1898 report shows only twenty. A touching photograph of two Syrian children accompanying the same article (and used on the cover of the school's 1898 financial report) shows a girl of about eight years of age in a calico dress and a scarf tied under her chin, next to a smaller boy (Yusef Malouf) in short pants and a soft bow tie and a little fez (Figure 13-1). Both look off to one side and seem a bit melancholy, perfect poster children for the school in its perilous state. In 1898, an article referred to the day school for children and the night school for adults as fulfilling the Syrians' "almost pathetic desire for education," which was seen as a means to only one end: getting rich.[20]

Miller doesn't mention the school in his summary of children's school attendance, but an article about it in 1906 bewailed its still-rickety finances; at that point, Ameen Haddad was serving as both teacher and director of the school.[21] The Society survived until at least 1912, when it was housed at 21 Washington. Ameen Haddad was still its secretary.

Two letters to *Kawkab America* signed by "an Ottoman" heralded the formation of a group called the *Arabic Society* or *Arab Brotherhood* in June 1893. Its first (and last) meeting took place on July 1, 1893, at 61 West Street (we don't know whose residence this was). Its aims seem to have been mainly literary, but it was also meant to foster a sense of solidarity among all the scattered Syrians. No attendees' names were mentioned.[22] A letter from another (anonymous) reader expressed his approval of the formation of such an association,

[17] "Helping a Worthy Society," *New-York Daily Tribune,* February 24, 1893.
[18] State Board of Charities 1898: 461–462.
[19] "Occidental Orientals," *New-York Daily Tribune,* October 27, 1897.
[20] "New York Letter," *Oswego* (NY) *Daily Palladium,* February 10, 1898.
[21] "Syrian Society's Work," *The* (NY) *Evening Post,* February 23, 1906.
[22] *Kawkab America,* June 23, 1893; June 30, 1893.

repeating again the problems caused by disunity among the Syrians.[23] The group was apparently unable to agree on a leader, which caused its immediate demise.

The *Syrian Orthodox Benevolent Society* was founded in November 1894; George Coudsy was named president. The members of the executive committee were Abraham J. Arbeely, Nageeb Arbeely, Salim A. Fadel, Abdow Lutfy, Najeeb Mallouk, Ameen Halaby, Antoni Tadross, Constantine Biskinty, Kalil Freije, and Nicola Awad.[24] Coudsy gave the opening speech, saying that the purpose of the Society was to help all Ottomans, who were all part of one body, and Abdow Lutfy compared their modest charitable impulses to the great generosity of the sultan.[25]

It was this group of men that arranged for Archmandrite Hawaweeny to be sent to New York to serve as their priest, and the Society may have been formed for just this purpose, although it wasn't mentioned in its mission statement. When Hawaweeny arrived in 1895, he became the de facto president, taking the place of Abraham Arbeely, who had replaced Coudsy. The Society had already rented space at 77 Washington to serve as the church.

In addition to being concerned with church matters, the Society also had as its mission to help the poor, by giving them a ticket home, a helping hand to tide them over, or advice, as needed. Notwithstanding their lofty goals, it seems unlikely that they extended help to non-Orthodox, as there was a Maronite organization helping its coreligionists. At the beginning at least, they held monthly meetings on Saturday evenings, either at the home of Nicola Awad, 40 Washington Street, or at the Tadross Brothers' store/home at 77, and later 79, Washington.

The Society encouraged people to be good citizens, as all the Syrian associations claimed to do. More practically, it organized a medical dispensary, presided over by Dr. Najib Barbour, located above their church at 77 Washington.[26] During all the trials, tribulations, and fisticuffs that took place during the first five years of the twentieth century, however, the Benevolent Society was not mentioned. It may have folded by then or decided that discretion was more important than valor.

The *Syrian Maronite Charitable Organization* had its first meeting in

---

[23] *Kawkab America,* August 4, 1893.

[24] Anonymous 1895: 34.

[25] *Kawkab America,* November 16, 1894.

[26] "The Syrian Colony in New York, an Interesting Element There," *Springfield* (MA) *Republican,* March 26, 1899.

October 1895 at the home of Salim Ganim (at 19 Washington). The forty members present contributed a large amount of money to kick-start its charitable activities.[27] Entries in various New York City directories imply that the organization had actual offices throughout the decade, but these were probably simply the addresses of its members, in whose homes the meetings were held.

The Organization was active in providing funds for indigent Maronites, hiring lawyers for the defense of Maronites accused of crimes, including successfully defending Elias Farhat Kfoury against a murder charge, and upholding the moral standards of the Maronite community. It donated the sign for the Maronite Chapel at 83 Washington Street. Its first president was Salim Elias, and its earliest officers were Salim Ganim, Joseph Hanna Geha, and Michael Abousleman. Other members included George and Joseph Malhami, Petrus Saad, Joseph Abi Lama (Bellamah), Dominic Joseph Faour, Peter Khoury, Nahoom Hatem, Tanious Abdoo, Namallah Abraham, Ameen Gorayeb, Souma George el Hayek, David Hederi, Pedro Caram, Abdulmassih Mussawir, and Ghattas Faris. It received frequent coverage and unremitting support in the pages of *Al Hoda*, as is to be expected, but we do not know how long it lasted. The Organization put on the grand celebration for the twenty-fifth anniversary of Peter Korkemas's ordination in August 1899.

A second Maronite organization, the *Maronite Youth Association*, was founded in New York on January 9, 1899.[28] Emir Joseph Shehab was named as president, with Abalan Tanuri as vice president, Daniel Faour as treasurer, and Mikhail Khoury as secretary. Its first charitable act was a donation to St. Joseph's Maronite Church. In 1901, it had offices at 93 Washington and in 1902, at 1 Carlisle Street. It lasted until at least 1908, when it was based at 53 Washington.

In 1900 or earlier, the Maronite Youth Association established an affiliate called *Al Jamiat el Haykel el Watanieh*, for the purpose of raising money to build a Maronite church and school. The members named Father Khairallah Stefan as president, Salim Elias as vice president, Joseph T. Moshy as treasurer, and Elias Abousleman as secretary. People were urged to send money to Father Stefan at 57 Washington Street.[29]

[27] *Kawkab America,* October 18, 1895; October 25, 1895.

[28] *Al Hoda,* February 21, 1899.

[29] *Al Hoda,* October 27, 1900.

To me, one of the most interesting clubs was the *Syrian Young Men's Association*, founded in October 1895. It was a high-minded club similar to that started by Rihbany and Arbeely earlier. Founding members included Michael Abousleman (president), Rizkallah Deeb, Joseph Moshy, treasurer, and Cesar Sabbagh. Meetings were held at Petrus Saad's "Syrian Shop" at 59 Washington. Although its founders were Maronites, it seemingly welcomed men from all sects. *Kawkab America* published a long account of its eighth session on Sunday, December 29, 1895, at which Alexander Yazaji made opening remarks, Cesar Sabbagh gave an overview of "The West," Ameen Rihani delivered a speech in English on the subject of individuality, and Rizkallah Deeb and George Hobeika debated the question, "Is Syrian Immigration Beneficial to the Syrian Nation?"[30] Deeb represented the affirmative and won the debate. Both Raphael Hawaweeny of the Orthodox Church and Yusef Yazbek, the Maronite deacon, were in attendance. We also have an agenda (Figure 13-2) for a meeting that took place on Wednesday, September 2, 1896, the Society's fortieth session. There was an opening speech, the reading of the minutes, a speech in Arabic on "Our Advantages and Disadvantages," a speech in English on "Current Affairs in America," and a discussion of "Whether a Woman's Status Improves More with Money or Education."

The Association was responsible for the performance of *Andromache* in Arabic that fall (see chapter 8), and fifty young Syrians (both Maronite and Orthodox) attended its second annual meeting held on November 11, 1896, at 59 Washington. At that meeting, Michael Abousleman lectured in Arabic on "Turkey, Past, Present and Future," Nageeb Arbeely gave a speech in English praising America, and Nicola Nasser spoke about "Arabia." Then a debate was held on the question, "Have Foreigners Benefited Syria or Not?," with Said Shoucair taking the affirmative and Najeeb Diab the negative. The meeting wound up with a recitation of Arabic poetry.[31]

The *Syrian Women's Union* was established in 1896 by a number of prominent women in the community who served as its first officers: Najla Moghabghab, Nemnour Hayek, Ramza Macksoud, and Shafika Lutfy. That first year there were about thirty-five members. The women spent their first six months investigating conditions in the Colony and thinking about what they wanted to do.

At the end of the year, the forty members of the Union held a reception at Trinity House on Trinity Place at which they introduced the Union to the

[30] *Kawkab America,* January 10, 1896.

[31] "Young Syrians in Debate," *NYT,* November 15, 1896; *New-York Tribune,* November 15, 1896.

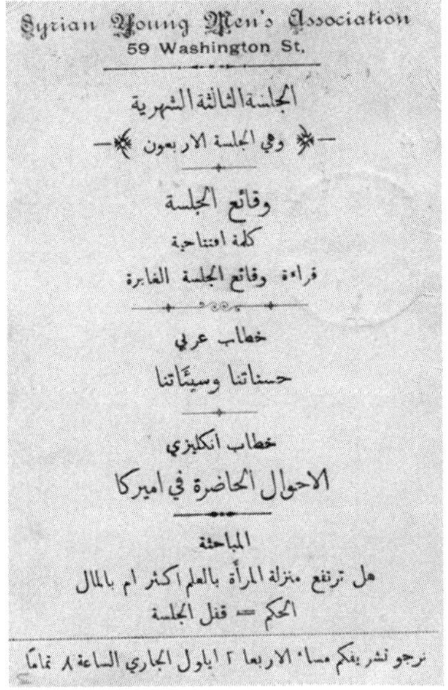

Syrian Young Men's Association
59 Washington St.

الجلسة الثالثة الشهرية
وهي الجلسة الاربعون

وقائع الجلسة
كلمة افتتاحية
قراءة وقائع الجلسة الغابرة

خطاب عربي
حسناتنا وسيئاتنا

خطاب انكليزي
الاحوال الحاضرة في اميركا

المباحثة
هل ترتفع منزلة المرأة بالعلم اكثر ام بالمال
الحكم = قفل الجلسة

نرجو تشريفكم مساء الاربعا ٢ ايلول الجاري الساعة ٨ تماما

13-2. Postcard announcing a meeting of the Syrian Young Men's Association, 1896 (collection of the author).

community. An article reported that 400 people came (although this seems unlikely given the size of the community), and that they gained many new members. The entertainment consisted of speeches by Mrs. Moghabghab ("The Position of Women"), Mrs. Maloof ("The Love of Country"), Bishop Hawaweeny, Nageeb Arbeely, and Dr. Mussawir. George Jabour sang, as did Miss Macksoud. Mrs. Saadi recited a poem. They held a debate on the topic, "Should Men and Women Be Equal?"[32] Throughout 1898, the women met together weekly and sewed, raising money for the poor of the community. They elected new officers for 1899, reelecting Najla Moghabghab and Ramza Macksoud and electing Almas Halaby, Maneera Moshy, and Jamilie Zainey. In December, they put on a fair that raised $400 toward their plans to build a crèche. In 1899, they made this plan a reality, as described previously.[33]

Organized by and for young, literate Syrian women, *Daughters of Syria* aimed to raise the level of the Syrian Colony in general, and its women in

[32] "Union of Syrian Women," *New-York Daily Tribune,* February 5, 1897.

[33] "Nursery for Syrian Babes," *NYT,* May 21, 1899; "Syrian Babies," *NYH,* June 9, 1899.

particular.[34] They first met at 95 Washington Street (the home of the Syrian Society school) on 12 October 1896, when they elected officers: Fareeda Flutie, president; Mariam Reesha, vice president; and Martha Haddad (the teacher at the school), treasurer. Supported by membership fees, it offered free English classes for members (and for nonmembers at a nominal fee) and hoped to open a circulating library and reading room for women. Unlike the Syrian Society, the members accepted donations only from other Syrians.

Two years later they elected new officers: Mariam Reesha, president; Martha Haddad, vice president; Jamilie Milkie, secretary; and Malake Saleeba, treasurer. Three older women were added to the executive committee: Mrs. Lian Kattini, Labeeby Saadi, and Louisa Hakim. Meetings were held at the tenement at 25 Washington. One of their projects was making an American flag to present to the 22nd Infantry Regiment (a New York City regiment), which was active in the Spanish-American War. Mariam Reesha's photograph in the *Tribune* shows a formidable and serious-looking young woman, wearing a voluminous Victorian garment with mutton sleeves and a white corsage at her shoulder.[35]

Early in 1898 Nageeb Arbeely, Najib Diab, Selim Kisbany, Joseph Moshy, Ameen Rihani, Saleem Moghabghab, and George Jabour founded the *Syrian-American Club*. Yusef Arbeely was named honorary president. This Club was seemingly able to transcend factional differences: Maronites, Orthodox, pro-Turkish, and anti-Turkish individuals were on the founding committee. It will be recalled that George Jabour, in a letter to the *Times*, protested that he was not anti-American, his proof being his membership in this Club and being a member of its naturalization committee. The mission of the Club was to "educate Syrians in American citizenship by weekly lectures."[36] Whether such lectures ever took place is unknown. The Club pledged all of its "3,000 members" to vote for Theodore Roosevelt and held a reception on Greenwich Street for the Syrian men who had fought with Roosevelt in the Spanish-American War.[37] The number 3,000 was clearly an exaggeration, as there were no more than 1,500 Syrians in the city. The membership was probably closer to 30 than to 3,000: it "admits only those who have become naturalized, and no one can

[34] *Butte* (MT) *Weekly Miner*, November 13, 1896.

[35] "The Daughters of Syria," *New-York Tribune,* June 1, 1898.

[36] "A Syrio-American Club," *NYT*, February 6, 1898.

[37] "Syrian Roosevelt Club," *The* (NY) *Sun*, October 17, 1898. The article claimed that 350 Syrian Americans fought in the war. We know the names of only three of these soldiers from New York: Khalil Asswad, Gabriel Farah, and Najeeb M. Saleeby. Saleeby remained in the army in Cuba until at least 1900.

hold office who does not read, write, and speak English,"[38] which must have considerably limited the number of eligible men.

The 1890s saw the formation of Syrian associations in other American cities as well, but it was not until the 1920s that Salloum Mokarzel attempted to unify all of the clubs into a national association. The effort failed, and to this day there are no national associations that can be said to represent all Arab Americans (or even Lebanese Americans) in this country. A salient exception to this disunity was the effort made by the Syrian diaspora to have Syrians declared legally "white." The battle began in 1909 and mobilized Syrians all over the United States (and in other countries) across sectarian lines. They mounted a legal and a public relations battle, which they won,[39] but this unity did not last.

## Politics

As is true today, the majority of Syrian entrepreneurs were Republicans: supporting Teddy Roosevelt, fighting for him in the Spanish-American War (although there was some debate about where the Syrians' duty lay in relation to this war), and stumping for Republican causes. Nassib A. Shibley was the most public of these men, being on the dais at many Republican events, before he killed himself in 1908. In 1906 he was featured in a guide to prominent Republicans. Ameen Haddad, as mentioned, was the only Syrian member of a committee to reform the New York Republican Party; he was referred to as "that eminent Republican" in more than one newspaper article. The Syrian-American Club pledged all of its members to vote for Theodore Roosevelt. Alexander Yazaji spoke for many members of the Colony when he wrote to the editors of *The New York Press* to congratulate the paper's editors "upon your brilliant work and that of other Republican newspapers which brought about the election of our favorite candidate, Colonel Roosevelt."[40] When McKinley was shot, Salim Sarkis, the editor of *Al Mushir*, told the *New York Times* that "the hearts of the New York Syrians go out to [his family] in sympathy."[41]

[38] "The Syrian Colony in New York, an Interesting Element There," *Springfield* (MA) *Republican,* March 26, 1899.
[39] Gualtieri 2009: 3.
[40] "Thanks from a Syrian Friend," *The New York Press,* November 11, 1898.
[41] "Resolutions and Messages," *NYT,* September 8, 1901.

Seemingly at the other end of the political spectrum, but with the participation of some of these same Republicans, the *Suriya el-Fetat* (Young Syria Party) was the only purely political association formed by Syrians in the nineteenth century. Modeled on the Young Turk Party in the Ottoman Empire, it was founded to encourage (and help implement) the overthrow of the Ottoman regime and recruit (Syrian-American) men who would go armed to the aid of their countrymen should such a revolution take place. Its founding proclamation was supposedly written by each and every one of its thirty members so as to spread the responsibility and blame evenly. Some people feared retaliation from the Ottoman authorities or their proxies. It was meant to be an anonymous group: members' names and addresses were not supposed to be published. The founders' names, however, were reported in several articles: Nassib Shibley (a lawyer and Republican stalwart in a Turkish revolutionary party!), Esau el-Khoury (a newspaper editor and the husband of Marie T. Azeez), Shibli N. Dammous (another newspaper editor), and Najeeb Sawaya (a merchant and future editor of *Al Kawn* newspaper).[42]

The first meeting, on May 11, 1899, was widely covered in the American press, which referred to the Party as a "junta." The founding document was translated and published, its language biblical and stirring: "How long shall they [the Syrians] suffer ignobly under the blasphemous oppression of Turkish rule?"[43] The group met again on July 28 in an "open-air meeting" on the corner of Rector and Washington. In August, newspaper editor Salim S. Sarkis, newly arrived from Egypt, was the keynote speaker at a "mass meeting" in Madison Square, where he denounced the Ottoman sultan from the podium.[44] This article's subtitle, "Warships to Be Bought," and the revolutionaries' claim that 25,000 Syrians around the world were ready to fight in a war for independence, make it clear that the group's rhetoric had run ahead of the reality.[45]

The two priests, Korkemas and Hawaweeny, both seem to have been working to suppress the Young Syria Party at the behest of the Ottoman government. They claimed they were only doing their duty, while party members said the priests had sold them down the river for a mess of pottage, in the form of medals of honor awarded to the priests by the Ottoman Porte.[46]

[42] "Young Syria Holds a Meeting," *NYH,* August 11, 1899; *NYT,* August 11, 1899.

[43] "Syrians to Revolt Against the Sultan," *New York Herald,* May 12, 1899.

[44] "Speaker Denounced Sultan," *Boston Herald,* August 25, 1899.

[45] "Syrians Plan Revolt," *The Morning Star* (Glens Falls, NY), May 13, 1899.

[46] "The Syrian Revolutionists," *NYT,* March 18, 1900.

Naoum Mokarzel, through his newspaper *Al Hoda*, criticized the very premise of the party. Yousef Delbani, one of its members, had written an open letter to the paper decrying the Syrians' suffering, to which Mokarzel responded that no one in Syria had anything to complain about.[47] Shibli Dammous used his newspaper *Al Islah* to support the revolutionaries, as did Sarkis in *Al Mushir*. Norman Duncan satirized the formation of the party by relating how each and every member would fight to kiss the hand of the Ottoman ambassador when he appeared in New York.[48]

George Jabour, ever the royalist (and, if one can believe his enemies, in the pay of the Ottoman government), scoffed at the idea that 25,000 Syrians would rise to revolution. On the contrary, he claimed that the more than 150,000 Syrians in America were all loyal to the Sultan.[49] The fact that both groups could express their positions and see them reported in the press, though, must have provided a heady whiff of American freedom.

One moving story ends our narrative regarding the Syrians' faith in the American system of government. We have seen several instances in which Syrians or Arabs had an audience with the president of the United States. It seems incredible to us now that the president could have been so open to visits from the rank and file. After they had been in America only a few years, Yusef Arbeely and his son Nageeb (then twenty-one) paid a visit to President Garfield in the White House with two purposes: "to receive the President's salutation and to ask his aid in their effort to secure from the Mohammodan *[sic]* Government of Damascus the little sum of $10,000, an indebtedness created in the shape of a forced loan some twenty years ago. In both missions they were successful."[50]

---

[47] *Al Hoda,* June 13, 1899.

[48] Duncan 1900: 137-168.

[49] "Now There Is a Syrian Junta," *NYH,* May 13, 1899.

[50] "A Syrian Patriarch's Story," *Galveston Weekly News,* June 2, 1881.

Chapter 14

# Conclusions/Oppositions

*No newcomer in New York is more ready to adopt American customs than the young Syrian.*[1]

## Coming and Going

Whether traveling around the state as peddlers in their early years, setting up branches of their business in other cities, traveling to Europe, the Caribbean, Mexico, and the Far East for business, or going to Syria for a visit or to stay, the New York Syrians were constantly on the move. This is one of the reasons why it is so difficult to fix the population of the Colony in the nineteenth century. This peripatetic existence began with the trip to the United States itself. It was long and arduous, involving at least two sea voyages and land travel on both ends of the voyage. The trip could take a month or more from departure to arrival, and it cost a significant amount of money, despite the fact that almost all traveled steerage. It is amazing that so many came, week after week. Think too of those traveling from Beirut to the Chicago World's Fair in 1893: they not only had to make the trip to Beirut (from wherever they resided), to Marseilles, Le Havre, New York, and finally to Chicago, but they had to bring along their wares: people, goods, costumes, building materials, whatever they thought was needed.

Once they settled in the United States, their seemingly endless "coming and going"[2] began. Peddlers traveled all over the country; witness my grandfather's presence in Texas and Colorado in 1890. The relatively new railroad system facilitated this travel. Some of those who went far afield to peddle ended up settling down in these other places, but many eventually returned to New York and settled down there.

---

[1] "Colonists from Lebanon," *The* (NY) *Sun,* April 22, 1894.

[2] This phrase comes from the title of a weekly feature in *Kawkab America.*

Wholesalers eventually set up depots in other towns where they would ship goods by train and wagon to resupply their peddlers. These depots quickly turned into stores that would serve as wholesale and retail outlets, echoing the structure of the parent store in New York. Suppliers sent many of those who manned these depots out from New York; others set up their own businesses in towns in which they had already settled. Some of the former type eventually returned to New York; others stayed where they were and built lives and families there. Said el Hayek, for example, went to Waco, Texas, in 1892 to open a branch of el-Hayek Brothers Jewelry and the Tadross Brothers sent Elias el Hajj to open a branch of their dry goods business in New Mexico; both eventually returned to New York. Elias Halaby's son Najeeb opened a branch in Dallas, Texas. The brothers Joseph and Najeeb Maloof co-owned Oriental goods stores in San Francisco and New York, respectively, but Joseph eventually moved to New York to start the newspaper *Al Ayyam*. All of these suppliers had varying degrees of connection with their New York home businesses.

Another model was that of the supplier who ran retail outlets in other cities. Abdow Lutfy, partly because he dealt in fancy goods rather than notions, had retail shops in Saratoga, New York, and Cleveland, Ohio, that he supplied from his base in New York; he constantly traveled to these outposts with goods. Yet he was still able to set up concessions at the Chicago, New York, and San Francisco world's fairs and send his family on lecture tours throughout the United States.

Many Syrian businessmen in New York also had a network of international contacts by the early 1890s. Rahaim and Malhami had a business arrangement with Said Hashim, who opened a store in Yokohama, Japan. Najeeb Mallouk and Brothers and Elias Mitry Abdelnour worked as importers and exporters between Colombia and New York. One of the Rahaim brothers lived in Paris and shipped Parisian goods to New York; he and his brothers were constantly going back and forth. Salim Elias also had a store in Paris very early. There were active Syrian communities in Haiti and Cuba: New York merchants traveled back and forth to the islands regularly. Several families, such as the Sadallahs and the Mokarzels, had branches in Mexico where they did business. My maternal grandfather had relatives representing him in China, Portugal, and Italy, and he had contracts with factories in England, Belgium, and Ireland. Like Abdow Lutfy and many other merchants, he maintained wholesale establishments in New York and Chicago and owned a seasonal retail shop in Petoskey, Michigan, which was supplied out of his

Chicago warehouse. He visited all these places on a regular basis and still managed to make several trips to Syria in his lifetime.

Manufacturers, like exporters, had customers all over the world and had to travel to maintain these relationships. "Najeeb Mallouk and Brothers" and Elias Mitry Abdelnour worked as exporters to South America, and many Syrians sold American or Oriental goods in Europe.

The Moroccan entertainers constantly traveled, moving from one city to another on both sides of the Atlantic. The Syrian priests also traveled extensively, by necessity, in order to minister to all their flock, and they used these trips to raise money across the United States for the churches in New York. Those Syrians who lectured or preached moved from city to city every day, covering the whole of the United States. The performers—belly dancers, vaudeville acts, strongmen in the Wild West shows, or "Arabs" in the circuses—were constantly moving; many of these men and women had no real home.

And of course many of the immigrants went back to Syria on a regular basis. As we have mentioned, the number of Syrians who went back home for good remains unknown; estimates ranging from one-quarter to one-half make them meaningless. We do know that returning was a major part of the "going" of the community; every week at least one businessman was wished Godspeed by the editors of *Kawkab America* when he left for the homeland. A missionary in Hadath described that town's returnees: they would come back with their accumulated wealth, build a house, live for two years on their savings, and then go back to the United States to earn another fortune. He says that several of the villagers had made the trip four times.[3] They were called "birds of passage" with good reason. When the French steamship *La Bourgogne,* sailing from New York to Le Havre in July 1898, sank off the coast of Halifax, it was carrying sixty-six Syrians heading home (most were in steerage). How many of them were planning to stay in Syria and how many were just visiting we don't know. Sixty of the sixty-six perished.[4]

My paternal grandfather's trajectory was the antithesis of this pattern, as must have been the case with many others. After a protracted life of wandering and peddling in the 1880s and 1890s, he settled down in Brooklyn with his family in 1904 and never left.

[3] *Presbyterian Letters,* Harris to Ellinwood, September 25, 1893.

[4] *Al Hoda,* July 12, 1898. People thronged the French Line office at 3 Bowling Green trying to find out information. One unnamed Syrian was reported to have said, "No sir, I not French or Italian. I Syrian. I know friend of mine with whole family on this ship, six people, father, wife, three children, all with him. I guess all gone." "At the French Line Office Sad Scenes among Inquiring Relatives," *NYH,* July 7, 1898.

## Success and Failure

Stories of success came naturally to the Syrian immigrants and to their descendants; the "rags-to-riches" myth was and is the controlling narrative. Unsurprisingly, failure was not much talked about.

### *Wealth and Prominence*

The Syrians did prosper. Shibli N. Dammous, the editor of *Al Islah*, claimed that during the "so-called famine of 1893, no Syrian applied for help to the Charity Commission." He estimated that "our wealth here in this city represents no less than $50 per capita, and while there are none of us that are millionaires as yet, I assure you that we are in as good a condition morally, intellectually and financially as any foreign born people within your boundaries."[5] An 1894 article in the *Rochester Democrat*, citing an article in *The* (NY) *Sun*, stated that during the recent hard times, Syrians pooled together donations for one of the bread funds, and "not one cent of that money found its way to their countrymen. As a matter of fact, most of these Syrians are quite well to do."[6] Miller agreed: "The Syrians do not become public charges and they mind their own business. The variety and usefulness of his commercial enterprises, the ability with which he prosecutes them, the industry which insures their success, and the sobriety and politeness that accompany them, make clear that he is a valuable addition to our economic strength."[7] In the English pages of *Kawkab America*, meant for American readers, Arbeely claimed, "The public records show that they make good citizens, and that they become valuable adjuncts to the communities in which they settle."[8] In response to a query submitted to *Kawkab America*, Nageeb Arbeely estimated the total amount of business done by the Colony as 2.5 million *rials*.[9]

Were there evident economic strata in the community? Yes, there were. These strata can be discerned in several ways: the frequency of their appearance in documents such as business directories; their appearance in the American or Arabic press; the nature of their businesses; and where they lived.

[5] "Turks Menace Syrians in New York," *NYH*, March 12, 1899.
[6] "A Syrian Colony: An Oasis of Quiet 'Midst the Busy Bustle of New York," *Rochester Democrat and Chronicle*, February 27, 1894.
[7] Miller 1903: 41.
[8] *Kawkab America*, April 29, 1892.
[9] *Kawkab America*, February 14, 1896.

This book has mostly been the story of the successful members of the Colony because they are the ones who leave documents; we will attempt to tease out the stories of the less successful in the next sections. To name again some of those men who have had a prominent place in our story and summarize their accomplishments:

- John Abd-el-Nour, an importer of fine embroidery, was called the "Boss Arab Peddler of the Country," when he posted a bond of $25,000 for forty-two Arabs whom he contracted to work for him.[10] His path to success was dramatic, despite spectacular setbacks. It's interesting that Abd-el-Nour never seemed tied to the Syrian neighborhood. His first apartment was at 285 Hudson Street, which was also the location of his store. His next apartment, at 27 Charlton Street, was in a brick row house on a tranquil and leafy street. In 1895 he moved to 105 Waverly Place, in Greenwich Village, which was fitted out in Oriental splendor: "gold embroidered portières hung between the two parlors. Richly worked table scarfs and hangings were scattered through the rooms. Heavy rugs of the finest textures were on the floors."[11] This is the apartment he lived in when he was being hunted by the police for smuggling. The richness of the apartment was somehow taken as proof of his dishonesty. The opulent interior of his "country retreat" on Eltingville Lane on Staten Island—said to sit on 250 acres—was pictured in Miller's 1903 book with the caption, "The Syrian as a Capitalist."
- The Faour Brothers, founders of the second Syrian bank, were also real estate investors. They owned their large bank building at 81–85 Washington Street, three five-story buildings that they must have joined together. When Daniel Faour died, he left an estate worth $60,000.
- Joseph Oussani, who made his money in tobacco and dry goods (and a Turkish smoking parlor), ended up owning an estate in Pocantico Hills, several apartment buildings in New York City, a vineyard in California, and a mansion in Hastings-on-Hudson; he bought and sold real estate all his life.
- Abdow Lutfy was a prominent fancy-goods importer and big man in the community whose sons were also successful businessmen. Abdow's daughter Shafika married Elias J. Macksoud, another successful im-

[10] "Backsheesh Extorted from Them," *The* (NY) *Sun*, January 8, 1888.
[11] "He Did Big Business," *Fort Worth* (TX) *Gazette*, December 8, 1894.

porter of embroideries in 1899. Macksoud himself came to be known as the "Kimono King," having one of the largest factories in this exclusively Syrian sector.

- Najeeb M. Mallouk, one of seven Mallouk brothers, made a small fortune in importing cutlery from Germany and England and had business interests in New York and Colombia.
- At first a successful importer of Oriental goods, Joseph Ayoob later began manufacturing them here. He also owned, or sold shares in, a large goldmine in Cripple Creek, Colorado.
- The five men of the Presbyterian Merhige family were importers of embroideries.
- Both of the Tadross Brothers, although they separated early, became successful. They traveled around the country seeing to their business interests, and both were mentioned frequently as taking the lead in Orthodox events in the community.
- The Moshy Brothers were prominent commission merchants who rented or owned a large building at 59 Washington.
- Salim Elias, in partnership and alone, was one of the largest dry goods wholesalers in the country. He was also active in the Maronite Church, serving several times as president of the Maronite Youth Association, as well as chairing the committee charged with raising money to build a new church.
- The three Awad brothers—Essa, Gabriel, and Nicola—were suppliers of Oriental goods.
- On his naturalization papers, Salim Barson called himself a "brush man," but he soon began to manufacture suspenders and aprons at 60–62 Washington. He may have been one of several Aleppan Jews who were considered part of the community, including Ezra Sitt, Anton Simon, Salim el Kuku, Mohammed Dwek, and Mourad J. Shemtob.
- Another dealer in Oriental goods was Maroon Fagher, who supplemented his income from trade by renting out rooms at 5 Carlisle.
- Although not based in New York, the Ferzan Brothers—Fares and Elias—were intimately involved with the Washington Street Colony. They were important members of the Maronite Youth Organization and were often called on to provide aid to other Maronites, including arranging funerals for those who had no people here.
- Assad George Khoury was a real estate magnate as well as a cigar manufacturer.

- Marie T. Azeez el-Khoury, really the only woman entrepreneur among the first immigrants, designed and sold fine jewelry at her store on upper Fifth Avenue.
- Muossa Daoud managed a succession of boardinghouses, was a peddlers' supplier, and became a ticket agent and real estate broker. Although lionized by the American press, it is not at all clear that he was ever wealthy, having never owned property, and he ended his days in rented quarters in the neighborhood.
- Abraham Sahadi, Tamer K. Maloof, and the Zalloums were successful wholesale grocers; Maloof also invested in real estate.
- Beshara Ganim started in partnership with Antoine Sadallah (both Maronites from Baskinta) importing and exporting Oriental goods. Ganim moved into wholesale groceries and finally, with his son Salim, became a manufacturer of sweaters and neckties. Sadallah joined forces with his cousins and went on to become a very prosperous businessman with a branch in Mexico.
- The four Rahaim brothers and the Malhamis—Maronite families from Jezzine—immigrated to the United States from Egypt and joined forces to start a religious goods business, first selling Holy Land objects and then moving into ecclesiastical articles (rosaries, vestments, etc.). In 1896 it was reported that they had bought the four-story building at the corner of Rector and Washington (97 Washington), and *Kawkab America* reported in 1896 that the company's annual turnover was more than 200,000 *rials*.[12] The company lasted in a somewhat attenuated form into the twenty-first century.

Other success stories were brothers Elias and Michael Abousleman, Kalil G. Freije, Antoine and Habeeb L. Khoury, Aref Khoury, Peter Khoury, Assad G. Khoury, Najib S. Maloof, Tanous Mansour, Selim Marrash, the Moghabghabs, Abraham Mouakad, Elias Moussi, Hatem Nahas, Najeeb Naja, Shakir Nasser, Petrus Saad, Nicola Abu Samra, Najeeb Sawaya, Assy Shaheen, Mansour Sharbel, the Shohfi brothers, and Nasrallah Souraty.

Was economic success covalent with being a community leader? Not entirely. The newspaper editors who have been mentioned several times in this writing (Naoum Mokarzel, Najeeb Diab, Nageeb Arbeely, and others) were powerful men by virtue of both their editorial power and apparent charisma.

[12] *Kawkab America,* February 14, 1896.

They were, in the early days at least, among the relatively few who were literate in English and Arabic, and thus were able to play a mediating role between the Syrian community and the Americans. Through their newspapers, they promoted American values, while romanticizing the culture from which they came. Arbeely was quoted in American newspapers countless times, as an interpreter of Syrian life and as an expert on immigration (by virtue of his position at Ellis Island), but he also seemed to be the center around which many events of the community coalesced. These editors became spokesmen for the community both within and without. It is indicative of their influence that the editor of *Mira'at al-Gharb* was asked to give a speech at the 1913 Arab National Congress in Paris, and that Naoum Mokarzel represented his constituency at the Paris Peace Talks in 1919. They bear a large responsibility for both the tensions that divided the community in the nineteenth and early twentieth centuries and for whatever fellow feeling the Syrian-Americans had for one another as a people.

The professional men—doctors, lawyers, pharmacists, and the like—were also held in high esteem. Some of these men were also recognized in American circles; Ameen Haddad helped found the Syrian Society with "American" men and women, was in demand to give talks throughout New York, and was named as a member of the "Committee of Fifty-three," charged with the task of reorganizing the Republican Party in New York City. He was the only Arab on this committee.[13] Nassib Shibley, before his suicide, represented several Syrians and many Americans in court cases, and was a pillar of the Republican Party. He did not live in the neighborhood and married an "American."

The Syrian religious leaders, of course, were deeply revered: Peter and Gabriel Korkemas and Khairallah Stefan among the Maronites, and the Orthodox Raphael Hawaweeny. Elias Saadi, the Presbyterian, was here for such a short time that we don't know much about him. Abraham Beshewate, the Melkite priest, seems to have had a checkered career, but he served the Melkite community for almost three decades.

### *Financial Hardship*

What about those immigrants who did not fit the stereotype of the poor immigrant made good, yet stayed in America? Our information about them is scanty, but telling. The three Forzly brothers—Selim, Solomon, and Tan-

[13] "To Reorganize the Party," *NYH*, December 18, 1897.

nous—must all be counted as "failures," at least as far as the Syrian dream was concerned. Their early successes in England were never repeated here. Selim was forty-eight when he arrived in New York; he and his sons went to the Chicago fair and opened a confectionery stand in the Tunisian Pavilion. After that, he apparently never again found any work at which he could succeed. The family moved households a half-dozen times, and he and his wife ended up living apart; I don't know whether they were estranged or were forced by circumstances to live separately. He died in the Home for Incurables in Brooklyn in 1921; her death followed soon after. He lies in the only unmarked grave among all the other Forzlys at Mount Olivet Cemetery.

Selim's brother Solomon (my great-grandfather) had a number of jobs in a number of cities, all of which were lowly: shoemaker in Philadelphia, cutter in a cotton mill in Putnam, Connecticut, fruit stand in Worcester, Massachusetts. His wife ran a confectionery shop in Worcester. The third brother, Tannous (called Thomas), who came much later than the other two, didn't really work after he arrived. The men of the next generation—their sons—were cautionary tales as well.

We have described the sad career of Selim's son George, whose bank failed in 1899 and who died in 1902. His brother, Nicholas Forzly, who as a young man had had a lackluster career as a cashier and a manager, became a notorious racetrack "plunger" (a person who took big risks) known as "Nick F." He won and lost several large fortunes in his career: it was said that he won over $500,000 gambling in New Orleans in the winter of 1920, but lost it by summer. Although he and his wife, Daisy McLean, were living large in the Claridge Hotel in 1928 when he died, he was broke. Two other members of the family, my great uncles Al and Elias Forzly, Solomon's sons, were not men who made and lost fortunes, but men who never made them. Al was a notions salesman and died young. Elias, although he loved to buy newly invented gadgets and drive fancy cars, worked as a salesman for a silk mill in Pennsylvania, managed a linen shop, and then sold postcards. The sons of the third Forzly brother, Thomas, worked as manual laborers and salesmen, first in Worcester, Massachusetts, and then in Brooklyn; all were failures when held up to the myth of the Syrian self-made businessman.

Nohman, Salim, and Kalil Ghiz were some of the earliest immigrants, all arriving from Beirut in the early 1880s. They had a modest success when they opened a bicycle shop on Lispinard, but its trajectory was troubled, with numerous moves, reorganizations, and finally bankruptcy.

As I mentioned, my paternal grandfather peddled or set up stands in a number of cities for nearly two decades before settling down, dragging his growing family from town to town. He had a small success after that in the straight razor business but went broke in the early twenties. Assad Balesh, who immigrated with his wife in 1893, worked as a peddler for two decades as well, with a short interval as a grocery clerk. None of this work represented the kind of success that was expected in the Colony.

In other cases, we know that a person stayed in a position that we might classify as lower middle class, whether or not self-employed: bakers (George Jureidini), barbers (Beshara Daher and Cesar Abdelnour), bookkeepers and clerks (two dozen of them), factory workers, truckmen, waiters, shoemakers (Habib Salloum), carpenters (Ameen Sirgany), and small shopkeepers (too numerous to list). That the Ghiz brothers and many of these others owned their own business and worked for themselves did not mean that they were wealthy. Other Syrians may have still grudgingly called them successful, but their status was definitely considered lower than that of the merchants and manufacturers.

How do we recognize a failure? In some cases we know about the bankruptcy of a company: in the nineteenth century, George Forzly's bank in 1899 and Zahi Azar's variety store at 40 Washington, which was shut down in 1897 by the sheriff for nonpayment of a debt of $175 to Assy Shaheen.[14] Numerous other businesses must have gone bankrupt in the nineteenth century, but as the failures were not recorded or reported in the newspapers, we do not know about them. Other nineteenth-century immigrants who went bankrupt in the twentieth included Najeeb N. Maloof and George Jabour in 1903, Deeb Lutfy and the Garzouzi brothers in 1907, Thomas Rahaim and Alexander Yamin, Ashi and Coury, Naoum Hatem, Richard Korkemas, the Abousleman brothers, and Nicola Dibs all in 1909; Lutfy and Macksoud, Sabah Nasrallah, and the Khoury brothers in 1911; Salim and Filomena Ghiz in 1914; and my grandfather in about 1920. The Faour Bank failed in the depths of the Depression in 1933, as did many other businesses. Some of these individuals emerged out of bankruptcy, regrouped, and began again; others did not. Given the almost sacred aversion to debt that most Syrians claimed to feel, many of them worked for years to pay off their creditors, whether or not they were legally obligated to do so. My grandfather's family, for example, never recovered financially from his business failure; all of the daughters worked for many years to keep the younger sons in school and pay off their father's debts.

[14] "Business Troubles," *The* (NY) *Sun*, September 11, 1897; *Trials*. Assy Shaheen v. John Azar, 1897: A-17.

The family's pride in this probity perhaps substituted for pride in business success that the patriarch hadn't achieved.

In his article on Syrians' impressions of New York, Michael Suleiman describes one Khalil Sakakini who came to New York in 1908. He "faced a life of penury and humiliation. He despised having to peddle or work in a factory when the job was literally backbreaking."[15] He returned to Syria for good, and unlike others in his situation, Sakakini left a record of his distress, writing a 1918 article called "The Way Americans Live" in the Egyptian newspaper *As Sufur*.[16] Others wrote disheartening and disheartened articles about the United States, but few would admit they could not make a living here.

### *Poverty and Its Effects*

These stories of economic failure are relative; there were people much worse off than those who owned a barbershop or who peddled for years on end. We have the odd story in the American press that alludes to Syrians being hungry; no such stories appeared in the Arabic press, and both the Syrian and American observers would have us believe that this was a rarity, if it existed at all. One story concerned the theft of a small beefsteak by a Syrian woman named Deborah (Deebie?) Malouf. After being arrested, she was stricken with stomach cramps, apparently caused by hunger.[17] Another story concerned one George Druby (?), who was arrested for peddling, leaving his son Zufeik (Toufic) in the care of the Children's Aid Society. The reporter said the child was "ragged and hungry and half frozen from exposure."[18] Abdallah Saad was found stranded in Brooklyn; he was sent to the hospital where he was found to be suffering from malnutrition.[19] How many of the Syrians were actually hungry? Everyone agreed that even during tough economic times, the Syrians never turned to the government for help. Instead they took care of their own. This, in any case, is what they would have us believe. The number of children in care (about 4 percent of the Syrian population), if we are not to interpret it as a cynical ploy by Syrians to offload a financial burden onto the state, as it was interpreted by many American observers, is probably the strongest indication that poverty was endemic in the early Colony. The number of children

[15] Suleiman 2002: 33.

[16] Cited in Suleiman 2002, note 18.

[17] "Deborah Seized a Steak," *BDE*, February 28, 1894.

[18] "Druby the Syrian and His Boy," *BDE*, December 20, 1890.

[19] "Abdalla Saad Stranded," *BDE*, September 5, 1901.

retrieved from care, however, shows that many of these same Syrians were able to improve their lot.

Infant and child mortality must have been high, although we have only a very few cases that were reported to the city. The Trinity Commission gives the 1910 infant death rate in the neighborhood as an incredible 320 per 1,000 live births, which must have been the same or higher in the nineteenth century. Of the fifty Syrian deaths before 1902 for which we have records, twenty-one were children three years old or younger. The cases of tuberculosis in 1902 were charted on a map of the neighborhood; the biggest concentrations were on the east side of Washington between Battery Place and Carlisle—exactly where the Syrians had been and were still living.[20] In the eight years between 1894 and 1902, there were 200 reported deaths from consumption in the Syrian Quarter.[21] Bear in mind that these statistics applied to the whole neighborhood; Syrians were not called out separately. We do know that tuberculosis must have been endemic in the Colony; Dr. Baddour specialized in its treatment. Diphtheria and yellow fever were also common, but the most common cause of death seems to have been bronchitis and other illnesses related to the damp and cold seeping into the walls and floors of the tenements—perhaps simply another way of describing consumption/tuberculosis. Several of Norman Duncan's characters die of "lung trouble."[22]

Some infant deaths were attributed to marasmus (severe malnutrition) or the consumption of (criminally) adulterated milk, which was a pernicious problem in all slum neighborhoods of New York. Adult deaths resulted from gastroenteritis, cholera, diphtheria, and the usual run of heart attacks, cancer, and childbirth. As in other immigrant communities, it seems that if you lived past infancy, childhood, and childbirth (in the case of women), your chances of living to old age were rather high.

Three Syrians were inmates in the Alms House on Blackwell's Island in 1900, including a seventeen-year-old Syrian girl who died there in 1903—our only examples of adults in institutions. The 1914 study by the Trinity Church Men's Committee presents a bleaker picture. Of the 818 families registered with the charitable Health Society in lower Manhattan, 30 percent were Syrians, twice the percentage of Syrians in the studied population. The

[20] Trinity Men's Committee 1914: 57.

[21] "Results of Twelve Years' Battle with Consumption," *NYT*, August 2, 1903.

[22] Duncan 1900.

two doctors (Rasheed Baddour and Abdulmassih Mussawir) who offered half-price or free services to Syrians must have done so because there were Syrians who could not pay their fee.

### *Suicide*

The most extreme form of despair manifested itself in the suicides that occurred in the Colony. Not all took place in the nineteenth century, but all the ones described in this book involved nineteenth-century immigrants. These sad people leave few traces apart from the suicide itself. The first that we know about was twenty-one-year-old Elias Akkawee (Ackary?), who was working as an ironmonger in Plainfield, New Jersey. He had moved from New York to be near his lover, the daughter of a blacksmith. The father would not agree to the marriage and urged Elias to go back to New York and look for work there more appropriate to his education. We don't know what his education was, but his suicide note was written in French, indicating some learning.[23]

Khalil Sawabeeny shot himself at Tannous Shishim's restaurant at 91 Washington Street in 1894. He had made a good profit selling Oriental coins at the Chicago fair but apparently was not able to make a living in New York. He was twenty-five years old. Rasheed Baddour and Shukri Rizkalla, the doctors who declared him dead, found one-and-one-half *rials* in his pocket, along with a receipt from a Chinese laundry. More than two dozen men ("and some of the ladies") collected forty dollars for his burial.[24] Only two weeks later another Syrian man, Yanni Mukhbat, committed suicide by shooting himself in the head. He lived on 7th Avenue and 27th Street, but the news spread quickly around the Washington Street neighborhood. Lotfallah Atta and Elias Ferzan went and made arrangements for the funeral.[25]

After his first foray into business as a restaurant owner in the 1890s, Alexander Abukalil, elder brother of restaurant-owner Gabriel, spent the better part of his life as a student. In July 1902, he had had to be committed to an insane asylum in Astoria, Queens, after causing a disturbance at the Waldorf Astoria. His brothers attributed this breakdown to too much study.[26] In 1903, after reportedly being admitted to Harvard, he shot himself at Lipton's Hotel

[23] *Kawkab America,* December 23, 1892.

[24] *Kawkab America,* April 6, 1894.

[25] *Kawkab America,* April 27, 1894.

[26] "Waldorf's Disturber Crazed by Overstudy," *NYH,* December 28, 1902.

on Cortlandt and Washington streets, where he was visiting his brothers.[27] He was thirty-five.

We have already discussed Naseeb Shibley, who killed his young wife and himself in despair over not being able to provide well enough for her.

A Syrian man who was being sent back to Europe killed himself by jumping overboard, and a young Syrian girl who had been refused entry at Ellis Island, and was refused again when she tried to enter from Canada, also killed herself. As the reporter had it, "Death seemed preferable to turning back to the old home she had left, preferably with a boast of the good fortune which would be hers as soon as she had crossed the ocean."[28] That must have been a relatively common occurrence, but went largely unreported. After all, what did the future hold for those who were debarred: being stranded somewhere in Europe with no way to get back to Syria or return to the United States?

A man called George Georgis was killed by a train at Jamaica, Long Island. People thought he had committed suicide because he ignored all warnings as he crossed the tracks, but it is more than likely that he simply didn't understand what was being shouted at him. He left a family in Syria and an eleven-year old daughter who, when last heard from, was peddling religious goods in New Jersey.[29] The fact that other Syrians assumed it was suicide speaks to the relative frequency of the occurrence. A young Syrian man, Basel Saheb (Saab? Saib?), who was a student at Columbia University, shot himself in 1901. According to the article, he was despondent over his inability to solve the mystery of perpetual motion.[30] A suicide for which we have no information other than the death certificate, was that of Sophie or Shafia Maloof, who was twenty-eight years old when she drank carbolic acid in the sanitarium where she was confined. Certainly this small number of suicides does not indicate an epidemic of despair, but it is those that went unreported that frighten us.

The unlucky and unsuccessful were, to a certain extent, winnowed out. Every day people left for Syria. It was never made clear whether they were going to visit or intended to stay, but we can be sure that those who had nothing to come back for did not come back.

Buried deep within the success stories of the immigrants, if one listens

---

27 "Harvard Syrian a Suicide," *The* (NY) *Sun,* July 10, 1903.

28 "Light and Shadow in Immigrant Office," *Rochester* (NY) *Democrat and Chronicle,* October 10, 1902.

29 "Wife Sick and Children Starving," *BDE,* September 2, 1890.

30 "Wheels Caused His Suicide," *NYT,* May 24, 1901.

closely, are the stories of failure and the accompanying shame. In my immediate family, typical in many ways of the upwardly mobile stereotype, there were at least four bankruptcies, an abortion, a pregnancy before marriage, a family and business betrayal, long-held grudges and jealousies against other family members. In our community, business failures were equated with personal failures, and families rarely recovered.

## Women and Men

Perhaps the most interesting opposition, and one for which there is little information for the nineteenth century, is the gender question. We have seen throughout this book that women were important contributors to the economic well-being of the Syrian community, active participants in civil society, and imparters of knowledge about the Middle East to American audiences, either through dance or lectures. Yet they are largely silent in the historical record. With few exceptions, we do not hear them speak, we do not read their words, and we do not know them as individuals. Some of the books about Syrian communities in other parts of the country have given voice to these women by recording their stories as told by their descendants; what is lacking are contemporary records of their lives in their own words. If 54 percent of them could read and write, as indicated in the 1900 census, where are their stories, letters, journals, articles, and books? The few published letters and articles we do have, by Marie Azeez, Hanna Korany, and Jamilie Milkie (and much later, Afifa Karam), give us just a taste of what might be hidden or lost. One of our jobs should be searching out these documents, assuming they exist at all.

Those who wrote *about* Syrian women include American reporters who were fascinated by their exoticism, but to a much greater extent than the men, women were described in stereotypic terms. Syrians also tended to talk about their women in stereotypic terms, but as paragons of virtue. They contrasted their behavior with that of American women, whose morals were, to say the least, suspect. The Syrians had a somewhat schizophrenic attitude toward their women. On the one hand, women came alone to this country and/or went out in large numbers to peddle, lecture around the country, or entertain in Coney Island with the acquiescence or approval, if not the urging, of their husbands or fathers. These women out on their own were subjected to criticism or even improper approaches by American men, which in turn dishonored the Syrian community as a whole. Some Syrian writers went so far as to criticize the husbands and fathers of these women and urged them to protect their women from the dishonor inherent in such activities. There is no evidence that the men paid attention to these admonitions, as long as it was economically necessary for their women to work.

It seems that, contrary to what my great-aunt claimed about work being liberating for Syrian women, most women gave up peddling as soon as they could; they either settled down as housewives (perhaps doing piecework at home) or worked alongside their husbands in a shop. The source of dishonor, then, was not earning money per se, but being out among strangers unsupervised. As in most communities, the ultimate proof of a husband's success was that his wife could stay home, with servants to take care of the drudgery—a state that many eventually achieved.

An amusing and telling comment in *Kawkab America* referred to the recently installed Statue of Liberty in New York Harbor. Arbeely advised his fellow Syrians, "Contrary to what your women are telling you, Lady Liberty's finger is not pointing to the sky in a gesture of liberation for women to do as they please." The Lady had apparently been used as a cudgel by Syrian women to keep their husbands in their place, saying, "Shame on you, haven't you seen the pointed finger?"[31] Of course there is no pointed finger, but a woman holding a torch that, for some Syrian women, lit the way to freedom.

Any debate about the role of women in Syrian-American society played out between the lines in *Kawkab America*; it was rarely overtly discussed. It was not until the mid-1920s in the magazine *The Syrian World* that this became an open topic for discussion in the Syrian diaspora, and women like the journalist Afifa Karam weighed in on the subject.

### *Mixed Marriages*

Everyone was thrown together on Washington Street: Orthodox, Maronite, Melkite, and Protestant, people from cities and people from villages, men and women, illiterates and literates, successful businessmen and their drummers. Sometimes strangers would end up sleeping in the same room in a crowded tenement. Of course there was self-selection taking place: people of like faith would form partnerships and associations, socialize together and worship together. But they got to know people of the opposite sex with whom they

[31] *Kawkab America,* February 14, 1896.

might never have come into contact in Syria. The social arrangements in which they found themselves led to relationships that no one could have predicted. Neither of my grandparents' marriages, for example, could have taken place in Syria: my paternal grandparents' because of the difference in faith, my maternal grandparents' because of the distance of their villages from each other. On the streets of New York, much was possible and more was permitted.

We have documentation for 134 Syrian marriages in New York City in the nineteenth century but have city marriage certificates for only thirty-six of them. Why some people chose to register their marriage with the city and others did not is a mystery. Twenty-five (18.6 percent) of the 134 known nineteenth-century marriages were to "American" women; only two Syrian women married "American" men in that period. As is usual in this study, the term "American" is placed in quotation marks, because any non-Syrian was considered by the Syrians to be an American, no matter from where she or he hailed. In the Melkite marriage records, if the wife was not Syrian, that fact was noted.

Joseph Oussani was one of those who married out. Already somewhat of an outsider (an Iraqi Chaldean who ran the Cairo and Chibouk cafés, both notorious joints in the Tenderloin), he married a young Irish woman, Margaret Shea, at St. Stephen's Catholic Church on May 23, 1896. She had worked for him at the Chibouk and testified on his behalf when he was arrested. Abraham Beshewate officiated, and Azeez Khayat, the antiquities dealer, Margaret's sister, Joanna, and John Oussani, Joseph's brother, were witnesses. Just before the wedding, Joseph wrote a touching letter to his parents in Baghdad, begging their indulgence for marrying an "American Catholic girl," saying she was from a respectable family and was "beautiful in looks and character." "I found in her," he wrote, "all that conforms to my character and nature as I had wished."[32] The couple ran the two cafés together, had two daughters, and seem to have had a harmonious marriage. Unfortunately, Margaret died in 1907 at the age of 29, and in 1911, Joseph married his children's British governess, Gladys Holmes. Their marriage was tumultuous, despite or because of his great wealth.

Another "American" marriage took place between Khalil Beshewate, the brother of the Melkite priest, and Helena Shamendov in 1898; his brother performed the ceremony. Her German nationality was noted in the Melkite registry. In 1887, Hajji Tahar married Julia Doyle in New York. After their divorce in 1892, Tahar married another American, Florence Hunter, in 1899. Gabriel and Said Abukalil, the restaurant owners, both married Americans,

---

[32] *Oussani Letters,* Joseph Oussani to his parents, May 5, 1896.

14-1. Wedding portrait of Joseph Oussani and Margaret Shea, New York, 1896 (courtesy Gail O'Keefe Edson).

as did the tobacconist and real estate mogul Assad G. Khouri; his first wife, Annie Sheeny, died in 1900, and he immediately married another Irishwoman, Katherine Callahan. Two Arbeelys married non-Syrians: Abraham married Anna Marie LaFetra, whose father owned a hotel in Washington, DC, and Nageeb married Marie Dilopoulo, a Greek woman whom he met in Egypt. Abraham Samaha, who, along with the Ferzan Brothers, had an Oriental goods business on the Boardwalk in Atlantic City, attended the Southern Exposition in Louisville in 1883. There he married an American named Issa Stigger and brought her back to New Jersey. The four Baddour brothers all married Americans.We know of only two Syrian women who married "American" men in the nineteenth century, one of whom was Selma Uniss, a Greek Orthodox woman from Abeih. She came here with her brother George in 1899. She peddled when she first arrived to pay her way through school so as to become a missionary in Syria, or at least that was what she said when she sold her goods. But she met and married Byron Guy Warner, the owner of a sporting goods store in Brooklyn, and gave up her plans, if plans there were, to return home. Sadly, she died in 1905. Norman Duncan, in his "Correlated Stories of the Syrian Quarter," related the story of a Syrian girl, "Haleem Khoury," who married an Irishman, "Jimmy Brady," much to the despair of her Syrian boyfriend, her father, and her "uncle," "Khalil Khayat." The story ends with Khalil going to the father to beg him to forgive (and perhaps reclaim) his daughter.[33]

Although the overwhelming number of marriages carried over values and traditions from Syria and joined families of the same faith and class, if not village, some interfaith and intercultural marriages did occur. These may have been mainly opportunistic—in the early years of the Colony the choices of a mate were limited—and occasionally romantic. It took courage to go against custom and marry someone outside your traditional cohort.

Apart from the American marriages mentioned above, we don't know how frequently interfaith marriages occurred in the Colony (and of course we don't know, in the case of marriage with Americans, how many of them were considered interfaith). Alixa Naff interviewed Helen Uniss Khoury, who described how her father, George S. Uniss, met her mother Alice (Liza) on Washington Street in the nineteenth century.[34] Ameen Haddad had brought Alice Frinch over from Abeih to teach at the Syrian Society School he had helped found in 1892. Like the Haddads, she was a Protestant and had attended Miss Brown's American school in Sidon.

Alice lodged with the Haddads on 48th Street in South Brooklyn, because she had no people here. Khoury continued, "He [Khoury's father, George Uniss] saw her lifting a window at the Syrian School on Washington Street and fell in love. That's how an Orthodox and Protestant got married. He asked Dr. Ameen for her hand." They married in Brooklyn in 1900.

Nabeah Shammas also came from a mixed Protestant–Orthodox marriage. The parents had "admired each other in Tripoli," but married here in the Greek Orthodox Church in Brooklyn. Shammas claims there was "an affinity between Orthodox and Protestants, who intermarried a lot."[35] One Orthodox man, Nageeb Arbeely, married Mary Diapolo in the Melkite church; was that because she was Greek Catholic? We don't know. Gabriel Saba, also Orthodox, married Adelia Shahdan, a Maronite, in 1902. It was his second marriage; his first (Orthodox) wife had died, possibly in childbirth, in 1900.

[33] Duncan 1900: 77-104.

[34] *Naff Interview,* with Helen Uniss Khoury, January 26, 1986.

[35] *Naff interview,* with Nabeah Shammas, June 26, 1988.

Like Orthodox and Protestants, Melkites and Maronites had an "affinity" for each other, as Maronite children often had Melkite godmothers or godfathers.

My paternal grandparents' marriage was certainly not representative, piling anomaly on anomaly, but it must be mentioned, because they were part of the nineteenth-century community. My grandfather, Joseph Jacobs, a Maronite, came to this country in about 1888 from Beirut, apparently escaping after committing some crime in Mount Lebanon. According to family lore, Joseph met his wife, Affifie Forzly, in Putnam, Connecticut, where he was peddling. The Forzly family was Orthodox. Raphael Hawaweeny officiated at their marriage in the Orthodox church at 77 Washington Street in 1897, yet after her marriage, she converted and became a devout Catholic. Affifie (also called Effie) was only fourteen years old when they married; Joseph was twenty-nine or thirty. Perhaps her parents allowed her to marry a Maronite and someone much older because they didn't have a choice: Affifie was five months pregnant (which meant she had conceived when she was thirteen), presumably, but not necessarily, by Joseph. Their first child, George, was born in Jersey City, New Jersey, and died as an infant in Philadelphia; if the family story is accurate, she accidentally rolled over on him in bed and smothered him. Their next four children were each born in a different city, as the family traveled around.

Although my paternal grandparents' marriage may have taken place out of necessity, my maternal grandparents apparently married for love. Fayad M. Jabara saw Katherine Milkie on the ferry to Manhattan, and it was love at first sight. He contrived to find out her name and spoke to her brother; they married six months later. Of course it was a suitable marriage because they were both Orthodox, and there was nothing on either side to object to. One imagines that her mother would have felt more comfortable if she had married someone from Bishmezzine, but there was no one eligible in New York from there. The letters he wrote in Arabic to my grandmother in the summer before their marriage were filled with declarations of love, little jealous vignettes, and a desperate longing for her to return to New York, his arms, and their wedding. Of course this may have been pure lust, but how are we to differentiate the two from this distance? She was peddling in upstate New York with her mother and sister, so he had to be decorous in these declarations, but the feeling of lovesickness is very apparent. Marrying for love did not, of course, guarantee a happy marriage any more than an arranged marriage was bound to be unhappy. It is just that the pool of potential marriage partners had greatly expanded when the Syrians moved to New York, which allowed the possibility of romance.

### *Syrian Weddings Celebrated in the Press*

A few Syrian weddings were reported in the American press, but why they chose these particular weddings over others is a mystery. They all sound splendid, well attended, and highly exaggerated, and although the principals were not necessarily the wealthiest or most prominent of the Colony members, they were reported as if they were. Of course the attraction for the American public was not the sumptuousness but the exoticism: whether it was the weird language used in the service, the rifles fired by young men, or the poems delivered in the church, the reporters never tired of relaying every exotic detail.

The earliest mention of a Syrian marriage in an American paper was that of Nicola Abo Samra and Mariam (Abo) Reehan, second cousins who were married at Trinity Church on May 7, 1893. Father Christopher Jebbarah (the Orthodox priest who was on his way to the Chicago fair) married the couple, assisted by Nageeb Arbeely. The wedding took place only a month before Jebbarah consecrated the new Orthodox Church at 157 Cedar Street. Saad Khoury was best man and Adma Nasser matron of honor. Abo Samra had immigrated from Hasbaya in 1889 and had built a "thriving silk business." The Reehans (Mariam, her brother Khalil, and their father Joseph) came from Jdeideh Marjayoun in 1891, and they lived with Abo Samra at 74 West Street until the marriage. After the wedding, the couple caught the nine o'clock train for the Chicago World's Fair.[36]

The new Maronite Church at 81 Washington Street was the scene of the 1894 wedding of Fares A. Ferzan, a fancy goods dealer on the Boardwalk in Atlantic City, and Sassool Maloof, daughter of Naaman Maloof and sister of Najeeb N. Maloof. According to one reporter, "The diamond studded watch and rich jewels worn by the bride seem to indicate that there is plenty of wealth in the family."[37] Peter Korkemas, who was assisted by the Melkite priest, Abraham Beshewate, married them. The bride and groom were attended by Elias Ferzan, the groom's brother, Salim Elias, and Hafeza Ayoob, herself recently married. Several men in the congregation read poems to celebrate the marriage, including Ameen Rihani, Asad Milkie, Naoum Mokarzel, and the groom's brother, Elias; all were recognized poets and orators. The couple went to Niagara Falls for their honeymoon.

---

[36] "Syrians Married by the Greek Service in the Fashionable Episcopal Church," *NYH*, May 8, 1893.

[37] "By a Syrian Priest," *Syracuse* (NY) *Daily Standard*, October 29, 1894; "Syriac Wedding Service," *NYT*, October 29, 1894.

Like Nicola Abo Samra, Nahoum Daher Merhige was a prosperous silk merchant when he married Yinna (or Minnie) Kaydouh at Trinity Church on November 22, 1896. Yinna was the sister of Michael Deeb Kaydouh, first a dry goods merchant, then the owner of a cigar store on Battery Place, and finally the owner of the Annex Restaurant and Café. Merhige was one of three Protestant brothers from Tripoli who had immigrated in 1893, all of whom had separate business interests. "Nearly 2,000 Syrian friends of the couple, from Washington, Boston, Philadelphia, Jersey City, and Brooklyn filled the church."[38] The number of guests seems highly exaggerated. After the wedding, Nahoum and Minnie moved to Florida and ran Merhige's Oriental Bazaar, first in Jacksonville and then in St. Petersburg. After she was widowed, Minnie continued to sell kimonos and dressing sacques at the bazaar under the name "Mme. Minnie D. Merhige."

Miriam Azar, who had recently arrived from Jaffa, and Touma (Tannous/Thomas) Elia were married by Archmandrite Raphael Hawaweeny on October 17, 1897, in the Syrian Orthodox Church at 77 Washington Street. "The wedding was a great event for that part of Washington Street, for a block on each side of Rector, and especially in the five-story tenement at 105 where Miss Azar and her mother occupied a room on the third floor."[39] The article stretched to a whole column as the writer described the strange Oriental customs attaching to the service. Thomas Elia was said to be handsome and well-to-do, trading in notions and dry goods. Prominent businessman Abdow Lutfy sponsored Miriam, who had no father. Unfortunately we have no further information about either of them; the only possible trace is a Thomas and Mary Alias and two children in St. Louis, Missouri in 1900; he was a notions peddler. If this is the same couple, Thomas may have been simply a peddler when he married, and he probably was not as well-to-do as reported. Whether this was the reporter's gloss or the family's is impossible to say.

The wedding of Elias Macksoud and Shafika Lutfy has already been alluded to. Father Beshewate, the Melkite priest, married them at St. Peter's Church on Barclay Street. Americans were in attendance. "She was dressed in a white satin gown and wore a long white veil with a pearl necklace and diamond pendant" and was given away by her father, Abdow Lutfy. They went to Washington, D.C., for their honeymoon.[40]

---

[38] "Syrians Wed in Old Trinity," *NYT,* November 23, 1896.

[39] "Wedding in Pure Arabic" *NYT*, October 18, 1897.

[40] "A Syrian Wedding," *NYT*, February 7, 1899.

An interesting wedding reported in *Al Hoda* was the double wedding of New York merchants Ibrahim and Antoine Sadallah to Nemnour Abdoo and Barbara Karam, respectively, which took place in Utica, New York, in 1900. The Karams lived in Utica. Yusef Mandour, a Philadelphia cigar merchant and the Sadallahs' brother-in-law, was best man for Ibrahim, and Ibrahim was best man for Antoine. The brides adopted the same arrangement: Barbara was maid of honor for Nemnour and Amelia Maroon was Barbara's maid of honor. Many New York Maronites attended the wedding, including Salim Elias, Beshara Ganim, and Issa Saloomy; the four newlyweds returned to New York.

Elias Elias, son of the prominent New York Maronite merchant Salim Elias, married Princess Eugenie Shehab in Marseille in 1900. Her uncle, Prince Yusef Shehab, gave her away. The article about the wedding, perhaps because the bride was an aristocrat, took up six columns in *Al Hoda*,[41] and several subsequent issues printed poems submitted by readers in praise of the couple.

### *Divorce*

The great majority of these marriages—whether interfaith, interethnic, arranged, or based on love—lasted until the death of one or the other of the couple, and many, I'm sure, were happy. There is little information about these marriages in the Colony, while unhappy marriages, particularly those that involved the police or the courts, were regularly covered in the press.

A rather spectacular early example was that of Frasina Hayek (or Rosa Jacob, depending on which account one reads), who sued the Hayek brothers and Msgr. Korkemas for forcing her into a marriage against her will. She had come to the United States in 1889 and lodged with the Hayek brothers at 1 Carlisle Street; they were distant relatives. She and Joseph Hayek married in Texas, where he had been sent to pursue the brothers' jewelry business. But Joseph's brothers opposed the marriage, and they allegedly lured her back to New York and forced her to marry Nassif Elias, a marriage at which Korkemas presided. They tried to consummate the marriage by locking the bride and groom together in a room. The newlyweds were then placed on the train to Concord, New Hampshire, where he had been peddling. She escaped, came back to New York, and took refuge with her mother at 73 Washington. She not only blamed the Hayeks, but accused the priest of aiding and abetting

[41] *Al Hoda,* October 31, 1900.

them (he claimed he didn't know she was already married). Unusual as the case was, even more unusual was that she hired a lawyer, Adolphus D. Pape,[42] to represent her. The judge appointed Abraham Ashie as her guardian,[43] and gave her permission to sue to obtain damages from the priest and her brothers-in-law. The story makes little sense, but it does point to the conflicting values—love and duty—which confronted the immigrants here. Unfortunately the outcome was not reported, nor is the case documented in the archives.

Hafeza Maloof married Joseph Ayoob, the importer and novelties dealer mentioned several times above, in May 1893. Shortly afterward, he was arrested in New Haven for smuggling.[44] Hafeza went to New Haven to plead his case with the wife of the customhouse collector, but she was unsuccessful. He was held on $4,000 bond and apparently stayed in jail until he was finally able to raise the money for bail. He was found guilty in both the criminal and civil suits against him and was liable for the duty on the goods plus all court costs for both the criminal case and civil case, paying $1,300 in fines.[45] He was then sued by his lawyer and was forced to pay him an additional $1,100 in fees. No wonder Ayoob got out of the importing business and began manufacturing Oriental goods in Queens.

This must have been a lot to handle for Hafeza, his new bride. Despite all the turmoil, Hafeza and Joseph had a daughter, Gabel (Isabella) in 1894. In 1895, they had a son Fareed. Ayoob went into a new business, selling shares in a goldmine in Colorado, a rather radical change in career for someone who had been an importer of Oriental goods. Hafeza separated from Joseph that same year,[46] but apparently had returned to him, because she was pregnant with their third child when eight-month-old Fareed died in March 1896 of bronchitis. She sued Joseph for divorce in June on grounds of cruelty.

On June 15, 1896, as part of her divorce suit, Hafeza petitioned the court for custody of their daughter, Isabella.[47] Ayoob was apprehended trying to flee the country with the child, and was arrested on $1,000 bail. "A part of the Syrian Colony was in the Supreme Court yesterday when the habeas corpus proceeding brought by Hafeza Ayoob against her husband, Joseph, to obtain

---

[42] As we have seen, Pape represented a number of Syrians in civil suits.
[43] "Forced to an Illegal Marriage," *The* (NY) *Sun*: December 22, 1891.
[44] "Ayoob Still in Custody," *New Haven Register*, June 17, 1893.
[45] *New Haven Register*, October 4, 1894.
[46] "Unusual Number of Lost Children," *NYH*, May 27, 1895.
[47] *Trials*, Hafeza Ayoob v. Joseph Ayoob, June 15, 1896: WR A-1127.

possession of their child, came up before Justice Andrews."[48] Several Syrians were called as witnesses to prove that Ayoob's cruelty and jealousy had forced his wife to leave him. He was ordered by the judge to pay his wife's legal fee of $100 and eight dollars per month for alimony. She was given custody of Isabella, and Ayoob was put in Ludlow Street jail in default of the $1,000 bond—his second jail term in three years.

In October 1896, Hafeza gave birth to her third child, Halim, who was also called Patrick. In the 1900 census, she is listed as head of household (and married, rather than divorced or widowed) with her two children, Isabel and Patrick. She was living with her sister Rosie Barak at 32 Willow Place in Brooklyn; they both worked as dressmakers to support the household. In the same census, however, Isabella Ayoob is also listed as an inmate in the Home for Friendless Women and Children, a sign that the mother must have been desperate and wanting. Like the two Maloof girls—Adele and Emma, who were Isabella's aunts and who were in the same orphanage—Isabella was listed in the census twice, which must imply a reluctance on the part of the mothers to admit that their children were in care. All three girls were listed as being "Austrian." Was this a simple mistake on the part of the orphanage or a deliberate lie by the parents? Sadly, in 1905, both Isabella and Halim were in an orphanage in Yonkers.

Other notable divorces include the rather extreme case of Naoum Mokarzel, the publisher/editor of *Al Hoda* and the future leader and spokesman of the Maronite community. As mentioned above, Mokarzel came from Freike to the United States with his cousin Abdow Rihani and Abdow's nephew Ameen Rihani in 1888. He had held a number of jobs after he arrived including the ill-fated store he opened with Abdow, teaching at Xavier College, and publishing a short-lived newspaper called *Al Asr*. He was also embroiled in a running feud with the editors of *Kawkab America*.

In 1895, while living in Jersey City, New Jersey, he was named as a co-respondent in an adultery case brought by Tannous Shishim against Shishim's wife, Sophie (Shafika).[49] Shishim, Sophie, and Sophie's father, Habeeb Daoud, had immigrated from Zahleh together in 1889. In the years leading up to the suit, Daoud and Shishim ran a boardinghouse/restaurant together at 91 Washington Street, but Daoud moved to Texas in 1893, leaving Shishim with the boardinghouse.

[48] "Many Syrians in Court," *NYT*, June 17, 1896.

[49] *Trials,* Tannous Shishim v. Sophie Daoud Shishim, June 29, 1895: S-79.

14-2. Studio portrait of Sophie Daoud Shishim, 1895.

In the suit, Shishim accused Sophie of having had an affair with Mokarzel. *Kawkab America* quoted from the trial transcript as follows: "That in the month of April 1895, the defendant commited [*sic*] adultery and had sexual interecourse *[sic]* with one NAOUM MOCARZEL at a house known as No. 177 Third Street Jersey City [Mokarzel's residence] in the State of New Jersey."[50] *Kawkab America* published the scandalous proceedings on its front page in both Arabic and English (even though the paper was exclusively Arabic by this time), with Mokarzel's name in boldface across the full column width. The editors went to the trouble of translating the judge's verdict into Arabic. This extensive coverage seems less a journalistic ploy than an act of revenge against Mokarzel, who had published some inflammatory words against *Kawkab America*'s editor Nageeb Arbeely in his newspaper *Al Asr* the year before.

Mokarzel and Sophie had lived at the Third Street residence for only two weeks before the trial, and their landlady, Mabel Wilbur, testified that she

[50] *Kawkab America,* August 9, 1895.

had seen Sophie and Naoum in bed together. These two facts suggest that the adultery may have been a performance put on by Sophie and Tannous to obtain the nineteenth-century version of a no-fault divorce. Subsequent revelations prove that suggestion false.

Sophie and Naoum had actually married in April 1895; their marriage certificate is on file in Trenton, New Jersey. They were living together in Jersey City, then, not in sin but as a married couple. But if the dates are to be believed, she had married Mokarzel *before* her divorce from Shishim was granted in July 1895, making her a bigamist, which must have been at least as great a sin as adultery. Neither Shishim nor the editors of *Kawkab America* mentioned the marriage; they either did not know or purposely suppressed it.

As was customary, Sophie did not appear at the trial, and therefore the judge found against her, awarding Shishim the divorce as well as court costs.[51] After the trial, Sophie and Naoum moved to Philadelphia; Mokarzel started *Al Hoda* there in 1898. Although Mary Mokarzel claimed he moved there to start his paper in the "Cradle of Liberty," I suspect they moved to get away from the scandal in New York.

In 1899, nearly four years after the lawsuit, Naoum and Sophie published a remarkable joint defense of the legitimacy of their marriage in a four-page supplement to *Al Hoda*. It was not just a personal defense but also a sustained attack on the editors of *Kawkab America*. At the top of the first page, Mokarzel reproduced their New Jersey marriage certificate, dated April 11, 1895. Pages of vitriol followed, with Mokarzel accusing the paper of slandering them. Sophie took over from Naoum to offer a chronology of events leading up to their marriage, in which she insisted that she had left Tannous in 1893, because he had been cruel to her and refused to support her. She spent two years peddling in the Midwest and filed for a divorce in the Oklahoma Territories. She claimed that she was granted the divorce partly because Shishim did not show up for the trial and partly because she had witnesses who attested to his abuse of her. One wonders how she was able to get witnesses in Oklahoma to attest to his cruelty in New York. She was awarded the divorce, making Tannous the "guilty" party. She insisted that the marriage to Mokarzel was perfectly legal and the editors of *Kawkab America* had lied and slandered the couple.[52]

A letter from her Oklahoma lawyer, which is inserted in the New York

[51] *Trials,* Shishim v. Shishim, July 3, 1895: S-79.

[52] *Al Hoda,* January 17, 1899.

divorce trial transcript, confirms her story, although it came too late to affect the verdict. He wrote that Sophie was an upright and respectable woman who had been treated badly by Shishim, and he was sorry he had not known about the trial before it happened. The judge wrote him for more details saying that if what he wrote was true, Shishim had committed perjury. Shishim was specifically asked, as was required in such cases, whether any action for divorce had been brought against him, and he replied in the negative. Did he lie to protect his reputation and to be sure he was the injured party? Is it possible he had not been informed of the Oklahoma divorce, either by design or negligence? If so, how could he have not known when Sophie returned to New York and married Mokarzel?

Inconsistency piles on inconsistency. Although it seems to have been normal practice for the defendant in an adultery trial not to appear, why didn't Sophie appear at the New York trial to present evidence for her previous divorce and defend her present marriage? Why did she allow Shishim to win the suit by default? She claimed she was in Oklahoma during the trial and had been for ninety days, yet the Mokarzels' wedding and the "adultery" took place in Jersey City in April, less than three months before the beginning of the trial. And too, Moussa Zalka testified that he had personally served papers on Sophie in New York on April 22 (eleven days after Sophie's marriage to Naoum). If she did go to Oklahoma before the trial; why did she? Why not stay and defend herself?

And, most puzzling, why did the Mokarzels wait almost four years before presenting the evidence? Mokarzel was never shy about expressing his opinions in print; the founding of *Al Hoda* in 1898 gave him the vehicle to do so. This article was, however, an extraordinary departure from the normal Syrian tendency to keep one's private life private. One can only imagine that it was partly motivated by the wish to discredit the editors of *Kawkab America*, which he did on every page. Although Naoum's vitriol was of a general sort, accusing *Kawkab America* of lying, misleading the public, and insults, Sophie was cutting in her presentation of the evidence, inserting phrases such as, "on April 11, 1895, I was married to Naoum Mokarzel, and you accused me of adultery in the month of May (which is after the month of April...)." She even attributed this reporting to jealousy on the part of the editors of *Kawkab America* because their circulation was decreasing, while that of *Al Hoda* was increasing.

Ironically enough, despite this public airing of an unseemly event and their apparent solidarity in their joint response, the Mokarzel's marriage did not last; they separated shortly after the publication of the joint defense. Sophie Mokarzel was already on her own and back in New York by May 1899. We know this because she sued one Mohammed Deweek (or Dwek) for the return of property she had left in trust with him: "one pair solitaire diamond earrings, one diamond breast pin, one diamond ruby ring, one diamond marquise, one five stone diamond ring, and one gold ring with stone...plus a deposit passbook with the Bowery Savings Bank of NYC containing entry of credits to plaintiff of $210."[53] Naoum was not mentioned in the suit at all. She won the case and was paid $1,200 by Deweek, who had apparently sold the jewelry. Like some other women in the community, she seems to have had money of her own, perhaps from her years as a peddler. It is interesting that she left her assets in trust with Deweek, apparently keeping them separate from those of either Shishim or Mokarzel.

In any case, Sophie must have finally broken with Naoum by 1900, because she had opened a boardinghouse in Brooklyn that year (Naoum was still living in Philadelphia). She must have funded the enterprise with the money just recovered from Deweek. Sophie actually appears in two 1900 censuses: one has her still part of Naoum's household in Philadelphia; in the other she is living with her sisters Emeline Axem and Sarah Birdsall, their children, and Sarah's husband in Sunset Park, Brooklyn.[54] Sophie is listed as married in the Philadelphia census, single in the New York census, and as the widow of Naoum in a 1900 city directory. In addition to running the boardinghouse, Sophie once again turned to trade. She set up a seasonal shop in the Burlington Arcade in Richfield Springs, New York, in which she sold kimonos and Venetian laces. She and Naoum were legally divorced in December 1902, but she continued to use the name "Sophie Mokarzel."

After the divorce, Sophie and the Birdsalls (her sister and brother-in-law) moved out to Los Angeles and the two sisters opened a fine linen shop. She also invested there in a Syrian-owned confectionery shop and married its owner, Beshara Cressaty, in 1905—her third and final marriage. She had no children by any of her marriages.

Naoum and his brother Salloum meanwhile continued to live and publish *Al Hoda* in Philadelphia; their widowed sister Catherine arrived in 1899 to keep house for them in place of Sophie. In 1903, the brothers moved the

[53] *Trials,* Mokarzel v. Deweek, May 3, 1899: D-188.

[54] This duplication, along with several other instances cited in this book, cautions us once again about putting too much faith in the accuracy of the census.

household and the newspaper to New York. In May 1904, Naoum married Sa'ada Rihani, Ameen Rihani's sister, at Ameen's house at 32 Willow Place in Brooklyn. According to Mary Mokarzel, Rihani had begged Naoum to marry his sister, who was on her deathbed, and Naoum agreed to this "marriage of mercy."

Sa'ada did not die: far from it. Soon after their marriage she went back to Syria and lived for many decades. Perhaps because the marriage may have been agreed to out of pity, it did not last. The couple divorced in Brooklyn in 1908. She was addressed as "Miss Rihani" ever after. In 1910, Naoum married for the third and last time. His new wife, Rose Abi Lama (Bellamah) had been living with relatives in New Bern, North Carolina, which is where Naoum met her. He was 44; she was 22. On the marriage certificate, he only admitted to one previous marriage, which must have been the one to Sa'ada. Was that marriage annulled or the previous one annulled? Perhaps it was unnecessary, as none of his marriages was performed in the church. The Abi Lamas were an aristocratic family from Matn, and one can tell simply by looking at Rose's picture that she was an upright, moral pillar; she was well upholstered and well corseted and looked like butter wouldn't melt in her mouth. He lived with her until his death in 1932. He had no children by any of his wives.

Mokarzel, as we have seen, led a highly irregular personal life: three marriages (none sanctioned by the church), two divorces, co-respondent in a divorce case, and husband of a possible bigamist. As far as I can tell, none of this was hidden. He, perhaps, did not talk about his past, but anyone who wished to could have found out. Yet he was not only the editor of the most influential Arabic newspaper in the United States, he was also a spokesman for the Maronites, deferred to as their leader, a famous orator, and esteemed throughout the diaspora. How was he able to put this checkered career behind him and become the pillar of the Maronite community that he undoubtedly was?

The third case of divorce in the Syrian Colony was that of another Shishim, George, who married Frida (Farida or Fatneh) Freike in New York in 1896. George was only eighteen years old when they married; she was a widow of thirty-four and had a five-year old son from her first marriage who also happened to be named George.[55] Frida had come over for the Chicago fair in 1893; perhaps she worked in one of the Turkish cafés, because after the fair

[55] In her naturalization papers, which she signed in Arabic, she gave a birthdate of 1875, which would have made her a bride at seven years old.

she opened a café on Bushman's Walk in Coney Island. The family lived above the store. In 1904 George sued her for divorce, alleging adultery. The suit describes in specific detail the men she slept with, where, and when: "During October, November, and December in 1903 and January 1904, and especially on or about the 22nd day of January, 1904, the defendant had intercourse with one Neklis Vavegotes in rooms occupied by her at 58 Dey Street." She also had intercourse with Joseph Abojlad in January 1904, and "committed adultery with diverse persons between October 12 and the commencement of this action." The lawyer for the plaintiff questioned the witnesses closely on whether they had seen a man in a state of undress in her room; they all answered in the affirmative. "Undress" in this case meant he was not wearing his waistcoat or shoes. As if this weren't enough to win his case, George also claimed that Frida was a bigamist, having married Kalil Freike "on or about March 10, 1882" in Syria. Shishim had been led to believe that Freike was dead, which he later found out was untrue, at least according to his testimony.[56] The detailed accusations were required by law or custom, as the divorce of Tannous and Sophie Shishim also specified the date and place where the adultery had occurred and had an eyewitness to Sophie and Mokarzel in bed together. Both trials give the feeling of a rote recitation, which may imply that the witnesses said whatever was necessary to make the divorce go smoothly. Like Sophie, Frida opted to stay away from the trial, and the divorce was granted George.

Frida must have already been living apart from her husband before the divorce suit since her alleged adulteries took place in her rooms at 58 Dey Street. In 1903, she owned her own cigar store on Kensington Walk in Coney Island. She was naturalized that same year and, although we know nothing more about her, she must have been able to support herself and her son on her own. Perhaps her filing her naturalization papers meant that she planned a trip back to Syria. She died in Brooklyn in 1931. Her ex-husband George moved to California, first working as a private guard for an amusement park in Santa Monica and then as a policeman in Venice. His name was in the news because, although he had been in the United States since 1894, his application for naturalization in 1909 was denied because he was deemed "not white," and therefore barred from citizenship.[57] His job was at risk. He hired

[56] *Trials,* Shishim v. Frik and Shishim v. Shishim, 1903: GA 1903-1698 S-4.

[57] This case and others related to the question of whether Syrians were "white" are covered in Gualtieri's 2009 book.

a lawyer who argued that Syrians were Caucasians, and he won his case. He remarried—this time an American—and had two sons.

The divorce proceedings become wearingly similar: in 1898, Abdallah Nassar sued his wife, Martha, for divorce. They had married in Syria in 1887. He accused her of committing adultery with one Magal Caram in their home in Rondout, NY.[58] The usual witnesses were called to testify that they had seen his wife and a man in bed together. As usual, the defendant did not appear, and Abdallah was given his divorce.[59]

The Moroccan actor and theater manager Hajji Tahar married Julia Doyle in New York in 1887, and they had a daughter, May, the next year. Tahar must have met Julia in San Francisco while traveling with the Buffalo Bill show; his naturalization papers were filed there. Perhaps Doyle was a performer as well. They divorced in San Francisco in 1892 and custody of May was awarded to the mother. In 1898, another Moroccan theater impresario, Hassan Ben Ali, sued Tahar for custody of the nine-year-old girl, claiming that Julia had apprenticed her to Ben Ali for seven years to learn the circus trade. He asserted that Tahar was keeping May restrained at his (Tahar's) home at 108 Eighth Avenue, and that he was planning to take her out of the country.[60] Tahar, for his part, accused Julia of indenturing the girl for seven years to Ben Ali, who is "engaged in theatrical pursuits of the lowest order," and who "has made infamous attempts to corrupt the morals and chastity of the infant, and induced said infant to sleep in a bed while said Ben Ali committed fornication with a belly dancer."[61] It is clear that committing fornication with a belly dancer was a more heinous crime than committing fornication with just an ordinary woman. This accusation would be laughable if it didn't involve a child. And Tahar's characterization of Ben Ali's work as "theatrical pursuits of the lowest order" is ridiculous, since Tahar was engaged in exactly the same pursuits.

Despite Tahar's lurid accusations, the court ordered the child to be given to Ben Ali's sister-in-law, Henrietta Cheriff, of 432 E. 16th Street, to be cared for and educated at Tahar's expense, which must have been a bitter pill for Tahar to swallow. Henrietta was the American wife of Hajji Cheriff, another Moroccan performer/impresario. In 1900 May was living with two American ladies, Mrs. Harris and Mrs. Young, on 90th Street, so perhaps Cheriff

[58] Rondout was the port serving Kingston, New York, the residence of a small group of Syrians who worked in the brickyards.

[59] *Trials,* Abdallah Nassar v. Martha Antonia Nassar, April 2, 1898: GA-1531 N-2.

[60] "Says Tahar Restrains Her," *NYH,* December 25, 1898.

[61] *Trials,* Ben Ali v. Hajji Tahar, December 22, 1898: WR A-285.

had given her up. She was eleven then and had certainly been shunted from household to household over the course of her short life.

Tahar married Florence Hunter in 1899; she was sixteen, he was forty. In the 1900 census, the couple and their baby son were living on East 33rd Street, while he also lived, at least part time, with his theatrical troupe at the apartment he had had for years at 108 Eighth Avenue (at 15th Street). In 1900, he was brought to trial for sodomy for raping a young member of his theater troupe. On the night in question, Tahar's troupe had performed at Koster & Bial's Music Hall at 34th Street and Broadway and gone back to Tahar's residence on Eighth Avenue. Living in Tahar's flat was a sixteen-year-old acrobat named Albert Richards, one of two young British acrobats in the troupe. The attorneys cross-examined the witnesses closely on the sleeping arrangements in the three-room apartment. It seems that Tahar had been in the habit of sleeping in the front room with one of the American girls who performed with the troupe, and the two acrobats had slept in a single bed in the back room. A Filipino couple, also part of the troupe, slept on trunks in the kitchen. As one of the girls was ill that night, she had slept in Tahar's bed with another girl, and Tahar, according to testimony, had gotten into bed with Albert Richards and raped him.

Defense counsel did a good job of convincing the jury that Richards had made up the whole story simply because he was angry with Tahar for not sending him home to England as he wished. Defense also implied that the boy had been encouraged to make trouble for Tahar by the Gerry Society (the New York Society for the Prevention of Cruelty to Children). The actual complainant in the case, Thomas Agnew, was probably a member of the Society. The Gerry Society was not only active in trying to punish child molesters, but it was also concerned with child labor, particularly in the theaters. There were stories circulating as early as 1880 of children being sold or indentured to Arab acting troupes,[62] which was the main accusation in Tahar's custody case, described above. In the present case, perhaps the Gerry Society saw a chance to score two victories, against child slavery and child molestation. But Tahar was acquitted. We find him listed in the 1910 census, living alone and managing a restaurant in San Francisco; he died in New York in 1938 at the age of 78. We do not know what happened to his second wife and baby son. Nor do we know what happened to poor Albert Richards; did he ever make it home to England?

[62] "Hadj Ali's Apprentices," *NYH*, December 7, 1881.

"Abdalla Hamati Loses His Wife," proclaimed a headline in the October 7, 1892, issue of the *Brooklyn Daily Eagle*. Abdallah ran a boardinghouse at 71 Washington. Amalia Hamati eloped with one Abalan Booharap (Aboarab?), taking $700 of her husband's cash, and Hamati swore out a warrant to have them arrested when they landed in Europe. They must have escaped his grasp, because six months later he published a notice in *Kawkab America* stating he was divorcing her due to her "inappropriate and dishonest behavior," to which the Colonists could bear witness.[63] Hamati married Zarifa Abraham in 1896.

After immigrating in 1884, Selma Gobreen worked for the Syrian Mission of the Presbyterian Church in New York, acting as an interpreter at Castle Garden and appearing as a lecturer around New York. John Abd-el-Nour had been in America since 1880 and was quite successful; we have seen that by 1888, he was able to guarantee a number of new arrivals by posting a large bond. The couple married in Boston in 1889 (he was fifteen years her senior), and they took first-class passage to Europe for their honeymoon.

They worked together importing silks and embroideries, and they lived an opulent life in Manhattan and in their country retreat on Eltingville Lane in Staten Island, which became their permanent residence in 1899. They were involved in a well-publicized smuggling case in 1895 (described previously), but the "differences between the accused and the Government were adjusted and the woman was freed."[64] They seem to have resumed their lives soon after. This apparently settled existence was not to last. In 1905, Abd-el-Nour accused his wife of plotting to murder him; she accused him of cruelty. Her father and Tewfik Lewis (?), a man sometimes identified as her brother, who were living with the couple in Staten Island, weighed in against Abd-el-Nour and tried to have him arrested for assault; he in turn accused them of being accessories in the murder plot. Selma moved out of their home in Staten Island to the Murray Hill Hotel with their son, Hector, where she occupied "one of the finest apartments, being a wealthy woman in her own name."[65] Gobreen even went to court to ask permission to carry a revolver in order to protect herself and her son. She claimed that she was afraid of her husband and afraid that he would kidnap their son. The judge refused her request, telling her she should ask the help of the police.[66]

---

[63] *Kawkab America,* May 19, 1893.

[64] "After His Syrian Clients," *The* (NY) *World,* March 23, 1896.

[65] "Syrian Stories Differ," *New-York Tribune,* September 20, 1905.

[66] "Wife Charged with Seeking Husband's Life," *The* (NY) *Evening World,* May 24, 1905.

Abd-el-Nour was arrested but freed on $500 bail. She proceeded to sue him for divorce, claiming cruelty and assault. Abd-el-Nour accused Archmandrite Hawaweeny of instigating the divorce suit, which the priest denied, but which may have added fuel to the factional fight that broke out that year between the Maronites and the Orthodox. Gobreen named Fadwa Jabaly, the wife of Abd-el-Nour's business partner at the time, as the co-respondent in the case, and Fadwa sued her for slander. Abd-el-Nour countersued Gobreen for custody of Hector, claiming he was not her child.[67] It was a lurid story all around.

They apparently did not divorce, as they were reportedly living together in Staten Island in 1910; Gobreen's other sister Chasine (Shahineh), who had immigrated in 1895, was living with them. In 1914, Abd-el-Nour moved to Tientsin, China, for business, working for (or proprietor of) the Philippine Embroidery Company. He may have stayed through the twenties, as he is listed on a 1922 ship manifest returning to San Francisco from Hong Kong. His 1916 passport shows a distinguished, white-haired gentleman with a luxuriant handlebar mustache. Gobreen stayed in New York with Hector. We find Abd-el-Nour finally in the 1930 census, a seventy-eight-year-old widower living with his son in rented quarters in rural San Diego, California; Selma must have died sometime in the twenties. Father and son were involved in a scheme to raise silkworms on a large scale,[68] but John passed away in 1931 at the age of 79. Hector died in 1947 at the age of 51.

A breach of promise case was brought against Yak Oussani in 1899. According to the suit, he had promised to marry Rosa Kara (Karam?), but broke off the engagement one week before the wedding. His implausible claim was that he had been threatened by three men he didn't know and forced to break the engagement. He thought they must have been friends of a woman named Fatima (one of the belly dancing Fatimas?), with whom he had lived in the past. Rosa sued Yak for $20,000.[69] She was a forty-year old dressmaker and it seems unlikely that Oussani, who was only thirty-six and wealthy, had been engaged to her, but it is possible; he never denied the charge. The outcome of the case was not reported. He never married, however, and died in 1903. A young woman named Sarah David,[70] who owned a restaurant on Whitehall Street, sued Kaisar Yamin, an importer of rugs and Turkish goods, for breach

[67] "Syrian Sues for Child," *NYT*, May 25, 1905.

[68] The California Building at the Columbian fair featured, as one of their products, silkworms raised in California, which excited the interest of several of the Syrian merchants.

[69] "Pretty Syrian Girl Sues for $20,000," *Evening Telegram* (NY), January 24, 1899.

[70] Was this Sophie Shishim's sister, who later married Fred Birdsall?

of promise in 1893. She asked for $10,000 in damages; he did not dispute the fact that he had courted her but claimed in his defense that his sister objected to the match. Again, we do not know the outcome of the case, but Yamin married someone else a few years later.[71]

I have described Ameen H. Batal in the context of the formation of the Melkite church in New York City. His letter to Archbishop Corrigan apparently spurred the archbishop to bring the priest, Abraham Beshewate, to New York. Disputes between Batal and Beshewate were decided in Batal's favor, but they perhaps encouraged Batal to leave New York to join relatives in Lawrence, Massachusetts, in 1892. In March of 1895, a charge of sodomy was brought against him by someone, presumably a Syrian, in New York. The alleged crime was said to have taken place in 1892, which may be another reason Batal left New York. That charge was dismissed when it was apparently proved that Batal was in Massachusetts at the time the crime was committed. Also in March, he petitioned the Superior Court of Massachusetts for a divorce from his wife of four years, Rosa Estefan. They had had a child in 1892 or 1893, and then twin girls were born in July of 1895, four months after he filed for divorce. The family was said to be living at Hamati's boardinghouse at 71 Washington Street then, although Batal had filed his petition in Boston and claimed to have lived in Massachusetts since his marriage. Both girls died of "inanition"—exhaustion due to lack of nutrition or general weakness—a month later, attended by Ameen Haddad. The divorce petition accused Rosa of committing adultery with one Abraham Borahm (?) "and with other persons at present to your libellant unknown." The twins were born eight months after the alleged adultery; perhaps Borahm was the father (although Batal is named on both birth certificates). Or perhaps Batal abandoned her after impregnating her. Whatever the truth, the petition went uncontested, and Batal was granted his divorce in October of 1895, two months after the death of the twins. We don't know what happened to Rosa or the surviving child, but Ameen married a widow named Salima Hobeika Tenn in Boston in 1901, and they had four children.[72]

These cases of divorce are clearly not the norm: there are so few of them, and each is more baroque than the one before. In the nineteenth century, men

[71] "Yamin Says His Sister Objected," *The* (NY) *Sun,* July 15, 1893.

[72] This reconstruction comes from a number of newspaper articles, documents, city directories, and vital records. See, for example, "They Want Batal," *Boston Journal,* March 22, 1895, "Ameen Batal Can Stay," *Boston Journal,* March 27, 1895, and legal notices in the *Boston Daily Advertiser* of March 7, 13, and 18, 1895.

could divorce if they proved their wives had been adulterous, while women divorced men for cruelty. The "guilty" party was then forbidden to marry again while the ex-spouse was alive—a cruel fate for those Syrian women divorced by their husbands. Sophie Shishim was a remarkable exception in having remarried (twice) after apparently being convicted of adultery. One wonders if the oft-referred-to cruelty or adultery actually took place, or whether most of these divorces were "collusive," where both partners acted the charade required of them. The language and circumstances of the divorce proceedings are so similar that they do seem pro forma. One also wonders how many men (or women) escaped an unhappy marriage by simply abandoning their spouse.

A subject that was completely invisible was unwanted pregnancy. Before the availability of birth control this was a constant worry for all women. My two grandmothers both had unwanted pregnancies: one married, the other had an abortion. We have one other story of Hanna Yusef and his wife, who were accused of aborting their child. *Kawkab America* claimed they were innocent; the wife was not charged, but the husband was sentenced to ten years.[73] By twenty-first-century standards, this is an unusual outcome. With the help of his fellow Syrians, however, an appeals court released Yusef after only one year. How many more abortions were there? The procedure must have been a necessary and perhaps frequent part of the Syrian midwives' business, but of course went unreported.

## Assimilation and Resistance

The mixed marriages described above can serve as a symbol of the divided opinion on the question of assimilation. Those men who married "Americans" did so either because there were not enough Syrian women to choose from or because they made a considered decision to "marry into" American culture.

There were pros and cons to the American way of life; whether the Syrian should assimilate or try to preserve his culture and whether America was or should become home, were topics debated in the newspapers, cafés, and meetings of the various societies as well as at home. The debate began, at least as far as the Syrian newspapers were concerned, with a question posed

[73] *Kawkab America,* July 13, 1894.

by *Kawkab America* about the influence of American missionaries in Syria. Reactions from the reading public were mixed, with some citing the good schools and American values the missionaries brought, and others citing the corruption and dishonesty of the missionaries themselves. Then the debate moved its focus to life in the United States as immigrants began to look at the "Americans" around them and judge them. As I mentioned, many of these so-called Americans were new immigrants themselves, but the Syrians generally ignored that distinction. The behavior of Americans they encountered touched all aspects of the immigrants' lives, and the Syrians' ambivalence about their hosts was profound.

One aspect of American society that troubled Syrians immensely was the perceived moral laxity of the Americans, notwithstanding the fact that the Syrians, like everyone else, often profited from these lax morals. In 1893, an anonymous letter writer addressed the readers of *Kawkab America*. According to him (I presume the writer was a man), Syrian children were forced to live in poor conditions, hear bad language, and witness violence among their Irish and American neighbors (the writer called the latter "villains" and "lowlifes"). Their minds, he felt, were not being nurtured but instead being corrupted by the gangs of thugs on the street throwing stones, harassing women, attacking others, and getting adults involved in trying to break up fights. "These are daily scenes," he said. He urged Syrian parents to spend time every day to improve the behavior of their children and nurture them with curiosity and knowledge.[74] It wasn't just that the Irish gangs were preying on the Syrians, but that they also set such a bad example for the children.

There were complaints in letters to the editor about American men saying suggestive things to Syrian women, including something that sounded like "Ducky" to the Syrians (but which may have been "Dago"). Even pregnant women were spoken to in this manner, which angered the Syrian men. Although Syrians themselves drank *'araq*, they were appalled by the drunks coming out of Irish and German saloons on Washington Street. American women were condemned for being too free, drinking beer like the men, and marrying "slaves" (blacks). New York was home to 5,000 bars and 43,000 prostitutes, according to *Kawkab America*.[75] The newspapers were quick to qualify these condemnatory comments by saying that not all Americans were like that; there were a few bad apples in every barrel. It was clear, however,

[74] *Kawkab America*, June 2, 1893.

[75] *Kawkab America*, November 18, 1892.

that this moral laxity on the part of the Americans greatly troubled the Syrians and affected their feelings for the country.

On the occasion of the Orthodox bishop Nicholas's departure from his post as head of the North American Church, he exhorted his fellow Orthodox to keep their children out of American schools: "You see yourselves how bad is the education given in the public schools of this country: most of the children who have attended them come out of them not only without the fear of God, but without the customary sense of shame." This lack of shame is manifested in "disrespect toward their elders; too light a view of duty, in the family, the community and the state; a chasing after easy gain, pleasures and recreations."[76] American newspapers treated this speech with derision, but it reflected the ambivalence that many Syrians felt about their adopted country.

At the same time, the Americans' perceived success in business—as a result of their work ethic, ambition, cleverness, and even their trickiness—was worthy of emulation by the Syrians (but not, the editors hastened to add, at the expense of honor). The difficulty of separating admired business practices from repugnant personal behavior was one that plagued the Syrians for many decades. Which aspects of the American way of life were worthy of emulation? Interestingly, mention was rarely made of the aspects of American life that we deem important: freedom of religion, democracy, and multiculturalism. Syrians only talked about such things for the benefit of American reporters. Those characteristics were neither touted nor debated in the Syrian papers. Instead, the newspapers praised the Americans' no-nonsense approach to life and their sharp business practices. Lest it be thought, however, that the Syrians were abject in their praise of American acumen, we should remember that many Syrians who returned home to Syria bragged about how easy it was to cheat them and how gullible they were.

Conversely, what parts of Syrian culture could and should be retained? The issue was treated only glancingly in the pages of *Kawkab America*, when it extolled the "beauty" of wearing the fez or reminded people of the beauty of the Arabic language. The difficulties of choosing must have been manifested within the family as well as in the community; at a much later date the debate was brought to the public (in English) in the pages of *The Syrian World*.[77] George A. Ferris, a Syrian American lawyer, wrote, "does it [the success of the Syrians] not point unerringly to the conclusion that as our contacts broaden

[76] "Another Critic of Our Schools," *The New York Press*, January 3, 1899.
[77] Mokarzel 1928: 36.

we are bound in the process of time to lose our racial identity?"[78] As the initial epigraphs to this book suggest, the process of assimilation was seen as a loss of Syrian or Arab culture. Gualtieri[79] treats this process as a correlate to Syrians seeking to be seen as "white."

The Syrians were fully aware of and deplored in print the moral failures of Americans, but they also criticized their own. The eminent men of the community tried hard to curb the worst of their countrymen's behavior because they believed that Americans would generalize the bad behavior to all members of the Syrian community and they were extremely anxious to be accepted in their new land. Sharp dealing by Syrian businessmen was not condemned, but their cursing in public was. Almost every admonition from the *Kawkab America* and *Al Hoda* editors, as well as those from letter writers, concluded with the sentiment, "We must not behave like this because Americans will generalize this bad behavior to all Syrians and think the worst of us." Presbyterian missionaries in Syria were aghast at the Syrians' deceptive business practices in the United States, believing that they had been "corrupted" in America.

Much as American reporters would like to have seen the exotic in this population, in fact there was not much to report. The exotic aspects of the culture that the Americans did see were ones that were out in the open: the fez-wearing men smoking *narghile*s and playing backgammon amid tapestry-covered divans; the odd food served in their restaurants; the women with their muslin veils; and the Oriental goods they sold. Many of these Oriental touches were put on for the purpose of beguiling the Americans; the Syrians knew full well how interested the reporters and tourists were in these aspects of Syrian life. They also knew that publicity was good for business; if strangers came down to Washington Street to see the men in fezzes, so much the better: they might also buy goods. The Syrians also offered to the unsuspecting American a much more flamboyant version of Orientalist fantasy in their smoking parlors, Turkish theaters, Streets of Cairo, Mohammedan Wedding Ceremonies, and Holy Land goods (whether or not manufactured on Greenwich Street). They "played east" whenever it suited them.

Syrians thus responded to the Americans' stereotypes in two ways: they strove to prove them wrong about their foreignness by becoming more American than the Americans, and they exaggerated that foreignness by playing

[78] Ferris 1929: 7.

[79] Gualtieri 2009.

east for the sake of selling themselves or goods (or a bill of goods, whichever the reader prefers). In this first generation, both these performances required practice: they studied the American way of life in order to emulate it, and they boned up on the "Oriental" way of life in order to exploit it.

Yet story after story attests to the rapid dilution of Middle Eastern culture within the Colony. In one rather sad article in *Kawkab America*, a Syrian advised other Syrians to lose many of their conversational habits, such as asking people about their families, making small talk, or asking people about how they are doing financially. The Americans, he said, are too busy for such niceties and want to get straight to the point.[80] The second generation of immigrants often spoke no Arabic, attended American churches (perhaps because they could not understand services in Arabic), went to American universities, married for love, and moved to the suburbs or the West. Arabic newspapers in New York lasted only as long as the first generation of immigrants stayed alive; new immigration was reduced to almost nothing after the 1924 quota went into effect, essentially preventing new Arabic-speaking peoples from entering, so the audience for anything in Arabic decreased precipitously. Very few first-generation immigrants were concerned with teaching their children Arabic, and the children were anxious not to stand out in American schools. At the same time, the Orientalist fad of the late nineteenth century quickly faded, and Syrians' presentations of their Arab selves disappeared, leaving only the assimilated part.

Many immigrants kept close ties to their homeland; they went back and forth regularly and sent money to their villages to build schools, install electricity, pay for children's schooling, or simply to supplement the income of family members who stayed behind. Many Syrian American families proudly tell a story about what their patriarch did for the home village. The Immigration Commission sent a delegation to Syria in 1907; the report stated, "They [the Syrian immigrants] send more money per capita than the immigrants of any other nationality. Between Beirut and Damascus, one sees more houses built with American money than one sees in a trip in South Italy five times as long."[81] A Presbyterian missionary in Hadath said, "Three-fourths of the present village people are living in homes built with American money."[82]

In this country, the immigrant's household became a magnet for other

[80] *Kawkab America,* October 5, 1894.

[81] Quoted in Ansara 1931: 44.

[82] *Presbyterian Letters,* Harris to Ellinwood, September 25, 1893.

family members from the old country, not just the immediate family who may have followed the first immigrant but also extended family: in-laws, cousins, nephews, and nieces. At various times in my maternal grandfather, F.M. Jabara's, house in Brooklyn, for example, the following people lived with the family for extended periods of time: one of F.M.'s brothers when the brother was still single; the same brother and his wife after he married (they had their first child there); a nephew (the son of one of my grandfather's brothers who had stayed in Syria); my grandmother's sister; my grandmother's niece (the daughter of a sister who stayed in Syria); her sister's sister-in-law; and (for more than two decades) my grandmother's mother. My grandfather was recognized as the best situated member of the two families, and it was his duty to house, take care of, and find jobs for these relatives. Many of the young men who passed through ended up working for him in one capacity or another, and my grandfather safely married the girls (whether of his family or my grandmother's) to appropriate young Syrian men.

Other immigrants apparently cut all ties. The "plea" section of *Kawkab America*, in which people advertised for information about their lost relatives, poignantly attests to this. Just to give one extraordinary example, George Saba, a New York merchant hailing from Amioun, had lost touch with his brother Nicola for twelve years. George told the story in American newspapers—where he claimed that Nicola was due for a large inheritance, if he could only be found—and in *Kawkab America*. Lo and behold, he was found, alive and well and doing business in Texas. George was overjoyed and looked forward to their reunion, but it never took place. Nicola later reportedly shot and killed another Syrian at the 1904 St. Louis World's Fair in a dispute over twenty cents and fled to Cairo. Perhaps he had never wanted to be found.

My paternal grandfather, Joseph, was another one who cut all ties with his homeland. He was never naturalized, apparently because he didn't need a passport. He never visited Syria—never left the United States for that matter—and never spoke about his relatives. He apparently had a brother in Denver and a sister who remained in Syria, neither of whom were ever mentioned; my father found out quite by chance that he had a cousin. No family members came to visit or to stay.

It remains a mystery as to why some people did cut all ties. Were they escaping some cruel Muslim overlord, as many claimed, a criminal prosecution in Syria, or some family problem? Or were they simply declaring their independence from the world they left behind and immersing themselves, heart and soul, in their adopted country? Did this cutting of ties lead to, or correlate with, more rapid or more complete assimilation in this country? It is hard to know. Certainly if one compares my father's family with my mother's, there were striking differences. There were many more "American" marriages on my father's side (there were none on my mother's); the family lived some distance from the South Ferry community;[83] the women of the second generation became professionals to support the family; and several of the men of the second generation followed career paths that were unusual in the Syrian milieu. But there is no obvious causal relationship between severing ties and assimilation, and a sample of one is too small to draw any conclusions.

## Myth and Reality

It is not surprising that the stories told about the Syrian immigrant experience by the Syrians themselves contain elements of both truth and falsehood. To call them all myths, however, trivializes the very real successes that the Syrians achieved. There is no doubt that an inordinate number struck out on their own, established businesses, bought houses, and made satisfying lives for themselves and their families. Were these successes as great as their descendants believed? Probably not. In the first place, the wealth in the community was never more than modest. No member of the nineteenth-century community became a millionaire, much less a multimillionaire, the breathless prose of American commentators notwithstanding. In the second place, their wealth was in many cases ephemeral, both during the entrepreneur's lifetime and over the course of the succeeding generations. The second and third generations, although they sometimes moved into professions such as law, engineering, and medicine, rarely maintained or achieved the kind of self-made success that seemed to distinguish our ancestors from many other immigrant groups. Their much-touted entrepreneurial spirit and trading acumen that were said to derive from their Phoenician heritage were not much in evidence in the second generation.

The first-generation Syrians in New York then, despite their self-ascribed exceptionalism, were not much different from other immigrant groups who came to the United States. They succeeded or didn't, became more or less assimilated, and stayed or went home. They lived together until they no longer felt the need to do so.

---

[83] "We had moved away from the Lebanese ghetto of Atlantic Avenue...." Jacobs 1991: 25.

Like all immigrants, though, they were remarkable men and women who traveled 5,000 miles to face an uncertain future and make new lives for themselves and their families. If the nineteenth-century Syrian Colony produced no Carnegies or Conrads, it did leave a lasting mark both on the Middle East and on the members' adoptive country. Lebanese villages still have houses built by money sent from America. More important, the Syrian diaspora helped catalyze the intellectual ferment—both political and literary—that took place in the Middle East in the early twentieth century, and in that way changed the course of history of the region, for good or ill. The Syrian pioneers also opened the American door to Arabs; they managed to keep that door open in the early twentieth century when immigrant groups from Eastern Europe and Asia were effectively barred. They accomplished this by working together and never giving up. Newer immigrants from the Middle East continue to be able to walk through that door, despite the convulsions of September 11th. New York's fabric is made up of the warp of its citizens and the weft of immigrant groups, and the nineteenth-century Syrians were one unbreakable thread in that fabric.

## Biographical Sketches Of People Mentioned In The Text

Note: This list includes only those people who lived in New York City in the nineteenth century; marriages that took place after 1900, or family members who came or were born after 1900 are not included. Family members living outside of New York City are not included. Some people mentioned in the text, but about whom we have little or no information, are not listed. A forward slash (/) represents alternative names, dates, and/or religions. See http://bit.ly/LJacobs for a complete list of nineteenth-century residents.

**ABALAN/ABLAN Assaf** *Born*: 1859 (Batroun). *Imm:* 1889. *Wife:* Affify Abu Khatar. *Rel:* Maronite.

**ABBOUD Moussa/Moses** *Born*: 1867 (Jaita?). *Imm:* 1890. *Wife:* Mary.

**ABDELNOUR Cesar D.** *Born*: 1883. *Imm:* 1897. *Parent(s):* Dimitri Abdelnour, *Sibling(s):* Abraham, Basil, Nicola, Mary Hinkaty.

**ABD-EL-NOUR John** *Born*: 1852 (Damascus), *Died:* 1931 (CA). *Imm:* 1880. *Wife:* Selma Gobreen, *Child(ren):* Hector. *Rel:* Orthodox.

**ABD-EL-NOUR Selma Gobreen** *Born*: 1866 (Zahleh). *Imm:* 1884. *Husband:* John, *Child(ren):* Hector, *Sibling(s):* Assad, Tewfiq, Hannah Maloof, Chasnie/Shahineh. *Rel:* Orthodox.

**ABDOO Tanious George** *Born*: 1867 (Baskinta). *Imm:* 1890. *Wife:* Zahia Elias, *Parent(s):* Gelantrona, *Sibling(s):* George. *Rel:* Maronite.

**ABOUSLEMAN Elias R.** *Born*: 1860 (Baabda). *Imm:* 1888. *Wife:* Yasmine Abousleman? *Child(ren):* Mariam, Nassif, Marie, *Sibling(s):* Michael.

**ANDALAFT Alexander Gabriel** *Born*: 1870 (Damascus), *Died:* 1929 (MO). *Imm:* 1888. *Wife:* Frieda Seidensticker, *Child(ren):* Edward. *Rel:* Orthodox.

**ARACHTINGI Alexander J.** *Born*: 1867 (Smyrna). *Imm:* 1896. *Parent(s):* Mary, *Sibling(s):* August, Jeanne, Corinne, Mary, Henry, Michel.

**ARBEELY Nageeb Joseph** *Born*: 1861 (Damascus), *Died:* 1904 (NYC). *Imm:* 1878. *Wife:* Marie N. Dilopoulo, *Parent(s):* Yusef and Mary Arbeely, *Child(ren):* Isabel S., Marguerite, Olga, George, *Sibling(s):* Abraham, Khaleel, Fadlallah, Habeeb, Nasseem, Amelia. *Rel:* Orthodox.

**ATTA Lotfallah** *Born*: 1864 (Beirut/Tyre). *Imm:* 1886. *Rel:* Maronite.

**AWAD Gabriel/Gibran** *Born*: 1869 (Homs), *Died:* 1948 (NYC). *Imm:* 1896. *Wife:* Zakia Shogri, *Parent(s):* Atouf Shweiry, *Child(ren):* Wadie, William, *Sibling(s):* Rafika, Essa, Nicola, Aref. *Rel:* Orthodox.

**AYOOB Joseph** *Born*: 1870. *Imm:* 1890. *Wife:* Hafeza Maloof, *Child(ren):* Isabel/Victoria, Fareed, Halim/Patrick. *Rel:* Melkite.

**AZEEZ Tannous** *Born*: 1850 (Beirut), *Died:* 1905 (NYC). *Imm:* 1891. *Wife:* Julia Thabet?, *Child(ren):* Marie el Khoury, Alice Azeez. *Rel:* Protestant?

**BADDOUR Rasheed/Richard S.** *Born*: 1862 (Hamana), *Died:* 1934 (NYC). *Imm:* 1895. *Sibling(s):* Joseph, Louis, Sultana. *Rel:* Maronite.

**BALESH Assad** *Born*: 1862, *Died:* 1934 (NYC). *Imm:* 1892. *Wife:* Amelia, *Child(ren):* Jameel.

**BALESH Yusef** *Born*: 1868 (Zahleh). *Imm:* 1888. *Wife:* Anjoul, *Child(ren):* Fouad, Elias, Jacob, *Sibling(s):* Shafika Balesh Geha.

**BARBOUR Najib G.** *Born*: 1860 (Beirut), *Died:* 1949 (NYC). *Imm:* 1880. *Rel:* Orthodox.

**BARDWIL George Elias** *Born*: 1880 (Zahleh). *Imm:* 1892. *Sibling(s):* Ameen. *Rel:* Melkite.

**BASHA Tanious Ghannoum** *Born*: 1845 (Baalbek), *Died:* 1925 (NYC). *Imm:* 1885. *Wife:* Mariam Salloum, *Child(ren):* Rose, Shafik, Mountaha, Faddouk. *Rel:* Melkite.

**BATAL Ameen H.** *Born*: 1860 (Damascus), *Died:* 1948 (MA). *Imm:* 1888. *Wife:* Rosa Estefan, *Child(ren):* Esther, Isabel. *Rel:* Melkite.

**BEN ALI Hassan** *Born*: 1863 (Agadir), *Died:* 1914 (NYC). *Imm:* 1884. *Rel:* Muslim?

**BESHEWATE Abraham** *Born*: 1852 (Zahleh), *Died:* 1923 (CA). *Imm:* 1889. *Sibling(s):* Khalil, Salina Sayeg. *Rel:* Melkite.

**BISKINTY Constantine G.** *Born*: 1860 (Hesbaya), *Died:* 1916 (NYC). *Imm:* 1888. *Wife:* Martha Ghosn, *Child(ren):* Thomas/Tawfeeq, Mary, Selma, Gabriel, David C., Emilia, *Sibling(s):* David *Rel:* Orthodox/Protestant.

**BOUTROSS Makhoul/Michael** *Born*: 1838 (Zahleh), *Died:* abt 1916. *Imm:* 1889/1894/1899. *Wife:* Mariam, *Child(ren):* Najeeb, Emily, John, George, Nellie, Peter, Paul, Amelia, Hannie. *Rel:* Melkite.

**CHERIFF Hadji** *Born*: 1860 (Sus). *Imm:* 1883. *Wife:* Henrietta Athelda. *Rel:* Muslim?

**DAAS Abdallah S.** *Born*: 1868 (Rashaya), *Died:* 1962 (NYC). *Imm:* 1891. *Wife:* Helen, *Sibling(s):* Bedawiyeh. *Rel:* Orthodox/Protestant.

**DAHER Beshara** *Born*: 1853 (Zahleh). *Imm:* 1890. *Wife:* Cecilia Haddad, *Child(ren):* Affifie Ganim, Marie, Solomon, Yusef, Shafia, Elias, Emily, George, *Sibling(s):* Elias? *Rel:* Maronite.

**DAMMOUS Shibli Nassif** *Born*: 1871 (Zahleh). *Imm:* 1889. *Wife:* Mary Beshara. *Rel:* Orthodox.

**DAOUD Habeeb** *Born*: 1843 (Zahleh). *Imm:* 1890. *Child(ren):* Sophie Shishim Mokarzel Cressaty, Sarah Birdsall, Emeline Axem, *Sibling(s):* Heilani, Muossa? *Rel:* Maronite.

**DAOUD Muossa A.** *Born*: 1869 (Zahleh), *Died:* abt 1945 (NYC). *Imm:* 1889. *Sibling(s):* Heilani, Habeeb?

**DAVIDS Nellie C.H.** *Born*: 1873. *Imm:* 1891. *Husband:* Clarence, *Child(ren):* son.

**DIAB Najeeb Moussa** *Born*: 1870 (Rumieh), *Died:* 1936 (NYC). *Imm:* 1893. *Wife:* Katherine Saba, *Child(ren):* Athena, Rosa, Dora, Ida. *Rel:* Orthodox.

**DOWALIBY Salim Abadalla** *Born* 1878 (Zahleh), *Died* 1936 (NYC). *Imm:* 1896. *Wife:* Yasmine George, *Child(ren):* Hanna, Najla, *Sibling(s):* Michael A. *Rel:* Melkite.

**ELIAS Salim** *Born*: 1851 (Baskinta), *Died:* 1911 (NYC). *Imm:* 1885. *Wife:* Shamooney, *Child(ren):* Salim, Abdalla, Angela, Camille, Elias, Eugenia, Joseph, *Sibling(s):* Zakia Elias Abdoo. *Rel:* Maronite.

**FAGHER Maroon T.** *Born*: 1867. *Imm:* 1890. *Wife:* Wardiah Acoory, *Child(ren):* Antonio, James, Charles, *Sibling(s):* Tannous. *Rel:* Maronite.

**FAOUR Daniel Joseph** *Born*: 1867 (Hadath al Jaba), *Died:* 1919 (NYC). *Imm:* 1891. *Wife:* Filomena Coury, *Sibling(s):* Dominick, George. *Rel:* Maronite.

**FERRIS Khattar/Charles** *Born*: 1847 (Tyre). *Imm:* 1890. *Wife:* Amelia Edeb, *Child(ren):* Eddie, Emma, Eva, Fred, George, Mary, May, Myrna. *Rel:* Maronite.

**FERZAN Fares Anton** *Born*: 1864 (Zahleh/Zouk). *Imm:* 1884. *Wife:* Sassoul N. Maloof, *Sibling(s):* Elias. *Rel:* Maronite.

**FLUTIE Elias Assad** *Born*: 1876 (Beirut). *Imm:* 1893. *Sibling(s):* Fareeda A. *Rel:* Protestant.

**FORZLY Selim Mansour** *Born*: 1843 (Damascus), *Died:* 1920 (NYC). *Imm:* 1893. *Wife:* Selma Daoun, *Child(ren):* Beatrice, George, Margaret, Nellie, Nicholas, *Sibling(s):* Solomon, Thomas. *Rel:* Orthodox.

**FREIJE Kalil G.** *Born*: 1865 (Zahleh). *Imm:* 1892. *Sibling(s):* Nageeb. *Rel:* Orthodox.

**FULEIHAN David A.** *Born*: 1868 (Ain Zehalta), *Died:* 1959 (NJ). *Imm:* 1892. *Sibling(s):* Naoum. *Rel:* Protestant.

**GANIM Beshara** *Born*: 1873 (Baskinta). *Imm:* 1889. *Wife:* Rasheeda, *Parent(s):* Salim Beshara, *Sibling(s):* Shakir, Asad. *Rel:* Maronite.

**GEHA Khalil J.** *Born*: 1860 (Bishmezzine). *Imm:* 1889. *Wife:* Labiba Azra/Azar? *Sibling(s):* Spiridon, Gabriel. *Rel:* Orthodox/Melkite.

**GHIZ Nohman** *Born*: 1864 (Beirut), *Died:* 1940 (NYC). *Imm:* 1881. *Wife:* Malake Bonnet, *Child(ren):* George, Adele, *Sibling(s):* Kalil, Salim. *Rel:* Orthodox.

**HADDAD Ameen F.** *Born*: 1865 (Beirut). *Imm:* 1888. *Parent(s):* Wadieh, *Sibling(s):* Saleem, Nayef. *Rel:* Protestant.

**HADDAD John** *Born*: 1850. *Imm:* 1892. *Wife:* Emmel Shehadi, *Child(ren):* Salem, Helen, Wassila, Najeeb.

**HADDAD Rizq Gantous** *Born*: 1873 (Jdeideh Marjayoun), *Died:* 1943 (NYC). *Imm:* 1900. *Rel:* Orthodox.

**HAJJ, Elias el** *Born*: 1874. *Imm:* 1891. *Sibling(s):* Yusef.

**HAKIM George** *Born*: 1853 (Aleppo). *Imm:* 1899. *Wife:* Allina, *Child(ren):* Adma, Christina, Edmund, John, Mary, Michael.

**HALABY Elias** *Born*: 1844 (Damascus), *Died:* 1897 (NYC). *Imm:* 1892. *Wife:* Almaz, *Child(ren):* George, Habeeb, Camille, Najeeb, Rosie, Isabella. *Rel:* Orthodox.

**HAMMWY/HAMOUI Khalil O.** *Born*: 1860, *Died:* 1900? (NYC). *Imm:* 1885. *Wife:* Catherine, *Child(ren):* Jamilie Tadross, Isaac, Adla, Lizzie? *Rel:* Orthodox.

**HASSEY Habib** *Born*: 1866 (Zahleh). *Imm:* 1893. *Child(ren):* Farid. *Rel:* Maronite.

**HATEM Nahoom** *Born*: 1879 (Hamana), *Died:* 1943 (NYC). *Imm:* 1897. *Rel:* Maronite.

**HAWAWEENY Raphael M.** *Born*: 1859 (Damascus), *Died:* 1915 (NYC). *Imm:* 1895. *Sibling(s):* Selim. *Rel:* Orthodox.

**HAWIE Ameen S.** *Born*: 1873 (Al Shobr). *Imm:* 1895. *Sibling(s):* Michael, Nahoom.

**HAYEK Souma George el** *Born*: 1872 (Baabda). *Imm:* 1888. *Sibling(s):* Said, Tannous, Fatneh, Mary Mattar, Joseph, Anissa. *Rel:* Maronite.

**HOMSY Nahmy E.** *Born*: 1871 (Tyre), *Died:* 1929 (NYC). *Imm:* 1894.

**ISAAC Michael** *Born*: 1872? (Hesbaya), *Died:* 1913 (NYC). *Wife:* Sayeda Wahby, *Child(ren):* Jameel, a daughter. *Rel:* Orthodox.

**JABBOUR Abdallah** *Born*: 1858, *Died:* 1938 (NYC). *Imm:* 1891. *Wife:* Bahiyyeh.

**JABOUR George** *Born*: 1875 (Constantinople). *Imm:* 1893. *Wife:* Julia Moutran. *Rel:* Maronite.

**JACOBS Afiffie Forzly** *Born*: 1883 (Zahleh), *Died:* 1949 (Buffalo). *Imm:* 1890. *Husband:* Joseph Jacobs, *Parent(s):* Solomon Forzly and Mary Malek, *Child(ren):* George, Margaret, *Sibling(s):* Rose Forzly Trad, Elias Forzly. *Rel:* Orthodox, converted to Maronite.

**JUREIDINI Said Khalil** *Born*: 1866 (Beirut). *Imm:* 1891. *Sibling(s):* Michael.

**KALIL, Alexander Abu** *Born*: 1868 (Mashgara), *Died:* 1903 (NYC). *Imm:* 1889. *Sibling(s):* Shikri, Sophie, Gabriel, Said/Sydney, Helen. *Rel:* Protestant.

**KAYDOUH Michael Deeb** *Born*: 1880 (Tripoli), *Died:* 1931 (NYC). *Imm:* 1891. *Parent(s):* Mariam Tadross, *Sibling(s):* Yinna/Minnie Merhige, Bahia, Nadia. *Rel:* Orthodox.

**KHAYAT Azeez** *Born*: 1876 (Tyre). *Imm:* 1894. *Wife:* Mariam Farah, *Child(ren):* Victor, Lucy, Suzette, *Sibling(s):* John. *Rel:* Melkite.

**KHOURY Antoine L.** *Born*: 1878 (Tripoli). *Imm:* 1891. *Sibling(s):* Habeeb.

**KHOURY Aref H.** *Born*: 1880 (Homs). *Imm:* 1895. *Wife:* Saleemy Nasrallah, *Sibling(s):* Naji.

**KHOURY Assad George** *Born*: 1860. *Imm:* 1885. *Wives*: Annie E. Sheeny and Katherine Callahan.

**KHOURY Esau/Issa M. el-** *Born*: 1879, *Died:* 1904 (NYC). *Wife:* Marie T. Azeez.

**KHOURY Peter** *Born*: 1873 (Jezzine). *Imm:* 1889. *Parent(s):* Mary.

**KIRDAHY Elias Tannous** *Born*: 1875 (Tyre), *Died:* 1929 (NYC). *Imm:* 1894. *Rel:* Maronite.

**KISBANY Selim Habib** *Born*: 1870 (Kefr Shia), *Died:* 1951 (NYC). *Imm:* 1893. *Wife:* Anissa. *Rel:* Protestant.

**KORANY Hannah Kisbany** *Born*: 1871 (Beirut), *Died:* 1898 (Beirut). *Imm:* 1893. *Husband:* Ameen. *Rel:* Protestant.

**KORKEMAS Peter/Boutros/Petrus** *Born*: 1848 (Ghiballah). *Imm:* 1890. *Nephews*: Gabriel, Estefan. *Rel:* Maronite.

**KORKEMAS Richard** *Born*: 1879 (Ghiballah?). *Rel:* Maronite.

**LIAN Anissa** *Born*: 1870 (Zahleh), *Died:* 1925 (NYC). *Imm:* 1899. *Husband:* Abdullah, *Child(ren):* Abraham, Raji, Nabiha, William, Wadeah, Helen, Sahid. *Rel:* Melkite.

**LUTFY Abdow** *Born*: 1845 (Zahleh), *Died:* 1923 (NYC). *Imm:* 1888. *Wife:* Tarkman/Marta, *Child(ren):* Shafika Macksoud, Ameen, Antoun, Deeb, Michel, *Nephew*: Abdullah, *Sibling(s):* Ramza Lutfy Macksoud. *Rel:* Orthodox.

**MACKSOUD Elias Joseph** *Born*: 1873 (Zahleh). *Imm:* 1893. *Wife:* Shafika Lutfy, *Parent(s):* Joseph and Susane Macsoud, *Sibling(s):* Abraham, Gabriel, Alexander, Albert, Jebdeh, Lutfy. *Rel:* Orthodox.

**MACSOUD Saleem N.** *Born*: 1852 (Beirut). *Imm:* 1899. *Wife:* Malake/Mary, *Child(ren):* Nicolas, Wadie, Jamilie, George, Adele, Adma, Jean.

**MALHAMI George J.** *Born*: 1850 (Jezzine), *Died:* 1929 (NYC). *Imm:* 1889. *Wife:* Jameely Rahaim, *Child(ren):* Gabriel, Charles, Hortense, David. *Rel:* Maronite.

**MALLOUF Hannah G.** *Born*: 1864 (Beirut). *Imm:* 1888. *Child(ren):* Najeeb, Naseem.

**MALLOUK Elias N.** *Born*: 1884 (Damascus). *Imm:* 1892. *Parent(s):* Nicola Mallouk and Marie Homsy, *Sibling(s):* Andrew, Constantine, Joseph. Rose, Saleem, Salma, Shafia. *Rel:* Orthodox.

**MALLOUK Elias M.** *Born*: 1856 (Damascus). *Imm:* 1891. *Child(ren):* Tewfik, Anthony, James, Joseph, Mariam, *Sibling(s):* Najeeb, Cesar. *Rel:* Orthodox.

**MALOOF Joseph/Yusef Namaan** *Born*: 1870 (Zahleh). *Imm:* 1892. *Parent(s):* Namaan Maloof, *Sibling(s):* Joseph, Habeeb. *Rel:* Melkite/Maronite.

**MALOOF Najeeb S.** *Born*: 1865 (Zahleh), *Died:* 1916 (NYC). *Imm:* 1891. *Wife:* Affifie. *Rel:* Melkite.

**MALOOF Tamer Kanaan** *Born*: 1875 (Kafr Aqab), *Died:* 1953 (AZ). *Imm:* 1900. *Child(ren):* Eileen. *Rel:* Orthodox.

**MANSOUR Nassif** *Born*: 1864. *Imm:* 1888. *Wife:* Sultana Habeeb Lutfy, *Child(ren):* Elias, Rose, Shafika, Ibrahim. *Rel:* Melkite.

**MANSOUR Tannous** *Born*: 1856. *Imm:* 1883. *Child(ren):* Kalil, Marwa Rizk.

**MEJDELANI Wadie** *Born*: 1880. *Imm:* 1895. *Sibling(s):* Elias. *Rel:* Orthodox.

**MERHIGE Solomon Daher** *Born*: 1863 (Tripoli). *Imm:* 1893. *Wife:* Mary, *Child(ren):* Nistas, Jameely, Aneesa, Jad. Raji. Rizkallah, Julia, *Sibling(s):* Nadjim, Nahoum, Lydia Tadross. *Rel:* Protestant

**MIKWEE Salim J.** *Born*: 1868. *Imm:* 1889. *Wife:* Lucia Ghattas Herro, *Child(ren):* Assisa, Azeez, Lillie. *Rel:* Melkite.

**MILKIE Foutine Hayek** *Born*: 1852 (Bishmezzine), *Died:* 1937 (NYC). *Imm:* 1897. *Child(ren):* Asad George, Abla, Katherine, Jamilie. *Rel:* Orthodox.

**MOGHABGHAB Faddoul** *Born*: 1866 (Ain Zehalta), *Died:* 1956 (FL). *Imm:* 1892. *Sibling(s):* Naoum. *Rel:* Protestant.

**MOGHABGHAB Saleem Assad** *Born*: 1876 (Ain Zehalta), *Died:* 1930 (PA). *Imm:* 1893. *Wife:* Nabeeha Moutran, *Sibling(s):* Rasheed, Najeeb, Kaleel, Mariam Habib. *Rel:* Protestant.

**MOKARZEL Naoum Anton** *Born*: 1866 (Freike), *Died:* 1932 (France). *Imm:* 1889. *Wife:* Sofia Daoud Shishim, *Parent(s):* Barbara Akl, *Sibling(s):* Salloum, Catherine, Elizabeth Rahid. *Rel:* Maronite.

**MOSHY Joseph/Yusef T.** *Born*: 1870 (Jezzine). *Imm:* 1890. *Wife:* Habouba/Amma, *Sibling(s):* Maneera Moshy Rahaim, Saad. *Rel:* Maronite.

**MOUAKAD Ibrahim H.** *Born*: 1865 (Damascus), *Died:* 1943 (NYC). *Imm:* 1888. *Wife:* Adele Zainey, *Child(ren):* Abraham, Violet, *Sibling(s):* Ibrahim, Elias. *Rel:* Melkite.

**MOUSSI Elias M.** *Born*: 1860. *Imm:* 1888. *Wife:* Mahabe, *Child(ren):* Mikhail, Charles, Thomas, Nellie, Anne, Naomi, Annie. *Rel:* Maronite.

**MUSSAWIR Abdulmassih G.** *Born*: 1869, *Died:* 1940 (NYC). *Imm:* 1891. *Wife:* Mohalla/Julia? *Rel:* Maronite.

**NAFASH Malake Cassatly/Assatly** *Born*: 1878 (Damascus), *Died:* 1939 (NYC). *Imm:* 1896. *Rel:* Orthodox.

**NAHAS Hatem** *Born*: 1875 (Hama), *Died:* 1940 (NYC). *Imm:* 1898.

**NAJA Najeeb** *Born*: 1872 (Bayt Shebab). *Rel:* Maronite.

**NASSER Shakir** *Born*: 1862 (Shweir), *Died:* 1916 (NYC). *Imm:* 1889. *Wife:*

Adma Yassoos, *Parent(s):* Katia, *Child(ren):* Michael, Adele. *Rel:* Melkite.

**NOHRA/NOAH Joseph** *Born*: 1860. *Imm:* 1884. *Wife:* Mary, *Child(ren):* Frank, Mary, Winnie, Norah, Nicholas. *Rel:*Maronite.

**OUSSANI Joseph T.** *Born*: 1866 (Baghdad), *Died:* 1934 (NYC). *Imm:* 1893. *Wife:* Margaret Shea, *Parent(s):* Catherine, *Sibling(s):* Theresa, Yakoob, John, Peter, Gabriel. *Rel:* Chaldean.

**PETRAKIAN Habeeb** *Born*: 1863. *Imm:* 1891. *Sibling(s):* Arteen. *Rel:* Armenian.

**RAHAIM Shukri Salloum** *Born*: 1874 (Jezzine). *Imm:* 1895. *Wife:* Maneera Moshy, *Sibling(s):* Tannous, David, Jameely Rahaim Malhami, Joseph. *Rel:* Maronite.

**RAHAL Elias M.** *Born*: 1879, *Died:* 1939 (NYC). *Imm:* 1895.

**REESHA Elias L.** *Born*: 1880. *Imm:* 1897. *Sibling(s):* Kaleel, Miriam Reesha Daher, Asma.

**RIHANI Fares A.** *Born*: 1855 (Freike), *Died:* 1902 (NYC). *Imm:* 1889. *Wife:* Anissa Tohmeh, *Child(ren):* Joseph, Ameen, Saada, Adele, Assad, Albert, *Sibling(s):* Abdow. *Rel:* Maronite.

**RIHBANY Abraham** Mitry *Born*: 1869 (Shweir/Betater), *Died:* 1944 (CT). *Imm:* 1891. *Rel:* Orthodox/Protestant.

**RUSTUM Mikhail** *Born*: 1849 (Shweir), *Died*: 1922 (NJ). *Imm:* 1891. *Wife:* Rougana, *Child(ren):* Asad, Wadie, Ernest, Shafik.

**SAAD Boutros/Petrus** *Born*: 1865 (Baskinta). *Imm:* 1887. *Wife:* Bader Nematollah, *Child(ren):* George, Rose, Milia, Salha. *Rel:* Maronite.

**SAADI Elias** *Born*: 1840 (Tripoli), *Died:* 1902 (NYC). *Imm:* 1899. *Wife:* Miriam, *Child(ren):* John, Josephine, Nessim, Nayeff. *Rel:* Protestant.

**SABA George** *Born*: 1869 (Amioun), *Died:* 1902 (NYC). *Imm:* 1885. *Sibling(s):* Daniel? Nicola. *Rel:* Maronite.

**SADALLAH Antoine Joseph** *Born*: 1878 (Baskinta), *Died:* 1947 (NYC). *Imm:* 1892. *Wife:* Barbara Karam, *Parent(s):* Joseph, *Child(ren):* Yusef, *Sibling(s):* Asad, Ibrahim, Jacob, Jamilie Mandour. *Rel:* Maronite.

**SAHADI Abraham Abdullah** *Born*: 1869, *Died:* 1951 (NYC). *Imm:* 1888. *Wife:* Zakia, *Sibling(s):* Ameen, Najeeb, Salim.

**SAMRA Nicola Abo** *Born*: 1869 (Hesbaya), *Died:* 1922 (NYC). *Imm:* 1899. *Wife:* Mariam Abo Reehan, *Child(ren):* Philip, Victor, Victoria, *Sibling(s):* Said, Sophie. *Rel:* Orthodox.

**SARBOUKH John/Hanna** *Born*: 1848 (Zahleh). *Imm:* 1892. *Wife:* Mary, *Child(ren):* Boutros, Monie, Moussa, Salem, Wadeah.

**SARKIS Salim S.** *Born*: 1866 (Beirut). *Imm:* 1899. *Wife:* Bahiyyeh, *Child(ren):* Najla.

**SAWAYA Najeeb A.** *Born*: 1870 (Damascus). *Imm:* 1897. *Wife:* Labiba Rizk, *Child(ren):* Nazaly/Mariam. *Rel:* Melkite.

**SHAHDAN Mannie Adaimy** *Born*: 1840 (Beirut). *Imm:* 1887. *Child(ren):* Elias, Adelia Saba, Nozha. *Rel:* Maronite/Melkite.

**SHAHEEN Assad/Assy** *Born*: 1850 (Gharbaniya). *Imm:* 1887. *Wife:* Habous, *Child(ren):* George, Assy, Tewfik/Thomas, Wadiah, Mannie. *Rel:* Maronite.

**SHEHAB Joseph** *Born*: 1871 (Bisbani), *Died:* 1933 (NYC). *Imm:* 1886. *Wife:* Natalie. *Rel:* Maronite.

**SHIBLEY Ameen A.** *Born*: 1867 (Beirut), *Died:* 1918 (NYC). *Imm:* 1893. *Parent(s):* Marah/Mary, *Sibling(s):* Anees, Samuel, Wadie, Nassib. *Rel:* Maronite.

**SHISHIM George** *Born*: 1880, *Died:* 1978 (CA). *Imm:* 1883. *Wife:* Frida Freike, *Child(ren):* George Freike (stepson).

**SHISHIM Sofia Daoud** *Born*: 1871 (Zahleh) *Died:* 1964 (CA). Imm. 1889. *Husbands*: Tannous Shishim, Naoum Mokarzel, *Parent(s):* Habeeb Daoud, *Sibling(s):* Emeline Axem, Sarah Birdsall. *Rel:* Maronite?

**SHOHFI John C.** *Born*: 1869, *Died:* 1930 (NYC). *Imm:* 1898. *Wife:* Rahmy Merhige, *Sibling(s):* Salim.

**SIRGANY Barbara G.** *Born*: 1845 (Zahleh), *Died:* 1905 (NYC). *Imm:* 1890. *Child(ren):* Ameen, Michael, Malake BouKhater? *Rel:* Melkite.

**SROUR Habib J.** *Born*: 1850. *Imm:* 1892. *Wife:* Almas Balesh, *Child(ren):* Wadiha, Najeeba Basha, Michael, Najeeb, *Sibling(s):* George.

**TADROSS Antoni/Tannous Rawady** *Born*: 1866 (Tripoli), *Died:* 1913 (NYC). *Imm:* 1884. *Wife:* Jamilie Hammwy, *Parent(s):* Farha Hayek, *Child(ren):* Nellie, Kaisar, Victoria, George, *Sibling(s):* Nami, Abdo, Helen Zahloute, Mariam Kaydouh, Catherine. *Rel:* Orthodox.

**TAHAR Hajji** *Born*: 1860 (Sus), *Died:* 1938 (NYC). *Imm:* 1883. *Wives*: Julia Doyle, Florence Hunter, *Child(ren):* May, Nora. *Rel:* Muslim?

**TANURI Abalan Abraham** *Born*: 1869 (Baskinta). *Imm:* 1888. *Wife:* Aziza, *Child(ren):* Abraham, *Sibling(s):* Sliman. *Rel:* Maronite.

**UNISS George Solomon** *Born*: 1875 (Shweifat). *Imm:* 1893. *Wife:* Alice Frinch (Protestant), *Sibling(s):* Selma Uniss Warner. *Rel:* Orthodox.

**YAMIN Kaiser S.** *Born*: 1869 (Sidon). *Imm:* 1888? *Wife:* Marie Dayrel, *Parent(s):* Solomon? *Sibling(s):* Habubi? *Rel:* Maronite.

**YAZAJI/YASAJI Alexander Selim** *Born*: 1874 (Damascus). *Imm:* 1892. *Rel:* Orthodox.

**ZAINEY Jamilie/Rusina/Regina** *Born*: 1868 (Egypt?). *Imm:* 1897. *Husband:* Abraham, *Child(ren):* Elias, Henry. *Rel:* Maronite.

**ZALOOM Farjallah A.** *Born*: 1848 (Aleppo), *Died:* 1903 (NYC). *Imm:* 1890. *Wife:* Adele, *Child(ren):* George Besheer, Joseph, Nasry, Salim, Alice, Clementine, Josephine. *Rel:* Melkite.

**ZREIK/ZUREIK Elias Kanaan** *Born*: 1860 (Mazah/Beirut), *Died:* 1933 (NYC). *Imm:* 1892. *Wife:* Nagham Nassar. *Rel:* Orthodox.

## BIBLIOGRAPHY

Abdelhady, Dalia. "Representing the Homeland: Lebanese Diasporic Notions of Home and Return in a Global Context." *Cultural Dynamics* 20.1 (2008): 53–72.

Abdou, Nagib. *Dr. Abdou's Travels in America and Commercial Directory of the Arabic Speaking People of the World.* Ed. Nagib Abdou. N.p., 1907–1910.

Abohatab, Georgette. "Reflections of the Syrian Orthodox Church while under the Russian Jurisdiction." April 1976. Unpublished ms.

Abraham, Sameer Y., and Nabeel Abraham, eds. *Arabs in the New World: Studies on Arab-American Communities.* Detroit: Wayne State University, Center for Urban Studies, 1983.

Akarli, Engin Deniz. "Ottoman Attitudes towards Lebanese Emigration, 1885–1910." In *The Lebanese in the World: A Century of Emigration*, ed. Albert Hourani and Nadeem Shehadi, 109. London: Center for Lebanese Studies, 1992.

Al Akl, F.M. *Until Summer Comes.* Springfield, Mass.: Pond-Ekberg Company, 1945.

American University of Beirut. *Directory of Alumni, 1870–1991.* Beirut: American University of Beirut, 1992.

Andrews, Mary. "The Syrians in America." MA thesis, Columbia University, 1951.

Anonymous. *American Newspaper Directory.* New York: Geo. P. Rowell & Company, 1894.

———. *Official Guide to the California Midwinter Exposition.* San Francisco: George Spalding & Co., 1894.

———. *Portrait Types of the Midway Plaisance.* St. Louis: N.D. Thompson, 1894.

———. *Nickerson's Illustrated Church, Musical, and School Directory.* Vol. 1. New York: Nickerson & Young, 1895.

———. *Yearbook.* New York: St. Bartholomew's Parish, 1901.

———. *Catalog of Copyright Entries, Part I, Books, Group I.* Volume 9, Issue 2 (1912).

Ansara, J.M. "The Immigration and Settlement of the Syrians." PhD dissertation, Harvard University, 1931.

Arbeely, Abraham J. *Al-Bakoorat al Gharbeyat fi Taleem Al-Lughat Al-En-*

*glezeyat (The First Occidental Fruit for the Teaching of English)*. New York: Oriental Publishing House, 1898. http://catalog.hathitrust.org/Record/011223258.

Arida, Nasib, and Sabri Andria. *Al-Taqwim Al-Suri Al-Amriki Wa-Dalil Al-Muhajirin (The Syrian American Directory Almanac)*. New York: Arida & Andria, 1930.

Atiyah, Edward. *An Arab Tells His Story: A Study in Loyalties*. London: John Murray, 1946.

Babbitt, B.T. *Grocers' Directory for the State of New York: Washing Made Easy, by the Use of B.T. Babbitt's Trademark Best Soap...for Sale by Grocers Everywhere: Manufactured Only by B.T. Babbitt, 64, 65, 66, 67, 68, 69, 70, 72, 74 Washington Street, New York*. New York: The Firm, 1870.

Baedeker, K. *Palestine et Syrie: Manuel Du Voyageur*. 2nd ed. Leipzig: Karl Baedeker, 1893.

Benson, Kathleen, and Philip M. Kayal, eds. *A Community of Many Worlds: Arab Americans in New York City*. New York: Museum of the City of New York; Syracuse, N.Y.: Syracuse University Press, 2002.

Bernstein, Rachel Amelia. "Boarding-House Keepers and Brothel Keepers in New York City, 1880–1910." PhD dissertation, Rutgers University, 1984.

Bier, Jess. "How Niqula Nasrallah Became John Jacob Astor: Syrian Emigrants aboard the Titanic and the Materiality of Language." *Journal of Linguistic Anthropology* 18.2 (2008): 171.

———. "Mapping the Archive for Arab American Women and Labor in the New York Metropolitan Area, 1880–1930." Unpublished ms. 2009.

Bishara, Kalil A. *The Origin of the Modern Syrian*. New York: Al-Hoda Publishing House, 1914.

Boosahda, Elizabeth. *Arab-American Faces and Voices: The Origins of an Immigrant Community*. Austin: University of Texas Press, 2003.

Buel, J.W. *The Magic City: A Massive Portfolio of Original Photographic Views of the Great World's Fair and Its Treasures of Art, Including a Vivid Representation of the Famous Midway Plaisance*. St. Louis: Historical Publishing Co., 1894.

Buonaventura, Wendy. *Serpent of the Nile: Women and Dance in the Arab World*. New York: Interlink Books, 1998.

Bush, Brian S. *Louisville's Southern Exposition: 1883–1887*. Charleston and London: History Press, 2011.

Carlisle, Rodney P. *The Arab Americans (Multicultural America)*. Facts on File, 2011.

Carlton, Donna. *Looking for Little Egypt*. Bloomington, Ind.: IDD Books, 1994.

Catlin, Louise Ensign. "The Americanizing of the Syrian South Ferry Colony." MA thesis, Columbia University, 1915.

Çelik, Zeynep. *Displaying the Orient: Architecture of Islam at Nineteenth-Century World's Fairs*. Berkeley: University of California Press, 1992.

Civantos, Christina. *Between Argentines and Arabs: Argentina, Orientalism, Arab Immigrants and the Writing of Identity*. Ed. Jorge J.E. Gracia and Rosemary Geisdorfer Feal. Latin American and Iberian Thought and Culture. Albany: SUNY Press, 2006.

Cole, William Isaac. *Immigrant Races in Massachusetts: The Syrians*. Boston: Massachusetts Department of Education, 1922(?).

Dillingham, William Paul. *Immigrants in Cities*. Vol. 2. Washington, D.C.: United States Immigration Commission (1907–1910), 1911.

DiNapoli, Mary Ann. "The Syrian-Lebanese Community of South Ferry, 1900–1977." MA thesis, Long Island University, 1977.

Dix, John A. *A History of the Parish of Trinity Church in the City of New York, Part V*. New York: Columbia University Press, 1950.

Duncan, Norman. *The Soul of the Street: Correlated Stories of the New York Syrian Quarter*. New York: McClure, Phillips & Co, 1900.

———. "A People from the East. " *Harper's* 106.631 (1903): 553–562.

Ekinci, Mehmet Ugur. "Reflections of the First Muslim Immigration to America in Ottoman Documents." In *Turkish Migration to the United States*, ed. A. Ceniz Balgamis and Kemal H. Karpat, 45–56. Madison: University of Wisconsin Press, 2008.

Elias, Leila. "The Impact of the Sinking of the Titanic on the New York Syrian Community of 1912: The Syrians Respond." *Arab Studies Quarterly* 27.1 (2005): 75–87.

Epstein, Lawrence J. *At the Edge of a Dream: The Story of Jewish Immigrants on New York's Lower East Side, 1880–1920*. San Francisco: John Wiley & Sons, 2007.

Farah, Mounir A. "The United States' Identity from Its Origin to 1876 in Syria." PhD dissertation, New York University, 1987.

Farshee, Louis. *The Way of the Emigrants: Badawi and Catherine Simon in America*. Bloomington, Ind.: AuthorHouse, 2010.

Fawaz, Leila. *Merchants and Migrants in Nineteenth-Century Beirut*. Cambridge, Mass.: Harvard University Press, 1983.

Feld, Allison, ed. *Middle Eastern Diaspora Communities in America: Proceed-*

*ings of the 17th Annual Summer Institute of the Joint Center for Near Eastern Studies of New York University and Princeton University*. New York: Hagop Kevorkian Center for Near Eastern Studies at New York University, 1996.

Felton, Ralph A. "A Sociological Survey of Syrians in Greater N.Y." MA thesis, Columbia University, 1912.

Ferris, George A. "Syrians' Future in America." *The Syrian World* 3.11 (1929): 3.

Foner, Nancy. "New York City: America's Classic Immigrant Gateway." In *Migrants to the Metropolis: The Rise of Immigrant Gateway Cities*, ed. Marie Price and Lisa Benton-Short, 52–67. Syracuse, N.Y.: Syracuse University Press, 2008.

Forzley, Bashara Kalil. *An Autobiography of Bashara Kalil Forzley*. Ed. Philip Forzley. Worcester, Mass.: [B.K. Forzley?], 1958.

Gilfoyle, Timothy J. "City of Eros: New York City, Prostitution, and the Commercialization of Sex, 1790–1920." PhD dissertation, Columbia University, 1987.

Gualtieri, Sarah. "Gendering the Chain Migration Thesis: Women and Syrian Transatlantic Migration, 1878–1924." *Comparative Studies of South Asia, Africa and the Middle East* 24.1 (2004): 67–78.

Gualtieri, Sarah M.A. *Between Arab and White: Race and Ethnicity in the Early Syrian American Diaspora*. Berkeley: University of California Press, 2009.

Haddad, Ameen F. Midhat Pasha Perfume; Young Lady Perfume. US Patent 43,008; 43,009. June 14, 1909.

Hagopian, Elaine C., and Ann Paden, eds. *The Arab-Americans*. Wilmette, Ill.: Medina University Press International, 1969.

Hatab, Helen Regina. "Syrian-American Ethnicity: Structure and Ideology in Transition." MA thesis, American University of Beirut, 1975.

Hawie, Ashad G. *The Rainbow Ends*. New York: T. Gaus' Sons, 1942.

Hay, Bryan. "Mishaps Brought Lebanese to Easton." *The Morning Call*, August 15, 1988.

Hitti, Philip Khuri. *The Syrians in America*. Piscataway, N.J.: Gorgias Press, 2005 (1924).

Houghton, Louise Seymour. "Syrians in the United States. Part I: Sources and Settlement; Part II: Business Activities; Part III: Intellectual and Social Status; Part IV: The Syrian as an American Citizen. " *The Survey* XXVI and XXVII (July 1, 1911; August 5, 1911; September 2, 1911; October 7, 1911): 480–495; 647–665; 786–803; 957–968. New York: Charity Organization Society.

Hourani, Albert, and Nadeem Shehadi, eds. *The Lebanese in the World: A Century of Emigration*. London: Centre for Lebanese Studies, 1992.

Hourani, Guita. "'Aqlah Brice Al Shidyaq: A Woman Peddler from Northern Lebanon." *Al Raida* XXIV (2007): 50–54.

Industrial Commission on Immigration and Education. *Reports of the Industrial Commission on Immigration, Including Testimony with Review and Digest, and Special Reports and on Education, Including Testimony, with Review and Digest, Vol. XV*. Ed. James H. Kyle. Washington, D.C.: US Government Printing Office, 1901.

Ipek, Nedim, and K. Tuncer Caglayan. "The Emigration from the Ottoman Empire to America." In *Turkish Migration to the United States*, ed. A. Ceniz Balgamis and Kemal H. Karpat, 29–43. Madison: University of Wisconsin Press, 2008.

Ismaeal, Hani. "Creating an Imagined Community: Self-Representation in an Arab-American Journal, The Syrian World, 1926–1935." PhD dissertation, Southern Illinois University, Carbondale, 2003.

Issa, Andre G. "The Life of Raphael Hawaweeny, Bishop of Brooklyn: 1860–1915." MTh thesis, St. Vladimir's Orthodox Theological Seminary, 1991.

Issawi, Charles. *The Fertile Crescent, 1800–1914: A Documentary Economic History*. New York: Oxford University Press.

Ives, Halsey. *The Dream City: A Portfolio of Photographic Views of the World's Columbian Exposition*. St. Louis: Published weekly by N.D. Thompson Publishing Co., 1893.

Jacobs, Joseph J. *The Anatomy of an Entrepreneur: Family, Culture, and Ethics*. San Francisco: ICS Press, 1991.

Johnson, Alfred Sidney, et al. *The Cyclopedic Review of Current History*. 3 Vols. Garretson, Cox & Company, 1893–1894.

Karpat, Kemal H. "The Ottoman Emigration to America, 1860–1914." *International Journal of Middle East Studies* 17.2 (1985): 175–209.

Kasaba, Kathie Friedman. "'To Become a Person': Immigrant Women's Experiences of Gender, Ethnicity, and Work, New York, 1870–1924." PhD dissertation, State University of New York at Binghamton, 1992.

Katibah, Habib Ibrahim. "Syrian-Americans." In *One America, the History, Contributions, and Present Problems of Our Racial and National Minorities*, ed. Francis J. Brown and Joseph S. Roucek, 291. New York: Prentice-Hall, 1945.

Kayal, Philip M. *An Arab-American Bibliographic Guide*. Belmont, Mass.: Association of Arab-American University Graduates, 1985.

Kayal, Philip M., and Joseph M. Kayal. *The Syrian-Lebanese in America: A Study in Religion and Assimilation.* New York: Twayne Publishers, 1975.

Khalaf, Mona. "Male Migration and the Lebanese Family: The Impact of the Wife Left Behind." *Journal of Middle East Women's Studies* 5.3 (2009): 102–119.

Khater, Akram Fouad. *Inventing Home: Emigration, Gender and the Middle Class in Lebanon, 1870–1920.* Berkeley: University of California Press, 2001.

Khater, Akram F. "Like Pure Gold: Sexuality and Honour amongst Lebanese Emigrants, 1890–1920." In *Sexuality in the Arab World*, ed. Samir Khalaf and John Gagnon, 85. London, San Francisco, Beirut: Saqi, 2006.

Kherbawi, Basil M. *History of the Syrian Emigration.* New York: N.G. Badran, 1913.

Knight, William Allen. *The Song of Our Syrian Guest.* Boston: Pilgrim Press, 1904.

Latcheva, Rossalina, and Barbara Herzon-Punzenberger. "Integration Trajectories: A Mixed Method Approach." In *A Life-Course Perspective on Migration and Integration*, ed. Matthias Wingens et al., 121 New York: Springer, 2011.

Macdonald, Duncan B. "Arbeely's Arabic Grammar," *American Journal of Semitic Languages and Literatures* 15:3 (April 1899): 181–182.

Makdisi, Ussama. *Artillery of Heaven: American Missionaries and the Failed Conversion of the Middle East.* Ithaca, N.Y.: Cornell University Press, 2007.

Maloof, Joseph N. *Kizanat Al-Ayyam Fi Tarajim El Azam (Biographies of Great Men).* New York: Jaridat al-Ayyam, 1899.

Markel, Howard. *Quarantine!: East European Jewish Immigrants and the New York City Epidemics of 1892.* Baltimore: Johns Hopkins University Press, 1999.

McCabe, James D. *The Illustrated History of the Centennial Exhibition: Philadelphia, 1876.* Philadelphia: National Publishing Company, 1975 (1876).

McKay, James. "Religious Diversity and Ethnic Cohesion: A Three Generational Analysis of Syrian-Lebanese Christians in Sydney." *International Migration Review* 19.2 (1985): 318–334.

Melki, Henry M. "Al-Shihafa Al-'Arabiyah fi Al-Mahjar Wa-'alaqatiha bi Al-Adab Al-Mahjari (Arab-American Journalism and Its Relation to Arab-American Literature)." PhD dissertation, Georgetown University, Washington, D.C., 1972.

Miller, Lucius Hopkins. *A Study of the Syrian Population of Greater New York.*

New York: n.p., 1903[?].

Moghabghab, Faddoul. *The Shepherd Song on the Hills of Lebanon.* New York: E.P. Dutton & Company, 1907.

Mokarzel, Mary. *Al-Hoda, 1898–1968: The Story of Lebanon and Its Emigrants Taken from the Newspaper Al-Hoda.* New York: Al-Hoda Press, 1968.

Mokarzel, Salloum A. "Can We Retain Our Heritage?" *The Syrian World* 2 (1928): 36.

Mokarzel, S.A., and H.F. Otash. *The Syrian Business Directory, 1908–1909.* New York: Al-Hoda, 1909.

Moses, John G., and Eugene Paul Nassar. *Annotated Index to The Syrian World, 1926–1932.* Ed. Judith Rosenblatt. Saint Paul, Minn.: Immigration History Research Center, 1994.

Moss, Frank. *The American Metropolis: From Knickerbocker Days to the Present Time. Vol. 3.* New York: Peter Fenelon Collier, 1897.

Naff, Alixa. "Becoming American: Peddling and the Syrian Immigrants to World War I." Unpublished ms., n.d.

———. *Becoming American: The Early Arab Immigrant Experience.* Carbondale: Southern Illinois University Press, 1985.

———. *Lebanese Immigration into the United States: 1880 to the Present.* Ed. Albert Hourani and Nadeem Shehadi. The Lebanese in the World. London: I.B. Tauris & Co., 1992.

Naimy, Nadim. *The Lebanese Prophets of New York.* Beirut: American University of Beirut, 1985.

Nance, Susan. *How the Arabian Nights Inspired the American Dream, 1790–1935.* Chapel Hill: University of North Carolina, 2009.

New York Juvenile Asylum. *Annual Reports, Vols. 47–49.* Albany, N.Y.: James B. Lyon, State Printer, 1899–1901.

Orfalea, Gregory. *Before the Flames: A Quest for the History of Arab Americans.* Austin: University of Texas Press, 1988.

———. "On Arab Americans: A Bibliographical Essay." *American Studies International* 27 (1989): 26–41.

Owen, Roger. "The Study of Middle Eastern Industrial History: Notes on the Interrelationship between Factories and Small-Scale Manufacturing with Special References to Lebanese Silk and Egyptian Sugar, 1900–1930." *International Journal of Middle East Studies* 16 (1984): 475–487.

Peterson, Jaffray. *Sixty-Five Years of Banking and a Record of New York City Banks (The Rise of Commercial Banking).* New York: n.p., 1980.

Pizzitola, Louis. *Hearst over Hollywood: Power, Passion and Propaganda in the*

*Movies*. New York: Columbia University, 2002.

Portes, Alejandro, and Ruben G. Rumbaut. *Legacies: The Story of the Immigrant Second Generation*. Berkeley, New York: UC Press, Russell Sage Foundation, 2001.

Quataert, Donald. "Ottoman Women, Households, and Textile Manufacturing, 1800–1914." In *The Modern Middle East: A Reader*, ed. Albert H. Hourani, Mary C. Wilson, and Philip S. Khoury, 255. Revised ed. New York, London: I.B. Tauris, 2004.

Rihani, Ameen Fares. *The Book of Khalid*. Beirut: Librairie du Liban, 2000 (1911).

Rihbany, Abraham Mitrie. *A Far Journey: An Autobiography*. Boston and New York: Houghton Mifflin Company, 1914.

Riis, Jacob A. *How the Other Half Lives: Studies among the Tenements of New York*. New York: Charles Scribner's Sons, 1890.

Rizk, Salom. *Syrian Yankee*. Garden City: Doubleday, Doran & Co, 1943.

Rustum, Asad M. *Al Rustumiyat*. New York: Eagle Press, 192?.

Rustum, Mikhail. *Al-Gharib fi El Garb (Stranger in the West)*. Vol. 3 [3rd Ed.]. New York: Commercial Printing House, 1909 or 1914?.

———. *Kitab Al-Gharib fi El Gharb (Stranger in the West)*. Beirut: Dar al Hamra, 1992 (1895).

Saliba, Najib. *Emigration from Syria and the Syrian-Lebanese Community of Worcester, Massachusetts*. Ligonier, Penn.: Antakya Press, 1992.

Samra, Bishop Nichola. "Era of Missionaries: Economos Abraham Beshewate, BSO." Unpublished ms., n.d. (2012).

Shadid, Anthony. *House of Stone: A Memoir of Home, Family and a Lost Middle East*. Boston and New York: Houghton Mifflin Harcourt, 2012.

Shadid, Michael A. *A Doctor for the People: The Autobiography of the Founder of America's First Cooperative Hospital—and How He Successfully Defended It against the Attacks of the Medical Trust*. 2nd ed. New York: Vanguard Press, 1939.

Shakir, Evelyn. *Bint Arab: Arab and Arab American Women in the United States*. Westport, Conn.: Praeger, 1997.

Sherman, William C., Paul Whitney, and John Guerrero. *Prairie Peddlers: The Syrian-Lebanese in North Dakota*. Bismarck, N.D.: University of Mary Press, 2002

State Board of Charities. *Annual Report of the State Board of Charities for the Year 1897*. 2 Vols. New York and Albany: Wynkoop Hallenbeck Crawford Co., State Printers, 1898.

Suleiman, Michael W. *Arabs in America: Building a New Future*. Philadelphia: Temple University Press, 1999.

———. "The Mokarzels' Contribution to the Arabic-Speaking Community in the United States." *Arab Studies Quarterly* 22.1 (1999): 71–88.

———. "Impressions of New York City by Early Arab Immigrants." In *A Community of Many Worlds: Arab Americans in New York City*, ed. Kathleen Benson and Philip M. Kayal, 28. New York: Museum of the City of New York/Syracuse University Press, 2002.

———. *The Arab-American Experience in the United States and Canada: A Classified, Annotated Bibliography*. Ann Arbor, Mich.: Pierian Press, 2006.

———. "A History of Arab-American Political Participation." In *American Arabs and Political Participation*, ed. Philippa Strum, 3. Washington, D.C.: Woodrow Wilson International Center for Scholars, 2006.

———. "La Experiencia de la Immigración Arabe." In *Arabes de Norteamerica*, 7. Madrid: Casa Arabe-IEAM, 2011.

Syrian Socicty of the City of New York. *Annual Report*. New York: n.p., 1893.

———. *Financial Report, from April, 1893 to January, 1897*. New York: n.p., 1898.

Tannous, Afif I. "Social Change in an Arab Village. " *American Sociological Review* 6.5 (1941): 650–662.

———. "Acculturation of an Arab-Syrian Community in the Deep South." *American Sociological Review* 8.3 (1943): 264–271.

———. *Village Roots and Beyond: Memoirs of Afif I. Tannous: Written at Intervals between 1972 and 1985*. Beirut: Dar Nelson, 2004.

Tannus, Afif I. "Trends of Social and Cultural Change in Bishmizzeen, an Arab Village of North Lebanon." PhD dissertation, Cornell University, 1940.

Trinity Church. *Year Book and Register of the Parish of Trinity Church in the City of New York, A.D. 1888*. New York: Authority of Trinity Church, 1889.

Trinity Church Men's Committee. *A Social Survey of the Washington Street District of New York City*. New York: n.p., 1914.

Truzzi, Oswaldo. "The Right Place at the Right Time: Syrians and Lebanese in Brazil and the United States, a Comparative Approach." *Journal of American Ethnic History*, 16.2 (1997): 3–34.

Vandor, Paul E. "Joseph Oussani." In *History of Fresno County, California*. Los Angeles: Historic Record Company, 1919.

Walker, Francis A. *The World's Fair, Philadelphia, 1876: A Critical Account.*

New York: A.S. Barnes & Co., 1878.

Ward, Gabriel E. *Kitab Al-Jundi Al-Suri fi Thalath Hurub (The Syrian Soldier in Three Wars)*. New York: Syrian-American Press, 1919.

Women's Foreign Missionary Society of the Presbyterian Church. "Syria." In *Historical Sketches of the Missions under the Care of the Board of Foreign Missions of the Presbyterian Church*. 3rd ed. Philadelphia: Women's Foreign Missionary Society of the Presbyterian Church, 1891.

———. "Work among the Moslems in the Turkish Empire." In *Woman's Work for Women* 16.12 (1901): 327.

Younis, Adele L. "The Challenge of Commerce: The Syrian American Directory Almanac by Naseeb Arida and Sabri Andria, 1930." Unpublished ms., n.d.

———. "The Growth of Arabic-Speaking Settlements in the United States." In *The Arab-Americans*, ed. Elaine C. Hagopian and Ann Paden, 102. Wilamette, Ill.: Medina University Press International, 1969.

———. *The Coming of the Arabic-Speaking People to the United States*. Ed. Philip M. Kayal. Staten Island, N.Y.: Center for Migration Studies, 1995.

Zacks, Richard. *Island of Vice: Theodore Roosevelt's Doomed Quest to Clean Up Sin-Loving New York*. New York: Doubleday, 2012.

Zelditch, Morris. "The Syrians in Pittsburgh." MA thesis, University of Pittsburgh, 1936.

# INDEX

**Bold** indicates figures and maps.

© Rafael Salazar

Linda K. Jacobs is a New York-based scholar and author. She holds a Ph.D. in Near Eastern Archaeology/Anthropology and is the author of *Digging In: An American Archaeologist Uncovers the Real Iran*. Dr. Jacobs is the founder of KalimahPress and sits on the boards of several Middle Eastern organizations. All four of her grandparents were members of the New York Syrian Colony.